The President and the
Council of Economic Advisers

Westview Replica Editions

The concept of Westview Replica Editions is a response to the continuing crisis in academic and informational publishing. Library budgets for books have been severely curtailed. Ever larger portions of general library budgets are being diverted from the purchase of books and used for data banks, computers, micromedia, and other methods of information retrieval. Interlibrary loan structures further reduce the edition sizes required to satisfy the needs of the scholarly community. Economic pressures on the university presses and the few private scholarly publishing companies have severely limited the capacity of the industry to properly serve the academic and research communities. As a result, many manuscripts dealing with important subjects, often representing the highest level of scholarship, are no longer economically viable publishing projects--or, if accepted for publication, are typically subject to lead times ranging from one to three years.

Westview Replica Editions are our practical solution to the problem. We accept a manuscript in camera-ready form, typed according to our specifications, and move it immediately into the production process. As always, the selection criteria include the importance of the subject, the work's contribution to scholarship, and its insight, originality of thought, and excellence of exposition. The responsibility for editing and proofreading lies with the author or sponsoring institution. We prepare chapter headings and display pages, file for copyright, and obtain Library of Congress Cataloging in Publication Data. A detailed manual contains simple instructions for preparing the final typescript, and our editorial staff is always available to answer questions.

The end result is a book printed on acid-free paper and bound in sturdy library-quality soft covers. We manufacture these books ourselves using equipment that does not require a lengthy make-ready process and that allows us to publish first editions of 300 to 600 copies and to reprint even smaller quantities as needed. Thus, we can produce Replica Editions quickly and can keep even very specialized books in print as long as there is a demand for them.

About the Book and Editors

The President and the Council of Economic Advisers: Interviews with CEA Chairmen
edited by Erwin C. Hargrove and Samuel A. Morley

Interviews with ten former chairmen of the Council of Economic Advisers--from the Truman to the Carter administrations--are gathered in this book to examine the relationship between economic advisers and the president and the institutional relationships among the CEA, executive departments, and federal financial agencies. The interviews also reconstruct major presidential decisions since the establishment of the CEA, such as the 1964 tax cut, the 1971 wage and price freeze, and presidential strategies for managing inflation and recession. In a preface to each interview, the editors analyze the conditions for CEA effectiveness, look at how well the advice of the Council has conformed to the presidential world view, and pinpoint the distribution of responsibility for policy analysis and advice within successive administrations.

Edwin C. Hargrove is professor of political science at Vanderbilt University and is director of the Vanderbilt Institute for Public Policy Studies. Samuel A. Morley is professor of economics and business administration at Vanderbilt University and is a consultant for the World Bank.

The President and the Council of Economic Advisers
Interviews with CEA Chairmen

edited by Erwin C. Hargrove
and Samuel A. Morley

Westview Press / Boulder and London

Copyright © 1984 by Westview Press, Inc.

Published in 1984 in the United States of America by
    Westview Press, Inc.
    5500 Central Avenue
    Boulder, Colorado 80301
    Frederick A. Praeger, Publisher

Library of Congress Catalog Card Number: 84-51229
ISBN: 0-86531-866-2

Printed and bound in the United States of America

10 9 8 7 6 5 4 3 2 1

Contents

Foreword

This volume contains oral history interviews with ten of the past chairmen of the Council of Economic Advisers.* Eight of the interviews were conducted at Vanderbilt University in the 1977-78 academic year. They were conducted in the historical sequence in which the chairmen were in office, beginning with Leon Keyserling and concluding with Alan Greenspan, with two exceptions: Arthur Burns was interviewed in July 1980 and Charles Schultze was interviewed twice, in 1982 and 1983.

With the exceptions of the Burns and Schultze interviews, all of the sessions were conducted at Vanderbilt University as faculty seminars in which a small number of faculty members met for a full day with each guest. Each discussion lasted approximately six hours. A faculty seminar was a good way to elicit responses because the general conversation would stimulate unforeseen insights and reflections. The membership of the seminars varied slightly, but a core of steady participants was always present. Erwin C. Hargrove and Samuel A. Morley took principal responsibility for the questioning, with Hargrove focusing on institutional and political questions and Morley devoting his attention to the contents of economic policy and the contribution of economics to policy. Professor Ivar Berg suggested the seminar format initially and was a regular and valuable participant. Professors Avery Leiserson and Dewey Daane contributed greatly to the entire project. Professor Lester Seligman of the University of Illinois participated in several of the seminars. James Gardner, a recent doctoral graduate in history from Vanderbilt, prepared background essays on the chairmanship of each guest as preparation for the seminar members. These edited essays will be found in this volume preceding each interview.

The sessions were recorded on tape and transcribed. The former chairmen reviewed the transcriptions, made additions and subtractions and gave their approval for publication. An edited version was then prepared for publication by Kay Hancock, a Research Associate at the Vanderbilt Institute for Public Policy Studies. Scarlett Graham and JoAnn Bennett, also of the Institute, did further editing to reduce the length and enhance reada-

---

*Edwin G. Nourse, the first chairman, had died when we began our work, and the project stopped with the Carter administration.

bility. Mrs. Bennett also supervised the final preparation of the manuscript for publication. The original, approved transcripts are on file at the Institute and may be read by students and scholars who receive the permission of the men whose materials they wish to examine.

Louise Patton did a very efficient job of transcribing the tapes. Janice Jones and Cheryl Solometo helped with additional typing. Diane Sircy retyped the entire manuscript in preparation for photocopying. Lottie Strupp, of the Institute staff, managed the project and kept track of tapes, materials and successive editions of transcripts.

The project was supported by the public policy committee of the Ford Foundation, the University Research Council of Vanderbilt University and the Vanderbilt Institute for Public Policy Studies. Vanderbilt University contributed to the publication of this book with a subvention.

Erwin C. Hargrove and Samuel A. Morley
Institute for Public Policy Studies
Vanderbilt University
May 1984

Introduction

The Council of Economic Advisers was created by the Employment Act of 1946 and received its mandate from that Act. The most important motivation for the Act was the memory that the problem of unemployment had not been solved in peacetime. The political determination to prevent unemployment in the postwar period was joined to the acceptance of Keynesian theory by many prominent American economists.[1]

The Council was to apply economic science to policy problems in behalf of maximum employment. The term "full employment" was struck from the original bill because there was insufficient support, in Congress and among the active interest groups, for governmental planning to achieve full employment in hard times.[2] The goals of "maximum employment, production and purchasing power," as expressed in the language of the Act, were joined with the goals of "free competitive enterprise."[3] Thus, a balance between government intervention and reliance on the market was struck. The CEA was to march alternately under these two banners in the ensuing years.

The emergence of the CEA as the vehicle for economic analysis was in accordance with the grain of history which produced the Brownlow committee of 1937 and its recommendation that "the President needs help."[4] The earliest Senate drafts of the bill had given the Fiscal Division of the Bureau of the Budget the responsibility for preparing the "National Employment and Production" budget under the president's guidance. But the drafters feared departmental opposition to increased powers in the Bureau and, therefore, placed the activity in the Executive Office of the President without specifying any organizational form. The Senate sponsors of the bill agreed that the president should be free to develop administrative modes in consultation with his cabinet.[5]

The idea of a small unit of economic advisers had originated with a suggestion to Congressman William Whittington, Chairman of the House Committee on Expenditures in the Executive Departments, which was handling the bill, that an independent economic commission be created.[6] The Secretary of the Treasury, Fred Vinson, opposed such an independent unit as not being sufficiently responsive to the president and Whittington reduced the independence of the body.[7] However, as the bill went to conference, Vinson prepared a revision which would replace the CEA with a cabinet committee under the direction of the Secretary of the Treasury.

President Truman gave the Vinson draft to his assistant, John
Snyder, who did not forward it to the Committee. Stephen Bailey
suggests that the reputed long standing friction between Vinson
and Snyder may explain this inaction.[8]

The House-Senate conferees eventually settled on a council of
three "expert" advisers who would work for the president in consultation with the departments and the Budget Bureau. There were
to be no operational responsibilities. No existing agency, such
as the Treasury or the Bureau of the Budget, was to have the lead.
The president was to be given "help" without tying his hands. The
assignment was clear. The "experts" were to advise the president
on economic trends and suggest ways to promote the health of the
economy.

The CEA was the first of a succession of advisory units that
were to burgeon within the Executive Office of the President, all
in the spirit of the Brownlow report.[9] Each of these units has,
over the years, developed its own configuration of expertise,
organization and politics. But they all depend on the president
for their influence. If he does not use them, they fall idle.

With one exception, the thirteen CEA chairmen from 1947 to
1984 have been professional economists, and only two have not been
university professors of economics before or after their appointments. There have been three council positions, including the
chairman, from the beginning and the professional staff of economists has remained at about fifteen in number for the entire time.
The similarity in composition of successive CEAs has been matched
by stability in structure and function. The CEA has remained a
small unit in the Executive Office of the President which has
carried out analytic and advisory activities for the president
with a great deal of continuity of operation. For example, because staff members are on leave from their universities for the
academic year, they usually continue to serve the Council of a new
president of a different party from January to June following the
presidential election year. This is one small indication of the
high level of professionalism and stability that characterizes the
Council.

This continuity and stability invite study of the CEA as a
presidential institution in its own right. All chairmen, but two,
are alive. They have met as a group to discuss the CEA as an
institution on anniversary occasions.[10] The great availability of
former chairmen and the apparent high level of self-conscious
agreement among them about the mission of the CEA engaged our
interest and stimulated the development of this project.

Purposes of the Study

The project was undertaken for three reasons: (1) we wished
to develop an approach to conducting oral history interviews; (2)
we wanted to better understand the functioning of the presidency,
as an institution, in regard to economic policymaking; and (3) we
hoped to contribute to the historical record about the making of
key economic policy decisions of each administration and to generalize about the varying relationships between presidential politi-

cal strategies and the uses of economic knowledge. We will consider each of these purposes in turn.

Oral History

The oral history interviews carried out by the several presidential libraries seldom have as their purpose the understanding
of the presidency as an institution. They are not grounded in the
literature on the presidency. Rather, individual interviewers
pursue idiosyncratic themes with individual respondents without
the reader's ever knowing why the questioning is proceeding on a
given course. There is no organizing framework for such interviews beyond the interests of the questioner. There are two
complaints: first, that the interviews are not designed to discover how the institution functions, and second, there is an
absence of comprehensiveness in the interviews covering a given
administration. Some subjects are touched repeatedly and other
topics are omitted altogether. It was our intention that the
interviews with the CEA chairmen would overcome both deficiencies
by illustrating how to uncover knowledge of an institution and how
to achieve comprehensiveness.

We covered what we regarded as the most important questions
about the functioning of the CEA in government. There were three
primary themes: (1) the relationship of the chairman of the CEA
with the president; (2) the intragovernmental relations of the CEA
with other economic policy advisory bodies; (3) the relationships
between presidential politics and economic knowledge in the making
of economic policy. Anyone who interviewed future CEA chairmen
would wish to cover these themes. We neglected other possible
topics, such as the public role of the chairman and relationships
of the CEA with the economics profession. Therefore, we cannot
claim to be fully comprehensive, but we have moved beyond an
idiosyncratic approach. If future interviews were grounded in the
literature on the presidency, as we think is the case with our
work, the questions would surely vary in response to historical
changes, but there would be that grounding. The libraries are
devoted to presenting individual presidencies rather than the
presidency as an institution, but interviews could be based on the
literature without sacrificing a special concern with particular
periods of history.

Our approach can be employed by scholars, quite apart from
the work of the presidential libraries. Of particular interest
here is the analysis of a governmental office by comparing the
words and actions of individuals who have held the same position.
This is seldom done. But, what we have attempted with the CEA
could be done with any or all of the established positions within
the White House or Executive Office staff, such as press secretary, director of the Office of Management and Budget, etc. The
advantage of such an approach is that one is able to disentangle
the temporary from the enduring in an institution, chart changes
and speculate about their causes. It is also a very useful way to
understand the relative importance of personalities in government,
both of presidents and economists, as compared to political and
institutional forces.

Schultze was interviewed by two people, Burns by three interviewers and all the rest met with a small group of faculty members who acted much like students in a seminar, asking questions, making comments of their own and disagreeing with each other and the teacher. Most of the record of the seminar has been edited out of this published version. Each approach has its advantages and disadvantages. The fewer the number of interviewers the greater the continuity of questions and answers. A seminar provides more opportunity for serendipity at some cost to continuity. Several of the respondents remarked that the seminar discussion so stimulated their thinking that they added ideas they might not have otherwise expressed.

Finally, we cannot claim that all of the factual statements made by these former chairmen are accurate nor can we compensate for what are surely personal interpretations of historical events. Such efforts would be endless. That is the weakness of oral history. But it is only one approach and must be supplemented by additional interviews and documentary research.

Understanding the Institutionalized Presidency

Our inquiry about actual patterns of behavior was guided by a normative question. Is the presidency organized so that the president receives the best available economic advice? Since presidents shape the formal and informal patterns of advisory relations in the relatively unstructured institution over which they preside, we wished to know how the styles of authority of individual presidents influenced advisory patterns in economic policymaking. To what degree do these patterns vary according to presidential taste, as the literature often claims, and to what extent are they institutionalized so that personal style is less significant for the giving and receiving of advice?[11]

A second question asks about the relationships of the CEA to other advisory bodies, such as the domestic policy staffs, the Office of Management and Budget, the Treasury and other departments. Do these bodies collaborate in a way to provide complementary kinds of knowledge for the president? For example, OMB program examiners possess a great deal of knowledge about the actual functioning of programs that can complement the more theoretically based micro economic analyses of CEA staff members on issues like farm subsidies, minimum wage, employment and training programs and health care costs. The Treasury brings an expertise in international economic questions, and a departmental perspective as well, that the CEA must both rely on and, at times, challenge. How are these different strands of knowledge woven together in the development of policy alternatives to be presented to the president? Are there criteria for evaluating the efficiency and effectiveness of different ways of organizing and directing such activities? Are the more "optimal" patterns institutionalized or do they depend upon the disposition of individual presidents? Are there unresolved, and perhaps intractable, problems because no one mode of organization can serve all goals? Are there similarities and differences among the patterns and problems of structuring decision processes in economic, national security

and social policy? Have accepted and valued processes of economic
advising been placed under strain by new sets of economic policy
problems?[12]

A third question asks about the best ways to organize and
staff the CEA itself. The interviews reveal near unanimity among
the chairmen that the Council should have a small professional
staff composed primarily of faculty members on leave from universities for one or two years and that their work should consist of
analysis, with the CEA avoiding administrative responsibilities
for the coordination or implemention of policy. Both the national
security and domestic policy staffs have grown larger in recent
years. The CEA, however, has not grown since 1946, and its tasks
have not varied greatly. Does a small, highly talented, academic
group of professionals have a comparative advantage in the rough
and tumble of government and, if so, what is it? Are there disadvantages as well? Can such a small group cope with the great
range of economic policy questions and, if not, how does it best
multiply its capacities by collaboration with OMB and other agencies? These questions have not been explored in the literature in
regard to the CEA, but they permeate the general writing on presidential staffs. The CEA appears to have worked out an acceptable
division of labor with other advisory bodies, such as OMB and
Treasury, that eludes both the national security and domestic
policy staff units. If this is the case, why is it so and are the
lessons transferable to other units?

The Relationships Between Presidential Politics and Economic Know-
ledge in the Making of Economic Policy

What are the relationships, in presidential decision making,
between broad political strategies, for re-election, congressional
and constituency support, and economic science? Formal economic
knowledge and theory may enhance political strategies if presidents receive reliable advice about how economic policies may
permit them to achieve both policy and political goals. Since the
theory and knowledge may be inadequate to the policy problem in
some cases, what do presidents do in the absence of such help?
Economic science may also conflict with what presidents wish to do
or feel they can do in the face of political constraints.

We were interested in particularly crucial decisions such as
Lyndon Johnson's reluctance in 1966 to recommend increased taxes
to Congress to pay for the Vietnam War and Richard Nixon's imposition of wage and price controls in 1971. But, the reconstruction
of such decisions was primarily regarded as raw material for the
larger question of whether the expert knowledge of economists is
congruent with the political knowledge of presidents. Perhaps the
two kinds of knowledge are complementary for certain kinds of
situations, especially expansionary periods. There is also the
question of whether formal economic science can adequately explain
and prescribe for contemporary problems of inflation, low productivity and persistent underemployment. It could be argued that
the blend of neoclassical and Keynesian theory that has guided
most Councils is not suited for these problems and that new intellectual capital is required. Or one might answer that there is

nothing wrong with economics except the hard choices it presents to politicians and presidents in a time of inflation and declining economic growth when strong medicine must be administered and some interests damaged. If this is the case, any eclipse of the CEA would be explained by politics rather than the deficiencies of economics. Of course, both economic theory and the political resources with which to face new problems may be weak, and one can only speculate what would be required in the development of knowledge and political invention to strengthen the capacities of government to deal with new problems.[13]

I. The Organization of Macro Policymaking

The CEA, Treasury, OMB and the Federal Reserve Board are the four agencies responsible for macro economic policymaking in the United States. We now examine the descriptions of the chairmen of the institutional relationships that have developed between these agencies. In doing so, we first make a distinction between fiscal and monetary policy. The so-called "Troika" composed of the CEA, OMB and the Treasury together advise the president on fiscal policy. Monetary policy is decided independently by the Federal Reserve Board.

The Troika: A Division of Labor

1. The functional division of labor among Troika members which began to develop informally in the 1950s took structured form during the Kennedy administration and has continued much the same since that time.

The Treasury made revenue estimates, the CEA estimated how the private economy would function, and the Budget Bureau anticipated federal expenditures. Presidential choices for the year ahead were extracted from these analyses. The creation of a formal Troika structure brought explicit collaboration of three sets of staffs and regular meetings of their principals to analyze and assess economic trends. Heller says that either Douglas Dillon, Secretary of the Treasury, or Sam Cohn, a Budget Bureau official, invented the Troika idea.[14] Okun attributes parenthood to Cohn, who was determined to create a situation in which the agencies advised the president on the basis of common information.[15] Authorship is less important than the shared view that a structured division of labor was in the interests of the president.

Keyserling was the only chairman to insist on the preeminence of the Council, in theory and fact, among the economic advisers to the president. He opposed a formal group which would give everyone equal standing.[16] But, he also emphasized that the CEA was continuously involved with the Cabinet departments in estimating economic trends in relation to administration goals.[17] Thus, while he denies a division of labor, Keyserling affirms the principle which eventually led to a formal division of labor—the need to verify, structure, and simplify the picture of the economy to be presented to the president.

Saulnier contends that an incipient Troika was established informally during the second term of the Eisenhower administration when he, the Secretary of the Treasury and the Chairman of the Federal Reserve Board met regularly but informally with President Eisenhower.[18] Differences were discussed in front of the President, who liked to engage in such collegial discussions.

The Kennedy administration formalized that Troika, added the principle of staff work and differentiated between the Troika and the Quadriad, the latter including the Chairman of the Federal Reserve Board. But both Saulnier and subsequent chairmen reported that whether the organization was informal or formal the search for agreement was continuous and differences, while present, were seldom sharp and divisive.[19] Stein even asks if the existence of the CEA, and a structured advisory process, might reduce the range of sources from which the president receives economic advice and make the presidency more ingrown.[20]

By the early 1960s, a broader division of policy roles among the Troika members was established which has continued to the present. The secretary of the Treasury is the chief presidential spokesman for economic policy with both Congress and the public. The OMB, its director and the program divisions are the chief advisers to the president on the relative effectiveness of departmental programs. The CEA serves as the chief analyst of economic trends and explicator of alternatives for the president. Each role is grounded in what each institution can do best. The Treasury secretary has statutory obligations and is the chief financial officer of the administration in accountability to Congress. As a member of the president's "Inner Cabinet," which also includes State, Defense and the Attorney General, he is well attuned to the politics of economic policymaking and, therefore, is a logical choice for chief spokesman. The program divisions of OMB exercise continuing oversight over departmental operations and are in the best position of any presidential advisory units to assess the effectiveness of programs. A natural collaboration between CEA staff members and the OMB program officers develops in the stance which both often take toward unsupported departmental claims, but the CEA can only identify and deal with a few of the many issues raised by OMB. Finally, the Council is best equipped to relate economic analysis to policy alternatives.

2. Questions of macro economic policy are the exclusive province of the Troika plus one or more other senior advisers within the administration. The departments which represent strong constituencies (Labor, Commerce, Agriculture, etc.) are not invited to the decision making table.

Ackley remembers the jealousy of the CEA expressed by the secretaries of Labor and Commerce. They resented his access to and their exclusion from discussions of fiscal and budget policy.[21] He adds:

...on fiscal or monetary policy, tax policy, size of the budget...[The Labor and Commerce Departments]... didn't really have much to contribute. Their ideas about these subjects were ill-formed; it wasn't that

there weren't people in their agencies who were intelligent in respect to these issues, but that they were
farther down; the principals spent most of their time at
a big administrative job and couldn't really get into
the analysis of these issues.[22]

Ackley suggested the idea of a Department of Economic Affairs
that would incorporate Commerce and Labor and perhaps subdue
constituency representation.[23]

Other chairmen reaffirmed the lack of credibility of the
constituency departments because they were perceived by presidents
and the Troika as representing specific interests and as lacking
in the broad viewpoints and capabilities required for questions of
macro economic policy.[24]

The suspicion of the constituency departments by Troika members is just as strong on micro matters. But, the political
resources of the departments may be greater. Arthur Okun remembers a former secretary of Health, Education and Welfare:

> Wilbur Cohen could get almost anything he wanted
> out of Johnson, tremendously persuasive. He knew exact-
> ly how to approach the President. Califano would have
> these carefully constructed task forces and the Assis-
> tant Secretary of HEW would be there and never be able
> quite to say what Wilbur would go for or what he
> wouldn't go for....Then before the task force report was
> on the President's desk, you'd hear that Cohen had
> gotten a commitment from the President to do thus and so
> in the January budget. It was clear that Johnson didn't
> care that much about things rising through channels and
> his getting the income maintenance task force report.
> Wilbur sounded like he had a very good idea and the
> President bought it. Califano would tear his hair
> out.[25]

However, Ackley reports that Johnson preferred that Ackley
and Califano discuss agricultural policies for him with the Secretary of Agriculture.[26]

The tentative conclusion to be drawn is that the Troika
easily dominates the advisory process for macro policy but that
the patterns are more variable in micro policy matters.

3. Each of the three Troika agencies have predictable policy
orientations whether the administration is Democratic or Republican. McCracken best expressed it:

> ...The CEA will probably tend to be a little more
> concerned about...the level of unemployment...the cen-
> tral banker [Treasury] is going to be a little more
> concerned than the CEA chairman...about inflation...
> [OMB] has an institutional bias that might be character-
> ized as you've got to prove it to me, because the aggre-
> gate of all the good proposals add up to an excessive
> amount.[27]

There was general agreement that the Treasury takes a less expansionist view of economic policy than CEA. It must service the national debt and worry about the effect of the international balance of payments on the dollar. No one argued that Treasury positions were taken in response to the views of the banking community. The Treasury was not perceived as a "constituency" department. Rather statutory obligations were cited as the basis for Treasury "conservatism."

In most administrations, the CEA has been more expansionist than Treasury.[28] Saulnier was more expansionist than Humphrey, the Kennedy-Johnson chairmen were to the left of the Treasury. The one exception is Greenspan, who, while agreeing with the general proposition, reports a high degree of policy agreement and collegiality within the Ford Troika.[29]

The Budget Bureau was not characterized in terms of a policy orientation but by an economizing mode of thought which sought to develop priorities and efficiency in government spending.[30]

All participants reported that agreement on policy was greater than disagreement among Troika members. Government is a continuous conversation and the Troika structure is one in which disagreements are progressively lessened as issues reach the top. Only two areas of continuous disagreement were identified. The Treasury jealously guards policy areas which it sees as its exclusive preserve, for example, debt management, international economic policy and relations with Congress. There was ample testimony that the CEA cannot compete with the Treasury on inter-agency committees on matters chaired by Treasury civil servants who are past masters at bureaucratic management.[31] Second, the relative influence over macro policy of the Treasury and the Council was shaped by presidential politics and policy. If presidents were inclined to move in an expansionist direction, the CEA would have greater influence. If presidents were more inclined to put brakes on the economy, the Treasury would be more influential.

4. The period of consolidation of the Troika has given way to a new institutional pattern which still lacks form. These changes have been caused by new economic policy problems which make it difficult to disentangle macro and micro policy.

The first sign of this development began in the Nixon administration, with the formation of a collegial body that would consider the interrelationships of macro, micro and international economic policy. It was felt that economic questions were too important, substantively and politically, to be considered in a fragmented manner. In 1969 the CEA suggested setting up a Cabinet Committee on Economic Policy to give the constituency departments a forum. It did not want them in the Troika but felt that controlling inflation went beyond the capacities of the Troika and fiscal policy. Some machinery was needed that would give an opportunity for consideration of other kinds of anti-inflationary policies. This committee operated for almost a year, but it was too big a group, discussion was not focused, the President became bored with it and it faded away.[32]

However, there was still a feeling that things were at loose ends because policy coordination was weak, particularly on inter-

national questions. Nixon felt the need for guidance and centralization and turned to John Connally as his new Secretary of the
Treasury.[33] During the 1970-72 period, Nixon had the same relationship with Connally and could discuss matters more easily with
him than with others. Connally did not have a collegial style but
the degree of exclusiveness between Nixon and Connally faded when
the Cost of Living Council was established to administer wage and
price controls in 1971. Connally operated with the advice and
consent of the Cost of Living Council. He lacked "strong preferences about policy" and simply wanted to make decisions.[34]

George Shultz became Secretary of the Treasury in 1972 and
received the same delegation of authority that the President had
granted to Connally. However, his style was collegial. He worked
through a committee system. The Troika was expanded to include
the chairman of the Cost of Living Council and the President's
Assistant for International Economic Policy.[35] The other departments were not part of this expanded Troika, but they were brought
into it to discuss specific questions. For example, since food
was a big part of the inflation problem, the Department of Agriculture was consulted. State was brought in to discuss international monetary questions.[36]

This committee structure presented the President with the
options that synthesized the arguments objectively. Stein reports
that Nixon had observed Shultz as Secretary of Labor in meetings
of the Cabinet Committee on Economic Policy and noted his facility
for taking everybody's thinking into his consideration before
reaching a conclusion. The President could have confidence that
Shultz as coordinator of economic policy was not grinding his own
axe.[37]

Despite Nixon's penchant for working through strong lieuten-
ants who would coordinate others, more fundamental forces were at
work in this shifting search for mechanisms of policy coordination. The interlacing of international, macro and micro policy
was joined to presidential politics and policy in ways that went
beyond the Troika structure and beyond the fiscal policy that had
been the primary focus of the Troika.

Evidence that more than presidential style was involved came
with the development of the Economic Policy Board in the Ford
administration. The Secretary of the Treasury chaired the Board;
its secretary was the Assistant to the President for economic
policy and the membership included the CEA, OMB, the State Department, the constituency departments and the Chairman of the Federal
Reserve Board. The function of the EPB, according to Alan Greenspan, was to permit conflicts within and between departments to
surface and be resolved and to develop comprehensive options for
the President.[38]

Despite these trends, the testimony is clear that the members
of the Troika appear to have worked around larger bodies on key
macro questions.[39]

None of the three Republican chairmen saw a dimunution of CEA
influence with the president as a result of these collegial
bodies. All argued that so long as the CEA had direct access to
the president and won credibility for its technical competence it
could always obtain a hearing for its analysis. Greenspan remem-

bers that, in 1975, the fear of a recession was looming and Congress was pushing the administration for a tax cut. He was convinced that it was only an inventory backlog and spoke to this
effect in Cabinet meetings. The data were unequivocal, which is
unusual, but:

> That gave me a strong conviction, and since I was
> the only analytical economist in the senior operation, I
> could hold sway on that question.[40]

The Carter administration replaced the EPB with an Economic
Policy Group consisting of virtually the same membership as the
EPB, but the President and its members found it too large and
unwieldy and discussed macro policy through an EPG Executive
Committee consisting of the original Troika members, the vice-
President, the Assistant to the President for domestic policy and
the director of the Council on Wage and Price Stability.[41]
Therefore, by 1977 the membership of the original Troika had been
expanded to include other presidential advisers who needed to
participate in discussion of macro policy questions. The analytic
division of labor of the staffs of the original three Troika
members continued as before, supplemented by the work of a small
EPC staff.

The Coordination of Monetary and Fiscal Policy: Relations Between the Troika and the Federal Reserve Chairman

As we have mentioned earlier, monetary policy, the other key
macro policy variable, is not determined in conjunction with
fiscal policy in the United States. Rather, it is determined
independently by the Fed. That means that in one important sense,
monetary and fiscal policy are not coordinated if, by coordinated,
one means determined simultaneously. Rather, monetary policy is
set by the Federal Reserve Board, and then fiscal policy is tai-
lored to that monetary policy and to the economic projections of
the Troika, often after a great deal of consultation with the
chairman and staff of the Federal Reserve Board. That, in an
important sense, gives primacy to monetary policy, for the structure of decision making is such that the makers of fiscal policy
have to adapt to monetary policy, but the reverse is true to a
lesser degree. Of course, it is the case that, if fiscal policy
resolutely produces large budget deficits as has happened in the
period since 1980, the Federal Reserve Board has to take this into
account in setting monetary policy. But the important point here
is that, although there is a good deal of consultation and generally close relations among the four agencies of the "Quadriad,"
there is no true coordination of policy in the sense we have just
defined. Furthermore, if one believes that monetary policy is
more important than fiscal policy in determining the level of
macro economic activity, the administration does not control the
key macro policy lever.

In our system, the Federal Reserve Board has been given a
special independence in order to insulate it from political pressures for undue expansionary policy or irresponsible manipulation

of the nation's monetary system. It was created by Congress and
it is, in the final analysis, a congressional rather than an
executive agency. As such, it has always maintained an arm's
length relationship with the CEA and the Treasury, and there have
often been tensions between the Fed chairman and the administration.

As students of macro policymaking, we were interested in the
perceptions of CEA chairmen about the relationship with the chairman of the Fed and, particularly, about the administration's lack
of control over a key policy instrument, monetary policy. By and
large, we found no sentiment for a change in the current arrangements. Chairmen implied that the pressure for expansionary policy, regardless of the inflationary consequences, is very great.
They feared that there would be no way to resist the pressures to
excessive expansion of the money supply if the Fed were forced to
coordinate its policy in the sense we have defined it. By maintaining the belief that the Federal Reserve is independent, the
Troika has ammunition to resist excessive deficit spending. Thus,
in summary, although there were periods when monetary and fiscal
policy have worked at cross purposes, such as 1966 or 1975-76, we
found no strong sentiment among the chairmen for a change in the
current institutional arrangements.

The Changing Role and Influence of the CEA

The CEA, as we have seen, was created by the Employment Act
to assist the president in the design and evaluation of programs
aimed at creating employment opportunities and to "promote maximum
employment, production and purchasing power." In practice, CEA
functions appear to have changed considerably from this initial
description. While a good deal of time is still spent on macro
functions, increasingly the CEA has become involved in micro
issues. It has moved away from its original function of advocating and helping design macro policies to being an all-purpose
staff of economic advisers to the president. Since, many economic
problems faced by presidents are micro in nature, the CEA has
shifted its focus in order to continue to be useful to the president and to be influential in the government.

As Stein put it:

At some point in the history of the Council...the
Council changed. The initial idea of the Employment Act
was that all you needed to do was determine the size of
the deficit and, once you knew that, then everything
else would follow....But, at some point, the Council
changed from doing that to being a kind of all-purpose
economic analysis staff and developed some capabilities
in a lot of other fields, particularly agriculture....I
think of it as coming probably around Heller's time.
Now you need an energy man and someone who can deal with
environmental health problems.[42]

The trend noted by Stein, no doubt, has been intensified by
the increasing awareness of the importance in the macro sphere of

monetary policy over which the executive branch never had much influence.

The CEA has proved to have several powerful advantages to a president as an adviser on micro issues. First and foremost, it is perceived as working for the president and no one else. Unlike the departments, it has no other client.

Successive presidents are described as distrustful of recommendations which came to them from the departments with strong constituencies like Labor, Commerce and Agriculture. Eisenhower would never let a decision that affected housing be made without its being reviewed by the CEA because he was not sure of the Home Housing Finance Administration and its constituencies.[43] Kennedy's White House staff learned that the CEA could improve departmental proposals that were to go to Congress so the Council was asked to comment.[44] The Secretary of Agriculture in the Nixon administration got a proposal to increase price supports for soybeans on the President's desk where CEA Chairman Paul McCracken only discovered it by chance. But he was able to stop it. After that, the President asked the Secretary to send all his memos through the CEA.[45]

The CEA establishes credibility with presidents and wins disputes within administration councils in both macro and micro policy only by providing convincing analyses and arguments. The analyses of the Council must be shown to be valid, either by data or subsequent events.[46]

Another source of credibility with the president is the capacity of Council analyses to protect the president from arguments against his policies which are made in technical and expert terminology. For example, Heller and Ackley taught Kennedy to explain to congressmen and lay audiences how planned deficits could stimulate economic growth.[47] Ackley and Okun supplied President Johnson with arguments for a tax increase to combat the inflation cause by deficit financing of the Vietnam War. Johnson delayed the decision too long for political reasons, but he understood the arguments, and they were available for public use once he had decided to ask Congress for the surcharge.[48]

Presidents learn that the CEA is politically useful to them because political fortunes ride on the state of the economy. The mission of the CEA, as defined by the Employment Act of 1946, coincides with the responsibilities of the president more closely than that of any other unit of government. The president is clearly responsible for maintaining high levels of employment and price stability, to paraphrase the language of the Act. The CEA is his principal adviser in this task. The Treasury and Budget Bureau share that responsibility, but their official responsibilities are more specific and limiting. Thus, the CEA's substantive mission coincides with presidential political accountability. The president has a strong incentive to seek good economic advice on the theory that knowledge is to be preferred to ignorance. It does not follow that the president acts on the advice; there may be short run political reasons not to do so. But, the politics of choice is still enhanced by knowledge. The president should know and want to know both the economic and political costs and benefits of alternative choices.

However, it is not immediately obvious to presidents that their economic advisers can help them politically. Walter Heller reports that Theodore Sorensen and other key members of President Kennedy's White House staff were initially skeptical about whether economists could help the President. But he adds:

> Once we won Sorensen's respect and once he saw that what we would do for the President in economic matters would improve not only economic policy but would improve the President's chances of achieving his objectives, there was no further problem, and he had independent confidence in all three of us—in Tobin, Gordon and myself—and that had a great deal to do with our access to the President.[49]

Heller remembers acting to weave a web around Kennedy by writing memos that all the principal White House domestic policy advisers would read. This reaped benefits because the others came to accept economic analysis as crucial to the general success of the President.[50]

Eisenhower may have acted against the short-term electoral interests of the Republican party in his willingness to tolerate temporary recessions in favor of fiscal probity. But, he saw balanced budgets and a stable dollar as the chief basis for the popular approval of his domestic policies. He sought economic advice on how to best achieve his policies. John Kennedy initially resisted the Keynesian thesis that a tax cut would stimulate the economy. He told his economic advisers that the Republicans would hurt him politically if he did not advocate and produce a balanced budget.[51] However, when a lagging economy threatened to produce a "Kennedy recession" in the 1964 election year, the President changed his mind and put Heller to work on the tax cut.[52]

Johnson and Nixon both thought about economic policy in political terms and often rejected the ideas of their expert advisers for political reasons. But, even in these cases, presidents had to consider the economic consequences of political choice. Such consequences may hurt politically in the long run. Nixon's 1971 decision to establish wage and price controls was made for political reasons against the advice of his CEA chairman. But the President also believed, from advice, that controls had to be temporary. No president could have safely ignored such information.

President Ford was more like Eisenhower in seeing a congruence of ideology, politics and economics. He thought that a "sound" economy was the best politics and used economic advice as an instrumental tool.

It is clear that presidents look for the political consequences of economic choices and often disregard expert advice. But it is also true that presidents must consider the economic consequences of political choices lest their politics be short sighted. The belief that economists understand how the economy works and how to influence it binds them to presidents.

As we have seen, the president needs the Council for the analysis of questions of macro economic policy even when he disregards advice. The Council is his guide to understanding the world and the teaching function is well established. But, it was agreed that there are only five or six major presidential decisions a year in macro economic policy, covering taxes, deficits, budgets, coordination of fiscal and monetary decisions and international economic questions.

The Council and its staff spend most of their time on micro economic matters where their comparative advantage is weaker. We have already discussed the function they perform for the president in knocking down ill-advised proposals from the constituency based departments. When that analytic function collides with a strong presidential constituency, represented through a department, the Council has few, if any, resources to invoke. For example, both Democratic and Republican Councils have regularly opposed large increases in the minimum wage, often without success.

It has become an accepted role for the Council to take issue with ill-advised departmental proposals in the micro economic area. That responsibility has increased with the subsequent expansion of government policy in health, energy, environment and diverse welfare policy areas. But the CEA is at a disadvantage much of the time vis-a-vis the departments:

1. There are "many micros" and the decisions in these areas are so decentralized, often escaping presidential attention, that a CEA professional staff of fifteen cannot keep up.

2. Presidents may not even request "hard-nosed" micro economic analysis from the Council if they are going to oppose it for political reasons. It could be embarrassing to them if the fact of the advice becomes known.

3. OMB is more knowledgeable on many micro matters than the CEA through the close relationships of its program desks with the departments.

4. The CEA may succeed with micro analysis if it can link such work to important macro questions, for example by showing the inflationary impact of specific proposals. This can be done through aggregating particular issues into a general theme such as the need for deregulation. However, the political resources available to presidents for such broadly conceived innovations are weak. The costs are borne by specific groups, and the benefits to publics are diffuse and invisible.

Nevertheless the Council persists in the micro analytic role because it is useful to presidents and is something that economists know how to do well. There appears to be virtual agreement among these Democratic and Republican chairmen that economists of all persuasions examine micro issues with similar theoretical and ideological perspectives which favor markets and competition and oppose subsidies and restraints on free economic activity.

In summary, the CEA now appears to perform the following six functions for the president:

1. Preparation of the annual Economic Report of the president as a statement of presidential policy in relation to current economic problems.

2. Forecasting of economic conditions which may rely on formal economic models.

3. Continuous education of the president about what economic science can and cannot do in behalf of policy.

4. Assessment of departmental proposals in accordance with presidential policies.

5. Advocacy for presidential policy with Congress, interest groups and the public.

6. Defense of presidential policies from technical attacks.

How the CEA Should be Organized

There was virtual unanimity among these chairmen about how the CEA should be organized and how it should conduct itself in order to maximize its influences over policy. The following propositions appear to be logically consistent:

1. Stay small.

The Council has three members assisted by fifteen or so professionals. The working norms of this group are academic rather than bureaucratic. A high premium is placed upon close and intensive discussion of issues. It is feared that internal communication would be stifled by a large staff and that more thoughtful work comes from a nonbureaucratic, collegial atmosphere.[53]
By the same token, it is assumed that these eighteen people will be more knowledgeable and will work harder than their bureaucratic counterparts. Civil servants who are going to be around year after year are not inclined to work twelve- and eighteen-hour days. This is expected of CEA members and staff. Arthur Okun remembers asking a high ranking career official in the Bureau of the Budget to help him prepare a memo for President Kennedy by the following morning. The response was as follows:

No, no, if he's [the President] going to get a memo tomorrow morning, I'm not going to write it. I've been here a long time, and I've seen a lot of presidents ask for a lot of memos, and they don't read them when they get them....You guys come down here for fourteen months and you're full of vim and vigor and don't mind these eighty-hour weeks. I can't do that.[54]

2. The CEA should avoid administrative responsibilities.

The performance of administrative tasks would require increases in staff, create a bureaucratic atmosphere, embroil the
Council in disputes with the departments and increase the distance
between it and the president.[55]
Without exception, it was agreed that important functions
such as the administration of wage and price guidelines and controls and the settlement of specific wage disputes should be
performed by other bodies. There was no support for the view that
the CEA should generate its own data by assuming responsibility
for the Bureau of Labor Statistics in the Labor Department or the
Bureau of the Census in the Department of Commerce. Rather, the
Council should get its data from them.
Two other advantages for the CEA were cited by the chairmen
on this question. The CEA had the capacity to respond more quickly to presidential requests than the departments. White House
requests of departments for information on analysis of a problem
were captive of department chains of command, and answers were
slow in coming. The CEA, on the other hand, could go to the
proper source in a department and acquire the answers quickly.[56]
Second, the CEA was able to respond to such requests because it
limited its scope to those issues important to the president and
avoided administrative responsibilities.[57] There is a trade-off
between proximity to the president and the performance of continuing administrative obligations.

3. Academics make the best staff members, with some qualifications.

It is generally believed that university scholars are the
best economic policy analysts because of their intelligence and
knowledge. These are the kinds of people who will work on the
most challenging problems.[58] However, this view is qualified in
two ways.
First, not all academic economists work well in government.
Only those who can think and write clearly and quickly under tight
deadlines and who are willing to draw inferences for action from
incomplete knowledge need apply.[59]
Second, economic analysts from universities who come to
government temporarily suffer from a lack of knowledge about how
government works. This is particularly true of those who work on
micro economic questions. They must learn about the departments
and develop friendly ties with departmental staffs. The macro
policy analysts have less need of this.[60]
Because the time of service is short and the learning period
is long, several past chairmen suggested that it would be good for
the Council to have a small number of permanent staff members who
would be ongoing sources of institutional knowledge.[61] This injunction has been heeded only to a limited extent. Most of the
Council and staff members have been academics who have served for
limited periods.
A few have returned, graduating from staff to Council membership. One could conclude that the pressures favoring a small,

academic collegial body are stronger than the perceived need for institutional knowledge and memory.

4. Write clearly.

Economists have technical language that few of their clients in government understand. Therefore, the ability to write clear, brief memos, especially for the president, is crucial. Clarity is essential for the teaching function which several cited as the appropriate role for the CEA chairman in relation to the president. McCracken remembers choosing Herbert Stein for the Council because Stein wrote so well and he describes the Council as having a literary task.[62] Ackley and Okun recall learning how to write memos for the president from Heller. They also report that it is not simply a question of clarity; memos must be articulated according to themes that appeal to the president.[63]

Presidential Style and Policymaking Patterns

To the degree that advisory processes and decision making patterns are well institutionalized, the leadership styles of presidents are less important in the shaping of those patterns. The transcripts suggest that economic policymaking is well institutionalized. Regardless of variations in presidential styles of consultation and decision making, successive presidents appear to have received the best available economic analysis and advice. The relationships among presidential economic advisers have not varied that greatly across administrations, and the division of labor among them has fairly represented the different institutional stakes within the Executive branch, such as Treasury, the Budget Bureau, the CEA itself and the several departments. The transcripts also make quite clear that presidential beliefs, political insights and strategies, and modes of persuasion in regard to Congress, interest groups and the public are extremely important for economic policy. But, these factors are more important for the content of decisions and the implementation of leadership strategies than for the actual decision process.

The transcripts make very clear that the presidents described had quite different ways of seeking advice, thinking about economic questions and generally dealing with their advisers. But, these different styles do not appear to have affected the decisions made in any significant sense. Truman is described as seeking single recommendations with a minimum of debate. Eisenhower, Kennedy and Ford are characterized as enjoying the analysis of alternatives and as being particularly curious about modes of economic reasoning. Johnson is described as seeking to learn only enough about his economic choices in order to proceed to the more important and interesting political questions of desirability and feasibility. Nixon was bored with economic questions and chose to work through single intermediaries, John Connally and George Shultz. Carter was frustrated by macro economic analysis because it seemed so inconclusive but very much liked to address micro questions because they were clear, usually carried implications for action and often had moral content. However, one searches the transcripts for any indications that these different styles enhanced or prevented the individuals in question from receiving the best advice available.

Comparison of Advisory Systems

The process of economic policymaking appears to be more highly institutionalized than those for either national security or domestic policy. There also appears to be less internal conflict within the economic policy system than within the other two systems. The literature on national security policymaking is filled with descriptions of the variations among presidents of the influence of the presidential assistant for national security policy and his staff in relation to the secretaries of State and Defense and their staffs. This issue has become highly controversial, not only in academic debate, but in the practice of government itself. There does not seem to be a similar kind of tension between the chairman of the CEA and the secretary of the Treasury. However, something of that conflict appears in the relationships between the CEA and the constituency-oriented departments such as Labor, Commerce and Agriculture. How does one account for these differences and similarities? In the first place, the macro economic policymaking system has produced a clear division of labor among the main participants. The Secretary of the Treasury is clearly the public spokesman because he must go to Congress. The CEA does not attempt to assume administrative responsibilities. The Office of Management and Budget has demarcated duties that are quite different from either those of Treasury or the CEA. Controversies within the national security system have arisen when presidents have given operational responsibilities to the assistant for national security and NSC staff members. This has produced the confusion of two state departments--one in the White House and one in Foggy Bottom. In addition, the NSC assistant and his staff do not apply a single discipline to the analysis of problems, as is the case with economics, but range broadly across a large number of topics as do State Department officials. In short, the analytic methods and responsibilities of both sets of actors in foreign policy lead to clear jurisdictional conflicts.

The economists of the CEA, on the other hand, do not claim the institutional knowledge available to Treasury mandarins about national banks and the banking system, international organizations and financial institutions. The division of labor is enhanced by the fact that the CEA is staffed by professional economists. However, these propositions do not seem to hold in the relationships between CEA and the constituency departments, but the tension there is not between the CEA alone and those departments. It is between the Troika institutions and the departments, and it is a matter of presidential versus departmental perspective. This conflict cuts across all areas of government and encompasses both economic and foreign policymaking. However, it is not present, at least to the same degree, in macro economic policymaking. In that instance, the main advisers work from a presidential perspective.

The White House domestic policy staffs have taken various forms in different administrations, but there has been a gradual process of institutionalization under an assistant to the president for domestic policy. There is considerable overlap between social policies, dealing with education, health and welfare, and micro economic issues such as regulation, environmental policy and energy policy and, therefore, between domestic policy staffs and the CEA. The central difference between the two staffs is that presidents have authorized their assistants for domestic policy to coordinate and, at times, arbitrate among departments in preparation of presidential policy proposals. This has been an organizational necessity since cabinet departments are not good at leading or coordinating each other. The decision of how much authority to delegate to such assistants varies from president to president. However, that issue is not applicable to the CEA which has avoided administrative and coordinating responsibilities. The assistant for domestic policy is by virtue of the leadership role entrusted to him a political, as well as a substantive, adviser to the president. Again, this is less true of the chairman of the CEA. Tensions between the assistant for domestic policy and the departments are, therefore, likely to be even greater than between the CEA and the departments because the Council plays primarily an analytic and, therefore, more limited role.

These comparisons are tentative and somewhat speculative, but they suggest fruitful avenues of inquiry.

II. The Economic Context

Before we analyze the advice given to presidents by the CEA, it is important that the economic context for which that advice was being formulated is understood. Figures 1-3 help to do that. They give a visual picture of the historical pathway of gross national product corrected for inflation and the rate of unemployment. These are the three main variables which it is the job of macro policymakers to control. All three, of course, can take on a wide range of values. The target at which policymakers generally are aiming is the "full employment or capacity level of GNP." This is a hypothetical construct which is defined as the amount that the economy could produce if it were operating at full employment. Full employment, in turn, means that the labor market is in full equilibrium. This does not mean that everyone has a job; rather, it means that any unemployment that exists is voluntary or frictional.

In a large and complex labor market, it is inevitable that a certain number of people will be between jobs. These people are called frictionally unemployed by economists. This sort of unemployment is voluntary and consistent with the notion of full employment. Another definition of full employment is the unployment rate at which the inflation rate is stable. We show the hypothetical estimates of full employment and of full employment output in the figures. As the reader can see, there has been a significant increase in the estimate of the full employment/unemployment rate from around 4 percent in the early 1970s to 5.5 percent by 1980. The reason for the increase is the rise in the percentage of teenagers and women in the labor force. Since each of these groups has a higher unemployment rate than adult men, the average unemployment rate of the entire labor force has increased.

Comparing the actual and the full employment output level, we can see that the U.S. economy has been through a number of cycles in the postwar period, some mild, others severe. The period between 1945 and 1950 was a return of the economy to a peacetime structure after the abnormally high levels of output during World War II. After an initial burst of postwar inflation, prices were brought under control and the unemployment rate rose from 2 percent in 1945 to almost 6 percent in 1949. The Korean War (1950-53) returned the economy temporarily to low unemployment rates and supernormal levels of output. Inflation was controlled by a relatively successful system of wage and price controls.

Subsequently during the Eisenhower and Kennedy periods, the economy went through a long stabilization phase in which the rate of growth of output was relatively slow and the level of unemployment was relatively high. There were short booms during the period (1955-56, 1958), but they were not long enough to bring the economy back to the full employment level. This was a period when the predominant concern among macro economic policymakers was controlling inflation, particularly in the period after 1956. During those years, monetary and fiscal policy were both contractionary. The full employment surplus, a measure of the thrust of fiscal policy, was positive all the way from 1954 through 1962, except for two quarters during the recession of 1958. Between the end of 1954 and 1960, the nominal money supply increased at an average rate of 3.1 percent per year, which meant that the real money supply was growing at less that 1 percent per year, not enough to provide for very much real growth in the economy. The result of this contractionary mix of policies was a six-year period of slow growth (1956-61), high unemployment and idle capacity in which the inflation rate was brought down to around 1 percent per year.

The second cycle was triggered by the passage of a large tax cut in 1964. This tax cut, advocated by Walter Heller and pushed through Congress by President Johnson, was probably the most successful macro policy ever proposed by the CEA. Based on Keynesian principles, it aimed at reducing what was called the fiscal drag which had kept the economy from reaching its full potential during most of the Eisenhower period.

Helped by supportive monetary policy, the economy moved toward full employment by 1965. At just that moment, the United States became enmeshed in a costly war in Vietnam. But we no longer had the men or machines to supply the extra output required by that conflict. For reasons that continue to be debated by historians, there was no effective reduction in demand until about 1968 when a tax surcharge went into effect and monetary policy finally became more restrictive. The result was a four-year period (1965-68) during which demand grew far faster than the capacity of the economy (except for a short period of monetary restraint in 1966). The inevitable result was a demand-pull inflationary boom as output rose above the full employment level, unemployment dropped to 3.2 percent, and inflation accelerated.

22

Figure 1

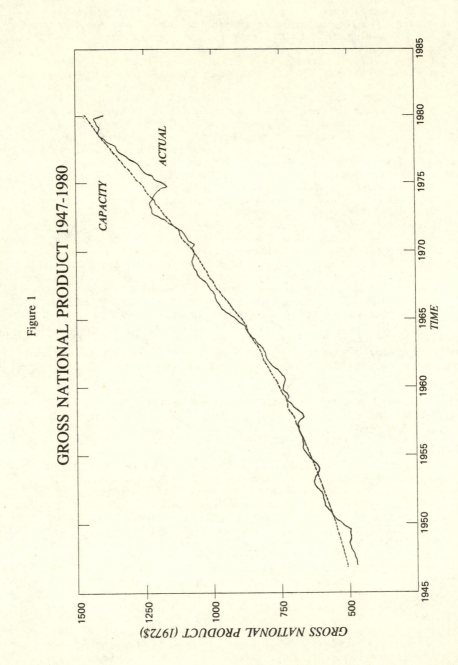

GROSS NATIONAL PRODUCT 1947-1980

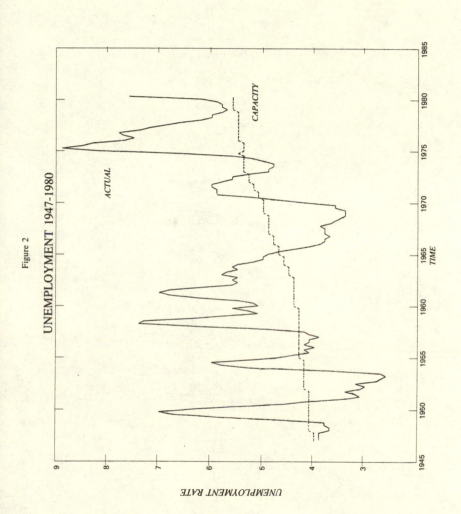

Figure 2

UNEMPLOYMENT 1947-1980

ACTUAL

CAPACITY

UNEMPLOYMENT RATE

TIME

24

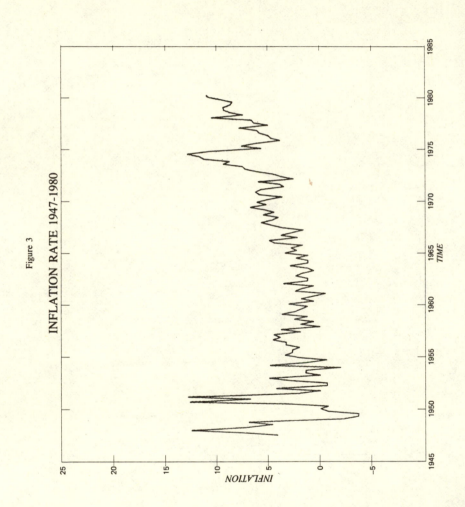

Figure 3

INFLATION RATE 1947-1980

When the government belatedly made an attempt to stabilize the economy by raising the tax rate and limiting the growth of money in 1968 and beyond, the economy almost immediately went into a recession. Unemployment rapidly rose from 3.4 percent in 1968 to 6 percent in 1971. But prices continued to rise, presumably as a result of the lagged adjustment of worker expectations.

Frustrated by the slow gains being made against inflation and worried about the 1972 election, President Nixon cut short the stabilization phase in August, 1971 by imposing the first peace-time wage and price controls in our history. At the same time, both monetary and fiscal policies became far more expansionary, and the economy moved rapidly back to full employment by the end of 1972.

At just this time, two momentous events hit the economy simultaneously: President Nixon lifted wage and price controls and the world experienced a crop failure. During the first quarter of 1973, food prices rose by almost one-fourth, and then nine months later, OPEC embargoed its oil and then quadrupled the price. The effect on the economy of such supply shocks depends critically upon what happens to demand. As it happened in this case, the United States chose not to validate the supply-side price increases. Demand management was neutral to contractionary. The fight was led by the Fed. For each of the three years, starting in 1973, the money supply fell in real terms, and even by the end of 1978, M/P had not regained the value it had reached six years earlier. This contractionary monetary policy was reinforced by fiscal policy in the key years of 1973 and 1974.

The result of contraction in the face of a supply shock was a severe, but short, recession accompanied by accelerating inflation as workers demanded compensation for rising food and energy costs. The recession, which occurred under Greenspan, did not fully eliminate inflation, but it did succeed in limiting the inflation-ary damage from the oil price hike. Essentially the oil price hike led to permanently higher prices, but the economy returned to its original rate of inflation.

The only way to cut inflation further would have been an even more prolonged period of recession to force domestic factors of production to accept lower real wages and profits. But the politi-cal will to endure such a recession had evaporated. Indeed, the severe recession and uncertain recovery during his presidency probably cost Gerald Ford the election in 1976. Jimmy Carter was elected, at least implicitly, with a promise not to fight infla-tion any further with recession. As a result, after his election, fiscal policy became somewhat more expansionary, and the economy returned slowly to full employment, restrained by a still contrac-tionary Fed under Arthur Burns.

Fighting Inflation and Recession

We turn now to the actual policies advocated by the CEA and the administrations they served as revealed in our interviews. We will confine this discussion to the two macro problems of infla-tion and recession because these are the subjects of most of the discussion in the transcripts.

Except for a short period in the early 1960s, all the chairmen worked in an environment in which inflation was at least as great a concern as recession. As a result, recession remedies were advanced cautiously and often were not accepted by other advisers to the president. It was generally the case that the CEA, true to its charter, was the most expansionist of the four principal macro policymaking agencies.

Under Eisenhower the economy went through three recessions and was below the full employment level for most of the period he was in office. The gap was particularly large during his second term. There is no doubt that his first priority was to fight inflation and preserve the integrity of the dollar. That meant a willingness to tolerate levels of unemployment that would not have been acceptable to most Democratic administrations. However, the record suggests that, if anything, Truman was more conservative than Eisenhower in this regard. In response to the onset of recession in 1949, Truman vetoed a Republican-sponsored reduction in taxes in 1948 and in mid-1949 expressed opposition to any tax reduction despite a recession as deep as that of 1954. Despite Keyserling, the administration did nothing, and it was automatic stabilizers that brought the economy out of the recession on its own prior to the Korean War.

To say that the Eisenhower administration was primarily worried about inflation does not mean that no action would have been taken in the face of a really severe recession. Consider how the administration reacted to the 1954 recession. By mid-1953 Arthur Burns was predicting a recession. Eisenhower watched the situation closely and ordered an acceleration of spending of already approved projects.[64] This may appear to be a less than vigorous response to the downturn. However, one should remember that a major tax bill reducing Korean War taxes took effect on January 1, 1954, and that monetary policy had become easy during the summer of the previous year. Under these circumstances, it is easier to understand Burns' caution in 1954 in backing a more expansionary policy despite the public outcry that something be done. Burns was convinced that the downturn was going to be fairly mild and self-correcting. He was right. By April 1954, he was reporting signs that the bottom had been reached and that the upturn had begun. Eisenhower and Burns stood ready to take action against a major downturn, but they did not think that active fine-tuning to counteract small cycles in the private sector was either wise or necessary.

The performance of the CEA in the downturns of 1958 and 1960 has been more controversial. By mid-1957 the economy was clearly in a recession. Saulnier urged that immediate steps be taken, but the Federal Reserve maintained a restrictive credit policy. There had been an outbreak of inflation between 1955 and 1957 and a weakening of the dollar which strengthened the hands of Humphrey and Martin.[65] Although observers at the time claimed that Saulnier was in disagreement with George Humphrey's resistance to intervention through countercyclical fiscal actions, Saulnier himself denies this interpretation. He was never an advocate of fine-tuning, because he did not think that our knowledge or our degree of control was good enough to instantaneously correct downturns in spending in the private sector.[66] As Stein has noted, the 1958 CEA Report suggests no active intention to intervene nor even any contingency plans in case the recession got worse.[67]

Looking back on his record, Saulnier does not strongly regret the failure to respond with countercyclical policy. When asked specifically whether he had tried to get the Federal Reserve to adopt a more expansionary policy in the 1959-60 period, he replied: "These were not sharp differences of view. It was a shade of view, between ourselves and the Fed. Our position...more inclined [than Martin's] to an easing of...[policy]. But it was not as strong a difference...."[68]

What action there was in both 1958 and 1960 was neither tax reduction nor public works, but rather a lengthening of unemployment benefits, more liberal mortgage insurance and a speed-up of already approved government spending programs.

It is clear from the transcript that Saulnier's primary concerns were inflation and the deteriorating position of the dollar. When he took over in 1956, inflation was running 3 to 3-1/2 percent per year and the trade surplus was declining. However, that does not mean that Saulnier favored fighting inflation with unemployment. No one thought exactly in those terms.[69] No one deliberately engineered a recession to keep inflation down. But the concern with inflation did mean that there was a reluctance to run government deficits or to increase anti-recessionary spending. Perhaps more important, the administration was quick to reverse whatever expansion it had permitted with the first sign of improvement in the economy.[70]

If there was a policy error during this period, it was not the failure to act more decisively in either the 1958 or 1960 recession. After all, the Federal Reserve turned expansionary by late 1957, and the economy bottomed out shortly thereafter. Rather it was the rush to renewed contraction in 1959-60. Eisenhower and Humphrey pushed hard for an end to government deficits. By mid-1959 discretionary anti-recession actions were sharply reversed. The Full Employment Surplus rose by $15 billion in 1960, and monetary policy resumed its contractionary stance. The result was that the economy never fully recovered from the 1958 recession and slipped quickly back into recession by 1960. Burns, outside the government in 1960, warned of another recession and called for expansionary policy. But both Anderson, the new Secretary of the Treasury, and Saulnier refused to go along.[71]

This is perhaps the only time in the entire postwar period when the CEA chairman failed to be a vigorous advocate of a full employment policy. Yet looked at from Saulnier's point of view, the inaction can perhaps be justified. First, he really was concerned with inflation. Second, he was forced to contend with an extremely conservative Federal Reserve. The Federal Reserve felt that it had made a serious error in overexpanding after the 1954 recession and was determined not to repeat the mistake. Hence, it very quickly reversed its expansionary policy and was contractionary by mid-1958. That left Saulnier the unpalatable choices of either doing nothing or proposing deficit spending despite the Federal Reserve. Everyone knew that this would drive up interest rates and choke off private investment. As Saulnier himself has said, "It would have been irresponsible to have undertaken to offset the restraining effect of tight money by cutting taxes."[72]

Secondly, of course, one should remember that the government budget was still in deficit. The concept of the full employment surplus was not then completely understood or accepted and one can imagine that the Secretary of the Treasury would not have been amenable to an increase in the actual deficit just because the hypothetical surplus was increasing.

Finally, there was a good deal of uncertainty about the facts themselves. The economic picture, according to Saulnier, was confused because of inventory adjustments after the big 1959 steel strike. It was not obvious at the time whether the economy would pull out of this adjustment on the upside or the downside, hence whether special action was needed.[73]

The next two recessions of 1970-72 and 1975-76 are more properly part of the story of the struggle against inflation and will be discussed in that light. Both were intentionally caused by deliberate downward countercyclical policy. In all the previous recessions we have discussed, the slump occurred either as an unwanted side effect of balancing the government budget or because of fiscal drag.

All the recession cures discussed so far were countercyclical remedies, proposed because the economy was thought to be temporarily below full employment. The tax cut of 1964 was something else, a remedy for a structural defect in the United States economy.

Because of our progressive tax system, economic growth tended to increase tax revenues faster than government expenditure was growing with the result that over time a fiscal drag (in the form of rising full employment budget surpluses) would tend to keep the economy below full employment. The solution proposed by Walter Heller was a permanent cut in the tax rate both for individuals and corporations.

When the tax cut was passed in 1964, it more than lived up to Heller's promises. The economy rapidly went to full employment, almost completely silencing the talk about structural unemployment problems which had been so prominent in the 1950s. Furthermore, because it was aided by permissive monetary policy, the tax cut produced a growth rate in income so great that tax revenues actually went up rather than down. The success of the tax cut was such that the reputation of the CEA and of macro economics in general was propelled to its highest levels ever.

The Struggle Against Inflation

A far less cheerful story is the struggle against inflation. After 1965, as the United States became more deeply involved in the Vietnam War, the old inflation problem returned to center stage. Unlike the two earlier outbreaks of inflation during the Korean War and the capital goods boom of 1955-57, policymakers, from 1965 to 1980, were unable to ride the economy of rising prices. Despite three recessions and ten years of almost constant slack, the rising rate of inflation was a chronic problem. Some part of that inflation was due to external shocks such as the rise in the price of oil. But a large part appears to have been due to economic mismanagement, confusion and delay. Let us look behind the scenes as the perceptions of the chairmen who were involved in this long and frustrating battle.

The economy by 1965 was already at or close to full employment. This was not a time when a major new government spending program could be introduced without either a contraction in some other area or an increase in taxes. President Johnson was unwilling to cut his Great Society programs to pay for the war. Thus while defense expenditures were rising by 47 percent in the period 1965-68, federal transfer payments were rising by a not much smaller 51 percent. By 1965 Ackley and Heller were pushing hard for a surtax of some sort. Johnson was unreceptive because he did not think that he could sell a tax politically in Congress. In December 1965, the Federal Reserve, which didn't have to worry about Wilbur Mills, Chairman of the House Ways and Means Committee, and the Congress, moved to a sharply more contractionary monetary policy. The discount rate was raised and credit was contracted, much to Johnson's anger and dismay. Interestingly, the Council was against the Federal Reserve's move. The reason, according to Ackley, was that the entire economic team was trying to orchestrate a campaign to push through a surtax, and they felt that the Federal Reserve had jumped the gun.[74] Johnson could have used the threat of tighter money to help him sell the surtax. In any case, the restrictive monetary policy went on for the first half of 1966 and was followed six months later by a clear softening in the economy. As it turned out, this mini-downturn enormously complicated the job of policymakers. It fooled both them and the public about the strength of inflationary pressures in the economy and the need for further restraint.[75]

In January 1967, the government formally asked for a surtax. However, because the economy was in the midst of the mini-recession, no one, not even the CEA, wanted the tax implemented immediately. The idea was to send the tax proposal to Congress but not to ask for action until the economy showed signs of heating up again.[76] Meanwhile, in what we can now see was a major policy error, the Federal Reserve changed from contraction to expansion. The money supply which had only been allowed to grow at 2.2 percent in 1966, grew by 6.6 percent in 1967 and a further 7.2 percent in 1968. Despite the political difficulties of raising taxes or cutting expenditures, there was apparently little attempt to substitute monetary for fiscal policy. An outsider would imagine that the principals might have agreed that if demand could not be dampened through the surtax, then they should fall back on monetary policy. However, judging from Ackley's comments, there were no specific joint plans or close cooperation. Ackley said:

> There had never been any effort to coordinate formally either analysis or policy recommendations between the Fed and the Troika. There were informal discussions,

but there was no joint staff work and there was never a
piece of paper signed "We recommend" by the Quadriad.[77]

Also the slowdown in 1967 was confusing. It was not obvious
at the time that underlying demand was so strong. The macro
models predicted that the surtax would slow down the economy far
more than it actually did. As Okun said "If anything, we were
pushing them [the Federal Reserve] harder for more easing, and we
were off. (Italics added)."[78]

In terms of the Phillips curve, they thought that higher
unemployment was the necessary medicine required to lower wage
demands and thus keep price increases to an acceptable level. In
the late 1960s, it was thought that simply eliminating excess
demand would be sufficient for this task. Later, with the discovery of the importance of inflationary expectations in worker wage
demands, economists came to accept the necessity of a period of
higher than normal unemployment in order to bring inflationary
expectations and wage demands to a permanently lower level. In
either case, eliminating inflation means consciously accepting and
even taking measures to bring about a recession. To see perceptions about the role of recession in stopping inflation, we asked
each chairman whether he had opted for recession in order to
control inflation. Here is what they said:

Burns:

Q: Did you ever think in terms of engineering a recession in
order to combat inflation?
A: I should say not.[79]

Saulnier:

Q: ...did you discuss those recessions (1958 and 1960) as
necessary in terms of controlling inflation or slowing it down?
A: Never. The idea that a recession was ever engineered for
the purpose of helping to control inflation is, I think, a really
scandalous charge against the administration.[80]

Ackley:

Q: I gather that your aim, to put it in Phillips curve terms,
was not to generate a recession in order to stop inflation. It
was simply to cool off the boom, to go back to a sustainable level
of output?
A: Yes, we certainly had no desire to create a recession
...at no point were we willing to contemplate the possibility of
risking a recession.[81]

Okun:

Q: It was never your intention to generate a more significant recession?

A: Sure wasn't our game plan. I don't think that it was the
McCracken-Kennedy game plan in 1969. Gradualism was still the
name of the game....I think that the perception was still, "Yes,
we want unemployment to go back from 3.6 percent to 4.1 percent
but 2 percent growth for a couple of quarters is the way to do
that."[82]

McCracken: (Discussing his statement before the Joint Economic
            Committee in 1969)

The thrust of [the statement] was that...we would have
to move steadily in a restrictive direction....On the
other hand we wanted to avoid locking the brakes and
producing a serious decline in business activity...to
pursue demand management policies that would provide for
an essentially lateral movement in the nominal volume of
economic activity....

Q: How long did you think that the slowdown would take?
A: At that time I think we would have visualized it beginning around the middle part of the year...but upturn again by
somewhere around...the middle of the next year.[83]

Stein: (Discussing his goals as a policy of contraction began
        again early in 1973)

Q: Do you think in retrospect that [the restrictive monetary
and fiscal policies in 1973] may have been excessively harsh...?
A: These questions are very hard to answer. Of course, we
did not at all foresee that the unemployment rate was going to
rise to 9 percent under this policy....Nobody then foresaw the
unemployment rate rising above 6 percent....If we had known that
it was going to go to 9 percent perhaps we would have retreated,
but I'm not sure whether that would have been the wise thing to
do.[84]

Greenspan:

Q: Could you give us an idea of how you were going to fight
this inflation? Were you going to be gradualist versus shock
treatment? Were you aiming at a soft landing on a 4 percent
unemployment rate?
A: It was a soft landing scenario. Our general view was
that you have to defuse the inflationary pressures very gradually....It was considered that 7-1/2 percent would be a large
increase in unemployment. You wouldn't be able to continue....The
choice wasn't a real choice especially with our type of system, so
we concluded that the only way to do it was to support a marginally lower rate of monetary growth....It was always a gradualist
approach.[85]

Despite the commitment to gradualism by all the chairmen,
there is a clear difference of viewpoint between Stein, Greenspan
and the earlier chairmen. For Ackley, Okun and McCracken stabili-

zation meant eliminating excess demand, nothing more. But by 1973, a rate of inflation of 5 to 6 percent had become embedded in the wage demands of the labor force. The economy had moved to a higher Phillips curve. Both Stein and Greenspan thought that a period of much lower growth, involving rates of unemployment of at least 6 percent (Stein) and 7-1/2 percent (Greenspan), would be necessary. When they spoke of gradualism, they meant moving out to these rates of unemployment gradually rather than in a sharp recession. In Greenspan's case, it seems clear that the 7-1/2 percent rate was a ceiling imposed by essentially political considerations. That is what he meant by his comment that one does not have any other choice in our system but gradualism. In other words, Greenspan was willing to accept the 7-1/2 percent unemployment ceiling as the price to be paid for continuing a policy of slack in the economy for a longer period of time.

Each chairman had an unemployment ceiling which he did not want to exceed. He tried to hit the ceiling by a limited contractionary policy. The ceilings were gradually raised as the inflation rate worsened. However, in no case were the tools of monetary and fiscal policy delicate enough to manage the "soft landing" successfully. The economy overshot in every case, going into a deeper recession than desired. That is why each chairman pushed for expansion even though each saw himself as fighting inflation. For example, by the latter part of 1969, Paul McCracken became concerned at the restrictiveness of monetary policy and wrote a memo to the President warning of the danger of an overkill or a deep recession due to the combination of tight money and the surtax.[86] Fiscal policy remained restrictive throughout 1970 but monetary policy eased. By early 1971 Stein and McCracken were pushing hard for an easier fiscal policy. They thought that there had already been sufficient recession to control the inflation and planned a way to get back up to full employment.[87] In other words, the two years' recession which bottomed in late 1970 with an unemployment rate of 6 percent was seen as enough time spent to the right of the long run Phillips curve.

The same phenomenon occurred in the 1974-75 recession. In early 1975 Greenspan supported a tax cut to stimulate the economy, even though others in the administration urged Ford to veto the bill put together by Congress. In Greenspan's case, the transcript suggests that his reasoning was essentially pragmatic. He thought the pressure for an even more expansionary policy would have been overwhelming if the administration was not seen doing something about the unemployment rate which was then rising to 9 percent in the worst recession since the 1930s.[88]

Differences Between Democrats and Republicans

It has often been said that the Democrats fight unemployment and the Republicans fight inflation. This generalization is incorrect, except in one special sense. The record really suggests that each administration fights the problem that it confronts. As it happened, the Nixon and Ford administrations confronted a serious inflation, while Kennedy and Johnson faced high rates of unemployment and low rates of inflation. It seems exceedingly likely that McCracken would have pushed for expansion had he been in Heller's place, and we know that Okun and Ackley pushed hard for contraction during the last three years of the Johnson administration. Under Eisenhower the situation is less clear since inflation and high rates of unemployment occurred together. In that case, the Republicans did choose to make inflation the number one problem. A Democratic administration might have moved earlier against unemployment. However, when Kennedy took over, he did nothing of the sort for well over two years.

What is different is the method of fighting inflation and unemployment under Democrats as opposed to Republicans. Except for Truman, the Democrats tried too hard to fine-tune remedies for inflation. Understandably they wanted the smallest possible recession. As a result, they opted for the least restraint that their models told them would slow down the economy. Thus, we find the Johnson economists advocating a surtax coupled with a more expansionary monetary policy. They were sure the tax would be enough to reduce excess demand and get back to the 4 percent unemployment rate; and they did not want a contractionary policy to overshoot their target. Unfortunately, they over-estimated the controllability of the economy, and the accuracy of their econometric models. The same thing happened again in 1979. The effect has been some very costly delays in eliminating inflationary pressures.

The Republicans, on the other hand, because they seem to abhor inflation more and unemployment somewhat less, tended to adopt stabilization strategies which, if anything, erred on the side of overkill. Under all three Republican administrations, they tended to hit the economy hard with restraint and then bring the patient back to life with stimulus if that was needed, as it always was.

A real difference between Republican and Democratic economics stems from a difference of opinion about the responsiveness of prices to demand: in technical terms, the shape of the aggregate supply curve. Economists in Democratic regimes have tended to believe that the supply curve is flat, particularly at less than full employment. This means that they have not been enthusiastic about using recession to cure inflation, and they have not been as fearful as Republicans of the inflationary potential of demand stimulus. This is why they tend to be reluctant to push the economy into recession and quick to cut taxes or use expansionary monetary policy at the first sign of recession. They see recession as pure waste. It causes a fall in output with little impact on prices if the supply curve is flat.

Republicans, by contrast, see the supply curve as relatively steep. They think that variations in aggregate demand have a big impact on prices, and less of an impact on the level of employment and output. Perhaps this is why they have been less afraid of contraction than the Democrats. They grant that contractions cause recession, but they think that the process will quite rapidly reduce the inflation rate. Thus, the cost in lost output is counterbalanced by significant gains in lower inflation. The same contrast extends to the willingness to expand the economy to get out of recession. If the supply curve is upward sloping, any

expansion can be inflationary, even one from low levels of output.
Hence, Republican administrations have typically been quite cautious in engaging in such expansion. As Burns put it:

> Take, for example, the notion...rising when you reach,
> or almost reach, full employment. Historically, of
> course, the price level began rising around the trough
> of the business cycle, not the peak....Keynes came along
> in 1936 and taught economists to believe...that the
> price level begins rising only when full employment is
> reached. That sort of nonsense goes a good distance in
> explaining why we became so complacent about infla-
> tion.[89]

Policy Errors and Model Failures

One of the reasons for talking to policymaking principals is
to find out why certain decisions were made which subsequently
appear to have been mistakes. What comes across from these conversations is first, the inflexibility of the fiscal machinery of
the government and second, the importance of forecasting errors.
Over the last thirty years, economists have devoted a good deal of
money and time to the building of macro economic models. These
models were expected to give policymakers the ability to fine-tune
the economy, making small adjustments in taxes, spending or monetary policy to keep the economy on the path of non-inflationary
full employment. These hopes have not been realized. In several
cases, the models failed to predict the strength of private sector
demand which lulled policymakers into the belief that contractionary measures were sufficient to control inflation. In other
cases, the models failed to forecast the severity of recession.
One of the most widely noted errors in macro policymaking in
the United States was the failure to take steps to contract aggregate demand under President Johnson. This failure has generally
been ascribed to politics. The story goes that Johnson knew a
surtax would not sell politically. He refused to sacrifice his
Great Society programs in a deal with Wilbur Mills to get a surtax. Granted the political difficulties and also some misinforma-
tion on the extent of the military buildup, there are still some
awkward questions to be answered by policymakers.
Why did they not fight harder for the surtax, and why did
they allow monetary policy, after the 1966 credit crunch, to
become so easy that it offset whatever fiscal restraint there was?
The answer appears to be that the economists were misled by the
mini-recession of 1967 into believing that it would be easy to
slow down both aggregate demand and inflation. Okun said:

> The economy did have this period in which it was really
> flat [1967]. People were talking about recession and,
> as it turned out, that was a sort of lovely cooling off
> period. In fact, I think that misled us a lot later,
> because it really looked as though a little tap on the
> brake brought the inflation rate interest rates down.[90]

and then, speaking of the effect of the surtax:

> I expected much more cooling off from the taxes than did
> take place. The debate, in retrospect, is whether the
> patient had a higher fever than we realized, or whether
> the aspirin did less good than we'd expected. I would
> still say that the surcharge made a real dent in aggre-
> gate demand and consumer demand. But basically the
> overall economy was a lot stronger and by this time
> private demand really seemed to have a lot of momentum
> and just kept forging ahead.[91]

In other words, the failure to react more strongly against
rising demand was partly a failure of forecasting. The economists
did not know how rapidly the economy was moving out of the 1967
lull and they clearly underestimated the impact of expansionary
monetary policy and the reinstatement of the investment tax credit
in March, 1967. They thought the chief danger was recession, not
inflation.[92] In retrospect the effort to fine-tune the slowdown
caused a very costly delay in the coming of recession.

Another error of overexpansion occurred during 1971-73. Expansionary policy to bring the economy out of its engineered
recession was applied in 1971-72, along with wage and price controls. In retrospect it now appears that the total stimulus was
excessive. The economy moved rapidly toward full employment and
even excess demand by the spring of 1973 just at the point when
the administration moved to a voluntary wage-price system. When
asked why such a rapid expansion had been permitted, Stein replied:

> Although there is a lot of complaint now that the policy
> in this period was too expansionist--and I think it
> was--the criticism then was that we were stepping on the
> brakes too soon...we were accused of slowing down the
> economy before we were up to full employment.[93]

Then in response to a question on the very expansionary
monetary policy pursued in 1972 by the Federal Reserve, Stein
replied:

> My explanation of it all is that we all made the same
> mistake. We all thought, `We're a long way from full
> employment, we still have a lot of room for expanding
> the economy, and the inflation rate is low.` We misin-
> terpreted. Before we went into the controls, we argued
> many times that one of the great dangers of the controls
> was that they tempt you to an expansionist fiscal mone-
> tary policy. That had been the universal history of
> controls. We fell into that trap again even though we
> said we never would.[94]

Once again the buoyancy in the economy and its sensitivity to
monetary policy were underestimated. Arthur Burns confirmed the
difficulties. In 1972 the Federal Reserve was criticized for

being too restrictive, not too expansionary. In addition, the data the Fed had to work with were both late and misleading about actual conditions in the economy.

It is quite clear that an underestimation of the strength of private demand occurred in 1978-80. The forecasters and the model builders were predicting recession for both 1978 and 1979, but the recession did not arrive until the beginning of 1980 because of a significant shift in consumer behavior. Either because of inflationary expectations or because the value of housing was rising (enabling consumers to afford more), people lowered saving and raised consumption thus forestalling the contractionary effects of higher taxes. The point is that the administration, misled by the belief that a recession was coming, did not push for more contraction. In its desire to fine-tune its response and not overkill, it failed to administer enough contractionary medicine. As in 1968, the effect was a two-year delay in contractionary recession.

A contractionary error was the cause of the very deep recession of 1975. With the oil embargo and crop failures of 1973, prices exploded upward in 1974. Everyone agreed restraint was needed. No one, however, expected anything like the decline that actually occurred. When Ford came into office, Stein says:

> But nobody then foresaw the unemployment rate rising above 6 percent....If we had known it was going to go to 9 percent, perhaps we would have retreated....[95]

Greenspan, coming to Washington to assume the chairmanship, said:

> The last forecast I made from my model before I left for Washington was for a mild recession in 1975. And I thought I was a pessimist.[96]

When asked why there were such forecasting errors, Greenspan answered:

> In all instances the models were wrong. You cannot construct what happened in the next year [1975] or the next six months from the structure of any model then extant. All of our models now have been rejiggered to factor in that sequence and the effect has been to increase very dramatically the effect of monetary policy in the models....
> ...As it turned out, there was a massive shutdown of the capital investment process. All of a sudden capital investment collapsed and that triggered the inventory collapse...what was missing in all of the models was the ability to see what risk premiums could do to capital investment.[97]

All these examples illustrate the extreme difficulty of forecasting with sufficient accuracy to enable the CEA or anyone else to fine-tune the economy. The difficulty seems to lie with the macro models. These models are based on and, therefore, reflect previous experience. When there is a basic change in structure,

or when a variable changes which never has before, the models
cannot adjust. Their forecasts will be wrong.

In 1967-68 inflation expectations were becoming an important
factor on the supply side for the first time. Since there had
never been an inflation which had lasted long enough to activate
this variable before, the models incorrectly measured its effect
as insignificant (i.e., they showed the short run Phillips curve
as shifting less than it actually did). In the Carter presidency,
the models failed to forecast the positive effect of rising housing prices on consumer expenditures because that had never happened before. And throughout, there seems to have been too low an
estimate of the effect of monetary policy. Perhaps from Keynesian
bias, policymakers tended to assign the larger impact to fiscal
policy, the smaller to monetary policy. Because the estimated
models are based on past experience, it has been difficult to get
an accurate measure of the effects of the two policies separately
simply because there have not been many observations of the two
moving in opposite directions in the postwar period. Hence policymakers underestimated the effect of tight money in the 1950s, of
easy money in 1967 and 1968, and of tight money in 1974.

Finally, of course, the models were unprepared for the extent
of downward inflexibility of wage and price inflation in the face
of unemployment and slack markets. As Okun has said, that is
probably the biggest forecasting error of the period, and the one
which has left economists with the greatest perplexity both about
the inflationary process and about the appropriate cure for inflation.

Perhaps George Jaszi was being only slightly too pessimistic
when he said:

> I doubt that there has been any genuine progress at all
> in our ability to foresee essential developments in the
> economy. Our record has always been poor and has re-
> mained so. Nor do I see hope for improvement in fore-
> casting performance. This conclusion is based in a
> general way on the great complexity of the economic
> system, on the possibility of indeterminacy, or the
> existence of old-fashioned free will. On the contrary,
> I expect a deterioration. In essense, forecasting is
> the tracing of the effects of exogenous factors on the
> basis of the extrapolation of past relationships. In
> the conditions of rapid change we are likely to face on
> an increasing scale, it will be even more difficult to
> foresee the exogenous factors, and the past relation-
> ships on which we rely to tracing their consequences
> will tend increasingly to break down.[98]

Arthur Burns made the same point. He was asked whether we
have made any progress in forecasting. His answer was:

> What the models do is to average together very different
> periods....They tell us that if we had a substantial
> increase in unemployment, that would be accompanied by a
> negligible reduction in the inflation rate. But if you

38

go back and study the record historically you will find
that it isn't so. If you take different kinds of
periods together and average them out, you get some kind
of mish-mash....I think that relying on economic
history, on close statistical studies of an historical
sort will yield better forecasts than relying on econometric models. These models are bankrupt.[99]

Conclusion

This essay has characterized, and, to an extent, analyzed the
interviews with the ten CEA chairmen who served from 1949 to 1981.
Their reports of CEA advice and presidential policies and styles
have been set against a summary of economic conditions during
those years. What do we conclude about the questions with which
we began? Has the Council met the needs of presidents for bringing the best available economic knowledge to bear on decisions?
Are the institutional arrangements through which presidents receive counsel about macro and micro policy choices structured to
provide clear and accurate policy alternatives? And finally, how
adequate has economic science been to the responsibilities assigned the CEA in the Employment Act? Our answers to these questions are tentative and, like the transcripts themselves, point
the way to further inquiry.
We devoted the beginning of each interview to a characterization of the manner in which each president sought economic advice,
including the relationship between president and chairman. The
objective was to learn whether variations in presidential styles
of authority have an independent effect on the relations among
advisers and the advice given. On the basis of the transcripts,
we could not perceive such an independent effect on the relations
among advisers and the advice given. On the basis of the transcripts, we could not perceive such an independent effect which
might bias what presidents learn. Despite a great diversity of
styles, all of these presidents appear to have been presented with
a wide range of arguments and the best available economic advice.
Of course, former CEA chairmen are likely to make such claims, but
the descriptions of presidential decision making make clear that
presidents understood the major alternatives and their consequences before they acted.
The economic policy advisory system as it has developed
appears to be well institutionalized. This would account for the
diminished importance of presidential style in comparison with
other policy areas. There is a stable division of labor, within
the Troika and the Fed, and between the Troika and the constituency departments. This advisory system appears to present presidents with adequate knowledge of both economic choices and possible political consequences.
If institutions do not obstruct the development of economic
analysis, the next question becomes "how good is that analysis?"
The key to CEA utility for presidents would seem to be the economic knowledge and theory available to it. Of course, there is no
guarantee in any advisory system that political leaders will
follow the advice of experts. Politics has its own imperatives.

But, if the knowledge of experts is deficient, the question of their utility is never put to the full test. What do we conclude about the utility of the CEA to presidents in this respect?

The chairmen felt, without exception, that CEA analysis and advice on micro questions were sound. They understood when it could not be followed for political reasons. The analysis of micro questions by the CEA appears to be derived from axioms of economic science about which there is little controversy in the discipline.

There was much less certainty about knowledge and advice on macro policy questions. This is particularly true with respect to controlling inflation, but it also applied to the use of demand management in general to offset economic cycles. Economists know how to use demand management to avoid recession. Yet throughout much of the postwar period, so great has been the concern over inflation that these remedies have been applied cautiously if at all. Yet there was little sense among the chairmen that they had advocated or done too little in fighting recession. There are two reasons for this. First, they were worried about inflation. Second, they were convinced that the recessions they faced were going to be short lived and self-correcting. There has been a decline in economists' faith in their ability to fine-tune the economy to achieve full employment through continuous demand management. As a result, there is consensus that short recessions should be left to work themselves out without major shifts in fiscal policy. So far, this judgment has been correct. Fluctuations have been relatively minor, and there have been no self-feeding downward spirals in the postwar period that should have been met with a more decisive response than the one taken. In this sense, the advice of the economic advisers has been sound.

Advice on how to control inflation has been less useful. Economic science has been unable to agree on a policy less costly than lengthy recessions to break inflationary expectations and the wage spiral. Such a policy is politically unpalatable and the inflexibiltiy of prices and wages to downward pressure is such that the necessary recessions have proved to be far more prolonged and costly than most economists expected. Because such an inflation cure is politically unpalatable, presidents have tended to leave it to the Fed. As a result, in periods when inflation is the main macro economic problem, the CEA has tended to be less central to macro economic management.

There is then a congruence of politics and economics. Economic science has discovered how to foster politically popular expansion. The discovery, in both politics and economics, of how to cope with inflation without pain eludes us.

Erwin C. Hargrove and Samuel A. Morley

NOTES

1. Stephen K. Bailey, Congress Makes a Law, the Story Behind the Employment Act of 1946. (New York: Vintage Books, 1964) pp. 17-18.

2. Ibid., pp. 122-23; 221-25.

3. Ibid., pp. 224-25.

4. Ibid., p. 228.

5. Ibid., pp. 167-68.

6. Ibid., p. 169.

7. Ibid., p. 170.

8. Ibid., p. 222.

9. Erwin C. Hargrove and Michael Nelson, Presidents, Politics and Policy. (Baltimore: The Johns Hopkins Univ. Press, 1984) Chapter 6.

10. Gerhard Colm, ed., The Employment Act, Past and Future: A Tenth Anniversary Symposium. (Washington, D.C.: National Planning Association, 1956.) U.S. Congress: Twentieth Anniversary of the Employment Act of 1946, An Economic Symposium and Supplement to Hearing before JEC, Invited Comments JEC, 89th Congress, 2nd Session, 1966.

11. Stephen Hess analyzes the effects of presidential style on staffing in Organizing the Presidency. (Washington, D.C.: Brookings Institution, 1976); Lester Seligman has developed the concept of "institutionalization" in "Presidential Leadership: The Inner Circle and Institutionalization," Journal of Politics, p. 18 (August 1956).

12. Roger B. Porter deals with alternative ways of organizing economic policymaking in Presidential Decision Making, The Economic Policy Board. (New York: Cambridge Univ. Press, 1980); I. M. Destler covers the same ground for national security policy in Presidents, Bureaucrats and Foreign Policy. (Princeton, N.J.: Princeton Univ. Press, 1972.)

13. Edward Flash has given us the best analysis of the relations of experts and politicians in his Economic Advice and Presidential Leadership, the Council of Economic Advisers. (New York: Columbia Univ. Press, 1965.)

14. Walter Heller, p. 189.

15. Arthur Okun, p. 286.

16. Leon Keyserling, pp. 72-73.

17. Ibid., p. 58.

18. Raymond J. Saulnier, p. 135.

19. Raymond J. Saulnier, p. 135;
     Gardner Ackley, p. 237;
     Arthur Okun, pp. 288-89.

20. Herbert Stein, p. 382.

21. Gardner Ackley, p. 237.

22. Ibid., p. 240.

23. Ibid., p. 241.

24. Paul McCracken, p. 332;
     Alan Greenspan, p. 433.

25. Arthur Okun, p. 278.

26. Gardner Ackley, p. 240.

27. Paul McCracken, p. 335.

28. Arthur Okun, p. 290;
     Paul McCracken, p. 335.

29. Alan Greenspan, p. 439.

30. Gardner Ackley, p. 239.

31. Ibid., pp. 237-38.

32. Herbert Stein, p. 368.

33. Ibid., pp. 368-69.

34. Ibid., p. 369.

35. Ibid., p. 370.

36. Ibid., p. 372.

37. Ibid., p. 371.

38. Alan Greenspan, pp. 427-28.

39. Ibid., pp. 428-29.

40. Ibid., p. 449.

41. Charles Schultze, pp. 467-68.

42. Herbert Stein, p. 379.

43. Raymond J. Saulnier, p. 146.

44. Walter Heller, p. 187.

45. Paul McCracken, p. 338.

46. Walter Heller, p. 187.

47. Gardner Ackley, p. 223.

48. Ibid., pp. 252-54.

49. Walter Heller, p. 179.

50. Ibid., p. 176.

51. Ibid., p. 178.

52. Ibid., p. 201.

53. Leon Keyserling, p. 73;
    Raymond J. Saulnier, p. 147;
    Gardner Ackley, pp. 243-44;
    Herbert Stein, pp. 379-80.

54. Arthur Okun, p. 283.

55. Walter Heller, p. 183.
    Arthur Okun, p. 296.

56. Gardner Ackley, p. 244.

57. Arthur Okun, p. 296.

58. Ibid., pp. 283-84.

59. Alan Greenspan, pp. 426-27.

60. Arthur Okun, pp. 281-82.

61. Leon Keyserling, pp. 68-69;
    Raymond J. Saulnier, p. 145.

62. Paul McCracken, p. 320.

63. Walter Heller, p. 185; 187;
    Gardner Ackley, p. 227;
    Arthur Okun, p. 284.

64. Flash, op. cit; p. 154, and Robert J. Donovan, Eisenhower: The Inside Story. (New York: Harper, 1956), p. 217.

65. George L. Bach, Making Monetary and Fiscal Policy. (Washington, D.C.: The Brookings Institution, 1971), p. 94.

66. Raymond J. Saulnier, p. 138.

67. Herbert Stein, The Fiscal Revolution in America. Chicago: Univ. of Chicago Press, 1969), p. 327.

68. Raymond J. Saulnier, p. 137.

69. Ibid., p. 150.

70. Herbert Stein, Fiscal Revolution, op. cit; p. 321.

71. George L. Bach, op. cit; p. 101.

72. Raymond J. Saulnier, "Anti-Inflation Policies in President Eisenhower's Second Term," (Paper delivered at American Historical Association Meeting, December 1973), p. 8.

73. Raymond J. Saulnier, pp. 29, 76; and Wilfred Lewis, Jr., Federal Fiscal Policy in the Postwar Recession, (Washington, D.C.: The Brookings Institution, 1962), p. 246.

74. Gardner Ackley, p. 248.

75. Ibid., p. 253.

76. Ibid., p. 302.

77. Ibid., pp. 256-57.

78. Arthur Okun, p. 307.

79. Arthur Burns, p. 119.

80. Raymond J. Saulnier, p. 150.

81. Gardner Ackley, p. 257.

82. Arthur Okun, p. 308.

83. Paul McCracken, pp. 341-42.

84. Herbert Stein, p. 420.

85. Alan Greenspan, p. 444.

86. Paul McCracken, p. 343.

87. Herbert Stein, p. 394.

44

88. Alan Greenspan, p. 447.

89. Arthur Burns, p. 122.

90. Arthur Okun, p. 304.

91. Ibid., p. 306.

92. Ibid., p. 308.

93. Herbert Stein, pp. 395-96.

94. Ibid., p. 396.

95. Ibid., p. 402.

96. Alan Greenspan, p. 442.

97. Ibid., pp. 441-42.

98. George Jaszi, "The Role of the Economist in Government: An Economic Accountant's Audit," paper delivered at a conference on the role of the economist in government, Royamont, France, 1974. Quoted in David Naveh, The Political Role of Professionals in the Formation of National Policy: The Case of the President's Council of Ecnomic Advisers, Ph.D. thesis, 1978, University of Conn., pp. 168-69.

99. Arthur Burns, p. 121.

Participants in the Vanderbilt Faculty Seminars

GA   – Gardner Ackley
IB   – Ivar Berg, Professor of Sociology and Economics
AB   – Arthur Burns
DD   – Dewey Daane, Professor of Banking, Owen Graduate School of Management
RF   – Rendigs Fels, Professor of Economics
TAF – T. Aldrich Finegan, Professor of Economics
JG   – James Gardner, Research Assistant and Graduate Student in History
DG   – Dewey Grantham, Professor of History
OG   – Oliver Grawe, Graduate Student in Economics
AG   – Alan Greenspan
EH   – Erwin Hargrove, Director, Institute for Public Policy Studies, Professor of Political Science
WH   – William Havard, Professor of Political Science
WWH – Walter W. Heller
LK   – Leon Keyserling
ML   – Melvyn Leffler, Associate Professor of History
AL   – Avery Leiserson, Professor of Political Science
PM   – Paul W. McCracken
McS – Samuel T. McSeveney, Associate Professor of History
SM   – Samuel A. Morley, Professor of Economics
AO   – Arthur Okun
RS   – Raymond J. Saulnier
CS   – Charles Schultze
LS   – Lester Seligman, Professor of Political Science, University of Illinois
JS   – John Siegfried, Associate Professor of Economics
HS   – Herbert Stein
BW   – Benjamin Walter, Professor of Political Science
DW   – Donald Winters, Professor of History

1
The Council of Economic Advisers Under Chairman Leon H. Keyserling, 1949–1953

Summary History

It is not possible to fully understand Keyserling's chairmanship without knowledge of the first years of the Council under the chairmanship of Edwin G. Nourse (1946-1949). Keyserling was a member of the first CEA and his actions as chairman were shaped by that experience.

President Truman's selection of Edwin G. Nourse as Chairman of the three-man council was considered an indication of his desire to appoint a person of professional standing rather than partisan loyalty. At the time of his appointment as Vice-President of the Brookings Institution with which he had been associated since 1923, Nourse was a well-respected, moderately conservative economist with a background in academics and a specialization in agricultural economics. He had not served in government before and prided himself on his objectivity and nonpartisanship. Truman then chose for his colleagues two men of very different backgrounds and economic philosophies. In his early sixties, John D. Clark was of Nourse's generation but quite different otherwise. He had originally been a lawyer and had followed a business career until his resignation as vice-president of Standard Oil of Indiana when in his forties. He had then moved on to an academic career after receiving his Ph.D. in economics in 1931. In addition to teaching, in the ensuing years he served one term in the Wyoming state legislature and became a close associate of Senator Joseph O'Mahoney of Wyoming, one of the sponsors of the Employment Act.

Vice-Chairman Leon H. Keyserling was at thirty-eight the youngest of the three. He had also had a rather varied background, beginning as a lawyer, then pursuing a Ph.D. in economics until he went to work for the Roosevelt administration in 1933. He became an ardent New Dealer, working in the Agricultural Adjustment Administration and various federal public housing agencies assisting in the drafting of a range of legislative proposals including the Employment Act of 1946, and working closely with Senator Robert F. Wagner of New York, another sponsor of the bill. The most liberal of the three, he was also probably the most politically sensitive because of his years of government service. The differences between these three men were to become clearer as the Council set about its work.

The major disagreement within the Nourse Council centered on the nature of its duties and responsibilities. Nourse viewed the Council's role essentially as one of providing the president with expert and objective advice. This meant that the CEA would refrain from any political considerations in its deliberations and avoid advocacy or policymaking roles. Keyserling and Clark, however, felt that public advocacy and defense of the administration's economic policies was central to their role in the same way that it was for other officials and agencies. The focus of the disagreement was whether or not the Council should yield to requests and testify before congressional committees on the administration's economic program. Since Truman had not expressed his views on the subject, it was left to the Council to formulate its policy.

Although the main concern was to be whether to testify before the Joint Committee on the Economic Report (a committee also established under the 1946 Employment Act to review the President's Reports), the first request for testimony came from the Senate Foreign Relations Committee in November 1947. That committee was then conducting hearings on the Truman administration's Marshall Plan for European Recovery. Since Nourse had chaired one of the three committees that had developed the plan, the Senate committee asked him to testify. The CEA Chairman refused to do so, insisting that appearance before a congressional committee would subject him to questions that might damage the confidentiality of his advisory relationship with the President. He also felt that the CEA should restrict its role to advice and avoid an advocacy role that would call into question the objectivity and scientific expertise of the Council. This same argument was then used in early 1948 against testifying before the Joint Committee on the Economic Report. Both Keyserling and Clark disagreed with Nourse and felt that trusteeship of the administration's program was part of the advisory relationship, but the two yielded to the Chairman's wishes and did not testify. The issue became public, however, when Nourse discussed it in speeches and openly criticized his colleagues' difference of opinion.

Truman was up for re-election in 1948, and his call for a special session of Congress in the interval between the summer political conventions and the November elections was directed toward that goal. He endeavored to make the Republican-controlled Eightieth Congress responsible for, among other things, the failure to curb inflation. It was felt that CEA testimony in support of the President's eight-point anti-inflation program would help make this a strong political issue for the Democrats. Nourse still did not believe it a proper function of the Council. His two colleagues were, however, increasingly concerned that the refusal to testify was costing the Council much in terms of congressional support; the cuts in the CEA's budget by Congress appeared particularly threatening. Keyserling and Clark were eager to repair relations with Congress and protect the CEA's future. On August 3, 1948, Truman finally made his own position clear; he encouraged but did not require Council members to testify. With the President's approval, Keyserling and Clark made their first Congressional appearances on August 4 at hearings of the Senate Banking and Currency Committee. From then on, they agreed to give testimony when requested on pertinent administration programs, appearing regularly before the Joint Committee on the Economic Report beginning in 1949. Nourse, however, refused ever to make such an appearance.

Dissension within the CEA became more open by late 1948, with Nourse and Keyserling publicly acknowledging their conflicting views. While the three economists had managed earlier to work out their difference over economic policy in order to produce a unanimous report to the President, the Mid-year Review in 1949 contained for the first time a minority statement written by Nourse. The three members were increasingly independent and sent individual, often conflicting, messages to the President. There was some question as to whether the CEA could operate effectively. The Hoover Commission's Report of the General Management of the Executive Branch in January 1949 suggested that part of the Council's difficulties was due to the ambiguous relationship of the chairman to the other two members; the chairman was only the first among equals and had no real authority or power. Consequently, the Commission suggested that the CEA be replaced with an Office of Economic Adviser with a single head.

For his part, Nourse saw resignation as his only possible course of action. He sent a first letter of resignation to Truman in December 1948, but the President did not respond and Nourse stayed on. Then in October 1949 as the conflict and controversy continued, Nourse again notified Truman of his intentions and resigned effective November 1, 1949. The former Chairman never concealed the reasons for his resignation, publicly criticizing both the direction the Council had taken away from the objectivity and scientific expertise he felt essential to its advisory role and the indifference of President Truman to the Council's advice.

The public debate between Chairman Nourse and Keyserling over the nature of the Council's role was a central aspect of the Council's early development. Yet it was not always clear that this was the entire problem, for many observers sensed an underlying conservative-liberal ideological conflict. The Chairman basically had little sympathy with the Fair Deal and freely voiced in public speeches his criticism of the economic policies advocated by Truman and his CEA colleagues. Keyserling, on the other hand, had been an ardent New Dealer and was just as committed to the Fair Deal, a position clearly evident in his speeches to such partisan groups as the Americans for Democratic Action. Although Keyserling has insisted that there was basic agreement within the Council about what were the proper economic policies and goals, the public conflict between the two appeared the more significant for the Council's future.

Keyserling became acting chairman of the Council of Economic Advisers in November 1949, upon the resignation of Nourse. He was told by friends in the White House that President Harry Truman had indicated that he planned to appoint Keyserling as full chairman, but the appointment did not come for six months. John Clark continued as a member of the Council and the other position was filled by the appointment of Roy Blough, an economics professor at the University of Chicago. Another academic economist, Robert C.

Turner, replaced Blough for the last year of the Council under the Truman administration.

The Keyserling CEA generally avoided the bitter dissension that had focused so much attention on the Nourse Council. This is not to say that there was total agreement among the three concerning either the CEA's function or economic policy. While Blough was willing to join Keyserling and Clark in testifying before Congress, he had a more limited view of what this would involve. Blough would not testify on policy and insisted that a CEA member should only give objective testimony on economic trends and data that would not compromise his relationship with the President or his standing in the profession. When in doubt, he felt silence was the wisest course. Also, there was not as much concern in the Keyserling Council with presenting an outward consensus on economic issues, but rather each member made separate statements when they disagreed with the CEA's Review or Reports, a development particularly evident on issues related to Korean War mobilization.

Keyserling also did not have the problems his predecessor had had with the limited statutory role of the chairman, for he simply asserted a more central role for the chairman in the Council's operations. While he advocated delegation of duties and responsibilities, he was also insistent on maintaining control of the CEA's Reviews and the President's Reports. Staff committees compiled memos and advice was sought from administration officials, but it was Keyserling who in the final analysis wrote the CEA Reports.

Keyserling was also more involved in staff organization than Nourse had been. As chairman, he continued to coordinate the largely career staff, supervising the informal division of labor and overseeing a series of staff committees on statistics, editing, long-range projections and requirements, manpower, public works development, housing, and the like. Relations within the CEA were generally informal, with frequent intermingling of CEA members with staff and staff involvement in substantive issues and policy. Since all were basically Keynesian expansionists, compatibility was not a problem. Keyserling was more conscious than Nourse had been of the need to work with other departments of the government. He circulated his draft Reports and encouraged staff contacts outside the Council. A number of inter-agency committees chaired by CEA staff were established to facilitate such contacts. Keyserling himself headed an inter-agency Committee on Economic Stabilization. After the Republican congressional victories of 1946, Keyserling was one of the major participants in the "Ewing group," a caucus of liberal Truman supporters within the administration. With the 1948 election in mind, this group attempted to formulate policies and programs that would give the administration a more liberal cast. Keyserling also had a more public role in supporting the Truman administration through his testimony before congressional committees. Unlike Nourse, Keyserling perceived the CEA as trustee for the President's economic programs in Congress. He rejected Nourse's claims to objectivity and nonpartisanship, claiming instead that the Council was part of the administration and should act accordingly.

As chairman, Keyserling developed a closer relationship with the President than did Nourse and had no trouble arranging to meet privately with Truman as often as was necessary. Keyserling was also more effective in working with the White House staff than Nourse had been, continuing to keep in close touch with Presidential Counsels Clark Clifford and (later) Charles Murphy. He did not get along with Assistant to the President John Steelman's more conservative views. Steelman also apparently sought to increase his own power at the CEA's expense, in late 1946 unsuccessfully attempting to rewrite the Council's draft of the President's Report and during the Korean War preparing his own economic reports for the President. Open conflict between the two was avoided only by the actions and influence of advisers like Clifford and of Truman himself.

Keyserling also moved beyond the formal duties and responsibilities of the CEA chairman. Working with the President and his staff, he wrote drafts for speeches and messages. Eager to assist the administration in whatever way possible, he was made a de facto member of the Cabinet and the National Security Council, especially after the advent of the Korean War. Meetings with advisory groups representing business, labor, agriculture, and consumers were held frequently to extend the CEA's contacts outside government. The Chairman also made frequent use of the media to publicize the Council's work and defend the administration's economic policies. Keyserling had been in government service long enough to know the value of contacts both within and outside government.

The CEA Chairman did not hesitate to articulate his own economic views whenever possible. Although known as a supporter of the New Deal and Keynesian economics, he was increasingly critical of both. He insisted that the United States must move beyond a New Deal perspective on economic policy. According to Keyserling, too much emphasis had been placed on government action when business-government cooperation was the most logical path to economic stability. The government alone simply could not control the economy. As for the actions the government had taken, Keyserling found them too crisis-oriented. He felt long-term goals—not forecasting or planning, but goals involving trust and cooperation —were essential. Specifically, he advocated a "National Prosperity Budget" that would clearly set forth reasonable goals of economic growth and expansion, the keys to eventual economic stability. Balanced economic growth should not be sacrificed to maintain short-term price stability; some inflation was inevitable with expansion and would simply have to be tolerated as the price for long-run stability.

The CEA Chairman was also critical of more specific policies. He considered tax cuts as generally regressive and to be avoided. If compensatory fiscal policy was needed, he preferred an increase of expenditures. He thought the Keynesians had put too much emphasis on macro economics, and urged a combination of both aggregate and structural approaches. Government policies should be selective and reflect micro economic analysis as well, an approach evident for example in the CEA's studies of the steel industry.

Keyserling had many critics, particularly among the New Dealers who could not accept many aspects of expansionism. His reliance on voluntarism was especially unpalatable to many liberals who had long since abandoned any expectations of rational economic action by private interests and had come to see government action and responsibility as essential to attaining economic prosperity and stability. Despite Keyserling's emphasis on the need to couple economic and social needs, liberals also suspected that his expansionism was a "trickle down" theory, avoiding any attempts to bring equity to the distribution of wealth by simply insisting that economic growth alone would solve the problems.

The Keyserling Council was responsible for only one Report and Review before the Korean War broke out and changed the entire economic situation. Written during the 1949-50 recession, both documents acknowledged that there would be a period of adjustment in the economy but focused on more optimistic goals for economic growth. They did not seek large tax cuts or increases in Federal spending. A balanced budget and debt reduction were still urged in the years to come. The Republican minority on the Joint Committee was highly critical of what it termed the "political" use by the administration of the Report to continue to deny responsibility for the recession. They were also somewhat skeptical of Keyserling's expansionism as a cure for economic ills. According to its critics, the Report lacked the focus and clear objectives and policies that were essential to renewed growth and prosperity.

By the time the 1950 Midyear Report and Review came out, the entire situation had changed as the Korean crisis forced the nation to shift its focus from overcoming the effects of a recession to mobilizing and expanding the economy to meet urgent defense needs without yielding to destructive inflationary pressures. When the nation actually became involved in Korea, Truman embraced Keyserling's policy of expansionism, as opposed to controls. The President was not eager to have to deal with the political reaction to controls and wanted to avoid any exaggerated response to the Korean crisis that would indicate to the USSR that the U.S. expected an extended involvement. Keyserling's expansionism suited these needs well, for his basic approach was to accept short-term wartime inflation and to concentrate on long-term economic expansion. Although the CEA was willing to work for indirect controls such as higher taxes to pay for defense needs, consumer credit controls, and allocations, direct price and wage controls were to be avoided in order to allow maximum economic growth. The assumption was that government action of the latter kind would not be necessary since the war would be short and the expanding economy would be able to handle the necessary mobilization. Others, such as Dean Acheson, however, felt strong direct controls were essential for economic stability and were highly critical of what they termed the "relaxed" view taken by the expansionists toward the war. But with the mobilization structure not yet formally developed and Truman endorsing expansionism, Keyserling and the CEA were able to take a position of leadership in the early mobilization effort, beginning with a persuasive argument for the expansionist program in the 1950 Midyear Report and Review. Although the 1950 Defense Production Act signed by

Truman on September 8 did provide stand-by wage and price controls, the expansionist title of the bill and the President's
refusal to use the new control powers clearly indicated the influence of Keyserling's economic theories.

Expanded defense production urged on by the CEA helped maintain price stability for a time. But with the escalation of the
war with the entry of the Chinese into the fighting in November
1950, the economic situation worsened and Keyserling's expansionism seemed an insufficient response to the situation. Many
alarmed observers warned that the war would not soon end and that
without some form of controls the inflationary wage-price spiral
would continue with disastrous consequences for the economy. The
Council began to consider gradual controls, but its support of
such action was unenthusiastic at best. As a result of this
failure to respond quickly to the changing situation, the CEA by
January 1951 began to lose its influence. By then the various
mobilization bodies (Office of Defense Mobilization, Defense Mobilization Board, Defense Production Administration, and Economic
Stabilization Agency—Office of Price Stabilization) which Keyserling had sought to direct expansion were capable of taking over
the mobilization effort. The CEA was forced to yield, and price
and wage controls were established.

Although the inflationary spiral was essentially under control by March 1951 because of the end of the scare-buying, higher
taxes for Truman's pay-as-you-go defense program, credit restraint, and tax incentives for business expansion, liberal fears
still continued and Truman pushed for continued controls and
higher taxes. Keyserling continued to push for expansion and
mobilization to meet defense needs. However, with production requirements already straining capacity by December 1951, and Congress' refusal to raise taxes, the administration had little
alternative but to stretch out mobilization over the next two
years.

The Keyserling Council also sought to influence the outcome
of the debate within the Truman administration concerning monetary
policy. Keyserling, Truman, and the Treasury Department all insisted on the necessity of easy credit policies to encourage
investment and keep government financing costs down. At that time
the Federal Reserve was operating under an agreement by which it
supported the price of outstanding government bonds, a policy
which effectively set a ceiling on the interest rate. The Fed
wished to be freed from this obligation so that it could pursue a
more anti-inflationary monetary policy. The conflict between the
Treasury and the Federal Reserve became so disquieting that in
February 1951 Truman appointed a committee headed by Charles
Wilson, Director of the ODM, to look into it. Keyserling, Secretary of the Treasury John Snyder, and the Federal Reserve Chairman
Thomas McCabe were the other members. The group, however, had
only one meeting before the Treasury and the Federal Reserve Board
announced independently of the committee on March 3 that they had
reached an accord that freed the Federal Reserve from its market
support commitment. Keyserling was angered that the Council had
obviously been excluded from the negotiations of a basic economic
policy. Neither the Treasury nor the Federal Reserve Board was

willing to allow interference from Keyserling or the CEA in what was considered their problem.

The CEA's active role in economic policymaking under Keyserling was the object of increasing criticism from conservatives within Congress. The Republicans on the Joint Committee on the Economic Report repeatedly criticized both the President's Reports and the Council's Reviews for their political overtones and propagandizing. In 1952, when Congress considered the 1953 fiscal year budget, it seemed that the CEA's opponents would finally have their way when the Council's budget was cut by 25 percent. Although other agencies were also cut, animosity toward the Council's advocacy role was clearly an important factor. With the help of Senators Maybank, Ellender, Saltonstall, and Taft, Senator Joseph O'Mahoney managed to have a provision included that allowed the CEA to spend the remaining funds in the first nine months, the time left for the Truman Council before Dwight Eisenhower took over. The CEA was then able to operate fully for the remainder of Keyserling's tenure. The fate of the Council after that was left to Eisenhower and his Council chairman.

Oral History Interview

The President and Economic Policy

EH: Last night I was reading a book edited by Craufurd Goodwin, _Exhortation and Controls_, in which he quotes someone as quoting President Truman. Professor Nourse wrote a first memo to Truman; it was an "on the one hand, on the other hand" memo, and Truman said, "By God, if I could just get a one-armed economist." What did Truman expect the Council to do for him, as you perceived it, from the very beginning? And how did that change?

LK: I knew Truman long before he became president. When testifying before an Appropriations Committee in late 1944, I was asked a number of questions by the distinguished Senator from Tennessee, Mr. McKellar, Chairman of the Committee, by Carter Glass, who was then on the Committee, and by others. Just as I was walking out, I was asked one question by Senator Truman; I still remember, although it's forty-three years ago, what went on in my mind as I went out of the door: "My God, think of a Senator asking a question like that." A few months later he was president. Well, between my experience with the Appropriations Committee and before the Democratic convention, I went to see my old boss, Senator Wagner. He said, "I have just had a visit from the junior Senator from Missouri, Mr. Truman." I said, "What did he want?" He said, "Well, we don't know whether Roosevelt is going to run for a fourth term, and Harry was in here, recommending that if he didn't the senior Senator from Missouri, Bennett Clark, would be a great standard bearer for the Democratic party." I said, "Well, what do you think of Bennett Clark as President?" And he looked at me without smiling and said, "Well, Leon, somebody's got to be president." And then I said, "How about Harry Truman?" He laughed and said, "Nobody would think of that." That was about two months before he got nominated for vice-president.

I tell this story to illustrate the tremendous growth in Harry Truman after he became president. It was phenomenal. And he had a very pronounced concept of what he expected the Council to do for him. Dr. Nourse felt that when he went to see the President, the President should have the same kind of seminar with him that he had with us over in the Council office. The President of the United States cannot do that. Truman was always well informed about the operations of the government, probably more so in detail than any past or subsequent among the eight presidents who were in Washington while I was. He had a knowledge of the government comparable to Al Smith's knowledge of New York State and a definite concept of the Council's role, which was very different from Dr. Nourse's; Nourse wanted it a quiescent and statistical gathering body in giving the president alternatives. A president is terribly hurt if he gets from three members of a Council three alternatives as to what he should do. He can't

pick between alternatives in that manner. If he values at
all a three-member Council, it is because of its capacity to
give him one view that represents the synthesis of three
views. Anyhow, his perception of the role of the Council was
illustrated by the fact that when I became Chairman he immediately said, "This is really about the most important job in
the government." Well, he was prone to a little exaggeration
of that type. He said, "It is so important that you've got
to be much closer to the Cabinet people," and from the beginning of my chairmanship he made me a full participant in the
Cabinet and National Security Council meetings. I didn't
come in there and brief them on the economy, or come in and
leave, or answer questions about the economy. When there was
going to be a Cabinet meeting, I was called upon to be there,
and I was there the same as everybody else. But this was the
view that Truman had of the Council.

Second, Truman fixed responsibility and he either upheld
the men--there weren't many women at the top then selected
because they were women--listened to them and supported them,
in accord with the functions of their job, or he fired them.
He didn't have a Secretary of State in the State Department
and another Secretary of State in the White House, as we've
had since. He didn't have, as we had during the Eisenhower
administration, a chairman of the Council of Economic Advisers in Arthur Burns and another economic adviser to the
President in the form of a man whose name I forget at the
moment, but who is now Chairman of the Hanover Trust Company.

EH: Hauge.

LK: Hauge, thank you. Truman didn't do that. From the time I
became Chairman, I can't think of any important instance
where Truman didn't follow my advice. Whether it was right
or wrong. Truman saw the role of the Council as opposed to
the advice of others, emperors of provinces like the Treasury
Department--I say province because it deals with a segment of
economic policy, not with the whole. After all, presidents
had always been sending economic programs to Congress, but
their advisers had been segmental people; the very idea of
the Council was to have an economic general staff that
synthesized and winnowed out the segments and put them together into one program. I can't recall any important instance
when he didn't follow my advice and took instead the advice
of people like John Snyder, who were, in a personal sense,
much closer to him than I was. (Actually, Snyder and I very
seldom differed.) He took that approach for two reasons:
first, because of his theory of supporting the person he had
chosen in accord with his sense of what that person's job
was; second, because he felt the need for that kind of instrumentality, and third, there was also what might be
called, in the main, a natural sympathy between my economic
views and the economic views of Harry Truman. After one
economist told Truman that 3 percent unemployment was right
and another told him that 5 percent unemployment was

right and another that 7 percent unemployment was right, he
was asked by a reporter, "Mr. President, what is the right
level of unemployment?" And Truman snapped back, "It depends
on whether or not you're unemployed." Now, some people may
look at that as a wisecrack, but I don't. I look at that as
a very profound philosophy; the main problems of unemployment
are the unemployed people. If economists would remember that
a little bit more, I think we'd have a better economics and a
better public policy. Truman, more than any president I
knew—with the possible exception of Roosevelt—really believed, not merely as a dogma or a slogan, his statement that
"there are 110,000 people in Washington serving every interest; I'm the only man in the country who is charged with the
responsibility of representing all the people." I think he
tried to do that. I think this entered into his economics as
he saw it. I suppose that everybody says that is their
economics, but he believed in it by directly helping the
average citizen rather than by the circuitous process of
helping them indirectly by helping somebody else with the
thought that in that way they will be helped equally well;
that is another basic conflict that runs throughout economic
thought and action. He was, generally speaking, in favor of
the small man, because he had been a small man. The one
economic policy that he understood best was money policy. He
had been made bankrupt by the tightening of money and the
lifting of interest rates. He really understood it thoroughly, and he was always for what one calls an "easy money"
policy—that is not entirely a descriptive term—and for low
interest rates. And he succeeded until the accord between
the Treasury and the Federal Reserve in 1951 and 1952, which
was one of his great oversights; I'll come to that later.
Until then he succeeded in maintaining, through his influence, the traditional low interest rate policy that had
prevailed from the beginning of the Roosevelt administration;
I think with very desirable results.

EH: What was his formal knowledge of economics? To what extent
     did he have an understanding of the discipline?

LK: My answer would be: he understood economics as well as, if
     not better than, every other president I knew anything about.
     If you define formal economics in one way, it wasn't very
     much. But Harry Truman understood economics more than Roose-
     velt, about the same as Lyndon Johnson, about the same as
     Nixon—I'll skip Ford and Eisenhower out of charity—and
     perhaps more than Jimmy Carter. Asking how much a president
     understands formal economics is like asking how much a presi-
     dent understands the techniques of weaponry, even though he
     has to make a decision as to the composition of the Armed
     Forces. He doesn't and he can't. He has to have people who
     do understand it, and how well he succeeds depends upon
     whether his judgment is right or wrong. That's competence
     and public dedication. I think Truman had that. Coming back
     to money policy, he understood money policy very thoroughly.

He understood how it worked, had definite views on it, and there he was a competent economist, whether one shares his views or not. He was not a technical economist, a formal economist. He had the level of understanding that one might expect, shaped by certain profound views that were fundamental to economics and to public policy. He was easy to talk to; he was more of a listener than a talker. Except on subjects that were novel, he usually had a very, very clear and firm notion of what his policy was and usually stated it on many matters. And this arose from his knowledge of the government, from his intimate and constant connection with the federal budget, and from the nature of the man. When you brought new ideas to him, he listened. He usually was receptive for the reasons that I have given.

RF: Does this mean that when you had some economic ideas to get across to him he grasped them readily and you didn't have any difficulty making him understand what you were saying?

LK: This gets first to the nature of my contacts with Truman and the nature of my influence on Truman. The problem was easier for Truman because he really had only one economist, right or wrong, who he thought was the government's chief economist, from whom he thought he should get his basic advice. We had a system whereby we got the benefit of the news of the departments. We always circulated the Economic Reports we drafted initially and the Council's Reports to them. We had interconnecting committees with them in every field at the staff level. I was frequently with them at the top level, as well as being in the Cabinet. So what they had to say was brought into the picture, and they, of course, had the privilege of going to Truman if they disagreed with me. He was also extremely accessible, partly because he didn't have so many people to whom he had to be accessible. If I called on Matt Conally at any time and said, "Can I get to see the President?" he never said, "I'll call you back." He said, "Eight o'clock on Wednesday, ten o'clock on Thursday," and I had half an hour, alone. This was one line of contact which I did not abuse, but which was very easy. That type of meeting occurred maybe twenty times a year. The second line of contact was through the Cabinet meetings, which I have already described. The third line of contact was that, rightly or wrongly, Truman used me for other purposes, out of the ordinary line. I helped with his speeches on economic subjects and on other subjects, and this brought me around the table with a little group that included Clark Clifford, David Lloyd, and Charlie Murphy. Truman was not the same during the first couple of years of his presidency that he was later on. During the first two years he was somewhat provincial without much cosmopolitan grasp. And he also had less adequate advisers then. For example, he was using a judge by the name of Collett somewhere in Missouri; later he used Judge Vinson. As you may recall, the first two years of his economic policy were far less than satisfactory, although he was mainly hamstrung by the premature abandonment of controls, which he couldn't prevent. But after the election of 1946, when the Republicans took control of the Congress, he woke up to policy as well as to politics; he appointed a small group that met every Monday night, from 1947 on into 1952 when he decided not to run again. This small group was chaired by Oscar Ewing, the head of what is now Health, Education and Welfare.

EH: You're saying that Truman appointed the group?

LK: Yes, not technically, but I believe in the sense that he authorized it and that the names of the participants were probably known to and checked with him.

EH: I thought they had just taken it upon themselves to meet informally.

LK: Oh no. We couldn't have taken it upon ourselves; it was too important, too well formalized.

EH: Clark Clifford has been quoted as describing this tremendous struggle for the mind of the President between the liberals and the conservatives, saying that the President didn't really know what was going on. But the suggestion that Truman appointed the group is slightly different.

LK: Well, I don't think it's inconsistent. What Clifford was describing was the struggle to convert Truman; that struggle took place substantially through the instrumentality of the group. That Truman didn't know what was going on was true in the sense that he didn't attend the meetings and didn't know what was happening. But it was always my view that this was authorized by Truman. It is hardly likely that anyone would have risked—certainly I would not have gotten into that kind of thing without believing he had so authorized, and I think he also passed upon who attended the meetings. The group was composed of Oscar Ewing; Clark Clifford, the President's Counsel; me, which in itself was a recognition of the role of economic policy in the whole picture; Charlie Brannan, who became Secretary of Agriculture; David Morse, Under Secretary of Labor; Jebby Davidson, Assistant Secretary of the Interior; and one or two others. It was a small group. We met every Monday night for dinner and three hours of discussion at the home of Ewing at the Wardman Park. These meetings dealt with matters of high policy, what Truman should do. One of the first things that came up, fortuitously, was what he should do about the Taft-Hartley Act. But we ranged over the whole field. This committee, through the individuals on it, had a great influence in many ways. It provided a unified position on the part of the people who saw Truman, and it helped Clark Clifford, who saw him more than anybody else. I tried to delineate who was more important in this, Clifford or I. Clifford had a great deal more to do with persuading

the President, and I had a great deal more to do with what
Clifford persuaded him on. I don't know which is more important. I don't think that anybody other than the extremely
gifted Clark Clifford would have gotten as good results. I
do not think that somebody else as Chairman of the Council
would have gotten the same results. I got to see him frequently too, and through that process, there was a pronounced
shift in the accent of the policies of the Truman administration, beginning with his State of the Union message of 1947
and carrying on from there. So there were many ways in which
access to the President was maintained.

AL: Was the Ewing group self-selected, and were there ever any
conflicts within the group? Any really genuine differences
of opinion?

LK: I can't really know how the group was selected, because I
didn't select them. I don't know how I was selected. Whether Ewing discussed this with the President and the President said go ahead, and then Ewing phoned a number of people,
or whether Clark Clifford did this, or whether each choice
was cleared with the President really isn't a matter of great
importance. The group functioned in a given way, performed a
purpose, and achieved results. People brought Truman the
ideas as developed, that I know, and he approved them. He
was kept informed in a general way of what was going on. The
President didn't come to the meetings and didn't know what
was happening in most of the meetings. The results reached
him later. Whether the individual names were cleared with
him, my informed guess would be that they were. Certainly, I
think he would have been asked whether he wanted the Chairman
of his Council of Economic Advisers to be on a group like
that. In fact, I was Vice-Chairman at the beginning of that
time; I became Chairman later. So that's about how I think
the group was formed. As to whether there were differences
within the group--of course. How can any intelligent group
of people get together and discuss issues without having
differences? But the differences were not really as to basic
philosophy or purpose. They were differences as to means,
differences as to timing, differences as to the relative
priorities. But those didn't result in fracases, or result
in break-up. They didn't result in going to the President
and saying, "Give us the answer." They were worked out with
a surprising degree of accord. The success of a presidency
depends upon getting people of different views but not in
fundamental disagreement. You couldn't have a workable economic council composed of Milton Friedman and me. The members of the Ewing group weren't people in basic and fundamental disagreement. Charlie Brannan, and Jebby Davidson and
Oscar Ewing and Clark Clifford and I, as of then, were basically like-minded people. This also says something about the
President's method of selection.

EH: Does this indicate, that the Cabinet was in fundamental disagreement and that is why this group was set up?

LK: No, it wasn't because the Cabinet was in fundamental disagreement, but because a Cabinet is a limited instrumentality. What is the reason for bringing the Postmaster General, when he was in the government, and the Secretary of the Interior together once a week on any particular issue that you might discuss?

EH: There were conservative people in the administration: Snyder, Sawyer, John Steelman later, but they were not an organized clique, were they?

LK: I think they were, to a degree in substance, not formally. They were an established clique that gathered around John Steelman to a degree. There's an interesting story, which illustrates Truman. When I was first appointed Vice-Chairman of the Council, Truman hardly knew me at all. I immediately had a lead article in the New York Times Magazine, and was on the television taking positions. Some of the conservatives got up a great big book of clippings and took it to the President. Clark Clifford called me and said, "You'd better go over and see the boss." So I called up Matt Connally and there I was. I thought this was going to end me. I walked into the office and Truman said, "Sit down." He put his hand on this huge book and said, "Leon, I have read every goddamn clipping in this book, and I haven't found anybody who accuses you of disagreeing with the President of the United States, so let's forget about it." That was Truman. Later on, of course, I got to know him much better and that's how I got these 40 letters after he left the White House. That conservative group was substantially sidetracked. In the battle between Clifford and Steelman in the White House, Clifford won so completely that Steelman became a man who was asked mainly to help with the settlement of labor disputes, which was what he had been doing in the Department of Labor, and to perform housekeeping chores. Yet, he was an honest, able, and hard-working public servant.

EH: This was Truman's decision to sidetrack?

LK: Nobody else could do it.

EH: So, you're saying Truman didn't put confidence in those people the way he did in you and Clifford and others, ultimately.

LK: Absolutely. Most of the history can't get written because so much of it is oral, but I think the available record is clear.

EH: Of course, Snyder and Sawyer stayed in their jobs.

LK: Sure, they stayed in their jobs. First of all, Snyder was a very close personal friend of the President, but beyond that Snyder was a very honest man, an able man who ran the Treasury well. But Truman didn't believe it was his job to participate extensively in the making of overall economic decisions, even if they involved taxation, because that is an overall economic decision, not simply a matter of the Treasury. So he sidetracked them only to the extent of relegating them to their proper functions within the government structure.

JC: Where did Edward Nourse fit into this? I understand he worked more with Steelman in the White House than with Clark Clifford. Was Nourse more conservative?

LK: He didn't work with Steelman rather than Clifford for that reason. At the very beginning the President designated Steelman to make contacts with the Council of Economic Advisers. This didn't mean that we didn't go to Truman. From the beginning Truman had the three members of the Council come before the Cabinet and brief them on the economic situation. We met with Truman from time to time. But the idea of having this arrangement with Steelman was agreeable to Nourse because he did not want to get involved, did not want to get affiliated with policy decisions. This was consistent.

EH: Did President Truman really want a recommendation rather than alternatives laid out, by and large?

LK: He didn't want alternatives laid out. He wanted a one-armed economist. What does a president do when alternatives are laid out? What does a president do if his chief economist comes to him and says, "Well, there are three possibilities. You can do this, or you can do that or can do that. This might have that consequence, that might have this consequence, that might have that consequence." Truman would say, "Go back and tell me which you think is the most desirable of the three policies." One may think that was right or wrong, but that was Truman. Simply from the viewpoint of the mechanics of the presidential operation, it is very hard to do it any other way though there may be exceptions to any rule.

EH: What did he do if the Secretary of the Treasury and you were not in agreement?

LK: When we disagreed, he in a majority of cases took my advice. But our disagreements were not many, after we had discussed the matter.

EH: Would that be a general formula for Truman? When you disagreed, he would just come down on the side that was congenial to him?

LK: I don't think it was simply a matter of a recommendation being congenial to him, because the matters on which the Secretary of the Treasury and I disagreed were matters of the President's overall economic policy or the parts that are related to the whole. Quite apart from his reactions to the views of the two individuals, he felt that I was in a better position to give him advice than the Secretary of the Treasury.

EH: You would argue the Council has no institutional stakes of its own, other than disinterest.

LK: That was why it was created; it is free because it is not the ruler and administrator of a particular province or segment of economic policy. Even the Treasury Department is a claimant agency. The Treasury Department is usually, and in the main, close to the financial community.

EH: Does this mean that Truman regarded his White House staff as disinterested in that sense and therefore different from the people out in the government?

LK: Well, first, CEA was not White House staff; White House staff was Clark Clifford and Murphy, and others. CEA was really an "independent" agency in the Executive Office of the President, but independent to the same degree, and to the same degree only, as the Bureau of the Budget. Yes, he regarded us as being subject to human limitations, but freer from group alliances than the claimant departments. I think that was proper.

AL: The technical adviser has to make up his mind as to whom he is working for in our system of government. It's got two heads here, at least. Congress thinks it's equal with the president. In the presidential staff there should be no doubt that they are working for the president. Yet I detected in your earlier period the feeling that when things were controversial, the viability of economic policy depended on the Joint Economic Committee and when Congress wanted, the economic adviser had to go over and get on record publicly with Congress and its committees in order to make the policy viable. I gather you thought it would have been better if the CEA Chairman had followed the policy of the Bureau of the Budget Director and said, "How I advise the President is between him and me not between the congressional committee and me."

LK: You have a lot of different questions in here that are distinct and do not overlap. And this necessarily involves the differing views of Dr. Nourse and me. Actually, Dr. Nourse and I did not disagree greatly on economic policy. In fact, as distinguished from some of the Keynesians, Dr. Nourse and I were in agreement as to the importance of decisions in the private sector and of the price-wage processes: with two-thirds or more of the economy in that sector, they could cancel out any fiscal and monetary policy by an antithetical pattern of behavior. Therefore, we believed--not through controls but in various other ways--that bringing that consideration into the picture was very important. We didn't have many disagreements on economic policy. We wrote five published Reports of the Council, as required by the statute and they were published. Later Councils abandoned that practice. We were unanimous on all of them and they related to economic policy. We submitted advice to the President in the form of drafts of something like thirteen or fourteen economic reports sending them up in the middle as well as at the beginning of the year. There were only one or two minor instances in all that time where we had to carry differing views to the President. We also sent quarterly private reports. We differed on whether or not the Chairman of the Council or the Council should testify before the Congress, before the Joint Economic Committee. Dr. Nourse's view was that if the Chairman of the Council testified before the Joint Economic Committee, what would happen if he disagreed with the President? Manifestly, since he couldn't testify contrary to the President he would be stultifying himself. As many have pointed out, it was an inconsistent view, because he did go around the country making speeches to groups, and at times even disagreeing with the President. It was inconsistent. Second, it was a false concern, because that is a problem common to all men of integrity in top positions of the government. Once one assumes that the Chairman of the Council is functioning as a Cabinet officer relating to general economic policy--if he is not that, then the agency will have sunk into desuetude and will have no influence, and he won't have performed the function that the Act requires. There is no problem of integrity in the Chairman of the Council of Economic Advisers going before the Congress, before the Joint Economic Committee, or in the Secretary of State's doing that, or the Chairman of the Joint Chiefs of Staff. What if they disagree with the president and are men of integrity? If the difference is small, you submerge your holier-than-thou pride and say the government has to work, and you can't fight with the president on everything, and it isn't enough to bother about. If the difference is large enough, you resign: there's no other way out, if you're a man of integrity. To create the impression with the public that you are the Chairman of the Council of Economic Advisers and having your cake and eating it too when you disagree with the president on fundamental things--that doesn't seem to be integrity. In addition, the statute that established the Council of Economic Advisers established a parallel Joint Economic Committee, which held hearings. Now to Walter Lippman, who had warned me that I shouldn't go up there and testify because I would get into trouble, I said, "Walter, the President sends his most important domestic program to the Congress. Somebody has got to be the trustee for it. If we are not, who should be?" He said, "That's a powerful question. I can't answer it. I change my mind."

And what happened before we did it? The President first sent Paul Porter, then Averill Harriman, then Charlie Brannan to the Joint Economic Committee to discuss an Economic Report of the President that the Council of Economic Advisers had helped him prepare and that had written on it "prepared with the assistance of the Council of Economic Advisers." This was chaotic and impossible. Now you come to the question of how Truman handled it, how we handled it, and how the trouble in the papers got started. Nourse took the position I have described. John D. Clark and I, who believed profoundly the other way, went along with Nourse for two years and didn't bring it to public attention. As a matter of fact, on a matter of procedure, the general rule in the three-man body when the Chairman is first among equals, is to take a vote. If two out-vote one, then the procedures are determined by the views of the majority. Despite the fact that we went along, Nourse went before the public, said we were just political supporters of the President, threw the whole thing out into the open, so that we, on the one hand, were going along with him, and, on the other hand, suffering all the blows and arrows of being called politicians because we had a concept of the functioning of government that was so in accord with reality and practice. Subsequently Arthur Burns finessed it by saying he would testify before the Joint Economic Committee, but only in secret session. Every subsequent Chairman has recognized the obligation to educate the public and the Congress on the President's program, to support the program, and my view is that if he can't do that, he has to resign. Everyone has done it, and has received acclaim for doing it, because of the trail that was blazed during the time of the Truman Council. And here is one instance where Truman--I don't want you to get the feeling that I think he was superhuman--fell down on his job. Whether or not the Council should testify before the Joint Economic Committee was not an issue of high economics, it was an issue of how the government operated. Truman clearly thought that the Nourse position was unrealistic and that Clark and I were right. But instead of making a decision on that and saying to us, "This is the way it should operate," in which event Nourse wouldn't have resigned but would have said, "All right, let the Vice-Chairman go up," Truman said, "I'll leave it alone for a while." Then in 1948, when it became so hard because Nourse was speaking to the public anyway, and the fiasco of sending up Averill Harriman et al. to represent the Economic Report before the Congress became so clear, the President said, "The member of the Council who wants to do it can do it," and Clark and I went up. That's how it happened. But it blazed a trail, and nobody has questioned it since the period after Burns.

It is very interesting that Nourse, in the talks we had before the 1946 congressional elections, raised no objection to our testifying on the Hill. The 1946 elections came along and the Republicans took over the Congress, and he was absolutely certain--most people were--that Thomas E. Dewey was going to be the next president. Nourse had an interest in continuity and survival beyond the Truman administration. He was honorable, but utterly naive to think that a job at that level could or should be independent of who was president. But that was his view. Before the 1948 elections—this came to Truman's attention as well as mine—Nourse wrote a letter to Taft saying that he would like to discuss how he could continue and what changes should be made in the Council when Dewey became president. Taft replied that that was none of his (Taft's) business. This came to Truman's attention, and I suppose was a factor in Nourse's resignation in 1949, though Truman didn't in any way force his resignation.

Now you also asked if I represented the President or the Congress. I represented the President. You next come to the question: what does representing the president in that kind of a job mean? Representing the president involves understanding the climate and problems of government. You can't represent the president at that level unless you maintain good relations with him and are sufficiently aware of congressional possibilities in the advice that you give.

IB: Did you find yourself in discussions with the rest of the Council and the President about the kinds of logic that would support the reasonableness of the positions that were being presented to the JEC?

LK: We appeared before the Joint Economic Committee. The President never discussed with us what we should say.

IB: Was there any consensus about the style of the presentation so that there would be some consistency between what he was saying to the press and what you were saying to Congress?

LK: There had to be consistency, because it is not the function of a cabinet officer of the president to take positions that are inconsistent with his position. You resign if there is that conflict. All of my testimony before those committees is available in the printed record. It is inconceivable that Harry Truman would have read that in advance or participated in the development of the arguments. It is also obvious, from reading the testimony, that they are sheerly and purely economic analyses and have no element of politics in them, except in the larger aspect that all government is a political process. They were strictly economic arguments in support of positions that I believed in and had recommended to the President and he had accepted. If there was some small item on which we differed, I just didn't treat it. The Joint Economic Committee is made up of Republicans and Democrats. Never once was I embarrassed by being asked what I had advised the President or whether he had accepted my advice. Those people played by the rules of the game. They didn't expect me to tell them what I had advised the President or how I had differed with him. That was not their business.

Their business was the President's program and what I was saying in support of it.

EH: Crauford Goodwin, in <u>Exhortation and Controls</u>, talks about the search for stabilization policy in 1951. He writes, "It's noteworthy that during this period the CEA under Keyserling often found itself presenting the political dimensions of issues to supplement the mainly economic interpretation offered by economists in other parts of government. Keyserling's characteristic reply to the stabilization administrators was 'your policy was impossible in terms of labor's reaction to it.'" Goodwin is saying here that Keyserling had both institutional knowledge and political knowledge. Walter Salant made the point to me that the interesting thing about the staff in your time was that a lot of them were career government people who had a lot of institutional knowledge. You have noted that it's a shame that the Council became a place in which academic economists co-opted each other—in other words, people without institutional knowledge.

LK: Why shouldn't the Council members all be picked from universities and picked by professors rather than by the president? I don't want to argue the personal merits of various people. But how did Harry Truman pick his Council of Economic Advisers? He picked one man (Nourse) who was an academic economist and head of the Institute of Economics at Brookings and a former president of the American Economic Association. Truman got what he asked for. He picked one man (Clark) whom people hadn't heard of. A lawyer, a former member of the Wyoming legislature, a businessman and later vice-president of Standard Oil of Indiana where he made a fortune leading James W. Girard to list him as one of the twenty wealthiest men in America. Clark had sold his stock holdings just before the Great Crash and had gone to Johns Hopkins to study economics, bought a house there, took his Ph.D. in economics, and then became Dean of the Business School of the University of Nebraska. This was pretty varied experience. He picked someone (Keyserling) who, not exactly with the knowledge of the economics profession, had completed all of the requirements for the Ph.D. in economics at Columbia, including passing the exams, but hadn't written a thesis coming instead into government, believing that was more important than writing a thesis at the beginning of the New Deal. I would not have been "qualified" in the eyes of some of these academicians to be on the Council of Economic Advisers because I had gone into the government and participated during the most parlous period in our history in the big economic problems and decisions and had a great deal to do with writing most of the important statutes that even today are regarded as the bedrock of our stability.

When I was first appointed Vice-Chairman of the Council, Truman didn't know me except from the Senate, but not at all well. I was appointed on recommendation of others. Some

economists and Nourse, in his book, say that the fact that
Senator Wagner recommended me for appointment showed that it
was "political." I had worked for or helped Wagner for
thirteen years. He had estimated my abilities. He had
nothing to gain when he hired me. I wasn't even from New
York. He had never met me before. His recommendation of me
was the same as George Norris' recommendation of the first
head of the General Accounting Office. Wagner recommended
somebody who had worked for him whom he knew and whom he had
tested. What's wrong about that?

But the Council of Economic Advisers has hardly ever
really been selected by any president after my time, which,
among other inbred effects, means that you get a type of
person who comes there for a while to burnish his reputation
and then leaves. You hardly ever had anybody who stayed
there more than two or three years. Is this the way to run
an important enterprise? I couldn't conceive of myself leaving the job of Chairman of the Council of Economic Advisers
to go back to any other job. I was "voted" out of the job in
November 1952. What else could I do that was more important?
What greater opportunity could I have? But we since have had
a constant churning and rotation and the job has been de-
meaned to the point that it is merely an opportunity to get a
little experience for two or three years and then go on to
brighter heavens. I think it is too bad.

The Structure of the Council

EH: With high turnover there's little continuity or historical
memory. What kinds of knowledge do you think are part of the
kind of economics that you have been practicing which are not
found in academic economics, and how do you see the operation
of the Council in your time and since?

LK: I have not been protesting so much against academic economics
as against the nature of current academic economics, and that
is an entirely different thing. I don't think I could possibly have done whatever I did, right or wrong, without as
thorough an academic training as one could get. The fact
that I didn't write a thesis has nothing to do with it. I
got all the training. I'm not denying the need for academic
training. I'm merely saying that academic training ought to
be improved. It has serious flaws. Nor did my period on the
Council deny it. Nourse was an academic economist, so was
Clark although he had an immense amount of other training.
He was a Ph.D. from Johns Hopkins; he was dean of a business
school. I was an academic economist. And on the staff,
which I helped to select, there wasn't a single one at the
top level who wasn't a Ph.D. in economics and trained in
academic economics. We had Paul Homan, who had been the
editor of the American Economic Review; we had Walter Salant,
who had worked with Burns at the National Bureau. We had
Fred Waugh, who was a top agricultural economist from the
government. Running all the way down the list they were all

academic economists. But they happened to be people who, largely through work in the government, had something added to their academic training.

EH: What was that?

LK: An interest in the solution of actual problems and the knowledge of how problems had been approached successfully and unsuccessfully, which is adding a lot. For example, a man who was in the Office of War Production during World War II learned something about how and by what methods production was accelerated and enlarged that he could not learn by the conventional processes of academic teaching in the university. Or somebody in the Social Security Administration learned something about the problems of old people and the problems of a workable system of social insurance that he wouldn't learn at a university. I myself, working on housing laws, the studies underlying them and the reports surrounding them and most of the public work laws and the collective bargaining laws, learned things that I wouldn't have learned if I had stayed at Columbia.

EH: What have been the consequences then of virtual takeover of the Council by academics?

LK: I don't judge entirely by results, although I judge mainly by results. First, I think it is bad government for officials at that level to select each other rather than being appointed by the president. And that is what has happened. Second, I think it bad government to have a three-man Council when two of them are in effect reduced to the level of top staff officials because they owe their appointments to the Chairman and have been selected from his circle of like-minded people. Should you have a one-man Council or a three-man Council? I favor a three-man Council for reasons stated. But I think there is no point in creating a public impression that you have three equals or two equals and one first among equals who are contributing to the job, when in fact you have one Council member and two top-ranking staff members who never see the president, who don't get into the picture, and who are really only helpers to the Chairman. I think it's bad government for people to be selected by a process that essentially produces inbreeding. There are changes if there is a change in administration, but if you have an eight-year administration, that's really bad. And the Chairman picks his successor and the Chairman picks the other members. Burns in reality picked Saulnier; Heller in reality picked Ackley as a member of the Council, then in reality picked him to be Chairman. I think this produces an excessive concentration of members of the Council to one school or one approach or one group of people who have helped each other. The combination of this process, with the high rotation, with the flaws that I find in the nature of a considerable part of the academic environment especially at the schools from which it appears these people are most likely to be chosen--those few places with their accent upon what I regard as the unreal and remote. The policies they follow have frequently been wayward. The pragmatic results are that they haven't been able to produce. We haven't had full employment since 1953, or a decent stabilization of prices since 1966. That's a long time. Something must be wrong.

BW: You said that one of the happiest things about the Nourse-Keyserling-Clark Council of Economic Advisers is that all three of you were so close in diagnosis and description. Now you seem to be objecting to the Chairman's designating the other two, on the grounds that it breeds excessive like-mindedness. Is there something of a misperceived tension between these two statements?

LK: No, I think those two positions are entirely consistent. I think there would be all the difference in the world between nine judges on the Supreme Court arriving at a unanimous opinion and having a chief justice who picked the other eight judges and then having them arrive at the unanimous opinion. I think there is a great value in three men of widely differing backgrounds and experiences--although they have to be within a broad spectrum of sympathy with the administration--arriving at a unanimous opinion and three people arriving at a unanimous opinion when one of them picks the other two. I think there's all the difference in the world.

EH: What are the consequences in effectiveness of staff members if, in fact, they had personal knowledge of the government, in their prior working with other government bureaus?

LK: When Burns became Chairman he made a big play of the fact that he for the first time was appointing a troika that indicated interrelation among the heads of different agencies. When I was Chairman of the Council, at a Cabinet meeting, President Truman said, with respect to Sawyer and Snyder, "You know these people started out critical of you, now you've won them over completely." And I said, "Well, Mr. President, I had to sell my shirt to do it," and he said, "Oh no, you didn't." But never did a Chairman of the Council of Economic Advisers work more closely with the Cabinet people, formally and informally. My being in the Cabinet, which hasn't happened since, had an effect on that. Never were there more complete coordinating groups at other levels. We had working committees within the Council. We had a committee on stabilization, a committee on wage-price relations, a committee on economic developments. We had a so-called "round up" committee (which was a committee on the business situation forecasts) and a policy committee. We had the counterparts of all of those committees in interdepartmental committees, implicating the Treasury, the Commerce Department, the Labor Department, Agriculture Department and the Bureau of the Budget--I think those were the main ones--at the top staff level. In every case, the person who was chairman of our own committee was the chairman of the inter-departmental group, and they were meeting all the time. So we had a continuous, year-round, formalized, working set-up.

EH: Is it important for Council staff to know how the government works at the bureau level?

LK: No person could have been an effective chairman of this interdepartmental group if he hadn't known the government. He could not have been as effective if he had been suddenly called in from some remote place.

JG: Do you think that the CEA staff should be involved in policy decisions?

LK: It depends on what you mean by policy decisions. When we were submitting drafts of Economic Reports to the President, which is his basic policy document, the Council, not the staff, was responsible for the view that went to the President. So in that sense, the staff didn't participate in policy. In another sense they did. We didn't ask them merely to bring us statistics, we discussed policies with them. We got their views on the Reports. Actually, the President's Report was prepared first by making an outline. Parts of it were assigned to various people on the staff who wrote memos and then tried to put the memos together into a document. I then took the document and edited it any way I saw fit and questioned anything I didn't think was right. It then went to the three members of the Council who met on it, and the staff people were brought in. Staff still could say, "Keyserling changed this in a way we didn't mean or something got left out that we thought ought to be brought in." It was argued out. The Council members could decide to put it in, leave it out or change it.

After we had been through this process and the Council had the Economic Report draft, it was sent to all the relevant Cabinet people and discussed with them if they wanted to, so their views were considered. But again I didn't sit around the table with them and take a vote, because it was our CEA job, not theirs. But it was discussed with them; sometimes they affected our views, sometimes they didn't. Then it went to the President. If any Cabinet officer wanted to disagree, he could still go to the President. When it got to the President, the White House staff--Clifford (later Murphy) and others--took a look at it. The White House staff never intruded upon our policy. That hasn't always been the case since. They never believed that they were our equals in policy. They asked: "Are these words in the form that the President would like to have attributed to him? Does it square with certain other things that the President may have decided or done recently?" They didn't change it; they called specifics to our attention. Very frequently they had very helpful suggestions. After that stage, the Council and the White House Staff people would sit around the table with the President, and he would read the whole Economic Report and discuss it. And even at that stage, the President looked predominantly to the CEA.

EH: You said that you sat with the Cabinet and think that's been important. Why is it so important? You also sat regularly with the NSC. Why do you think it's so important that the Chairman meet with those two bodies?

LK: There are many reasons. It gives the chairman a chance to see the president more frequently and to converse with him a little bit apart from the meeting. It gives him the chance to influence the president through the comments he makes at those meetings. It gives him a chance—and this is probably most important—to gain the confidence, understanding, and friendship and help of the members of the Cabinet. It is his continuous responsibility to try to get them in agreement with what he is recommending to the president, because they can't be ignored. Those kinds of contacts are most important because they improve your relations with the Cabinet and with the president. Those are the bases that bring you closer to the president, give you more chance to influence him, give you better relations with the other Cabinet people, and give you an alert awareness of certain problems that come up, and at the same time tell these others, even the president, that certain problems are within your bailiwick and that you have an interest in them. Being there, you know that this is happening and you have a chance to assert yourself. There are all kinds of ways in which it is important that the CEA Chairman be a _de facto_ member of the Cabinet.

EH: Was there even informally in your time either a Triad or Quadriad, as that term was used in Heller's time? Regular meetings of the four...

LK: No.

EH: Should there be?

LK: I have mixed feelings about it. I had frequent contacts with Secretary Snyder, with the Budget Director, with the Secretary of Labor and with the Secretary of Commerce, with McCabe as Chairman of the Federal Reserve Board—Martin didn't become Chairman until very late. I had contacts with most of them in Cabinet meetings. The other approach is a very good idea in theory and can work very well in practice. There's one trouble with it. That trouble has become acute in the Carter situation. He calls it an Economic Policy group. This arrangement tends to give all of the members of the group ostensibly equal standing with respect to overall economic policy, which is wrong for the reasons previously given. Any group of that kind also tends at that level and at that degree of responsibility, if it is done that way, to produce a vying for leadership—who is the most influential of the group and who in effect is the chairman?

AL: Don't these considerations argue for a single economic adviser rather than more?

LK: Could be. But I would say that if I had to make the choice I would prefer to have three people. "Sharing" a responsibility which should be CEA's with others is very different from the responsibility of the CEA being shared by three CEA members. Nobody is all-knowing and nobody is all-wise and nobody has all the technical equipment or all the practical equipment. It is valuable to be able to sit down and talk with two other very competent people to get their judgments. It had a great influence on my thinking.

JS: During the past year there was a lot of discussion of increasing the size of the Council.

LK: I can't pass upon whether it should be five or three. I am inclined to think that three strikes a good balance between having too few and having too many.

JS: How about on the staff side?

LK: That's a matter of the work load. If the Council assumed the work load that I think it must assume, it would need a bigger staff than it has. With its current work load, writing one Economic Report a year rather than two, asserting, as Okun asserted and as it is still asserted, that it isn't the CEA's business what happens about foreign policy or transportation, I don't see why they need twice as many people as we had.

EH: The Council is now very dependent upon analytic work done in the departments.

LK: This is why the Council can and should remain a small staff. The Council should be a small agency, doing the kind of work I am talking about; now to do that they have to get a great amount of statistics and analytical work and advice from the departments, and have to ask for it, naturally. But there is an even more important job that the recent Councils have fallen down on entirely to the best of my knowledge; suggesting to the departments some of what they ought to be doing. Let me illustrate what I mean. When I became Chairman of the Council, the Department of Commerce was stating all of the GNP and component figures only in current dollars. This was meaningless; you can't tell what the rate of growth has been; or what really happened in current dollars. You have to have constant dollars with different deflators. The Secretary of Commerce said this would cost too much and he didn't see why we should do it. I had to go to the President. The result was that the Secretary of Commerce was ordered to do it in constant dollars as well as current dollars. This has been

one of the biggest sources of information for economists and
everybody else; now you get the picture in constant dollars
and in current dollars with the proper deflators. That's one
example. Income distribution is another. I don't understand
how economists could think, no matter what their views are,
that income distribution isn't a vital aspect of economic
analysis. The Department of Commerce with hundreds or thou-
sands of economists and research people had one girl alone
working on gathering new information on income distribution.
I protested it repeatedly...didn't get far with it. It was
only when the poverty problem came to be a great issue that
they began to recognize that there was a problem of income
distribution because different people had different incomes.
They began then to set up quite an adequate service for
getting income distribution figures. Now the government has
started making various other studies. The Department of
Agriculture, as we all know, had more economists and statis-
ticians and research people than almost any other department.
But they weren't asking the right questions for the purpose
of national economic policy. When I asked the questions that
I wanted to use in writing a pamphlet on the farm problem, or
that I would have wanted to use if the work of the Council of
Economic Advisers were properly expanded to take in the
agriculture problem in the sense that I have discussed it,
they weren't even working on these matters. The Council of
Economic Advisers should have the authority and obligation to
indicate to the departments those lines of inquiry, to be
conducted through their larger staffs and their expertise,
which are directly relevant to the making of a comprehensive
and integrated national economic policy. They should say to
the Department of Agriculture, to Commerce, to Labor or
Treasury, "Here's what we are going to need from you."

Bureaucratic Politics and Economic Policy

EH: How would you characterize the relations of the Council with
the Bureau of the Budget when you were Chairman?

LK: Excellent.

EH: But in terms of some sort of overall view of the economy?

LK: Well, suppose the budget is going to be submitted in January.
A full year in advance the Budget Bureau would ask us for a
complete portrayal of likely economic developments and broad
outlines of what size budget was compatible with these prospective developments and with our targets for the economy.
That was asked for at the very beginning of the year. That
involved continuous relations over the course of the year
between our people and the Budget Bureau people. In that way
our economic responsibilities and projections and goals and
prospects entered into the making of the budget itself. It
was done on a very harmonious and useful basis. It was not
done sufficiently well because we still had some who held to

the notion that the main economic policy is budgetary policy and that you use your Economic Report to defend the budget. Actually, budgetary policy is an aspect of economic policy.

AL: Would you say that the business of the Chairman of the Council is not primarily to represent the economic thinking of the profession in order to maintain relations with it, but the primary responsibility is to the president and to the economy as a whole?

LK: That's easy. It is never the primary responsibility of anybody, under the system that I approve of, to represent anybody but himself. Let me tell you what I mean. I don't think it is the function of a congressman or a senator to vote what he thinks is the view of his constituents at the moment by taking a poll—this is corruptive. It is his duty to vote his best thinking on the grounds that the people elected him to represent them and to carry out the process. Now in the final analysis, my job as Chairman of the Council of Economic Advisers is to give the president my thinking and not an average of the thinking of everybody else. Actually it is my job to tap in proper ways the thinking of others and to take it into account in formulating my judgment. I could not go to the President and say, "This is what I think, but, on the other hand, the majority of the members of the Economic Association feel differently." Truman would have said to me, "Well, should all of them be my economic advisers?" No, you have got to give him your views, after proper and constant benefiting from the views of others in formulating your views. Now as to whom I am responsible, I am trying to respond to the interests of the country first, the interests of the president second, in that order. But I am, in a managerial sense, responsible to the president, and to him alone.

Reconstructing Policy Decisions

EH: I'd like to shift gears now and reconstruct some policy decisions. Why don't we begin with the tension between inflation and recession and the postwar questions that the early Nourse Council faced. What were we looking at after the war? Fear of recession? Problems of inflation? The problem of wage and price controls?

LK: You have to remember that the Council of Economic Advisers, appointed late in 1946, did not really function until the beginning of 1947. We weren't even appointed until very late in 1946, a good many months after the Act was passed. Our first preparatory work for the President's Economic Report related to 1947. A lot of the big problems of postwar inflation immediately connected with the war came and were resolved, I think rather poorly, before we came in. However, I must say one thing about my own analysis of the causes of that inflation. There were many. The main cause was that

half of the war was financed out of taxation and half out of
borrowing. When you borrow money for productive investment
purposes, there is a productive asset to match the money when
it's spent. When you borrow $50 billion a year to finance a
war and blow it up in explosives, there is no productive
asset. The public is misled in the belief that they are
saving when it is merely euphemistically called "saving."
The real cost has been paid for out of the current product,
which you can't shift to a later time. My view is that the
main factor in the inflationary problems shortly after the
war was the release of this tremendous volume of accumulated
savings, which had been blown up. To the credit of the
Roosevelt administration, it did not want to finance the
entire war out of taxation; it would have been ill advised to
do so. It did want to finance a larger part of it out of
taxation than actually took place, but Congress was opposed.
Anyway, by the time CEA came in, effectively in 1947, I would
say that the difference between Nourse and the other members
of the Council arose in 1948 because Truman was trying to get
legislated an anti-inflationary program at a time when we
were on our way into the 1949 recession. Many economists and
others very much objected to injecting an anti-inflationary
controls program at a time when we were moving toward a
recession. And that was a difference betwen Nourse and the
other members of the Council. The difference did not arise
out of a difference of views as to where we were moving. It
arose out of an entirely different consideration, which is
thoroughly revealed in about 10,000 words of testimony that I
gave to the Senate Banking and Currency Committee in the
middle of 1948 that an inflationary problem can arise at any
stage of the business cycle and that you really ought to have
effective weapons to deal with it at all stages. Inflation
isn't something that goes away when you have a recession or
comes when you have full prosperity. If you will take a look
at that testimony, you will see laid out the entire basis of
my challenge to the operation of economic policy and economic
thinking for most of the last fifteen or twenty years with
what, I think, are very disastrous results. In that testimony I said: First the problem is not just the level of
prices or where they are moving. The problem is the relationships among prices and between prices on other factors,
such as money incomes. I can look back to 1922-1929. We had
an amazingly stable price level, except for falling farm
prices, yet we ended with the greatest crash in history. A
stable price level does not in itself resolve the problem of
the relations between growth in productive power through
investment and ability to consume. What had actually happened was that there was a big advance in profits, investment
and technology and productivity, while workers' income and
farm income fell so far behind that you had a fundamental
maladjustment under a stable price level. The position I
took as early as 1948 was that you had to look at the relationships and I saw many imbalances which were corrected.
Second, in a highly "administered" price system, there is

very little correlation between the level of demand related
to capacity and price trends. Large corporations raise their
prices faster when we are in a recession because they have a
profit target and because productivity goes way down. It
goes down to zero or negative, so the per unit labor costs
rise. In an effort to compensate for the lower productivity
and the inadequate markets, they raise their prices faster
than when the economy is in good shape. For all these reasons I argued in 1948 that we needed, not the imposition of
the controls, but the addition of them to the armory; I still
say that. That was the difference between me and many other
economists at that point. Of course, until the Korean War,
we didn´t get the controls.

Now, the more important issue, by far, the one that is
more relevant to our situation today, was on the general
question of how to strike a balance between the prevention of
inflation and the full use of the nation´s resources. This
became acute with the Korean War. There were people in the
government, and there was Mr. Bernard Baruch, insisting that
the war ought to be fought out of the current product. In
1950 they put on a big campaign that the war ought to be
fought out of the current product, that inflation was a
greater danger to us than the aggressors, and that we should
undertake extremely strenuous cutbacks in civilian supplies
and put the whole nation under rigorous controls. I took a
diametrically opposite position. In the first place, I
argued that this isn´t going to be just a war of four years;
this is going to be a long struggle, hot or cold. In a long
struggle, when the war is far away and not at home, and not
the kind of a big war that we had with the Germans and the
Japanese, you can´t hold the people´s support for a program
of permanent denial. They won´t support your effort. I
suggested second, that the best way to take care of the
inflation was to build the industrial base rapidly, deal with
selective shortages through a great many measures including
special amortization programs. My expansionary or growth
position and the restrictionist position had a furious battle. My viewpoint won out. I even took the position represented in the last of the published pamphlets of the Council
of Economic Advisers entitled, "The Economics of National
Defense," that if we rushed into the controls (in addition,
before the Chinese entry into the war, it´s dubious whether
the controls would have been needed because, economically
speaking, the war didn´t amount to much) as the cure-all, we
would just forget all these other problems and that we first
ought to establish priorities and goals similar to what we
had done in World War II; that we should get this out of the
way without becoming obsessed, rather than properly concerned, with the matter of inflation. I think this is the
reason why the average rate of inflation during the seven
years that I was on the Council was only 3 percent, which is
incredible now. It was down to 0.8 percent in the last year.
I don´t think the main reason was the controls. They were
needed after the Korean War expanded with the Chinese inter-

vention. But I think the expansionary approach was the basic
reason why the rate of inflation was held down and why it did
not burst forth for a number of years after 1953. We took
the position that the best economic policy fully uses and
distributes the economic product of the nation. We took the
position that not only in war but equally in peace, the
incremental value of used rather than unused resources tremendously outweighs a tendentious and uncertain hypothesis as
to which will yield more inflation. After all, the real
reason why people suffer when you have the kind of inflation
we have had recently--Paul Samuelson pointed this out,
strangely--is because there is less distribution of goods and
services per capita. The price behavior is merely one factor
in how that is taking place. In addition, the policy I urged
was immensely successful in restraining inflation.

SM: Did you propose raising taxes substantially during the Korean
War?

LK: Not only proposed it, we did it. We raised them greatly.
Certainly. That was the difference between what we did and
what was done during the Vietnam War. Certainly, we raised
taxes greatly.

SM: Then you relied on selective controls or some selective
increases or attempted selective increases in productive
capacity to deal with the expected inflation that might have
occurred.

LK: We had a total economic approach in the nature of government
planning. Now I'm not talking about government planning of
the private economy; I have been very moderate on that. I
don't want the government to make the myriads of decisions
involved in the operations of the private economy. I think
we have got the best system on earth, although we can do much
better and need to do much better. You know, it's a funny
thing that now I am accused of being an inflationist when the
Truman administration made a better record against inflation
than any administration since, especially when one looks at
the price trend from the first to the last year. I am accused of being a reckless government spender, yet the Truman
administration was the only one to average a surplus budget
among all the administrations between Coolidge and now. And
I am accused of wanting to control the whole economy when I
dragged my feet on controls until we got other things done
first. I never regarded them as important as the other
things. It isn't important just to have goals for reduction
in unemployment. Here's where the misapplication of the
Keynesian economics and all the subsequent policies have
fallen down. When they think the economy needs to be stimulated, they say, "Pour in," and they don't care where you
pour in. Even Paul Samuelson and Walter Heller said to me,
"X billion of stimulus will have the same effect whether it
is tax reduction or whether it is spending or no matter where

you put it." I said, "You're like a man driving up to a gas station and saying, `fill `er up,´ and the attendant says, `Shall I put the water in the gas tank and the oil in the refrigerator and something else in the tires?´ and the driver says, `What's the difference? Haven't you ever heard of Lord Keynes?´ " Well, there's all the difference in the world. The whole basis of economic analysis is to analyze where your resource maladjustments are, where allocations are going wrong, where your income flows are going wrong. And you correct it by applying the stimulus or the restraint at the right points, which really gets back to what I said in 1948 to the Senate Banking and Currency Committee. We don't have the kind of economy where you can just throw a blunderbuss at the whole thing. Here again, the economists are beginning to say that we need micro economic as well as macro economic policies. Well, that's exactly what I meant when I talked about the driver and where you put the oil, except that the macro as well as the micro needs to be selective. That's all it comes down to: policies to deal not only with the structure of the labor force, but the structure of national product and the structure of national income. The government shouldn't plan that for the whole economy, but since every national policy affects that, whether it be tax or money or anything else, how can you arrange these policies without having a full tableau of what you are trying to do and why? Otherwise, you set it all off in the wrong direction. What we were doing during the Korean War was deciding what kinds of tax increases where. We were combining tax increases with selective tax benefits with regard to specific shortages relating to various commodities. We were combining an anti-inflationary effort, which was successful, with a growth effort, which was also successful.

EH: Could we go back and talk about the war, 1950 right on through 1952, and how economic policy changed in the beginning and then at mid-point when the concern was for stabilization and slowing down production?

LK: As soon as the Korean War broke out, we began moving on the front that I have talked about, after debate, and the debate didn't take long, because Truman saw it that way. He established Charlie Wilson, General Electric Charlie, as the mobilizer, and the CEA helped to set priorities and to build these practical quantitative models for the proper allocation of resources, some of which were to be implemented by general monetary and fiscal policies. For more micro policies, on the monetary side, for example, we had regulation X, regulation Y and so forth, which dealt with selective restrictions. We never went along with Arthur Burns' unsuccessful idea that monetary controls, so to speak, can be only aggregative. We went for selective controls on the money supply and credit, on the simple ground that use of the nation's money should be related to economic balanced priorities of need. We did the same thing on taxation, when we came to consider how taxes

should be raised, where the burdens should be imposed. By
the time of the Chinese entry in late 1950, which was unexpected and which was only a few months after the war started,
it was clear that the war was going to be a much bigger war
than we had earlier foreseen. I am not prepared to say that
we would not have put on price-wage controls anyway, even for
a smaller war. I don't think they would have been necessary,
but they might have been. However, the war did get bigger.
We did put on the price-wage controls, and in the sequence
that seemed to be desirable. When we put the controls on,
there was no way of deciding, of defining their exact scope.
We had a quite full panoply of instrumentalities. We had a
stabilizer; we had a wage-price board; we had mobilizer
Charlie Wilson; and we had at one time two stabilizers aside
from the wage-price board. We had Allen Valentine and Eric
Johnson. Though I don't remember exactly what their respective titles were, their activities were very carefully and
harmoniously reconciled with the overall planning of the
Council of Economic Advisers. I would not have become in any
way subordinate to Charlie Wilson; I worked for the President. But I did sit as a member, an adviser, on his mobilization board all the way through, and this gets again back to
how President Truman handled things, because he was the one
who decided this. Once a week he also had me brief his
mobilization advisory board, also chaired by Wilson, which
was different from the mobilization board. The mobilization
board was in the government structure as an operating agency.
The advisory board was composed of labor, business, and the
general public--William H. Davis was there from the general
public. William Green, George Meany, Walter Reuther and Phil
Murray were there from labor. People were there from business. President Truman had me brief them every week with
charts. So we moved into the controls and had all these
arrangements for controls, and the controls were fairly wide.
We had a fairly large nation-wide staff in control administration. I have never had an aversion to controls, and I've
never accepted most of the constantly-repeated objections to
them. Naturally, they couldn't work under Nixon, since he
changed his mind every few months and announced when he put
controls on that he didn't believe in them and was going to
take them off pretty soon. They worked remarkably well in
World War II and during the Korean War. Sure, people said
that there were black markets, and undoubtedly there were
some. Controls created black markets just as traffic laws
create violators. But related to the whole picture, they did
bring about the desired restraints; they did get the goods
where they were needed; they accomplished redirection of
resources along desirable lines in accord with an established
plan. They worked very well.

JG: Did the Truman administration's decision in late 1951 to
stretch out the mobilization program over another year reflect a decline in your influence with Truman?

LK: I think it was later--in 1952. It indicated some decline in my influence--this is rather thoroughly traced in Edward Flash's book--and naturally, I thought it was a wrong policy. It was a wrong policy for two reasons. First, regardless of whether or not we should have gotten into the Korean War, we were in it. I regarded it as a definitive war, that is, once we were in it, the whole purpose was to show the people whom we denominate as the aggressors that we were strong enough to get a win. (And this doesn't mean MacArthur's view of going to war with China.)

I was in the Cabinet when General Greunther came in weekly to brief us. We had been told before the war that we were so superior industrially and in tools and that, even though we had a smaller population, we could always out-gun and out-fly and have a larger mass of material anywhere in the world. And here Greunther was briefing us that the Koreans, who were getting their supplies from distances that logistically were as difficult or more difficult than getting them from the United States, had faster planes, more planes, and were out-gunning us. I said, "How come?" I am talking about these later stages. So this involved one of my colloquies with the man Truman called the greatest of Americans (that was one of Truman's misjudgments) General George Marshall. It ran like this. We were talking about making cutbacks and the argument for the cutbacks was not military; the argument was economic. Marshall was one of a very many military men who got all their knowledge and thinking on economics from big business. So there was a slight reversion to business as usual. We were told that unless there were cutbacks in the defense program we would have to close down the automobile industry, close down the housing industry. My goodness, a little while after those cutbacks, the housing and the automobiles were just falling out of our ears. The idea that we would have to close down the automobile industry and the housing industry to fight that limited war after the big buildup and taking into account the marginal difference between before and after the cutbacks was ridiculous. But we did it. I was sitting across the table from George Marshall in the Cabinet meeting. He looked at me and said, "Young man, you don't understand. In World War II, we did things very inefficiently. Sometimes the engines got to the field before the crates. You know, the crates mean the bodies. And sometimes the bodies got there before the engines. This time we are going to spell it out. We're going to do it more efficiently. We are going to do it slower." I said, "General, war is wasteful. So is a fire engine. A fire engine is the most wasteful car or motor vehicle that you can imagine. But it needs to get to the fire and it needs to get there fast." And Harry Truman was a little nonplussed by this disagreement on war policy between the greatest living American who had led our war efforts in World War II and me. But then he came to realize in discussions I had that we were talking economics and not war strategy and that George Marshall didn't know very much about economics, but nonetheless there was a cutback and I think that was a mistake.

EH: Why did the President go in that direction?

LK: I think it was a mistake, but I can't explain why he went in that direction. I think at the time he may have blurred a little in his own mind. My informed guess would be that we went in that direction, not because he didn't understand what I was saying, but because the generals were assuring him that you could make the cutback and still do very well and win the war anyway. Look at the advice President Johnson got, for a while, about Vietnam, which has nothing to do with the merits or demerits of that war.

OG: Do you feel that your Council might have differed in its effectiveness if it had been established at the beginning of an administration and not in the middle of an ongoing administration when relations among people in the Executive had been set?

LK: I don't think that is the case, because I was so much more part of the administration, of the machinery of the government process, than my successors who came in at the beginning of an administration. But long before there was a Council, I was very, very much a part of the Truman administration and of the Roosevelt administration. I had risen at the start of World War II to the position of acting administrator of the agency which was building millions of units of war housing a year and which Truman, as the head of the Senate investigatory committee, said was doing one of the best wartime jobs in Washington. I had actually written three platforms on which Roosevelt ran for re-election as President, because I was then working for Senator Wagner and he was the Chairman of the Platform Committee. I affected many of the government's shots from 1933 forward; for example, I had worked on much of the early New Deal legislation. I had been in the Executive branch, I had been in the congressional branch, so I was very much a part of things for almost two decades, from March 1933 forward. It was fortuitous that the Council was established in the middle of an administration; I assume that if it had been established at the beginning of an administration, if there were a new president, he would have gone out and found the members of the Council the way they have been found most of the time since, from the outer world—people regarded as generally within his political framework—and they would have been newer to the situation than I was. I think, though, that the controlling factor is the nature of the president and the nature of the people he is dealing with, rather than just when they come in.

AL: I have read Rex Tugwell's story of the experimental Roosevelt, and Vannevar Bush's Pieces of the Action. Both deal with the relations between the President and the succession of his advisers--how people whom he relied upon very closely at some stage have a way of revolving out. How long can a man stay in that job?

LK: My record of longevity in the government was a monument to endurance. But seriously, another explanation for this again goes back to Truman. There are many reasons why people gradually lose their influence with the president and gradually get pushed out. One of the most important reasons is that when they acquire a prime influence, there are a lot of other people in the government who start working against them and often "get them" in one way or another. But Truman was remarkably adept at not allowing that to happen. I think this is an important factor in the situation.

JC: To what extent did you feel you were exluded from the Treasury-Federal Reserve negotiations in 1951?

LK: Well, technically, I wasn't excluded. Truman appointed a committee of Charlie Wilson and myself, John Snyder as Secretary of the Treasury, and Thomas McCabe as head of the Federal Reserve Board. John Snyder went to the hospital and was replaced by William McChesney Martin who was Under Secretary of the Treasury. These were the four. As I indicated in my very lengthy monograph on the Truman administration, which was part of the meetings of the Truman group this year and which is now in the Truman library--you see, some of the stories I told you indicate that I admire Truman; I don't and never worshipped him--this was where he fell down very badly, because he surrendered command, just as he had surrendered command, despite his usual assertion of command and his usual decisiveness, when he didn't decide right away whether or not the Council of Economic Advisers should go on the Hill. It was intolerable to leave that matter undecided. And he surrendered command toward the very end on this monetary thing. I can't give psychological reasons, I am not a psychiatrist. I can't go back to first causes, but he surrendered command, despite the fact that earlier he had asserted himself rather strongly. In fact, he had called Alan Sproul, the head of the Federal Reserve Board of New York, down to Washington, and held a meeting at the White House--I was there--in which he said: "I am going to withdraw the money out of the banks just as Andrew Jackson did." He was very strong about it, but in connection with this accord, he surrendered command. First, he surrendered command in making Charlie Wilson chairman. It just wasn't correct for the mobilizer to be chairman of this committee. This was not a war mobilization matter; this was one of the most important issues of general and long-term economic policy. President Truman should have made the chairman of the Council of Economic Advisers the committee chairman, which has nothing to do with who held the job, although it happens that the person who held that job, myself, was fully in accord with Truman's policies on this and always had been, quite independently of

Truman. Anyhow, this was the first thing, and Wilson didn't
listen to anybody but his banker friends on what the monetary
policy should be. You see a tremendous campaign was going on
then. Marriner Eccles, who had helped the best financing of
a war in our history by following a liberal money policy and
had been a radical banker in the early days of the New Deal,
.later suffered the great sea change that many people do. He
became an arch-conservative and started shouting all around
the country that the Federal Reserve Board policy had been an
engine of inflation during and immediately after World War
II. I said, "The Federal Reserve Board wasn't the engine of
inflation; the war was the engine of inflation. We had much
more inflation during wars when there was no Federal Reserve
Board. How can you say that the Federal Reserve Board was
the engine of inflation?" Accompanying that was the argument
for Fed "independence" on the ground that it should be non-
political. I said, "Look, I'm for independence in its place,
but monetary policy isn't any more important than tax policy.
Should tax policy be in the hands of an independent group of
experts drawn largely from the banking community? Shouldn't
wage-price policy during World War II, which took money out
of everybody's pocket, be in the hands of management and
labor?" It is an anachronism--not only an anachronism but
inconsistent--to claim that the money power of the nation
should be "independent" in the central bank.

EH: What about the Ewing group and the contribution of your
      economic thought to the development of the Fair Deal program?

LK: I think it was large. I think that the Ewing group was
      largely responsible for the totality of the shift in the
      President's policies and undertakings. I think the first
      major manifestation of what is called the Fair Deal program
      was in the 1947 State of the Union message and that was very
      substantially a product of the work of the Ewing group.

EH: How did your ideas develop in that group and what were the
      economic underpinnings of social policies?

LK: In the first place, I cannot possibly draw a dichotomy be-
      tween social policy and economic policy. I just can't. Is
      having people employed rather than unemployed a social policy
      or an economic policy? What about providing decent housing
      for slum dwellers? Or minimum-wage laws, or income redistri-
      bution? In a sense I agree that anything which requires use
      of economic resources is an economic problem. The dichotomy
      between economics and morality, if you want to call it that,
      has been one of the banes of national economic policy. But I
      don't mind your saying that these are social programs. I
      happen to think that careful examination of the American
      economy from the viewpoint of balance would indicate that if
      I drew on that board the five or six major elements in main-
      taining a full economy, which is an economic problem narrowly
      conceived, and drew on another board ways to meet the main

social and moral needs of the nation, that the two lists
would be almost the same. The reason that we have had such
enormous departures from a full economy is because we haven't
paid much attention to the fact that for technological and
many other reasons there is no way of using the economy fully
without developing more fully those particular sectors.

EH: I really want to go back to that Ewing group. I didn't mean
to suggest a dichotomy in my question, I think that economic
and social thinking are interrelated. What I want to do is
ilustrate that. You met for two years?

LK: We met from 1946 until 1952 when Truman announced he wouldn't
run again. Now we have to remember another thing. While the
Ewing group was a quiet and select group, it was in no sense
apart from the government. Who were the people in the Ewing
group? There was Clifford, who was really the chief man in
the White House, especially on domestic policy, the Chairman
of the Council of Economic Advisers, the Agriculture Department, the Interior Department and the Labor Department, and a
few others. So the Ewing group really was a small group of
people in the top domestic policy fields. We developed the
ideas by discussing them. I did find, to a certain extent,
that I had to sell some of the economic ideas by indicating
that they were also politically advantageous. I wouldn't
believe it at all appropriate to advocate the passage of a
law that I thought was economically undesirable on the
grounds that it was politically saleable. But if I thought
that the passage of a law was economically desirable, as well
as politically profitable, I would certainly not hesitate,
with the President and others, to bolster my economic argument with the argument that this is also going to help in
other ways. What could be fairer?
    Again, they have nothing to do with whether one agrees
as to the merits or not. The first example, clearly, was
Taft-Hartley. I don't have to prove whether I was right or
wrong, but having drafted the Wagner Act, my general position
is that I wouldn't have regarded the Taft-Hartley Act as a
good law. I was profoundly against it. When every member of
the Cabinet, except the Secretary of Labor, was urging the
President to sign that law, I didn't hesitate to argue in the
early meetings of the Ewing group why it was substantively
undesirable, pointing out the position of the labor groups in
the political structure, how they felt about this, and that
it would be politically advantageous for the President not to
sign Taft-Hartley but to veto it and politically disadvanta-
geous for him to sign it. So that was the first example.
Then we moved into a great variety of other areas. We dealt
with the Brannan plan, which, broadly speaking, I favored,
not to have price supports that help mostly the big farmers,
but to have farm prices find their own level and to support
farm income. I really said that a farm program ought to be a
genuine anti-poverty program to help disadvantaged farmers
apart from those who move into other types of occupations.

We moved into the whole question of health insurance, which
at that time focused on the Wagner-Murray-Dingle bill. In
that way we moved seriatim into all the fields that were the
major areas of national economic policy. Then our confusions
flowed back to the President in two ways: through the natural channels of contacts with the President--through me as
Chairman of the Council of Economic Advisers, through the
representation of the Labor, Agriculture and Interior Departments, and through Ewing of HEW, I mean, the forerunner of
HEW--it was Federal Security originally. They also flowed
back to the President through Clark Clifford and Charlie
Murphy, because they were the men who were right there in the
White House, were on the President's staff, and met with him
every day and who, as is always the case, were brought into
the discussions in most areas.

EH: Would it be possible to compare and contrast the influence of
the Council and Heller on the Great Society social programs
with your approach to social program development? Could you
return to the Ewing group and the Fair Deal program and
suggest how your strategy differed from Heller's?

LK: We had different programs in many respects. They were different in that under Truman there was aid toward an improved
distribution of income rather than a regressive distribution.
The Kennedy-Johnson tax program, especially, was regressive
on net balance; so was acquiescence in tighter money and
higher interest rates; so was the tightening of the domestic
outlays in the Federal Budget while defense outlays were
increased. The Truman administration put high accent upon
priorities of human and social needs and then economic
balance. The idea of the Ewing group was that there had to
be a reconstruction of Truman's policies, though we took the
position that this would help him in other ways. There had
to be a reconstruction of policies formulated when he was
influenced by the Fred Vinsons and others in 1945 and 1946.

EH: What were your contributions to some of these policies?

LK: Well, the policies were founded in the idea, first, that at
all times the economy should be fully used and I have stated
the reasons for that earlier, the economic growth argument.
Second, was the idea that it was not enough for wealth to
accumulate and men decay, but that growth had to be properly
directed toward meeting the priorities of needs, including
social justice, which is a little bit different from most
priorities. Mass transportation is a priority, even though
you don't usually think of it as social justice. The aboli-
tion of poverty is both a priority and social justice. That
was the second principle. In fact, I have one publication
put out by Indiana University called <u>The Three Basic Purposes of an Economic System</u>, condemning positions which I
have repeated over and over again. It developed the idea
that the three great purposes of an economic system are not

the restraint of inflation, which you can have on a desert island, but growth, priorities and justice. That's my whole economic philosophy, and the three objectives interrelate and fortify one another. So that was the second principle. Embodied in that principle was the idea that we wouldn't even think of a trade-off between unemployment and inflation, because there is none and, even if you got one, it would be wrong. It's wrong to disemploy people on the theory that the employed person will be able to do a little better as to prices.

You know, these things don't change so much. This idea I've heard recently in all quarters--Paul Samuelson had an article that the economic problems are now so complex that to indict the economists for not making any progress in solving them is like blaming the doctors for not having found the cure for cancer. That's a mighty poor analogy. Under Truman, we had to deal, in a larger degree, with all of the later problems. We had the problem of getting away from World War II, a transition which, incidentally, most of the economists forecast would lead to eight million unemployed. I had an article in the _Times_ in 1947 saying that the transition would not lead to eight million unemployed. We made a smooth transition. Within a year or two after World War II, we reduced the military budget from about $100 billion to about $12 billion--just imagine--with hardly a ripple effect on the economy because many things were planned and done. We had that problem. We had the problem of the Korean War. We had tremendous inflationary pressures resulting from the accumulated wartime savings. We had acute shortages when the Korean War started. The problems between industry and labor, and inflation, and maladjustments--we had them all. I don't see any great new problems. The policymakers today don't realize sufficiently that any job is a national economic asset, and any unemployment is a national economic liability. It isn't simply a matter of the individual, it's all along the line. It wasn't a difference in the external economic environment. Most of all, we applied the idea of the planning of government programs. We had models in the Council of Economic Advisers, not econometric models, but quantified goals and timetables for the economy. We stated every year what the goals for production and employment were, but we realized that it meant nothing to say that you'd have so much employment, so much production, unless you stated the component goals, both on the product side and on the income side, so that you could get the balances that relate to the achievement of these goals. Now Arthur Burns would say economics doesn't know enough to do that. If so, how can you devise policies, because every time you change the tax laws or every time you change the spending rate you are affecting both aggregates and components. You are making a reallocation of resources and of incomes. How can you do it if you don't define what the goals and relationships are? And if you define wrongly, you correct every year. This is just the difference between flying blind and having your eyes open.

If you go the wrong way, you try to get back on the track. Those are the natures of the differences between what was done during the Truman period (and even more stringently during World War II) and what has been done later on. This explains the differences in the results obtained. The Humphrey-Hawkins proposal pours successful experience into one vessel. But this is a subject in itself.

2
The Council of Economic Advisers Under Chairman Arthur F. Burns, 1953–1956

Summary History

When Dwight Eisenhower became president in 1953, he had to decide the future of the Council of Economic Advisers. Although statutory authority for the Council remained, the drastic cut in the CEA's budget in 1952 jeopardized the continued existence of the advisory body. Congress had provided only sufficient funds for operation of the Council through the completion of Truman's tenure in office; after that, it was up to the incoming Eisenhower administration to decide whether to continue the Council. Although Republicans had been the strongest critics of the Council, Eisenhower and his advisers decided that the economic advisory system should be salvaged. The President then had the choice of either asking Congress for a supplemental appropriation to continue the three-man Council or attempting to restructure the whole system of economic advising. A one-man advisory office had been proposed in the 1949 Hoover Commission study, but some CEA critics felt internal restructuring of the Council would be sufficient. Eisenhower's own position was not clear at first, but advisers Gabriel Hauge and Sherman Adams apparently spoke for the President when in early 1953 they sought simple continuation of Council funding for the remainder of the fiscal year. Despite this, the House and Senate in a series of conflicting actions denied the requested appropriation. Funds were provided for the remainder of the fiscal year, but for only a single economic adviser.

On the advice of Hauge, his assistant on economic matters, Eisenhower selected Arthur Burns to fill this position. A Democrat-for-Eisenhower, Burns' reputation as an academic economist was based on his work on business cycles while Professor of Economics at Columbia University and head of the National Bureau of Economic Research. Burns responded to Eisenhower's request to study the problem of what to do about the CEA and proposed that the administration support continuation in the next fiscal year, but only if the Council were reorganized. Burns suggested that many of the Council's problems had been due to its weak internal organization. He proposed that the chairman be given administrative authority over the body and be made responsible for reporting to the president. The vice-chairman would be eliminated. Critics insisted that such reorganization would produce further problems by calling into question the prestige and independence of the

other two CEA positions. But whether or not this would solve the
Council's problems, the reorganization proposal would eliminate
the weak chairmanship that Burns found personally uninviting. The
President's Reorganization Plan No. 9 was subsequently accepted
by Congress, and the Council once more resumed its activities in
the late summer of 1953 with full appropriations for the coming
year.

The other two members of the Council were Neil Jacoby and
Walter W. Stewart. Jacoby was an academic economist who had been
Dean of the Graduate School of Business at UCLA prior to his
appointment to the CEA. Stewart did not have a Ph.D. but had
established a solid reputation as an economist in government
service. In contrast to Truman's policy of deliberately appointing men with varying backgrounds and interests, Eisenhower initiated the practice of accepting the recommendations of the Chairman for the other positions. So in addition to strengthening the
chairmanship through reorganization, Burns was able to insure CEA
colleagues of his own choosing.

The staff also had to be reconstituted essentially from the
ground up. Because of the confusion over the future of the Council, only three staff members remained by the summer of 1953. Any
concept of neutral competency or a career staff had vanished in
the transition from the Truman administration to the Eisenhower
administration. Getting new staff members was no simple matter,
due to Republican patronage needs, the anti-government reactions
of many academics to McCarthyism, and the timing of the recruitment just as a new academic year was beginning. Burns was forced
then to recruit staff on a temporary basis of one or two years,
with a resultant high turn-over as staff members moved back and
forth between academics and government. This system proved important in keeping the CEA in touch with the academic profession, but
it did not allow the establishment of the contacts and continuity
often essential to operating effectively in government.

This was less a problem for Burns, perhaps, than for later
chairmen, for his concept of the duties of the staff did not
require experience, contacts or continuity on their part. While
Keyserling had encouraged policy considerations by the staff,
Burns felt the staff's role was simply to advise him, providing
him with whatever information he needed to make the necessary
policy decisions. He wanted a completely objective support staff.
He also controlled all staff contacts with other departments and
agencies, a policy that contrasted with his predecessor's encouragement of the development of the intra-government contacts basic
to a well-functioning career staff. But like Keyserling, Burns
still insisted on doing most of the work on the annual Economic
Reports himself, personally drafting large portions and reviewing
or rewriting all other sections. The organization of the Council
clearly reflected Burns' conception of the chairman as chief
spokesman and administrator.

Burns developed a strong working relationship with President
Eisenhower. Eisenhower approved of Burns' emphasis on a return to
a non-political role for the Council. He wanted a confidential
adviser, and his CEA Chairman insisted that was exactly what he
intended to be. The clearest indication of this change in the

CEA's role from the Truman years was in the structure of the annual Reports. While the Truman Councils had published their own reviews under their own names, the Eisenhower CEA receded into the background, aiding the President in preparing the Reports but theoretically not authoring them. While the Council did in reality routinely write the Reports, they always went out under the President's authorship, a situation that some critics felt opened up the possibility of distortion and confusion over their objectivity. Burns at times expressed himself in the annual Reports as an advocate for administration policies and even made occasional pro-administration speeches, but he still sought to avoid giving public testimony in congressional hearings and avoided both criticizing the President and adopting extremely partisan positions when forced to testify. Burns felt such a stance was essential if the Council's prestige were to be restored after the years of criticism under the Truman administration.

Eisenhower approved of Burns' concept of the CEA's role. The President had other economic advisers, including Gabriel Hauge and Secretary of the Treasury George Humphrey, but he maintained a close relationship with Burns. Hauge's duties involving economic policy were more administrative and political, essentially serving to shield Burns and the Council from issues irrelevant to their duties, such as appointments to the Federal Reserve and the administration of tariff regulations. Although also participating in important economic policy decisions, Hauge rarely disagreed with Burns. Humphrey, however, often did not agree with the CEA Chairman on fundamentals of economic policy. A conservative businessman, Humphrey, in contrast to Burns, was more insistent on such fiscal orthodoxies as a balanced budget and more opposed to countercyclical actions by the government. Moreover, Humphrey was a potentially more influential adviser as both Secretary of the Treasury and close personal friend of the President.

Although Secretary Humphrey often had the last word in economic matters, Burns' access to Eisenhower and the persuasion of his expertise made the CEA Chairman a powerful contender. Eisenhower respected Burns' economic advice and had him brief the Cabinet regularly on the economic situation. He also delegated to Burns a major role in the coordination of economic policy, making him Chairman in 1953 of the newly established Advisory Board on Economic Growth and Stability, an economic sub-cabinet made up of representatives of all agencies involved in economic policy, including Commerce, Labor, Agriculture, the Treasury, the BOB, and the Federal Reserve. A similar senior staff-level group, the "Tuesday Group," organized by the CEA's David Lusher, further enhanced the Council's role in policy formation. In addition, the Council set up various task forces and participated in other inter-agency groups such as the Cabinet Committee on Small Business. If the Burns Council was determined to stay out of the political spotlight, it nevertheless took an active role in policy formation that extended beyond the scientific expertise and neutral competency that Edwin Nourse had sought during his tenure.

Relations with Congress were strained from the start due to the conflict over the future of the Council. Burns' resistance to open testimony before the Joint Economic Committee did not improve things. While he was willing to appear, he insisted on testifying in executive session and asked the Committee not to release transcripts of his testimony. He would answer questions relating to administrative aspects of the Employment Act or technical matters, but refused to discuss any matters he felt would damage his advisory relationship with the President. His answers were often criticized as being deliberately obscure. The Committee was also critical of Burns' refusal to give numerical estimates of needed levels of employment and production. Burns felt that such predictions were useless, preferring instead broad guidelines and moral suasion. Nevertheless, the Joint Committee issued a unanimous report on the first Economic Report under Burns in 1954. Although later Committee reports were to be less favorable, the extreme partisanship that had characterized the JEC during the Truman years appeared for a time to have abated.

As one of the foremost authorities on business cycles, Burns' main concern was with developing the flexible programs essential to preventing major downturns in the economy. Unlike the Keynesians, he did not feel that it was the government's duty to prevent minor economic declines. However, he did see the value, in certain circumstances, of such Keynesian tools as deficits, tax cuts, public works, and easy credit. Such a view was in conflict with that of Eisenhower's more conservative advisers, but Burns managed to push Eisenhower into accepting a more active role for government. Rather than reversing the New Deal, the Eisenhower administration found it necessary to accept federal responsibility for the economy, especially when an economic downturn in 1954 brought on Republican fears of blame for another 1929.

In terms of economic policy, the Eisenhower administration hoped to reduce federal spending, balance the budget, cut taxes, and generally reduce the role of the government in economic activity. Its main concern was the danger posed to private enterprise by inflation and excessive government intervention in the economy. Since the Korean War was winding down, decontrol of the economy was one of its first moves. Although there was some debate about how quickly the Truman price and wage controls should be lifted, by late spring of 1953 most of these controls had been dismantled. Concern remained, however, about the possibility of postwar inflation. Accordingly, tight credit policies were instigated by the Federal Reserve Board in March, although this policy had to be reversed in early summer to accommodate a Treasury bond offering. The administration also resisted Republican congressional pressures for a tax cut and successfully pushed for continuation of the war-time excess profits tax. Avoiding a tax cut was essential to the Eisenhower campaign promise of balancing the budget. Although there was little real hope for a balanced budget for FY 1954, the administration worked hard to cut the Truman budget and managed to lower the estimated deficit from $9.9 billion to $3.9 billion.

Burns and his colleagues did not play a significant part in the formulation of these anti-inflation and retrenchment policies, however, for they were still in the process of organizing. But by September 25, 1953, Burns had news on the economy for Eisenhower and it was not good. According to his study of a series of economic indicators developed by the National Bureau of Economic Research, the economy was in the midst of a decline or readjustment. Pointing to the decline in the stock market, the increased number of business failures, a dropping off in the volume of orders for durable goods, evidence of excessive inventories, and other factors, Burns concluded that the nation was in the midst of a recession that had begun perhaps as early as July 1953. The decline was probably due to a combination of the cutback in government spending on military goods and the adjustment or reduction of business inventories to current sales. While some insisted the tight money policy pursued earlier in the year had some role, the other two factors appeared more central.

Despite fears of another downturn like 1929, the first reaction of the Cabinet was to try to ride out the recession without taking any extreme actions. The Council of Economic Advisers had, however, begun consideration of more positive action that would still be consistent with administration goals to minimize federal activity. The Federal Reserve´s easing of the money market in the summer probably cushioned the decline somewhat, and Burns worked with Fed Chairman William McC. Martin to continue a policy of monetary ease. Impending tax cuts on January 1, 1954, while not countercyclical in intent, could also be expected to help offset the effects of the downturn. Since Congress had earlier set the date for the expiration of Korean War excess profits taxes and increased personal income taxes, all the administration had to do was yield, an action nevertheless firmly resisted by financial conservatives such as Humphrey.

Burns´ first Economic Report in 1954 affirmed the principles of the Employment Act of 1946, stated the administration´s confidence in the resiliency of the economy, and laid out its anti-recession strategy. The Report emphasized the role that built-in stabilizers such as social security payments and farm price supports would play in stimulating the economy. But proposals were also included for liberalization of housing credit, broadening of old age and unemployment benefits, tax incentives for investors, and an expanded highway program. There was much resistance within the administration to these proposals. Secretary of the Treasury Humphrey adamantly insisted that restraint was still essential in order to maintain stability and opposed Burns´ efforts to ease housing credit. Although the Housing Act of 1954 did not give the President the discretionary authority sought by the CEA on government-guaranteed loans, the administration was able to ease credit policies sufficiently to revive the home construction industry. Humphrey was also resistant to plans for further tax reductions that might increase the budget deficit and lead to inflation in the long run. His view again lost out, for Burns was able to convince Eisenhower of the necessity of such actions in order to strengthen the economy. Focused on excise tax reductions and tax reform, the administration´s proposals were criticized as too pro-business, too late, and too moderate to offset the damages done by the administration´s 1953 budget cuts. But the tax reductions also indicated that Humphrey´s fiscal conservatism was not dominant in the administration, and that even a Republican administration was now willing to accept, however unenthusiastically, tax cuts and an increased budget deficit as basic counter-recessionary measures.

As a last resort, federal spending was considered as a possible alternative. Republicans had long criticized the New Deal-Fair Deal Democrats for their attempts at "pump-priming" through large government expenditures, and were determined to put off such actions. One alternative was to step up the rate of government expenditures while not increasing the actual amount spent. Burns felt such budget flexibility could prove an important countercyclical tool. By February 1954, pressure from labor and congressional liberals forced Eisenhower to consider developing new public works projects. He sought to avoid rash action and entrusted to Burns the actual planning and coordination of a "shelf of public works" that could be put into operation if the economic situation warranted. Neither Burns nor anyone else in the administration was enthusiastic about this possibility and all were greatly relieved when recovery of the economy in late July 1954 removed the necessity for such action.

With recovery, the Eisenhower administration returned to its emphasis on restoring "free competitive enterprise," an interpretation of the Employment Act of 1946 that contrasted sharply with the Truman administration's efforts "to maintain employment, production and purchasing power." This meant a less active role for both the Council and the government. The two remaining Economic Reports of Burns' tenure and Eisenhower's first administration emphasized the role of the private sector in economic development. Burns continued to push for liberalization of housing credit, expansion of the public highways program, and aid to chronically depressed areas, but the dominant tone of the administration in financial matters remained conservative. While the government was acknowledged to have a role, it was only as a partner with private enterprise in establishing the proper environment for economic growth and stability. According to the administration and its supporters, this meant that government should be primarily concerned with achieving the stability essential to economic growth, even though critics insisted that this preoccupation with anti-inflationary measures would damage chances for full recovery and long-term growth. Rather than emphasizing full employment and growth, the administration focused on such anti-inflationary policies as tightening monetary policy, opposing further tax cuts, and once more trying to bring the federal budget into balance. In Eisenhower's second term, under a new Council chairman, this conflict between the goals of growth and stability was to remain the central issue of debate.

Oral History Interview

The President and Economic Policy

EH: President Eisenhower called you to Washington in 1953 to reconstitute and lead the CEA. Why did he want a CEA? What did he expect it to do for him?

AB: Eisenhower was by no means certain that he wanted a CEA. In fact, he was inclined not to continue it. He asked me to look into the advisory function in the economic area, and he expressed grave doubts about the Council of Economic Advisers. He suggested that he would prefer to have me alone as his economic adviser, but that he also wanted my best thoughts on the subject. I told him that just as he started with some prejudices, so also did I; that I strongly felt that a deliberative body would serve the President and the presidency better than a single economic adviser, no matter how competent he might be. I ended by saying, "You and I are on somewhat different tracks. However, I will look into the matter of the advisory function seriously. I will try to discipline my prejudices. And after talking to people in the government who have some interest and competence in this matter, and also to some of my academic colleagues and friends in the business world, I will come back and report. Is that what you would like," I asked, "a report with definite recommendations on the economic advisory function?" His answer was, "Yes, that is exactly what I want. But I must warn you, I don't want a long report, because I don't know how to read." And--I will explain in a minute why I remember this so clearly--I shot back, "Mr. President, since you don't know how to read and I don't know how to write, the chances are that we may be able to get along." That was the beginning of an extraordinary personal as well as professional friendship.

EH: Had you known him at Columbia?

AB: Oh no. I had met him at a faculty reception, passing through a line with hundreds of my colleagues, but he didn't know me and he surely didn't remember meeting me. Of course, I remembered meeting him.

EH: What did he expect? What did the report suggest, say, and why? He obviously accepted it.

AB: You can infer the content of the report from two objective facts. One is the Reorganization Act for the CEA that was recommended in my report and, second, the establishment of the Advisory Board on Economic Growth and Stability that was also part of my recommendation. Those two documents--the Reorganization Act and the Executive Order establishing the Advisory Board (ABEGS)--those expressed the essential recommendations.

EH: Did he become persuaded in this process that he needed an economic advisory group? Did you persuade him of that? You said he was uncertain about it.

AB: Oh yes. I took seriously the responsibility of studying the advisory function in spite of my prejudices. I owed it to the President. So I proceeded to consult with Senator Taft, Jessie Walcott, Paul Douglas, and other members of the Congress who had been active in the Joint Economic Committee. I consulted with Nelson Rockefeller, who then headed up a government organization committee. I consulted with the Attorney General, with the Director of the Budget, and other people who had some background in the field of government organization, particularly those who had some interest in the Council of Economic Advisers or, more generally, the advisory function within the executive establishment. Finally, once I had indicated that I had completed my study, the President convened a meeting in the Oval Office and I submitted my report. There were about ten individuals present--some of whom I named--I don't recall everyone; but it was a very significant group of government leaders within the executive establishment and the Congress. They liked and applauded the report.

SM: This was after Eisenhower had taken over?

AB: Well, I came on in early March as I remember. I obviously didn't have this meeting immediately. I would guess it occurred no earlier than May--possibly in June; but I have no specific recollection of the date.

SM: At that time you were simply an economic adviser to the President.

AB: What happened was this: the Council of Economic Advisers had an appropriation for only a nine-month period ending March 31. This was a very unusual action of Congress. My understanding was that in view of the uncertainty in both parties whether the Council as an institution should be continued, a mere nine-month appropriation was voted with the exception that the new president, whoever he might be, would ultimately decide what to do with the Council. So, to enable me to function at all, starting April 1st, a three-month appropriation was voted for an Office of Economic Adviser in the White House.

EH: Was there in this meeting in the Oval Office that you mentioned--was there a compelling argument, if you like, that carried the day?

AB: The compelling arguments were two. First, that the President defintely needed economic advice on a continual basis and on a professional level. Second, that a deliberative body would serve the President better than a single economic adviser.

EH: You are talking about three persons, right?

AB: Yes. Further, that the administrative authority within the
Council and the function of reporting to the President should
be centralized--that is, this should be the responsibility of
the Chairman. The reason for that recommendation was that
Truman had apparently had unhappy experiences with the Council. One can interpret the history one way or another; you
can blame the Council or you can blame Truman. Personally, I
am inclined to think that the Council rather than Truman was
to blame. My understanding is that the three of them would
walk into the Oval Office and soon start arguing with one
another. The president doesn't have the time for that,
particularly since he doesn't understand much of the vocabu-
lary. What he wants is advice and recommendations: where
are we, where should we be going, how soon can we get there,
and how? The Council, according to what I learned, was not
proceeding in quite that fashion.

    To return to my recommendations, the Reorganization Act
was designed to avoid such difficulties. I also recommended
that systematic ties be established with other agencies of
the government, so that instead of operating on a personal
level or through the grapevine, I and my Council colleagues
would have an organized method for communicating with the
leading economic agencies of the government and they in turn
with the Council. That was the basis for the recommendation
for the Advisory Board. Once we met, I put through the rule
very quickly that there would be no alternates at meetings of
the Advisory Board. Certain departments were included and
their representatives designated; they either came to the
meetings or they didn't. As a result I had, almost without
exception, perfect attendance at these meetings.

EH: Let's go back to your reading and writing comment. How did
you go about establishing a comfortable advisory relationship
with the President?

AB: I would attribute it mainly to accident, which means good
luck in this instance. I would attribute it also in part to
some planning on my part. Originally, I had no idea how to
go about advising the President. But, as it happened, I had
plenty to do for a time, being a business-cycle specialist.
I saw a recession coming, that was quite clear to me. Not
having any staff in that field, I had plenty to do in monitoring the developments that were leading up to a recession
and in formulating tentative plans for dealing with it. And
as for advising the President, I didn't know what to do, but
felt that something was bound to happen and then one day I
got a call from Eisenhower. He wanted to see me. This was
to be my second substantive meeting with him. The first, of
which I have already spoken, dealt with organization of the
advisory function. Well, I thought about what I would do
when I went in there to advise the President. To talk about
the economy, how things were developing, I didn't have to

prepare for that. It was clear to me that I would cover
that, either at the President's request or on my own initiative. But I kept asking myself: Was that enough? Here was
a President who came to his post by virtue of his military
record. His role at Columbia University was minimal. He
certainly had no special background, perhaps no background,
in the economic area. He must, therefore, be concerned about
proper handling of economic matters. To help him I would
have to teach him, but how do you teach a president? Obviously, I didn't know; but I felt that he must have some
interest in the size of the government--after all, he was now
heading it up. It might be desirable, therefore, to trace
for him the history of government--quantitatively--in terms
of employment, expenditure trends, revenue trends, etc. over
several recent decades. Then again, I might talk to him not
just about the current condition of the economy, but also
about the business cycle--some of its leading characteristic
features. And one or two other things about the economy
occurred to me--such as our tax system. So I just put together quickly some tables and one or two charts. I didn't
know how I would use this material, but I decided to take it
with me and somehow look for an opportunity to teach him some
things about the national economy, the kind of government he
was heading up, where it had been going, etc. Well, once you
have a fairly definite idea as to where you would like to go,
either opportunity will knock at the door or you will create
your opportunity. So, in the course of the conversation, I
found it expedient or wise, describe it as you will, to bring
out some of my charts and tables and talk a little about the
history of business cycles, about the growth of government in
terms of employment, expenditures and revenue, also to describe some basic facts about the structure of our tax system, etc. Eisenhower was deeply interested, and when I was
about ready to leave, he said, "You must wait a minute," and
he called in Tom Stevens, his appointments secretary, and
said to him, "I have just had a fascinating talk with this
fellow Burns"--you know it was Eisenhower's style to bellow
out his commands with enthusiasm--"Now, you put him down for
an appointment with me each week for one full hour, from now
on, never to fail." Well, that is how things got started.

EH: There was an intellectual curiosity there. He had a curious
mind.

AB: No question about that. These things are always, also,
matters of personal chemistry. We got along well during that
hour; and I think that the earlier brief interchange about
his not being able to read and my not being able to write,
also my telling him about my prejudices just as he told me
about his, all that helped enormously. The basic personal
chemistry was, by accident and luck, right.

EH: Did he come to understand economic analysis and your mode of
thought?

AB: I would say that he came to understand it superbly well.

EH: You would say he was a very intelligent man.

AB: No question. People develop stereotypes, such as that Eisenhower didn't have a brain and that all that he could do was play on the golf course—just as Reagan is now described by many as simplistic and even stupid—my sister has just added another item of description: he can't even speak English. No, Eisenhower was a highly intelligent man. As a matter of fact, I would put it this way. If you were to pick some eight or ten outstanding individuals in public life, put them in one room and include Eisenhower there; if you then walked in blindfolded and after a while tried to decide which of the men clearly stood out as being wise and well informed; the chances are more than fair that you would have picked Eisenhower out of such a group. Now that is not the typical description....

EH: No, although the literature now is making that very clear—the research on the presidency—making it very clear, reliable. Did his values, his fundamental values, his thoughts about the good society, shape his economic thinking? Did you become aware of that?

AB: I think philosophically he and I were on the same track. It certainly took no effort on my part. I am what I am, period. And I have no reason to think there was any special effort on his part. We were, to start with, on much the same track.

EH: Would you characterize that philosophy?

AB: Eisenhower himself characterized it very accurately by saying—I don't remember his precise phrasing—that in fiscal matters, he was uniformly a conservative, but that in dealing with human problems, social issues, he tended to be liberal. We're both inclined that way. During Eisenhower's presidency, we had great reforms of the unemployment insurance system, social security system, housing legislation, etc., and much—perhaps most of that—came out of the CEA. In any event, it won enthusiastic support from Eisenhower.

EH: But he didn't know this about you in advance. Why did he select you, do you think?

AB: I can answer that only in part. I will tell you all that I know. He went about selecting me, or found me, through a committee. The committee, I was told, consisted of John Williams, a professor at Harvard in money and banking, also Randolph Burgess. Randolph Burgess had been an officer of the Federal Reserve Bank of New York. I think that at that time he was with the First National City. In any event, he was a banker of some distinction and prominence. And the third member of the committee was Gabe Hauge, who had served as

Eisenhower's adviser in the economic area during the campaign. These were the three individuals and they recommended
me. Why, I don't know. It so happens that I didn't know
Hauge at all, I did know John Williams, and I did know,
although only superficially, Randolph Burgess. My guess is
that I was picked because of a certain position that I had
attained in the area of business-cycle research. I want to
add just a footnote. I had no political connections whatever. None.

EH: You were a registered Democrat, weren't you?

AB: Yes, we'll come to that. As I said, no political connections
whatever, and I had no interest in that job, really. I
wasn't quick to accept it. I made my conditions before I
did. The invitation came as a surprise to me.

EH: Did Eisenhower think about economic policy in a larger political reference? I don't mean politics in a narrow sense,
but in a larger sense of the interrelationship between politics and economic policy and the constraints on economic
action, or economic policy as a resource for politics, and
programs--what he wanted to do?

AB: Eisenhower did not neglect narrow, partisan political considerations. But he hated them. They influenced his thinking,
but they did not dominate his thinking. The future of our
society and the future of man, that was his main concern,
certainly on a conscious level.

EH: Did he see economic policy as a basis for electoral appeals,
for example, in the 1956 election year? Did he think of the
two as interrelated in some way?

AB: He did, no doubt. To give you an example. I was chairman of
a Cabinet Committee on small business, and I kept him informed of the work of the committee and where I thought we
were coming out. I had some difficulty in getting two members of the Cabinet to agree to the report I had written.
But Eisenhower was anxious to have that Committee's report,
first, because--I don't mean by that that was his leading
motive--he thought it was a sound report; and, second, because he thought very explicitly that it would help him in
the election.

EH: All right, so he was mindful of these things?

AB: No question about that.

EH: In a general way, would you say that the structure of economic advising in the White House--in the executive office and
the cabinet--was a function of Eisenhower's style, liking to
get everything well satisfied, collegial style--you know how
his style has been characterized in the literature--struc-

tured, everybody represented, lots of talk around the table. How would you characterize his style of authority, his administrative style and then fit economic policymaking into that?

AB: I find that a very simple question. Eisenhower came up through the military; he had had enormous responsibilities as an administrator in the military establishment and he was a first-rate administrator. I've worked with six presidents, no one even approached Eisenhower in that regard. He was a first-rate manager and administrator. The role of the Council of Economic Advisers in his administration, and my personal role again, were in large part an accident of his background and training. If he wanted military advice, where would he go for such advice? Clearly, to the Joint Chiefs of Staff. If he wanted economic advice, therefore, where would he go? The answer was obvious to him--to the joint chiefs of the economic staff. Truman was accustomed to thinking politically. Eisenhower, by virtue of his military background, was trained to think in professional terms, and that brought him to the Council of Economic Advisers.

EH: It is a General using staff, insisting on staff work, is that right?

AB: Exactly, and I don't believe it was something that he had thought through systematically; it was just a natural outgrowth of his military background and experience over many years.

EH: Who were the principal economic advisers to the President other than the Council? Who were the other actors?

AB: George Humphrey, the Secretary of the Treasury, was certainly one. The Secretary of Commerce, Sinclair Weeks; his role was very marginal. Arthur Summerfield, who was Postmaster General, played a certain role by virtue of the fact, certainly not by virtue of the department that he headed up, that he was a business man.

EH: It wasn't that he was sort of the chief politician for the Republican National Committee and so on, just business?

AB: I would agree that his role as a politician played a part. Charlie Wilson, Secretary of Defense, his influence in the economic area was marginal. There was Oveta Hobby in HEW to whom Eisenhower would listen with respect. And his first Director of the Budget--an extraordinary man from Detroit-- Joe Dodge, banker, was very influential.

EH: How about Jim Mitchell, when he became Secretary of Labor. Was he important in economic policy?

AB: Yes, he played a role. I'd forgotten about him. Yes, he

definitely played a role, always on the social side and always also with a certain political accent.

EH: Were there really two teams? Treasury and the CEA and the Bureau of the Budget, if you like, on the first macro policy team and then the constituency departments coming with their concerns of macro policy? Was it demarcated that way?

AB: I didn't think of it that way.

EH: There was no informal Troika, to coin a phrase? Of yourself, Humphrey and Dodge in the beginning?

AB: I saw Humphrey more frequently than any other government official. I think I saw Bill Martin of the Federal Reserve fairly frequently, about as frequently as Joe Dodge. I saw Sinclair Weeks with some frequency, but that was largely a personal thing. He was a New Englander, had a farm not very far from mine in Vermont, and we became personal friends. One could perhaps speak of an incipient Troika, yes, but it was not sharply...

DD: More on a one-to-one basis with you?

AB: Yes, on a one-to-one basis, largely. It was on that basis, I believe, precisely because I had the Advisory Board on Economic Growth and Stability. We will come to that later; it was a very useful agency in my day.

EH: Well, why don't you go into that and tell us about that.

DD: Yes, I am interested in that and particularly when I looked at the summary of your period after that, I was a little puzzled why—when that was set up. You recommended it obviously, spearheaded it. You picked not your peers, but the one level down since I am aware of the relationships. You didn't try to set up a cabinet group of a high-level group.

AB: I don't quite remember, but I think this is something that can be verified rather easily. I did not push for cabinet representation. What I think I pushed for was either the secretary or the number two man—one or the other. That is my recollection. And that I am right, at least in part, is indicated by the fact that Marion Folsom, who had served as the Treasury representative when he was Under Secretary of the Treasury, wanted to continue when he became Secretary of HEW. He liked ABEGS; he found it useful and important. I believe that Joe Dodge, the first Director of the Budget under Eisenhower, was also a member. He lasted a year only— well, that is the wrong verb—it may suggest that he didn't get along. On the contrary, Eisenhower was heartbroken over his departure. Dodge was an extraordinary man. I can tell you things about him that are tremendously important. No, come to think of it, he was not a member of ABEGS, but his successor whom I later brought into the government, Percy Brundage, did attend ABEGS meetings regularly.

SM: Did anyone from the Fed?

AB: Oh yes, Abbot Mills. He was the Federal Reserve representative.

EH: Now what was the business of the ABEGS, and why was it so useful?

AB: First, why did I originally think of ABEGS? I had looked into the history of the Council with some care. The Council encountered difficulties quite apart from a certain inability of members of the Council to get along with one another. There were clashes of personality, to be sure. But more important than that, they did not have systematic links to the rest of the government and therefore had frequently resorted to the grapevine. That sort of thing didn't suit my personality; it's not my style. I wanted something that was organized, formal in the sense of being subject to rules, something that was well understood, above board, also systematic, continuous, so that there would be steady communication between the Council and the other agencies concerned with economic matters. That was important not only with respect to actions being taken, but, even more important, with respect to actions that were being considered. I fully shared the thinking of the Council with my colleagues in ABEGS, whether we looked forward to two years or three months. To a very large degree, and I believe with equal candor, my colleagues in ABEGS shared their thoughts with me and with one another. Each therefore knew what the other was thinking and doing.

EH: This really encompassed all economic policy—macro and micro?

AB: Not quite. I made a decision on that early in the game, and I think my role as Council Chairman differed from that of my successors—certainly in recent years. At present the Council gets into everything; at least it so appears from the outside. I behaved differently. I made up my mind that there were only a few things that really mattered, that I thought were basically important to the economy, and that I would focus on those. As for other things, they would take their own course, or somebody else would attend to them. ABEGS therefore tended to concentrate on macro issues.

EH: And these are primarily macro matters in terms of the language of the Employment Act; were they—fiscal, monetary questions?

AB: Oh, yes.

DD: Arthur, how did that go in terms of—I came in late in the

Treasury--late in the Eisenhower administration--how did all
of this go in terms of Bill Martin on the monetary policy
side and the Secretary of the Treasury who has fundamental
responsibilities under the law, as chief financial officer?
Were there any--to put it indelicately--were there clashes?
You obviously had the lead role with the President.

AB: There were clashes. Not with Bill Martin; it's hard to have
a clash with Bill Martin. Yes, I had some clashes, serious
clashes with Humphrey. I had no problems, certainly never
any clash, with Bill Martin. There were differences, now and
then, but as a matter of fact only two of any consequence.
In 1955, I was pushing Bill hard, along with Sproul, to
pursue a tougher monetary policy because the economy was
heating up, and the Federal Reserve was not moving fast
enough in my judgment. That was also the thinking of Sproul
who was then quite influential in the Federal Reserve system.
Again, in 1956, around April as I remember it, when the
Federal Reserve wanted to raise the discount rate, my own
feeling was--since the economic indicators had flattened out
around that time--that it would be best to wait a month or so
and then judge the course of the economy. But the Federal
Reserve went ahead anyway, and raised the discount rate. I
was right in 1955 and Bill Martin was right in 1956, but we
had no clashes; with Humphrey it was different, there were
some serious clashes.

EH: Did Humphrey even understand the role of the Council? Did he
think of himself as adviser to the President?

AB: Well, that is a perceptive question. He very clearly thought
of himself in that capacity, and that came to a head in late
December 1955, or perhaps it was very early in 1956. Humphrey and I had one of our meetings. We had frequent meetings, but not scheduled meetings on a regular basis. Hum-
phrey--he was a blunt man, an honest man within broad
limits--said to me, "Arthur, we have to reach a decision, you
and I. You're giving the President advice on taxation; well,
that happens to be my responsibility. You're trespassing on
my function. Now the fact that you are doing it is bad
enough; the fact that your advice differs sharply from mine
makes things worse. This is an intolerable condition. The
President will have to choose between you and me." I said,
"George,--do you mean that?" He answered, "Yes, I have
thought about it carefully and I regret it, but that's my
decision." I said, "George, I don't understand what's wrong
with the President getting two views on fiscal policy. It's
his decision; it's not yours, it's not mine. We don't always
disagree. Right now we do disagree sharply on tax policy for
1956." He wanted a tax reduction then, and I didn't.
"What's wrong with two opinions?"

SM: He wanted a tax reduction? In 1956?

AB: 1956. Well, taxes were very high then. I had great sympathy
with his objective to reduce taxes. But to me the basic
question then was one of timing. Inflation was beginning to
heat up in 1955. It wasn't as yet reflected in the consumer
price index, but it had registered very clearly in the prices
of sensitive raw materials. Also, the broad wholesale price
index was already moving up. Therefore, I was opposed while
Humphrey was in favor of a tax reduction then. Doubtless,
political reasons also played a part in his thinking. In any
event, he had arrived at the conclusion about our respective
roles. So I said, "Well, you've reached your decision and I
must accept that; but I do want you to understand that I have
not been trespassing on your territory. Maybe the President
has to choose between you and me, but not because I have been
trespassing on your territory or authority. As Chairman of
the Council of Economic Advisers, I can't ignore fiscal
policy. I would not be discharging my responsibility under
the law if I did. You, of course, as the Secretary of the
Treasury, are inevitably involved in fiscal matters. What
the President does with your advice or with mine is up to the
President. But I certainly am not trespassing on your
authority and don't you ever forget that." He responded, "I
understand how you feel about it, but I think that it's
primarily the responsibility of the Treasury—in any event, I
have reached my conclusion." I said, "All right, you go
ahead and make an appointment with the President." I then
said, "I don't have to be there; it's your problem, it's not
mine." He said, "Well, I want to go about this in a thoroughly fair manner." I said, "All right, if you insist on
my being there, I will be there. You set up the appointment." Well, I had, as indicated earlier, a standing
appointment with the President; that appointment was coming
up, I think, the next day or two days later. Since the
chances were high that sooner or later in the course of my
conversation with the President, which often extended well
beyond an hour because Charlie Wilson, the Secretary of
Defense—he was the only other official with a standing
appointment with Eisenhower—who preceded me, was not very
popular with Eisenhower, so that he often got rid of Wilson
quickly and I therefore had some of his time as well as my
own. In view of the chances of tax policy coming up in the
course of my next conversation with Eisenhower, I wasn't
going to take advantage of my regular meeting with him. So I
made my excuses to his office and I didn't see Eisenhower
that week. Finally, as Humphrey had arranged, the two of us
arrived at 2:00 in the afternoon on the appointed day in the
Oval Office. Eisenhower greeted us with his customary enthusiasm: "My two friends, just the two men I wanted to see. I
just had a damn fool businessman in here saying that we ought
to lower taxes now, this at a time when inflation is beginning to heat up—to lower taxes! Can you imagine any idiocy
like that?" I took out a handkerchief and covered my
face...It was all I could do to control myself from bursting
out laughing. Well, there was talk about all kinds of things

for about an hour and a quarter. I did not say one word. I was waiting for Humphrey; but he never got around to the subject of the meeting.

EH: And you got along more or less well after that?

AB: I will tell you another story about Humphrey. We generally got along well personally, but this was not the case with the January 1955 Economic Report. I was the kind of damn fool chairman who himself wrote the President's Economic Report. Sure, I got assistance from my staff, but I did the basic writing. As you know, the season before the presidential messages come out is exceptionally busy. My days then were fully taken up with meetings of one kind or another, and so there was not time during the day to do any writing. I stayed in the office till 8:00 or so, then came home, had a late dinner, rested for an hour, and by 10:00 or 11:00 I would start working on the text of the report. I stayed at it until around 3:00, 4:00 or 5:00 in the morning. This went on for weeks. And, of course, by 8:00 I would be back in the office again. So, as you might guess, my nerves were on edge. Then, one bright morning, I got a phone call from George Humphrey, who said to me: "Art, I want to talk about the Economic Report." "Yes," I answered, "what is it?" I should note that I had previously sent around a draft for comment by the various agencies concerned. He then said, "I don't like it." I replied, "What's wrong with it?" His answer: "Well, it's socialistic." I burst out, "Socialistic? Gee, you don't mean that." He continued: "Yeah, it has to be scrapped." I had poured out my heart in writing that report. Actually, it was the best I had written. I think it stands up even today, which I discovered on re-reading it recently. I answered with some feeling, "It can't be rewritten; it stands as is." He persevered, "No, it's got to go." I finally said, "George, I poured out my heart on that report. You don't like it, you think it's got to go. But you're talking to the wrong man. I am not changing one word or one comma." That, of course, was an extreme statement. I couldn't have meant it literally, but being disturbed, I went on, "You're talking to the wrong man. You had better talk this over with the President. My report stands as is." He exclaimed, "You don't mean that." And I replied, "I absolutely do! Our conversation has come to an end. Goodbye." The next thing that happened was a phone call from Gabe Hauge. He said, "Arthur, there is a storm brewing. George Humphrey is angry about the Economic Report. He is organizing a cabal against you, and I want to sit down with you and plan a counterattack." I replied, "Gabe, you and I have always worked closely together. Please respect my wishes. You stay out of this. There may be a cabal, but there will be no counterattack. Let George Humphrey do what he wants, let him do his damndest. The President will either accept his judgment on the report or he won't. As for myself, I just don't want to interfere with that process, and I

certainly don't want you to get into the act." Gabe then
said, "But he is going to destroy you." I replied, "Well, if
George Humphrey can destroy me on a subject like this, then
he will do it, if not today, on some other subject a month or
two later. Eisenhower either has confidence in the work that
the Council is doing and in me personally, or he doesn't.
Let us leave it at that." Finally, the day arrived--I remember this so vividly--when I was to submit the Economic Report
for review by the Cabinet. This was in 1955. In submitting
the report, I could only summarize it, or read passages here
and there, since the report was fairly lengthy. At the
outset Eisenhower said to me, "Arthur, you have two pipes in
your hands. How can you smoke two pipes simultaneously?" I
didn't realize that until he mentioned it. So I just shot
back, "I'm well prepared this morning, Mr. President." And,
by Jove, I was well prepared, all keyed up. I felt confident
that I was going to carry the day in spite of Humphrey and
without having said a word to the President--he hadn't said a
word to anyone except Hauge. I had, of course, sent out a
draft of the document to various people, but I omitted Dick
Nixon, since there was no clear reason to send him a copy.
Yet, after I had summarized the report to the Cabinet, he
spoke up and said, "It is a beautiful report. It gives the
Republican administration a philosophy that it has lacked."
Then Oveta Hobby praised it, as did Jim Mitchell, and then
Arthur Summerfield spoke up. George Humphrey's cabal presumably consisted of the business types, Sinclair Weeks and
Secretary of Defense Charlie Wilson. I may be confused about
Arthur Summerfield. In any event, not one of the business
tycoons said a word except Sinclair Weeks who simply asked a
question; it was not a belligerent question, and it certainly
was not put in a belligerent manner. And that was all there
was to the Cabinet debate about the report. Then Eisenhower...

SM: Humphrey didn't speak to the report?

AB: Not one word. But he had spoken to Eisenhower previously,
you see. Then Eisenhower thanked me for the report and said,
"Arthur, what you presented here is of course a summary. Now
I would like--could you leave a copy of the whole report with
me? I want to read the report in its entirety." I replied,
"Yes, I would be glad to," and handed him a copy. That
afternoon, around 4:30, I got one of the most beautiful
letters I have ever had from anyone, from Eisenhower. As a
matter of fact, I had the opportunity to re-read this letter
just a few months ago. A fellow by the name of Ewald, who
was on the White House staff, is writing a biography of
Eisenhower and I dug out that letter for him. In this letter, besides praising the report, Eisenhower stated that some
would describe it as too radical, others as too conservative,
but that as far as he was concerned it was just right. After
this episode was over, I made no effort to conceal my feelings towards Humphrey. He had been so brutal in condemning

the report. He didn't make one specific criticism, besides calling it socialistic. I really doubt that he had even read it.

DD: My impression of Humphrey was that he never read anything more than one page. Or is that overly harsh? He conceded reading an entire draft of an Economic Report.

AB: I think what happened was that someone read it for him, and pointed out three or four phrases that were perhaps—or probably—careless, but which could be modified easily. But to condemn the whole thing as socialistic, that was outrageous. And so I made no effort to conceal my feelings, and for a time—when I saw Humphrey—I just looked the other way. This went on for about ten days. But our paths kept crossing, and while I never looked at him, he stopped me one day and said cheerfully, "Art, that report of yours was a great report." What do you make of all this? Here was a man who was brilliant in many ways. The trouble with Humphrey—he was indeed a very effective debater—the trouble with him was that he didn't know where his knowledge stopped and where his opinions began. For example, he was constantly down on the military, down on its spending, calling it waste, waste, waste. This finally got my goat. I kept asking myself, what does he know about the military? Sure, there is waste in the military, there is waste everywhere in the government. It is just a part of life. He kept thundering that we ought to cut military spending by ten billion dollars, by fifteen billion, that this was easy. One day I finally said, "George, your talk about expenditures of the Defense Department troubles me. After all, what is the first obligation of government? Is it not to defend the nation against enemies outside or enemies from within? In talking about military spending, you are talking about our nation's future, about our nation's security. What the hell do you know about military matters? What do you know that I don't know?" He replied quietly, "I know nothing about military matters. I am staying out of that." I continued, "But when you talk as you do, when you bang the table about waste in the military—you're a very persuasive gentleman—you may be misleading people." He answered, "Arthur, now that you have put it that way, I really don't know much but I just have a feeling it's wasteful. I ought to be more careful." A half hour later he was again banging the table about military waste, the same way all over again. He had his weaknesses, but he also had his strengths. I fundamentally liked him.

EH: Can I return to ABEGS for a minute? Were the constituency departments—Agriculture, Labor, Commerce, HEW—helpful to the Council on macro policy; did they have insights? A number of your counterparts have said they weren't too helpful—they just had special departmental interests.

AB: That is not an easy question to answer. I have to strain my memory. I have the impression we all worked harmoniously. You know what happens when you talk to people with whom you work well, you soon no longer know whether you are expressing your thoughts or their thoughts. The thinking tends to merge. I have the impression that they were helpful. Did ABEGS have representatives who could be considered outstanding architects of economic or macro economic policy? It did not; but yet I think that their information, advice, encouragement, if nothing else, was very helpful to the Council, and the entire process was constructive.

EH: Was the Economic Policy Board a re-invention or re-discovery of the ABEGS principle? Need for collegiality? Or was that inspired by something entirely different?

AB: I want to go back to the point about why ABEGS wasn't set up at the secretary level explicitly at the outset. My decision to be somewhat ambivalent on that was deliberate. I probably thought I would be overreaching myself and might not succeed, since I wanted to be chairman of it. That is, I thought the chairman of the Council of Economic Advisers should also be the chairman of ABEGS. But in my book on Prosperity Without Inflation, written in 1957 after I left the Council, I believe I came out in favor of elevating ABEGS to the secretary level.

EH: So the same impulses may have been at work there--the need for greater collegiality in economic policy in later years...

AB: To what extent ABEGS served as a model or to what extent people re-discovered the need for an Economc Policy Board, I just don't know. But there is a need for some instrumentality like that. I attended a good many meetings of the Economic Policy Board that President Ford set up. It was different. In the case of ABEGs, I had the right instinct of putting through the rule that there were to be no alternates, so that if a member of ABEGS couldn't be there, it was just too bad. Also, no minutes were kept--that too was deliberate. Therefore, if you were absent, you didn't know what happened, and they were all there at meetings--almost without exception. At the meetings of the Economic Policy Board under Jerry Ford, all kinds of alternates were present--the deputy, his alternate, the third or fourth man down. A lot of people were there at meetings. At my ABEGS meetings no staff was present. The meeting consisted of--I forget the exact number--six, seven, or eight individuals and that was it. I think it functioned better than Ford's board because it was better organized. I think that a major principle of organization is the one that I hit on by instinct--that is, no alternates or staff.

DD: Arthur, did Bill Martin come to your ABEGS meetings?

AB: No. It was Abbot Mills. Martin never came. He was not a

source of strength. Actually, what I learned about Federal Reserve policy and planning...I learned directly from Bill rather than from Abbot.

DD: In the later years under Jerry Ford when you had the Economic Policy Board and you went as Chairman of the Fed, did you have any feelings that you were really at a higher level than these other people and also you were always very jealous about the Fed's independence and so on? Did you have any feeling that you shouldn't be at those meetings? Or that they were really beneath you and you didn't want to share Fed system policy with them?

AB: I never did. I didn't share specific Fed plans with anyone. I did of course—and I am sure that was right—inform the Secretary of the Treasury and the Chairman of the Council and somebody in the White House in charge of economic matters about fifteen minutes before a public announcement of one of our formal decisions. That is, when we actually changed the discount rate, or reserve requirements, we would let others in the government know. The fact that it sometimes took us a week or longer to arrive at a decision, they never knew about it.

DD: The Economic Policy Board must have been a rather useless board, as far as the Fed was concerned.

AB: Oh no. What the Fed planned to do precisely, that was none of their business. We had to prevent leaks. I don't want to generalize or universalize—but that was my attitude, period. Just a word of further recollection about my part in the Policy Board—I was cautious about that. I had worked it out with Jerry Ford, so that I would not become a member of the Board, but serve instead as an adviser to the Board. I thoroughly respected the Fed's independence. But we were talking before about George Humphrey. I remember a cute remark of George's one day, namely; "We Republicans have been talking so much about the Fed's independence that if we keep it up the fellows over there may start believing it."

DD: What about your other Council members? They didn't come to ABEGS, did they?

AB: Yes, they came to ABEGS.

DD: But you were always the spokesman for the Council.

AB: Yes. I didn't do much testifying. It varied as to whether or not the record was disclosed. Actually, on this matter, I think I was wrong. I now feel my attitude about testifying was a mistaken one, and I lost a good friend in the process.

DD: By refusing to testify or only under wraps?

AB: Exactly. I insisted on closed sessions and no transcript.
At that time, I just didn't know how to work with Congress.
I felt, on the one hand, that I had to be honest as an
economist. I felt, on the other hand, that I must not do
anything to embarrass the President. And my compromise, or
my way of dealing with the problem, was to agree to testify,
but without a transcript, in closed session, etc. I now know
that was wrong--I reached that conclusion later on; but
that's another story. As I said, I lost Paul Douglas, who
was an old friend, on account of my insistence on procedure.
Once, when the Committee voted on my request for closed
meetings, etc.--I don't remember the details--every Republican on the Joint Economic Committee supported me, and so too
did three Democrats--Wilbur Mills, John Sparkman and Ful-
bright. Incidentally, those three Democrats have remained my
friends through the years. But Paul Douglas, the Chairman of
the Committee, lost the vote and he never forgave me. The
vote was on the issue of disclosure. What the technicality
was--whether it was to hold a closed meeting but also not to
have a transcript or something else--I do not remember. But
I was quite wrong at the time. I was looking at the procedural issue from a personal viewpoint. I paid too much
attention to my own inhibitions. I did not pay nearly enough
attention to the needs of the Congress. Its members need a
transcript. All that I can say is that I was then innocent
and ignorant of governmental processes. I didn't even realize that what goes on in a closed session is frequently
leaked, and you are better off with a record. Later on I
learned my lesson. By Jove, when I was at the Fed and when
there was some talk about closed session, I invariably insisted that I didn't want a closed session, that I wanted
everything to be in open session. All that is part of the
record.

The Structure of the Council

EH: What would you say are the comparative advantages and disadvantages of this small group of economists--the CEA--in
achieving influence in this world we have been talking about,
and what maxims for the structure and the strategies for the
CEA followed from them?

AB: The staff had largely disbanded when I arrived on the scene.
There were about two economists left, so I almost had to
start from scratch. I think I can give myself a little
credit here. I got on the telephone and I stayed on--it was
in August when I finally got an appropriation from the Coun-
cil--until I had assembled a very good staff.

EH: Would you give yourself credit for specializing that staff in
the sense that you are establishing the principle that it was
going to be academic economists?

SM: You set the standard for the Council, and assembled a small, extremely competent staff.

AB: Yes, but I don't give myself too much credit for that. I can't fully reconstruct what happened, but I don't think I had much of a choice. I was calling people in August, when everyone had made his commitment. How could I possibly get an academic man except on a one-year basis? Even that was difficult because a replacement would somehow have to be found.

EH: You could have gone with civil servants, though; you could have built up a permanent staff.

AB: Yes, but I wanted truly able people.

EH: What was your notion of a good Council and the composition of a good unit and what kind of people and...

AB: First of all, I paid absolutely no attention to a man's politics. I didn't know and I didn't care about that, and my judgment turned out to be right. I had on my staff fellows like Joe Pechman and Charlie Schultze; and they were devoted, thoroughly loyal, professional members of the CEA staff. As for their politics, they might or might not attend to that after hours. As you know, I came to the Council from the National Bureau of Economic Research, and I brought certain habits with me. Actually, I thought of the Council in very unrealistic terms at the beginning. I thought that the Council would be engaged to a significant degree in long-term research on the needs of economic policy, and that we would be devoting little time to short-run economic problems. But all that collapsed. A recession got underway in 1953, and we had to mobilize all the energy we could muster in developing plans for limiting the recession. Soon after that, a threat of inflation came along, so that the concept...

DD: At that time there was no international problem or then we didn't realize there was one in the making, did we?

AB: Yes, there were some stirrings. I remember Cabinet meetings where Randy Burgess in particular made detailed presentations of the deterioration that was taking place in our balance of payments. And this was in 1953 and 1956...

DD: That was Treasury's focus, not the Council's.

AB: I had an international economist on the staff from the start, but it was not a basic consideration in our endeavors.

EH: You said you wanted able people, you didn't want civil servants; give me some more maxims. Small staff, large staff, operating responsibilities, no operating responsibilities, so on. What are your maxims for a good Council? In terms of being effective.

AB: One thing I did which worked beautifully was to restrict the size of the staff. I wanted a small professional staff, partly because I was my own economist and I didn't have to lean on dozens of people. Partly also because I didn't place a high value on my managerial talents and I didn't want to be managing a large group, partly also because I had the good sense, again by accident, to realize that if I needed some large investigation, the chances were I could get one or another of the economic agencies to handle it for me. And they in fact did. I had a lot of work done by other agencies for the Council. Finally, I had some very definite ideas about how a professional staff should conduct itself in a sensitive political environment. I didn't want them to be leaking information to the press and so on. My problem was how to develop a useful ethical code. To accomplish this, I got hold of a former classmate who was on my staff. He was a public finance man out in Indiana...Louis Shere. He was a classmate of mine at Columbia, and had already served as a Treasury expert for many years. A Canadian by birth, whom I knew well. I said, to him, "Louie, I've got a problem. If I try to draw up a code of ethics for the staff, it would be resented. Suppose I appoint a committee and you be the chairman of it. You and I can talk privately, but the staff shouldn't know about our conversations. Let this committee work with the staff, so that the staff would itself finally work out a code of ethics, with you and the committee taking the leadership. Then a document suggesting a code would be handed to me." Louie agreed and that's the way it was done. It was a beautiful code. As a matter of fact, during my term we had only one leak that I know of out of my staff. I had appointed a deputy chief of the Corps of Engineers, General Bragdon, to work at the CEA on planning for public works. But I didn't want that disclosed. One day I heard this appointment announced over the air. So I sat down and asked myself, "How did this happen? Do I have a weak link in my organization?" And I had to answer, "Yes, I do have a weak link in my organization." Since he was a rather insecure man, I decided that he was probably responsible for the leak. I knew him as a thoroughly honest man, so I said to him, "News of the Bragdon appointment has been announced over the radio. Did you disclose that to someone in the press?" He answered promptly, "Yes, I did." "All right," I said, "Just don't do it again." Now that ethical code actually should have been disclosed, since it might well have become a model code. Why then did I make a secret of it? I suppose that the answer must be that I had a certain tendency to play my cards close to the chest. But it was a good code and it worked out beautifully. It must exist somewhere among my papers.

I will tell you something about a conscience problem of mine. I think I held on to some of my most valuable Council papers. I turned over several CEA filing cabinets to the Eisenhower Library, but some files I kept. They are in my basement now. They are mixed up with other files that have nothing to do with the Council. I wrote some months ago to the man in charge of the Eisenhower Library and told him about this. I just haven't been able to find the time--I really must do that--to turn over the papers to the Library.

EH: Let's go back to the role of staff. You had a staff of twelve which stayed about the same right along. Did they spend most of their time on micro matters or on macro?

AB: They worked on macro questions primarily.

EH: So they didn't have a lot to do with what I call the constituency departments--on the regular business of the constituency departments?

AB: No. As I commented before, many of these things are partly accidental rather than clearly thought out steps, deliberately taken. I didn't know Gabe Hauge at all at the start, but it so happened that he and I got along beautifully. He had an interest in micro matters and that was quite natural, since he was attached to the White House. Now and then I was drawn in on some micro issue, and now and then I took the initiative, though I can't now recall any case like that. The dairy farmers and the bicycle manufacturers had their special problems and Gabe Hauge worried about all that.

EH: But was one man enough to protect the President? From the claims of the Secretary of Agriculture or whatever? Somebody had to sit down and analyze those things.

AB: Gabe had a small staff. I think he had two assistants, no more than two. More important than that, he had access to specialists in my Council; he could talk to them whenever he wanted, and he certainly had access to many more specialists in the traditional government departments. He also would talk to me at times about some of these matters. Whether that was sufficient or not, I cannot be sure; but it seemed to work well.

EH: The Council, ever since the early 1960s, has been heavily involved in micro matters. The question--is it out-gunned?

AB: I think they are making a serious mistake by being all over the lot. That aspect of the Council's activity was deliberate on my part. I made up my mind at an early stage that some economic areas are of basic importance, that I would attend to those thoroughly, and that there were other matters that--while important in their own right--are more of a marginal character and that somebody else will have to attend to them. In other words, I was prepared to let such issues alone. I think there has been a trend toward involvement in every micro issue by Council. The members of the Council now seem to think that their prestige suffers if they do not get into every act. In my judgment they weaken their influence in the process, because they are spread much too thin. I deplore that tendency. I think it's a mistake.

SM: We got the impression from later Councils that the reason they did this was to maintain their influence with the president, that if they backed away from these issues they would be marginalized.

AB: I can understand that. No two presidents are alike. Some may expect an answer from the Council on every petty issue, while others are smart enough to keep down the number of issues in which they themselves get involved.

Bureaucratic Politics and Economic Policy

EH: It seems to me that the Council has or the government has a serious problem now and that somebody has to protect the president with micro analysis from the bombardment he is getting from all the departments and interest groups and so on. The Council is not staffed to do it if you've only got a handful of people. Is this a serious institutional problem?

AB: In my judgment, the White House staff, to begin with, ought to be reduced by about 90 percent--not by 1 percent or 10 percent but literally 90 percent. I think the president ought to rely chiefly on his cabinet officers and agency heads. What is happening now is that almost every problem is put on the president's desk, so that very soon many members of the White House staff, the Council of Economic Advisers, and the Bureau of the Budget get involved. Since the president rarely knows enough to make a decision on his own, in the end he is apt to echo the thinking of some staff member with whom he has a good and close relationship. I believe that some presidents have destroyed themselves because they lacked the ability to administer. A good administrator must know how to delegate responsibility.

EH: OK. So you would have him establish bonds of confidence with cabinet officers and put the monkey on their backs?

AB: Yes, right.

SM: Would you be in favor of the continuation of some person like Hauge in the White House who is the intermediary between the CEA and the president?

AB: This is a difficult question. Hauge and I got along beautifully. But I've been told that Hauge and Saulnier, my successor, didn't get along so well, that the relationship between them was tense. There was only one time when Hauge and I came even remotely close to having a significant difference. Hauge had undertaken to write an article on the economic situation for one of the weeklies. He sent me a copy of his draft and wanted to know what I thought of it.

This was in December, just before the presidential messages were due. "Gabe, your article is fine, but you are stealing the thunder of the Council of Economic Advisers, since our Report—which will soon be out—will analyze the economic situation along very similar lines." I don't think I really used that crude phrase—"stealing the thunder," but that was certainly the thought I expressed. Gabe promptly replied, "I think you are right, Arthur. I hadn't thought of that, but I should have. I will cancel that article." That was the closest we ever came...

Reconstructing Policy Decisions

SM: Perhaps you could take us through the measures that you used to react to the 1954 recession, starting in 1953.

AB: You will find that fully discussed in the January 1955 Report. There is also Donovan's book on the Eisenhower administration. He got hold of minutes of cabinet meetings. I had warned Eisenhower, back in 1953, that a recession was developing. Once it became a matter of serious governmental concern, he said to me, "Arthur, you are my chief of staff in handling the recession. You are to report every week at a Cabinet meeting on where we are going and what we ought to be doing." So that became the Council's responsibility. And Eisenhower rather liked the plans we developed. I remember his saying with enthusiasm—in some ways I hate to speak of this because it can be interpreted as boasting—after I had outlined a plan of action at one of these weekly sessions, "Arthur, what a chief of staff you would have made during the war." To Eisenhower, that was probably the highest compliment he could pay—he being a military man. That, in a general way, is how policies for dealing with the recession were handled. Of course, my Council got much help from other agencies.

But I would like to comment on a related matter. I don't know if any of that is in the record anywhere. I became concerned about potential inflationary trends at a very early stage. In the spring of 1955—perhaps it was close to mid-year—I therefore established a new informal organization, where representatives of various credit agencies of the government frequently met. This was designed to supplement what the Federal Reserve did in the area of credit restraint. The Federal Reserve was represented on this informal group. So, as we moved away from anti-recession policies, we lost little time in getting anti-inflation measures underway in the credit area.

This was a high-level group. The head of Federal Home Loan Bank Board was on it. Randolph Burgess, the number two man at the Treasury, the Under Secretary of Monetary Affairs, was on it. The FHA was included; at that time it was an important agency, but it's a dying agency now. The Fed was represented. I don't think Martin was on it. There were some ten or twelve individuals in the group. I'll tell you a fellow who has considerable knowledge of this activity. Saulnier worked with it. Here was an outfit that kept pushing for restraint on the part of the credit granting, guaranteeing, and insuring agencies of government, along with the Treasury and the Federal Reserve. It was moderately effective at the time. I felt a need for such a supplementary instrumentality to restrain credit expansion.

SM: Could we go back to the recession again? Was Humphrey on the side of not expanding as much or not running deficits? Did you have sort of a running battle with Humphrey in late 1953 or the beginning of 1954 as the recession was underway?

AB: No, at that time Humphrey was in favor of tax reduction and so was I. We were on the same track then, but, as a matter of fact, I was pushing even harder for tax reduction than George Humphrey was.

SM: You were slightly more expansionary than he was?

AB: I think the answer is probably in the affirmative, but I don't remember having difficulties with Treasury in 1953 and 1954.

DD: When you got into 1955 did you want to push a tax reduction?

AB: When we both favored tax reduction, he generally didn't go as far as I wanted to go. I remember his saying one day, "Why in the wide world are you always talking about cutting the high bracket tax rates? Here I am and I pay 91 percent"--that was the rate at the time--"and you don't, and yet I don't complain and you do all the time." I didn't like the logic of that pronouncement or its personal accent. So I told him, "George, this 91 percent tax that you pay and that I don't pay is a greater burden on my family than it is on yours." It took him some time to understand that.

DD: But within a year you had reversed roles. He was fighting for a tax reduction and you didn't want it at all.

AB: Different times.

EH: Did he understand economic theory at all--did he have an appreciation of where you were coming from as a theoretical economist?

AB: I think probably not.

SM: Did he understand countercyclical fiscal policy?

AB: I'd say probably not. Eisenhower became very good on countercyclical economic policy.

SM: And Eisenhower would have been willing to engage in a more interventionist policy if the recession had deepened?

AB: Sure, I think it was May 25 of 1954, when no signs of recovery had as yet appeared. They first came a month or so later, around June (I don't know how much of that is in the public record), but the order went out on that day to the Defense Department no longer to cut back on military spending, in fact to start increasing it by a substantial amount. Other agencies were also instructed to speed up their spending to some degree.

SM: Was there a difference between the relationship of Saulnier, or his relative power position relative to Humphrey? He was still at Treasury in 1958?

AB: No, I think he had left. I believe that Anderson and Saulnier were less interventionist than I had been. I think that's a fair statement.

SM: What was your view on fine-tuning? Or the extent of fine-tuning when you talk about intervention?

AB: I never believed in fine-tuning. On the other hand, I did believe that recessions should not be permitted to run their own course. This present recession should be allowed to run its course. But economic conditions are very different now. We had a stable price level in 1958.

SM: When you say you are against fine-tuning, you mean that you just didn't think it was possible to do it?

AB: Right.

SM: But when you got evidence that things were slowing down, then you moved and you moved in this kind of sequence because...

AB: As a matter of fact, I recommended a tax reduction in 1958.

SM: Well, let's go to the 1955-56 period. I gather as the economy gathered steam in 1955 your worries about recession were replaced by worries about inflation.

AB: I stopped worrying about the recession by mid-1954. In fact, I informed the Cabinet around June that the recession was over.

SM: We didn't have the Phillip's curve at that time and all that apparatus. How did you think about it, did you think we are going to have to slow things down or have higher unemployment to fight inflation? How did you view the inflation control?

AB: I did not think of higher unemployment. Unemployment reached about 6 percent, I believe, in the course of the recession of 1953-54. It started from a level of about 2-1/2 percent. My rough goal at the time was the conventional goal of 4 percent unemployment but the time to take restrictive measures was not when you had already reached 4 percent. The time to begin was soon after unemployment began falling, in other words, well before unemployment reached the 4 percent level.

SM: So they slowed down the speed.

AB: But hoping you'd get back to 4 percent unemployment, and yet not go lower.

SM: Did you ever think in terms of engineering a recession in order to combat inflation?

AB: I should say not.

SM: It was more just slowing things down so that you landed on 4 percent.

AB: There was no question in my mind toward the end of 1954 that a vigorous recovery was underway, and that inflationary forces would soon develop as they normally do in the course of a vigorous business-cycle expansion. Therefore, I felt that it was particularly important to take restrictive measures in the financial areas, and not trust solely to the Federal Reserve to do that. As I indicated before, I was critical of the Federal Reserve on the ground that they weren't moving fast enough in early 1955. I strongly felt that we would have to slow down the credit programs of the federal government quite apart from the monetary policy by the Fed. That is why the informal financial group, to which I referred earlier, was organized.

SM: Did you think about slowing down the fiscal side too, or is that simply too hard to do?

AB: There was no way of slowing down the fiscal side in sufficient time.

SM: So it was going to be monetary—mostly monetary—or fighting off tax reductions?

AB: The tax issue came to the fore towards the end of 1955, when we were getting ready for the 1956 program. It didn't become an issue until December of 1955 or thereabouts. But restraint could be exercised and in fact was exercised, quite early in the financial area. If I remember correctly, the first step was taken in December 1954 with regard to stock exchange credit. I think you will find a full recital of early financial actions in the Economic Reports of the President of January 1955 and January 1956. You might also check what I have to say on this subject in the chapter dealing with inflation in my book on Prosperity Without Inflation.

It was written in 1957, when I was still very close to the facts.

SM: It sounds as if you were coordinating quite closely with Martin at the time, that there was quite a lot of good discussion about how monetary policy ought to be operated.

AB: I don't like the word coordinated, because that may be unfair to the Federal Reserve or to Martin. I had frequent conversations with Bill Martin, and I did not hesitate to tell him what I thought and I felt that he was thoroughly candid with me.

SM: I don't quite understand the way the monetary and the fiscal authorities coordinate their policies together, though I guess you don't like the word coordinate.

AB: I do not. In practice, coordinate very frequently means that you are to think the way the other fellow thinks. I have been accused of not coordinating the Federal Reserve Board's monetary policy with fiscal policy. Those who talked that way frequently meant that I didn't go their way. Of course, if you mean by coordination frequent, honest consultation and communication, we certainly had that during the 1950s and we had it during my period on the Federal Reserve Board as well.

SM: That means that the Federal Reserve reserves the right, which it has, to run, to decide monetary policy. How does it inform the fiscal side so that they can adjust their policy to that?

AB: Let me speak only of my own period at the Federal Reserve. I never informed anyone of what precise actions I would recommend to the Federal Reserve Board or to the Federal Open Market Committee.

SM: Then how do the fiscal authorities operate their policies?

AB: I would inform them fully on what was in the public arena. I would also interpret what the trend of monetary policy has been—what the broad thinking currently was, but any...

DD: What he is saying is that if we were thinking about a discount rate change, he might give the broad thinking that the policy needs to be a little more restrictive, but he wouldn't say we are thinking about a discount rate change. Am I interpreting you right there?

AB: Yes, exactly.

SM: Now if the Treasury was coming out with a big debt financing, that presumably entered into your thinking.

AB: It now and then affected somewhat the timing of our actions, but no more than that. And after the Treasury shifted to an auction technique, it had almost no effect.

SM: You've had a tremendous experience with forecasting business cycles and following the macro economy and it seems to me that your ability to do that in the mid-1950s really was a lot better than what we have been seeing in the last five or six years. Do you think we have made any advances in forecasting, do you think we are going to be able to make advances?

AB: Retrogressed...

SM: If we have done that why have we done it? Have the models ruined us?

AB: I think that you have hit the nail on the head. What the models do is to average together very different periods. Look at what the models have been telling us about the inflation rate. They tell us that if we had a substantial increase in unemployment that would be accompanied by a negligible reduction in the inflation rate. But if you go back and study the record historically, you will find that isn't so. If you take different kinds of periods together and average them out, you get some kind of mish-mash. I wonder why people pay any attention to such results. On the other hand, if you make a straight-forward historical analysis along the lines of the National Bureau's business-cycle analysis, if you proceed to study tables and charts and data, actual turning points, you will find a clear-cut response of the inflation rate to the business cycle. The inflation rate as measured by the consumer price index was 12 percent on an annual basis in 1974 and came down to 4.8 percent in 1976. On a quarterly basis, the decline was still greater. The wholesale price level moved down from around 18 percent to 3.3 percent. Or take what's happening now. The business-cycle analyst who doesn't work with these econometric models will probably predict accurately the direction of the inflation rate, not its precise magnitude. Nobody knows how to do that. In short, I think that relying on economic history, on close statistical studies of an historical sort, will yield better forecasts than relying on econometric models. These models are bankrupt. But I've looked for guidance, looked for assistance and I haven't gotten much. I think economists have gone wild about models. They pay little attention to the real world. This craze will probably go on for another twenty or thirty years, but eventually they will wake up. These swings in thought take a long time.

SM: But people have a vested interest in all the techniques they have developed.

AB: They have vested interests psychologically. They have developed a set of habits, a way of thinking. These trends in economic thinking are interesting. For example, studies of the business cycle were long conducted in a sort of subterranean world. Who were the early students of the business cycles? Certainly not the major economists of the world. The major economists were concerned with equilibrium economics. The discovery of the limitations of that came late, notably during the Great Depression. All of a sudden Keynes became the great authority on the business cycle. Why? In large part because he used the language that academic economists were accustomed to. Keynes thus taught economists about the business cycle, but what he had to say about the business cycle--directly or indirectly--was in very large part wrong. Take, for example, the notion that developed that prices begin rising when you reach, or almost reach, full employment. Historically, of course, the price level began rising around the trough of the business cycle, not at the peak. In more recent times, this has been true of the rate of inflation.

SM: Is the rate of increase different in various parts?

AB: That is something else again. In the original study of business cycle indicators that Mitchell and I did in 1937, we had a wholesale price index as an early indicator. Keynes came along in 1936, and taught economists to believe--of course, they oversimplified Keynes and we really ought not to put too much blame on Keynes--that the price level begins rising only when full employment is reached. That sort of nonsense goes a good distance in explaining why we became so complacent about inflation.

3

The Council of Economic Advisers Under Chairman Raymond J. Saulnier, 1956-1961

Summary History

When Arthur Burns resigned the Chairmanship of the Council of Economic Advisers effective December 1, 1956, his successor was one of his colleagues on the Council, Raymond J. Saulnier. Saulnier was also a Columbia economist and had been Burns' associate at the National Bureau of Economic Research. As an expert on finance, he had been asked by Burns to serve as a consultant to the CEA beginning in 1953. In 1955, he was appointed as a member of the Council.

Like his predecessor, Saulnier was insistent on an objective, non-political role for the Council. Saulnier was more inclined to delegate responsibility than Burns had been, sharing more of the burden with his colleagues, Joseph Davis and Paul McCracken. The new Chairman also depended more on staff assistance than Burns and preferred a more permanent, career staff, balanced by academics.

Saulnier, coming into an ongoing administration, did not initially have as close a relationship with Eisenhower as his predecessor. But although some observers have suggested that the President was increasingly isolated in his second administration, Saulnier appears to have had meetings with him nearly as often as Burns. He also attended all Cabinet meetings, participated in meetings with legislative leaders, helped brief Eisenhower for his press conferences, assisted in speech preparation, and recommended action on legislation sent to the President by Congress for his signature. Like Burns, Saulnier also maintained that the Council must take a "professional" stance above politics, but he was not as insistent on maintaining his confidential advisory relationship with the President when called to testify before Congress. Saulnier did not insist on testifying in executive session and was willing to allow the release of transcripts of CEA testimony.

Saulnier maintained good relations with White House Assistant Gabriel Hauge and his successor Don Paarlberg. He worked more easily with Secretary of the Treasury George Humphrey than Burns. He got along even better with Humphrey's successor Robert Anderson, for the latter was more flexible and less dogmatic in his approach to economic issues. Saulnier also maintained the other inter-agency contacts that Burns had developed during his tenure. Although the Advisory Board on Economic Growth and Stability was reportedly less important in Eisenhower's second term of office,

Saulnier continued to chair its weekly meetings and set up an
expanded ABEGS that included the heads of all credit agencies. He
was also Chairman of the Cabinet Committee on Small Business and
the Cabinet Committee on Government Actions Affecting Costs and
Prices and served on the Committee on Price Stability for Economic
Growth and the board of directors of the Federal National Mortgage
Administration.

Perhaps the major innovation of this period was the arrangement of informal meetings of Saulnier, Hauge, Anderson, and
Federal Reserve Chairman William McChesney Martin. Eisenhower
insisted on strict observance of the Fed's independence, but it
was essential that there be some coordination between its actions
and the administration's overall economic policy. There was some
coordination, since the Fed was represented on ABEGS and Council
members met frequently with Federal Reserve officials. But by the
early fall of 1957 Saulnier and Anderson felt that there needed to
be a regular meeting of the major economic policy advisers with
the President, particularly to develop better communications with
the Fed. Consequently the four began to meet informally with the
President in what was known variously as the "Little Four" and
"the financial committee." This was one of the most important
forms of inter-agency communication established during the Eisenhower administration and proved valuable in working out the administration's anti-recession policy in 1957-58. This was the predecessor of the Kennedy administration's Troika and Quadriad.

Saulnier became Chairman in late 1956 as rising prices (due
to a capital goods and consumer durable goods boom) made inflation
the major concern of administration economic policy. The consumer
price index was rising at the rate of 3.5 percent a year, a rate
viewed with alarm by the administration. In the 1957 Economic
Report, the first under his chairmanship, the same basic arguments
were presented as in earlier administration Reports about the need
for limited government intervention in cooperation with the private sector in order to provide the proper stable environment for
a free competitive economy. Although doubts were expressed about
the efficacy of tighter monetary policy in holding down inflation,
the administration proposed no alternative government action other
than trying to balance the budget, but the size of the proposed
budget for the next fiscal year led conservatives to doubt the
sincerity of the administration on this point. The Report focused
more on exhorting business and labor to take responsibility for
the nation's economic welfare and to exercise voluntary restraint
in price and wage decisions. In its report, the JEC insisted this
was not drastic enough action. Secretary of the Treasury Humphrey
also indicated that perhaps more budget cuts were called for.
Thus encouraged, Congress cut another $4 billion from the budget
despite administration resistance.

By May 1957, economic indicators indicated that the boom was
over and that anti-recession not anti-inflation policies were in
order. Yet other evidence indicated that the economy was still
booming, with GNP, personal income, and employment all up. Although he would not predict a recession, Saulnier did begin efforts to persuade the Federal Reserve Board to loosen its credit
policy, but Fed Chairman Martin, Hauge, and others in the adminis-

tration continued to focus on the problem of inflation. Credit was tightened even further with a raise in the discount rate in August.

In October 1957, Anderson, the new Secretary of the Treasury, set up the first of what were to become a series of meetings between himself, Saulnier, Martin, Hauge, and Eisenhower. Saulnier received little support for his advocacy of less restrictive monetary policy at the first meeting, but in mid-November the Federal Reserve took steps to ease credit. Beyond that, however, the administration did not develop an active anti-recession program. Despite Saulnier's effort to convince the administration that the low budget estimates for FY 1959 by Bureau of the Budget Director Percival F. Brundage were neither defensible from an economic standpoint nor acceptable in light of post-Sputnik military needs, the administration still pushed for a surplus, although it never materialized. Eisenhower feared that tax revenues would not be sufficient for an expanded budget and that a deficit would lead to disastrous inflation in the long run.

Pressure increased on the administration to act more vigorously to stem the recession. Both the AFL-CIO and the National Association of Manufacturers insisted a tax cut would give the sagging economy the boost it needed. Eisenhower's previous CEA Chairman Arthur Burns also urged the President to endorse a tax cut. Former Secretary of the Treasury Humphrey was, however, opposed to such action, as were Anderson, Martin and others. Saulnier was not an ardent advocate of a cut in taxes, but he was more willing than others in the administration to accept such action if the recession did not bottom out soon. Although there was some indication in March that the administration might advocate a cut just to keep the Democrats from making political capital out of it, Anderson used his influence with the President to block such a move.

There was little change in spending plans to counter the recession. Aside from defense, the only major spending hike supported by the administration was an extension of unemployment insurance compensation benefits. Otherwise, there was strong opposition to any expenditures for public works (resulting in a veto of a Democratic-sponsored rivers and harbors bill), although there was acceleration of scheduled projects and planning of emergency projects. However, easier monetary policy and the limited fiscal measures proved sufficient to halt the recessionary trend by the summer of 1958.

The 1959 Economic Report reviewed the 1957-58 recession and recovery but again the administration's primary concern was inflation. While critics felt that the economy had not sufficiently recovered from the economic downturn to merit a shift to anti-inflation policy, the administration was alarmed over the fact that inflation had continued throughout the recessionary period. This was a "new inflation" different from any experienced before and particularly ominous to conservatives who emphasized price stability as the primary requisite for economic growth and development. If Keynesian-liberal economists were willing to accept a measure of inflation as simply the cost of achieving full employment, the Eisenhower Republicans were not so inclined. Arthur

Burns advised Eisenhower that the administration should not be so consumed with this fear of inflation, but others, including Raymond Saulnier, were apparently more influential with their emphasis on the need for price stability. The depth of the Eisenhower administration's concern was evident in the President's endorsement in the Report and in his State of the Union Message of a proposal to amend the Employment Act to specifically include "price stability" as a central economic goal. The proposal did not pass Congress, but Eisenhower took other actions of his own to focus attention on the inflation problem. In January 1959, at the recommendation of a special Cabinet committee, he set up the Committee on Government Activities Affecting Prices and Costs (CGA) which was chaired by Saulnier, and the Cabinet Committee on Price Stability for Economic Growth (CCPSEG).

In the policy area, the administration's major objective was to balance the FY 1960 budget, emphasizing stability over growth. Anti-recession and recovery actions were stopped in favor of reductions in expenditures and elimination of the recession-based deficit. Democratic critics on the Joint Economic Committee insisted that this would mean unnecessarily sacrificing the growth essential to lowering the high unemployment rate (6 percent), but Eisenhower maintained that budget deficits only competed for private savings and retarded economic growth.

Eisenhower and his economic advisers were also concerned that continued inflation and government deficits would undermine foreign confidence in the dollar. By 1958 the U.S. had a deficit in its balance of payments. In addition to expanding the resources of the International Monetary Fund in order to strengthen international financial institutions, the administration considered a stable domestic economy and confidence abroad in the U.S. dollar as essential to correcting this imbalance. Consequently, anti-inflationary policies were bolstered by concern over the balance of payments problem.

The 1960 Economic Report and the JEC's Report again reflected partisan disagreement over the goals of stability and growth. The administration attained its $1 billion surplus in FY 1960, continued to resist tax reductions or easing of monetary policy, and planned an even larger surplus for FY 1961. Their plans for stability, recovery, and growth, however, were quickly thwarted by a recession similar to the 1957-58 downturn. Although Saulnier considered the delay in easing of credit the central cause of the recession, the administration's attempt to shift so quickly from a deficit to a surplus also seems to have been instrumental in the 1960 downturn. Although the administration tried to obviate the political effects of the recession by simply not recognizing that a problem existed, dissatisfaction with Republican economic policies played a role in the party's 1960 defeats. The Eisenhower administration had managed to slow inflation but only at the cost of continued unemployment and limited economic growth.

Oral History Interview

The President and Economic Policy

EH: Why don't we begin with the President and the Adviser in the White House and ask you to talk about Dwight Eisenhower? What was your perception of what he knew about economics when you first began to observe him and how he thought about economic questions?

RS: In almost all respects he was very different from his public image. Let me illustrate that. In 1952, just before he was to run for President, a group on the Columbia faculty, mainly from the Graduate Faculties, undertook to build public opposition to his candidacy. He was then president of the University and they were speaking irreverently, to put it mildly, of their president, to build opposition to him on the ground that he was a military man, a militarist, and that he would be dangerous in the presidency. Now, oddly enough, the record is pretty much the opposite of that. He's memorialized now for his farewell talk to the country in which he spoke very feelingly about the so-called military-industrial complex. That illustrates something of the difference between the man and the image—in this case he did not live up to the image of him projected by my university colleagues. He is also frequently pictured as a man who had no great competence in handling economic matters or interest in them. Nothing could be further from the truth. He was not a trained economist, but had a great deal of experience with economic matters in military services. He'd had a good deal of exposure to business and finance in the period between his military service and his presidency—he was on the board of a number of companies. In Germany he had been closely connected, of course, with reconstruction after the war. Jean Monnet—father of the Economic Community—was one of his great favorites. He was very interested in the way Erhard had moved to free up the German economy after the war, and had a great admiration for him and for Erhard's philosophy, which was, as you know, a free market, free enterprise philosophy. So when you talked to him about economic matters, there was no need to start from the bottom and explain yourself. He had a good start on these things.

As far as interest is concerned, I used to see him frequently. When I was briefing him on what was happening to the economy, I would come in with a whole sheaf of charts and tables. He would go over them, piece by piece, and if he were looking, say, at a chart on housing starts, he would say: "Well, now, I'll tell you where that'll be next month." And he would make his own forecast and mark it on my sheet. I'd later have an opportunity to discuss with him how his forecast turned out.

EH: Was he conversant with economic theory? Did you ever need to get into certain theoretical questions with him?

RS: I wouldn't say so, at all. If you talked to him about the acceleration principle, he would ask you to explain what you were talking about, and properly so. I remember one State of the Union Message that had come to me late at night—as these things always do—in its last appearance. I'd gone over it, and I went to him in the morning—just before he was to read it to the Congress. I saw him about 11:00, maybe 11:15; his secretary was soon telling him that it was nearly 12:00, and looking daggers at me, I had said, "Mr. President, there are some things here I'd like to see you change." So we went through it, and he made changes. I was cleaning up the economic references, so that nobody could pick it up and say: "Look, he doesn't know economics." When we finished, I said: "Now, Mr. President, nobody is going to fault you on the economics." He looked at me benignly, and said: "Steve, I don't expect to talk like an economist, or to write like an economist; all I want is for people to understand me." That was his purpose: to be understood; and, incidentally, he was telling me something about economists!

Another example of how he differed from his public image: he's often pictured as rather irascible, quick-tempered, pounding the table, saying "Goddamn it!" I saw a great deal of him: attended every Cabinet meeting through my whole incumbency; every meeting of the legislative leaders; numberless conferences; individual meetings with him, not every week, but certainly every two weeks—and I never once saw that red-faced, out-of-control personality that's often pictured. He was typically a calm and collected person; he could grit his teeth over something—and the President has a lot to grit his teeth over—but he was not a difficult person to work with. There was nothing difficult in his personality as I saw it. The public iamge, in just about every respect, doesn't match my knowledge of him and my experience with him.

McS: Was it established from the beginning by the President or some member of his staff just what it was that he wanted you to do? Were there questions or major points that provided a framework for these briefings and beyond that, what kinds of questions interested him enough to raise during the course of your regular meetings?

RS: You might group the meetings into two categories: first, occasions when your object is to talk about a specific problem: a housing bill, for example. If it were that kind of question, you would be there with the other persons in government who had a reason to be there. If it were agriculture, you can be sure there would be somebody from Agriculture present. He was very much the staff man, the staff-using man. And just as I would be offended if I were not there when some matter was under discussion that I thought the Council had a reason to participate in, so also would Agriculture be offended if I were there talking about a Sugar Bill, for example, and they had no voice in it. Let me say as a footnote that he operated—unlike President Carter, but

like most presidents--with a Chief of Staff, first Sherman
Adams, then Jerry Persons. On such an occasion you would
normally go first through those people, and they or someone
of their people would normally be there when you were with
the President.

Now, the second category: What's the economy doing? Is
it slowing down? Are we headed for troubles? What's the
pitch of activity, the drift of things? This is a business-
cycle and business-analysis problem. In that kind of case I
would typically be there by myself, and we would sit down and
go over the numbers. You may be familiar with Business
Conditions Digest, which was started while I was at the
Council. The underlying materials were brought together on
my initiative, and I got Julie Shishkin, who is presently
Commissioner of Labor Statistics, to assemble the material on
economic indicators that had been developed at the National
Bureau of Economic Research. Having been a member of that
staff for many years, though not on business cycles, I was
familiar with the data. We started using the indicators to
follow what was happening in the economy. The data were
published later--we didn't publish the material. I would go
in with a whole batch of these things and we'd sit down
together. No one set this up. If I wanted to see him, I
would ask my secretary to see if the President would have
some time. And I never asked for time without getting it
within a day or two, and if it were an emergency, you'd
simply say it was that, and you would walk across the street
and be there.

McS: How long would you have with the President during regularly
scheduled meetings?

RS: Well, you have an appointments secretary sitting outside--
believe me, he is chopping up that time to a fare-thee-well--
and if you want more than 15 minutes you have to have something important on your mind. In the general briefings, I
would have about half an hour. But he would become so interested in the subject we would usually run over the allotted
time. I was never there that we weren't interrupted--the
appointments secretary would come to the door. The President
would grunt a little bit, and I'd have to get up and walk
around, and finally we'd break it up, and that would be it.

EH: When it came to a major decision, say something to do with
what to do about a possible recession in 1953 or 1954--I mean
a major question--the different economic ways of looking at
this are theoretical; there are different theories about what
to do. Now you wouldn't go in and present theories to him,
but you would present alternatives that were grounded in
theory, wouldn't you?

RS: Yes.

EH: How would you explicate those alternatives?

RS: A question of that kind, of course, would have been under discussion very actively outside the Oval Office before it got to him. When we were there, you had a chief--the Assistant to the President--and you would sit down around the table with him, with the Budget Director, somebody probably from Commerce, and someone certainly from Treasury, and that's about it.

SM: What about the Federal Reserve?

RS: No, no, not the Federal Reserve. I'll come to that in a minute. You'd be sitting around the table discussing the question, "Do you need to do something?" Now that is not a matter of alternative theories, that is a matter of judgment of an economic situation. Is something happening in the economy that's going to lead us into a downturn or not? It's a matter of looking at the numbers, studying them and knowing them. Then the question is, "Something is building up. What do we do about it?" There, of course, you can get differences of opinion. Some people might accent money policy; some people might accent tax policy. Those would be the two major differences. I don't really see that, necessarily, as a clash of theories; more often it involves things at a practical and institutional level.

EH: You are saying then that you really didn't take options to him, or alternatives that were couched in theoretical terms at all. The president doesn't really need to be educated in economic theory--just deal with practical alternatives.

RS: In any case he will consider alternatives.

EH: Did he want options or did he want recommendations?

RS: It would depend on the problem. If you could work the problem out at a staff level, you might come to him and say, "Mr. President, we think this bill ought to be vetoed." Incidentally, you could never recommend a veto to him or to Sherman Adams or Jerry Persons, without having already written the veto message. It's a very good idea because it cools off many people. They would never be able to write a veto message because they couldn't articulate--nor could anyone else articulate--a defensible reason for vetoing the bill. Now if the staff agreed that it ought to be vetoed, and you had all the people with a need to know and a need to be involved in it and they all agreed, you would come in and say, "Mr. President, here's legislation that we are proposing be vetoed." "Well, what are your reasons?" So-and-so lays out the reasons. He'd want to know the other side, and he probably would already have been massaged, intellectually, on the subject by people interested in it one way or another. On the other hand, I can recall cases when we just couldn't agree. I remember one case where I simply could not agree with the staff, and we had to bring it to the President's

office. We got in, and so-and-so put his case, and I put my
case. I was for vetoing the bill. Eisenhower looked at me
and said, "Have you written the message?" "I happen to have
one here," I said, as I pulled it out of my pocket. He took
the papers home and probably spent a good part of the night
on them. In that kind of case there would be alternatives,
and he would have to choose from among them.

IB: Was it your sense that the question he put to you about the
reasons for supporting or vetoing legislation was of the
quality of economic judgment that one, for example, meets in
boards of directors and banks?

RS: Better. Yes, really very good. I never left a meeting with
him without saying to myself, "He has taught me something
about this question; he's brought out some aspects of it,
thrown some light on it, that hadn't been thrown on it
before."

EH: Was that primarily teaching you about politics or something
about American life or about the government or was he teaching you about economics?

RS: Well, it certainly would not be politics. I really don't
have all that much recollection of having talked politics
with him. His attitude was, "What's the best thing to do?"
As he said many, many times, "What's best for all Americans?"
What should the Republican Party be doing, or what are those
Democrats doing...that sort of thing wasn't in the picture.

EH: But surely he had political considerations in mind, did he
not?

RS: Well, I'll tell you a story about political considerations.
When I went to my first meeting with him as incoming Chairman, I remember his looking at me and saying, "There's only
one thing I want from the Chairman of the Council of Economic
Advisers. That's economic advice. I don't want political
advice. I have too much of that already, most of which is no
good." His attitude toward the Council was, what does the
professional economist have to say about the questions? It
didn't make any difference who was hurt, or who was benefitted. The question was what was the national interest in the
thing?

IB: Did he ever probe the extent of consensus among economists on
those issues with you?

RS: I don't recall any occasions when that was discussed in any
systematic way, or any need for it.

EH: The President would say to you, "Let's do what's best for the
country."

RS: Yes.

EH: That kind of choice is guided by values of some kind. He had a free-market ideology. He had biases in certain directions. Did you notice that he was filtering advice and processing it in terms of his own values?

RS: Definitely. Always. His philosophy is known; I don't need to describe that for you. The individual was at the center of his philosophy. He was a dedicated advocate of a basically individualistic type of system, an essentially democratic system, an enterprise system, private property and the market. You didn't have a sense that he was a great evangelist pushing the market system, but he was a man who had definite values and wanted to do things consistent with those values. I would hope that it would be clear from what I have said how he would react. Suppose, for example, that it was a question having to do with the railroad system. The railroad system has been a problem in this big country of ours for a long, long while, a highly regulated system. Here's a man who believes in the competitive system and is faced with that kind of situation. If a piece of railroad legislation, or questions about regulation, came before him he would be disposed toward developments that would strengthen the competitiveness of the system. Would he have gone as far in deregulation as they went under Nixon? I was a member of the Board of Governors of the American Stock Exchange while this was going on, and I could see the destructive, and, I felt anti-competitive, effects that were going to result from what the SEC and the Congress, with White House backing, were looking for in the setting of commission rates in the securities business. I looked at this and said, "You're going to redo the whole securities business. You're going to get a few giant firms. The smaller, regional firms are going to go out of business. You're going to get lower rates for the big buyers of securities and higher rates for the little fellows, like me." I argued that there were no economies of scale, and the deregulation would move us toward consolidation, and be anti-competitive. I wouldn't have had any trouble selling that to Dwight Eisenhower. He had sense enough to know that that would happen, and his innate conservatism would have said, "Let's go slow here; maybe this is the right direction, but let's not go overboard on this." Well, he went overboard. And what has happened? All of the predictable results. Eisenhower believed in the competitive system; but he was a very practical man and a very realistic person, and thoughtful of what the next move would have to be. If you asked him to do something, he would look at you and say, "Well, if I do that, what do I have to do next?" That question might be very embarrassing to the proponent. Eisenhower probably would have moved less rapidly on deregulation than you might think, considering his position on the essential values of competition.

EH: There's a presidential perspective that no one adviser, no single adviser, has, in other words. The president's job is not like that of anyone else.

RS: He has been through a number of fires, and so he did have an advantage over me. I hadn't organized the invasion of Europe, and hadn't controlled masses of men, or dealt with heads of state all over the world. There wasn't anybody in the whole governmental organization who could match him and his tremendous experience.

AL: You said that the general staff system--working through Sherman Adams--did not prevent you from getting access whenever you felt it was necessary to get to the President.

RS: It did not.

AL: How did the Adams type of general staff operation function with respect to the White House staff, and how did it differ specifically on matters of economic policy from Nixon's relation with Haldeman and Ehrlichman. Haldeman, I always thought, carried that principle of general staff much, much further than Adams did.

RS: Yes, I think it is probably true that the White House situation under Adams was more open than it was under Haldeman or Haldeman-Ehrlichman, probably also more than it was under Haig. But I doubt that you could show the difference organizationally on a blackboard, with boxes and lines. I think it's a matter of personality. Jerry Persons, for example, as Chief of Staff, was perhaps a more accessible, approachable chief than Sherman Adams. Sherman was from New Hampshire, and a pretty cold fellow. But I never had any occasion to see him when I was turned down. Still, you didn't just roam into his office. You wouldn't really roam in on Jerry Persons either, but there was a more open feeling under Persons. Maybe that's because I was an old hand by that time. And that's the personality difference.

AL: The way Eisenhower saw it--and the way Adams worked it--was to make sure that nobody got to the President on a policy matter that involved action by the President or Executive Office without being sure that all bases had been checked.

RS: That is correct.

AL: That is one sense. Another thing is to isolate the president so that the effect of clearance in the carrying of recommendations to the president is just that--only what the chief of staff wants gets to the president.

RS: Exactly. That is the risk. And there are risks on both sides.

134

JG: Wasn't there some controversy over a letter written by Secretary Humphrey in late 1956, indicating that he felt the President should have called for a larger cut in appropriations for the next year, and Congress then reacted to that?

RS: There was an argument about the budget that went up in January 1957. Humphrey was off somewhere when the budget was finally wrapped up, and it involved a larger increase in expenditure than he thought was right in the circumstances. And he gave that famous press conference in which he said, "If you keep this up, you'll have a recession that will curl your hair." Now, that reflected George's rather colorful speech; he was a very colorful fellow, and had very definite ideas on things. There was extensive Cabinet discussion on the question, but it is an example of a case where things didn't clear through Sherman Adams. I want to say when I speak of staff that I am not talking about the Treasury. I am talking about the White House staff, in which the Council operates, because the Council by statute is organized as an adviser to the President. We're not an independent agency, nor are we a separate Cabinet-level agency.

Bureaucratic Politics and Economic Policy

EH: Were there other White House staffs with which you did collaborate closely? Leave aside the Bureau of the Budget because I know you were involved with them.

RS: Bureau of the Budget you were involved with all the time. Now, Gabe Hauge, as you know, was in the Eisenhower picture before anyone else. Not longer, but before. He was associated, first, with Elliott Bell when Elliott was working for Tom Dewey, and then he went onto the campaign train with Eisenhower. When Eisenhower went to the White House, Gabe went with him, and Gabe had a very important role there. Gabe's functions were, first of all, that presidential appointments with an economic aspect would filter through his office. No one would be appointed to the Federal Reserve Board, for example, without having gone through the office of the Special Assistant to the President. Second, Gabe would have responsibilty for much of the legislation in the domestic policy area that would come before the President. But if the legislation dealt with, let us say, minimum wage, he would not make an analysis of the economics of that; that would go to the Council. Then there was a certain amount of speechwriting. But that'a different set of functions than those assigned to the Council of Economic Advisers.

AL: Under Eisenhower, Hauge was the White House man and Eisenhower saw to it that Hauge and the Council worked very, very closely together.

RS: We had very close connections with Gabe Hauge and after Gabe, with Don Paarlberg. It was work done not in a line of command, so to speak, but on a par; with a different mandate, but on the same level.

EH: The President put his confidence in you as his economic adviser. There has to be a relationship of trust and confidence, doesn't there?

RS: Of course. but you're not the only one. After all, he has the Treasury Department, among others. Now let me return to the Federal Reserve, if I may. There were two ways in which the Federal Reserve got in the picture. One of the first acts of the President was to establish what was called the Advisory Board on Economic Growth and Stability, the initials made it ABEGS. It met every week in the office of the Chairman of the Council of Economic Advisers, under the chairmanship of the Chairman. I sat on it all the while I was a member, and, of course as Chairman when I was Chairman of the CEA, which extends over a period of about six years. On ABEGS was always a representative of the Federal Reserve Board, and in ABEGS most of the major economic questions would be thrashed out. Second, in 1957, when the economic situation began to tighten up a bit, there was activated at the President's initiative a small group that would meet late in the afternoon in the Mansion with the President. There would be the Secretary of the Treasury, sometimes with his Under Secretary; I would be there, as would Gabe Hauge or Don Paarlberg, when he succeeded Gabe; Bill Martin, Chairman of the Federal Reserve; and the President would be there. That's my second example of the Fed in the picture. Those meetings would almost invariably start with the President looking to me to describe the economic situation. Then if the Fed saw it differently, or the Treasury saw it differently, they had an opportunity to make their views known. I don't remember any cases in which there were really sharp differences.

SM: Was that group set up specifically because of the tightening up in the economy in 1957?

RS: It had a more general utility but if there were something like 1957 in the works we would meet more frequently than if there were not. It continued throughout the presidency.

McS: Who would have been presenting the President with alternative views on economic policy?

RS: Possibly the Treasury. The Commerce Department would not be a likely source. When things get really interesting they typically get taken out of Commerce and are made independent, like the Small Business Administration. Commerce, perhaps, but more likely Treasury. Bill Martin would make his views known. The Fed was on ABEGS and the Fed was in the same White House group, and then I would meet regularly--whenever it was necessary, but certainly at least every two weeks--

with Martin. He'd usually have Candy Baldeson, his Deputy
Chairman, with him. We would talk about the economy, and if
the Fed had a different view, they would state it, but the
Fed tends to be not very communicative. Incidentally, on the
matter of Fed independence, the President had a definite
position. He would say to me, "This is an independent agency
and it's going to stay that way. We're not here to tell them
how to run the Federal Reserve System. But I want to be sure
of one thing: when they make their decisions I want them to
know how we feel about the situation. That should be part of
the information they have to work on." That was my job, to
be sure they had that information. But going to your question, they would also have an input to us.

AL: What about the representatives of the expansionist, the Keyserling philosophy?

RS: We had cyclical problems, but our problems at the time were
not those of an economy that seemed to have run out of gas.
When I became Chairman of the Council, at the end of 1956, we
were in a business-cycle expansion. Capital spending was
rising somewhere in the neighborhood of 25 percent per annum,
and there was no price inflation to amount to anything in
that there was a capital boom going on. We had had a boom in
automobile sales in 1955, carrying into 1956. We had had a
really traumatic change in the terms for extension of consumer loans, when the average maturity went from about thirteen months to twenty-three.

IB: This was after the X and Y credit controls had run out.

RS: Right. They'd all run out. So our thoughts were more on the
correction of imbalances than on stimulating a lagging economy. Now, in another day, in another time, the same Eisenhower, dealing with different problems, where would he be?
Would he be an expansionist or not? My guess is yes. His
methods might have been different, but there is nothing I am
conscious of in the man's makeup that would have prevented
him from playing an activitist-expansionist role.

SM: But during the last three years--1958, 1959, and 1960--didn't
a progressively larger gap open up between the full employment output of the U.S. economy and the actual output, except
for the short-lived expansion in 1959?

RS: Yes. Right. Incidentally, we didn't have any numbers on that
at the time. We're talking about 25 years ago, and gap
concepts, let alone statistics, had not been developed to the
degree that they came to be in the 1960s--not that we weren't
conscious of operating at less than the full capacity of the
economy. Of course we were concerned about that, but we were
also concerned about establishing balances in the economy
that would make it possible to pursue safely the expansionist

policies, if you will, that would reduce the amount of any gap that did exist.

SM: The interesting year for that strikes me as being late 1959 or 1960. Was there an argument in the administration about the advisability of a more expansionary stance?

RS: I wouldn't say an argument. I don't know whether I can call the money policy tight, but it certainly was not easy. It was a tight policy by most standards. Incidentally, this has a bearing on the tax questions. Were we supposed to be in a tug-of-war with the Federal Reserve--trying to undo with tax cuts what the Federal Reserve was doing with money policy? Where could time be best spent? Working on the Federal Reserve, and maybe getting a little easier policies from them? Or trying to get a tax cut? In the spring and summer of 1959 and extending into 1960, the situation was complicated by the fact that we had a long steel strike, which started in the middle of 1959 and didn't end until the end of the year. I was in the middle of that all along; I wrote the economic part of the government's brief to the Supreme Court, and it was in the Supreme Court that we finally got a Taft-Hartley action to end the strikes. We came out of it with a big surge of inventory accumulation, so that it was very difficult in the first half of 1960 to see whether you were dealing with a backlash from the steel strike or whether you had a cyclical problem on your hands. If you'll look at the numbers, you will see that they were not the typical pre-recession numbers.

Second, the Fed, under Bill Martin, was very much concerned about the inflation rate, our international payments position, and the dollar. And the President was not disposed to take risks with the position of the dollar. He understood the importance of the dollar as a reserve currency, and felt strongly that the greatest contribution we could make to world stability and growth was to have a dollar in which there was confidence. So there was support, you see, for a cautious money policy; perhaps if we'd been in an easier position internationally we could have had a more stimulative money policy. In any case, that's the context in which arguments were made.

SM: Did you agree with that Federal Reserve policy or did you in fact try to get them to adopt a more expansionary policy in that 1959-60 period?

RS: These were not sharp differences of view. It was a shade of view, between ourselves and the Fed. Our position on the question--and I want to be entirely fair to Bill Martin--was more inclined to an easing of the situation than his. It was not as strong a difference as there might be in some circumstances, but it was still a real difference. And remember that an easing movement was underway fairly early.

SM: It's also true, as I remember, that in 1960 there was a substantial increase in the surplus of the federal tax system, the fiscal side went towards contraction, too.

RS: Well, that depends. There are theoretical questions here. The budget for the fiscal year 1960 went to a small surplus. Something like $200 million, went to this from a deficit, so some would say that there was a contractionary effect. I would differ on that. We would have to be here several days to exploit this point fully, but I believe the fiscalists and those who put the accent on the so-called "full employment budget" take an unduly narrow view of the economy. The important question is whether the whole credit system is operating so that there is a contractionary or an expansionary influence on the money supply. The federal budget is important in that, but the private sector is also important. If you are moving toward a surplus or toward a balance from a deficit on federal accounts, I have a right to ask: What is happening to the household account? Are households moving from a big deficit in their accounts to a balance, or are they going in the other direction? And what is happening on the business side of the economy? Is it moving toward a surplus or deficit in its accounts? I am the real macro economist in this game; the Keynesians are narrow and myopic, in my view. I don't deny the importance of the federal accounts; I am simply saying that they are not the whole picture. We felt that by lowering the federal government's borrowing requirements interest rates would be lower than they would otherwise be, that the effect of this on the private side of the economy would be expansionary, and that it would be beneficial.

SM: Since you couldn't control the Federal Reserve and since they were using a fairly tight policy, it sounds very much as if you took that as a datum and adjusted your policy around that.

RS: I wouldn't say so. If we felt money policy was excessively tight, so much so that it threatened recession, or threatened to reduce unduly the rate of growth of the economy, we would have no hesitation about saying so. The two times in which that situation arose in my incumbency were in 1957 and 1960, and I would say I made my views known clearly in both of those cases. The differences were not as great as it's often convenient in professional writing on the subject to make them—certainly not as great as it's usually convenient in popular writing on the subject to make them—but there were differences of judgment. Certainly we did not take money policy as a datum. But once they'd acted, what could you do then?
     And other things could happen within our own family. In 1957 the Treasury came out with a refunding issue at a rate so high it seemed to me they would surely draw money out of the thrift institutions, raise mortgage rates, depress home

purchases and thus home construction, and be contra-cyclical in their effect. And they did it without my knowing it. Well, believe me, when I heard that, I went over to the White House to protest it. Sherman Adams was there then. He had somebody with him--I remember the occasion very well. He was on the telephone but finally he asked me to "state my business," a favorite expression of his. I told him what had happened, and why I thought it was wrong. He was very sympathetic and would have taken it up with Treasury had I wanted him to do so. But I preferred to do it myself. They were tightening the whole credit situation on me--it wasn't the Fed. You know, people don't know enough about the institutional structure of the economy. If I could reform the economic curricula of the university system, I would reform it in the direction of a fuller, more factual training in the nature of our institutions, especially our financial institutions, and how they operate. It's a lot more complicated than one would judge from reading the principles of macro--or for that matter--micro economics.

EH: Was the Adams staff system designed to pull together points of view not only within the White House but throughout the government on questions like this? Did he take that responsibility--to get you and Humphrey together?

RS: Yes, he might. The Treasury thing was a lapse. They ought to have consulted the Council. Maybe they thought it was not that important, which was a bad mistake on their part.

EH: But that was one of his responsibilities--to staff out these important questions--beyond the orbit of the White House itself?

RS: Definitely.

EH: But you were also structured on your own initiative in ABEGS and other ways, weren't you?

RS: Right. And this should have been discussed at ABEGS. We have tax policy; we have expenditure policy; we have monetary policy. And we have a fourth and fifth policy. The fourth is debt management policy. The fifth consists of all the things the great federal establishment does that affect costs and prices. This has been rediscovered recently, though I never see a sign in the discussions that it had ever been known before. In 1960 Eisenhower established, and I was Chairman of, a Cabinet Committee on Governmental Actions Affecting Costs and Prices to take responsibility for that.

AL: How different is this fifth category from something we used to call labor policy?

RS: It involves labor policy but much more than that. True, the Labor Department does a lot of things that have an effect on costs and prices, not the least of which is setting minimum wage floors, what you can pay a carpenter or a steam fitter in any community affected by federal contract work. And their scales are constantly being raised.

EH: The Council, unlike the Labor Department, is almost the only entity in this world that lacks a constituency.

RS: Oh, we have the whole nation as our constituency, and the president is our client. The Council's mandate and its object is to help the president promote the growth and the stability of the whole economy.

EH: All right, but when you get in a situation of disagreement between the Council and the Treasury or in the Quadriad, there are institutional stakes here and constituencies supporting these other groups. How can the Council be influential?

RS: By the force of its argument. By knowing more about the problem than anybody else. If it's an argument about the state of the economy, you trot out the numbers.

EH: So you would see examples in which you would actually sway people from the Treasury even though they had a different institutional stake?

RS: Yes, of course. Government is a continuous conversation, a never-ending conversation with your peers, your colleagues. You're with these people almost continuously, in one context or another. It isn't that suddenly you come together, and one fellow feels this way and another feels that way and you have a head-on collision.

EH: But when you did have disagreements, did they have to go to the President for him to resolve them?

RS: Indeed.

EH: Now a man like George Humphrey, as far as I can tell, really didn't know much about economics, but he had very strong economic views.

RS: Well, he wasn't an economist. If you asked him what an indifference curve was, he couldn't tell you. But if you asked him how consumers behaved, he'd be very perceptive; he could tell you a lot. And he had the ear of the President; he was very influential. The President respected him for his experience, for his judgment and for his intellectual capacity.

EH: Are there not, in fact, two teams? The first team is the Council, the Treasury, the Bureau of the Budget, maybe the Fed; the second team is then the constituency-oriented departments: Labor, Commerce--they're put in the back of the bus, aren't they?

RS: No. They weren't in the back of the bus as far as ABEGS was concerned, nor in the Cabinet. No, I think I'd take total, complete exception to that.

EH: I would think that the general view of political scientists would be that those are regarded in the White House--those two departments--as constituency departments, that everything has to be taken with a grain of salt.

RS: No, definitely not.

McS: Wouldn't you add Agriculture?

EH: Agriculture. All the distinctions drawn between the inner and outer Cabinet. The inner Cabinet are the people who are close to the president's regular important business: Treasury, Attorney General, State, Defense, and, of course, Bureau of the Budget. The outer cabinet is all the rest and the assumption is that all the rest are constituency-oriented, captured departments and more removed from the president, less in line, more looking to the Congress.

RS: Well, I just wouldn't push it that far. Agriculture does, of course, have a different standing in presidential business than Treasury or State or Defense. It is more focused on a special interest and a special sector, and that necessarily means that it won't be present at a lot of affairs where others will be involved. But that's not a reflection on their importance; that doesn't make them country cousins. It's just that they're not always involved.

EH: The mandate of the Council under the Employment Act perhaps would involve it day-to-day more closely with the Treasury, the Bureau of the Budget, the Fed, would it not? Did the Council have to make decisions about where to cut off its purview? You can't do everything.

RS: Well, you can't do everything, but I tried. And you'd be surprised how much you can do.

EH: Is it, in your view, within the orbit of the Council to involve itself in national security policy?

RS: Only where there's an economic aspect.

EH: Did you sit on the National Security Council?

RS: Yes, I did, when there was an economic question involved.

EH: Do you think it's important that someone from the Council sit on the National Security Council as a regular matter?

RS: I wouldn't think so. I think I would want to feel, however, that the President was alert to the need to have the Council involved in the discussion and development of policy positions where there was an economic impact. In our period, David Lusher was, in my recollection, a regular participant in the meetings of the National Security Planning group. At that time Bobby Cutler was the President's National Security Adviser, and there was a planning group where all of the agencies were represented. We were a regular part of that. The National Security Council itself would meet in the Cabinet room—they were Cabinet officers; the Planning Board was not—and if Cutler was to bring up a proposal that had an economic impact I would have been alerted by Lusher in advance, or by the White House, and I would be there.

EH: This is a good example of the positive side of Eisenhower's staff system, from your point of view.

RS: I think so. He was a "need-to-know" type of man. You aren't there unless you have a need to be there. It was not just a great community picnic, one day after the next, with everyone present, whether he had any reason to be there or not.

McS: It seems clear that you wouldn't be involved in crises such as Quemoy and Matsu unless they had a domestic economic effect. But what about petroleum during the Eisenhower years, where, for example, import quotas were...

RS: I was in it, and it was through my own intervention that words were introduced in the presidential order restricting imports of residual oils giving notice that if the effect of this was to bring about undue, unacceptable pay increases we would intervene. We also had a Council on Foreign Economic Policy presided over by Clarence Randall. I wouldn't be there, but some member of the Council would be. It dealt with problems of tariffs, trade agreements, and commodity agreements. Also with petroleum. We were always in those meetings.

McS: Since you were sitting on the NSC, would you deal, on something like petroleum, with the Department of Defense and the State Department?

RS: Sure, any time it wasn't that big a problem. In those days the East Texas oil field was opened up and Texas was, economically speaking, where the action was on oil, and where the millionaires were being made. You didn't have, fortunately, the balance of payments problems that the Middle East has. Petroleum was not really a big problem for us.

McS: But you did deal with the quotas and the residuals.

RS: We did, and this bears on those matters of inter-agency organization. The Council—and it's understood, of course, that I speak only of my own time--was a sort of neutral ground. There are adversaries in government. They shift, but there are certain continuing adversary relations, and one of those--I think it has standing as historic as any--is between Treasury and State. The Treasury has responsibility for the dollar, for the pocketbook, for meeting the bills, for keeping your financing in order. State, on the other hand, will often have interests that do not conform with that, are inconsistent with that. So you can get differences, even conflicts. For a time, under my chairmanship, many meetings involving Treasury and State that had to do with our connections with the OECD were held in my office. The Council was able to play a mediating role. This has some bearing on questions of structure; also some bearing on how we would get into foreign economic policy matters.

EH: Those two parties did not see you as an advocate, at least not in the first instance?

RS: Not to the extent that they saw each other.

EH: Are those two roles of arbiter and gatherer of information, on the one side, and recommender and adviser ever in conflict for an analytic staff?

RS: I suppose they could be, yes. I don't want to picture the Council as an agency that tries only to find the middle ground, because there are many times when, believe me, you must feel very strongly on one side or the other. But you could mediate where it was necessary. In my time I don't know that any other agency in government could have done it.

EH: I suppose that really is the point. Somebody has to do it and the other agencies need it done, whether they want it done or not.

RS: I should amend that statement to this extent: we had an Office of Defense Mobilization--it's gone under many different names over the years--and it was run when I was there by Arthur Fleming. We had that because we were deeply involved in stockpiling critical minerals during and after World War II. This also led to a system of accelerated depreciation allowances for industrial plants which were viewed as especially useful in the correction of metal shortages. I, or some member of the Council, regularly attended meetings of ODM. George Humphrey would be there, as would be the Under Secretary of Commerce, Interior, etc. So there was a place where these various parties could come together, and where a point of view could be reached, or a difference of viewpoint could be crystallized. Then we had the Council of Foreign Economic Policy, which was much the same. But if I at the Council, and Arthur Burns before me, felt that something came out of ODM or the Council on Foreign Economic Policy that we were genuinely unhappy with--something we had argued against

and lost--there would have been no impediment to our going in
to see the President about it. We would have gone through
the Assistant to the President, and would have said that we
dissented, and for what reasons. If we had not done that,
the President would have thought we were derelict in our
duties.

The Structure of the Council

EH: Perhaps you could reflect for a moment on your chairmanship
of the CEA and how you sought to organize the Council.

RS: When Arthur went down in 1953 he asked me to come down as a
consultant. I didn't become a member of the Council until
1955. Then in December 1956 I became Chairman. By that time
I was pretty savvy about government machinery.

EH: What skills do you believe that a Chairman of the Council
would need to be an effective Chairman?

RS: The Chairman of the Council has to have first-rate economic
training, analytically, and considerable experience. He
ought to have a fully adequate understanding of the institutional structures of our economy. He ought to be sensitive
to public feeling and be able to translate political and
broad, community-type responses to actions. He ought to have
a good memory, and an ability to work with people.

EH: Isn't there a loss of institutional memory on the Council
every time there's a turnover of administration?

RS: Yes. One question that that raises is the organization of
staff. There are two ways you can go on that. One, you can
put the accent on continuing members of a Council staff. The
other is that it can be a rather transient place, where
academic fellows come and go. It's always been a blend of
the two. I don't know any case where they've had one or the
other. My own preference would be to have that blend rather
heavier on the side of the continuing staff, for reasons that
I expect are obvious. A number of people on the staff, or in
the picture, when we came there were not Republicans, but
they continued and worked very effectively on our staff. Of
course, when Eisenhower came, the whole question of there
being a Council of Economic Advisers was up in the air. The
outgoing Congress had appropriated only enough money to keep
the Council going until January 31. That's why Arthur Burns
came into the picture to study the question whether they
ought to revive the Council. There wasn't much carry-over
staff, but there were two or three: Frances James, who was
in charge of statistical work, and David W. Lusher, who died
about five years ago, who was the forecaster. Shortly after
it was determined that Dave would be staying--that we had a
budget that afforded that--he enlisted Charlie Schultze as

his assistant. The third was Joseph L. Fisher, now a member of Congress.

EH: But a career staff would have much greater institutional knowledge about the government, about the agencies, about the agency biases, than would a group of academics, wouldn't they?

RS: It's especially useful in areas where the government is deeply involved, such as housing. Very little happens in the housing business and in the home mortgage financing business in the United States that isn't deeply affected by the federal government. I had a leg up on that because at the National Bureau I had studied housing and written extensively on its credit aspects. This helped me understand the institutions of the housing market. And institutional knowledge can be hard to come by. You can reach into the universities and find people who are very knowledgeable about the banking system and the monetary system and can step right in and work on monetary policy very effectively. And you can find people who know labor economics without knowing much about the labor movement. In short, there is a need for institutional as well as theoretical competence. A good career staff person has perhaps a better chance of proving this than someone on short-term leave from a university. But you need both.

JG: Were there any staff level inter-agency groups parallel to ABEGS?

RS: There was the group that met under the chairmanship of Dave Lusher. It brought together people from Commerce, Treasury, and maybe Labor. They were responsible for GNP forecasting. When a GNP forecast for the next three quarters or so was needed that group would develop it, and then it would go through the Council. The Council members would have to agree with the judgments that had been made.

EH: There's now a domestic policy staff under Eizenstat that supersedes the Domestic Council, which was abolished, but it includes essentially the same kind of staff people. Before that Califano had a domestic policy staff, before that I suppose it was Sorensen. Then you have to jump back to Clark Clifford. Was there a comparable group or person in the Eisenhower White House responsible for domestic policy?

RS: No. ABEGS was the nearest thing to that, which meant that the focus was at the Council of Economic Advisers. Gabe Hauge, who was on the White House staff, sat as a member of that Council. On the other hand, in the cases you mention in other administrations the focus of power and influence was in the White House. This was not so under the Eisenhower Council.

EH: Does it follow from what you say that the Council really worked in the area of social policy--aid to education, health insurance proposals, interstate highways, if you want to see that as social policy; it's economic policy, too?

RS: We were deep in it.

EH: Because there wasn't anyone else to work on those questions, you were the analytic staff?

RS: There were competent departmental staffs, on which the Council could draw, but in the end the work centered at the Council. But I've seen these things develop differently since 1960. I testified against major features of the Nixon proposal for a Domestic Council, which I thought was a bizarre proposal. The Council of Economic Advisers seemed to me to have an entirely subordinate role in it, and in the first listing of its membership the Director of the Budget was not included. I don't mind having [a domestic council] other than the ABEGS type, but I would insist that the Chairman of the Council of Economic Advisers be a member of it. I would not push his being the Chairman--though I certainly wouldn't resist that, and in many situations I would think that a good idea--but I would insist that the staffing--the analytical work--be done by the Council of Economic Advisers. Otherwise you build another organization in the White House that duplicates what the Council ought to be doing.

AL: What is happening is that the institutionalized agencies in the executive office, which at one time were symbolized by the Director of the Budget and the Chairman of the Council and the Chairman of the National Security Council, gradually had been displaced by people whom we used to call the White House staff. By virtue of its being closer to the President, the White House staff started building up a staff and a policy machinery that pushes the institutionalized agencies in the executive office out one step.

RS: That's correct. That's exactly what is happening.

AL: In the old days the president wanted people who cut across several departments because those people shouldn't become too closely identified with a distinctly departmental view.

RS: Yes. Eisenhower would never sit still for a decision that affected, for example, the housing business--and there were many of them--without its having gone through the Council of Economic Advisers. And why? Because he was not altogether sure that what would come out of the Housing and Home Finance Agency was the right thing. They had their constituencies: either the home builders, or the Savings and Loan Associations, or the Mortgage Bankers Association, and so on-- perfectly respectable constituencies, but still constituencies. I suppose what he admired about the Council was that it didn't have a constituency in that sense. It served him, exclusively.

EH: Would it follow from your argument that the Council should be the center of domestic policy, the analytic work—that economics is sufficient as a social science to develop domestic policy?

RS: Well, I have sketched ideas in my own book on how this might be done. I think there is a need—I could see it in my day—to focus cabinet-level discussion onto social and economic questions. Indeed, that was the mandate of the Cabinet Committee on Growth and Stability, as I saw it. However, it became the Nixon Committee, and through that became a partisan campaign instrument. I would like to see the secretaries of Treasury, State, Defense, Commerce, Labor, and so on, brought together in a cabinet-level group for setting strategy—with the president having the last word, of course—on economic matters. As I have said, the chairman of the CEA might serve as the working director of such a group, under the president's chairmanship, on the model of Eisenhower's National Security Council. I think it would be desirable to have the CEA chairman in that position because of his relative independence and his relative lack of commitment to agency or constituency interests. In any case, the Council of Economic Advisers should provide the staff work for such a group. I think it can do this just as well for HEW as it can do it for Labor or for Treasury or what-not. This doesn't mean there would be no participation by department staffs. If you're the person at the Council of Economic Advisers responsible for financial work, for example, you're working with the Treasury; if something financial is to come before that top committee, you would work it out first with your Treasury colleagues, and then it would go through you to that top group, where the question could be discussed directly by the secretary.

EH: The implication is that the Council staff doesn't need to be much larger than it is. Or if you're going to do this properly, do you have to have a larger Council staff?

RS: We had a staff that was adequate, and I would avoid like the plague the multiplication of that staff. You have to learn to work with the agencies—Commerce, Treasury, State, etc.—through a highly qualified person on the staff of the Council. You don't need more than a dozen.

EH: What are the virtues of a small staff?

RS: Manageability. You know what people are doing; you get more intellectual content—less mechanical, bureaucratic content. You get a collegial atmosphere. For staff meetings, you don't need a whole auditorium; you can get your people around a table. You can walk into each other's offices at any time; you know one another.

IB: The assumption being that the mass of statistical material that has to feed into thoughtful judgment is generated by the operating agencies and can be distilled by lower-level people elsewhere in the pipeline.

RS: I think it's better to have that done outside. You get more thoughtful, more reflective, work with a smaller group than you do with a big group.

EH: As you know, there ha e been proposals over time for a Council of Social Advisers. The problem is that nobody has ever been clear what disciplines should be represented or whether the other social sciences can get a hold on it. Economics is certainly necessary; I wonder if it's sufficient, though, in this area.

RS: Well--I want to be perfectly candid with you--I didn't feel there were any significant gaps. Of course, I have to look back on it now from a world in which we have many new theoretical formulations; more than that, we have a richer body of data. We don't have, really, any newer problems--and I'll stand by that statement--but I'm tempted to say that I would strengthen the forecasting side of the operation. Now, that really doesn't do justice to Dave Lusher. Working with the kinds of material that were available when Dave was working on them, I think we did a very creditable job--better than anyone else was doing in the federal establishment--and we were right, which, after all, is the test. We were right about the turnaround in 1958, and I was right about the turnaround in 1961, in both cases in the face of a widespread opinion that we would be wrong. But I think if I were there now, I would strengthen that side of the work.

Reconstructing Policy Decisions

EH: Let us reconstruct some policy decisions. President Eisenhower was very proud of the interstate highway act and you've said that you thought it was a very important piece of legislation. Could you take us through that and illustrate the role the Council played?

RS: Yes, I will, but I must tell you that although it was underway while I was a consultant to the Council, that was before I became a member and I was not really in on it. Lucius Clay was organizing the effort and developing the legislation. I think I'm correct in saying that that whole exercise originated after Eisenhower got there. But, you know, these things don't come out of the blue, and I would not want to have to demonstrate that Eisenhower was the first to think that it might be a good idea to have a better interstate highway system. I couldn't prove that. Anyway, the exercise began early in the administration. Arthur Burns can speak for himself on this, but I know that he was deeply involved in it. There were important questions of financing, of costing it out and the effect on the economy. When I got onto the Council the system was underway, and then the question was the timing of expenditures, a story in itself.

EH: Was there any anticipation of the consequences the highways might have on our cities and our population flow--draining the cities of people, strengthening the suburbs and so on?

RS: I think it was pretty evident that it would increase the mobility of people, that it would tend to spread the population, tend to expedite the development of less developed areas of the country. In general, these were considered to be good things. I would say that they have been good things. The problems of New York City are due less to the interstate highway system, believe me, than to the machinery of New York City's government and how the city has managed its financial affairs. But there were things happening in the 1950s that had to do with the pattern of development through the country--the movement of population through the country--and the interstate highway system helped promote them, at the time and subsequently. Movements that I would say were far less well appreciated then than they are now. As academic people, we ought to be able to understand that; we do learn things as we go along. But the movement of population itself was a bigger thing than anyone realized at the time. The change in the age distribution of the population that was taking place was a bigger thing than was realized at the time.

EH: Did agricultural policy--moving people off the land--have an effect on population movement, particularly in the South?

RS: Of course, there has been a long-standing drift of population off the farms and into the cities and the villages. In general, that was considered by most people as a beneficial movement. Among other things, it helped accelerate increases in productivity. Productivity improvement was faster in agriculture than in industry, but the level of productivity was higher in industry, so the shift out of agriculture lifted the average.

EH: So another illustration would be a criticism of urban renewal which drove people out of the central cities.

RS: On the contrary, early in the 1950s we took steps to extend the operations of our federal housing programs, including urban renewal. FHA was invented to aid the financing of single-family, owner-occupied homes, and I regard it as one of the great social inventions of our time. And so it developed from 1934 through the 1940s. But by 1953 we saw we had inadequate facilities for federal aid to projects of the high-rise, multi-family, inner-city type. And so urban renewal was invented. It really is a little odd for me to read, as I do frequently, that we were wrong in the 1950s for assisting urban renewal programs, which we did in a big way. Some of them came to grief, but this was due to administration, not concept.

SM: At the time of the recession of 1960 or 1958, did you discuss those recessions as necessary in terms of controlling inflation or slowing it down?

RS: Never. The idea that a recession was ever engineered for the purpose of helping control inflation is, I think, a really scandalous charge against the administration.

SM: Subsequently all this literature on the Phillips curve was developed. I guess that article was published in 1958. So it couldn't have been part of the mainstream of that time?

RS: Not in the sense it subsequently came to be.

SM: So there never was any talk of trade-offs between inflation and unemployment as we subsequently got in the 1960s?

RS: Nowhere near as much. I don't want to say there never was any conversation about this, because that would be wrong. But never to the extent that we had it later. If you will read the Economic Reports published under my chairmanship, you will see numerous discussions of how some approaches to eliminating inflation would impact adversely on unemployment, and how to avoid or minimize that kind of effect.

SM: In 1957 when you became aware that a recession seemed to be underway, did you consider it reasonable to have a small recession to slow down this inflation rate? Did you think of it in those terms?

RS: No, never. Definitely not. The recession in 1957 was an unwanted, uninvited intervention in our affairs. So was 1960-61, which was far less severe. I could go into the reasons why we got into recession in 1957--they have to do mainly with things that were done to get out of recession in 1954. The recession of 1953-54 was followed, as I say, by a very vigorous and unsustainable increase in capital goods expenditure, in consumer spending for durables, and also in governmental expenditure. One of the things that was done early in 1954 was to activate in the White House a program to plan and to push public works expenditure. There was a fellow in the White House, Colonel Pike, whose job was to expedite public works spending to spur recovery in 1954-55. As is typical of such efforts, the expenditures didn't come until long after the problem was over. We got the peaking of those construction expenditures in 1956, when the economy was already overheated. I used to say that it was my lot to have entered the picture on the wrong side of Pike's Peak. I came

151

in when those expenditures had mounted to the point where
they were all out of line with budget allotments, and steps
had to be taken to bring the thing under control. And that
helped produce the 1957 downturn. I think people have the
idea that running the government is like driving a nicely
tuned, neatly engineered automobile, in which, if you move
the steering wheel a little bit to the left, your car will
simultaneously move, just as you wish, and that you can pull
yourself out of any situation without any difficulty. Well,
believe me, neither government nor the economy operate that
way. It is more like operating a line of cars connected by
chains of varying lengths, and varying degrees of responsiveness; you slow the front car but you can't tell when the end
car will be affected. The 1957 incident came about, in part,
because our economy was a victim of just that kind of reaction.

Yes, the causes of recession in 1957-58 were partly of
the government's own making. A great easing of credit took
place in 1955-57, and it probably went too far. It was in
that period that installment credit terms went from something
like twelve months on the average to twenty-three. And debt
management had a role in it. In retrospect, the Federal
Reserve would have been better advised to have stripped the
system of reserves to the extent that it did in early 1957--I
believe I'm correct about that date. They changed their
signals on this and they began to move into an easier posiion
earlier, so it wasn't that we didn't respond to it, but I
think money policy helped bring it on. But, you know, when
you go through a great capital goods boom, you are going to
pay for it. It's an unsustainable rate of increase; it's an
imbalance in the economy that is not viable.

There were indications by the middle of 1957 that something was building up, though that view was not shared by
everybody. But when things turned down they turned down fast
and the argument was quickly over. We went into recession in
mid-year and by January automobile production was off 30-35
percent. The question then was: Should you cut taxes? You
might think the tax cut question would have been resolved on
the basis of theoretical considerations. Those were discussed fully, but there were other considerations, too.
First, I was confident that the economy was going to turn
around early in 1958. That's vital; that's absolutely crucial. I was not thinking of a decline that would cumulate
downward out of control; rather, I believed it would be
checked fairly soon. That gave me confidence, and it gave me
a sense of having some elbow room, some working time that
otherwise I would not have had. Second, we had some taxes
that we didn't want to have expire. We had a telephone
excise, for example. If we were going to have a tax cut, it
wasn't going to include taking the excise off telephone
calls. We had other excises scheduled to expire and we
figured we would ask to have them continued and then, if
needed, we would ask for a tax cut on personal incomes. So a
message went up to the Congress asking for the extension of

the excises. I think you'll find that that was in late
February, maybe even early March. We didn't ask for a tax
cut because we didn't want to open up that box until we got
the excise thing settled. Who could say what would happen
if, along with a suggestion to extend the excises, we had
asked for a general tax cut. But when the message went up,
it was worded to leave the door open to a later tax cut
request. And this was done, of course, with the President's
complete support. It was only a matter of a couple of weeks
before we had numbers that showed the economy turning up:
industrial production was up, personal income was up. So, we
didn't have the embarrassment of having to call back a tax
proposal that had been made prematurely. Did theory have
anything to do with this? Economic forecasting did. Did
politics have anything to do with it? Certainly the parlia-
mentary process had something to do with it.

McS: How did you arrive at your estimate that the downturn would
be short-lived? How did the Council function in generating
analysis for you? Did theory play a role there? And was
there consensus on the Council?

RS: Yes, there was consensus. On how one did it, I can only say
that you study the numbers very closely, applying well-known
cyclical tests. What's the inventory situation in the economy? What's the situation with respect to new orders? The
volume of shipments? The amount of backlogs? These things
give you clues as to whether you have a cumulatively declining situation or something that has a chance of correcting itself. We didn't have all the data at that time that is
available now, but we had a good deal. I initiated an exercise in which I compared what was happening to what had
happened in earlier cycles. But this was a hand tabulation
job. Shortly thereafter, I got Julie Shishkin, who had been
at the National Bureau working with data processing equipment
on business cycle analysis, to computerize the whole operation. Eventually it became this [Business Conditions
Digest]. I had Geof Moore down from the National Bureau to
give me his judgment of the economic situation. We would
discuss it in ABEGS. Then we had our own Council: Paul
McCracken, Joe Davis and myself. If we had had a disagreement, Paul would have had to see the President, but all the
time I was at the Council I was never in a situation in which
other members of the Council needed an audience to express a
view contrary to mine. I met with the President and stated
the Council's views, which were consensus views.

SM: What caused the 1959 episode?

RS: Well, 1959 was not a cyclical problem. The steel strike was
in 1959, and you can't really discuss anything but the steel
strike in 1959.

IB: When the steel strike in 1959 occurred, were there sentiments expressed in and around the White House and to the White House and the executive agencies about the wisdom of the steel companies having struck out in the correction of the work rules, in tighter contract language, in the repossession of management's rights? Was this seen as an unfortunate strike situation?

RS: Not at all, it was seen as a quite proper move on the part of the steel companies. There was no reservation about trying to settle this strike at any time, from the beginning to the end. There were no reservations about the position that the steel companies took, which was that they had to get more control over their work rules if they were going to get any chance whatever to achieve productivity improvements.

IB: Were there discussions about whether it would be judicious to facilitate the solution through the injunctive process rather than letting it run a little longer?

RS: Well, the Taft-Hartley law does not allow you to intervene, to gain an injunction, until you can show that a national interest--health, safety, security of the country--is jeopardized by the action. Now, you couldn't show that in July.

IB: You couldn't even really show that there was much demand left for steel because the steel sales for the year of the strike had alredy reached what they had reached for the year before?

RS: Right, so we got through the summer and into the fall before the thing began to grip. But by September it was clear that you had a problem. All the while we had Commerce putting together numbers on inventories--they were far less adequate than they are now. A Justice Department lawyer and I wrote the brief that went to the Supreme Court. We were able to show that it was having a national security impact. So 1959 was not a cyclical problem. You have to talk about 1960. We went into recession in 1960 in good part because of inventory liquidations.

IB: How big a part of the previous recovery was attributable to the inventory buildup, which then was liquidated to contribute to the 1960 turndown? Does the inventory figure in both sides of your assessment?

RS: I'd like to go back and look at the numbers and refresh my recollections. I haven't studied that recently, but that would be part of a typical scenario. We were growing at a relatively low rate in 1960 and it was a 50-50 proposition whether we would pull out of it on the up side, or would move down. And we lost it. I remember meetings in the fall of 1960 when it became clear that businesses were holding back on year-end purchases. There was no clear reason why it was happening. True, the Fed was not pushing on the economy but it was helping; mainly it was working to get our trade balance into an improved situation.

SM: Was the Fed being contractionary through that whole year?

RS: Not through the whole year, no. Net free reserves went from plus 500 millions in 1958 to a minus 500 millions in the summer of 1959, but then started back to a plus, and they moved back to a plus 500 millions, actually a little more than that, which they reached at the end of 1960. So there was an easing process in money policy from mid-1959 right through the onset of recession, and through recession, to the beginning of recovery in 1961. You might argue that the fault here was to have gone as far as the Fed went in mid-1959, namely to minus 500 million. In any case, a major factor in those decisions was the international position of the dollar.

SM: Did you disagree with that policy [of contraction] at that time?

RS: Did we disagree? We didn't go over and say, "We won't stand for it." We went over and said, "Don't go too far."

IB: And their logic was what? Out of anxiety about inflation?

RS: Yes, and a feeling of concern for the international position of the dollar.

McS: In 1960 did you find pressure and opinions coming out of the Committee on Growth and Stability or anywhere else to shape the Eisenhower administration economic policies in order to enhance Mr. Nixon's chances of election to the presidency that fall?

RS: I had no impression of that at the time. None whatever. I had no notion that there was any dissatisfaction on the part of Nixon or the personnel of the so-called Nixon Committee that the administration was laggard in what it was doing. It wasn't until very much later that I read a story to that effect. A person on Nixon's 1968 presidential campaign staff was interviewed by someone from, I believe, Fortune magazine—I'm not sure—and the question was put to him: What about unemployment? Would Mr. Nixon respond as quickly to the threat of unemployment as Senator Humphrey? The response was that he thought Nixon would be less disposed to move in this area. This is a question of how fast you move, of judgment, of timing and effort. Well, the papers picked this up because it was what a lot of people were looking for. It made it possible to picture Nixon as a passive fellow, and Humphrey as an activist; Nixon as one who didn't care about unemployment; Humphrey as one who did. This got a lot of publicity, and his campaign strategists figured it was going to hurt Dick Nixon's campaign. Arthur Burns either volunteered or was enlisted to give an interview with one of the Washington writers--Hobart Rowen--and the account that Arthur gave was that this wasn't at all the kind of person Dick Nixon was; that he would move vigorously and early to offset any such threat; that, in fact, he would have done so in 1960, except that Saulnier as Chairman of the Council of Economic Advisers and Anderson as Secretary of the Treasury "stonewalled" this move on the part of the administration. The interview went on to point out that the story of this incident was told in Dick Nixon's book, <u>Six Crises</u>. The book had not been on my reading list, but it was in my library-- incidentally, autographed by Mr. Nixon--and I leafed through it, and quickly found the reference. It was a fairly innocuous statement to the effect that he had been pushing for a more activist policy in 1960, but the White House staff--I must say it didn't identify me, didn't identify anybody--had resisted this. Now I'll tell you what the history was. The President said to me, very early in the game, when Nixon started his campaign: "You do what you can--provide such briefings as the Vice-President needs." And about once a week I would go to the Vice-President's office and talk with him about the economy, about what was happening, and what we were doing about it. I explained to him that I was responsible for a White House, executive branch group that was meeting regularly at that time to do what could be done to assist the economy. We were doing so because the economy was not growing to the extent that we wanted it to grow. You raised this question earlier: sure, I was dissatisfied with the growth of the economy, and we were doing everything we could to stimulate it. Well, I would explain that, meeting after meeting, to Mr. Nixon. Never once did I have a word out of him that he was dissatisfied. And then, eight years later, I read that I'm a "stonewaller." One of the reasons I have been really aggravated by the charge--that we were not too willing to see anything done about resisting the onset of a slowdown, let alone a recession, in 1959 and 1960--is the history of money policy we have been discussing. Take a look at those free reserves and tell me if a change could have been made faster than it was between mid-1959 and mid-1960. How would it have been possible? And we were supposed to have been "stonewalling."

Evaluating the Economic Decision Making System

SM: It seems to me that you are really illustrating very strongly the difficulty of running economic policy when you have a Federal Reserve that may well be pushing or pulling in a different direction than the one you'd like. And the Treasury, too.

RS: Sometimes it's the Fed; sometimes it's somebody else who's not doing quite what you'd like to have done. But I feel very strongly about the desirability of depoliticizing, to the extent we can, the making of stabilization policy. That is what we have done in the Federal Reserve System. I have testified repeatedly for a continuation of that, and I have written extensively, as you see in the literature of the Senate, against the recent effort of Parren Mitchell to make the term of the chairman of the Federal Reserve Board coterminous, within a year, with that of the president. And I think we would be better served to have tax policy determined by an impartial, depoliticized board than having it determined, as it is, on a basis that is often highly political. I have strong feelings on that, so I don't want any reservations I might have about money policy in 1959-60 to mean that I think we ought to have money policy made in the White House.

AL: Depoliticization in political terms means to establish an independent and usually nonpartisan policy board separated and working against centralization. And this whole notion that you referred to pejoratively as "fine-tuning." How does this go with the notion of gradual direction of economic policy, which implies, intellectually, at least, the coordination of fiscal, monetary and budgetary policy?

RS: Very difficult. I am essentially a parochialist. I believe in spreading power. I'm a small "d" democrat. I'm a pluralist. A parochialist in the sense that I believe in things coming from the bottom up instead of from the top down. I'm concerned about centralization and, accordingly, I have trouble, as you necessarily will, with the problem of coordination of policy in a decentralized policymaking apparatus-- decentralized in the sense that you've got the Fed over here, the Treasury under the White House, and the Congress up here. I don't want to be understood as advocating centralization of all that, because that would go against my democratic grain. You resolve this problem by establishing good working relations among these centers of influence--between the Federal Reserve and the White House, and the Treasury, and the Council, and so on. And that's not impossible. It's easier to do if you have a balanced, and relatively stable economy. My object when I was there was to achieve that balance. And I think we did. By 1961 we no longer had a big foreign economic deficit. We had stable prices. We had a budget that was at or close to balance. In that context one could move more easily to the solution of all these problems. That's a major reason why the first half of the 1970s was a good period. It's a shame that it was undermined, but it was undermined, after 1965, for reasons that I think could have been avoided. I can't say there's no inconsistency here: I just don't want my bent for consistency to lead me to support a degree of government centralization that would be inconsistent with my pluralism.

AL: If the government, and especially the administration, is going to be ultimately responsible for the state of the economy, does this not call for the coordination of as much economic knowledge as we have, including the coordination of debt, expenditure, and monetary policy, so that you don't have one asserted as more important than the other? If the Federal Reserve's interest in the international position of the dollar or a certain level of monetary supply is asserted as a primary goal of policy, that part gets higher priority than, let's say, the interest of the Congress and the American people or the same economy, in a certain level of unemployment and rate of inflation...

RS: First, let me say that I don't want to give the impression that I ever had any feeling that Martin, as Chairman of the Federal Reserve Board, was not concerned about employment and unemployment conditions. He was just as much concerned about it as anyone else. He had, in addition to that, a responsibility for the management of the nation's money. He carried out those responsibilities always on the basis of open discussion and conference with the Council, with the President, and with Treasury. I know of no time when there was any feeling that our interests were in conflict here. True, you could have differences in judgment, and you have to respect the judgment of the leadership of an agency until it's been demonstrated that that judgment is defective. And that was never demonstrated of Bill Martin. Now, do you need common goals? Well, I have testified repeatedly against that. I'm not sure that government operates best in a fishbowl. I'm not sure, however, that it operates best in a context of pre-arranged, pre-fixed arithmetic, numerical goals that are set with political interests in mind. What becomes the object of policy? The balance and welfare of the economy, or the validation of your political interest in mind? What becomes the object of policy? The balance and welfare of the economy, or the validation of your political commitment? The latter will take precedence, and in the process the public welfare is lost. Naturally, you should run the government so as to promote the welfare of all the people, and if you fail, they'll throw you out. But, you need flexibility in order to function effectively. Fixed goals, especially numerically-stated goals, can deny you that flexibility.

AL: The old Nourse, Burns and your position is that it would be best if the Council just stayed thoroughly anonymous and gave professional economic advice to the administration. Yet every one of the former Chairmen of the Council, including Herbert Stein, who was one of the most conservative, say that the Council cannot confine itself to internal, anonymous professional advice to the administration; they've got to go out and engage in the public education, as Mr. Saulnier has very eloquently expressed.

RS: If I had my way, the Council of Economic Advisers would be anonymous; it would be organized on the basis that Franklin Roosevelt had in mind when he said his advisers should be men with a passion for anonymity. Most men do not share that

passion, but he was right. But, then, I have to remind
myself that there's a fault in that. It's very difficult for
a person to sustain great influence in the inner circles of
government if he's anonymous, especially when he's head of an
agency, or is Chairman of the Council of Economic Advisers.
The interpretation of the world is that the fellow who has
influence is the fellow who was in the last edition of the
New York Times. If you don't get enough publicity, you will
find that your clout in government is receding, and some
other fellow will get it. So, you have to have a certain
amount of exposure in order to have influence. I regret
that, but I recognize it as a necessity. Unfortunately, the
more exposure you get, the less likely you are to be talking
as a professional economist. That's really at the bottom of
this--that's basic to it.

McS: Even the professional economist would be bringing to his
position a set of values. If carried to the extreme you
think the president and his administration do bear the final
responsibility for the economic welfare of the whole nation.

RS: Right, but the Chairman of the Federal Reserve Board is not
exonerated entirely from these things.

McS: The president is held accountable. Without discussing the
merits of the issues, President Carter finds himself with a
Congress that is nearly two-thirds of his own party--not like
Mr. Ford facing a Democratic Congress.

RS: Right.

McS: The president has enough trouble translating his policy
wishes into legislation in a Congress of his own party. He
now faces the chairman of the Federal Reserve Board, with
whom he may not be in conflict according to his latest statement, but who is not responsible directly to the electorate
in the same way. At the same time, Mr. Burns or any chairman
of the Federal Reserve Board is just as much a political
creature as the others; I don't see how you can separate the
actions of men in the Federal Reserve or any appointments
from politics. All of this has to relate in the final analysis to political decision making.

RS: Well, there's high politics, and there's low politics. And
there's middle politics. No one can say that he is entirely
exempt. Certainly, no one says he doesn't come in with
values. When I wrote Strategy of Economic Policy, I dealt in
the first few pages of that book with what I call "national
purpose," and with what national purpose means for the place
of the individual in our society. I hope you will look at
those pages. I'm not saying that I came in with no views or
"values," with no political convictions--I had them--so did
Eisenhower. He came in with very strong convictions on these
things. But I would like to see government freed to the

extent possible from the partisan political competition that is often so prevalent in a democratic, multi-party system.

McS: You are saying that economic decision making is so central and so crucial that it should be insulated as far as possible from this very system of representative government.

RS: I wouldn´t put it in those words, because economic decision making is not exempted from the influence of representative government. Certainly, the Council of Economic Advisers is not; it is directly an instrument of the president, serving only at the pleasure of the president. In the case of the Federal Reserve Board there clearly has been an effort to depoliticize the activity, but it still functions within a context that permits the interlacing on the Board of appointees of successive presidents, and the choice of presidents in our world tends to swing from one party to the other. The position of the Chairman is not an excessively long one-- seven years. He has one vote. If he carries the Board he has to carry it by virtue of the strength of his argument. I´m not saying that these things couldn´t be improved, but I don´t think one can say that you have in present arrangements at the Fed an institution that is not responsible to the community generally or to politial parties through the appointment process. Again, this is one of these cases in which you have to strike a balance between responsiveness, politically speaking, on the one hand, and insulation from partisan political influence on the other hand. Every now and then I am faced with that question. I was faced with it in commenting on Parren Mitchell´s bill, and I wrote a long letter to him in which I came down on the side of leaving the arrangement where it is, because I thought that the changes that would have been made by his bill did not significantly improve the institution that we already had in being--which after all is performing pretty well. It´s a very respected organization. Its work is greatly respected, not only here but around the world.

SM: Don´t you think the issue is really the opposite? I think there are a lot of people who say it´s too powerful. In fact, there are many people who think that really all that matters is the money supply and so the really important organization directing economic activity is the Federal Reserve.

RS: You have the monetarist school, which came to prominence three or four years ago. There was a period here in which it was fashionable to argue that you just manage the money supply and let the chips fall where they may. Now, that view has receded some because there is a better appreciation now of the limitations in our institutional arrangements for the nice determination or management of money supply. And even if we could nicely determine or manage money supply, what would we aim to manage? We still don´t have a satisfactory, or altogether acceptable, concept of what money supply we are trying to manage. I think these are the reasons why we have seen a kind of recedence of the monetarists, and are now much more eclectic about these things. In the process we have developed all the monetary targets, and Burns acts a lot more like a monetarist than William McChesney Martin did, but Arthur is a very sage and capable person and, incidentally, a man who uses language very carefully. He went before the Joint Economic Committee, or the Senate Banking Committee, yesterday to give his periodic accounting of his stewardship. And what did he say? That they were reducing the targets for M2 and M3, nothing about reducing the M1 target. Well, now what's the situation? But the M1 target is 6-1/2 percent per annum and M1 has been growing at 9 to 9-1/2 percent per annum. Of course he doesn't want to reduce the target—it would throw the whole economy into a tailspin if he did. So he was silent on that, and said they were reducing the targets for M2 and M3, which are already increasing less than, or about equal to, target. And why? Because the M2 money supply, for reasons we don't have to go into, is tending to shift into the M1 account. So we're not talking here about a finely-engineered, well-understood system for managing the economy through the money supply, and anyone who thinks we are is either uninformed or is simply romancing with himself. We just don't have that degree of control over the system.

SM: And yet look back at 1957 and look, in your own time, how the changes from either expansion to contraction or contraction to expansion preceded by not too long a period the movements in the economy.

RS: I agree with you. I am not saying that the money supply is not important. It is. But I feel we should have more respect for what we don't know about this whole process. I'm not against tuning the economy—because I'm an activist in that—but don't try to persuade me that the chairman of the Council of Economic Advisers or the chairman of the Federal Reserve Board or the president or the secretary of the Treasury or all of them in concert have got a set of levers they can operate—and that they can make the economy do what they want. They can't.

EH: You have said in your oral history for the Columbia Library that you are an economic determinist—in your view conditions determine economic policy to a great extent.

RS: Yes, I think I could say that.

EH: Does that mean that you would think that the different economic policies of Democratic and Republican administrations are a function of conditions rather than ideology or political constituencies in two different kinds of administrations?

RS: No, I wouldn't go quite that far. Republicans tend to have

strong feelings about orthodox values. They tend to believe
that financial things ought to be kept buttoned up pretty
tightly--tidily is the best word I can use. Democrats tend,
on the whole, to be rather different in this respect. They
articulate mainly an interest in people, in active social
programs, with less accent on the fiscal side. One of the
reasons why people are so mixed up today is because the
traditional position of the Democrats has come to grief. In
one case after another we find ourselves faced with real
financial difficulties, and robbed of an ability to spend our
way out of the problem, we are left rather empty-handed. Now
the Republicans' hands are not all that full in this case,
either, but it's not because the values of fiscal orthodoxy
have been disproved. There are other reasons. But differences do exist. Eisenhower used to say, "In fiscal matters,
I'm a conservative; in humanistic matters, I'm a liberal."
And he would try to make the two consistent with one another
through sound financing. It is often said of Republicans
that they don't know how to do anything except balance the
budget. I think the community is better off, on the whole,
if it is operating at or close to a budgetary balance, but
that doesn't mean I am against spending more for people. It
means only that I don't want the spending paid for simply by
printing more money, because that will eventually get you
into trouble. If you want to spend more, be sure it is paid
for out of additional revenues. But these are the differences between people in political parties. I guess we're
fortunate that we have these differences, and have opportunities to express them.

EH: Those differences--do you think they are carried over in more
formal economic thought?

RS: Yes. When you get into econometrics the reasoning gets very
tight, but in most economics you can see the values, and
perceptions of the world, that are influencing the way the
author writes and understands it all. I have had a vision
always of the possibility of moving out of a highly cyclical
type of economy to a stable economy, but the first step would
be to achieve what I like to call a "pause-advance" or
"advance-pause-advance" economy in which we would substitute
for cyclical movements periods in which we might for six
months have a slow rate of growth and then move again to a
faster, more satisfactory rate. Even in that kind of situation, pump-priming doesn't help, because you can't turn the
faucet on and off that well. And how well does it work in a
cyclical society? My experience is that it doesn't work well
at all. You always have to try, but there are limits on what
you can do. Money policy, in the end, is going to have to do
it. Money policy is by far the most flexible, adaptable,
usable instrument for achieving economic stability. I am
satisfied to have that in the hands of a competent, experienced, so far as feasible depoliticized Federal Reserve
Board.

4

The Council of Economic Advisers Under Chairman Walter W. Heller, 1961–1964

Summary History

President-elect John F. Kennedy's announcement of his appointment of Walter W. Heller, a Minnesota economist, as Chairman of the Council of Economic Advisers came in December 1960 as he was also announcing his Cabinet appointments. Heller was well-respected within the economics profession and could be expected to reflect the liberal economic views associated with the Kennedy candidacy. Heller then recommended for the other two positions James Tobin of Yale and Kermit Gordon of Williams. While Heller was an active chairman, there was a division of labor, with Tobin responsible for monetary policy and Gordon in charge of industrial organization and incomes policy.

Heller was basically an activist concerned more with policy application than with theory. He saw nothing wrong with the CEA publicly advocating the policies it felt to be economically wise and educating the public in the "New Economics" espoused by himself and his colleagues. If JFK was more cautious and perhaps conservative in his economics, he still encouraged Heller and his associates to take advanced positions on economic issues. Consistent with this desire for consensus and his sense of political vulnerability, Kennedy preferred that his advisers feel out and educate the public on more unorthodox policies such as a tax cut to stimulate growth even with the economy on the upswing. He was thus able to avoid risking his own position on less popular policies while still trying out new ideas and retaining the image of a liberal administration.

Kennedy supported open testimony by the Council before congressional committees. While there was at first much concern that the CEA be cautious and not violate its advisory role in testifying, Kennedy soon recognized the educative value of such testimony as well as the importance of cultivating a friendly Congress. Along this same line, Heller and his associates also made speeches around the country to mobilize popular support. For instance, in 1962, after the steel crisis, Heller's frequent speaking engagements were part of the administration's strategy to win business support. Interviews and articles that could build support for administration policy were also encouraged.

Heller and the Council helped prepare Kennedy for his public appearances. In addition to working on the President's major

economic messages, Heller was a member of the group of close
advisers that routinely met with JFK to brief him prior to press
conferences. The CEA prepared lists of possible questions and
answers for Kennedy to study, and then Heller would follow up with
an oral briefing at breakfast the day of the press conference.
And of course, the Council's memos were not confined just to press
conference briefings. Hundreds of often rather lengthy memos were
sent regularly to the President on various issues. While Kennedy
did not often specifically acknowledge the CEA's memos, he apparently did read them, for the Council was frequently pleased to
find the President later using a particular concept developed in
the memos.

Kennedy preferred to deal with small groups whenever possible
and only with reluctance held large formal cabinet meetings.
Believing in the value of expertise, he did not want advice from
agency heads outside their own jurisdictions. He preferred in-
stead to consult only with those directly involved in the issues.
In economic policy, this meant meeting with what Heller termed the
Quadriad. Set up at the request of the CEA, the Quadriad con-
sisted of the heads of the CEA, the Treasury, the Bureau of the
Budget, and the Federal Reserve. Its meetings were not regularly
scheduled, and they usually met only when Heller suggested to the
President that a particular problem needed to be discussed by the
President's top economic advisers. Perhaps more important was the
Troika, the same group but without representation from the Fed.
The Troika did not meet with the President but rather reported to
him confidentially on the state of the budget, revenue, and the
economy. Although there was at times internal disagreement over
such matters, the Troika attempted to reach a measure of agreement
before reporting to the President. Functioning at three levels
(staff, sub-cabinet, and cabinet), the Troika became an important
mechanism for coordinating economic policy during the Kennedy
years. One other group was set up at Heller's suggestion in
August 1962 in order to work out inter-administration differences
over the proposed tax cut. This Cabinet Committee on Economic
Growth was made up of the CEA chairman, the BOB director, and the
secretaries of Treasury, Commerce and Labor. Under the Johnson
administration, this committee's duties were expanded to include
consideration of wage-price policy. Johnson also continued the
Troika and the Quadriad.

The basic concern of economic policy in the early 1960s was
the conflict between economic growth and stability that had dominated the Eisenhower years. While most Republicans and conservatives remained committed to the necessity of a balanced budget in
order to maintain the price stability essential to economic growth
and a favorable balance of payments, many liberals and Democrats
felt that fiscal activism to achieve economic growth and lessen
unemployment should take precedence over anti-inflation policy.
When he entered office, Kennedy was forced to deal with this
divergence of opinion. In addition to his own doubts about the
validity of liberal economics, Kennedy realized the potential
political problems of pursuing expansionist policies. His narrow
victory in the presidential race had scarcely been a mandate for
the "New Economics," and the control of Congress by conservatives

of both parties indicated that an orthodox approach to economic policy would be politically wise. The new President was also concerned that he not be branded fiscally irresponsible and that his policies be consistent with his campaign call for sacrifice by the people. Political considerations simply outweighed economic reasoning.

The clearest example of this acceptance of orthodox economics was Kennedy's anti-recession program in early 1961. Some sort of recovery program was essential, and his liberal advisers urged a tax cut or possible increased spending. They were not prepared for his commitment in his State of the Union Message to fighting the recession within the confines of a balanced budget. His advisers were not concerned so much that JFK's political concession to the budget balancers would prevent recovery but that it would mean a sluggish recovery short of the economic potential of the nation. Although the anti-recession program worked out by the CEA within Kennedy's guidelines was fairly conventional and stop-gap (centering on administrative acceleration of expenditures and legislative proposal to broaden government welfare transfers), the President's promise to re-evaluate his anti-recession program in mid-April held out the possibility of a more expansionist policy. But recovery by March 1961 made fiscal activism even less justifiable than before.

Kennedy continued to insist on the necessity of maintaining a fiscally responsible program throughout the first year of his administration. Despite the arguments of his advisers, he remained unconvinced of the wisdom of a deficit except during a severe economic downturn. A tax cut when the economy was on the upswing was not justifiable despite arguments about the need to move beyond sluggish recovery and the slack economic growth of the past decade. Accelerated defense spending did provide some stimulus to the economy, but Kennedy tried to offset such expenditures with drives for economy and efficiency. When the Berlin crisis of July 1961 threatened to increase the deficit, Kennedy considered even more drastic action. Concern over avoiding inflation, balancing the budget, and emphasizing the sacrifice expected of all Americans led to a move within the administration to seek a tax increase to finance the cost of U.S. involvement. Secretary of Health, Education and Welfare Abraham Ribicoff, Secretary of Labor Arthur Goldberg, Attorney General Robert Kennedy, Secretary of the Treasury Douglas Dillon, and Theodore Sorensen were some of the supporters of this action. Kennedy had apparently approved the proposal and was preparing to announce it, when the Council intervened with the assistance of Paul Samuelson and Kenneth O'Donnell to change the President's mind. Using national income accounts figures, the Council convinced JFK that a tax increase to cover the cost of the Berlin crisis would damage the already sluggish economy and that a small deficit would probably help the economy. But he was still not willing to abandon his emphasis on fiscal responsibility and made clear his commitment to a balanced budget in FY 1963.

In addition to his concern with his image of fiscal responsibility, Kennedy's budget balancing was rooted in a fear of inflation. While the Council and the other liberal advisers repeatedly insisted that other problems were more pressing, the new President remained concerned with the inflation problem much as his predecessors had been. The most pressing reason for pursuing an anti-inflation program was the balance of payments problem that had been the focus of concern within the Eisenhower administration since 1958. According to more orthodox economists like Federal Reserve Chairman William McChesney Martin, the deficit in the international balance of payments and the subsequent gold drain required government action in the form of tight money policy and a balanced budget that would insure confidence in the dollar abroad. Expansionist policies were deemed irresponsible and inflationary. Although the Democratic platform in 1960 had called for monetary ease and the Heller Council had subsequently urged that policy, Kennedy feared the international repercussions of easing credit and was reluctant then to use monetary policy as an anti-recession device. This concern also restricted fiscal policy and was partially responsible for his commitment to a balanced budget. A number of actions were taken to reduce government expenditures abroad, restrict civilian spending, and expand export trade (the Trade Expansion Act of 1962), but the major innovation was the monetary "twist" that provided high short-term interest rates and low long-term rates in order to encourage domestic investment and reduce the outflow of gold. Although Martin, Dillon, and others emphasized such policies to stabilize the dollar, the Council eventually gained support for its own proposals for reforming the international monetary system in order to lessen pressure on domestic policy. Although the balance of payments problems continued to trouble the Kennedy and Johnson administrations, efforts to ease monetary policy were sufficiently successful due to Dillon's influence with Martin, and the traditional conservatism of the Fed did not hamper domestic programs.

Even the CEA, however, came to accept the necessity of an anti-inflation program. Although Democrats had long criticized Republicans for their preoccupation with inflation and failure to focus on the need for growth, the Kennedy administration appeared to be doing the same thing in late 1961 and 1962. Although the CEA pushed for fiscal activism, it soon realized that some program to insure price stability was politically necessary before any plans for expansion could be realized. The CEA became active in the development of wage-price stabilization policy in 1961. In June it convened an "Economic Consultants' Meeting" under Kermit Gordon's direction to consider the problem. The division of opinion over the scope of government intervention was made clear in the meeting, and Heller, in a private memo to Kennedy, made clear the conflict over the proper policy and suggested his own framework involving productivity guidelines for price and wage changes.

Guidelines had not yet been established, however, in the fall of 1961 when contract negotiations in the automobile industry and the possibility of a steel price rise arising from earlier contract negotiations required administration action. The administration intervened publicly in the latter case to influence public opinion against action by the steel industry. The CEA took a particularly active role, encouraging Senate debate on the issue

and pushing Kennedy to issue public statements critical of a price
rise. There was no price increase, but it was not entirely clear
how much credit could be given to administration actions.

The administration's labor advisers and specialists could not
reach agreement on proper wage-price stabilization guidelines
because of internal conflicting interests, but the Council of
Economic Advisers with Kennedy's support went ahead anyway and
published the "Guideposts for Non-inflationary Wage and Price
Behavior" in the 1962 Economic Report. Calling for non-inflationary price and wage actions within the limits of changes in
productivity, both within the industry and within the economy as a
whole, the guideposts (written by Kermit Gordon) were non-binding
and dependent up administration persuasiveness and public opinion
for enforcement. Kennedy did not even specifically endorse the
guidelines. As expected, the reaction was not favorable. Labor
considered the guideposts too restrictive and questioned the assumption that income distribution would remain constant; management insisted compliance would cut severely into their profits and
restrict expansion; critics on all sides questioned the practicality of the rather vague criteria and doubted that the guideposts would be applied consistently; and even the Council's own
staff feared the new policy would result in direct controls and an
end to collective bargaining.

Despite such criticisms, however, the administration was
determined to enforce the policy and set about applying it to
contract negotiations in the steel industry in 1962. Heller
assured Labor Secretary Goldberg in late December 1961 that a non-
inflationary wage settlement within productivity gains could be
negotiated, satisfactory to both labor and management. With CEA
support, then, Goldberg and Kennedy successfully pushed a settlement that met labor demands without necessitating an inflationary
price increase. Both labor and management seemed willing to
follow the guidelines. Then on April 10, U.S. Steel announced
there would be an across-the-board price rise. Seven other major
steel companies followed suit. Kennedy was incensed by U.S.
Steel's actions and insisted that the company had committed itself
to holding prices down. Having gone out on a limb to convince
labor to accept a modest settlement, Kennedy was determined not to
allow steel's actions to jeopardize his labor support. Beginning
with an April 11 press conference in which JFK bitterly criticized
the price rise, the administration undertook to force a roll back.
The FTC and the Justice Department began pricing investigations,
the Defense Department shifted contracts to smaller companies that
had not raised prices, administration advisers telephoned everyone
they knew in a position to influence the decision, sympathetic
congressional leaders prepared to begin their own investigation,
and the Heller CEA worked around the clock to prepare a "White
Paper" denying steel's insistence of a cost-price squeeze as the
basis for the price increase. When Bethlehem Steel yielded to
administration action and rolled back prices, all others, including U.S. Steel, followed suit within 72 hours. The administration
had enforced its wage-price policy, but only by using strong-arm
tactics that further alienated already suspicious business interests.

The wage-price guideposts remained in effect after Lyndon Johnson came to office. Although there was debate within the CEA and the Cabinet Committee on Economic Growth about how actively to apply the policy, Johnson specifically endorsed the guideposts in the 1964 Report, an action the politically cautious Kennedy had always managed to avoid. Under Heller's guidance, machinery was set up to identify major problem areas. An inter-agency watch-dog committee, headed by CEA member John P. Lewis, focused on automobile industry negotiations as the major target. The basic problem was that United Auto Workers would accept the wage guideposts only if the price guideposts were also enforced, an action that would mean price cuts in line with increased productivity. Despite administration reluctance, Heller and others tried unsuccessfully to get the industry to accept the price cut, but in the end their major accomplishment was simply preventing further price increases. Although the wage-price guideposts proved less effective than planned, the Kennedy-Johnson administration could at least point to a period of relatively stable prices, with inflation less than 2 percent through 1965.

Persistent unemployment (8.1 percent in February 1961) was recognized from the beginning of the Kennedy administration as perhaps the major economic problem, but the President's concern with maintaining an image of fiscal responsibility had limited his ability to act. Yet even if Kennedy had been willing to move beyond his concern with the budget, there was no clear consensus about just what was the nature of the unemployment problem and how it should be dealt with. The more conservative view (held by Arthur Burns and Federal Reserve Chairman William McChesney Martin) was that an increasing proportion of the unemployment was due to structural factors. This view rested on the assumption that at least 4 percent, and probably more, of those unemployed could not find jobs because of lack of training or obsolete skills, and that efforts to stimulate the economy and create more jobs would only aggravate inflation and not deal with the bottleneck of the structurally unemployed. What was needed to lessen unemployment was vocational education, manpower retraining, and other programs, but within the confines of a balanced budget. The opposing view held by most liberals was that some sort of fiscal stimulus to encourage economic growth was needed to combat the problem.

The problem of the past decade, according to these economists, was that the economy had simply not been operating at its full productive potential. While not opposed to structural programs or meeting social needs, these economists insisted that the focus of economic policy should be on stimulating aggregate demand in order to close the gap between real and potential output. Increased production would then mean more jobs and less unemployment. Tax reduction in order to eliminate fiscal drag on the economy was the main tool. Countering the criticism of conservatives and structuralists, these liberal economists insisted that the resultant budget deficit would not be inflationary, for there was so much slack in the economy. And in any case, existing high rates of unemployment were more danger than potential inflationary pressures. The aggregate demand theorists insisted that the addi-

tional economic output would lead in the long run to even greater
revenue for important public needs.

From the first Cabinet meeting, Heller pressed his argument
that recovery alone would not eliminate excess unemployment. In
his March 6, 1961 statement to the Joint Economic Committee,
Heller insisted that the economy was operating at least 8 percent
under capacity and at a growth rate of only 3.5 percent. An
expansionary fiscal policy was needed in order to stimulate growth
sufficiently to bring unemployment down to the target of 4 percent. To deal with the sluggish recovery, Heller advocated in the
spring of 1961 both a stand-by public works program and a $10
billion tax cut, but recovery and political considerations eliminated them from JFK's program. Kennedy was more concerned that
spring and summer with his commitment to the American space program and growing defense needs. While such spending undoubtedly
helped the economy, it satisfied neither the advocates of spending
for public needs nor the proponents of the aggregate demand thesis. The two groups actually came into direct conflict over the
Berlin crisis, for one feared a cut in domestic programs if there
were not a tax increase, while the other feared the damaging
effects of a tax increase on the already sluggish economy.

A more politically acceptable aspect of the growth thesis was
an emphasis on encouraging industrial modernization and expansion.
The Treasury's proposals in 1961 for tax incentives to investment
included liberalized depreciation and a 7 percent investment credit. Even these measures met resistance and were not passed until
1962. Although these tax policies were directed at long-term
growth, they reflected more conservative concern with the investment rather than the consumer side of the economy.

More liberal growth measures were ruled out until mid-1962
when fears of a "Kennedy recession" finally convinced all but the
most conservative within the Kennedy administration of the necessity for action. John Kenneth Galbraith still emphasized the
importance of spending, but Kennedy considered such a policy
politically impossible. The Heller Council had been pushing for a
tax cut since the spring of 1961, and their arguments were increasingly convincing. Although Treasury Secretary Dillon had
been an opponent of a tax cut and an advocate of a more fiscally
responsible program, even he became convinced that a tax cut would
be beneficial, especially when accompanied by the tax reform
proposals he had long been advocating. After the May 28 stock
market crisis, Kennedy also became convinced and on June 7 finally
announced his commitment to tax reduction in 1963. He followed
this up with his June 11 speech at Yale in which he attempted to
lay bare the myths and illusions that had limited economic policy
decisions. If Kennedy had disappointed the liberals in 1961, he
no longer did so by mid-1962.

Heller and the Council wanted a "quickie" temporary cut as
soon as possible in 1962, but Kennedy was not convinced to go that
far. He realized that congressional conservatives such as Wilbur
Mills would simply not accept a temporary cut in less than an
emergency situation and that an attempt to secure such action
might in the long run damage the structural reform. But it was
not until Kennedy read Michael Harrington's The Other America in

1962 that he began to realize that the problem was more than just individual or area poverty but was widespread and not diminishing. Beginning in 1963, Kennedy began to reconsider the administration's efforts in this regard. In the spring of 1963, a CEA analysis by Robert Lampman confirmed Harrington's findings on the persistence of hard-core poverty. In June of that same year, the Council, with BOB assistance, began planning a comprehensive poverty program. In November 1963, shortly before his death, Kennedy told Heller to continue work on the program for inclusion in the 1964 legislative package.

When Heller told Johnson about the anti-poverty proposals on November 23, just after JFK's assassination, Johnson was enthusiastic and adopted the program as his own. In contrast to the tax cut and civil rights legislation, the other two priorities of the Johnson administration in 1964, the poverty program was to be Johnson's own program. With CEA facts and figures backing him up, Johnson then declared in early 1964 his "War on Poverty." Although the resulting program was hampered by bureaucratic infighting, limited funding, too many slogans, and not enough planning, it became central to Johnson's goal of a Great Society and the development of a national consensus as the 1964 election approached.

Walter Heller resigned from the Council soon after the 1964 election. In the four years of his tenure on the CEA, Keynesian fiscal activism had achieved a new level of acceptance in the making of American economic policy. In 1961, a balanced budget and price stability had been the goals under the prevailing orthodoxy, but under CEA guidance standard administration policy was refocused by 1964 on the problems of unemployment and balanced economic growth.

Oral History Interview

The Selection of the Chairman

EH: Would you like to comment briefly on how you came to be appointed Chairman of the Council?

WWH: I´ve been told by people that I went down to Washington-- somebody wrote something on this--knowing that I was going to be asked to be Chairman of the Council, but I had no idea. Well, excuse me, that´s not quite right. For all I knew, I was going down there for a consultation about positions. Sarge Shriver, Kennedy´s brother-in-law and chief recruiter, called me. He came into the DuPont Plaza to meet me and he got a call the moment he got there. I heard him say, "Yeah, yeah, I know we need a woman. Yes, yes, I know we need a black." So as I met him for the first time, I said, "I have my burnt cork and a wig and I´m ready to go." But I really didn´t know. Somebody from a Chicago paper had called me and said, "Do you know that you´re going to be offered the chairmanship of the Council?" My reaction was, "C´mon, you have to be kidding." My assumption had always been that if Paul Samuelson...wanted to be Chairman of the Council, he could have been. He is and always has been one of my heroes. But I think the role he played as outside adviser may have been an even more effective one than he would have played as chairman, just in terms of the range of his interests and his desire or lack of it on the administrative side.

EH: Do you think it was his recommendation to Kennedy on your behalf that led to your appointment?

WWH: It was one of them, I´m sure. It was Samuelson, Galbraith, Orville Freeman, Hubert Humphrey--a combination, of economic and political backing. But it was, as I say, a surprise to me. I did not know that that was the job he was going to offer me....
   Hubert Humphrey recalled that he talked with me about the Council and that I said that I would not take a position on the Council as a member, but that I would be very much interested in the chairmanship. It´s a conversation that I shouldn´t have thought I would have forgotten, but apparently there is a strong belief in the Humphrey camp that that´s the way it came about. All I can tell you is that I recall vividly that I ran into the Dean of our Graduate School on the plane on the way back to Minnesota and told him of the surprising offer I´d just had and added, "I don´t know whether I´m going to do it or not." He said, "You´re going to stew, and you´re going to weigh all the pros and cons and then you´re going to say yes." He was right, of course. I just cite that as an indication that I was not at all privy to the fact that I was going to be offered the chairmanship of the Council.

The President and Economic Policy

EH: Let me ask you now to talk about the two presidents you worked with. Perhaps you could either compare them or deal with them individually as we go down this list of questions. What were their casts of mind, their modes of thought, how did they think about economic questions, about the Council?

WWH: How did the two presidents think about economic questions? How did they link their values and ideology to economic questions? How did they think politically about economic questions? I think I would describe both Kennedy and Johnson as quite eye-minded, that is, they both liked to read. We did do 300 and some odd memos for Kennedy during his presidency, and Kermit Gordon often said, "You should just publish those memos sometime." Kennedy was capable of digesting rather lengthy and fairly penetrating memos, and it was Ken Galbraith who tipped me off on that early in the game. Ken had some very good pieces of advice and some bad ones. One was not to assault Kennedy with the whole Council, but rather to hold the reins tightly in my own hands. But I had decided from the very first to have a kind of coordinate Council. I knew that I couldn't keep or attract people like Tobin and Gordon and, as staff members, Okun and Solow and Arrow, unless they shared in the decision making and policymaking process. We had it so organized that I quite frequently had Kermit Gordon or Jim Tobin carry things all the way up to the President without my being there. Now that was, perhaps, the exception rather than the rule, but it happened often enough, and it tells you something about Kennedy. Once he had confidence in a person, he didn't care about protocol. What he was interested in, by God, was getting to the essence, the facts, the analysis, and he really did have a steel-trap mind. We were often amazed at his capacity for understanding a particular set of relationships in economics; I think he probed more deeply than Johnson ever did and had the ability to grasp it. I guess our favorite example—certainly Jim Tobin's and mine—was the session we had on the balance of payments not so very long before the assassination. We sat in the Cabinet room and he tripped up Bob Roosa, of all people, on a couple of questions relating to the balance of payments. He said to Roosa, "But I thought you told me a month ago or so that it was the other way around?"

DD: By the time of his death, he knew the balance of payments as well as anybody at the Treasury.

WWH: Well, I don't think you should condemn the Treasury. There were still things that he didn't understand as well as we thought he did. To illustrate this is to zero in on my first meeting with Kennedy in Minneapolis in October of 1960. Since Kennedy was running about an hour and a half late on his schedule I concluded that I wouldn't have a chance to meet him. I had already gone back to my car to go home. I thought, "You know, that's kind of stupid. I really ought to meet the candidate." So I went back, and by good luck, Hubert spied me, grabbed me by the elbow and ran me right past the Irish mafia--O'Donnell and O'Brien, O'Dungan and O'Sorensen--and marched me right into the presence. There was Kennedy, standing between the rooms of the presidential suite with his shirt half off--not what I would regard as a propitious time for an economics discussion. I really did think that he would just dismiss me and say, "Send in your ideas through Archie Cox or Ted Sorensen." But the way Hubert introduced me, he couldn't just dismiss me. He said, "Jack, I want you to meet the finest economist west of the Mississippi." Well, we made it by just six blocks, but if we had met in St. Paul, Hubert would have said something equally dramatic. Kennedy, who, as I say, was way behind on his schedule, stopped right then and there and the entire room fell dead, dead silent. He said, "Well, now, if you're such a good economist, tell me, can we really achieve the 5 percent rate of growth that we promised in the Democratic platform?" I said I thought it would be extremely difficult; that, when you are talking about growth rates, you are talking about the basic growth in the economy's potential and that involved investment in human beings and plants and equipment. But if you are talking short-run expansion, the main barrier is on the demand and not the supply side. It was going to be very hard to make 5 percent. My answers there aren't important. What are important are his questions. He went on to say: "Seymour Harris tells me that we can't grow all that fast with these high interest rates. But then I'm told that Germany has been growing very fast with a 5 percent interest rate. How about that?" Well, I discussed that. He had 5's on the mind, and his first and third questions, in particular, are significant. He said, "You know, Paul Samuelson tells me that I can turn a $500 billion economy around with about a $5 billion tax cut. How is that possible?" "Well," I said, "of course, you are only working on the gap. First of all, you know, there's a $50 or $60 million gap and there's the multiplier"--imagine discussing the multiplier with a man who's standing there half-dressed. He went through about five questions. I wrote the discussion up (in a memo of October 4, 1960) and sent it to the people who were closer to him--Samuelson, Galbraith and Harris-- because I wanted them to get some feel for the trend of his thinking. But the questions were so well put that I neglected to emphasize the fact that he didn't know the answers. Of course, if he had, he wouldn't have needed an economic adviser.

There are two sequels to the story: about three weeks or four weeks before the assassination he turned to me once and said, "Walter, how well have we done on economic growth-- how fast has the economy grown since I've been president?" and I said, "Well, Mr. President, we have actually expanded at a rate of 5 percent a year, but you have to distinguish between what part of that was growth in the economy and what part was closing the gap." He stopped me right there; he said, "Walter, in politics we don't make such fine distinctions." As far as he was concerned, he had his 5 percent growth rate, but it wasn't the growth of economic potential, obviously; it was the expansion of the economy.

The other sequel was that all the way through to the time when John P. Lewis was vetted as a member of the Council, he still asked that question about how you can turn a $500 billion economy, then a $600 billion economy, around with a $10 billion tax cut. I say that because we mustn't really fool ourselves, as we sometimes do. A president has to think about one or two things other than the economy; in between times some of the things that he has grasped at one point slip away from him, and he needs to have them explained to him all over gain. There can be instant understanding, but there is not necessarily retention.

DD: Are you saying that President Kennedy really thought more substantively about economic questions than he did politically, or was there always a political dimension as well?

WWH: There was always a political dimension. You remember that quote that I used in New Dimensions in which I note that when we met at the Carlisle in New York on January 6, 1961, he said to me something like; "Professor, I want you to use the White House as a pulpit for economic education, but always remind them that the recession started in the Eisenhower administration." Now this is so typical of him; he'd say that with a wry smile or a wink.

He really did not want to use the word "recession." When I went down to father Joe's place in Palm Beach for the announcement of my appointment (December 23, 1960), we were just going out on the veranda when Kennedy asked, "What are you going to tell them?" I said, "I am going to tell them that there have been seven months of recession, three years of slack, and five years of slow growth." He said, "Recession--do you have to use that word?" "Well, Senator," I replied, "I have to tell you that it is a recession. Business Week and the Wall Street Journal call it a recession, why shouldn't you call it that?" He said, "Well, I'm very much concerned about the psychological impact of that." I persisted, "But that bridge has been crossed; you're really beyond that." And he said, "Well, I don't like it. However"--that was always a little signal with him; when he said, "However," you knew you were in--"go ahead and call it a recession." So I did. We spent further time persuading him that confidence came first from recognizing the facts and showing that you had a program to deal with the facts--not suppressing the facts, not glossing over them. He was basically very responsive to that kind of argument. He was, in general, just a total pleasure to work with. He caught on fast.

Hardly a session with him went by where there wasn't some humor introduced into the picture, where he wouldn't be laughing a little bit at himself. Ego—they say every president must have a towering ego, but I did not see that in Kennedy. For example, in the famous or notorious speech of August 13 or 14, 1962, when he said that we wouldn't have a quickie tax cut—but we would have a sizable net tax cut in 1963, he used some terrible, dull charts that we in the Council of Economic Advisers, of all people, had gotten together for him. He was talking in his office to the country at large on a TV program. I was sitting there in the Oval Office with him, and at the end you always feel inclined to say something nice, and I said, "Mr. President, that was just a great speech." He said, "No it wasn't. It was dull." He knew it. And that was right. It was a pretty dry, pedantic speech. Now, it's true that he could get angry—indeed furious, on occasion if the _office_ of the presidency was slighted. I saw him just a moment after the Business Council refused to stand up for him when he went into the East Room after the steel crisis. When he came back into the room—I was waiting to see him about something—he said, "You know, those bastards sat on their hands and didn't get up when the President of the United States walked into the room." Now you could interpret that, if it were LBJ, as ego; not in Kennedy's case. It was the presidency—and I feel quite firm in this judgment—that was being insulted, not John F. Kennedy.

One has this marvelous sense all the way through that he was getting it, that you didn't have to draw him detailed pictures. Of course, he thought instrumentally about economic questions: how would the economic advice that we were giving him and the economic measures that we were recommending serve as instruments for his broader ends? Like all modern presidents, he recognized that a laggard economy could thwart him on a lot of his other objectives. That was the biggest thing we had going for us, once he understood that the Council's recommendations could improve what happened in the economy, could get it moving again. Ted Sorensen said to me, "You know, you were going back to Minnesota at the end of three and a half years. Kennedy would not have let you go, because he said yours was the one part of the program that one could really point to and say that it had gotten the country moving again; the economy was moving again and was helping to make possible all the other things he hoped to do in his second term." So, he recognized economics as a terribly important instrument and we felt he was very disciplined. We had lots of evidence that he read our memoranda because he would say something in a press briefing, or in a discussion with a foreign economic dignitary, or just in a meeting with us that he couldn't have gotten anywhere else but from our memo. Working in the Kennedy administration—with rare exceptions—was sheer joy. You always had the feeling that the most competent ideas would win out.

AL: Before we leave the question of how presidents think about economic questions, perhaps you could offer a comparison or contrast with LBJ.

WWH: Yes, I should like to. Let me just add one other thing about writing memos to the two presidents. With Kennedy, one really could write out a narrative account—one could have a ten-page memo and not feel that his interest would flag. One device we used with Kennedy, but not with LBJ, was some humor or quip or something in quotes; I used to try to put at least one into every memo, because I sent them not only to Kennedy, but to Dungan, Sorensen and O'Donnell, to Pierre Salinger, the Vice-President and Arthur Schlesinger. I was trying to weave a "web of interest" around Kennedy, and I wanted them to read those things. An important part of our eventual open access to the White House was that all of these people essentially got on board.

In Kennedy, however, you also had a president who was willing to penetrate and find out what lay underneath some of the recommendations. Let me give you an example of how we introduced economic analysis and theory into the President's thinking. After the first uptick in the economy in June 1961, Bill Martin said, "Mr. President, you've got to look out now for inflation." We said, "Mr. President, we don't have to worry about inflation. There's no chance of having inflation in this slack economy." And in those days, long before "stagflation" and "momentum inflation," there really wasn't. He would ask, "Why not?" Then we would give him the simple, Keynesian arithmetic of the gap, which we had developed at that time and after which came Okun's law. At the same time, we got in a plug for doing something about cost-push inflation on grounds that the only real threat to price stability at those low levels of operation might come from business and labor groups with excess market power. In a very simple way, we were giving him little lessons in economic theory, economic performance, how these things work.

Putting things, goals, in quantitative terms was a terribly important part of this undertaking. In his Buxton lecture, Jim Tobin brought out the importance of quantitative goals—the role that those played in getting the president committed to an expansionary economic policy. All during the Eisenhower administration, they talked about full employment but never defined it. We got Kennedy to accept 4 percent as our full employment goal. We were condemned by some as being heartless for having such a high unemployment goal—using unemployment to beat inflation. We were condemned by others for being so dumb as to think that you could ever get down to 4 percent unemployment with all that structural unemployment around. We were vindicated on the latter: we were down to 4.4 percent unemployment in mid-1965 just before escalation in Vietnam with no sign of inflation. That was one goal. He could understand something like that. Or the notion of the gap as I mentioned, he had some trouble with that and had to be reminded of the logic. After all, that was teaching him some of the structure of economic thinking.

Let me give you another example of Kennedy's interest in contemplating issues. Very shortly before the assassination,

I was going up to testify before the Senate Finance Committee on the tax bill. I prepared testimony and tossed it in with JFK's reading matter. Because it was raining and he was out at Camp David (or was it Atoka?) he read the whole thing from A to Z and called me. We talked for some 25 minutes about the testimony. He understood the progression. "Walter," he said, "first we're going to get your tax cut and then we're going to get my expenditure programs." He understood that he had to get the tax cut to stimulate the economy, that the revenues from a prosperous economy would later enable him to get the programs that he wanted. He had come to understand that expenditure programs would have to wait until his second term.

With Johnson you had to be much more staccato in your style. Bill Moyers said to me, "Walter, you can't just load everything into a wheelbarrow and bring it over here. The President wants to have it in bang-bang-bang fashion." Then Johnson told me, "Now I don't like long memos; those Treasury memos put me to sleep. I don't like these long, drawn-out affairs. I want them so that there are generals and majors and sergeants and privates." So I developed a staccato style with the indented bullets and the indented dashes. One day, after he'd been president for maybe three months, he took one of my memos and held it up in a Cabinet meeting and said, "This is Walter's memo and this is the way I want you all to write your memos." I thought, "What a good way to lose friends and alienate people." Johnson reminded me of someone whose name may be totally unfamiliar to you: Randolph Paul. When I worked in the Treasury in the 1940s, Randolph Paul was the General Counsel in charge of tax legislation and tax reform, one of my lifelong interests. Paul made it a point to learn just enough about a subject to enable him to draw from it the essential things that he needed to make a decision, leaving details to others. I always marvelled that he was able to come out right so often without more depth penetration. It was more fun to work with Kennedy on economic matters because of that depth penetration, but I'm not sure he needed to go so deeply into some of these things to make valid decisions on economics. Johnson was quick, surprising in what he absorbed. It was always amazing what he would bring out in these head-to-head sessions with small business or big business or labor or university presidents. What he suddenly had at his fingertips was incredible. I don't think the country ever understood that. LBJ, however, wanted his memos in staccato form, not lengthy pieces. He insisted on our three-times-a-week economic news notes, so he always had something in his pocket to haul out when he had a meeting with somebody or a press conference or an interview. Like Randolph Paul, LBJ learned enough about the central issues and relations and facts to make intelligent decisions on economics, but wasn't interested in going beyond that. In that sense he wasn't as much fun. But he listened. The inputs of the Council, if you had to put weights on them, actually weighed more heavily with him relative to those from the Treasury than they did with Kennedy. He relied on us even more than Kennedy did, and LBJ and I had first-rate personal relations. In that sense, he was a pleasure to work with.

EH: Was that because of the different values of the two men?

WWH: Good question. Kennedy was a pragmatist. Kennedy's Yale speech revealed his feeling that we were getting to the point where most of the questions of economics were technical. That Yale speech was remarkable. All kinds of people claim credit for it--if you ask Galbraith, he wrote it; if you ask Schlesinger, he wrote it; if you ask Sorensen, he wrote it. If you ever asked me....The truth of the matter is that it was crafted the way so many of these things were. First, Ted Sorensen asked us for twenty shibboleths or myths in economics that needed to be destroyed or exposed and then he drafted it or it was redrafted. On the plane to Yale, Kennedy, with the Wall Street Journal on one side--I didn't see this--and with the London Economist on the other, rewrote parts of the speech. So I always say Kennedy wrote it. In it he said that we had reached the point where a lot of the great philosophical debates had been resolved; now we had to learn to push away these shibboleths blocking policy, such as worries about deficits, public debt, and rigid budget balance, and attack the problems themselves. You can see why that would be a major economic policy departure for a president.

Now, what about his basic values? I think his reaction to the poverty problem tells you as much about how those values evolved as anything else. He obviously was deeply concerned, far more deeply than President Eisenhower had been, with the plight of the unemployed, with wasted resources. At the same time, he was somewhat politically bound by the balanced budget concept and the criticism by Nixon. He'd say time and again, "Nixon will slaughter us if we go the expenditure route." At the beginning, therefore, we had to have a balanced budget or seem to.

Even before the inauguration, he said, "You [the Council of Economic Advisers] have to get me an anti-recession message within ten days." With the speech scheduled for February 2, that was an incredible order, but, of course, we were delighted. We didn't have a new staff really put together yet, but we had enough to start with. My office was the command post for that and we worked until three, four, five o'clock each morning. We had an anti-recession message put together very quickly. As you recall, tax cuts were ruled out because of the sacrifice doctrine. He had told me in the house in Georgetown, "I know you're for a tax cut; I know Paul Samuelson's for a tax cut. I can't come in on a platform of sacrifice and the very first thing hand out tax cuts to people. That just won't wash." So we had to work out an anti-recession program without a tax cut.

We also had to fight the anti-recession battle, as I mentioned before, within the bounds of a balanced budget. As economists, we were shocked when we were told that in one of our first White House meetings. I think the distinction you have to make is that Kennedy knew it didn't make any sense to balance the budget. Later in 1961, at a briefing breakfast before one of his press conferences, Kennedy said he wished he had Eisenhower's ability to run big deficits without damaging his image as a budget-balancer. He knew—again it's terribly important to separate shadow from substance—as far as appearances were concerned that he had to have a balanced budget; as far as economic substance was concerned, he fully understood that you do not have to balance the budget when the economy is slack. With the Council's help, the commitment to do so was watered down to read in the State of the Union message: "Within that framework, that is of the Eisenhower spending and revenue estimates, barring the development of urgent national defense needs or a worsening of the economy, it is my current intention to advocate a program of expenditures which, including revenues from a stimulation of the economy, will not of and by themselves unbalance the earlier budget!" Now, that was a work of art. We counted seven escape hatches. And that, again, was one of the pleasures of working with the Kennedy group.

At the first, we economists were very suspect in the administration, because it was largely peopled with lawyers. One of the great banes of the existence of this republic is the fact that, with all due respect, lawyers have such a hold on the Congress—the House, Senate—and the White House, as of that time. Those lawyers didn't really, honestly believe—Ted Sorensen, I'd say, first among them—that economists could think straight, and present logical, sequential arguments. It took a while to capture Ted Sorensen, and it's always terribly important to capture the man who is closest to the president, and that meant Sorensen, and then Moyers, and then Califano. There, by the way, you had real coordination of policy: all three of them, utterly superb in my opinion in pulling things together for the President and bringing them to him, not prejudicially, not angled the way they wanted them, but honestly bringing the President, when we didn't do it directly, the pros and cons, the give and take.

EH: Do you think the president needs a generalist?

WWH: Oh, absolutely. I hope that Carter will make more use of Stu Eizenstat this way, because Stu is first-rate. He knows how to get the essence of the issues and how to present them. Once we won Sorensen's respect and he saw that what we would do for the President in economic matters would improve not only economic policy but the President's chances of achieving his objectives, there was no further problem and he had independent confidence in all three of us—in Tobin and

Gordon and myself--and that had a great deal to do with our access to the President.

EH: Let's go back to the point you were making about Johnson and the Treasury and the Fed and the difference in values between the two men.

WWH: I think Kennedy's values evolved a great deal during the time he was president. He first became very conscious of the poverty program quite early in the game in connection with Appalachia and went out there, looked at things, and was deeply concerned. Then around Christmas of 1962, he read Dwight MacDonald's poverty articles in the <u>New Yorker</u> that helped get him started. Then he asked to see some other things that had been written. I brought him Keyserling's and Harrington's books one day (and never got them back). He asked to see these things, read them and was obviously deeply affected. When he gave his first three-network interview where Sandy Vanocur and two of the other top people inter-viewed him, he did bring in this whole question of poverty and his concern about it. Then Kenny O'Donnell told me one day in March of 1963 that I shouldn't worry about the tax cut; it would pass. I should worry about other things. I began to worry and got Bob Lampman to worry that while the tax cut could open up opportunities, there were lots of people mired in poverty who couldn't possibly take advantage of them and that therefore we had to have a separate poverty program. So first of all I had Bob put together the things he had done--the best work on the subject in the United States--namely measuring what had happened to poverty, what the sources of poverty were, what groups were impacted, why people were mired in poverty. We gave Kennedy this factual account about in March of 1963. Then something triggered my political interest in it: in June it was said that some Republican group--I've forgotten which Republican policy committee--was going to zero in on the poverty problem. At that point I wrote my basic memo to Kennedy saying in effect, "You really should have in your 1964 program an attack--(I didn't call it a war on poverty, but an attack)--on poverty, and here are the kinds of things that it might include. Unless you tell us not to, we're going to go ahead and work on them." We worked on them through the summer and--this, I think, is well known--the very last thing I talked to him about--three days before the assassination--was the poverty program, and he said, "It's going to be part of my program." We didn't know how big it was to be. I think that does address itself to the values question...

DD: Some people say that Johnson was more effective in trans-lating economic ideas and shaping issues with Congress than was Kennedy.

WWH: He went about it differently. They had very different in-struments of persuasion. Kennedy's conviction was really a dedication to the democratic process. He really, honestly, felt that you had to persuade the public or at least the major movers and shakers, policymakers, men and women of affairs; they had to understand. He felt that he was building this base of understanding in his first term and that he was going to capitalize on it in the second. Johnson's idea was quite different. Johnson's idea was to bring the key policymakers, the key power centers, into the room and strike a bargain with them. For example, he finally got aid to education through by saying in effect, "Now, you can't have all you want. You Catholics will get this, you NEA will get that, and you up there in Congress will get this. Now, are we going to have this program or aren't we? If you'll stick together on the general dimensions of the agreement that we have around here, we'll get it through." As the London Economist once put it, it was the end of ideology. The idea was to get your objectives straight, then get to the key power centers out of the public eye, and strike a bargain that would ease the path of the legislation through Congress. That's the way he got the aid to education through. With regard to the tax cut, he always kept telling me--I didn't know how much of this was flattery and how much was truth--but he kept telling me, "Walter, I'm going to go for this tax cut, because you're for it and because you say it's going to help the economy and it's not going to create inflation and it's going to balance the budget. But you know, if it doesn't do that...."He had some very expressive suggestions as to what my fate would be. His idea was that the success of the measure would itself be the education device. Kennedy was quite different. He felt the people had to be persuaded that this was the right way to go and then you could move.

EH: So, Kennedy wanted the Council out front, a public role, whereas Johnson didn't want you up front for fear you would queer the deal.

WWH: I think that's a fair way to put it, in part. But I don't want to imply that Johnson curbed our public role all that much or that he tried to politicize the Council--he didn't. Once a position was firmed up, he was glad to have the Council explaining it. And Kennedy didn't want us terribly far out front, just a little bit. He didn't want us so far out, and he didn't want different people in the administration popping off the way they do in the Carter administration! The idea was to work out those differences in a rational manner, in a sense behind closed doors, get all the actors into the play. But once the agreement was reached, then everybody--this was Kennedy, now--would go out and be on the same basic wavelength. He would say, "Walter, you can go out ahead of me. You can test some of these ideas." I have described that as "riding point." Riding point is a very honorary position, a very exposed one--I got hit over the head a number of times for that. But it was a different way of proceeding. Johnson held tight--in fact, tighter than I

liked--and you really had to stay on Johnson's wavelength.
He had as his end goal the party line. Kennedy was never so
afraid. He might go out this way and test a little bit more
about wage-price guideposts or about monetary policy. But
you knew about where the curbs were, that you couldn't go
beyond a certain point. I think it's fair to say that the
Kennedy administration gave the feeling of a coordinated
policy.

Now, the two presidents also had different ways of
handling "outriders." Whenever Kennedy wanted to see Paul
Samuelson, he would call me and say, "I'd like to talk with
Paul. Can you find out when it's convenient for Paul to come
in?" I don't mean to say that there was never a case where
the gap between Hyannis Port and Cambridge was bridged without my knowing it, but Kennedy had a sense of propriety about
organizational relations. LBJ, in contrast, had Bill Moyers
call me at the end of December 1965 to say, "The President
wants you down at the ranch tonight." This was around noon.
I'm in Minneapolis. I said, "Well, there's no transportation
to the ranch." He replied, "Oh, yes, there is. He's diverted a jet there and Colonel So and So and Major So and So
are piloting it. You be out at Wold-Chamberlain Field at
such and such a time and they'll take you down there." Then
Bill said, "And no one else is to know about this." I asked,
"Bill, are you saying that he doesn't want Gardner Ackley to
know?" "Yes, for the time being." That is no way to operate. So on this occasion (with a bit of a lag) and on others
when LBJ asked me to spend a day or two at the White House,
I'd make sure that Gardner knew what was going on in advance.

Now let's continue with values. LBJ had a deep, deep
gut feeling for the underdogs, the Blacks, the Mexican-
Americans, the poor, the unemployed. The language he would
use would absolutely curl your hair. He might talk about
"nigras" and what-not in private--whether for shock value or
simply being true to his native tongue, I just don't know--
yet he did more for civil rights and the Blacks than anybody
other than, say, Hubert Humphrey. Now Kennedy had made a
good start. LBJ deeply felt the fate of the Hispanic Americans; he was so proud of the fact that the first place he
ever taught was in that little town down there in Texas,
where they could hardly speak English, and of his civil
rights record and his appointment of Blacks in the administration. When we were at the ranch six days before his
death, he told us that his civil rights advances were his
proudest accomplishment. He could be as crude and as earthy
as you please and still, from his NYA days and from his
beginnings, he really had a deep, genuine commitment to the
cause of the underdog.

DD: Did LBJ's interest in some of these issues and approaches
      change as he got more and more preoccupied with Vietnam?

WWH: Remember, he thought he was doing the right thing in Vietnam.
      He constantly claimed that if he knew how to get out of it he

would, but he didn't know how. This would preoccupy him but don't forget that at the same time he was launching his Great Society program. He felt that he could do both, but if he raised taxes to finance Vietnam maybe it would impinge on his Great Society programs. So it's very hard to generalize on that--very hard.

The Structure of the Council

EH: Why don't we turn to some institutional questions?

WWH: Let me start tangentially by talking about the attempt to give the Council some line functions. Early in the game--as a matter of fact, down there in Palm Beach in December 1960-- Kennedy said, "First of all, we want to restore both the spirit and the letter of the Employment Act of 1946, which has been observed more in the breach than in the observance." This was language that we were prepared for--our license to operate. He added that he would like to have the Council also be sort of a watchdog of consumer interests, perhaps getting into public works or transportation as well. I did get partly into the consumer movement, and for a while I had the Consumer Advisory Council attached to me. At that time, in early 1961, would you believe, we wondered whether we were going to have enough to do? After the way the Council had progressively fallen--I'm sure that's not the way Steve Saulnier saw it--after its star had progressively declined in the Washington firmament, you really wondered whether CEA was to have enough to do. That seems incredible in retrospect, but I thought, "Well, maybe it would be good to take on a little thing like the consumer business." Well, there is no way that the Council of Economic Advisers should take on any line functions. That consumer business, much as I was personally committed, was beginning to get us caught in all kinds of crossfire. Obviously that interferes with the staff function that the Council should perform. Once I felt rather like the mule skinner in that joke who drove a pair of mules for the first time in his life; he came to a gate he had to open and didn't know how to keep the mules under control and still open the gate. So he wrapped the reins around his waist. When he woke up in the hospital, he said, "I hadn't been drug fifty feet before I realized my mistake." That was my experience with the consumer advisory function. I realized it had been a mistake on my part to take on such a responsibility and we eventually divested ourselves of it.

The other thing that was in the nature of a line function was the wage-price guidepost administration. That, too, got the Council involved in things that complicated its jobs; it was the object of criticism and opposition, and that interfered with the fundamental job of providing economic advice to the President. At the same time, the guidepost issue is more central to macro economic policy, and there was no other appropriate agency to handle it for the President. Still, it was diversionary. I just wanted to clarify that organization issue--that I really believe the Council has to stay away from that kind of operational responsibility.

EH: This is perhaps one of the reasons why the Council has been free from the criticism extended to other White House staff for overreaching its prerogatives.

WWH: No question about it.

EH: Could you describe CEA recruitment and staffing patterns?

WWH: I did not find that a big burden. We were always recruiting--this was the essence of what I called the use of "in and outers." I have always thought of that as a great asset. Sure, you want a few people--especially the statistical types--who are there right along and who represent continuity. Of the staff Steve Saulnier left behind, David Lusher was, in spite of some difficulties, the most valuable member. There were a couple of others. I saw what the Republicans did in 1953 when they came into the Treasury. They made the most egregious errors by just cleaning out the whole stable. They threw out superb people simply because they had been in the Truman administration. What they did was pretty brutal. In spite of the fact that CEA professionals don't have Civil Service protection, I was bound and determined to give them all the time they needed to find another job. So I called them in one by one and said to Dave Lusher and a couple of others, "If you'd like to stay, you're welcome to." Dave, of course, stayed. One of the other two did and one of them didn't. To the others I said, "I think it would be better if you would look for another job, but you can have as long as you want to find that job." Most moved quickly, but one staff member took two years.
We had very little trouble recruiting people because of the basic attraction of the Kennedy administration. Kennedy's charisma, plus the general quality of the Council we had, made the recruitment problem a lot easier than it might have seemed. We tried to draw in a very wide range of people as either special consultants or general consultants. So recruiting wasn't a very big problem. It did take new appointees several months before they really got rolling. We tried to get them for a minimum of fifteen months, and that worked pretty well.

EH: Don't they have to develop tremendous institutional knowledge in a hurry?

WWH: Well, yes and no. If you have savvy members of the Council, you can have some people on board who are not all that savvy, institutionally. One of our boys from Minnesota is on Charlie's staff now, and institutional sense is not his long suit. But they consider him invaluable. He's terribly good on econometrics and on a lot of applied stuff, even though he isn't very politically attuned. So you need balance for that.

One other attribute that I must stress is the ability to express yourself clearly in the English language. That is a characteristic much higher on the priority list than you might believe. The Chairman of the Council and the members of the Council have to be able to express themselves clearly in English or they are just not much use to the president. Arthur Okun would draft memos from me to the President and I would revise them; then Art would come and pick them out of the wastebasket--not quite literally--and see what changes I had made in his memoranda in order to school himself better on what was "presidentialese." It doesn't do very much good to send mathematical formulas to the President (even though we did teach him the multiplier).

I have spoken elsewhere about the advantages of not staying in government too long--that was in my first Godkin lecture. One reason that I had planned to spend at most another year--even before Kennedy's assassination--was that I do think you begin to give hostages to the political environment. You may not know it, and you tell yourself you are not doing it, but four years just struck me as long enough to be in Washington without beginning to lose your objectivity. To keep yourself honest, you have to get out. I hated to leave. I loved every minute--well, not every minute, there were some very bad minutes--but I hated to leave.

Bureaucratic Politics and Economic Policy

EH: You pointed out a little earlier that the key institutions here in implementing the Employment Act are the Council, the Treasury, the Bureau of the Budget, with the Fed in the wings, and the domestic departments to some extent in the background. Could you characterize the institutional stakes that are brought to bear here, the diversity of views, and describe how the Council develops political resources to work in this rough world and be effective?

WWH: Your question is, I guess, a dual one. If I'm interpreting it correctly, you're asking how we learned to operate in the political milieu and how we structured our operations. Operating in the political milieu meant primarily to me the very narrow political milieu called the White House.

First, it was, to my way of thinking, a matter of establishing our credibility and our judgment and sagacity not just with Kennedy but with the people around him. I spent a great deal of time on that. I gave you part of that answer earlier and that was in directing our memos and often following them up with conversations. When Sorensen began to see the nature of our reasoning and the way we sorted out the things for the anti-recession program, he was clearly pleased. He even suggested one time that economists could reason almost as well as lawyers! That was terribly important. Ralph Dungan, Myer Feldman, Pierre Salinger and Arthur Schlesinger were among others with whom we kept in touch.

The idea was to get all of these people to understand that we knew what we were talking about, that Kennedy would make better policy if he listened to us, that they ought to be clued in on what we were trying to do in spite of the fact that this was an arcane subject to a bunch of lawyers. In that sense, the first job was to become an accepted part of the inner circle. If I had simply stood on my dignity in my office as Chairman of the Council and said, "Let them come to me," I'd have waited a hell of a long time. One had to prowl the corridors of the White House, those corridors of power. I would go over and talk to various people there--Dungan, Feldman, Sorensen--about the importance to them of some of the things we were doing. I sometimes made a point of seeing that our memo was on the top of the President's night reading. Evelyn Lincoln cooperated with me on that. Thank heavens, early in the game Ken O'Donnell became an ally. He was a very important link in the chain of access to Kennedy.

Now in those days it was much more free-wheeling, too. Are you aware of how the physical configuration of the west wing of the White House has changed over these years? In those days you could walk into the White House and could walk up to either end of the President's office. There were separate accesses--one through Ken O'Donnell and one through Evelyn Lincoln--and I used the Evelyn Lincoln access in the evening. Between 6 and 8 p.m. the President was typically still in his office and if you couldn't get to him any other way during the day, you could call or go in then and say, "Evelyn, I really have something I ought to take up with the President." That's the way I went in to see him on November 19, 1963, the last time I ever saw him.

It was amazing that there was physically such easy access. Sometimes I'd be standing in the outer office, talking with Ken O'Donnell, and the President would come out for some reason or another and he'd say, "Oh, Walter, yeah, come on in." Johnson changed the physical configuration, so that the traffic through the White House no longer went past the President's office. There were then two levels to go through to get to Johnson, and it got even more protective under Nixon and stayed that way. Quite different, and it has an effect on access to the president.

Our access and influence were not foregone conclusions at the beginning. As I have said here, we were like a whistle stop and sometimes we'd blow the whistle and the damn train wouldn't stop. Recommendations would come in from anywhere in the government, involving primarily micro economics. There wasn't any question about macro economics--there wasn't any question that when it dealt with basic fiscal policy, monetary policy, even wage-price policy, that we had to be brought in. But when, for example, recommendations came from the Commerce Department to equalize the regulation of various types of carriers, that didn't come to us. It went directly to the White House and we had to get to Sorensen and say, "Look, we've got an input to make on this." What Commerce wanted to do was to rationalize it or equalize it by pushing the regulations on the less regulated carriers—trucks and airlines—up to the level of regulation of railroads, which is just the wrong way to go about it. We caught that because Kermit Gordon was vigilant. We got John Meyer as a consultant and they went to work on this and we turned it completely around. Before we were through we had a bill in Congress that proposed to deregulate rather than regulate.

EH: This is a good point at which to ask what the conditions are that cause the CEA chairman to be influential with the president on a given policy question.

WWH: First, you have to establish that you're right. Second, facts have to be facts. Nor can you afford constantly to put the brightest face on the facts. Third, I'd say the rationale must be plainly understood. It's something that Desai once told me when he was Finance Minister of India: "You know when somebody doesn't understand what I say, I never assume that he cannot understand. I assume that I have not made myself understood." An economic adviser just has to bring his stuff in a form that makes itself understood to the president. Fourth, don't bore him to death. The very last thing in the world to do is to bore the president. Fifth, make clear that pursuing the course you are recommending will help him accomplish his basic goals for the country and, if possible, that it will strengthen him politically.

      We were fortunate that we had a White House in which the people were dedicated to getting the best solutions, the right solutions. When they saw that running it through the Council of Economic Advisers improved the recommendations and gave them a sounder basis for what they took to Congress, then we were brought into the orbit. One of the most satisfying things that happened in terms of this inner political constellation was when we were brought into the year-end White House round-up of policies: all of the various recommendations from throughout the government had to be screened not just by the then Budget Bureau—now the Office of Management and the Budget—but by the Council of Economic Advisers. The team that screened all those recommendations, economic and non-economic, coming into the White House was Sorensen, Myer Feldman, who had something of a special interest point of view, Bell, Heller (also Kermit Gordon and Tobin, where their particular interests were involved), O'Brien, because of congressional relations, and, to the extent that they felt he needed to be informed, Pierre Salinger—but Pierre was there as an observer. This team, then, did the screening. We were at it all during December, and the week between Christmas and New Year's. We'd all go down to Palm Beach, spend nearly a week down there, working mainly with the President making final decisions between Christmas and New Year's.

I found out fairly early in the game that you couldn't operate just inside, that to get the kind of political leverage that you wanted on the President, you had to have an outside presence. After we got our feet on the ground, I began to accept television invitations. Kennedy encouraged me to do this and made a point of watching such appearances as those on "Meet the Press." I recall appearing on that program one time when the inquisitors included Vermont Royster of The Wall Street Journal, Richard Wilson (the conservative head of the Minneapolis Tribune's Washington bureau), and Larry Spivak, who wasn't exactly a patsy. The interview went well. Kennedy called me immediately afterwards and said, "You did us a lot of good today, but where did they dig up that murderer's row that faced you?" By the way, I had often wondered why anyone would voluntarily subject himself to those sharpshooters on "Meet the Press" and similar unrehearsed programs. What one discovers is that, especially with the proper homework, one knows a good deal more about 9/10 of the questions that come up than one's inquisitors. But to come back to the point, granted, the force of logic and understandable presentation, the adaptation to the President's values and the serving of his goals were critical. But some outside leverage was also important. Having the Council establish itself with the world at large, and having the President get feedback from that, strengthened one's position in the Kennedy administration.

DD: To what extent did he rely for economic advice directly and individually on you and the Council, vis-a-vis the rest of government?

WWH: Without question he brought in advice from a large number of sources, including some of his confidantes outside the government. He used to talk with David Rockefeller, for example. (Doesn't every president?) Certainly, Bobby Kennedy had his input, as did Clark Clifford, Bob McNamara, Arthur Goldberg, and, most of all, Doug Dillon. He did not give great weight to what came out of the Labor Department and the Commerce Department on general economic policy--a fate to which those departments are often condemned.

DD: Were the inputs from Bill Martin mainly in the Quadriad meetings?

WWH: Yes. If he wanted a meeting with him, he would tell Ken O'Donnell, "Get Walter to get the troops together and let's have a meeting with the Quadriad."

DD: But he might have had private meetings with Dillon?

WWH: Oh, yes. Dillon was the major counterweight to the Council, and we were the major counterweight to Treasury. Kennedy made that apparent when he brought me down to Washington to the house in Georgetown. He said, "I have Doug Dillon in the other room." This is when he popped the question with this kind of emphasis: "I want him to be my Secretary of the Treasury and my right bower, and I want you to be my Chairman of the Council and my left bower." It was clear that he perceived the desirability of some balance.

The Treasury is a terribly important part of this complex because, of course, the Treasury and the Budget Bureau had lots of line functions--everything in government budgeting had to go through the Budget Bureau, everything financial had to go through the Treasury. Things would go on that at times we wouldn't hear about right away, or on which the Treasury would have a different point of view. Dillon had an enormous amount of clout, both inside and outside the government, and there was, of course, continuous contention. No one should blink at that. On the surface we always operated very compatibly--Dillon was a gentleman; I hope I was, though we'd get awfully sore sometimes. We wanted to be more free-wheeling than Bob Roosa did. We had some contention in the debt management and balance of payments areas, where Jim Tobin, I guess, was a thorn in the Treasury's side as well as on monetary policy. But, as long as we're speaking very freely about the practical political science of policy advising, let me give you two examples of the kinds of things you had to do in the governmental structure. One was the question of who would head up our economic policy delegation to the OECD. Bob Roosa wanted to head it up, obviously. And I wanted to head it up, obviously. I was, after all, Chairman of the Council of Economic Advisers. What could be more logical? But you don't get that just by logic. What you do is go over to the State Department and say to George Ball, Under Secretary in Charge of Economic Affairs, "George, don't you agree it ought to be the Council rather than the Treasury?" And George said, "Yes." That was the decisive consideration. Then George Ball went to the President and said, "Look, those guys in the CEA really have a broad spectrum view of the economy that qualifies them to be head of that delegation," and it's remained that way ever since. On matters of that kind, we had to assert ourselves.

Another issue was how we would handle relations with the Federal Reserve. Before the inauguration, Kennedy asked me to go over and visit with Bill Martin to assess whether he would be cooperative or obstructionist. I'm sure he also had Bob Roosa or Doug Dillon do the same thing I was doing. I met Bill and was just enormously taken with him. He pledged, "I'm not going to give up the independence of the Fed." I said, "Well, I'm sure that's not what the President's going to ask you to do." But Martin added, "There's plenty of room here for cooperation." I went into Washington very dubious about the independence of the Fed, but I came out feeling that the Federal Reserve should be independent in a world that's fundamentally inflation-prone. It isn't so bad--even though it gets you awfully mad at times--to have somebody sitting there independently as a group of inflation fighters not subject to the political election process.

So much of it is the question of how you organize things. We had the Troika. That was not our idea; that was, I think, Dillon's idea or perhaps Sam Cohn's in Budget. Dillon handled the fiscal, financial, tax side, Bell handled the budget side; and the Council handled the economic forecast side. We really made that Troika work. It was tripartite, three-layered, in handling the basic analysis of the economy and what should be done about it.

The one missing link was Bill Martin. I think Steve Saulnier will have told you that Eisenhower used to have occasional meetings of all four agency heads, and I doubt that Steve thinks we established anything new by organizing that into the Quadriad.

Did you ever hear how I happened to name the Quadriad? The story was that we initially called it the Fiscal and Financial Group. Ken O'Donnell would call and say, "When do you want this Fiscal and Financial Group to meet?" Then one time he sort of swore and said, "Boy, you've got the Troika, but this has got the long, unwieldy handle--can't you think of something better?" So I went back to our 1947 Webster's Unabridged, which Ed Nourse had bought--that's really a little commercial about how frugal we were. By the way, I can expand on that: the Council staff today is the same size it was in 1947. We never got caught in Parkinson's Law. We never got involved in a lot of intra-office memos. We recognized that our customer was over there in the White House and that all our product should be aimed to go out of the organization to the President and to the people around him.

But anyway just to finish that little story, I looked this up in Webster's and found "quartet"--that would suit us, but was pretty dull. Finally I saw this wonderful word "quadriad"--"a group of four, rare"--and I figured that's us. I wrote Kennedy a memo and he liked it and so from then on we were the Quadriad. But the unkindest cut of all appeared in an article during the Nixon administration, which said, "The Quadriad, a group that was formed and named during the Eisenhower administration." Now here's my one contribution to posterity and it was almost stolen from me. The Quadriad worked out very well because it was a true dialogue. Bill would come in and tell us what he thought about fiscal policy, we'd tell him what we thought about monetary policy, and we really had good give and take. The main cause for calling meetings of the Quadriad was when we saw the purchases of long-term securities by the Fed flagging. Bill had agreed to the twist--this was more Bob Roosa's idea than ours--which was to try to boost short-term rates and thereby stop the hemorrhage of money flowing overseas.

DD: By having the Treasury put its issues out short and by having the Fed avoid buying short?

WWH: Exactly. In other words, to absorb short-term money and not to pump any short-term money back into the market, thereby lowering the supply of short-term funds and raising prices of such funds. The idea was to try to bring down rates for the long-terms because they were the ones that were important for housing, for investment and so forth. That was working fine. But the trouble is that we'd have a meeting with Kennedy--the meetings of the Quadriad were with Kennedy--and before the meeting Bill would be out there buying those long-term securities, but afterwards his buying would flag. It would go up before the meeting and go down afterwards. Jim Tobin would keep track of this and he'd say, "Walter, you'd better call Kenny O'Donnell and arrange another meeting of the Quadriad, because Martin isn't buying enough long-term bonds." So I'd call a meeting and sure enough the purchases would rise again, and Martin would be able to tell Kennedy, "We're doing everything we can." Jim plotted these purchases with the points on the chart being the dates on which we scheduled the meetings. Jim evolved the theory that you didn't need to hold the meetings, you just had to call them. But basically there was give and take; it was not just a one-way street with Martin.

EH: Is there more tension in a Democratic administration than in a Republican administration when the Council is likely to be conservative along with all the others? In a Democratic administration you're more against the grain of a conservative Treasury.

WWH: There's something to that, but we didn't feel that much against the grain. Well, sure, Kennedy, especially in 1961, was constantly protecting his flanks against conservative attack. He often referred to what Nixon would say and how he might ridicule what he was doing. Members of the Cabinet also weren't very sympathetic to tax cuts, because they did not really understand that that might give them more money, not less, if they waited a while. It's also true that Dillon was more conservative than we were. Martin is a lifelong Democrat but, as we all know, a conservative. But, at least, he was on the President's team. With Bill Martin it was understood that just as Martin could criticize our policies, we could criticize Martin's. In mid-1961, in fact, until fairly late in 1961, Kennedy was still thinking of replacing Martin, but as the date for reappointment or new appointment came up, Martin's standing in the domestic and international financial community kept rising--I'm sure Doug Dillon had something to do with this--and by the time the date arrived, Kennedy had decided to reappoint Martin.

SM: You said that the Council was always brought in on macro decisions and yet you really didn't have primary responsibility over these--over debt management, over monetary policy, or really over government expenditures either. How then could you really direct macro policy?

WWH: I didn't say we directed macro policy. I said that we were brought in on all macro policy questions. But the 1964 tax cut, for example, was born on my desk (in early 1962), and that was the most decisive macro policy measure that was taken. The Troika was one instrument for such policymaking. Our inputs were also sought on what the budget would be; this came as part and parcel--that's one reason I stressed it--of that year-end review in which we participated fully. Debt management, of course, was very much the Treasury's baili-wick, but that didn't have a great macro effect. They wanted to lengthen the debt; we didn't want them to lengthen it as fast as Bob Roosa wanted to lengthen it.

DD: He devised this technique to do debt lengthening without disturbing the markets by using advance refunding. You could even say that part of that was done because the Council sought to avoid financing in the long-term area. We didn't offer long bonds during that period either.

WWH: That's correct. In other words, Kennedy would have us dis-cuss these things together in his office.

DD: Even in monetary policy, didn't you set up luncheon sessions where the Council and Board members would get together and talk about these things? By 1963, we had this regular weekly luncheon session between the Council and the Fed.

WWH: True. We did have a good interchange. Once in a while we'd find some way to bring people over to the White House staff mess, but usually we would go over to the comfortable, well-heeled quarters in the Fed and have our sessions there.

A point that we haven't mentioned explicitly is that Kennedy did not believe in having meetings for the sake of having meetings. He didn't like big meetings, either. But Eisenhower, from what Steve has told me, would schedule regular meetings perhaps with the Chairman of the Council or some other group and would hold those meetings whether there was any special occasion for having it or not. That wasn't Kennedy's way at all. When he was involved in the Bay of Pigs, I might not see him for three weeks and then again I might see him three times in one day. His idea was to have a meeting when you had something to meet about and that meant a quite uneven schedule. But you always had access to him with memos. And he always brought the relevant parties together at the important meetings.

EH: This notion of how the Council develops the political re-sources inside the administration--would it be fair to say that these resources have to be redeveloped each time around?

WWH: Absolutely.

EH: The Treasury's always there, the Budget Bureau's always there. But any analytic staff cannot institutionalize itself in quite the same sense.

WWH: No, and that´s why I say at the end of that first chapter in
      New Dimensions that each president presumably recasts the
      economic advisory function or its organization in his own
      image and that I didn´t come out of those four years with any
      burning desire to change things very much. I did come out
      with the feeling that a national economic council--the coun-
      terpart of a National Security Council or Carter´s economic
      policy group--was pretty much a fifth wheel and not something
      that would be very helpful. That may be a bit myopic on my
      part, but I´m inclined to think experience is on my side.

EH: The Republicans went that way.

WWH: Yes they did, and so did Carter. And in Carter´s case it
      fell apart very quickly. It hasn´t worked and for the very
      reasons that I believed it wouldn´t work. I wrote a couple
      of memos to the Carter forces. One was, "Small is beautiful:
      keep the Council small." Larry Klein wanted to add a bunch
      of industry desks and roughly double the size of the Council.
      I wrote a two or three page memo saying, "No, that´s not the
      idea. The idea is to have this hard-hitting competent,
      small, overworked staff. That´s what you ought to have
      there." The other piece of advice was: Don´t set up this
      big amorphous group; of course, Commerce and Labor always
      want it, because they don´t know how to get in.

EH: Do they have a back seat because they´re seen as consti-
      tuency-oriented departments like Agriculture?

WWH: That´s part of it; part of it is that you just can´t have
      everybody in the act, and part of it is that they´ve seldom
      had the same economic competence in their staffs that you
      have in the Treasury and the Council. But, in good part, it
      is because they have special axes to grind, by their nature.
      That´s true of Agriculture. I had been Orville Freeman´s tax
      adviser (unpaid, but still very close, tax adviser) for six
      years in Minnesota before he went to Washington, where we
      were bound within a week to become adversaries--friendly
      adversaries, but adversaries--from the moment I became "eco-
      nomic adviser for all the people" instead of only those from
      the State of Minnesota. I was bound to clash with Orville
      Freeman on agricultural policy and with my old friends in the
      labor movement. It´s just part of the game.

EH: As you know, there´s this long history of tension between the
      assistant to the president for National Security Affairs and
      his staff and the secretary of State. In Kissinger´s time it
      was put in either/or terms. But that kind of controversy
      never develops around the Council in the sense of an institu-
      tional problem about where the authority is. I wonder what
      the difference is?

WWH: There has been a question about "layering" the Council.
      Under Eisenhower there was first Hauge and then Paarlberg

who, after all, were special assistants to the President for economic affairs. I did ask a couple of specific things of Kennedy; one, that I not be layered, that I would be not just the Chairman of the Council but the chief White House economic adviser. He said that was his intention. The second thing I requested was that, subject to his veto, I would select my fellow members of the Council. The question is raised, why shouldn't the president name those separately? Essentially, because to get the economic advisory work done, there must be close cooperation and harmony among the three members. And you have to have the kind of understanding between the chairman and the president that permits you jointly to pick the other two people. Though we were not layered, the White House did have Carl Kaysen as an economist specifically committed to the international dimension. Carl was working for Bundy, and he was a great ally to us. Bator didn't play quite the same role, but it was the same position. We never felt threatened in the least by either one of those. If he had said, "Here's my Chairman of the Council and here's Paul Samuelson (or someone else), my economic adviser," I would have said, "Thank you, but no thank you."

EH: I was thinking of the analogy between the NSC staff and the Council as coming between the president and the departments. The Council has great legitimacy, I think, for some reasons that need to be explored, which the NSC staff has never been able to develop.

WWH: Part of it is, of course, that the economic interest is so diffuse throughout the government that it is just inescapably true that the president needs somebody there to coordinate and bring together all the diverse threads. With only one really strong contender for the same role, namely the Treasury, those two can be paired off in a way that the president can manage rather nicely, so that we really never had that problem. I'm not sure that what I have said explains it terribly well, but I agree with your analysis that we did not get into that kind of crossfire.

AL: It seems to me the NSC and CEA are not at all the same, but they are in a sense. State and Defense are line functions, which really have a subordinate level of operation that has to be lifted out and brought up to the presidential level to get the policy considerations. That is quite different, I think, from the economic picture in which Treasury and the Federal Reserve Board have line functions, but both Budget and CEA are staff. In terms of the organizational relations, it seems that in your period the Fed was brought into the White House policy staff.

WWH: Yes. Of course, the Fed was not sending memos to the President as the Treasury and Council were. It wasn't a case of Bill Martin volunteering memos on, say, fiscal policy; his ideas were solicited in the course of our Quadriad meetings, but it wasn't a case of continuous input, as you'd get from OMB, Treasury, and the Council. So, subject to that footnote, I think your point is well taken.

Reconstructing Policy Decisions

EH: Perhaps we could begin with the preparation for the tax cut. You told me before we began that you had fresh material from your oral history at the Johnson Library that you would like to introduce into the record. Why don't we work through that: Kennedy's resistance to the politics of balanced budgets and your persuading him of the need for a tax cut, and then perhaps go on to wage-price guidelines and, if we have time, get into the poverty program.

SM: You might go through your whole campaign to sell the idea of expansion, which culminated in the tax cut. It started even before the inauguration.

WWH: Well, please interrupt, because I'm bound to stress the parts that I was involved in and tell it as I saw it.
  The campaign started the day I met Kennedy in Minneapolis in October. In that exchange I said something like, "You know, Senator, you're going to need to cut taxes after you're elected to get this economy moving." The next time I saw him was at the house in Georgetown in December when he offered me the job and pretty much foreshadowed his later firm decision to go against a 1961 tax cut because it clashed with his sacrifice doctrine.

SM: Wasn't there also the fear of the Nixon criticism--of being branded as a big spender, irresponsible?

WWH: The fear of Nixon was more on the spending and deficit side (though that's hardly unrelated). A tax cut fitted in better than expenditure increases.

JG: Was there any feeling that Congress simply would not go for a tax cut?

WWH: Well, there was a very substantial belief--and I'll come to that for 1962--that you couldn't move a tax cut rapidly through Congress--that these other things in the anti-recession program would move but that the tax cut would not move all that fast.
  Now, if I may to save time, I'm going to read to you from the interview for the oral history project at the LBJ Library. They have authorized this use of their material as long as due credit is given.* I'll intersperse quotes with summary or interpretive comments as I go along.

---

*Throughout the remainder of the interview Mr. Heller read from the interview conducted by the LBJ Library.

The questioner--David McComb--asked, "Where did this idea start? What's the genesis of the tax cut? I know it's back in the Kennedy administration, but whose idea is this, about a tax cut and the effect it will have on the economy?" And I say, very modestly, referring to the big 1964 tax cut (rather than an anti-recession cut in 1961), "This I suppose was as clearly a Heller idea as any purely economic measure in the Kennedy and Johnson administrations." McComb: "How do you get this idea? What goes into your mind that brings this up?" Heller: "Well, let me tell you how this developed. It goes back even before the Kennedy administration started. There was the Samuelson Task Force; the Task Force said that there ought to be an anti-recession program and if necessary a tax cut." I discussed this with Kennedy early on but, as I mentioned, he could not agree to it at that time. "By the end of 1961 we had begun, I thought, to get Kennedy fairly well educated on modern economics. And so, at least within the CEA, we were, in December-January, wondering whether we should still try to get the President to have an anti-recession tax cut. It was at that point that there was a big surge of GNP, a big surge of activity in the last quarter of 1961."

I remember this so vividly. I was trying to convince my colleagues that we needed a tax cut to get the economy up to full employment. Tobin and Gordon were adherents of the Cambridge-New Haven growth school. They wanted to have, if possible, an economy getting up to full employment with a surplus in the budget, that surplus to be transferred from the sizable pockets of taxpayers--in other words, taken away from consumer spending--and plowed into the capital markets by debt retirement in order to ease interest rates and the flow of capital. They wanted to tilt the economy toward plant and equipment investment and housing and, therefore, toward a faster rate of growth. Although, as a Council, we tried to arrive at almost everything we did by consensus--and were remarkably successful at doing so--in this instance there was a real difference of opinion among us. I was strongly for a tax cut; Kennedy wasn't getting anywhere with his expenditure programs. One talks about his increases in defense spending, but defense expenditures as a percentage of GNP dropped from 10 percent of GNP in the last year of the Eisenhower administration to 7-1/2 percent of GNP when the war in Vietnam was escalating. So we weren't getting the spending. I felt the only way to go was a tax cut.

Our discussion was part of the process of hammering out the Economic Report. On that front, let me digress to say that from the very beginning of working with Kennedy, it was my belief that we ought to go back to having a clear-cut presidential economic message that would have somewhat the same clout as a budget message. The brief economic message (twenty pages or so) would be the President's, and the rest of the Economic Report, ours. It seemed to me that that would make it a much more useful document, and would avoid the transparent fiction that the whole 200-300 pages was a presidential product.

So we were trying to formulate both the President's message and our analyses and statistics. The question was: Did we have any chance to get a tax cut? I thought we needed one but just at that point--mid-December 1961--we got the first estimate of the fourth quarter GNP in 1961 and, dammit, it was a great big jump over the third quarter. You can see why I say "dammit" about the "good news." Now the hand of the Cambridge-New Haven growth school was strengthened. It looked as if maybe we <u>could</u> do it after all. Maybe we could struggle up to full employment with this big overburden of taxes and get that big surplus, not to reduce the debt for any traditional shibbolistic reasons, if there's such a word, but to lubricate the capital markets--run a tight fiscal policy and loosen monetary policy--and thus have a more growth-oriented economy. That sentiment carried the day, mistakenly, as it turned out.

All right, now back to the LBJ transcript: "My partners on the Council who felt that we might make it to full employment even with what I regarded as an overburden of taxes, I must say, prevailed upon me. And we had a unanimous report saying it looked as though the economy could make it. We just goofed on the economic forecast for 1962. We were too optimistic....We thought we could make $570 billion in 1962, but GNP came in at only about $555 billion. And this is important for the genesis of the tax cut idea."

McComb then asks, "Let me push you back a little further...What I'd like to know is where do you get this idea [for a tax cut]? Now I know you implement it and so forth, but does this come out of research that you've done? Does it come out of a task force? Where does it come from?" And my answer was, "Fundamentally, it comes out of modern Keynesian economic theory and policy." "It builds on that?" "Right. The fundamental analysis on the basis of which the tax cut of 1964 was finally enacted really stems from Keynes' <u>General Theory</u> back in 1936. Now, it took a long time before that was translated into the specifics of economic policy. Let me modify that. In World War II we applied a lot of Keynesian economics. As a means of restraining purchasing power, we put in as many tax boosts as we could get through Congress. That was Keynesian, but under the pressure of the war. Then in the postwar period, already in the 1945-1950 period, you can find statements of economists--and one joint statement about stabilization and full employment policy in which leading economists agreed--that tax cuts and tax increases should be used for stabilization purposes: tax cuts in recession, tax increases to try to fight inflation. That's the basic theoretical analysis and research relating past actions to what then happened in the economy and so forth, all done back in the 1940s. Then in the 1950s there began to be some acceptance of this.

"By the way, Herbert Stein, in his interesting book on the fiscal revolution, attributes more acceptance of demand-

management economics in national policy in the 1950s and less
of a policy revolution in the 1960s than actually is the
case. As I view it, that doesn't begin to give the credit to
Kennedy and Johnson for providing the absolute essential of a
national policy revolution—namely, the conversion of the
President of the United States (and the conversion of leading
thinkers, men of affairs, opinion-makers) to those concepts.
That revolution did not take place until the 1960s. And
nothing that Mr. Stein adduces in his well-documented and
apparently careful historical work can establish, for me, the
proposition that the country had accepted the philosophy that
lay behind the great tax cut of 1964. I'm referring to the
philosophy and analysis and conscious use of budget expenditures and tax policy for economic stabilization, for full
employment and related policies." "Okay," says McComb,
"would you use that phrase that you just gave as a definition
of the `new economics´ (as the press called it) of the
Kennedy-Johnson days?" "Yes, in considerable part. The
conscious and active use of tax and expenditure policy—that
is, tax cuts and tax increases, spending speed-ups and slow-
downs, for purposes of trying to develop a full employment,
reasonably non-inflationary economy. That's part of it. But
you see, another thing happened during the 1960s that had
never really been part of the economics of the 1950s. It was
not only the kind of approach that was at long last adopted
by presidents, and consciously so, it also was the language
of the 1962 and subsequent presidential economic messages
that finds no parallel in earlier Economic Reports."

"I recall saying to Kennedy the first time I had drafted
language in which he openly espoused the use of deficit
financing under certain circumstances, `You are aware that no
president has ever said this before!´ "

It was in January 1963 that my draft of Kennedy's economic message had this deficit stuff in it. I never will
forget that encounter. We were both standing up in his
office and he had about a twenty-page double-spaced typescript in front of him and here's the way he went through it
(riffles pages). And he really was a speed-reader. He threw
it back to me—it was stapled—and said, "That's fine." And
I said, "Mr. President, you're sure expressing a lot of
confidence in your Council." He said, "Sure, why not?" And
I said, "Well, I have you saying some things in there that no
president has ever said before." And he said, "Show me." We
laughed about it. I went back and showed him where I had
written that there were good deficits and bad deficits.
Deficits that came as a result of positive action to stimulate the economy and would later largely pay for themselves
were good deficits. No president had ever dared say that a
deficit was a good thing. He did, then, modify one sentence.
That was all.

As I said in the LBJ Library interview, "Economists had
been talking about it for 25 years, but there's a vast gulf
between economists being able to do that and a president
being able to do it and not get penalized for it. That's

what I mean when I say that the `new economics` really took hold in the White House only in the 1960s. Eisenhower, in his final speeches, was still talking about the public debt imposing burdens on our grandchildren. President Nixon's approach was, `Oh, don't worry about $26 to $30 billion actual deficits, because we're going to have a balanced budget at full employment.` "

Nowadays, it's standard procedure to accept deficits. We introduced the balanced-budget-at-full-employment concept into White House rhetoric and thinking in 1961. "We also translated the `new economics` into specific numerical goals. It was done under Keyserling and Truman, but only fleetingly, and never fully accepted by Truman. But Presidents Kennedy and Johnson accepted 4 percent unemployment as an explicit goal; they accepted 4 to 4-1/2 percent growth rates as a goal. They pitched their economics, on our advice, to the growing full employment potential of the economy instead of worrying about every wiggle in the economy and trying to flatten out the curves of the business cycle. And this is a quite different orientation--a growth, expansion type of orientation that had never been accepted before."

Now let me return to the translation and implementation of the tax cut. In the first phase, you recall, we couldn't convince Kennedy to make a tax cut part of his anti-recession program. But in mid-1961, we began to get some of the philosophy underlying the tax cut idea accepted. The occasion was Kennedy's tentative decision to ask for a $3 billion tax increase to finance the $3 billion budget add-on for the emergency Berlin mobilization. His Cabinet was unanimously for it--both because they wanted people to feel a sense of participation through the tax boost and because they were more or less traditional budget balancers in believing that $3 billion of added expenditures should be matched by equivalent tax increases. This gives some credence to the proposition that, whether they were conservative or liberal in other respects, they were fiscally conservative.

Our attempt to kill the tax increase was a pretty exciting affair. I was in Dallas to give a speech when Jim Tobin called to say, "We just can't let this happen when there's so much slack in the economy." Jim persuaded me to talk with the President about it--which I did the moment I got back to Washington. And then, since it was Saturday and Kennedy was at Hyannis Port, I called Paul Samuelson to ask him to go over to see Kennedy. On Monday, Paul flew down to Washington with him. On the basis of our conversations and memos the President held an emergency meeting of the relevant Cabinet officers that afternoon. By the end of that meeting, I felt we had persuaded him to cancel the idea of a tax increase to finance the Berlin expenditures. It took a day or two before the issue was finally resolved. But Kennedy accepted the proposition that we pressed on him: with an economy so far below par, an increase of $3 billion in expenditures would do nothing but help increase activity, not inflation, in the economy and therefore didn't need to be offset by a tax increase.

As part of Kennedy's decision not to ask for a tax boost in July of 1961, he made a costly pledge that he would present a fully balanced budget in January of 1962. Some people think that this pledge caused us to raise the GNP estimate so that the President could project higher revenues for fiscal 1963. Subconsciously, this might have entered our forecast, but it certainly did not enter as a direct booster of the GNP forecast. I don't mean to say we were holier than thou about it. The range of forecasts we were talking about ran from $565 to $570 billion and we put it at the upper end of the range. Secretary Dillon was asked, "Do you think it is realistic or do you think it is optimistic," and he answered, "I think I'd call it optimistic realistic." This was a fair characterization of it.

It became apparent by about March or April of 1962 that our forecast was more optimistic than realistic. The economy was lagging. Let me return to the LBJ oral history: "By May 1, I was convinced that I had been right after all in late 1961, in my initial feeling that we couldn't struggle to full employment under this heavy over-burden of taxes. At the same time, we were failing to get economic stimulus by the expenditure route. The White House was butting its head against a brick wall as far as spending programs were concerned.

"This is something I underscore because some amateur historians say we just folded under and decided to give in to the conservative forces in the country and forego the expenditure route. Nothing could be further from the truth. The expenditure route had been tried again and again. Kennedy had said to me flatly, `Look, I'm not against spending money. If you fellows could figure out a way for me to get the programs out of Congress, let's go to it.´ This is directly quoting Kennedy. But (a) we were unable to do it that way; (b) it became apparent that we urgently needed some additional stimulus in the economy; and (c) it was true that with income tax rates still running up to 91 percent at the top and with rates at the bottom starting at 20 percent, the tax structure needed correcting. In the 1964 Act, it finally came out 14 to 70 instead of 20 to 91, which is certainly a more viable tax structure. There were a number of loopholes that needed closing. We didn't get much of that done in the 1964 Act, of course, because essentially the tax reform part of it got jettisoned fairly early in the game, except for a few remnants.

"Finally, we had to sell modern fiscal policy to an unbelieving and highly suspicious public. One way to sell it--and this, I guess, was a fringe benefit of going the tax route--was to get business on board to help sell modern economics through a tax cut, which was dear to the hearts of business. They'd always previously said, `You can't have a tax cut until you've got a surplus in the budget.´ Here we sold them deficit financing through a tax cut, and they in turn helped sell it to the country. It has taken me a while to cover this point, but I felt it necessary because there has been so much controversy about whether it was wise or unwise in the long-term perspective to have had that $12 billion tax cut in 1964 rather than boosting expenditures! I am completely persuaded that anybody who looks at the unsuccessful efforts to get expenditure increases out of Congress in that period has to conclude that if we foreswore tax cuts, we were simply condemning the economy to a long period of sluggishness and that full employment would have been a very distant objective. I had to say to Ken Galbraith one time, `The way to get to your objective of more expenditures most rapidly is through the tax cut route. This is one case where the long way around is the short way home.´ And Lyndon Johnson´s Great Society programs in 1964 and especially the 1965 expenditure expansion for domestic programs were based essentially on the expansion accelerated by the tax cut. So I feel that economic history has rendered its verdict on our side. But there are some observers--Galbraith, Lekachman, Keyserling, and others--who have not yet accepted that. That´s one reason I underscore it in this context."

EH: But it is a fact that the domestic programs of the New Frontier were not being passed because of it?

WWH: Because of the tax cut? No. The tax cut was decided on after we saw that we weren´t getting to first base on the spending side. They didn´t have the votes. "Okay, now to get back to specifics. The economy was falling well below its potential and well below the path that we had laid out. So in May of 1962 I wrote the opening-gun memo to the President saying in effect, `What I feared would happen and hoped would not is happening. The economy is falling well below its potential path of growth and well below our forecast. We aren´t getting anywhere with expenditure increase proposals, except for some military increases. It´s high time that we took the tax route. Perhaps a temporary tax cut would do, but nothing less than a sizable tax cut will do.´ At that time I wasn´t sure that I had fully persuaded my colleagues, Tobin and Gordon, but...we always worked by consensus in both the Johnson and Kennedy administrations and they were basically on board. There was never any conflict or problem. So we started plugging for a $10 billion tax cut by May and June of 1962. The President made his first commitment--in language that I worked out with Ted Sorensen--to a permanent net tax cut in a press conference of June 6 or thereabouts, 1962."

EH: What was bringing him around?

WWH: I believe it was in considerable part the Council´s persuasions, but it was also the fear of a Kennedy recession. Though politics was always a factor, I don´t think it´s unfair to say that we really had Kennedy pretty much on board

202

with modern economics by then. The political fear was that the steel crisis and the drop in the GNP might be followed by a drop in the GNP, and surely that helped him see the wisdom of that tax cut.

Back to the oral history: "Then we had a big battle about whether we should have an immediate tax cut. This is important because of the near-recession of 1962. I brought in people like Solow and Samuelson and others. We had a good go-around, and the President finally decided not to try the quickie first installment of a permanent tax cut, which I had been urging, but did decide to go for the tax cut in 1963. What I had been proposing was not a separate tax cut in 1962, but a first installment—which you could do through withholding and all the rest—to be finalized and folded into the permanent tax cut in 1963. But this was quite unrealistic on my part. Congress just hadn't been conditioned to move that fast on a measure like this. In that sense, I'm sure Kennedy made the right decision. He pledged, in mid-August, to have a major tax cut in 1963. That was the first real major commitment of a United States president to a truly modern fiscal policy involving tax cuts in the face of deficit financing, a rising budget, and a rising economy. That was simply unprecedented."

DD: Did the balance of payments have any effect?

WWH: One couldn't do as much as one might like to have done to stimulate the economy with monetary ease because short-term rates had to be held up to keep money from flowing overseas. To stimulate the economy, you just had to do it by fiscal policy, and tax cuts were the only promising path in Congress. The OECD people in Paris were part of our leverage on Kennedy. We had Van Leunep and others—Christensen, who was then head of the Secretariat—urging us to cut taxes in the U.S. rather than lower interest rates. So we got some leverage out of Paris and the OECD, and Kennedy was enough of an internationalist so that carried some weight with him.

"We had a running battle with the Treasury because they wanted only $2 or $3 or $4 billion of tax cuts to lubricate tax reform. I remember that so vividly because when I said ten, they at first said two. Steve Saulnier was quoted at that time as saying that anything like a $10 billion tax cut would be not only unwise, but `bizarre.` Tax reform was the Treasury's primary interest. They wanted to get the individual income tax base restored (something for which I'd been fighting for some twenty years).

"Our approach was, `Goodness, we hate to pass up any opportunity for tax reform, but the important thing here is to get a big tax cut for economic stimulus purposes.` We were always a little apprehensive about the excess baggage of the tax reform. Our heart was in it but not our head—in terms of the urgency of the tax cut to get the economy moving again. And eventually, interestingly enough, the Treasury shifted from the position that it wanted just enough tax cut

to lubricate tax reform to the position--I remember vividly
the way it was put--that tax reform would help to lubricate
the tax cut. Well, that was a reversal, which we didn't
mind, because our objective was to get that tax cut. But I
have no doubt that the tax reform part of the package slowed
it down.

"We ideally would have liked to have had--and I once
made this proposal to Kennedy--about $8 billion of tax cut
fast. Save the other $4 billion to couple it with tax reform
because we felt that we couldn't really get tough tax reform,
increasing some people's tax liabilities, without coupling it
with an overall tax cut. But what finally happened was (for
all practical purposes and to the anger and annoyance of the
Treasury and Mr. Mills) at a meeting with the Committee for
Economic Development (CED) only a few months into 1963,
Kennedy all but jettisoned the tax reform part of the program
when he, in essence, said, `That part is not the key part.
It's the tax cut.' "

Before delving further into the Johnson period, let me
explain right now about the Cabinet Committee on Economic
Growth. I remember its genesis vividly because at the end of
that pedantic tax briefing Kennedy gave on television in
August 1961, he asked, "Well, what do we do next?" I was
ready with a reply: "We now set up the Cabinet Committee on
Growth." He asked, "What for?" "First of all, to coordinate
policy on the tax cut, and some way or another it's got to
get reconciled. So why not have a Cabinet Committee on
Growth--for heaven's sake, don't call it a Cabinet Committee
on Taxes--and we'll hammer it out?" He did just that, set it
up by executive order within a few days. It was the Budget
director and the secretaries of the Treasury, Commerce, and
Labor and Heller. I was named Chairman. The principals did
attend that one most of the time. And it did broaden its
focus to the whole growth problem after disposing of the tax
issue. David Bell was still in the Budget Bureau at that
time, and was supportive, by and large. Dave was one who
played things very close to his chest, but I thought he
handled that job beautifully and that he had a good philosophy and a wonderful command for numbers as well as good
political sense. Let me give you an example. I got Kennedy
and Senator Clark of Pennsylvania together and Kennedy committed himself to Clark to have a public works acceleration
program, and that did go through the Congress. What made me
think of it is that David Bell went up with me to appear
before the Public Works Committee chaired by the powerful
Senator Kerr of Oklahoma. He would make a statement and say,
"Now is that right, Dr. Heller?" I didn't know Kerr well
enough to realize that what I was really supposed to say was,
"Yes," period. But I'd say, "Yes, except for so and so and
so and so," and then he'd ask me another question, and I'd
say, "yes, but also..." Finally Bell sidled up to me and
said, "All he really wants you to do is say `yes' and then
listen." And that was exactly right. Kerr was getting sort

of irritated with my thought that maybe I had something to contribute.

EH: The Bureau of the Budget, unlike the Treasury, has no predicted position on this, does it?

WWH: No, I think that's right. I think it took a less--doctrinaire isn't quite the term--but a less predictable point of view. Dave was a mild liberal and we felt we could count on him.

EH: There's no institutional position in the Bureau of the Budget quite as strong as that of a Cabinet department.

WWH: No, that's right, too. Now we had a Cabinet Committee on Growth and there we used a network of experts--the economists and tax experts in the Treasury, like Harvey Brazer, were on our side. They were sympathetic, on economic grounds, to a $10 billion to $12 billion tax cut. That was also true, as I recall, in Commerce and Labor. With their active cooperation, their principals gradually came around. Initially, we wanted about $11 billion and the Treasury wanted about $3 billion. We eventually "compromised" at $11 billion, and that's the kind of compromise I relish. But it should also be understood that Dillon then won an important victory when we went down to Florida for final decision making between Christmas and New Year's. He won the victory of, one, coupling sizable reform with the cut and, two, splitting it essentially into three parts. At first that tax cut was going to be phased in three stages. The gradual introduction was felt to be safer economically. What finally emerged was one bill enacted in 1964 with very little tax reform and phased in in two stages in 1964 and 1965.

SM: Could you expand a little bit on the opposition that you felt from the Treasury and, perhaps, from the Federal Reserve or what the Federal Reserve's position was in all this tax cut fight?

WWH: Well, Dewey might be helpful on that.

DD: Treasury was definitely--I think, it's predictable--they were not gung ho for this great big cut. They were really more concerned with the basic reform aspect. My recollection is that Martin on the Fed side was very pro the investment tax credit idea, wasn't he, Walter?

WWH: We should remind ourselves of the sequence of the tax cuts. In 1961, the Kennedy administration proposed the investment tax credit and liberalized depreciation guidelines, the latter being something that business had been seeking from the Eisenhower administration for years. These two measures added up to a 10 percent tax cut for corporations (and a cut also for unincorporated business). That finally went through in 1962. Since people occasionally credit me with being the father of the investment tax credit, I should note very clearly that it was a Treasury baby. At the very best I was a midwife, fully supporting it, and helping to sell it. But the proposal came out of the Treasury on the basis of work done principally by Professor E. Cary Brown, with the collaboration of Professor Richard Musgrave.

SM: Do you recall any significant fights with Martin in your Quadriad meetings over the tax cut?

WWH: Not really. It was the Treasury that was afraid of too big a cut, especially if it came all at once. Now, that also calls for a further point. We were applying the Keynesian multiplier analysis in determining the desirable size of the tax cut. We calculated that the gap between the actual level of GNP and the potential level was about $35 billion. We figured that an $11 to $13 billion tax cut was enough to close this gap. A pure consumption multiplier of about two buttressed by further investment and consumption effects would bring the total multiplier--we called it the "gross accumulator"--to about three. We went through this multiplier exercise in chapter 2 of the January 1962 Economic Report and then repeated it--in what was clearly a "first,"-- before the Joint Economic Committee. With appropriate charts, Gardner Ackley and I (we were temporarily a two-man Council) spelled out for the first time in history for a congressional committee just how the multiplier was going to work. Fortunately, as Art Okun's retrospective analysis later showed, the tax cut operated virtually on the schedule that we had projected in that analysis. Of course, one can't isolate economic cause and effect all that precisely. But Art's analysis is pretty persuasive.

EH: In the Fort Ritchie conversation, you or someone says that the moderate Democrats in Congress--I know that Mansfield was mentioned and others--were really not very excited about a tax cut because they didn't understand. They believed in balanced budgets--much the same point of view as that of the Cabinet officers.

WWH: Yes.

EH: It wasn't necessarily the conservative Southern chairmen--it was the mainstream of Democrats on the Hill?

WWH: Yes, we had a lot of trouble. Wilbur Mills had been a friend of mine since I first went to Washington in 1942. I went up and had lunch with him, tried to sign him on and had the devil's own time getting him to agree. He said, "Well, I'll go along with it if you have an equal cut in expenditures."

EH: He said that also to Johnson later.

WWH: That's right.

EH: Even though Mills was an intelligent, knowledgeable man, he really was not a Keynesian in this sense at all.

WWH: Oh, Wilbur Mills was not. No, that's right. And coming back to Martin—by and large, chairmen of the Federal Reserve Board have wanted things to be done that don't force them to run an easy money policy. I rather think that you'll find that we got either neutrality or support from Bill Martin because it meant that if we cut taxes, he would not be pushed as much to monetary policy. A far cry from the ease of the situation in the late 1970s!

SM: Reading the Fort Ritchie statements, it sounds as if the opposition to this kind of expansionary policy really came from the Congress more than from the administration.

WWH: Well, there were some very interesting lineups. In mid-1962, we were getting support from the U.S. Chamber of Commerce for a tax cut. And from Hubert Humphrey—I remember that vividly. He said, "It's high time to ease up on taxes." The more modern senators and congressmen were with us on the tax cut. But imagine proposing a tax cut that was going to increase the deficit in an economy that was already rising when the previous philosophy was always to lean against the wind.

SM: Was the basis of the opposition the fear of inflation?

WWH: No, it was more the traditional budget deficit—the budget balance problem.

SM: What about the role of some private groups, in particular, bankers and industrialists?

WWH: Well, we had this mixed picture, where the Chamber of Commerce came out early for a tax cut, where there was a lot of pulling and hauling and turmoil in the private community because they were licking their chops over a tax cut and scared out of their wits over the deficit. It really posed a terrible problem for them. I did a great deal of speaking in those days to business, to key business and financial groups, with this kind of a message: "Look, this tax cut will speed expansion and provide a substantial revenue feedback. As a result, it won't be long before you have smaller deficits than if you let the economy limp along without a tax cut. So in a sense you can have your cake and eat it, too." And indeed, without any significant step-up in inflation, the cash budget _fleetingly_ came into balance just before the July 1965 escalation in Vietnam.

IB: What carried the day with them? Was it depreciation allowances?

WWH: They already had those in the separate 1962 legislation. That, of course, had established the proposition that this Kennedy administration wasn't a wild-eyed anti-business administration after all, except that confidence took a big jolt from the steel confrontation in April 1962. Apropos of some of Kennedy's values, he really did once refer to big businessmen as "sons of bitches," as he himself admitted. And bankers. He came by that honestly from his father. It was very interesting to see that conditioning against the citadels of power that his own father had to assault. As a consequence, he was no great respecter and lover of these citadels of power.

EH: But he respected the political influence out there.

WWH: He respected the political influence but he was always trying to find some way to get around it. As I mentioned earlier, he said, "Lord, if I could only get away with huge deficits under the cover of a balanced budget philosophy the way Eisenhower did and paper over the deficits the way Roosevelt used to do by calling them emergency expenditures that didn't count in the budget or something like that." As far as we were concerned, he had the right economic vibes; he just wanted to proceed so that he had a kind of political screen behind which to make those policies go.

EH: Didn't he worry about business confidence?

WWH: Well, he did. I think I tried to indicate that I believe we fairly well persuaded him in 1962 that business confidence would come with high levels of demand and profits. And remember, corporate profits doubled from 1961 to 1965 while inflation was averaging just over 1 percent per year (and real wages were rising nicely, too). For quite a while, this business confidence issue bothered him, but then he stopped talking about that.

ML: Could you comment for a minute on the relations between various private groups and departments and the policymaking process? Did the Treasury have private groups that fed their pressures into the Treasury which in turn would then push them over toward the president and the White House?

WWH: Well, Dewey should answer this, but I'll just take a shot at it, then ask Dewey to speak to it. I think that it's fair to say that the Wall Street groups, with some exceptions, were very dubious about this tax cut in the face of a deficit and a rising budget. Even a financier who wanted to be friendly, like Andrew Meyer of Lazard, Freres, would knit his brows and be very, very dubious that this sort of radical procedure was going to succeed, but he, finally, I think, climbed on board, as did a number of other influential people. A very skillful job was done by Douglas Dillon in selling it. He was a marvelous buffer for Kennedy. This is one of the things about the Kennedy administration I keep coming back to: once you got everybody on board, we were really on board and we were all out selling that policy. But in the meantime, earlier, I think you're quite right. There was a constituency of the Treasury that was extremely dubious about this radical kind of measure. When Steve Saulnier as late as mid-1962 was saying that a $10 billion tax cut was not only unwise but bizarre, he must have been reflecting some kind of feeling in New York.

DD: Yes, the Treasury was always exposed at all times to this influx from the business-banking community, advising with Dillon and Roosa. Remember, we had advisory committees in Treasury, Walter. Theoretically they were debt management advisory, but they ranged all over the lot.

WWH: I always wondered about that, Dewey.

DD: Well, we had an advisory committee from the investment bankers and an advisory comittee from the commercial bankers. The top commercial bankers--the David Rockefellers, the head of the Bank of America, head of Continental in Chicago, that sort of group--and we had the principal investment bankers in. I don't remember precisely their position during 1963. But were I guessing, these committees would have been very concerned over the implications of a tax cut in the face of a big deficit or a rising deficit and they would have been concerned about the debt management aspect, just in their own narrow sphere--what you're doing is asking for more accommodation of markets.

WWH: Sure, I remember, now. Joe Fowler organized a business-financial coalition for the tax cut. Joe did an extremely clever job.

SM: But the problem was never the fear of inflation--it was how to handle the deficit, how to sell the bonds?

IB: There was fear of inflation. The argument was that anything you did could contribute to inflation, although a lot of liberal economists were arguing that there wouldn't be inflation; Eckstein was saying we have the inflation because steel has rigid pricing arrangements. Paper, after paper, after paper.

SM: Yes, but the argument, as you describe it, really wasn't over the inflationary implications of the tax cut.

WWH: I believe that's right.

IB: The argument was that the deficit would be inflationary.

WWH: I think that's the right way to put it--that deficits were considered to be inflationary. The focus was on the deficit, but the enemy behind the scenes was inflation.

EH: Are you persuaded that Kennedy had the consensus of the Congress and the country, the business community for a tax cut before he died? It would have gone through, do you think, regardless?

WWH: He still had this terrible obstacle of Harry Byrd.

EH: That was one of the first things President Johnson did. He had Harry Byrd to breakfast to talk about tax cuts?

WWH: That's right.

EH: Maybe we ought to go through some of the politics of the passage of the tax cut. Did it take Kennedy's death to achieve it?

WWH: I don't know, but I think it would have been achieved anyway, in the course of time, as Ken O'Donnell had said, but it didn't seem that easy. Remember that, in the first three months after the tax cut was proposed, there was just a barrage of criticism of the tax reform, the structural aspects, and there was a great lack of understanding of what we were really about. I'll never forget the day before the Joint Economic Committee when Martha Griffiths asked me how it was that here we were, trying to get people a tax cut, trying to do something for them, and yet they were resisting it. And without thinking, I said something like, "Well, maybe it's the Puritan ethic. Maybe they'd rather have debt cuts than tax cuts." I didn't think I'd said anything special, but I gather the pencils were going at the press table. The next morning: "Heller denigrates the Puritan ethic." The next day Johnny Byrnes, the ranking member of the Ways and Means Committee on the Republican side—very bright, very good sense of humor—went on the floor of the House and thundered, "I'd rather be a Puritan than a Heller." So I was keenly aware of the anti-tax cut sentiments.

EH: It was not resolved clearly.

WWH: It was not resolved. I'm trying to see whether I could shortcut again by reading a little bit from the LBJ Library oral history transcript. Let me just say that it was one of the first things that Johnson brought up with me when I met him that night. The interviewer, McComb, asked, "Was Lyndon Johnson informed about the tax cut prior to his presidency? Did he know what was in the works there?" "I have a little difficulty with your question. After all, the tax cut had been proposed in January of 1963, and we at the CEA had been fighting the battle for that from the spring of 1962 on. So yes, he had been in the act." McComb: "Your problem really wasn't to sell him on the idea of the tax cut." "Oh no.

Although in retrospect, he said--and this is Lyndon Johnson
the flatterer and ego builder--"The reason I accepted it was
because you were the author of it and I was convinced that
you knew what you were talking about" and so on. No, I think
he was thoroughly sold on the tax cut idea. My guess is that
he just felt it hadn't been handled too adroitly by the
Kennedy team, and he was going to see that it was driven
through by giving Harry Byrd what he wanted, namely, a budget
that didn't exceed $100 billion. You know, this totally
artificial administrative budget figure was just a will-o'-
the-wisp, but he was convinced that if he gave Byrd this
assurance on the budget side that he'd get the tax cut. And
he did."

"To what do you attribute Johnson's quick acceptance of
this [tax cut]?" McComb asked. "Now I know you mentioned
that you passed memos to him and apparently you were one of
the few people in the Executive Office at the time that was
doing that. Now is that part of the education process?" And
I said, "I think it is. And another part was the press
briefing breakfasts before President Kennedy's news conferences. I was just looking at my schedule of meetings a while
back and noticing how regularly the seven or eight of us
would meet in the President's little private dining room in
the mansion for breakfast."

For these off-the-record breakfasts, the standard group
was: Lyndon Johnson, Rusk, Sorensen, Bundy, Salinger,
Heller, Feldman. This group would meet at 8:45 and go till
about 10:00 and we'd review all the subjects that we thought
might come up at the press conference. About three quarters
of the time was spent on foreign policy and about a quarter
on domestic policy. I would always bring in a set of questions and answers for the President or would have sent them
over the night before and Lyndon Johnson expected me to hand
him a copy--that was a regular part of the ritual--and I
always sat next to him. At those meetings we often exchanged
a little intelligence on taxes, but in addition he was sitting in and listening to the discussion that went on at
sessions on the tax cut itself.

I want to say just one thing about the Kennedy tax cut.
We had sold Kennedy the tax cut on good, sound, long-run
reasoning--that this was an overburden the economy had to get
rid of if it was going to climb to full employment. Kennedy
felt that that wasn't a very persuasive argument with Congress, so a couple of times he jumped off the reservation and
said, "If we don't get this tax cut, we're going to have a
recession." We always regretted that because we felt that
that ran against the educational value of the tax cut. This
was not an anti-recession measure. This was a measure designed to achieve the full potential of the economy and
that's the way it eventually worked. But that's a relatively
small point.

As far as Johnson was concerned, he carried on a master-
ful charade saying he couldn't possibly get the budget below
$110 billion, then, maybe he could get it to $105 billion,

and finally, he actually brought it in at $98 billion or
$97.8 billion. Then Harry Byrd went along with it and the
tax cut quickly went through Congress. Well, it took a
couple of months (until March of 1964). And in fact the
budget, God knows, went up another $X billion above that
magic 100, but in retrospect it really didn't matter.

One instance I would like to share with you, though, just
to show you something about how Johnson worked. When we were
formulating the 1966 budget (really, the first truly Johnson
budget) in December of 1964, Johnson suddenly said to me (I
happened to be the one closest by), "Walter, I need a billion
dollars more; I need to cut the 1966 deficit in my budget by
a billion dollars." And I thought, "Well, that's very interesting." The next sentence, however, rocked me. He said, "I
want you to have the billion dollars here within one hour."
I'm not kidding. This is a paraphrase, but substantive: "I
want a billion dollars more revenue in my fiscal 1966 budget.
And I want it here within an hour."

Well, I remember Charlie Schultze telling me that if we
immediately reduced the withholding rate under the 1964 tax
cut to 14 rather than 15 percent we would get less revenue in
fiscal year 1965, but we would get more in 1966 because there
would have to be year-end make-up payments. So I called
Charlie and I said, "Charlie, how much was there in that?"
He said, "$800 million." I said, "A transfer from fiscal
year 1965 to 1966." Of course, Johnson felt he had no responsibility for 1965. And I said, "Well, isn't that great?"
We in CEA had wanted a 14 withholding rate because that would
give us about a billion and a half dollars a year more of
economic stimulus. Anyhow, I now have $800 million. Then I
called Kermit Gordon and said, "Kermit, here's my problem,
and I have $800 million of it." He said, "You know, it's a
funny thing. I was just recalculating miscellaneous revenues
and found an extra $200 million." I rushed back to Johnson's
office within the hour and said, "Mr. President, I've got
your billion dollars." Then I said, "Should I check it with
Doug Dillon? The Secretary of the Treasury ought to have
something to say about this." "No, no," he said, "He's down
at Hobe Sound; you're here." That was pretty free-wheeling.

EH: Have we left out large chunks in examining the Council that
we should be getting? What are we missing?

WWH: Well, the whole story--but you may be able to get that else-
where--of the wage-price guideposts and how those developed.

EH: Those essays in the Craufurd Goodwin book are based on docu-
mentation?

WWH: What you should probably do is look at the Goodwin book, see
if there's anything that seems to be missing. Bob McNamara
always considered our wage-price guideposts as the most inno-
vative thing that the Kennedy administration--in particular,
the Council--did. He believed deeply in them. They had their

212

genesis way back in 1961 when we began price and wage watching. Also, Walt Rostow had been urging Kennedy to undertake some kind of wage-price restraint. I brought Senator Gore to the White House one day to see Kennedy and plan a Senate rhetorical assault on the captains of industry in steel and other industries who would boost prices even in a slack economy. And thirteen senators, to our surprise, chimed in in August of 1971, condemning the ability of the concentrated industries to raise prices in weak markets. Then came the question of the steel industry perhaps raising prices in October 1961 because they were going to have their third installment of the previous wage bargain come in. That's when he wrote that letter, which I drafted with the help of Kermit, saying in effect, "Look, if you behave on the price side, we'll help hold steel wages in check." Meanwhile, we enunciated the guideposts in January of 1962. It was Kermit Gordon, Bob Solow, and Jim Tobin—Bob Solow, in particular—who provided a lot of the intellectual moxie for those guideposts. My greatest contribution was at four o'clock one morning when we were finishing off the Economic Report three days before it was to be published. We had left wage-price restraint to the last because it was most controversial. The big question was whether we should call them "guidelines" or "guideposts." In a major show of authority, I decided that they were to be "guideposts."

And then, of course, came the steel crisis. We were convinced, rightly or wrongly, that what really broke the steel price increase was economics. By that I mean Kermit Gordon's persuasion that if you held out as much as 15 percent of steel capacity, then the price increase would collapse. We did our work—I knew some people at Armco, others knew people at Inland Steel and Kaiser, and when those three (as I recall) promised to hold out, there was just no way that U.S. Steel could hold its price increases under those circumstances. Arthur Goldberg took the high road. By the way, he really did, by and large, work beautifully with the Council. He took the high road. He went to U.S. Steel and tried without success to get them to rescind the increase. We took the low road; we took the little ones and picked them off one by one, and we are inclined to think that in that sense economics broke the price increase.

EH: Was there anything else you wanted to add, perhaps on the revenue sharing story?

WWH: Yes, it's worth reviewing that story briefly, since it sheds light on how LBJ's Task Forces evolved, how things sometimes go awry in the White House, and how the White House and the press sometimes use (or misuse) each other.

EH: How did the idea surface, and why did Johnson turn against it?

WWH: As a student of state and local taxation, I had long felt that the federal government ought to couple with its detailed categorical grants a more general purposes grant without strings attached. The basic idea, which I had briefly described in the <u>Canadian Tax Journal</u> in 1957, was that the federal government should share a portion of the income tax with the states, not on the basis of origin--which would give most of the money to the rich states--but perhaps on a per capita basis, which would help reduce fiscal disparities among the states. In April of 1964, when economic prospects looked good after the passage of the tax cut and when the President seemed to be on the prowl for new initiatives, especially in connection with the 1964 elections, I decided to try out a couple of ideas on him. One had to do with making the income tax more cyclically responsive. The other was focused on revenue sharing.

EH: What kind of a proposal did you make?

WWH: Well, it was really very brief. The essence of it was that since the federal tax cut had now been enacted, the fiscal problems that most bore on people's minds and pocketbooks was the rapidly rising state-local tax burden. So we ought to explore some way of sharing the federal income tax with state-local governments in a new way that would not involve all the strings that are attached to grants-in-aid, that would help reduce inequalities among states, and that would at the same time promote state independence and vitality. I didn't even put it at that length in my initial memo, though I had a chance to back that up with some conversation with the President.

My memo asked the President for an expression of interest. He said, "Yes, tell me more." So, both on revenue sharing and on the more positive use of the fiscal system, I suggested that there be task forces to develop more definitive proposals. He gave me a green light on both scores.

When Kermit Gordon got copies of these memos, he told me that he had about a dozen subjects on which there ought to be task forces as well. Bill Moyers agreed, and we got Johnson's okay for about a dozen task forces in late spring, 1964. That's where the task forces were born.

EH: Were these inside or outside of the government?

WWH: These were outside task forces. In the case of revenue sharing, it was chaired and driven through by Joseph Pechman of Brookings. That's why it was called the Heller-Pechman plan. The President seemed to like the idea, and everything was going along just fine. Indeed, since Goldwater was proposing that we supplant the grant-in-aid system with a revenue-sharing system in which income tax monies would be returned to the states of origin--to him who hath shall be given--Johnson seemed to be particularly interested in having a plan that would distribute funds on a more equitable basis.

So in one of a series of economic policy statements, the

President, at our suggestion, stated that we ought to develop a new method of sharing revenues with the states in a way that would not only support state treasuries but promote their independence and reduce inequalities. We had revenue sharing in mind.

EH: But as I recall, the President repudiated the revenue sharing idea.

WWH: Not at first. But things did become unraveled. Shortly before the election, I decided that the issue was so sensitive and the President had seen so little of the task force report on revenue sharing—that is of the actual chapter and verse—in the pressure of the campaign, that I had better clear this with him. So I arranged with Walter Jenkins to see the President one summer night. Jenkins told me that he was having a number of people see the President for decisions that evening. Not hearing anything by 9:30 p.m., I finally decided to do a memo to the President. Referring to his campaign statement, I noted that it pretty clearly implied that we should have some sort of a revenue sharing system with such and such characteristics. At the bottom of the memo, I had the customary "approved, disapproved, tell me more." Still not hearing from Walter Jenkins, I finally called him at 1:15 a.m., and he answered just as if it were 1:15 p.m. This was typical of the Johnson administration. Jenkins told me that the President was tired and grumpy and didn't want to see anybody except him, so he acted as our agent in raising the various questions with the President. I asked him whether he had taken up the revenue sharing issue with him and had pointed out specifically the nature of the commitment. His answer: "Yes, I did, and the President said, okay, go ahead."

I never had a chance to follow up on this because the next day was when Walter Jenkins was apprehended and left the government because of homosexual activities. But since he had given me a firm answer, I tore up the memo to LBJ, which, in retrospect, turned out to be a mistake. Had I gone ahead and sent him the memo, the President would either have had the chance to stop me from going any further with this or he would have endorsed it in writing, and it would have been on the record.

But feeling that I had an oral commitment and then getting a message that he was anxious to differentiate his position from the Goldwater proposal, I moved ahead. In an off-the-record session with Ed Dale of the New York Times about the revenue sharing plan, Ed indicated that he had been getting some inklings of the revenue sharing plan from the task force, had a pretty good idea of what it was all about, but wanted to talk with me before he did his story. I made very clear that the ground rules were that he was not to divulge the source and that he was not in any way to suggest that the President had signed on to the specifics on this plan—he hadn't even seen them. I was double-crossed. The next morning, the headline story in the right-hand column of the <u>New York Times</u>, front page, went something like, "It has been learned that President Johnson has adopted (or endorsed) a revenue sharing plan along the following lines," and then he gave chapter and verse.

EH: What happend then?

WWH: All hell broke loose. George Meany and Secretary of Labor Willard Wirtz both called LBJ, violently objecting to the plan. Apparently, the feeling was that labor could do better in Washington than in fifty state capitals. The President was really sore. He claimed on several occasions that he rejected it because of this foul-up, that it was a perfect example of how not to get a policy adopted.

EH: Do you think this was his real underlying reason for opposing the plan?

WWH: Who knows? I think it is at least reasonable to assume that he felt he had so many things to do at the federal level, with the Great Society program and all that, that he wasn't about to hand the monies out to the governors and let them get the political credit for the expenditures, (and remember, this was before the escalation of the war in Vietnam). But he never let me forget--either through third parties or occasionally in mild personal reproofs--my "mishandling" of this issue. I wrote him a couple of memos about the issue after I left Washington, but that's a point on which he and I never agreed.

EH: It's ironic, isn't it, that a Republican president then adopted the plan that you Democrats developed.

WWH: Yes, and thereby hangs an interesting little tale. In 1969, when I was in the White House under the aegis of the League of Women Voters--I was a member of their national fund-raising committee--I met Richard Nixon for the first time. After a couple of comments on economic policy, he said, "Dr. Heller, I'm about to present your revenue sharing plan to Congress." After my enthusiastic response to that, he went on to say that it had to be a very modest beginning, only about $500 million a year. (A year or two later, he boosted his recommendation to $5 billion a year, which Congress eventually accepted.) Then he wound up his reference to his revenue sharing plan with the comment, "And the fellows around here all give you credit for it." My response: "Yes, Mr. President, and the liberals are giving me hell for it." Life as a liberal decentralist is sometimes hard.

5
The Council of Economic Advisers Under Chairman Gardner Ackley, 1964–1968

Summary History

Gardner Ackley took over as Chairman of the Council of Economic Advisers upon Walter Heller's resignation shortly after the November 1964 election. Although some change in style was expected, few observers expected any change in policies under the new chairman, who had served on the Council since 1962.

Ackley's main interests were economic growth, monetary policy, and the balance of payments. Remaining on the Council from the Heller period, Otto Eckstein focused on labor, manpower, wage-price guidelines, agriculture, and trade. After Eckstein resigned, James Duesenberry of Harvard took over his responsibilities. The newest member (and the youngest appointed to the Council up to that time) was Arthur M. Okun. Okun had been a senior staff economist for the CEA during the early 1960s and was responsible for the Council's forecasts and numbers generally. The staff remained small as before with only sixteen professional economists.

Ackley appears to have been relatively successful in influencing President Johnson. While he was not LBJ's only adviser on economic policy, Ackley's awareness of political realities and ability to deal with the President assured him of an influential role. He had full access to the President, speaking with him perhaps daily, frequently meeting with him, and sending him a steady flow of memos.

By the spring of 1965, the economy was in the midst of an unprecedented boom. The tax cut of 1964 had brought a $12 billion increase in the annual rate of private purchasing power. In May, the past record of peacetime expansion of fifty consecutive months was broken. The concern of Ackley and others was how to manage this sort of high employment economy. While policy decisions during the previous period of slack had been relatively easy, there was less room for error in an economy approaching full utilization. Economic growth and full employment remained central, but as the economy approached full productive utilization and 4 percent unemployment, the danger increased of excess demand, an overheated economy, and inflation. The expansionist policies of the "New Economics" had proven successful, but what remained to be seen was whether this balanced growth with high employment could be sustained without inflation.

217

As Ackley took over the chairmanship of the CEA, there was much dire speculation about the possibility of an economic slump in 1965 and how the new CEA would deal with it. But as it turned out, even the Council's optimistic forecast for the GNP in 1965 fell $14 billion short of the $672 billion finally reached. The GNP increase in the last quarter was the largest in history. Unemployment dropped to 4.0 percent, manufacturing capacity reached 90 percent, and plans for capital investment accelerated. The reason for the dramatic spurt in the economy was the sudden increase in defense expenditures in July 1965 as American involvement in Vietnam escalated. The increased expenditures added an unexpected fiscal stimulus to the economy that, when coupled with spending for LBJ's Great Society programs, pushed aggregate demand beyond productive capabilities and led to inflation. The CEA and economists in general were slow to recognize these developments. It was not until December 1965 that Ackley finally advised the President on the need for fiscal restraint in the coming year.

By that time, the Federal Reserve Board had already acted independently to restrain the overheated economy. Monetary policy had generally been accommodative to the expanding economy up through mid-1965. But beginning in December 1965, the Fed shifted to higher interest rates and a generally tight money policy. Johnson and Fowler were angered at the Fed's independent action and feared that this development would limit the administration's own policy alternatives in 1966. As it developed, monetary policy was the only real effort at restraint that year, as the Fed continued to raise interest rates from 4 percent in December 1965 to 5.75 percent by August 1966. Although Federal Reserve authorities were not eager to bear the whole burden of restraining the economy and realized the imbalances that would be created by an excessively tight monetary policy, the Fed was not willing to allow inflation to go unchecked in the absence of administration action. By late August-early September 1966, the Fed's policies seemed to be leading to a financial crisis. But at this point, the Fed was able to shift to a less restrictive policy because of signs of a slowdown in economic activity, and some moves toward fiscal restraint.

Throughout 1966, the CEA and the administration attempted to increase communication and coordination with the Federal Reserve Board. After the initial misgivings over the Fed's increase in the interest rate in late 1965, it was realized that the Fed's policies were all that prevented inflation, given Johnson's unwillingness to acccept the recommendations of his advisers for fiscal restraint. Ackley and others had urged a tax increase in 1966 to offset increased defense costs, but Johnson refused to consider such a policy. For one thing, he considered it politically impossible, particularly in an election year. He also feared that a request for a tax hike would only bring pressure for cuts in his Great Society domestic program that had just been launched in 1965 as the second stage of the 1964 tax cut brought increased revenue and hopes for increased domestic social spending. While he was willing to accept some limitations on nonmilitary expenditures as part of a program of restraint, he would only go so far. He was even less reluctant to yield on Vietnam costs.

While some advisers suggested the possibility of selling the tax hike as part of the cost of war, LBJ was apparently not yet willing to reveal to the public the extent of U.S. involvement in Vietnam. In fact, the CEA did not even know the extent and cost of involvement, expecting the war to end in June 1967 and not become a long-term factor in the economy. Whether through deception or simply lack of knowledge, U.S. involvement in Vietnam in 1966 ended up costing twice the budget estimate and exacerbating the inflationist pressures that had begun in late 1965.

The Johnson administration's program for fiscal restraint in 1966 was inadequate given the state of aggregate demand. There was no general tax increase and only minor reduction in non-defense spending. Johnson did support rescinding automobile and telephone excise tax reductions, speeding up the payment of corporate income taxes, and introducing graduated income tax withholding, but these programs were simply too piecemeal to be effective. Although the Fed's tight money policy served for a time to offset the administration's inaction in fiscal policy, by the fall of 1966 it was clear that the resultant dislocations in the economy (particularly in the housing industry) had to be alleviated. The Fed was able to ease its policies after Johnson, at the CEA's recommendation, sought temporary suspension of the 1962 investment tax credit and accelerated depreciation allowances when he sent his "mini-budget" to Congress in September 1966. Treasury Secretary Fowler and others felt the investment tax credit should remain a part of the permanent tax laws, but the CEA finally managed to convince them of the necessity of curbing inflationary business investment. In November Congress followed Johnson's recommendation.

As the spiraling costs of the Vietnam War became clearer in late 1966, it was evident that further restraint was needed to avoid further inflation. Few were willing to consider seriously direct controls or excess profits taxes, and there was general agreement that the Fed should not reverse its late 1966 easing of monetary policy. Johnson's advisers within and outside government insisted that a tax increase was essential to balance the war costs and cool down the overheated economy. As early as March 1966 the Cabinet discussed the possibility, but Johnson remained adamantly opposed to such a proposal for political reasons. Ackley, Schultze, and others continued to lobby for a tax hike and were joined by Heller, Samuelson, and the Cambridge Study Group. LBJ was finally convinced to include in his January 1967 Budget Message a proposal for a 6 percent surcharge on individual and corporate income taxes. The CEA then argued for the surcharge proposal in its Report, emphasizing the anti-inflationary effects of such a tax hike. No effort was made to sell the tax hike as necessary to pay for the Vietnam War. The problem, though, was that by early 1966 an inventory adjustment had cut the boom short, and there was more fear of a recession than an overheated economy. A Congress up for re-election later that year could not be expected to pass an unpopular tax hike simply on the basis of forecasts of economic problems. For that reason Johnson did not send legislation to Congress until August 1967, after the sluggish activity had ended and inflation had again become a problem. By that time, the economic situation was such that the proposed surcharge was raised from 6 to 10 percent. Johnson had evidently decided on this course of action as early as June 1967, but he had not been willing to announce his decision until August, despite the fears of Ackley and others that the Fed would again take independent action to curb inflation. Lyndon Johnson accepted the advice of the "New Economics" only when he wanted to. But LBJ's approval only removed on obstruction to the tax hike, for Congress still had to be convinced that the administration's forecasts were sufficient grounds for legislative action. It was not until after Ackley had left the CEA and Okun had assumed the chairmanship in 1968 that the surcharge finally passed Congress, but by then it was at least two years too late. During this period the balance of payments became an increasingly important problem for the administration. In a special message on the balance of payments in February 1965, Johnson proposed essentially a voluntary program centered on "quotas" to check capital outflow and attract foreign capital. While there was some subsequent improvement in the U.S. international economic position, the goods and services side deteriorated. By late 1967, the situation worsened as the capital outflow resumed after British devaluation, and at the same time the surplus of goods and services decreased dramatically. The fourth quarter payments deficit (annual rate-liquidity basis) in 1967 reached $7 billion. Rumors circulated that the U.S. would follow Britain's example and devalue because of its inability to meet its commitments in gold, but to dispel such rumors, Johnson asked the Congress to eliminate the 25 percent gold cover against Federal Reserve notes and free sufficient gold to meet international commitments. The problems within the international monetary system, however, remained, and the U.S. continued in 1968 to urge long-needed reforms to increase international liquidity and stop gold hoarding. Meanwhile, although an overall balance of payments program was developed with CEA assistance for 1968, the administration focused its efforts on fiscal policies to stem inflation and revive international confidence in the dollar.

Wage-price guideposts had been an important part of the Kennedy anti-inflation program, and they continued under Johnson. However, the boom in the economy changed their probabilities of success. Full employment gave labor the bargaining power to demand wage hikes. At the same time, there was less reluctance on business' part to raise prices to absorb such costs, since they were confident that the government would insure sufficient demands to make higher prices stick. By 1965, labor was also becoming increasingly sensitive to administration efforts to enforce wage-price guidelines, noting the 67 percent increase in corporate profits (after taxes) since 1960 while factory take-home pay had risen only 21 percent (13 percent real income). Union leaders felt that labor was being forced to bear the entire burden of the wage-price guideposts. As inflation raised the cost of living, labor became even less willing to accept the administration's 3.2 percent wage increase guideline.

In 1965, wage settlements in the aluminum, cement, glass, container, and automobile industries were among those that exceeded the 3.2 percent guideline. By fall, as inflationary pressures began to mount, the administration was determined to win at least one major non-inflationary settlement in order to demonstrate its wage-price policies. Since steel industry pricing was considered so crucial to economic stability, the CEA and the administration decided to focus their efforts on blocking an inflationary steel settlement that would lead to further price rises. Industry leaders insisted the settlement should be made on the basis of an estimated 2 percent productivity trend, but the CEA's estimate of 3 percent was finally accepted. With pressure from Lyndon Johnson, a settlement was finally secured in September 1965 that was placed by the CEA at exactly the 3.2 percent guideline. The administration was even more successful in pressing for industry compliance with the price guideposts. Ackley was particularly active in this aspect of wage-price policy and met frequently with industry leaders to urge compliance with administration policy. Arguments, however, often proved less effective in the long run than sheer pressure. Threatened disposal of government stockpiles was used to force the aluminum industry to rescind a price hike in November 1965, and similar pressure from the administration was used in negotiations with the copper and steel industries in late 1965 and 1966. The developments in 1965 showed that the administration would use force to back up its policies.

In 1966, the administration's success with its price policy continued as the CEA conducted private negotiations with some fifty different product lines. The administration continued to use its powers in government purchasing, stockpile sales, and foreign trade regulations to keep prices down.

However, by late 1966, it was clear that the administration's wage-price program was in trouble. In the early fall it had been only partially successful in forcing a rollback of automobile and steel prices. Labor specialists and the mediation profession found the CEA's "decimal point policy" unworkable in actual negotiations and contrary to collective bargaining. Labor had long felt that enforcement of wage guidelines without equal emphasis on the price side was unfair. Organized labor was particularly incensed in 1966 by the size of non-union gains the previous year and by the administration's rejection of the CEA's proposal to raise the productivity guideline to 3.5 percent. The turning point, however, was in the settlement of the airline machinists' strike in August 1966. The union had already rejected an arbitration board recommendation of a 3.5 percent settlement, when Johnson personally endorsed in July a 4.3 percent settlement, a clear violation of the guideposts and opposed by Ackley and the CEA. To Johnson's embarrassment, the union also rejected that offer and finally accepted a 4.9 percent settlement. The administration's capitulation and failure made further defense of the guideposts impossible. Subsequent settlements in excess of the guideposts made it clear that the policy was no longer workable.

The administration's wage-price policy shifted in 1967 and 1968. The CEA's Reports moved away from the 3.2 percent productivity standard and accepted the necessity of including cost of living factors, a clear concession to labor's demands. By 1968, the CEA did not even include a specific wage-price target.

The CEA was the central agency in carrying out the wage-price guideposts. This was in many ways unfortunate. CEA efforts to secure compliance hurt its image by putting it in an adversary relationship with business and labor and consumed much valuable time that should have been devoted to long-run economic problems. The emphasis on wage-price policy focused the Council's attention on micro economic policy at the expense of macro economic policy matters, and seemed to shift the blame for inflation away from excess aggregate demand where it belonged and on to price and wage decisions. Even worse, there was no way that a voluntary wage-price guidepost system could work in the overheated economy of 1967-68. A policy that may have made good sense in the slack economy of 1961-62 had been overtaken by events in the economy. Chairman Ackley realized the problems this had caused for the CEA and advocated shifting the responsibility for wage-price policy to a new Cabinet Committee on Price Stability. With endorsement from a secret task force proposed by Ackley to study the matter, a new Cabinet Committee was set up in early 1968, but the CEA retained a central role in wage-price policy throughout the remaining year of the Johnson administration.

Oral History Interview

The President and Economic Policy

EH: We will begin by asking Dr. Ackley to talk about the presidents with whom he worked. You were on the Heller Council and you have worked with John Kennedy and Lyndon Johnson. We're interested in several things: how did the president think about economics and economic questions; how was this thinking interlaced with his values, his ideology; how did this get mixed with political calculations and considerations; how did you find the best way to get to him?

GA: Both Presidents Kennedy and Johnson obviously knew that economic questions were of utmost importance to the success of their presidencies. Both of them impressed me as men who were always concerned with history's judgment of them--and it may be true of all presidents--and who were almost consciously thinking, "What will people remember me for, and how will this look five years from now?"

Let me describe Kennedy's approach to economic questions first so that I can contrast it with Johnson's. Kennedy had an intellectual interest in economic problems, although he really knew no economics when he started. I wasn't there during his first year of office, but I watched the process of his education after that. He was interested in the theory behind what we were trying to tell him and wanted to understand not just what the conclusion was, but the process by which that conclusion was supported, how it was derived.

One of my favorite anecdotes about President Kennedy relates to a day when Walter Heller was off on the road somewhere. Kennedy didn't usually call me over to talk to him, but this day I got a call saying I was supposed to come directly over to the White House. I picked up the papers that I assumed he was concerned with (at least, I thought I knew what they were), came into the office and he said, "Gardner, tell me again about the multiplier. I thought I understood it once, but now I can't reproduce the argument." So, in my best professorial way, I explained the multiplier to him. "Ah, yes, now I understand." And on several subsequent occasions, I heard him explain to congressmen or businessmen how it was that a $10 billion tax cut could produce a $20 billion increase in GNP; and that even though $20 billion isn't a terribly big number, you have to think about the gap between actual GNP and full employment GNP as needless waste. He really wanted to understand the logic and the chain of reasoning.

I don't think LBJ ever really got so deeply involved in the reasoning; it didn't interest him to be able to reproduce the argument. He was interested in the conclusion, and he was interested in alternative views of what the conclusion should be with respect to any particular question; he was apt to try it out on several people. He had the habit of trying it out on people who were not in government, or at least not in the executive branch of the government--often some of his friends in the Congress; but also on people who had no responsibilities in the economic area. LBJ was very impressed with Bob McNamara´s mental capacities and used to try out ideas on all kinds of economic questions on him. We were always delighted to have him do so because McNamara almost invariably supported our views on what the correct answers were. On major issues he would also call in people from outside the government--like Clark Clifford or David Ginsburg. He would let us brief them on the problem and the argument. Perhaps they would be given some documents or memoranda. Then we would chat with Clifford or whoever had been called in. If there were differing points of view, perhaps several of the protagonists would be invited to talk with Clifford; then Clifford would think about it and give LBJ his judgment. I don´t think that LBJ very often tried out questions on outside economists, except that occasionally he would check with Walter Heller, especially in the first year after Walter left.

The impression I increasingly had of the way LBJ approached economic problems and economic advice was that his first question about anyone who proposed to advise him on anything was to ascertain as best he could whether this adviser was giving it to him straight, or whether he had an ax to grind. He wanted to discover whether he was a Kennedy man, or someone who sneered at Johnson´s intellectual and social characteristics as he thought that all Kennedy people and Kennedy supporters did. Once he was convinced that the adviser was not out to stab him in the back, that he was not going to go out and talk to the press, that he was really devoted to the interests of the enterprise and loyal to him personally, then when complicated questions came up--and especially if the previous advice had turned out well--he developed confidence in his advisers. Within no more than a year, I think he did have that confidence in his Council of Economic Advisers. Once we told him what we thought he should do, this question no longer was "What would be the best thing to do?" but immediately, "Is that feasible?" When we told him that he really ought to do something, you could almost hear him immediately start to ask himself: "Is that feasible? Whom do I talk to about it? If it requires congressional action, are there the votes? What are the precise political maneuvers that would make this feasible?"

Often, of course, he knew at once that it wasn´t feasible to take our advice. Still, I would not have found working for him rewarding had I not been convinced that he did take our advice seriously, did make a real effort to consider whether it was feasible, or whether it could be made feasible. But the quick transition that he made, from deciding that your advice was a scientifically valid conclusion to thinking what can we do about it, was the most notable characteristic that I began to observe in his approach to economic problems. I suspect that that was true of his approach to many other problems....

He had a great power to take people apart, leave them spread out on the rug, but on only one or two occasions in more than three years did I ever feel that I was being reprimanded or treated in any way other than very courteously and respectfully. I think I had an advantage. He knew that I grew up in Kalamazoo, Michigan, that I went to a state teachers' college, as he did; I wasn't associated with the Ivy League; I wasn't one of those Easterners who sneered at his manners. He really did have a fear--it was a mixture of respect and antagonism--of people he associated with the Ivy League. He was sure they were very intelligent, probably more intelligent than he, better educated than he, probably knew a lot of the answers; but he always thought they were against him and out to get him, and he was very suspicious. I don't think that I ever encountered that suspicion, and I always had the feeling that he took very, very seriously the advice we gave. He didn't always follow it, but at least he didn't dismiss it casually or arbitrarily. He tried to see whether there was something that could be done. I decided that his testing out of our policy advice on other people was not so much related to the correctness of the advice but, again, to its political feasibility.

LBJ had little patience with people who tried to give him political advice. On one or two occasions I was indiscreet enough to suggest that I disagreed with him on whether some proposal was politically feasible, and he put me in my place in a hurry. I once told him that "We could sell that tax increase to the Congress. You just underestimate the power of logical argument. We can muster a lot of support from the banking community." He turned to me--one of the few times he really showed contempt--and said, "Who makes the political judgments around here? I pay you to give me economic advice."

EH: If you brought in advice that clearly was at variance with an obvious political structure or situation, he would point that out to you?

GA: Yes, yes. At one point we were trying to think of things to do that might have some downward pressure on the price level. Like all economists we thought that resale price maintenance was undesirable, on its own grounds, and abolishing it at this particular time might provide a little downward pressure on the price level. He could see the reason for our suggesting that, and he thought it was worth considering, but he said--he may just have been kidding us, I don't know--"I'll make an appointment for you to go up and talk to Wright Patman. If you can sell Wright Patman, I'll be behind it 100 percent." We went up and talked to Wright Patman, who was very polite--he was a sweet old guy--but he was not about to outrage one of his major sources of political support.

JJS: If LBJ were given alternatives that were both politically feasible, how did he compare them if he never really had the opportunity to hear the arguments?

GA: We always tried to give him the argument for our preferred course and against the others. I think that, in a very general way, he got the drift of the intellectual basis for the argument. But he wasn't really interested in it as an intellectual, academic exercise. He assumed that this was sound advice.

DD: Did he reach his conclusions quickly or slowly?

GA: Often very, very slowly. He was very fond of not giving any indication of how he was going to decide on a question. He may have made up his mind but he didn't want to let people know. Very often--certainly on the major policy issues, such as fiscal policy--he wasn't going to tip his hand. He had this phobia about being scooped in the newspapers and about people leaking his views in advance. He didn't want to read his decision in the newspaper until he had announced it. This often made it difficult to know how he was leaning on the major continuing problems. But he was certainly tremendously interested in economic questions.

DD: Did the whole Council get involved with him or was it just you as Chairman?

GA: He had some reluctance to have more than very small groups, or more than those really most directly involved. I used to try often to bring the other members in. I encouraged the practice, for a while, of having memoranda go to him directly over the name of Otto or Art. But I later got indirect word that he preferred to have all memoranda signed by me. Much of our contact with LBJ involved, or occurred through, Joe Califano, who had policy responsibility for domestic economic matters; Joe would relay messages both ways. Often we would discuss the questions with Joe in some length and detail before we discussed them with the President. My impression always was that Joe was a very faithful transmitter and that he never under any circumstances changed the message in either direction in transmission.

EH: In constructing the strictly social Great Society programs, did Califano perhaps play a more active advocacy role than he did on the economic side?

GA: That may be. Yes, I rather think that's right from the little I know about it. Actually, the Council's involvement in those Great Society programs tended to be quite marginal, and in most cases it was done at the staff level or by one of the other Council members. I don't recall ever having been involved in any crucial way in those programs.

EH: Walter Heller talks about the importance to him of Ted Sorensen and Ken O'Donnell in gaining access to Kennedy. Once they discovered that Heller could be useful to the President, they really helped him get in with the President. Would you talk a little bit about the other domestic policy staff in this regard?

GA: Of course, early on Ted Sorensen was around for a while; and Bill Moyers did this for a while along with his other duties. But after Joe came to the White House, as far as I can recall, all important economic questions funneled through Joe. The rest of the White House staff was not really involved at all, with one really important exception--the National Security Council. There Carl Kaysen was concerned with international economic matters and balance of payments problems; he was replaced later by Francis Bator. That channel on international matters was very much used, certainly when Carl was still there. It took a while for Francis to fill Carl's shoes.

LBJ encouraged us to keep sending him a maximum amount of information on economic questions. We often sent three or four a day, certainly fifteen a week, on the average, maybe twelve, at the minimum.

DD: Did you keep the style that Heller and you and others developed?

GA: We improved on that style, and this is one of the important things I wanted to refer to today. This is a speech that I have made many, many times and I almost know it by heart. The single most important requirement for access to power is the ability to write clearly, simply, understandably, giving everything that's necessary but nothing that's extraneous, in sentences of no more than ten words, in words preferably of no more than two syllables, arranged on the page with a lot of space so that you can see the organization of the argument by the arrangement of the space on the page, with dots and indentations and dashes and numbered points, and no solid paragraphs more than about three or four lines long. Then you don't have to read anything two or three times to figure out what it's saying. Very few dependent clauses. Qualifications belong in separate sentences, and qualifications that aren't really relevant to the issue should be omitted.

We knew that this was very important for our influence with the President because we observed it so often. For example, a memorandum would come to the President from the Treasury on some economic question. It was written in paragraphs that were six or eight inches long on the page, single-spaced, right out to the margins; full of long sentences, with a lot of modifying clauses; containing a lot of detail, some of which was pertinent and some of which wasn't. LBJ would look at those things and after about five minutes he'd send them over to the Council and ask, "Would you translate this for me?" That irritated us, of course, having to rewrite other people's memos.

He was a terribly busy man; he deserved to have communication that was as direct and simple and clear and to the point, as relevant to the question as could be achieved. We spent enormous amounts of time rewriting our memoranda so that they could be easy to digest. He would often carry those memos around in his pocket, pull them out, and read them to people. Three or four days or a couple of weeks later he would cite some fact out of a memo that you had sent him weeks ago, you couldn't have remembered it, but he had. He just ate that stuff up, called for more, and complained if he wasn't getting enough of it. There was usually one topic to a memo and if you could do it in half a page, fine. Ordinarily not several topics in the same memo. There were daily economic news updates, which tried to give him not merely the new numbers that came out that day, but what they meant, what their significance was, what their limitations were, but without going into any statistical complications. If you have to go into something that's complicated, just work like the devil to reduce it to its most clear, logical sequence, in short sentences so that he can read it and get the idea.

You know, we weren't the only economists in the government with our staff of fifteen or so. Dozens of people in the agencies knew much more about every question that we wrote to him about than we did. But it didn't take him very long to learn that if he asked the Secretary of Labor for information about some new statistic relating to unemployment, that memo would reach the Secretary, who didn't have the faintest idea of the answer; he would send it down the channel to the under secretary, who sent it down the channel to the assistant secretary. After a while it lands on the desk of the guy who really knows what the facts are. In going down the line, however, the question has gotten somewhat unclear, and the person receiving it is likely to answer a different question from the one the President asked. In any case, the answer will be in a very technical format. Then it takes several days to go back up the line and get cleared at each level and get over to the White House. If the President calls us up, within half an hour or an hour he has a memo on his desk that tells him exactly what he really needs to know, or that there are some things we don't know and will find out for him.

EH: Was there a question of an institutional bias that he might get from the Department of Labor? Did he feel that the Council was not biased in that sense?

GA: Well, we certainly believe that was often the case, too. But just the means of communication of information is very important. Bob McNamara used to say that the Council's memos were the best in the government, and that he was trying to get people in his Defense Department to write that way....Actually, it turns out that when you try to write that way, you find that it helps you sort out your objectives and clarify your own conception of the argument.

WH: How did the three members of the Council work in relation to one another?

GA: Actually, many of the memos were drafted initially by either a staff member or another of the Council members, but everything that went to the President I worked over very carefully myself, especially after the President let it be known that he preferred to have memos to him go over my name. I don't think even the shortest little note ever went over without being rewritten three or four times and being looked at by two or three people. Art Okun has a great gift for presentation of ideas. He has a nice sense of humor, an ability to think of very striking figures of speech, and in the memos he drafted he often put in things like that. I always left them in; they appealed to LBJ. I was never as clever as Art.

AL: What we've been talking about thus far is the channeling of economic intelligence and advice to the President. He wanted you and trusted you on this. But don't you get into a conflict of interest when the President looks upon you to do other kinds of things? One, to coordinate and develop economic policy for the administration on economic policy, which is quite a different function from the communication of intelligence on issues about the economy at large or particular problems. The other thing that Walter Heller kept emphasizing, which was so much in contrast to Nourse, Keyserling, and even Saulnier, was the task of explaining and attempting to influence public attitudes toward the economic policy or issues of the administration. In the Heller and Ackley and subsequent periods you seem to see much more the use of the Council to develop a coordinating policy.

GA: Certainly on some issues the Council did do some coordinating, but in the Johnson White House coordinating was done increasingly by the White House staff, and, in particular, on economic issues by Joe Califano. In a sense, that was his major responsibility: coordination of action and advice, rather than asking the Council to do that. Joe was tough as nails; Joe had no trouble at all calling a cabinet officer to task and telling him how it really was, and what he was supposed to do. I certainly had no talent at all in that respect. I suspect that this is one of the reasons why I rarely served as a coordinator. On issues of all kinds, Joe would very often get the agency people, the Council and other specialists within the White House staff who were interested together for endless meetings to thrash these things out, particularly where there were disagreements. We always reserved the right--perhaps it was our exclusive right--to report directly to the President on these issues while the discussion was going on.

The public advocacy problem is a quite distinct matter and certainly offers many of the greatest difficulties to the academic. Can someone who pretends to be a scientist advocate a policy with which he isn't necessarily fully in agreement? Should he go before a congressional committee, or talk to a reporter, or make a speech that advocates that policy when he has advised a somewhat different policy? That's a very tough question and the answer is not as clearcut as that way of putting it makes it seem.

Anybody with any humility must recognize that even on economic questions to which he has devoted his professional life, he doesn't know all the answers. There's always a large band of uncertainty around his best estimate. If, for example, you have insisted that a tax cut ought to be 10 percent and the president decides that it should be 8 percent or 12 percent—for reasons good or bad—you can't really say that it's a disaster if it's anything other than 10 percent. There is a second best, and if it is a second best that is better than a lot of other alternatives that might be adopted, I think you can, with all clear conscience, go out and say that we need an 8 percent tax cut, that the arguments against a tax cut are wrong, that these are the reasons why. You obviously have a problem if someone asks you what advice you gave the president on this question. The Council, as far as I know, has always taken the position: "That's a question we don't answer. We're sorry, but if we answered it on this, we'd have to answer it on every other question and we would lose our usefulness." I was never pressed on that at all. Nobody ever demanded to know, "What did you advise the president?"

On the other hand, suppose you're asked to go out as a public advocate of a position that you think is just dead wrong. Then you're in trouble, and the answer is, you don't go. You persuade the president that he doesn't want you to go. On only two occasions in four years was I more or less forced to say something publicly that I really didn't want to say. I also said some things publicly that I later regretted—a great many—but at the time I believed them.

One time, however, I was told to write a letter to the Chairman of the House Labor Committee, saying that a proposed increase in the minimum wage was consistent with the President's anti-inflation policy. I was ordered to write that letter, and under great pressure I did write it and then told them that if they ever asked me to do that again I would resign. Later, when I was off somewhere, Art Okun got a similar request and also wrote such a letter, and Jim Cochrane's history reports that on the carbon copy of that letter in the CEA files it is noted that the letter endorsing the increase was "written at Joe Califano's orders." I think those are the only two examples in my period in which we were told to take a public position that we believed was not in the public interest. But arguing publicly for second-best policies, it seems to me, is quite easy to do, and it doesn't have to compromise your professional principles.

DD: Do you think the Council should be out carrying the ball in legislative matters?

GA: Yes, I do. Not only in legislative matters, but also through speechmaking and newspaper interviews with journalists and so forth. For two reasons. One, there is an enormous opportunity for improving the quality of public discussion of economic issues. I think we have an important educational responsibility. Walter always used to say that this job was his greatest teaching responsibility, to educate (a) the president and (b) the public about modern economics. If you believe in modern economic theory—the kind I happen to think is appropriate and useful—I am prepared to use every opportunity I can to explain that and help people understand it. Second, if you do not participate to some degree in advocacy of administration positions with which you agree, or if you refuse to do so, you come to be seen as not a member of the team. There's a real point in the president's advisers being seen by the president and by the public as members of a team. There are certainly dangers here—dangers of being used as a captive "scientist"—parading a political view while giving it something of the "white-coat" advertising treatment. One must try to escape that danger. Your influence with the president, however, is going to be greater in achieving things that you really think ought to be done, if you are participating as part of his team. I haven't any problem with that.

I worked for Democratic presidents and not for Republican presidents not because the appropriate kind of economic analysis is necessarily different for them, nor because the Republicans didn't need it more than the Democrats, but because there are some value questions involved. There are Democratic economists and Republican economists; that relates hardly at all to differences in analysis, but to some ultimate values towards individuals, some probably vague ideas about income distribution and fair treatment. As a citizen, as well as a scientist, one can participate with a certain amount of enthusiasm in advancing the policies of an administration with whose basic objectives one is sympathetic.

EH: As a matter of fact, you wrote in one of the papers I read that economists, by virtue of their craft, are pretty experienced at thinking about hard value questions. Do you remember writing that?

GA: Yes, I do remember writing that and having said it a number of times. That's a somewhat different issue, although it's certainly related. The frequent—almost the standard—argument is that the economist should merely analyze the alternatives and describe as best he can the entire consequence of alternative policies in terms of alternative outcomes; then the policymaker should choose which of these outcomes he likes. If the policymaker believes your advice, if he likes outcome "a" then he has to take action "a." If he prefers outcome "c" he's got to take action "c." An economist is a technician who tells the policymaker the most efficient way to promote his objectives by particular actions. That is certainly part of his job. But the notion that the politician really has a well-developed analysis of values with respect to some of these complex questions is naive. Rather, the economist has in fact pursued these value questions in terms of their elements much further than a public figure is likely to have pursued them, and is trained in the analysis of the meaning of values, in a way useful for the policymaker.

EH: There has to be a congruence or a fit, though, doesn't there, between the two on basic values? Could you perceive Johnson's basic political values as he received your ideas?

GA: Yes--his interest in the little guy, his populism, his basic patriotism, his interest in the judgment of history about how he served the country, how he served its interests.

IB: Were those things accompanied by any kind of a shirt-sleeve economic theory?

GA: Oh, yes, he had all kinds of prejudices and ideas. Pro-farmer, pro-small businessman, anti-banker, anti-Wall Street. He was a real populist.

IB: Including a nascent model? That is, if he did these kinds of things these groups would benefit, and if he did those kinds of things, those others would benefit.

GA: Pretty unsophisticated, if there was any model.

ML: Did these values affect specific recommendations that came out?

GA: Surely, and we often had to fight him about this. For example, when he refused to go for a tax increase, the Federal Reserve tightened money and interest rates went up--which he thought was just usury and transfer robbery from the poor guy to the private banker. We had to fight like the devil to keep him quiet. And we did. One of the things I am proudest of is that in 1966 he sat still and took that rise in interest rates and that money crunch without ever saying a word. That wasn't like him, and it was very hard to keep him quiet.
     I remember one time around March or April 16, I got a memo--I don't think it was from Joe Califano, but rather from some other White House staffer--saying, "Shouldn't we have the President come out and condemn this tight money and these high interest rates?" I went back through my files and pulled out about ten different places in which we had said in so many words, "If you don't have a tax increase, one of the things you're really going to get is tight money and high interest rates. That is the choice you have to make." So I

said, "We told you so!" Never another word. But he did take it. He was very unhappy. It made him ill to think about those bankers collecting 12 percent interest.

ML: How did your own values affect recommendations? You emphasized a minute ago that you think that academic economists in some sense have greater sensitivities to the question of income distribution. How did that affect economic growth?

GA: Questions really don't often come up in such an abstract context. They come up in terms of should you do this, that, or the other explicit thing. One of your responsibilities in analyzing any policy proposal, whether it's somebody else's or your own, is to say what its implications are; among those may be implications for income distribution. You certainly set those forth to the extent that you can say anything about what they are. Very often, you can't.

JJS: Would the memos carry an explicit comment on distributional issues, aside from efficiency?

GA: There certainly were a number of times in which I distinguished for the President--and, as a principle, this always ought to be done--to what extent my advice depended on analytical propositions, and to what extent it depended on value propositions. I can recall in several cases saying, in effect, "The reason I prefer this to that is that it affects people differently, and different people, and that's a value question, and that is quite apart from my economic analysis of its effects." I don't know whether anybody appreciated that difference in the White House, but I know that I tried to make sure that the record showed that I recognized the difference.

EH: In referring to values in economic analysis you mentioned that Republican and Democratic economists are somewhat different. How are they different and why? Economists have common frames of reference; they talk to each other across these lines, and yet there are value differences. What are the essential differences? There is the ambiguity in the Employment Act itself about what values should be valid, employment versus price stability.

GA: Neither full employment nor price stability is a value in itself. It's associated with some kinds of benefits and costs to certain classes of individuals. I suppose that those who emphasize full employment tend to remember that the unemployed overwhelmingly have low incomes, that the burden of unemployment is not spread evenly throughout society: professionals, businessmen, executives, rarely become unemployed. Unemployment is a cost that, on the whole, is borne by the people of lower income; even skilled workers are unemployed less often than unskilled. There's almost a direct correlation between wage level and the exposure to

unemployment. So those who sympathize with the least well
off, I expect, put a higher value on employment.

The costs of inflation, whatever they may be and they
are very difficult to describe, are borne much more randomly
throughout the population generally. Indeed, the group that
is probably most hurt by inflation tends to be a relatively
distinct group, most members of it retired, and whose wealth
and income are associated with ownership of fixed income
securities. They tend to be fairly well off. I guess they
provide the principal political opposition to inflation. The
other retired people--the lower income level, people whose
income comes mostly from Social Security--are better protected against inflation, earlier through periodic adjustments in the rate schedule, and, later, through a formal tie
to the cost of living. To some extent the differences in
views about the importance to be attached to the goals of
full employment versus inflation--if it is a "versus," and
it's not clear that these always have to be alternatives--may
be somehow a matter of identification with the interests of
low income or with fairly wealthy retired people. And values
are reduced to, "With whom do you sympathize?"

Bureaucratic Politics and Economic Policies

EH: Let us look briefly at the Council's relations with other
parts of the bureaucracy. One of the first things Walter
Heller said when we asked him to compare Kennedy and Johnson
was that Johnson valued the Council even more highly than
Kennedy, particularly vis-a-vis the Treasury. Johnson was
less married to the Treasury than Kennedy was. Was there a
difference there? Kennedy did seem to defer to the Treasury
a great deal; he always was worried about the bankers.

GA: I think that in part represents the personal compatibility
between Dillon and Kennedy. They came from similar backgrounds, interests. Let's see, Dillon overlapped into the
Johnson era for a little while? I don't believe that their
chemistry worked quite as well. They didn't suit each other.
I think Joe Fowler, though, got along very well with LBJ and
they found each other very sympathetic. I also believe that
the Council was even more useful to LBJ than it was to Kennedy, but whether it served explicitly as a counterpoint to
the Treasury, I would not have...

EH: Why do you believe the Council was more useful to Johnson
than it was to Kennedy?

GA: Maybe it's just that the economic questions became more
predominant in Johnson's political situation. But also perhaps because he made less use of the White House staff in a
substantive way than Kennedy did. I believe the people
around Kennedy actually had important policy input. I think
that most of the people around Johnson did not have policy
input. He didn't look to them for that. He looked to them

for lots of other things. He worked them like dogs, and he sometimes treated them rather like dogs. Joe Califano, however, certainly was respected as a person who had important policy ideas of his own. But Joe was very, very careful, as far as I know, to give his own views only when asked, and never to confuse his views with the views of other people whose ideas he was supposed to be reporting and coordinating. I think he was extremely careful about that.

DD: Maybe you had a stronger Treasury under Kennedy?

GA: Yes, I think that's probably true. Not merely at the top, but the first several layers. Of course, Johnson was a terrific worker. He'd call you up in the middle of the night and ask you something or call you into a meeting at 2:30 a.m. in his office or in his bedroom. He really worked. He apparently took just a terrible pile of papers to his bedroom every night and really went through them. And we'd get them back with comments or questions or notes. Things we'd send over at 8:00 p.m. would come back in the morning with his handwriting on them.

IB: Was it your sense that President Johnson viewed the Council as more detached in contrast with the economic advice he was getting from Labor, Treasury?

GA: Oh, absolutely, yes. We were his people.

IB: Was there a discount applied to some of the departments' offerings on the grounds that they represented constituencies?

GA: Oh, no question. Yes, he very much believed that, and I think it's true. I think it's undeniable and unavoidable and perhaps not even undesirable. But the president does need a staff that has no constituency other than himself.

IB: Were these constituency representatives reminded in some subtle or obvious way that in fact their views would be contrasted with those of a "more objective" or "more dispassionate" or "detached" agency?

GA: There were some problems about the relation between our advice to him and that given by the cabinet secretaries; at times this became quite a serious problem. There was great jealousy of the Council on the part of Willard Wirtz and several secretaries of Commerce—in particular, John Connor—who resented very much our access to the President, which was so different from theirs, and complained bitterly that we were giving him a biased picture. We hoped we were not giving him a biased picture; we were trying to give him as unbiased and scientific a picture as possible. But there was a great deal of jealousy.

DD: He didn't use the Quadriad nearly as much as Kennedy or did he?

GA: No, he did not. The Quadriad didn't survive very long in any effective way. I guess as much as anything it was because he didn't like and really trust Bill Martin.

DD: Kennedy did like Bill Martin?

GA: I think so. I have that impression. But LBJ came to feel that Martin was not on his side, was not supportive. He was not necessarily secure in having questions discussed in front of Bill relating to matters on which he was still making up his mind.

EH: Does that mean that he sometimes would constrict the circle a bit too narrowly?

GA: At least at some stages, he often did. There were occasions, for example, when he explicitly requested that a memo that we were preparing for him on some important policy question not be sent to anybody else, but only to him, even though it was a memo for a meeting in which these other people would be participating. It had been our routine practice, if we were preparing a memo setting up the issues for a meeting that would involve Treasury and Budget Bureau and perhaps another agency such as Agriculture, to send an issues paper out in advance and also indicate what our views were. On a number of occasions he indicated that he preferred to receive our advice privately--at least in the initial stages. There were occasions, certainly, when he played people off against each other, and deliberately framed discussions so as to undercut one of the members. I never had the impression that we were being played off on much of anything. I think we really did have his confidence for, if nothing else, he really believed we were secure; we weren't going to leak, we really had his interest at heart, and we were trying to serve the presidency and not anything else.

DD: What about the role of the Fed as you saw it? You say he didn't like Martin. I still got the impression that Martin saw a lot of him.

GA: Yes, there were occasions when they saw each other--several occasions in which there were rather bitter arguments. It's awfully hard to know what LBJ really thought about anything; he was so complicated. I think in a way he rather liked Martin, but he didn't think he was a heavyweight and he didn't fully trust him.

DD: But the Council's relations with the Fed improved during your period.

GA: Yes, we made a real effort. I think the weekly lunch had started before I was Chairman, though I'm not sure, but we certainly tried very hard to make ourselves available to the Fed. We were never quite satisfied that they were constructive meetings, but at least they kept the channels open and if we had some message we wanted to give them, we could give it to them and vice versa. We had other channels to the Fed through staff, and some of our economists or some of our Council members and some of the top of the Fed did communicate unofficially a lot more, I think, than was ever known by the Fed, which tends to be pretty close about its policy discussions.

DD: What were your relations with the Treasury?

GA: Certainly on the majority of issues the top people in the Treasury, the Budget Bureau and the Council saw things essentially the same way; so far as possible our strategy was not to present the President with disagreements on which we had to give him divided advice. We tried to avoid that, particularly if the divided advice rested on different economic analyses or different interpretations of data or different forecasts. To ask the President to decide a question on the basis of an interpretation of economic data or theoretical argument is really unfair. He is certainly not as well qualified as his advisers to make the analysis, to interpret the data. It was very rare, I think, that an argument about a forecast or an interpretation or an analysis went to the President with more than one opinion. On policy advice, obviously, there were occasions when there were differences between the Budget Bureau and Council, on the one hand, and the Treasury on the other. It tended to divide that way, I guess, if for no other reason than because the Budget Bureau was headed by economists who thought essentially the same way we did and had essentially the same values. The Treasury had institutional positions on a lot of matters and its personnel were not prevailingly academic economists, and probably there were some value differences. But on most economic issues those three agencies were in the privileged position with respect to participation and discussion of policymaking. This, of course, was exceedingly irritating to the secretaries, particularly of Labor and Commerce, who were excluded, in effect, from the discussion about major questions of fiscal policy, tax policy, budget policy.
      The relations between Council and the Treasury were quite different from the relations between Council and the Budget Bureau. As I have just said, that's partly because of the different kinds of people you find on the Council and Budget Bureau, on the one hand, and in the Treasury, on the other. There were people like Dewey over there at the Treasury, occasionally, and Bob Roosa was something of an academic, but he'd already been corrupted by the banking community. The Treasury was much more to be feared, too, because it has a tremendous apparatus and able civil service over there, which is very, very cagey and knows how to oper-

ate. For example, on all those big inter-agency committees that Treasury chaired, nobody else really had a chance. They controlled the agenda, the minutes, the issue papers, and were just past masters of bureaucratic management. On the Balance of Payments Committee, for example, you could have all kinds of ideas about things that ought to be on the agenda and the report of the discussion never quite covered the points that you were most interested in.

DD: When Kennedy came in, there was such an electric feeling of excitement in organizing the administration that there was pulling and hauling and tugging between Treasury and Council as to who was going to do what at the beginning of that administration; you didn't really get that when Johnson took over under those unhappy circumstances.

GA: That's a good point. The circumstances in which Johnson came to power did pull people together. At least all except a certain group—the Kennedys.

WH: Wasn't there also a gradual accretion of prestige and esteem, greater visibility of the Council?

GA: Perhaps, yes. My Council benefitted a great deal from Walter and Kermit Gordon and Jim Tobin's miraculous performance.

SM: During at least a fairly large part of your chairmanship, your interests and those of the Treasury were fairly similar in the sense that you both wanted to slow down the economy. All the other people we've been talking to were often trying to pursue an expansionary policy, whereas the Treasury was really much more conservative and did not want to do that. Is it possible that your good relations with Treasury resulted from the fact that your interests coincided to a larger extent than they had for other Councils?

GA: I believe that's true, although at the beginning of 1965, the accent was still on expansion. We and the Treasury, as I recall, had no difficulty in agreeing on the repeal of the excise taxes. We did have a substantial tax cut at the beginning of 1965, which was entirely appropriate under the economic circumstance. I don't recall any real issues with the Treasury on that point. And, actually, the Treasury, at least under Fowler, and the Council had a generally similar view in terms of its disagreements with the Fed. Joe Fowler was as upset as I was by Dewey's discount rate increase in December of 1965. There was a period of several weeks in which Bill Martin and I didn't speak to each other. I was the one chosen to make some public comment, which I don't think Joe did. I gave the administration's views, probably in intemperate terms, about the lack of wisdom of it. And I know that Bill very much resented that.

EH: You don't think the Bureau of the Budget had the same kind of fixed institutional bias across time that the Treasury had?

GA: I don't know to what extent that's still true. In my day the BOB had a tremendously effective, very well organized staff. It tended several layers down to be dominated by, if not academics, at least academic professional types, economists, some of them career in the Bureau. Like the Council, they had no constituency other than the president. Their interest was in serving the president efficiently. They took as disinterested and coldly analytical a view of things that came out of Labor or Agriculture or wherever as we did. They promoted the rational analysis of economic questions in a rational way. I thought they were a very effective organization.

EH: You have discussed the primary position of the Treasury, in conjunction with the Council and the BOB, in economic policy-making. Treasury, of course, has an external constituency, has a bias and a mission--how does it get in the front row, unlike Labor and Commerce? What's the distinction?

GA: I think they have operating responsibilities--action responsibilities--in a number of very vital areas.

DD: The secretary of the Treasury is the chief financial officer of the United States. He feels that he has a special responsibility in anything you call financial.

GA: He's the one who has to work with the Congress on any legislation. The Council never was involved in legislative action. We testified before committees--and I'd be glad to explain the limitations on that testimony. But the operational responsibilities on taxes were in the hands of the Treasury, and also on debt financing, balance of payments, monetary operations.

EH: The president simply can't ignore the Treasury--he can ignore the Department of Labor for long periods of time?

GA: I think he can.

AL: Labor and Commerce have their contacts with organized labor and organized groups in business, but Treasury certainly has contacts with the banking community, which makes it also a constituency group different from the Council. Why has Labor, which deals with the working men on behalf of the working men and women in the country as well as organized labor, never been able to get that degree of recognition? These so-called interest group agencies or interest-identifying agencies are never included as part of the Troika or Quadriad.

GA: I think a couple of distinctions need to be made here. One is on the matter for discussion; in this period, most of the major issues were macro economic policy issues, which essentially means fiscal and monetary policy. This is where the action was. The anti-inflation business was another major activity; efforts were frequently made to bring Commerce and Labor into that "guideposting" activity, but they failed because of those agencies' lack of sympathy with the objectives, in part because of their constituent relations. Obviously, if it was a matter of action on labor legislation, Labor was involved. But even the minimum wage has important macro aspects and the Troika people had important input there. But on fiscal or monetary policy, tax policy, size of the budget, Connor and Wirtz didn't really have much to contribute. Their ideas about these subjects were ill-formed; it wasn't that there weren't people in their agencies who were intelligent in respect to these issues, but that they were further down; the principals spent most of their time at a big administrative job and couldn't really get into the analysis of those issues. They didn't really represent an independent source of ideas or advice, or didn't really have much to contribute, except perhaps prejudices or political notions. Wirtz had very strong ideas about the political desirability—or lack of it—of the tax increase, for example, and he always resented that he wasn't able to get to the President frequently to tell him what his views were.

As you say, not only Labor and Commerce have economists and responsibilities in the economic area—Agriculture, Interior, Housing, probably some others also do. Of course, when questions came up in these areas, not just Treasury, Budget Bureau and Council were involved. On agriculture questions, it was Agriculture, Council, and often Budget Bureau. On farm price problems Orville Freeman, Charlie Schultze and I had numerous sessions with the President, and especially with Joe Califano. I don't know whether LBJ disliked Orville Freeman, but he (LBJ) somehow liked to have most of these questions that involved Agriculture thrashed out through Joe Califano. We spent interminable sessions thrashing over agricultural prices with Joe Califano and Freeman.

DD: I think that those agencies have always been in a more political position.

GA: Sure, and they clearly have a constituency that they have some responsibility to protect.

AL: I'm inclined to think that the distinction you make—what you call macro and micro—has a great deal to do with it. The Treasury sees the financial situation of the United States as a whole; so does the Fed in a way and the Council, whereas the departments are looking at it somehow from the standpoint of a lower conceptual level, a particular approach to policy rather than the overall.

SM: How much of the Council's time was spent on macro matters, like taxes and balance of payments as opposed to micro matters like regulation or Great Society or agriculture?

GA: You'd be surprised at how much of the time of the Council went into micro matters, certainly if you take account of the staff work. The staff tended to spend much more of their time on micro matters; some of them worked exclusively on micro topics.

EH: They had desk assignments to be concerned about?

GA: Yes, those issues did not as often come up to the level of the Council or the White House because they were the kinds of things that usually got settled lower down in the government.

EH: Did they work closely with the BOB people?

GA: Often very closely.

EH: The Department of Labor? Labor economists would work with the labor program officers and they'd give a judgment on the agency?

GA: Right. We were frequently involved in agricultural questions. On the financial side, a fairly large investment over several years was made by the Council in financial reforms. The Financial Institutions Act. There were, I think, four big interdepartmental committees set up to consider the implications of the report of the Commission on Money and Credit. I think we chaired each of those committees.

EH: The Heineman Committee, as you know, toyed with the idea of a Department of Economic Affairs—it eventually went up in a message. The argument, I recall, was to overcome the constituency problem and elevate it. Would this have been a good idea, if it were politically feasible, which it was not? Would that have changed the tenor of economic policymaking?

GA: I was very enthusiastic about it and strongly supported it, for exactly that reason—that it would get rid of the constituency relations. Whether it would have worked, I don't know, but I thought it was, in principle, a great idea.

EH: What would combining Labor and Commerce have added that wasn't in the Council at that time in economic policy?

GA: It certainly would have added a more balanced view of the nature of problems from the national standpoint, rather than from the standpoint of particular interests. I doubt that you could have gotten rid of the Council with such a department; I think the president has to have at least a small staff of professionally trained people just to deal with the problems as they come to his office, quite apart from giving him major advice or developing policy alternatives. But it certainly might have been effective. If you could figure out whom to appoint to the position there--I'd assume that you would get lawyers, educators. It's hard to imagine who would be a secretary of Economic Affairs, embracing both Labor's and Commerce's responsibilities--possibly you could get a financial person. But at least you'd approach problems from a broader national standpoint, national interest.

ML: What was the nature of the interaction between LBJ and particular interest groups? Did you have a perception that interest groups had access to LBJ directly or did interest groups go through various Cabinet departments?

GA: LBJ strongly valued his ability to go directly to business groups and to labor organizations. He frequently consulted George Meany on questions. The chairman of the Business Council would often be questioned on his views on issues directly by the President with no intervention, but often also by somebody when the President asked to find out what so and so thinks. On a number of occasions, LBJ met with the leadership of the Executive Council of the AFL-CIO, with the executive committee or whatever it was of the Business Council. We often attended those meetings. LBJ, being concerned with the politics or the feasibility of economic action and never wanting to lose a battle, wanted to be sure he could win it before he got into it, to be as sure as one could be. He wasn't content to ask Bill Wirtz to find out what labor thinks of this; he often wanted to find out directly. Similarly, he didn't only ask Connor to consult with businessmen; he wanted to consult with them directly and very often did.

ML: Did interest groups ever approach the Council to push their viewpoints?

GA: Oh yes, sure. We could usually dismiss them fairly perfunctorily by listening to what they had to say and saying, "Obviously this question will have to be referred to the appropriate agencies." There was never any effort to put pressure on us. There wasn't any way to put pressure on us. One of your questions relates to the usefulness of having academics in these positions. I think that it's damned important because our careers are not in the government, our careers are not in industry or any place else. We could be as free as we pleased. We could quit tomorrow and walk out. That's one reason I think that the short-termers are desirable in these positions. You're really much more independent; if people do try to push you around, you don't have to take it. The other reason, of course, is that academics are willing to work ten times as hard as people who are career people. You're down there for two or three years and you think nothing at all of working an eighty-hour week and sometimes a hundred; you can't expect people to do that on a regular basis. That's why I think this kind of staff has to be short-term. Somehow I really believe there's a great advantage in the lack of commitment, the lack of career; your career is not going to be advanced by what you do there, your progression is in another area. Nevertheless, it's fascinating work; it's obviously very important; you work like the devil.

EH: Do you think that after a reasonable period of time you pick up the institutional knowledge required to function in the government?

GA: That is a problem. I have always thought that it would be desirable to have some continuing element in the Council staff. We always did try to have some. But it's very hard to find people who have been in the government to come to the Council on a one- or two-year loan. They've been in the government, they've become a little stodgy and somewhat willing to rely on the conventional answers to questions. But there are obviously some possibilities for finding really first-rate people in the government who can either have a continuing career in the Council or who can be brought in on call. I think the practice is continuing of trying to have a few such people, but it's difficult.

EH: Do you think it's a good idea for the Council to be a collegial body--three people, rather than one chairman and a lot of staff? What's gained?

GA: You gain the opportunity to recruit two very senior people, prestigious and able people, by having those two positions; I don't think you could get people of that quality just as staff members.

EH: When it comes to the actual work, the division of labor, three are stronger than one, I suppose?

GA: Oh, yes, you need at least three very good people. In fact, often some of our staff were better than the members of the Council: Ken Arrow, Bob Solow, and some of the young guys like Dick Cooper, who is just an absolute whiz. You need a lot of strength, but you don't need a big organization. I would continue to argue that, at least given the existing role of the Council, a professional staff of less than twenty is an advantage.

EH: Did you see the Klein memo that went to Carter in the summer of 1976 recommending that the Council virtually swallow up BLS and the Current Population Survey, and have micro sectors with big staffs?

GA: That would be a terrible mistake, especially giving it operational jobs in respect to the statistical work of the government. That doesn't make sense at all.

EH: The general argument was that the Council is undergunned and undermanned and just can't possibly compete with bureaucracies, can't possibly watch the economy carefully.

GA: I don't agree.

EH: Did you get the right kind of analytic help from the agencies?

GA: Yes, on the whole we did, almost always. One of the jobs of our staff people was to cultivate good relations with people who really counted in the agencies so they'd know where to go to get information. I don't recall any instance in which there was any withholding of statistical information. Always very cooperative at that point.

EH: Do you think that economists sometimes carry as part of their ideology an antipathy to bureaucracy because it's not a market mechanism?

GA: Yes, indeed.

EH: Does this sometimes carry over into dealing with bureaucracy?

GA: I think probably it does, yes. Perhaps the academics at the Council did tend to sneer a little at the bureaucrats. Maybe I did, too. Maybe some of them ought to be sneered at, I don't know. I believe that there was a little bit of a chip on the shoulder with respect to the quality of analysis in the bureaus, and the image of the bureaucrat—the guy who knocks off at 5:15 and goes home. We were much superior; we worked till midnight. That's part of the reward for being on the Council staff: you can feel superior to the guys who don't work so hard.

Within a short time, however, our Council staff located the really knowledgeable and imaginative people in the bureaus. Presumably it was part of the lore that was passed on from one man to his successor at the staff level. The staff members had very different effectiveness; they weren't all successful, but on the whole I think the quality of our staff was pretty good and they delivered quite well.

SM: What about the macro modeling side of the Council's work as a necessary input in making decisions? Were you getting advice from these great big models—the MIT model?

GA: The MIT wasn't operational in my day; it was still under construction. But there were big models. Commerce had a model that had been developed by Larry Klein; I guess he handed it over to Commerce. For a while the Brookings model was almost operational. There was one at Michigan. Since then, of course, there are several more of them. I think our view always was that we were very interested in what the big models were saying, but we had an independent judgment. By now the Council may have several big models going, I don't know. But certainly, in our day, the forecasts were based on relatively simple models, with a relatively small number of equations and a fair amount of judgment used in doctoring the equations or filling in their missing inputs. I guess I would argue--it may even still be the case--that a simple model, with a great deal of very good judgment, and with the input of a great deal of information that is not fully reducible to numerical form, still gives the best forecasts, at least for the big macro variables. What the large models can do is to generate output in much more detail than a simple model can.

SM: Were there some questions about what was going to be happening--for example, at the end of 1967--when you should push for a tax increase, the projections really must have been crucial. How did you go about trying to get some more input about the future under those circumstances?

GA: You immersed yourself in the information both qualitative and statistical. Incidentially, from the first Council I served on, I never was on the forecasting end. Art Okun had--still does have--tremendous judgment and intuition; Art was a staff member doing forecasting before he became a member of the Council. George Perry was also very good. David Lusher, who was our one civil servant on the Council, going back to the days of the founding of the Council, and who spent the rest of his life there, was that kind of forecaster--perhaps even more impressionistic than the others, but with a very fine sense for what was happening.

Reconstructing Policy Decisions

EH: I thought we might move now to a reconstruction of policy cases. We could begin with the question of the tax increase in relation to the war and inflation. The second big area would be wage-price guideposts. Of course, questions of relations with the Fed and questions about the balance of payments are interrelated with those. You may have other areas that you would like to talk about.

GA: I said a little earlier that in January, 1965 the economy was still well below full employment, and the view of the economists was that it needed stimulus. We advocated and got agreement on substantial removal of all of the manufacturers' excise taxes that had been adopted during the Korean War, which gave a substantial fiscal boost. It was our view, however--the view of the Council and, my memory is, of the Budget Bureau--that, in addition to the excise tax cuts, it would be desirable to have a somewhat larger expenditure budget than the President's guidelines had provided. At the end of 1964 and early 1965, I know that I made the case--I'm almost positive Charlie Schultze supported it--that there should be a couple of billion dollars more on the expenditure

246

side, primarily in education and, I think, social security.

EH: Did not the 1964 Samuelson task force make that recommendation?

GA: It's conceivable.

EH: More stimulus to the economy by spending.

GA: Yes, as well as the tax reduction. The alternatives obviously were whether or not to put a couple of extra billion dollars into education and social security with a macro economic objective. As I recall, the Treasury was opposed; the Council and perhaps the Budget Bureau were really the only ones interested in this idea. Of course, it would have further enlarged the deficit, which was still sizable. So the political dimensions of the problem were essentially the prejudices about the size of the deficit, versus the gains to be achieved--political as well as economic--by more rapid reduction of unemployment and faster increase in the GNP. The economic analysis contributing to it was a straight set of macro economic projections of the standard sort, which showed that the path of GNP with the extra budget expenditures would be somewhat higher, and the unemployment rate would fall somewhat faster. It was just a straight question of whether you want a more rapid expansion of the economy. And we advised the President to do so. This was either in early 1965 or at the very end of 1964--it was during the final stages of wrapping up the budget. The President was interested in our point of view and willing to explore it with us. I have a hunch that he had some consultation about it with people in the Congress, and perhaps also with personal advisers outside the government.

In the end he proposed a deal. He said, "Look, if you think this is so important, and in the interests of the country, let's set up two meetings within the next ten days--one with the Executive Council of the AFL-CIO and the other with the leadership of the Business Council. You can come to the meeting and make your case, and we'll see how it's received."

This would be additional fiscal stimulus. This is really the only case in which I saw the President allow an advocacy to be tried out on outsiders. It was a fascinating experience. I made my pitch, first to the AFL-CIO group, which was delighted to get in to see the President because they wanted to talk to him about repealing 14B of the Taft-Hartley Act. They had never been able to get him committed to the repeal of 14B. I made my pitch about how we could reduce the unemployment rate faster, and at the same time support education and the low-income beneficiaries of Social Security; I talked about the unemployed in particular. Not a single one of those guys even listened. As soon as I got through, they started to push the President about 14B. I was so disgusted with this group, which I had thought was so

proud of its liberal credentials. Incidentally, LBJ didn't
give them any comfort on 14B. But they weren't interested in
fiscal stimulus; they didn't even bother to talk about the
question. A couple of days later LBJ got the Business Council in the Cabinet Room. I presented essentially the same
pitch and there was discussion. A number volunteered the
view that this would be unwise: it would increase the deficit, increase the danger of inflation. LBJ went around the
circle and asked each one for his opinion. Only one supported it. Tom Watson thought that it might be a good idea
not to worry so much about the deficit, and get the economy
moving a little faster. But I had my chance to make my case.
It had no political appeal to anyone, so that was the end of
it.

EH: Johnson very much thought in terms of leaders as barometers
of opinion beyond them, didn't he?

GA: Yes, he did. I think he thought that by talking to a half
dozen business leaders he somehow got the views of the entire
business community they represented. I don't know whether he
felt the same way about labor leadership. He was not highly
enamored of Meany and those old guys on the executive council, but he recognized their political importance.

SM: Could you carry us through the tax issue?

GA: All right, tax increase issue at the end of 1965. I imagine
that this ground is fairly familiar to everybody, but I think
there are some misunderstandings about some aspects of it.
If you want to go through it systematically, the alternatives, I suppose, were whether the President should ask for a
tax increase. He had two other alternatives that really
weren't alternatives because, in a sense, they were ruled out
by his values. Alternatively, he might have substantially
cut government expenditures--non-defense expenditures--which
meant his Great Society programs. He just was not going to
do that. Those were his children, his babies--he used that
phrase many times. Those were what he'd be remembered for.
Another possibility--certainly one he wasn't ready to
consider--was to tighten monetary policy instead of fiscal
policy. His prejudices certainly did not allow that. Let's
define the period that we're talking about as between, let's
say, October 1965 and the time the economic, budget and State
of the Union messages had to go up at the end of January.
The discussion, of course, continued long after, but that was
the crucial period when LBJ had to decide whether he was
going to go for a tax increase. I believe it is frequently
assumed that at this period the Council of Economic Advisers
and perhaps other people were misinformed about some of the
facts, or what were later to emerge as facts, about the size
of prospective government expenditures, and that their advice
was handicapped by lack of understanding of what the real
questions were. I would like to try very hard to disillusion

anybody who believes that. In the first place, we knew what numbers were being talked about, and we also knew very well that, whatever those numbers, they weren't nearly big enough in terms of what was going to happen to defense expenditures. Certainly there was a period in the middle of the summer, July and maybe August, when there may have been a real effort by LBJ to conceal what he thought his commitment was to the Defense Department in terms of programs and what the cost of that would be. But he couldn't conceal that from the Budget Bureau, or from anyone who had been around Washington and knew something about what happens during wars. In any case, we had all the evidence we needed to conclude without any question, certainly by November or early December, that a tax increase was absolutely necessary if we were going to avoid substantial inflation in 1966. So the proposal for a tax increase was well formulated and strongly supported by Treasury, Council, and Budget Bureau in the late fall and throughout this period.

DD: Did you believe you knew the figures, Gardner, on the escalation of Vietnam spending?

GA: There is a famous memorandum--the only memorandum in this period that, so far as I know, has been published--in response to the President's request about what I thought of two alternative budget numbers. I don't remember the numbers precisely, probably $110 and $115 billion. This is the memo that LBJ put in his book, <u>Vantage Point</u>. It sounds as though the only sort of discussion that ever was held about the question of the need for a tax increase was whether a budget of either $110 or $115 billion would require a tax increase. I am reported as saying that the lower figure, whatever it was, very probably would require a tax increase and the higher figure certainly would. But the whole point of the exercise was that we knew damned well that neither of these figures was in the least bit accurate, that the real figure they were talking about--the military program that had been approved--was represented by a substantially larger figure. Nobody knew precisely what that figure was, but it was surely above the $115 billion. So there was cerainly no question about absence of sufficient information to reach a policy judgment, and the policy judgment was very definite and clear that we needed a tax increase. This discussion of taxes was interrupted by that little incident of the discount rate increase in December, which irritated all of us considerably. Our view--in the Council, at least--was that the question as to how we should meet the requirement for economic restraint should have been looked at <u>jointly</u> by the Fed and the administration, and all alternatives of monetary policy or fiscal policy or some combination ought to have been considered. Indeed, such discussions were informally underway, and we thought that the Fed had jumped the gun, essentially without notice, to foreclose the issue by resolving it themselves in terms of this action. The action was taken without consultation and may or may not have been the best way to go about it.

SM: Did you say that discussions were underway with the Fed just prior to that raising of the discount rate as to how to reduce the level of aggregate demand?

GA: Certainly at the staff level and at the level of the Council with the senior technicians in the Fed, this was under constant discussion. On the level of analysis, the top Fed economists were in continuous contact with the Council members and our fiscal staff. Certainly at some of our weekly lunches with the Fed during the fall, the question of tax increase came up, definitely.

EH: Dewey, you were on the Board by this time.

DD: Sure, I was on the Board--one of the four versus the three on the vote.

EH: You voted in favor of raising the discount rate?

DD: Yes. We started really thinking a little bit in that direction in July 1965.

GA: Which direction--the tax increase or the discount increase?

DD: The need for restraints, certainly. There was uneasiness. Martin had some sort of pipeline to David Packard. I had a gut feeling that the figures were going to accelerate a lot more and said so at a meeting. Martin called me into his office and said, "You know, I've been talking to David Packard and you're right." He said, "These things are going to go way beyond what the administration has admitted."

EH: And David Packard knew about war production?

DD: Yes.

GA: There was a period of a couple of months--six weeks maybe--in the summer, in which there was, I think, a deliberate effort not to let anybody know what was going on. But the people in Defense knew it, and the people in Budget and Council did not know it.

DD: Defense knew it, and Martin had some contacts there. Martin claims that he had a number of go-rounds with Johnson directly on this. He thought he had the President recognizing that this would be a first step because the President still hadn't come around to the tax proposal at all. Martin thought the President was really thinking, "Well, yes, maybe you fellows need to do something because then I won't have to step up to bat on that tax thing right away." Martin has always denied that raising the discount rate was such a great surprise to all concerned. If anything, the Fed moved too late on the need for restraint. It really should have been putting that in action earlier. Some of the governors who voted against it always said in retrospect that they felt we were right. Sherm Maisel, one of my other colleagues, has always made the point that Gardner is making that we should have waited until January and been part and parcel of a coherent program, but there was no assurance that we would get any restraint program in January at that time. Fred Deming in Treasury, for example, was acknowledging no need for any kind of restraint; he was not out fighting for a tax increase at that point.

GA: In retrospect, or even at the time, I would certainly agree that it might have been a reasonable proposition that the first step should have been a discount rate increase and that it should have come even earlier than it did. But it certainly came, as far as I'm concerned, as a surprise--not as part of any program that was discussed or rationalized in any way. And at a time when we thought we were having discussions about what the total government response ought to be. It's an interesting historical point. However, the protagonists in this discussion, once the discount rate increase was out of the way, certainly did not believe that the discount rate took care of the problem. We thought a tax increase was needed, and pushed as hard as ever. Actually, there was sort of a make-up meeting held down at the LBJ ranch in either late December or early January in which LBJ had invited down for the weekend the Troika members and Bill Martin. That was the first time that Bill and I resumed speaking. We sat around the pool part of the time, on the lawn another part of the time, and we had a long walk through the countryside, during which the subject of discussion was what kind of tax increase program should we have. At that point LBJ was very, very careful not to let anybody know how he was thinking. But I came back from that meeting with a clear conviction that he was ready to go on a tax increase of some kind.

DD: So did Martin.

GA: Yes, but that decision was not made at that point.

EH: This is before the budget has gone up?

GA: Oh, yes. Either the end of December or very early January. During the next couple of weeks there were many discussions. The groups were kept very small because LBJ was just paranoid, not only about letting anyone know how he was going to come down on this question, but even about people knowing it was under discussion. I was at a meeting with Wilbur Mills-- and I think only Wilbur from the Congress--in which LBJ put the question to Wilbur as to what he thought would be the desirability or the feasibility of a tax increase. I don't remember with absolute clarity what Wilbur said about the necessity or the appropriateness, but I do remember that he said absolutely it was a political impossibility, with no chance of getting a tax bill through the Ways and Means Committee. His answer was absolutely clear-cut: "A tax increase is out of the question."

EH: It wasn't just because it was an election year?

GA: I don't really think so.

JG: I understand he never had much faith in forecasts or any economic figures at all.

GA: There is something to that. Wilbur had his own private economist--by the name of Norman Ture--who throughout this period was violently opposed to a tax increase.

EH: Was he a staff person for Ways and Means?

GA: No, he was not a staff person with Ways and Means. Maybe at times he was a consultant. He was at that point a Washington-based economist, I think, in a private consulting firm. He was very close to Wilbur and one whom Wilbur trusted very much. Ture is one of the villains in the succeeding drama, I think, because of his influence on Mills. I'm sure that I remember LBJ also reporting conversations that he had had with business leaders about the question of a tax increase; this is long before that famous dinner in which he asked people to raise their hands if they thought the tax increase was desirable (and no one did). He did consult a lot of people. He was getting advice, strong advice, from outside economists, from Walter Heller and Paul Samuelson, I know. If I'm not mistaken we encouraged them to try to convey their views to LBJ. He included McNamara in this discussion; I'm sure Clark Clifford and probably David Ginsburg, who was a person he greatly trusted. He certainly included Clifford and Ginsburg in the later stages, but I believe they were already in it at this stage. I don't know all of what went through LBJ's mind in reaching his decision which was against the unanimous advice of his presumably principal advisers in this area: the Treasury, Council and Budget Bureau.

The political dimensions of it, as he described them, involved first his ruling out the alternative of a cut in his Great Society programs. His conviction was--he thought of himself as a political expert--that there was not a dream of a chance of getting a tax increase and he did not want to make a recommendation that would then be defeated and indeed perhaps even be ignored, in the sense that he couldn't even get the committees to hold hearings on the bill. There was some possibility that that would be the case, that hearings would not even be held. My impression is that Wilbur Mills, in my presence, told him that they would not hold hearings on a tax increase bill.

One always wonders to what extent Johnson believed that a request for a tax increase at that point would strengthen the opposition to his Vietnam policy. I think that later on that was an issue; but, at that time, Vietnam policy was still overwhelmingly endorsed by public opinion. I don't know whether he thought: "If we make people pay for this, then they'll change their view of how important it is to pursue it." I'm clear that McNamara expressed that point of view. He already saw the possibility--whether already in January or whether it was only in May--that the Vietnam War, popular as it was then, was not going to remain popular, and that a tax increase could hasten that opposition. Anyway, LBJ kept the issue formally open until the very last minute, and then he said, "We will not request a tax increase."

It was about the latest point possible to get it into the message. What he did finally agree to do was to go for some very minor tax adjustments, which were enacted--speeding up of collections on both personal income and corporate income tax and, I believe, postponement of the step decreases that had already been legislated in the telephone and automobile taxes. Those taxes had been scheduled to be reduced, and he recommended that the scheduled reductions be suspended. The one thing that we thought we got out of it was his willingness to put a lot of language into the 1966 Economic Report, and to let us start making speeches and talking to the press about the dangers of a <u>future</u> situation of excessive demand, and about the need to be ready always to reconsider fiscal policy. If you read even the President's Report, which is the first two pages of the 1966 Economic Report, you'll find that we got him to say some very strong things about how inflation in this new situation was a serious danger: "We have to stand ready to reconsider our fiscal policy at short notice. I will not hesitate if necessary to ask for a tax increase." Our report was full of it. We could start going around the country and saying, "This is a very serious problem. We've got to be ready to face up to it. It may be necessary to have a tax increase--not yet, of course, but that time may come. We've got to be alert." That's what we managed to get out of it. And at least for a while we managed to keep LBJ quiet about monetary policy-- quite an achievement--which then, of course, did proceed to tighten up rapidly.

DD: Martin had this great rapport with Wilbur Mills, and Martin never had any sense that there was the slightest possibility of a tax increase from LBJ. This may have been part of Martin's thinking when he was looking at the discount rate question and the further tightening by the Fed. There wasn't any alternative. Somebody had to do it.

EH: Mills had a very well-deserved reputation for never taking a question to the floor unless he knew he had the votes, and Johnson knew that.

GA: All right. The tax increase recommendation was not made in the January, 1966 budget. The issue remained open all during the year and the discussion continued with mainly the same protagonists, except that to a somewhat larger extent, and at various times, other people either tried to get into the act or were invited into the act. Moreover, as the problem became more obvious, the media and the interest groups began to take a greater interest in it than they had in 1965.

In 1966 you had the credit tightening and you began to have some inflation. The alternatives and the issues remained pretty much the same; it was only the evidence that was changing the record. We finally did get LBJ to recommend a modest package of fiscal measures in the late summer of 1966, which were quickly adopted: the suspension of the investment tax credit, some budget cuts, expenditure cuts. But these were obviously not highly effective. The real anti-inflation battle was being fought by monetary policy, which by the end of the year had pushed the economy to the verge of what we continued to refer to as a mini-recession. That made the first half of 1967 a very soft economy, with considerable easing of the rate of inflation and cessation of the decline in unemployment--maybe for a quarter or two a reverse, a slight increase in unemployment. The inflation then continued at a very high level, and the level of unemployment remained well below the 4 percent figure, which had previously been regarded as the inflationary threshold.

One of the more interesting, and discouraging, things to me was the role of the press during this period. Both the New York Times and the Washington Post strongly opposed any tax increase during 1966 when the question was debated as an essentially academic issue and even in 1967 after the President did recommend a tax increase. I don't know when they switched position--in 1968, if they ever did. The editorials in these two papers on the subject were written by two economists. Murray Rossant with the Times. I don't recall the name of the man at the Post. In any case, we considered their editorials not only wrong but very misleading, not only reaching the wrong conclusion, but very badly argued. We made several attempts to try to get the Times and Post to change their editorial policy in this respect. We used all kinds of efforts to get at the Times management; I was not directly involved in doing it, but various emissaries did try to do so.

DD: The Treasury was involved.

GA: Without any success. After one particularly offensive editorial in the Post, I wrote a letter to Katharine Graham and told her how disappointed I was and how mistaken I thought this policy was. I was somewhat carried away, I believe. She came back with one of the most scorching responses I have ever received on anything. Obviously she was not going to make any changes. That was his area--he was the editorial writer and she was not going to interfere. I don't know how important those editorials were, but it bothered us a great deal that the two best journals of opinion in the United States were on what was clearly the wrong side of a major public issue.

But within the government, the basic issue was still the same. It became more and more clear as the year wore on that the tax increase advice we had given in 1965 was right, that we would be a hell of a lot better off if we'd had a tax increase. The President was entirely convinced that he couldn't get it, that it would be a mistake to ask for it, and that it would boomerang in terms of substantial cuts in his social programs. He seemed obsessed with the conviction that he would be defeated if he insisted on a tax increase. As a political leader, he believed he couldn't afford to lose a major battle on a major issue of policy; his international stature and domestic ability to lead the country would be seriously weakened by a major defeat.

I am convinced that from the fall of 1965 on he had no question in his mind that the failure to raise taxes would have very serious results. He never questioned that. He might not have been willing to face up to it at all times, but deep down I think he was absolutely convinced of it; he never tried to argue that.

SM: But he never had the idea to let the Fed take the heat for a policy that was reducing demand, even though publicly he may not have been in favor of that policy?

GA: I can't imagine that he would have been satisfied to let that happen.

DD: I still think that, despite his initial, public blast, he might privately not have been so upset at the Fed's first move. But as that carried through you got extremely high interest rates and a credit crunch in the fall of 1966.

GA: Well, in 1967 he did recommend a tax increase.

IB: Facing the difficulties of Mills on the one side and not wanting a vote against the Vietnam War, was it essentially the President's belief that the war had to be prosecuted at the cost of inflation and economic disrepair?

GA: He was certainly prepared to accept that, yes.

EH: He wanted both. He wanted his programs and he wanted the war. He could have given up one or the other.

GA: No. You know, at the time, I thought that his political judgment was wrong. I thought that reason would succeed if we were allowed to present the case. But when he recommended it in January 1967 and didn't get it till July 1968, and this under circumstances in which the evidence as to what was happening was obvious to everyone, convinces me that his political judgment was absolutely right: he couldn't have gotten a tax increase.

EH: How did you turn him around in the fall of 1966?

GA: In the January 1967 messages he did make the recommendation. I'm not sure I remember the specific occasion on which he finally capitulated or what may have been the process. I suspect it was just the general buildup of the inflation and the unfortunate results of a monetary crunch. When he recommended it in January 1967, he was still very doubtful that he would get it, but at this point he believed that he had no alternative but to recommend what clearly was the right thing to do. At that point he began to get some opposition inside the government. For example, Bill Wirtz mounted a late initiative trying to turn him around and not recommend the tax increase. And I think there were some others. I think Califano was convinced at all points of the need for it. President Johnson made the recommendation in the January messages, but he didn't introduce the legislation because it was clear that there was a mini-recession underway in the first half of the year. He recommended the tax increase be legislated to become effective in October or something like that. Then in August, he sent up a specific bill, which was introduced and remained in the Congress until it was enacted with some further changes in July of 1968.

JG: In the summer of 1967 Johnson actually proposed the legislation for the surcharge. I understood that he had perhaps made the decision earlier, in June or July, and for one reason or another delayed until August actually sending the proposal to Congress. That might have had something to do with getting a report from McNamara on Vietnam. There were a number of delays and you encouraged him to go ahead with it perhaps in July, but he resisted until August.

GA: We wanted him to send up the legislation in January to become effective at the end of the year. He didn't do it. We weren't terribly unhappy about that because we didn't really need it in early 1967; and it gave a little more time for a climate that we considered would be more supportive. The first half of 1967 was a hard time to defend the case for the tax cut. We lost some of our strongest allies: Paul Samuelson, for example, came out saying it was too late. He did not support the tax increase, which I think he later very much regretted. Other private economists were speaking out against it, saying that tight money had already done the job.

SM: So the turndown in the economy in the first two quarters of 1967 really had an effect on the strength of your advocacy of tax cuts at that time?

GA: We certainly were not pushing to have them in effect at that time, but to go into effect later in the year--July or October.

JG: Wilbur Mills said you can't legislate on the basis of economic forecasts, that you have to legislate on the basis of reality, and he wouldn't accept forecasts.

GA: Right, and he kept calling the President's attention to the softness of the economy. One of my most poignant recollections relates to that period--apparently Mills was in the President's office talking with him about the state of the economy and being pushed by the President with the need to get ahead with tax legislation. I didn't know Mills was in the office and I got a telephone call from the President. Early in 1967 in the Economic Report we had, among other things, forecast that profits in 1967 would be essentially the same as in 1966. The President said, "Gardner, what about this profits forecast of yours? Some people are saying that it is much too optimistic and, in fact, profits are going to fall." I said, "Well, Mr. President, you know it's very difficult to forecast profits. My own guess is they'll probably be down a little bit, but we thought it was appropriate to say that they're going to be at about the same level." He sort of cleared his throat and said, "Wilbur Mills is here"--he had the squawk box on. So I continued to say, "But of course...." I was very embarrassed. That was unfair.

SM: By this time in 1967 the Federal Reserve had turned around on monetary policy, had they not? Was that entering your thinking about what was going to be happening to the economy and what you were going to have to be doing?

GA: I'm sure it was. We remained absolutely convinced of the underlying strength of the economy, that the demand explosion would renew itself, and that the problem was not solved. And we remained very strongly of the view that, even if monetary policy itself could do the job, it would be much more appropriate to have a major input from fiscal policy.

DD: The Fed was fighting at that time for the tax increase.

GA: Yes, strongly.

SM: To what extent was there coordination here between monetary and fiscal policy?

GA: It began to improve during that period. Actually, some institutional changes developed. There had never been any effort to coordinate formally either analysis or policy recommendations between the Fed and the Troika. There were informal discussions, but there was no joint staff work and there was never a piece of paper that was signed "We recommend" by the Quadriad--all four of us including Martin.

During that period we did work out a procedure whereby there would be formal joint staff work and agreed estimates—as far as there could be among the people at the technical level—and joint recommendations. Several pieces of paper went to the President with Martin's signature on them along with those of the Troika.

SM: How hard were you pushing the surcharge in the beginning of 1967?

GA: I think the recommendation made in January was that it be effective in October 1967. We would like to have seen the Congress get to work on it so there really would be legislation in place. But around the beginning of the year there was some reason to consider the possibility that there might be a genuine recession. I went down to see LBJ at the ranch in late winter. We talked about the state of the economy. I had brought down the first returns of the Commerce Department Investment Survey, which were very, very bearish, and we talked about whether there was really going to be a downturn in investment. It was a little disturbing to our point of view. We never backed away from our recommendation; but it was not the best time to be going public with this fight. We continued to make speeches pointing out that a tax increase was going to be necessary, that the inflation danger was not averted, that we had to get going on this. The thing was not formally pushed in the Congress. It was Treasury's job to get it up there and to get the hearings on it. I guess we probably were not pushing very hard. By mid-year, we could see that the recovery was coming and that the problem was soon to be back with us and then we really began to push.

SM: I gather your aim—to put it in Phillips curve terms—was not to generate a recession in order to stop the inflation; it was simply to cool off the boom, go back to a sustainable level of output?

GA: Yes. We certainly had no desire to create a recession. You ought to try to find out from Paul McCracken whether, in 1969, there was either a conscious effort to create, or a conscious willingness to risk, a recession in 1969 and 1970. At no point were we willing to contemplate the possibility of risking a recession, nor did we ever think that after that little soft period in the first part of 1967 there was any serious danger.

SM: Was there talk about a danger of getting a positive rate of inflation embedded in everyone's expectations? That came up later, but were you in 1967 talking about the dangers of getting to a higher level of permanent inflation?

GA: Yes, I think so. The theory had not been as well worked out at that point as it was later, though my personal views had long antedated the sort of general professional recognition

of the spiral character of inflation and the difficulty it
brings. That's an old idea of mine, which I had pushed for a
long time. It's hard to reproduce the thinking of those
days. I believe I noticed in Cochrane a memo of mine referring to the spiral character of inflation and the need to
stop it.

EH: You were Assistant Director of the Office of Price Stabilization during the Korean conflict. Would you compare the
Truman administration with the Johnson administration on the
question of war and tax increase? How did the Truman administration and Congress raise taxes?

GA: Congress raised taxes two or three times in the first year of
the Korean War. Truman's approach was not one of modern
economics, but one of old-fashioned patriotism--"We have to
give the boys what they need. We have to raise the money so
that we can fight the war. The patriotic thing to do is to
raise taxes because you have to have the money to spend."
Obviously it isn't so; you can borrow it. But Congress was
certainly very prompt to go ahead with that.

JG: Keyserling was against it. I think he wanted expansion.

GA: In general, that's right. Even during the war, he was a
great expansionist. But he wanted tighter price control and
rollbacks. I had a violent dispute with Keyserling on that
point and I believe that's described in one of the earlier
chapters of Craufurd Goodwin's book Exhortation and Controls.
I'm an old price control hand. I fought World War II in OPA.
I've been an inflation fighter all my life.

JG: Was that sort of argument used by the Johnson administration?
I understand that it wasn't that there was a deliberate
effort to avoid that sort of thing.

GA: Yes, I think so. First, we didn't want to use it because it
wasn't a scientific argument; and I don't think that he
wanted to use it because it seemed to invite opposition to
the war, or opposition to social programs, as much as it
invited support for the tax increase. If you could somehow
argue that the tax increase specifically fights inflation,
perhaps it suggests that it is not the total fiscal balance
that's at fault, and does not remind anyone that there are
other elements in the fiscal balance that could also be
manipulated, such as cutting social programs, or getting rid
of the war.

EH: Was the war-induced inflation a factor in the breakdown of
the wage-price guideposts? The government didn't have its
own house in order and business and labor could say so?

GA: Yes, that's right.

IB: And the sacrifice argument couldn't have been made very effectively in support of the expenditures in Vietnam in the face of the fact that the war was becoming increasingly unpopular.

GA: Yes. By 1967, certainly; 1968, definitely.

SM: Why was it that labor seemed to be so adamantly opposed to any kinds of guideposts or controls?

GA: Pure doctrine, ideology, conviction that such a program will be used to screw labor at the expense of business. It's not a very intellectual argument.

JG: In 1965 service professions had greater wage increases and unions then sought to catch up with non-union labor in 1966, and that's when the breakdown began, 1966 and 1967.

GA: Yes, but I don't know that that would account for their opposition. The labor movement has an institutional opposition to every form of control or interference in the wage level. It deals with their most vital function and purpose in life.

EH: In retrospect, what is your view of the president and the Council taking positions on given wage settlement and price increase controversies case by case?

GA: It was a mistake to have this function in the Council of Economic Advisers, and probably a mistake to involve the President in it so closely. To be sure, the President, and an agency that is known to be very close to him, have a lot more clout, simply because of that association; but I believe it was destructive of the role of the Council as an advisory agency, a kind of scientific, professional agency. And I believe that the President's close personal involvement in it was a political liability for him. If he could have been remote from it and complaints about a particular decision or effort, he could have said, "Well, you know, Harry's got that job, and it's a very important function; and I'm not going to second-guess him."

EH: Were you not moving toward a structure--a Cabinet Committee on Price Stability?

GA: The Cabinet Committee on Price Stability, I guess, actually wasn't even formed until after I left.

EH: Yes, but I think one of the points that Cochrane makes is that by the time Art Okun took over a structure was there and then it was dismantled by Nixon.

GA: In some things I've written, I've attempted to explore the notion of having a really prestigious, powerful organization that is tied to both business and labor organizations, as a sort of legislative arm and an executive center that is distinct from, but supported by, the president. Presumably he introduces the legislation, perhaps appoints the people, but he doesn't get involved in deciding whether this is a good time to fight a wage increase by the steelworkers. Let somebody else take that heat. The president can express full confidence in the machinery, and endorse its work in general terms, but that organization would have sufficient stature of its own to negotiate and attempt to enforce some kind of "social compact," without getting into the politial area of the presidency, and certainly not into the technical staff of the Council of Economic Advisers. I believe that the real failure of the guideposts is because that kind of reorganization never really evolved. To be sure, there was brought into existence under Kennedy--largely at the urging of Walter Heller and the Council--a Labor-Management Advisory Committee. The notion was that this would be the channel through which the incomes policy would get its legitimacy. The problem was that the Labor-Management Advisory Committee was set up with the Secretaries of Commerce and Labor as its joint chairmen, and both Secretaries of Commerce and Labor were opposed to using this machinery as supportive of an incomes policy. The committee even went out of existence for a while; its meetings were obviously unproductive with respect to supporting the guideposts. They talked about non-operational things like productivity, and it never got anywhere. At one point we did persuade Johnson to try to revive the LMAC, and it was briefly reviewed, but I guess it was too late. We did get some kind of general resolution out of them about the importance of the productivity principle in wage setting, but that was just too late. In the Nixon administration, there was a new Labor-Management Advisory Committee--I can't remember what it was called--under John Dunlop. The disaster there is that John Dunlop is completely opposed to any kind of incomes policy, so that the instrument was useless in terms of supporting an anti-inflation program.

SM: Did you assign Council staff to follow these industries where you were worried about prices?

GA: Actually, there was very little staff input into the guide-post business. Usually no more than two or three staff people were involved in that. But later on, as Cochrane described it, we did develop fairly systematic relations with Labor and Commerce to supply current information. For quite a while Labor, Commerce, Agriculture, and Interior, I guess, had an obligation to supply weekly price reports; these reports were supposed to report not merely price changes, as they actually occurred, but also ones that might be expected or anticipated for some reason. We hired essentially only one man to work on wage-price matters, and he was there for a couple of years.

SM: Perhaps you could tell us a little bit about the sorts of threats that the government or President Johnson was willing to use against companies or against labor unions that violated these guideposts you were proposing.

GA: On a couple of occasions, threats were made that I regarded as entirely inappropriate. I think it was not the general practice, though it tended to be in the later days when they got the lawyers into it. First, John Douglas, and later, Stan Ross. They pursued a very mechanical approach of looking for "handles." LBJ was not above using whatever handles he could get hold of. He didn't need to be encouraged. Joe Califano--I guess one of the few things I have ever criticized about Joe was that he was somewhat cavalier about his pressure tactics. As a lawyer, I think he ought to have been a little more careful about using extraneous issues, such as threatening antitrust action with respect to unrelated actions, to get companies to go along with a particular guidepost.

SM: What about the threat of imports or changing tariffs?

GA: That never bothers me at all, at least if you're willing to carry it out. Threatening to lower tariffs or remove import barriers--that's a market mechanism.

EH: Are the aluminum stockpiles the same thing?

GA: Yes. I never was bothered by the use of stockpiles. It seems to me that's what stockpiles ought to be used for. Sometimes, I think, rough threats were made about stockpile policy. Actually, we sometimes didn't even know until later just exactly what was going on there. The President never wanted to lose one of these battles; when he thought he might lose, he told the boys, "You just can't let me down; you've got to find some way to get them in line." This encouraged some people to look for some pretty extraneous kinds of weapons. I was never terribly happy making some of the condemnatory statements that I made. I would be embarrassed if I were to read some of those today. I think the idea of calling people names and questioning their patriotism is not a very good way of going about the government's business. Yet, to some extent, I was involved in that.

SM: The threats that you've mentioned are all on the side of pressure against management. Did you have equivalent threats that you could use on unions?

GA: Yes. Occasionally. In the end we never went through with them, although some people thought we should have. Cochrane describes the Webber case. Webber was the business agent or president of some construction union in New Jersey. I believe there was some evidence that there had been payoffs, or that he was engaged in bribery or something like that. There

was a long discussion, I remember, of whether it was appropriate to use that charge to try to beat down his union's
effort to get a big guidepost-busting settlement. I think in
the end we didn't do it, which I'm rather happy about.

EH: The machinists' strike against the airlines was a crucial
time. Did Johnson give in at that point?

GA: Once he got into it, I think he had no choice. The mistake,
I believe, was in building that up as a big issue. After
all, it was a handful of workers, and it didn't make a damned
bit of difference, in itself. We would have been so much
better off if we had never entered into a public fight. Once
we got into a public confrontation with them, we either had
to win or we took a very serious defeat. We made such a big
thing of it that we took a very serious defeat.

EH: Was it the President's doing to intervene in this one?

GA: I remember this was widely debated and all kinds of views
were sought. I suppose the final decision was made by the
President, but I think on most of the steps in which the
confrontation moved to a higher level, most of his advisers
agreed. He merely took their advice.

SM: Did Johnson push you into intervening in cases that you would
have chosen not to get involved in?

GA: On a few occasions, yes, I think so. We were as guilty as
anyone of looking for fights during that period. We didn't
have to be encouraged to try to find cases where we might be
able to beat down price increases. We got a little tired
after a while of being sent out on wild goose chases in that
respect, but we were looking for fights.

IB: How many of your efforts and interventions targeted on unions
were more symbolic than substantive in a world in which the
public sector wage bill was climbing considerably faster than
the private wage bill in the organized sector? Did you have
the sense that unions were a convenient target that might
help to discipline the rest of the workforce?

GA: We assumed that in the non-union area, wage decisions were
made by management, and we were trying to make very clear to
management what we thought they ought to do. On the other
hand, obviously, there were some pretty strong market pressures here and there that were pushing up some of the non-
union wages, where there was a real need for changes in
relative wages. There wasn't much point in trying to fight
those.

IB: Or any easy way to fight them.

GA: No, no easy way to fight them, even if you wanted to, but I don't think on the whole we wanted to. If you had a reasonably steady base in terms of the organized wages, or, let's say, the major settlements, you could permit a certain amount of change in relative wages, even though it's always on the up side rather than the down side. But we didn't have anything really to hang on to in the case of the big unions. I participated in the discussions with Walter Reuther on a couple of occasions, and with some others, too. In general, however, labor people were much harder to reason with than the businessmen.

AL: What we have lacked in our approach to labor policy is something more than simply approaching it in terms of jawboning techniques or guidelines. We assume somehow that economic policy is something the administration arrives at on a technical basis, but forget that we have a political problem of getting the participants actively to agree on what the formula will be.

GA: I couldn't agree more. I've written at some length that the basic failure of the guideposts is that they were dreamed up by some economists who said, "Here it is, boys," and we expected people to pay attention to them. It's a ridiculous way to try to get people voluntarily to adopt them.

DD: But you did have some principle here. You had the gearing to productivity and all of that.

GA: You should have made some effort to convince people that that was a wise principle and in their interest to accept it—and, indeed, if possible, give them a personal stake in the success of the principle.

EH: It's not clear that it is in their institutional interests, is it?

GA: To any individual group, it is not. It's only that it is in the interest of everybody if everybody should agree. It's not costly to labor if labor as a whole and management as a whole are willing to agree.

EH: Do we want to switch to international questions for a little while?

GA: I could make a few general comments with respect to the role of the Council. Clearly the international area is not one in which the Council was a major actor. The main role in all balance of payment matters was carried by the Treasury, by the Federal Reserve, and, in the White House, by the National Security Council—Kaysen and Bator. In general, the Council was pretty much in full agreement with the basic thrust of the ideas of Kaysen and Bator. I think we were usually quite willing to stand in the wings and be supportive, if necessary; but we were happy to let them carry the economists'

contribution to this discussion. Our special role, especially when Johnson was first coming into office, was to try
to help educate LBJ on the nature of the balance of payments
problem. I remember that we labored over a series of papers,
basically education papers to LBJ, in which we tried to
reduce international economics--which is one of the most
abstruse branches of economics--and balance of payments
analysis to a series of simple, easy lessons that he could
understand. We really sweated over those papers. I've never
worked so hard in a teaching situation.

EH: Did he first prefer to read and then discuss or could you go
in cold and discuss and educate in that way?

GA: He preferred to have a piece of paper.

EH: Then he would like to follow it up and talk?

GA: Yes, almost always. As the years went by--in the 1960s--I
think it became increasingly clear that the dollar was really
overvalued and that sooner or later we were going to have to
bite the bullet and devalue. At least that was our view.
One of the things we tried to do was to make clear to LBJ--
as, I think, earlier Walter Heller and Jim Tobin had tried to
do with Kennedy--that devaluation wasn't really the end of
the world. It was something you didn't want to do, but at
some point you very likely would have to face up to it. Most
economists in the government--particuarly at that time--would
have supported the case that floating exchange rates were
technically better and more efficient in the economic sense
than fixed exchange rates. But it was an exceedingly delicate situation for them; if it were ever mentioned or even
suggested that the President's economists were even dreaming
of the possibility that, at some point, gold payments would
have to be suspended and the dollar would have to fall, there
would have been an instantaneous crisis, which almost surely
would have forced that result to occur. So during this whole
period, most of our academic colleagues couldn't understand
why we wouldn't tell the truth openly: that the dollar was
overvalued and that we would probably either have to devalue
or float. But we recognized that if we ever suggested that
we were even thinking about that, events might well force the
decision, especially if it were attributed to economists who
were supposed to be quite close to the President. So one of
the dangers that always worried me was that some staff member
or Council member in an inadvertent way would admit this
fact, and would foreclose the decision simply by talking
about the possibility. This was recognized in the Treasury
and every other place in the government. We never publicly
even contemplated the possibility that there would be a need
for devaluation. The public posture was that we could patch
it up and muddle through. But as the war went on, as the
balance-of-payments deficits got bigger and bigger, and as
the overhang of dollar liability got greater and greater, we

were in basically an untenable situation. Looking back, I suppose it would have been better if that had been officially recognized several years earlier than it was. We got through the Johnson administration without ever coming to that point, and Nixon had to take the onus of finally closing the gold window in 1971.

All this meant that there was a certain air of unreality to economists about the exercises we were going through on balance of payments. In the Council, we generally loyally supported the Treasury view about the various kinds of efforts that we made to have exchange controls without really having them, to invent ways of enticing or persuading foreigners to hold dollars and not demand gold, and to keep patching things up--things like the Roosa bonds, and the special drawing rights, and all the other things that we were trying to invent to save what was probably an unsavable situation. We did attempt, as far as possible, to avoid the worst kinds of trade restrictions that some people were calling for, and we did get by without any serious trade restrictions. We did a lot of stupid things in the government account: we spent a hell of a lot of money to buy in ways that minimized the balance of payments strain; we shipped beer to Germany for our troops to drink over there and avoided every other expenditure that required foreign exchange. We developed these so-called voluntary capital controls, which I think probably didn't do a great deal of damage. Economists don't like them but they were administered in a way that gave them some flexibility and the possibility of dealing with particular cases.

But this is one of the areas where I, at least, believed that the scientific or professional involvement in the political process really involved some conflicts. I used to get letters from economist colleagues saying, "Why, it's obvious the dollar's overvalued and that you ought to float. Why don't you guys have enough sense to say that?" All you could reply was, "You know, it's not our job to educate the public. It's your job. If that's the way you feel, you're the ones to make that case." On the whole, the international policies of that period, in which the Council was somewhat involved, but the Treasury more so--dealing with the roles of monetary and fiscal policy with respect to the balance of payments-- were developed, and came to be accepted, in at least a somewhat more intelligent way than had previously been the case.

On the organizational front, I have already commented on the Treasury's ability to dominate the action program in that area through its control of the machinery, and I don't know that I have any other interesting observations to make on that side of it.

6
The Council of Economic Advisers Under Chairman Arthur Okun, 1968–1969

Summary History

The selection of CEA member Okun to succeed Ackley as chairman in January 1968 indicated a basic continuation of the policies associated with the Heller-Ackley Councils. At age thirty-nine, Okun was the youngest chairman in the Council's history. He was considered as articulate as his predecessors and as committed to the "New Economics." Basically a "numbers man," he had been responsible for the CEA's forecasts. James Duesenberry also remained on the Council and was joined by Merton Peck, one of Robert McNamara's "whiz kids" in the Defense Department in the early 1960s. With Duesenberry from Harvard and Okun and Peck from Yale, the CEA in the last year of LBJ's presidency had a distinctly Ivy League cast.

Okun had many of the same difficulties that Ackley experienced in dealing with Johnson. By early 1968, the problems in Southeast Asia were increasingly monopolizing the President's time. And when developments like the Pueblo incident, the siege of Khe Sanh, and the Tet offensive were not commanding LBJ's attention, his political problems engulfed him. The challenges from Eugene McCarthy and Robert F. Kennedy for the Democratic party nomination put LBJ in an increasingly vulnerable position. On March 31 that situation was eased, however, when Johnson publicly announced his decision not to seek renomination for the presidency. His plea to Congress at the same time to act on the surcharge proposal also raised hopes that the legislative stalemate might now be broken.

The 10 percent surcharge had never been popular with Congress or with the public. Rather than appealing for support on the basis of war needs, LBJ and his advisers had emphasized the importance of a tax increase to stem inflation, ease the credit situation, and avoid further balance of payments problems. The President's Economic Report and the CEA's Report in early 1968 had both been rather pessimistic about what would happen to the economy if Congress continued to delay action on the August 1967 proposal. Congress, however, was unmoved. Representative Wilbur Mills, Chairman of the House Ways and Means Committee that had bottled up the proposal, refused to consider a tax increase on the basis of forecasts of economic trouble, although he yielded on delaying cuts in automobile and telephone excises and speeding up corporate and personal tax collection.

The administration's predictions soon appeared to be coming true, however, as the GNP increased by $19 billion in the first quarter of 1968, inflation climbed to the 4 percent level, interest rates passed the 1966 peak, and the balance of payments problem worsened. Business leaders and the financial community joined the administration in pushing for the tax proposal. In particular, the failure to act on the surcharge was perceived by the international financial community as fiscally irresponsible and only served to further undermine confidence in the dollar. While the shift to the "two-tier" international gold system eased the situation, the threat of an international financial crisis increased support for the surcharge. What finally assured passage, however, was Johnson's concession to demands from Mills and others for a ceiling on federal expenditures. LBJ had resisted budget cuts because of his desire to maintain and expand his Great Society programs, but when it became evident that such cuts in domestic spending were the price that would have to be paid for passage of the surcharge, he yielded. The size of the budget cut was determined in negotiations between Congress and the administration, the House and the Senate, and Democrats and Republicans. As it was finally worked out, under the leadership of Treasury Secretary Henry Fowler, the surcharge and $6 billion expenditure reduction were added in the Senate to other tax legislation already approved by the House. Although this was an unorthodox approach, Mills yielded. Johnson signed the Revenue and Expenditure Control Act of 1968 on June 28, eighteen months after the surcharge had first been proposed in January 1967.

The surcharge was to be retroactive to April 1 on individual incomes and to January 1 on corporate incomes. Okun and other administration economists expected the surtax to slow down the economy and lead to a lower inflation rate. This would raise the unemployment rate temporarily about 4 percent. After the surcharge went into effect, there was some slowing of the economy, but the boom actually continued. The economists had apparently failed to clearly interpret the economic situation in the early months of 1968 and had underestimated the extent of the economic boom. Consumer spending did not moderate as expected, but actually increased by $5 billion in the third quarter of 1968. Home building had been in a slump early in the year, but the trend was reversed by late 1968. Plant and equipment spending also increased. The administration's fiscal policy appeared to have little effect on the economy. The tax hike had come too late and was too small to reverse the economic pressures that had been building since 1965.

Okun himself has suggested that such factors as expectations of long-term prosperity and the temporary nature of the surcharge probably moderated the impact of the tax increase. Perhaps more important was the Federal Reserve's easing of monetary policy. The CEA and most of the administration's other economists had approved of a more accommodative monetary policy because of their reading of construction industry trends and their fears of excessive fiscal restraint. But both their economic analysis and their fears proved wrong, and the Fed's policy only served to offset efforts at fiscal restraint and feed inflation. When the Fed shifted to a tightened policy later, however, the economy proved no more responsive than it had been to the administration's fiscal policy. The shifts in the Federal Reserve's policies from 1966 through 1968 brought criticism from Congress and increased interest in a monetary rule and closer Congressional control, but the Council backed the Fed in insisting on the continued independence of the board.

Okun had never claimed that the surcharge would end the nation's economic problems, but he had hoped that the government's fiscal restraint would set a good example for business and labor. Although LBJ had set up the new Cabinet Committee on Price Stability on February 23, 1968, little was actually accomplished in the wage-price field before passage of the surcharge simply because Okun and others were reluctant to push for business-labor restraint as long as the government did not itself follow such a policy. The CCPS did undertake studies of medical care prices, the construction industry, and regulated industries, but there was little in the way of specific wage-price action. Okun did manage to secure a CCPS statement critical of the construction industry settlement, but his efforts to stop a copper price hike were futile. No action was taken on the telephone settlement.

As inflation worsened and business-labor settlements continued to exceed administration guidelines, Johnson and others considered the possibility of direct wage and price controls, but Okun managed to convince the administration to continue its jawboning policy. On July 21, the CCPS released a statement, at the suggestion of the CEA, urging all major unions and companies to secure guidepost settlements. Before the November 1968 election the CEA managed to secure a price rescission on home heating oil, a cutback of a steel price hike, and a moderation of an automobile industry price rise (the latter two with the assistance of Defense Department pressure on the industries). After the Republican victory in the fall, the lame-duck Johnson administration was less active. In December, the Labor-Management Advisory Committee reaffirmed its endorsement of the guideposts, and the Cabinet Committee on Price Stability recommended new goals for wage and price negotiations, as well as a number of micro policies involving manpower development, trade, antitrust action, and the like. Okun for his part was less than enthusiastic about the administration's performance in this area. While he felt the guideposts performed an important service, he emphasized the need for specific numerical guidelines, consultation with business and labor, and separation of the responsibility for the guideposts from the CEA and the presidency.

In the last Economic Report of the Kennedy-Johnson years in January 1969, the Council noted the unprecedented economic growth that the nation had undergone since 1961. The Report acknowledged the inflation problem, but insisted that the failure to move to a policy of fiscal restraint soon enough indicated not the failure of the "New Economics" but the need for a more flexible policy that would give the president the authority to raise and lower taxes within prescribed limits without congressional approval. In calling for an extension of the surcharge with discretionary authority to his successor to eliminate it if the economic situation changed, Johnson himself affirmed the need for increased flexibility in fiscal matters. According to Okun, the inflationary problems of 1966-69 did not indicate the need to return to an inactive fiscal policy but rather the increased importance of acting to stabilize the impact of the government's fiscal policy in order to avoid a repetition of the same errors. Whether his successors would view the problem in the same light remained to be seen. What was clear was that the Kennedy-Johnson years had proved that prosperity was sustainable. What remained for the incoming Nixon administration was to deal with the continuing problem of inflation.

Oral History Interview

The President and Economic Policy

EH: Let us turn our attention first to President Johnson. When you became Chairman of the Council, you were dealing with him. Do you think he tried to structure advisory processes so that he would get the result he wanted?

AO: No. The focus of your question is, "Did he fix it so that he heard what he wanted to hear?"

EH: It's not really that; it's the sense that he really knew what he wanted to do right along.

AO: I believe he was more responsive to professional advice and judgment than that statement makes it sound. He listened. He did his homework. He didn't want to go through all the analytical reasoning. My perception is that Kennedy intellectualized problems much more than Johnson. That's partly based on Walter Heller's ability to make direct comparisons. Sounds similar to the analogy between the patient who wants to see the X-ray and the patient who wants to look hard in the physician's eyes when he renders the judgment. Johnson was the second type: he didn't ask to see the X-rays, but he did ask for the judgments and he was responsive to them. He did not play his own economist. He did call on people on the outside, by telephone largely, for reactions. I remember that he once explicitly cited something that Bob Anderson had told him. "I'm sure that's the way he sees it," I replied, "but Mr. President, he doesn't share your values on a lot of things." He said, "You're telling me he's a goddam reactionary, I know that. That's exactly why I called. I wanted to find out what the views of a sophisticated and thoughtful goddam reactionary are and that's what I use Bob Anderson for." He really did have a sense that everybody's advice was somewhat colored by an ideological position. He once chided me: "When you tell me that I ought to cut a Great Society program, I know you mean it because that's not where your natural inclinations are." He was asking what the doctor's bias was and how do you correct for it. But he really took economists and economics very seriously.

LS: If he wasn't interested in your analysis, did you stop giving him analysis?

AO: In the sense of giving him a less detailed presentation of how we arrived at a conclusion, yes. We did sketch roughly what a verdict depended on or why we thought something would be too stimulative. We also tried to give him a sense of the confidence with which we could say that something was dangerous or desirable, a sense also of why something might be controversial and why other people might come to different decisions on it.

LS: Then were all his responses simply to the political feasibility?

AO: It was more nearly: "Okay, you're giving me the best advice you can. If, after some questioning, I have no reason to doubt that this is the best advice I can get and my people are pretty well agreed on it, then I ask can we do it? What are the costs of getting it through?" If it was something legislative, this was a channel in which he operated very comfortably. He loved it. "If you write the bill this way, it'll go to this committee; if you write it this way, you may be able to get it through the Commerce Committee instead of that other one and that chairman is going to like it better. Let's see, we have got this many votes I can count on and there are two more people who may be interested in that. When is that FDIC appointment that this Senator's been trying to push on me? How bad would that be?" He would play his own legislative aide at meetings that had any kind of programmatic or legislative interest.

EH: This was all personal knowledge?

AO: Just personal knowledge. Who the people were, what they cared about. He saw these people a great deal, a big flow of congressional types, including the minority; very obviously very close personal relations with Dirksen were maintained. I heard him say kinder things about Jerry Ford than the ones that were typically quoted in the press when Jerry Ford was President. He thought of Ford as a guy who would be cooperative, who would sense a national interest that ought to be cut out of partisanship. But much of it came from his years on the Hill. He was a master of this notion of how to pass a bill.

EH: Was he less comfortable with the bureaucracy?

AO: Yes, I think so. I didn't see a great deal of it, but I thought that he had weak relations with Willard Wirtz, the Secretary of Labor, and just never really communicated well with him. I don't believe Connor or Sandy Trowbridge as Secretaries of Commerce had strong relations with Johnson; the exception was C. R. Smith at the very end, who had close and long personal relations with the President. For a period right after I became Chairman I was quite concerned that the President didn't seem to be calling me for special things nearly as often as he had Gardner [Ackley]. At one meeting in the White House at the end of April, two and a half months after I'd become Chairman, we really seemed to make a breakthrough. Thereafter I got a lot more requests.

This whole period between the beginning of 1968 and June was focused on the negotiations over the tax surcharge bill. It really looked as though that bill was going down the drain as of late April. The hassle was over how much of a spending cutback the President was willing to accept in order to buy

Mills' support for the bill. He sent him a rather bold memo--I remember signing it very nervously--saying that he needed to make one more try and show a little more willingness to compromise and get it on the public record. We were appealing to him partly on the basis that, in the perception of many of the press and many of the businessmen we talked to, the President's willingness to fight and really to compromise on the spending side to get the tax bill had not been established and that if the thing went down the drain, he would be blamed. We were making a political argument to him. We also reiterated in the memo how important we thought it was to get it, but basically said, "One more try in order to get it. But even if that doesn't work and even if you think there is a low probability of success, you ought to think in terms of the political benefits of getting on record and having made that try and of putting yourself in the position of being ready to pay a higher price than you have indicated at least publicly to date." The next day I was told there was going to be a meeting with Democratic congressional leaders in the cabinet room and that the Troika members were being asked to attend along with the President. He began that meeting by reading my memo with slight censorship of something that could have been interpreted as an unkind reference to Mills. It was apparently the first time he and the President had talked in this whole period and one of the few meetings I did a set of notes on afterwards. I don't know how momentous it was to him, but it was to me. All I know is that the next day I was asked to brief the Cabinet on trying to line up the agencies' support on the tax bill, explaining why we needed it so much and why they had to be willing to take expenditure cuts. Thereafter I had many requests to join the President in talking to congressional leaders, labor leaders, and business leaders, more than I had had in the preceding two months. So how seriously the President takes you is very important.

LS: Can we conclude that it was because you did such a good job of presenting your brief or because you were articulating what he wanted to do anyway?

AO: No idea, really. You always ask yourself, when the President comes down on your side, is it because that's the way he really wanted to go, you gave him the easy road, or because you gave him something.

LS: But you said you gave him a lot of good political reasons for doing it.

AO: Yes.

AL: Is it correct to infer from what you're saying that you did not share the very widespread attitude on the part of intellectuals that Johnson was repulsive, personally, and that this cut off somehow his ability to speak to or your ability to want to press upon him analytical and intellectual problems?

AO: I never had comfortable personal relations with him at all, and we had very different ways of thinking, but he was a damned good student. He was a student of a different sort. He would read a memo, he would cover it, he was proud that he did. On a few occasions he would say, "You told me that in a memo last week. You don't have to tell me that again. I read the memo." He was saying, "I really do my homework." He prided himself on that. If he didn't understand something or if he did hear a counter-argument that you hadn't anticipated, you would get it back. It became very important in writing him a memo or making a proposal to try to anticipate what the objections of a substantive nature would be. What was bold about that late April memo is that we were really trying to make a political point with him, which we very rarely tried to do, because he didn't need any advice on that game. The only time I can really remember his ever spending a significant amount of time intellectualizing and theorizing was on the connection between higher interest rates dampening down rather than intensifying inflation. Then he said, "You have to take me through this and explain why it works this way." He had clearly a very populist attitude toward this: "High interest rates are the worst thing in the world."

RF: Did you get it across?

AO: Yes, yes. He even joked about it. I remember his saying, "Well, maybe it is a lesser evil, but it's hard for a boy from Texas ever to see high interest rates as a lesser evil than anything else." He sensed his own populist attitude. But that was a rare occasion. When there were conflicts in the substantive judgments of his advisers, he would certainly want to know why somebody was giving him a much more bearish economic outlook than somebody else, but there was not a great deal of that.

JG: Did you manage to avoid becoming an object of Johnson's verbal abuse, which many advisers evidently went through at one time or another?

AO: No, I would not characterize that as a typical Johnsonian technique of cross-examination or devil's advocacy. I got bawled out by Johnson on a number of occasions.

EH: When he was a Senator, he had the reputation of being very hard to work for. Was he careful about whom he abused?

AO: Oh, I got bawled out on a number of occasions in a way that could be taken as abuse. His antipathy toward, preoccupation with leaks was something big. If he saw something in the newspaper and he immediately had a suspect, he got on the phone and said, "Why did you talk to him yesterday? Goddam it, why do I have to read these things in the newspaper? I didn't make that decision. It's characterizing my position. Will you stop talking?" Sometimes he'd be right and sometimes he'd be wrong, but once he'd decided it was you, you might as well spare someone else the agony of having to get the same phone call.

EH: Was it brutal or was it done with humor?

AO: Pretty brutal.

EH: But then he would forget about it. The next time you'd see him it might be quite different.

AO: Yes. Or he'd give you an assignment and say, "Do this on your own, because I don't want any of your goddam staff to be talking to the newspapers. I'm only telling this to you. If it comes out, it comes from you." It was impossible to carry out that instruction. If you did get one or more of your colleagues to work on it, they had to take the vow of secrecy.

He made unreasonable demands on your time. You would be trying to get out of the office at 7:15 when Jimmy Jones would call, "The President read about this in the Star; he doesn't understand what it is, and he'd like to have a memo for breakfast tomorrow morning on this." "For breakfast tomorrow morning?" "You heard me, Art, that's what he said. He wants a memo for breakfast." And he got a memo for breakfast, but it was just unreasonable.

That sensitivity about criticism, that tickertape in the office: AP 127 reports that the mayor in Dubuque says that something has happened to unemployment in Dubuque. "Find out if that's right; let's make sure it doesn't happen again. If it's wrong, I want a statement released to the press on this unfair crticism." Again you would be given two hours to respond. But why would it bug him whether the mayor of Dubuque was happy or unhappy?

EH: You talked about the interest rates—could you see his values influencing what he was hearing from you?

AO: Yes. You knew very clearly what his tendencies, liberties, biases were. For example, on all of his Great Society and social programs, it was always redistribution without divisiveness; the emphasis was, "We're giving to the disadvantaged," not "We're taking from the rich." He never wanted to look at that aspect of the redistribution. As long as the economy was growing rapidly and making progress, I believe he really did see an opportunity for shifting things to the public sector, for shifting the distribution of public services toward the disadvantaged without having anybody feel it very much because it would be sharing the gains rather than asking for belt-tightening. You had to put any proposal for income maintenance or job programs in that language. He loved turning tax eaters into tax payers. He privately expressed some quite reactionary views on welfare, concern about disincentive effects, concern about creating a mentality of being on the dole. He really loved programs, educational opportunities. His schoolteacher background came up all the time: this little Mexican kid who really got somewhere because he had the opportunity or who could have gotten somewhere if only he had had the opportunity. And that bizarre statement: "Up to 1963 we had only passed five education bills in the history of this country and now we have passed fifty in the last four years. We've made ten times as much progress in four years." That's another story--counting pieces of legislation as trophies he could hang on the wall, having signing ceremonies and giving you a pen. The only bill I know of that he didn't want to sign publicly was the tax surcharge when it finally went through. I never got a pen for that one. He had something of a small businessman, upward-mobility favoritism.

LS: This idea that you just mentioned--that he saw the fiscal dividend as being able to accomplish something--where did he learn that?

AO: The Council and the Budget Bureau probably helped to get him to focus on that. He picked up many things intuitively, in a way that he couldn't have explained, but he knew that when you had a good year, the revenues went up and the incomes went up and you had some elbow room to do something with it. We did not condition him in terms of categories and labels. Heller would write memos to Kennedy explaining what a fiscal dividend was. You didn't do that with Johnson.

EH: But you were able to moderate his world view, for example, on interest rates?

AO: Yes. He took that very begrudgingly.

EH: Any other examples of how the formal knowledge would moderate and soften his world view?

AO: I can think of one where he was unyielding, thank heavens, and that was on a free trade view. Joe Fowler once had a set of proposals involving some surcharges, and he said, "Joe, you ought to know better than to try to sell me a protectionist measure like that. I'm not going to buy that." Joe said, "Well, Mr. President, I think you would have to concede that that's only a little protectionist." Johnson replied, "A little protectionist is like a little pregnant."
  I don't know whether any of the Budget Bureau and Council efforts ever got him to focus on efficiency of federal programs in a concerted way. He had this tremendous optimism: "Give us some money. We define the problem. I've got all these good people; they'll find a good way of solving the problems with enough money." There really was an unreason-

able optimism about federal delivery systems. Budget Directors worked hard to get him to try to think in terms of what you could do efficiently and what you couldn't do efficiently.

EH: This goes back to his lack of feel for bureaucracy.

AO: Yes.

JJS: Did he ever get any feedback on analytical studies of these programs?

AO: The trouble was that there was very little program evaluation and all the efforts to get program evaluation often got aborted. I remember a couple of Labor Department efforts where they had very carefully put together a little group that was going to sit in the back room and do program evaluation. I remember hearing that the chief evaluator got appointed to be deputy director of the program. He came out of the back room and said, "You know what you guys are doing wrong?" And they said, "You may be right. Why don't you try doing it right?" I'm not sure whether that was a subtraction or an addition to the nation's welfare in having somebody with an idea put into the front line. But when there really seemed to be good program evaluators, they somehow got swallowed into the program.

JJS: Did the Council make any effort to push evaluation?

AO: Yes.

JJS: Did Johnson really want evaluation or did he believe these programs simply were going to work?

AO: That's not an issue that you can really raise at a presidential level. I suppose somebody could have proposed making an initiative or commitment to careful program evaluation. Of course, the PPBS initiative was supposed to be a systematic program evaluation across the board: getting agencies to define what their outputs were, what they were worth, and how much it cost to get them. I don't remember anybody other than Charlie Schultze getting a clear presidential mandate for agency cooperation with PPBS.

EH: You're really saying that the president is very remote from implementation. It's out in the departments.

AO: Yes, and if you told him that story about how the good program evaluator got made deputy director, he'd say, "That's wonderful. Gives us a better chance of making that program work."

EH: He did turn Califano's staff loose on the bureaucracy, but they were very frustrated and ad hoc.

AO: Yes. And there was bureaucracy and bureaucracy. Wilbur Cohen could get almost anything he wanted out of Johnson and knew exactly how to approach the President. Califano would have these carefully constructed task forces but before the task force report was on the President's desk, you would hear that Cohen had gotten a commitment from the President to do thus and so in the January budget. It was clear that Johnson didn't care very much about things rising through channels and his getting the income maintenance task force report. Wilbur sounded as if he had a very good idea and the President bought it. Califano would tear his hair out.

Another big problem we had was trying to find out what was going on in the national security end of things. There we had very little access. Califano didn't know what was going on--at least he always pled equal ignorance--so he couldn't help us. If he wasn't ignorant, he was putting on an awfully good act because he would ask us questions and we didn't know the answers to them. Francis Bator (of McGeorge Bundy's staff) worked very hard to try to get some connection between the national security decisions and economic decisions without much success.

EH: This was primarily because of concern about security?

AO: Concern about security, especially in the context of Vietnam.

EH: Could you point to policy mishaps that followed from that inadequate linkage?

AO: One incident always intrigued me when the Pentagon papers first came out. A critical NSC memo apparently was discussed and approved on, if I recall, April 1 or April 2, 1965; this seemed to be the real step toward the decision that the President finally made on July 28, 1965, for an escalation, which was really the first significant budgetary cost or economic effect of Vietnam. On exactly the same day or one day apart, the President agreed at a meeting to an excise tax cut, which had been foreshadowed in his budget but which he had not sent up explicitly at the time of the budget. In fact, he raised the ante, and he was the one who was pressing to raise the ante to make this a meaningful tax cut and not just a little insignificant one. He wanted it on page 1 and not on page 17. I don't think there was anyone at the NSC meeting who was also at that meeting on cutting excise taxes except Lyndon Johnson. I wonder now whether at any moment in that excise tax meeting it ever occurred to Johnson that there was some connection between this decision to build up troops in Vietnam and this decision to cut taxes as part of his domestic program.

AL: This is one of the tools of power of the top man: controlling those who are invited in or made a part of the policy decision. We tend as academics to assume that everybody knows everything so that everything is all of a piece, but that isn't the way it looks from the top.

AO: There are two hypotheses. LBJ may have been sitting there saying, "If these guys knew that defense spending was going up, they might not be as enthusiastic about an excise tax cut. I want an excise cut that's on page 1 and therefore they don't have to know what's going on in defense spending, and I don't have to get flak from my subordinates. In this way I keep control." That's not my bet as to what was going on in his mind. My bet is that he did not really put these two things together in a concerted way. He had a Vietnam problem and he had domestic prosperity; he wanted to capitalize on the domestic prosperity and, if anything, he may have thought, "Gee, if people are going to get bad news on defense spending, then they'd damned well better get good news on tax cuts." But I don't see that as a conscious, carefully constructed decision that "I know what's best," taking all things into account.

EH: Is the White House really quite separate compartments, without much interweaving, or does presidential style make a difference in interweaving?

AO: I think there was a remarkable degree of compartmentalization between the national security and the domestic policy operations.

EH: No matter who was president?

AO: Well, under Johnson—that's all I can speak for. He wanted it that way. Several explicit decisions had been made for escalation along the course of the Vietnam fiasco and at no time were we ever brought in on one of those decisions until early in March of 1968. One of the first important assignments I had as Chairman came in a secret memo with several alternative add-ons to the defense budget, and with a request for an assessment of what the economic implications of these alternatives would be. I think I smelled that one, that the reason this was coming our way and the previous ones had not was that the President knew very well that we were going to tell him this would have adverse economic implications, requiring either a larger tax increase or a bigger domestic spending cutback, and he wanted that ammunition. In the previous cases, he didn't want to be told—he knew what he would be told. This time he wanted to be told because he wanted to tell the generals that all his economists told him that it would be very bad to make these increases. It turned out that was right. That was the increase he rejected and the one that led to the announcement on March 31, 1968, that he was not a candidate for re-election. I was in on that speech all the way and walked to the television set to turn it off, because I knew where the end of the speech came, but he kept going. It was the greatest shock of my professional life to be told that I had ten more months on the job.

EH: Would you talk about the importance of the domestic policy staff as a gateway to the president for the Council: Sorensen, O'Donnell, and then later Califano.

AO: I have very little notion of the Kennedy era and what happened there. It was Moyers initially under Johnson. My contacts as Chairman were almost exclusively with Califano and as a member with some of his deputies, like Larry Levinson. I had very good relations with Califano, so I thought it was fine, but there was a great deal of power in that position. I remember Walter agonizing once about Sorensen advising him not to press a certain proposal on Kennedy at that point; the advice was couched in terms of, "You're just going to get a flat no. Maybe if you wait a while he'll be more receptive to it." Walter really had to ask himself whether Sorensen was giving him a straight forecast of what he thought Kennedy was going to do or was expressing his own view on this substantive issue of what Kennedy should do. Some loss of political capital was involved. He could have had that meeting if he wanted it, but we would have paid a price in terms of relationships with Sorensen. During my chairmanship Joe would say sometimes, "You don't want to push that now. The boss just isn't ready for that." You really do have to ask yourself whether you are getting a forecast or a prescription.

I always found it rather amusing that some agency heads just couldn't write a memo that the President would read. I heard repeated stories about Johnson getting livid over the long, turgid memos that Secretary of the Treasury Joe Fowler kept sending him, and it became standard practice for Califano to send a Fowler memo over to us and ask us to put it into a brief, English translation that the President would read. There was a little positioning on whether our briefing memo was to go the President as our memo or whether Joe was going to have his secretary do it and transmit it as his memo to the President. We pretty well established that if we were going to do a briefing memo to the President, he was going to know that it was our briefing memo, not one from Califano's whiz kids. In a way this was a chore. We were interested in making it unnecessary for Califano to want to have his own economist. We would do anything that he needed to have done. He didn't need an economics staff of his own. We managed to convince him several times when that issue came up. "You really don't need to recruit a young economist, Joe. We have all the young economists you need."

EH: This is in regard to Great Society programs primarily?

AO: No, it couldn't have stayed that way. He had young lawyers—Jim Gaither and Larry Levinson—covering what he needed in a programmatic area; an economist was to have a general purpose: "I wouldn't have to bother you when the President wants a memo to use when he talks on the great gains of the expansion." "Bother me!" We did a great deal of junk work, and the staff, the academics, didn't come to Washington to write puff memos on the great gains of expansion. They didn't like that chore. When they didn't like a chore, it usually meant that they didn't do it very well and when it was beneath the dignity of the staffer, the member or Chairman had to do it. But those relations are very important.

LS: Was this a club Califano held over your head?

AO: No, I don't think this notion of getting an economist was, in any sense, ever a threat.

Another task arising from inter-agency positioning also fell to the Council. The agencies were always trying to get the President to grab a piece of paper on the run and put into the record a statement of policy that was of major import and that would be picked up by the press as such. The White House speech writers and staff groups got quite sensitive to this, and they knew that sometimes they wouldn't know how to find it. They wouldn't know when the President was just expressing something that he was already committed to or when he was making a bold new controversial departure. So they would route these proposed speeches to us to make sure that there were no hidden, momentous decisions being made in the context of 4-H clubs.

EH: Heller described how important it was for him to gain the confidence of Sorensen and O'Donnell in order to establish credibility with the President. When Sorensen and O'Donnell learned that an economist could help the President politically, then it was easier for him. Did you have the same experience with Califano?

AO: Walter had established that. I think we all worked off the political capital that he had established. There was a need to reestablish personal relations each time.

The Structure of the Council

EH: Why don't we shift our discussion now to the Council staff. There's a brilliant staff in the beginning. You have Solow, Arrow, Dick Nelson, who came along later, and others. You're saying that these people were simply asked to be good economists. But did they have to acclimate themselves, develop some institutional knowledge, some skills of other kinds?

AO: Communicating is a layman's skill basically, a little knowledge of what other people were thinking in other agencies; it was more important for some than others. If you were responsible for social programs on the Council staff, you really could influence the world only by developing relations at HEW and HUD. That was less true for the macro types where the Council really had a well-defined responsibility. I believe that gets into some questions you raised about staffing and recruitment. I don't believe there was a high cost in relying on short-run academic staff. There were costs in recruiting, and those were not trivial. The Council members and the Chairman spent many hours putting together a priority list of who our first choice for covering money next year was and then spent many more hours interviewing and trying to persuade people to come when we found somebody we really wanted, who had problems of getting academic leave or moving the family to Washington.

EH: You selected primarily on the basis of academic criteria?

AO: Not exclusively. The academic criteria translated into capability of performing in terms of Council requirements. We'd hear stories about a very good academic who had a tendency to take a long time to think through a problem and was not likely, based on his past record, to be a good 24-hour memo writer. He belonged in academia or in some deep thinking part of the government, if such a place ever existed, and not on the firing line of the CEA. There were people who clearly tended to be too abstract, who had reputations for not being able to communicate. There was a tendency to draw heavily on people whom we knew. It wasn't an accident that Jim Tobin told Walter Heller that Art Okun ought to be on the CEA staff; I don't know that Walter had ever heard of Art Okun in 1961. Jim knew that I was somebody Walter would be comfortable with and have confidence in and who could function. It tends to be a rather inbred operation for that reason. It's a small professional world, when you come down to it, and personal contacts are fairly widespread; from professional meetings and conferences, you do know a fair number of people who are not in your university. Occasionally our forecasts about the ability of a person to shift to memo writing—a quick and dirty operation—were wrong. Some people who came down turned out to be excessively academic for the job. They couldn't give you the one-day or even the one-week memo. They needed three months to work on a problem, and by that time the decision would have been made. Occasionally we had some surprises: somebody who was initially seventh on the preferred staff list and had gotten only lukewarm endorsement from people we relied on for judgment turned into a cracker-jack, by energy, by enthusiasm, by ability to communicate. The ability to do quick and dirty is really terribly important.

EH: Is there a loss of intellectual capital along the way?

AO: Oh, yes. In a pure professional sense, there is total depreciation. Oh, you do learn something about the policy process, you get a new insight into how economics is used, but I'd have to look hard for qualifications for that—maybe in an understanding of the data system and the nature of federal statistics and the ability to create a little capital for future Council staff members by getting the Bureau of Labor Statistics or then the authors of Business Economics and Commerce to do something a little differently or give you a more systematic presentation. But I didn't have time to learn anything about the determinants of consumption while I was forecasting consumption on the Council.

EH: This suggests that as some staff members rise politically, you need turnover of staff members; it also suggests that a staff of civil servants wouldn't work so hard to be on top of things.

AO: I think that's right. Some of this may be just a function of personality, this kind of ethic that developed over time about long hours and hard work and that kind of backbreaking regime. Heller used to relate that Alec Cairncross always said that the Whitehall in the UK had managed to develop a quite opposite ethic where you had to apologize to your colleagues if you were ever caught working after hours or coming in on a Saturday—it showed that you really weren't up to handling your load—and that that was the right set of values to have in a bureaucracy, whereas the notion that in coming in on Saturday and working late you were showing how much you cared and how important your efforts were was all wrong. But, given the pace that did persist, I don't see how anybody could have maintained it over the long run.

There is a need for some continuity and some staff somewhere, and it was very helpful to have a Dave Lusher at CEA who did have a sense of the history and the continuity, a Sam Cohn in BOB. In fact, I remember Walter once coming off the phone from Sorensen, I think, and saying, "We have to do a memo for the President by tomorrow morning on this budget issue and its economic implications. Sorensen says get in touch with BOB. Let's do it. I'm going to call Kermit and suggest that you and Sam Cohn take it on." Ten minutes later I have a call from Sam saying, "There's no way the President's going to get a memo tomorrow." I said, "What do you mean? Sorensen says the President wants a memo tomorrow morning; we've got to get a memo tomorrow morning." "No, no, if he's going to get a memo tomorrow morning, I'm not going to write it. I've been here a long time and I've seen a lot of presidents ask for a lot of memos and they don't read them when they get them. You guys come down here for fourteen months and you're full of vim and vigor and don't mind these 80-hour weeks. I can't do that." You know that is just a completely different attitude. I think Walter got a reprieve on the memo.

But really you do get a different kind of talent on the CEA staff by drawing on academics who do not see government service as a career, but as an opportunity to get another perspective on the world. So you're just changing the set of professional talent you're drawing on, and you'll find that usually the best potential lies in the academic types, though

not always, by any means. The Council often got people on
detail from the Federal Reserve--some of that was really
quite good for inter-agency relations--but, given the way the
CEA functions, I don't believe the development of a long-term
civil servant staff is really a possibility. The legendary
long-termer was Francis James, the statistician on the Council; his was a self-contained shop and was not subject to the
same kinds of pressures or ideological problems. In some
areas some people just could not be comfortable working for a
Republican administration, or others working for a Democratic
administration. That does depend a lot on area. Tom Moore,
who is now at the Hoover Institution, is a very fine micro
staffer and I'm sure he never thought of voting Democratic in
his life, but the only micro problem he ever had any problems
with, in terms of the Council's position, was wage and price
jawboning; with issues like minimum wage and antitrust, there
was no real problem.

EH: The ideological barriers are not there?

AO: That's right. That's an area in which the degree of professional agreement is much greater than it is in the macro.

EH: Since you were a staff member, and then a member of the
Council, and then the Chairman, would you describe each role,
what you did at each level, and how one's perceptions change
as one moves from staff member to member of the Council to
the chairmanship. How do your skill and learning requirements change and how do you deal with a different class of
people at each level?

AO: I always considered my promotions on the Council a perfect
illustration of one of Parkinson's laws. I think I was a
very fine staffer for the Council, and I wouldn't be humble
about it at all. I much more than earned my pay as a
staffer, and I enjoyed myself because I was really working
almost entirely within my area of expertise, applying it in a
somewhat different way. I learned very early--sitting at
Walter's elbow in 1961, often between midnight and 2 a.m.--
that a big part of the game was communication. I concluded
that some of my success as staffer came because I was the
only one who could stay awake as long as Walter. But the
staff job was a nice transition from teaching because it did
keep me within the field of my expertise and did not impose
many additional chores and skill requirements beyond the
change in the communication dimension. As a member I got
plunged into responsibilities for international economics,
which is something I had never done anything with at all.
There I had to learn how to take advice from staffers, and I
got my first inkling of what it must be like to be a president, having to make decisions about things that you can't
possibly know very much about and having to rely upon advice
from others. I never felt nearly as comfortable with the
international set of responsibilities or some of the others

that I had as a member as I did just playing the GNP and unemployment games. The burdens of committee meetings and inter-agency relations were very large in the membership of the Council, larger than at staff level.

AL: What is the effect of the role the individual occupies in the central structure of executive policymaking, in terms of either technique or substance, of the role that you were required to play in policymaking at any given time. Walter Heller said it was the same, no matter what.

AO: Well, Walter started at the top. As a staffer, I didn't have the perception of what it took to win the heart and mind of the president, the problems of inter-agency negotiation, the whole question of the White House's perception of the legislative feasibility of recommendations. All of those things, I think, certainly are impressed upon you much more as you move up the line and closer to the point of giving advice to the president directly. This whole problem of access and interrelations with the White House staff really changes in order of magnitude when one becomes Chairman. In terms of decisions on what we really believed about the world or what we wanted, I believe the three members of the Council participated almost equally. In some cases, simply because the Chairman was diverted into more of the negotiating aspects of the job, the member had a greater influence in establishing the substantive position of the Council on the economic outlook or recommendations for how big a tax change should be, for example. The whole question of packaging proposals, putting them within the themes that appeal to the president, convincing him of the risks of not taking your advice, those are clearly things you're not asked to think about when you're doing the memo and interpreting this month's figures or the inflation and unemployment outlook for the next year.

Bureaucratic Politics and Economic Policy

EH: When you became a Council member, did you suddenly find yourself dealing with a different cast of political characters? Were you dealing with under secretaries and members of Congress all of a sudden, or even Cabinet officers? Who were your reference groups at this point?

AO: Yes, I think, I stepped up at that point. I was dealing with assistant directors of the Budget—Charlie Schultze for a short period of time while he was still an assistant director, then Charlie Zwick. At the Treasury, on the international side, it was Fred Deming, who was Under Secretary; Bob Wallace, who was the Assistant Secretary, was not an economist but he had this middle Troika function. I had a great deal of contact with Tony Solomon, who was Assistant Secretary of State, and with Francis Bator, who was then operating as the deputy to Walt Rostow on the National Security Council. Ties to Commerce, Labor were much less close; contacts with the statistical agencies were much more frequent than with anybody else in policy. So contacts were basically with assistant secretaries.

EH: Did you take on a public role at this time, such as beginning to give speeches?

AO: Oh, yes. I did a fair amount of speechmaking as a Council member. Members vary in this respect. By the time I became Chairman I had become one of the more visible Council members, partly by persistence. At that point I had been a Council member for more than three years. I didn't mind making speeches when I didn't have problems about the party line. During that period in 1966 I really tried to stay off the podium—and did so pretty successfully—so I wouldn't have to tell lies.

EH: What's the memo on which you wrote, "This was ordered by Joseph Califano?"

AO: I'm not sure. I think there were two. One gave something of a blessing to a minimum wage increase as being consistent with wage-price guideposts. Another gave the reasons against a tax increase in 1966, but that was very carefully worded in terms of the reasons one can legitimately have for not wanting one and then at the bottom, the reasons for having one.

EH: Those were memos to the President?

AO: The minimum wage memo was for use with Congress.

EH: That would go public.

AO: Yes. Gardner was away at that time, at an OECD economic policy committee meeting, I believe. It's surprising that that sticks in his memory. I was Acting Chairman, and he wasn't at all happy that I had yielded to the instructions, even though my own guess was that he would have done so. I had not been asked to tell lies, but had been asked to write a brief for a position that I would not have chosen on my own. I don't think I would be ashamed of any sentence in that memo, but I wouldn't have wanted to write it.

EH: You mentioned the burdens of inter-agency relations when you were a member of the Council. Did you also have horizontal linkages as a staff member with agency people?

AO: Oh, yes. The exciting development in 1961 was the development of the Troika as an explicit body. Sam Cohn, who was a civil servant in the then Bureau of the Budget, was probably the father of the Troika. He was determined to develop some kind of coordination among the Treasury, BOB and CEA on economic outlook and the fiscal policy implications thereof. He wanted some way to communicate with the President on a more or less regular basis—a system for coordinating the kind of information and advice he would get—leaving room for the differences among the agencies, but nonetheless assuring that these differences came out of some conscious discussion and not just from people telling the President different stories at different times about how they saw the world. The Troika was a three-by-three: it was three agencies and three levels. I was on the staff level of the Troika in 1961 and 1962, on the middle level between late 1964 and early 1968, and then on the top level as Chairman. That was the most important and continuing inter-agency element all the way through; from a fiscal policy point of view, that was the name of the game. The Quadriad, which was the Troika plus the Fed, did not have the same kind of articulated, coordinated staff effort, but there were a lot of staff linkages to the Fed. Those I didn't get into much in 1961 and 1962 as a staffer. Somebody else was covering monetary policy. But as a member I was responsible.

EH: You made a point in your book that the Kennedy administration and Johnson administration were blessed with economists. Each director of the Bureau of the Budget was an economist, the under secretaries of the Treasury were economists, and, of course, the Council, with the implication that there was a commonality, a way of looking at reality. Did that help to lubricate the Troika, or were there still institutional differences at each level?

AO: I think it helped. It's quite striking that people with common educational backgrounds, the same set of tools, can often look at the world very differently. Bob Roosa and Jim Tobin saw the world very differently, analytically and in terms of values and priorities, yet you couldn't string them on a very simple ideological or methodological spectrum. But it certainly helped a lot.

LS: Were there any changes in the Troika relations while you were a member of it?

AO: Yes, there was change in who was winning at various times. Between January 1961 and August 1962 the Treasury was calling the shots, or, to put it differently, the President was coming out on the side of the Treasury's advice. Whether because of that or for other reasons, the policy was much more Dillon than Heller. In August 1962 when Kennedy committed himself to a substantial tax cut and basically to a deliberate widening of the deficit, that was the turning point and from then until late 1965, fiscal policy was pretty much what the CEA was recommending. I don't recall big battles during that period. Heller was the father of the tax cut; the tax cut became the centerpiece of economic policy during 1963 and 1964, and that pushed the Council's role to the fore.

EH: What about the bureaucratic politics within the Troika?

AO: The Troika was important for a coordination of views, an exchange of views, and it created incentives for compromise and for presenting a united front when the differences were small. You´d make a decision whether the views on the outlook and on revenues and expenditures were sufficiently different among the three agencies to go to the President and say we disagree. You don´t want to confuse issues by elevating trivial disagreements, so there is a tendency to compromise. I don´t believe that tendency glosses over fundamental differences. It also helps to distinguish purely technical judgments on what the economic outlook is most probably going to be from what you should do about it through expenditures and tax policy. The way that funnels up through the staff, where people are basically operating as technicians, makes it harder for an agency that has decided it doesn´t want a tax increase or a tax cut to develop an intellectual position that really is a brief to support some predetermined policy view. You are getting a bunch of guys, whose incentives are to be as right as possible, to go through the nuts and bolts and argue those things out. Often the real question isn´t so much what´s likely to happen with a given set of policies, but which outlook is really more desirable all things considered; is some deviation from a preceding expectation big enough to justify the political capital of changing the budget program. There is a very big difference between the decisions that are made going into the beginning of the year budget program, where a lot of things are up for grabs anyway, and the decision to do something different from that initial program in April or July or October. But the Troika does force some reconsideration of that program, so that the president basically is forced in April, July and October to ask, "Are we still on the track that we thought we would be when we sent up the January program? Or has the deviation from the track gotten so big that I ought to do something explicitly to amend the program or to make up for something the Congress didn´t do that I asked them to do earlier?" You really are getting the best objective forecasting and revenue estimating and expenditure estimating, processes at a level that is not going to be excessively colored by the ultimate policy positions that an individual agency has.

EH: You said the incentive is to be right. Are you saying that these three agencies are somehow different in some degree from Commerce or Labor in the sense that they´re less special pleaders? Their credibility depends on being right. They´re not programmatic.

AO: There´s some of that, but it´s not so much that the agencies are free of these biases or positions. By having a level of technicians and telling them we want the best GNP forecast they can make, we have built in an inhibition about manipulating that technical staff, even when the agency has a commitment or a position or a bias of some sort that its head would like to see promoted. He can ask questions: "Aren't you really taking an awfully bearish view of investment or what makes you think it's not going to go up?" I think that's what you have built into this three-by-three system—as much objectivity as you can get at the low level.

EH: Would you describe the division of labor at the staff level; did that create different points of view and did those to some extent reflect different agency missions?

AO: You really had a division of labor even at the staff level. The Treasury is all geared up for revenue estimating. It has a large staff and basically they would prepare revenue estimates associated with some economic outlook. On occasion a Council staffer could say, "I just don't see how your profit taxes could be that low or that high," and then take them through it and occasionally even push them or bring to the middle level a disagreement on the revenue estimates. But the presumptive estimation was the Treasury estimation. Similarly, the Budget Bureau has many divisions that are tracking programs agency by agency. It takes a lot of guts for a Council staffer or a Treasury staffer to say, "You guys are just too low on defense or Medicaid," or something of that sort. But again he's subject to challenge on that. As things evolved, the Council forecaster took the primary role in doing the outlook for the private economy. Again, subject to challenge. We used to joke that the three-way division of labor was that the Treasury had the revenues, the BOB had the expenditures, and the Council had the deficits.

A staff effort would start during the year, as opposed to the end-year budget planning effort, if the middle-level guys thought that there was some programmatic decision to be made or some major contingency on whether Congress would or would not do something, and asked the staff to do alternative revenue estimates, expenditure estimates, and economic outlooks, based on these alternative assumptions. They basically supplied any new initiative or legislative outcome assumptions that they wanted to see staffed out. A week later they would get something out of the staff exercise, giving them a new set of economic paths, revenue paths, expenditure paths. Those would be reviewed. Again the middle-level guys might raise questions, although generally they would be sufficiently in contact with the staff so that they really wouldn't be surprised by the way things looked. But they might say, "Go back to the drawing board. You guys have been underestimating for three quarters in a row and you're doing the same silly thing again, etc." So a certain amount would again be subject to challenge by middle level.

Then the middle-level guys would generally draft jointly a memo for the signatures of the top Troika members to the president, consistent with the usual proposition that you never write what you sign, you never sign what you write. When I was on the middle Troika, Charlie Zwick, Bob Wallace and I would send a memo to Schultze, Fowler and Ackley, which was really a draft of the memo we expected them to send to the President. But they would want more information than would be included in the memo to the President, so the staff would draft the memo for our signatures to them explaining something in more detail, or whether there were compromises or doubts about the position--just why we took the tone we did in the presidential memo.

SM: In the other agencies that deal in macro policy--Treasury, BOB, and the Fed--there seems to be a constitutional bias towards contraction or at least rather conservative expansion, and the CEA seems generally to be on the outer edge of that. Do you agree with that?

AO: Yes, the whole notion of the independence of the Fed has to rest on the view that the political process is excessively susceptible to expansionary pressures, to inflationary pressures. If you don't believe that, you can't make sense of the whole thing: that there needs to be a safeguard so that when unpleasant medicine (in the form of high interest rates, which everybody hates) has to be administered, the decision is made by somebody who doesn't have to stand for re-election next November.

In general, you also have a somewhat more conservative, less expansionist attitude in Treasury than in either the CEA or the BOB. I think it is an institutional role. If you made the same man secretary of the Treasury or chairman of the Council, six months later you would detect a difference in the speeches of this same person. The signature on the dollar bill is a symbol of what the secretary of the Treasury is. He represents the whole set of international relations. His position produces a more conservative tendency, discipline, concern for balance of payments equilibrium. The Council was created by the Employment Act and not the Price Stability Act of 1946 and to that extent it has a somewhat expansionary tendency. That seems to have been persistent in most administrations. I suspect that Saulnier was to the left of George Humphrey.

EH: In your book you described the administration lobbying for the surcharge and you said that Fowler was out front. It is generally true that the secretary of Treasury is more likely to lead the political advance than the chairman of the Council?

AO: Oh, yes. I made remarkably few trips to Capitol Hill, had remarkably little contact with Congress in any role. It was really surprising. I believe there is more of that now. The real power of the Treasury lies in the fact that it manages most of legislation in nuts and bolts form to implement the revenue side of the budget. You can fight like hell with the Treasury about whether you want the line on equipment eligible for the investment tax credit drawn here or there, and

then they come back and say, "Well, we followed the party
line, but in this conference committee we just couldn't sell
it." There was always a tendency to find that the initial
position of the Treasury was more salable to the Congress
than any other position, and you have every reason to suspect
that they were using their power in the marking up and amend-
ing of legislation to try to push their own preferences. On
the international side, you had this second-level committee--
when I was a member of the Deming group--that was really
supposed to carve out the administration's position on the
Special Drawing Rights negotiations. When the Secretary was
doing the negotiation and had to give a bit, again it was his
discretion as to where he put priorities.

EH: The Treasury therefore had its antennae out all the time and
was bringing information back.

AO: Yes. It was really implementing these programs through the
legislative process. The basic thrust of the Budget Bureau
in the sixties was promoting rational government spending and
trying to improve efficiency and to develop a sense of priorities. It was not just a general attempt to hold down the
total; it was an effort to make the case for what could be
done on expenditures.

EH: Wouldn't the Bureau take coloration from the president, like
the Council?

AO: Yes. But in my time you had a really topflight civil service
staff with a very sharply defined sense of priorities. That
staff did not have a big turnover with administration
changes--even at quite higher levels. As long as their sense
of priorities among programs was getting some attention from
the top level, morale could be maintained; even if the guy
monitoring labor programs didn't think enough was being spent
on them or thought too much was being spent on them, somehow
his advice to his boss was reflected in the relative evaluation of separate programs and the pressures that were put on
the Labor Department. That was enough to maintain his
morale, to keep him operating. I found that very impressive.

EH: The Council didn't get into those questions of allocations to
programs within departments, did you?

AO: Not to a great extent, no. We were involved in the design of
income maintenance programs, jobs programs, the whole attitude toward model cities and housing efforts, but more at the
level of strategy, whereas the Budget Bureau really had a
voice in both strategy and tactics, right down to very small
programmatic decisions, which we would never want to get
involved in.
    There was a very strong alliance between the CEA and the
BOB. It may have had something to do with the fact that
there was a professional tie between the Council Chairman and

the BOB director. Perhaps there was a natural affinity in their being outside the Cabinet, meeting each other to rein-force their efforts to influence agencies. I don't know where that stands today, because Charlie Schultze is the only one who's ever seen this from the side of both the CEA and the Budget.

There is, I believe, some inevitable and natural con-flict between the secretary of the Treasury and the chairman of the Council. The secretary of the Treasury is the chief economic and financial appointed official of an administra-tion. Anything that challenges his position there is bound to lead to conflict.

LS: What accounts for the continuity of the Troika?

AO: I don't even know how much this institutionalization has continued. I don't know whether it's a regular quarterly reporting system today. But during the sixties it got insti-tutionalized. The Troika members themselves eventually said, "We're going to send a report to the president every quarter and if there is something of sufficient moment, we're going to ask for a meeting." This implied that there would have to be a staff exercise every quarter, and that in turn created a need for an enormous outgrowth of other contacts all focusing on this one link: "We're going to make the president read a piece of paper on where his fiscal policy is at least every three months, and also have a very explicit kind of budget policy operation in the fall." If people have to talk to each other, they know they have to work together. If some-body gets a piece of news that changes his view of the out-look, he wants to know whether his counterparts in Treasury and Budget are similarly impressed by this evidence. If they're not, he wants to convince them that it really is as important as he thinks.

LS: If that's what impelled it initially, what were some of the by-products that reinforced that continuation?

AO: Again, my only source of the history of the Eisenhower years on this was Sam Cohn in the Budget Bureau. He insisted that in one year the only communication among those agencies in the preparation of the budget was a 20-minute meeting at which the Council Chairman came in with a GNP figure, the Budget Director with an expenditure figure, and the Secretary of the Treasury with a revenue figure. Each had guessed what the other's figure would be and they hassled a bit and there was a little compromising and that was it. Almost a really shocking lack of a coordinated budget. It was this proce-dure, I would say, that led to the August 1962 middle-of-the-year commitment by Kennedy to a major tax cut. Never would have happened under Eisenhower, I suspect, because he was not getting this reconsideration of fiscal policy. Kennedy's proposal was a compromise of a split set of recommendations by the Troika agencies—the Council telling him to go for a tax cut, then and there, and Treasury telling him to do nothing. His decision, which was somewhere in between, was to commit himself to a tax cut, but one that he would propose in January.

Many small decisions grew out of this, when it was clear in a legislative process that Congress was willing to spend three times as much on a program as the President had initially recommended. The question was how responsive the administration should be: should it take a hard line, and should the negotiators tell the legislators that the President will veto a bill if it's much bigger? If other expenditures were falling below the track, if the economic situation was consistent with that, then the President would alter his tone of negotiation on the ongoing matters with the Congress in the direction of either putting a lid on very tight or making it clear that he was quite receptive to the add-on. Without really initiating a new program or changing your mind from January, there was that degree of fine-tuning which has become a very dirty word—just in terms of small attitudinal changes with respect to congressional implementation proposals.

Relations with the Fed really were built on the Troika plus one becoming a Quadriad. This grew into a good deal of importance. There was no doubt that Fed Chairman William McChesney Martin was very conscious of the Quadriad. As an in-house joke, a Council staff memo showed that for a couple of years, if you took the change in the federal funds rate in the week preceding Quadriad meetings, it was almost always negative, statistically significant. Martin was always bringing the President the present of a little lower interest rate than he'd run in the interim. Martin did a lot of bargaining in the Quadriad—a very different operating procedure from what apparently went on with Burns. He would have access to these fiscal projects and he would say, "That deficit is just a little bit bigger than we can handle now, Mr. President. We're going to try to do the best we can, but it's not quite manageable. I can't offer you very much assurance that we can manage that." He knew Johnson knew what he was saying and he knew what Johnson was going to do. Johnson would rise to the bait and say, "It's a little too big to be manageable. About how much too big to be managed?" If Johnson made a concession to Martin on fiscal policy in the range that Martin called euphemistically manageable, it damned well better mean that Martin wouldn't tell him that interest rates had to rise during the period. A lot of that went on. The Fed really did have power, but it was being used internally; it was being used essentially to try to negotiate a more harmonious mix of fiscal and monetary policy. I think in the past year the danger of a collision course between fiscal and monetary policy was very real, a very serious threat.

EH: But this was Martin's disposition. Are we really dependent upon the style and disposition of the head of the Fed for this kind of coordination?

AO: Yes, and the president, too. It clearly is very unformulated, very subjective, very much influenced by the personalities of the people there.

EH: Do you think this network is the best way to balance the accountability of the Fed with its independence? Are there alternatives?

AO: Oh, I think there should be some real changes in the present procedures. I think the dialogue between the Fed and the Congress, which is focused on monetary aggregates, has really turned into a smokescreen rather than a source of illumination. The first and foremost question should be whether the Federal Reserve accepts any economic targets that have been set by the administration as its guide to monetary policy. Is it working to promote and facilitate the economic part that the administration has set forth? It is difficult to interpret Federal Reserve policy in the last three years as an effort to implement the administration's economic policy. It has been an effort to hold down the economic path and to use monetary aggregates as a vehicle for doing that without ever talking about the objectives for the economy. We have managed to get ourselves into a discussion of whether the accelerator should be one-quarter or one-half down to the floorboard without asking how fast we ought to be going. In a dialogue between Burns and Bellmon in hearings with the Senate Budget Committee a few years ago, Bellmon pressed Burns harder than I've ever seen a Federal Reserve Chairman pressed on how he conceived of the exact scope of Fed independence: "Are you or are you not obliged to follow the targets set forth by the administration and the Congress?" "Well, I don't know what Congress' targets are. The administration sets forth targets and Congress doesn't." "Suppose we did set forth targets. Suppose we agreed with the administration. Would you be obliged to follow them?" Burns obviously didn't want to give him a very definite answer and there was some dancing around. Finally, he said, "Yes, if there was a congressional resolution with administration approval that put on record the intention that nominal GNP should grow 13 percent next year and the Federal Reserve thought that was a disaster, it would be our obligation to try to implement that program or resign." There is no way I know to construe the statute to imply that the Federal Reserve should be setting economic targets. The present version of the Humphrey-Hawkins bill would very explicitly commit the Federal Reserve to expressing its views on the economic target path. I don't think it commits it to implement the particular path that the administration sets forward, but it commits it to express its monetary policy decisions in terms of that path and essentially says, "If you're not going to do that, you've got to come forward and say it."

That is something which needs to be done and should be done. I think that's all I really would like to see done of any nature.

SM: Could you describe the differences in the CEA's relations with the Federal Reserve between the Heller, Ackley, and your years?

AO: I didn't see much of the Fed-Heller relations. There was some abrasion at the beginning, especially between Jim Tobin and some of the people at the Fed. Jim had a record of favoring major legislative reforms in the Fed's independence and that's no way to be popular at the Fed. He was also really enthusiastic about an easy money policy at that time, partly because he put more weight on monetary policy than some of the other people in the administration. My impression is that there was a very good flow of communication, information all the way through. When I heard a month ago that Burns called Schultze and Blumenthal within minutes before he called the press to tell them about a discount rate increase, I was shocked. The way Martin played it, the Treasury and the Council would have known that the Fed was thinking about a discount rate increase. He always managed to convey the warning; he didn't tell you to tell it to the President, and he didn't tell you not to tell it to the President. But the President never learned about a discount rate increase from the newspaper. For example, in December 1965, the President knew it was going to happen. The President told him then that he didn't want it, that he was against it. On that particular issue, I didn't want the Fed to do it, and Ackley didn't want the Fed to do it. We had a very different kind of motivation. We knew damned well that the economy needed restraint at that point. Our view was that our best chance of trying to sell a tax bill was if we could go to the President saying the Fed hasn't tightened but would have to tighten unless he went for a tax bill, and that he should tell the Congress that they had sixty days to show their conviction before the Fed tightened. Well, we were kidding ourselves. The President wasn't going to buy a tax bill on that basis any more than on any other basis at that time, I'm convinced. Martin's argument was that if the Congress did the right thing and the administration did the right thing on fiscal policy, he could reverse himself and he'd be glad to tell them. We did have a perception that we would be in a better bargaining position in fighting the case for fiscal restraint if he hadn't moved. But we knew he was going to do it. We started talking about this in September, that he thought that he would have to make a move unless things leveled off.

JG: Did Johnson know?

AO: Oh, sure. Johnson had a couple of Quadriads and lectured

Martin on how bad it would be to do that. Why did he want to destroy that nice prosperity?

EH: You have given us a picture of the institutions, and the stakes and the different perspectives. What resources does the Council have to make its way in this world with the president? When does it win and when does it lose?

AO: It's a small, free-wheeling staff, but it is not saddled with administrative chores; it doesn't have responsibilities for grinding out data. It has a great deal of flexibility in where it picks its crusades, apart from meat and potatoes fiscal and macro issues. I really do believe that this technique of recruiting and the closeness to the academic world does enable it to get some of the best and the brightest, if I may use that phrase. This whole question of when you win and when you lose--that's the roughest thing to evaluate.

EH: Let me try a proposition: that the Council is very strong for macro policy, because its perspective is the closest to the president, the broadest. Its responsibilities are akin to his, unlike the Treasury, which has a more limited perspective. Of course, on that theory, it ought to win every time. A companion proposition: that's not true in micro policy, because he [the president] has no incentive to get involved in micro policy and the Council has less influence with him on micro policy.

AO: Somebody claimed that the OMB organization team did an internal study early last year that sharply criticized CEA for becoming a pressure group for economic rationality. That would be the highest calling for the CEA. I believe that the CEA does have less of an interest group linkage than anybody else. You might expect the natural biases of the Treasury to be more in line with the natural ideology of a president in a Republican administration. But wherever the central tendency created by the president is, the secretary of the Treasury tends to go to the right-wing: Bill Simon, in relation to Ford, is probably as conservative as Dillon or Fowler in relation to Kennedy and Johnson. The CEA does seem to have this detached commitment to the public interest and professionalism that in principle impresses presidents as well as everybody else. The CEA calls it as it sees it, but with less inhibition about political feasibility and practicality. You can almost identify the periods when the Council wasn't winning on the macro side. Kennedy came in with a lot of criticism about not having an international perspective: all the rumors that he would break the link to gold; this whole ideology about budget balancing, against which he was being tested. I suppose every Democratic president starts with this concern about business confidence. I think that tends to make new Democratic presidents lean toward the conservative side and more likely in the direction of Treasury advice.

On the micro front the CEA is flying in the face of all of the political pressures, telling the president not to do what the secretary of Labor is telling him to do, what the secretary of Commerce is telling him to do, what the milk producers and the maritime unions and the AFL-CIO are telling him to do. The one eye-opener to me as a young man from academia coming to Washington was the intensity of these producer interest group pressures on all sorts of micro economic decisions. You can't feel them from outside or really see the difficulties of resisting these groups. The 200,000 milk producers beat 200 million milk consumers all the time. You go right down the line. Where a focused interest group is willing to put its vote, its campaign contributions, its influence on the line on that one issue, it really can influence policy. Almost invariably those producers' interests are contrary to the special interests of economic rationality. That's a big uphill climb. We tried to get a repeal of resale price maintenance advocated by Johnson in 1965. Humphrey got that memo and was absolutely livid about it because it affected fair trade for the small corner druggist. Then Johnson told Gardner that he would seriously consider recommending it if Gardner could get somebody on the Hill who would say that he even would hold hearings on it. We made a couple of pilgrimages to the Hill and got very negative reactions. As a matter of fact, that's about the one piece of producer interest protective legislation that has since been repealed. It used to be said that you would propose a bold initiative for restructuring agricultural programs and then be lucky if you held down the support price of corn by three cents. On these micro issues the CEA-BOB alliance was very, very strong. Almost every time there was an agriculture meeting, the staff would get together, would brief the principals together—basically a decision to go down in defeat together.

I don't know how I would characterize the victories and defeats. I guess the big victory in the micro area under Heller was the design of a poverty program, the commitment to a war on poverty, which came out of the Council. This was as much Heller's flair for packaging as anything else.

EH: It was also congruent with Johnson's sense of political goals.

AO: Yes. The commitment, actually, was made by Kennedy. But it fitted in very well with Johnson. I can recall CEA influences in nudging income maintenance, or job training, or housing, or HUD programs in certain ways, but not really a major thrust there. Understandably.

LS: What about minimum wage?

AO: It would have been worse if we hadn't been there. We told ourselves that every year. Actually, the minimum wage did not go up. I was thinking about micro activities over the

years--occasionally there were just thorny technical problems
that different agencies came to different verdicts on, and
the Council would get hauled in because it was respected for
being highly effective and professional and not having a
stake.   There were some big battles on what to do about
helium between Interior and BOB at one point, and the Council
got brought in as a technical mediator.   When I was Chairman,
Joe Peck took on an assignment for shepherding a workers'
compensation insurance study, because the White House staff
didn't believe some report that the Labor Department had put
in.   Those weren't so full of particular interest group
issues; they did come closer to being an evaluation of service functions of public sector activities of the government.
Just a matter of developing a data base and developing a
procedure for performing evaluation.

AL: The president has an interest in BLS, Census Bureau and CEA
and can be persuaded that he needs objective data.   He can't
deal similarly with the soil adjustment programs or agricultural adjustment price programs or tariffs or wage and hour
administration or occupational and health standards; you have
to let the groups have access to those issues. but you can
argue that for the sake of the government you have to have
detached and analytical evaluation.

AO: But your real safeguard there, I think, is professionalism.
Any politician who ever was nefarious enough to think that
he'd like to see the seasonal on the unemployment rate
changed in the month before elections so that it didn't
embarrass him knows that there are a dozen people in BLS who
have spent years trying to get the best possible method and
their commitment is to accuracy and they're going to blow the
whistle on him.   That deters him from messing around.   So,
yes, there's an interest in having some of these things done
right.

EH: Most of the analytical work on welfare reform was done in
HEW, not in the White House.   This is why I've asked every
CEA Chairman the question: Doesn't the president need a
Domestic Council policy staff?   Califano became convinced of
it after his experience in putting together the Great Socie-
ty.

AO: Yes.   He tried to operate by regularly putting together those
inter-agency task forces on a September through December
basis and feeding into the January budget program and then
occasionally making a larger or more continuing effort.   Part
of the problem was that Johnson just didn't accept that as
the operative way of making decisions and would accede to
procedures that allowed end-runs. The Chairman of CEA or the
Secretary of the Treasury would not have dared try to sell
something to the President in a one-on-one meeting with him.
That was clearly Troika responsibility. There was, in effect, a pact that every significant issue would go through

this process. There was never any such commitment in the social program area. I remember seeing Wilbur Cohen pull up to the White House and kidding him, "What are you going to end-run this time, Wilbur?" He said, "I won't sell the President anything that isn't good for the country, you know that." But nothing in that area had created a commitment by any of the agency heads to use an inter-agency procedure or a set of coordinated actions.

EH: Eizenstat now has what Califano really wanted. But such a staff is always at a disadvantage vis-a-vis·the departments because the issues are micro.

AO: Well, I'm not sure. I guess I'm questioning whether you really want to interpose still another staff of technicians. If you had the equivalent of a Troika with HEW and HUD and Labor and essentially the social program agencies and the Council and the Budget Bureau doing these micro analyses and priority analyses, I'm not convinced that you would need that extra layer of staff in the White House. You need to establish that this is the procedure by which things are going to go to the president, and you need a president who agrees that he will listen to proposals from his Cabinet officers only after they've gotten their seal of approval or seal of disagreement through this procedure.

AL: One also must determine whether the president wants to isolate himself to the degree that is necessary for, let's say, Treasury, CEA, and BOB to appraise objectively, detachedly, analytically the course of fiscal and economic policy. On these micro issues, especially in domestic politics, the president will let the parties, the producer groups, the effective people short-circuit them and wipe out the professional lives of the people who sacrificed themselves for something that they thought the president wanted. Because he's busy, because he has political pressures of his own, he says these guys are more important to him.

AO: Yes. It was a clear embarrassment to Carter last year when the press got wind of what was going on in the review of the economic impact of cargo preferences. Carter had made a promise in a speech in Baltimore that there was going to be cargo preference. He was committed to it. To have a staff saying that this is a very costly way to preserve some low productivity jobs and then leaking this to the press, that's costly. If these are going to be politically dominated decisions, then the president may well want somebody to whisper in his ear that this is terribly costly and he ought to think about it twice, but he doesn't want papers on his desk telling him that this is a terrible thing to do and that there's absolutely no rational defense for it, if in fact he's going to wind up doing it anyway, because he's made campaign commitments or because he's buying something else from George Meany by giving him this favor. In a way you have to ask what the president's higher rationality is.

EH: So a domestic policy staff has very few resources, because its domain is micro, and the Council has fewer resources in the micro than in the macro area. Does it follow that an effort by the Council to link the micro and the macro is somewhat abortive because of its limited influence in the micro area? For example, manpower programs, to my knowledge, have never been linked explicitly to macro policy or agricultural policy or deregulation.

AO: No. One linkage is obviously that if you do enough foolish things with micro policy, it begins to have significant inflationary effects or can even have significant macro growth effects. In the sixties Johnson was in the business of asking for price and wage restraints from business and labor; this was an important element in his willingness to accept some restraints for the federal government, whether it was on federal pay or even on proposals to raise price floors in agriculture. You could say, "Look, Mr. President, that's creating inflation, and you're asking all these guys to hold down in order to stop inflation." You couldn't say, "This is going to make the difference between a 3 percent and a 5 percent inflation rate," but basically, "How credible are you in asking for restraint by the private decision makers if you don't show some kind of restraint in the decisions you make, even if they're relatively small decisions?"

I think the way to try to control that area is to put it into some kind of focus in the totality of the cost raising and cost reducing actions of the federal government. In fact, this was initially Barry Bosworth's idea, when he was first there as a consultant to CEA and still at Brookings. He tried to get into that April 1977 anti-inflation program a procedure whereby the administration would come out with a quarterly report in which it reported on all of the cost raising and cost reducing actions engaged in by either executive discretion or legislation, including ones that were in the proposal stage in the Congress. As I heard it, the White House staff thought this was the craziest thing that they'd ever heard. He was asking the President to make confessions every quarter and would box the President in. When the President had good things to say, he could say them. Why should he commit himself to this kind of public monitoring of the sins of the federal government? I testified at the Senate Budget Committee this week and said, "You guys ought to ask CBO to do that on a quarterly basis." You should have some procedural way of highlighting these things, showing that these little expenditures add up—the famous Dirksen cliché, "A billion dollars here, a billion dollars there, and before you know it, it gets to be real money." But you cannot fight a farm program because it's inflationary. You can't fight the minimum wage because it's inflationary. You can't fight a payroll tax, because no one of these things is

big enough in itself to make the critical difference. But if
you show what is at stake in all the things that the federal
government is doing and if you start highlighting the opportunities for deregulation or reduced costs or regulatory
compliance on the plus side, I think you can create enough
visibility so that these little actions, which nobody understands except the pressure groups that really want them, will
get scrutiny from a different point of view. That's one
range of micro issues that latch into the macro by having an
effect on the cost-price level and hence on inflation.

LS: But it's a radical departure to think that way. Our government has always operated on the basis that you can pay off
all of these things and the extent that they overlap is just
a waste that the system can afford, as long as it's paying
off politically.

AO: Yes, I think that's a fair characterization.

Reconstructing Policy Decisions

EH: Why don't we turn to macro issues and talk about the surcharge and the intellectual and political questions there.

AO: The year 1966 was terribly frustrating for us. We started in
December 1965, even on the basis of substantial misperception
of just how much the defense buildup was going to be, to urge
strongly the need for a tax increase, got increasingly shrill
about it for several months and had very serious problems in
maintaining a public stance--Johnson expected absolute loyalty and no deviation from a party line--and at the same time
internally writing memos saying that the world was about to
come to an end. In that period, Fowler was not signing
Troika memos, not signing memos jointly with Ackley urging
tax increases. Normally one thinks of the secretary of the
Treasury as being quicker to hit the brakes than the Chairman
of the Council in terms of institutional biases and concern
about the international sector, as having a greater sense of
responsibility about protecting the dollar that bears his
signature. Whether Fowler really recognized that Johnson
just wasn't ready to accept a tax increase recommendation and
consequently didn't want to launch a crusade that was bound
to be ill-fated, whether his commitment to the Vietnam War--
he was just really an ardent hawk on the war--made him feel
that he didn't want to create any visible economic costs that
might have led to greater negative public response to the
war....
But just to give you the chronology, you had the failure
in December 1965 to get any action. Another initiative in
March 1966 focused on suspension of the investment tax credit. Another failure at that point. Then in September 1966,
Ackley did win the battle on the suspension of the investment
tax credit. He was hopeful at that time of also getting a
commitment by Johnson to a general tax increase in January.

He fought very hard, took a defeat on that very bitterly, was very upset about it, because he was very skeptical at that point of getting a January tax increase proposal in the President's program. Meanwhile, tight money had cooled off the economy, and we would not have wanted a major fiscal restraint to come on early in 1967 until there was some easing off from this money crunch pressure. We finally sold this formula for a January tax proposal that would be carried in the program but where the President would not be asking for action immediately, but be asking for action around the middle of the year, saying that he would send up the proposal when he thought it was appropriate, really taking into account that the economy did not then need further cooling off. This was a rather risky course on our part, because we were making a forecast that claimed to be able to see around corners. We were assessing the present outlook as quite quiescent, but saying we were going to get a spurt that would require further action. We were damned lucky that we were right. I think our batting average is better than 500 on this, but it isn't a thousand, and that was one of our better forecasts. It behaved just the way we called it in January 1967. The first half adjustment was an inventory correction and then the second half began to spurt.

I'm not sure that Johnson ever changed his mind. At least he kept telling us that he was for a tax increase at the earliest possible moment he thought it could conceivably be taken seriously, that you couldn't sell it on the basis of a forecast, that you had to wait for a little bleeding to take place before you volunteered to sew up the wound. I think quite honestly in Johnson's mind there was an evolution. Now I'm sure that part of his reason for not wanting to be on record for a tax increase in 1966 was this guns-and-butter notion that he didn't want to cut back his domestic programmatic and legislative objectives. He feared that once he said, "This is such a big problem that we've got to raise taxes for it," then he would be committed to restraining social programs. Congress would say that it wasn't the time to pass Model Cities. He had a great legislative agenda and I think he sensed that the Congress that had come in on his coattails in 1964 as he trounced Goldwater was going to be the most favorable environment for passing some of this legislation. With the war and other problems, he couldn't be excessively optimistic about the character of the next Congress. In every one of these discussions, he always said, "You guys keep sounding as though the war's going to last forever. I see that light at the end of the tunnel." I really believe that he kidded himself more than he kidded the country. I think the Halberstam view in The Best and the Brightest is more conspiratorial than it was. The administration and the national security types did really talk themselves into that light at the end of the tunnel.

When he made the actual proposal for action in August 1967, I believe he anticipated that there would be some demands for hold-downs and cutbacks in spending, but he obviously did not assess the magnitude and the vehemence of that. I think in his own mind, Wilbur Mills was the villain of the piece, that if Wilbur had gone along, the things could have been handled much more promptly and without a big flap on the spending side. The fact was, or at least so Fowler reported, that a very large number of liberal Democrats were not prepared for higher taxes, either because they didn't worry that much about inflation or because they didn't want to endorse the war. So the whole nose counting or head counting for the tax bill really depended upon a very significant Republican support for it, and almost all the Republicans insisted a price be paid in the form of expenditure restraint. Mills, in that emotional meeting that I referred to earlier, said he could have pushed the tax bill through Ways and Means, he could have put it on the floor in the fall of 1967, but it wouldn't have passed, it would have been killed, and that he had kept it on the back burner deliberately because that was the only way to keep it alive. If all of his efforts were really designed to pass that tax program at the earliest opportunity, he sure handled it in a very strange way. There were all sorts of conjectures about whether the failure of Johnson to accept an invitation to speak at a Chicken Day Dinner in Arkansas had more to do with the surcharge hang-up than many substantive arguments that were being offered.

There clearly was a division within the Troika in early 1968: Fowler would have paid any price, taken any cut in domestic spending to get the tax increase. If he had thought a repeal of Social Security was necessary to pass the tax bill, he would have been for it. Zwick really was dragging his heels on any significant expenditure cut, particularly on expenditure cuts that required the President to make the cuts. The whole process was really screwy. Congress was going to appropriate a hell of a lot of money, even more than the budget, but they were going to set a ceiling and the administration was going to have to commit itself to come in under that ceiling. The Budget Director found he couldn't live with that ceiling--being ordered to make a slash and try to hassle all the agencies--quite apart from what his sense of priorities was on the importance of federal programs. Incidentally, I understand that the most open cabinet meeting of the Johnson administration took place in May 1968--if that's the case, it tells me a lot about the other cabinet meetings that I hadn't attended in the earlier years. There wasn't really a very candid discussion of issues, but it was quite clear that the agency heads whose programs would have been gored by a spending cut did not see the same urgency in the tax surcharge that Fowler and I did. Or that Zwick did. In fact, several were prepared to tell the President that he shouldn't sacrifice a nickel out of his budget program, should not go along with any cuts. Fowler really was a master negotiator in a difficult position. With the Congress and with the President. He was pulling the two sides together, really, and he was trying to make the Mills-Mahon-

Johnson deal. A sharp antagonism had developed between Mills and Mahon because Mahon felt that Mills was really infringing on his turf in talking about spending cuts: "Mills' business is to look at revenue measures. Why is he talking about linking these to spending cuts? That's the Appropriations Committee." If we had had a budget committee, it would have been, I think, a much more rational process where we would not have had these ego conflicts on jurisdictional lines.

EH: You said earlier that Fowler was not enthusiastic about the tax program. What brought him around?

AO: All I know is that by January 1967 when Johnson was ready to go, he was gung ho and ready to go.

EH: What brought Johnson around to doing something? If he was always in agreement intellectually, what triggered the action?

AO: Well, the symptoms were there. In December 1965 we were talking about an economy that was generating fantastic good news—one and a half percent inflation rate, no problems in financial markets, the Dow was hitting a new high every day. "You guys are coming around trying to recommend an operation for a patient who is not only healthy but has just won the decathlon"—that was what I kept hearing from the White House. "What's the disease you're trying to cure?" By the end of 1966 I could explain very easily: it was 4 percent inflation, it was 6 percent interest rates. I think that was a big element. If my conjecture that the 1966 legislative program was an important deterrent to Johnson's moving earlier is correct, that would explain why he was more ready for it in early 1967. He sure hated high interest rates and he wanted to get them down, and Martin kept telling him, "If you can get the tax bill, I can back off on interest rates. I can't do it until you do."

SM: About monetary policy. It would appear that the monetary authorities started to ease up early in 1967, well before you were committed to a tax increase.

AO: Yes, that's true. The economy did have this period in which it was really flat. People were talking about recession and as it turned out that was sort of a lovely cooling off period. In fact, I think that misled us a great deal later, because it really looked as though a little tap on the brake brought the inflation rate and interest rates down. From a monetary aggregate approach, the Fed wasn't easing very much in the first half of 1967. Credit demands were slowing down. But by late 1967 they were raising interest rates again as the economy perked up.

SM: But the growth in the aggregates was pretty high, both in 1967 and 1968, and yet you were unable to make any progress on the fiscal side. Did you think about using the monetary side then, since the fiscal side was closed for political reasons?

AO: A very strong dose of monetary restraint had been administered in 1966 and that in fact did a lot of this cooling off. Even in the fall of 1967, Mills said, "I don't see this boom again. You're solving the problem of the first half of 1966 and here we are in August 1967." I believe there really was a conscious feeling at the Fed and a feeling on our part that you had to let the economy take on somewhat of a booming mood before the Congress would take you seriously. Once again you didn't have the symptoms of the disease. I think that the Fed was perhaps letting the economy have enough rope to make clear the danger that it would hang itself, and counting on the Congress to do something. But the interest rates were moving back up. The aggregates did move up rapidly, and if we had believed that there was just no way of getting a tax bill, greater monetary restraint clearly would have been in order. We were excessively optimistic; we thought there would be a tax bill by the end of 1967. Then we thought there would be one early in 1968. For a brief period we thought there wasn't going to be one at all. Somehow it got rescued. In a sense, Johnson accepted an expenditure cut that was bigger than he ever supported. He would not go over $4 billion as anything he would support, but when they did $6 billion he accepted it—he signed the bill. If at the beginning of 1968 he had been willing to call Mills and say, "I'm ready to go for $6 billion, if you're ready to tell me that you can pass that bill for me," perhaps it all could have been done much sooner. Johnson used to say, "You can't ask me to slaughter my own babies." He was committed to those programs, to the people who had pushed the programs for him.

EH: He did not go to work actively trying to persuade the Congress to make this tax increase. He left it to Fowler and stayed somewhat remote.

AO: He had some meetings with congressmen on this. It is my impression that he refused to get into the real negotiation on this linkage with expenditure cuts until very late in the game.

EH: But he didn't bring to bear all his armory of skills on this?

AO: No. The failure to communicate with Mills on this really is a vast puzzle. Something had to have happened personally between the two of them, because on every other piece of legislation, they were in constant communication. And what that was, I don't know.
    So much of staff effort, Council effort got focused on talking points, graphs to show what would happen, scare tactics, waving this international financial crisis. I was very impressed with that at the time.

EH: You said in your book that the international bankers were able to influence the Congress with the perilous state of the dollar. But just how did the Congress get the message?

AO: Fowler used to parade them up the Hill for one thing. When they came to Washington, he would arrange for them to have appointments with members of the Congress who were on the fence. Nobody really understood the connection between world prestige and this crisis, but it sounded terrible. Many congressmen were saying: "Tell me how I can tell my constituents back home that I did them a favor by taking money out of their paycheck." And they were serious. They needed simple-minded talking points about how it really helps you to pay higher taxes. The businessmen were volunteering for this, by and large.

EH: In your book you say that the economist has a role of public education, that this is the best remedy for this kind of problem. Is that a challenge beyond the capacities of an academic economist? How can you do it?

AO: You can get to a certain fringe group of sophisticated laymen by speech making and getting into the press and educating the columnists, but to get to the blue-collar level, it's extremely difficult. You almost go back to what could be done in our educational process starting in the high school to make people have a better understanding of some of the elements of economics and macro economics.

SM: In 1968, did you see the economy as operating at about the right level, or was it overheated?

AO: We saw it as somewhat overheated by late 1967 and early 1968. I expected much more cooling off from the taxes than did take place. The debate in retrospect is whether the patient had a higher fever than we realized, or whether the aspirin did less good than we'd expected. I would still say that the surcharge made a real dent in aggregate demand and consumer demand. But basically the overall economy was a lot stronger, and by this time private demand really seemed to have a lot of momentum and just kept forging ahead. Maybe there was something in the favorable psychology of passing the tax bill that helped businessmen to keep going with their capital spending commitments and automobile demand.

SM: Hasn't Milton Friedman said that the reason the surcharge took a long time to have any effect was that monetary policy was expanding too fast? In fact, the economy seemed to be following the cycles in monetary policy much more than in fiscal policy.

AO: Nineteen sixty-six showed that a sufficiently tight monetary policy could neutralize a sufficiently expansionary fiscal policy or upset it. People who had low money multipliers had to revise them upward and again in 1968. But this whole business of the temporary nature of that surcharge is a professional controversy I've spoken out on. That I don't think is the issue. In retrospect, I do think that the Fed's easing was clearly excessive. It was based on our expectations that private demand wasn't going to be as strong as it was. You had a fiscal tightening, you had a monetary easing, and you had an underlying state of private demand. I would still say the big error we made at that point was in assessing the strength of the underlying state of private demand rather than in underestimating the damper that the fiscal program would put on or in underestimating the stimulus that would be provided by monetary policy. That's a judgment matter. Capital spending didn't keep shooting up more than we expected because money was plentiful and interest rates had come down fifty basic points. That really showed there was much more vigor in the capital boom than we had anticipated. We were wrong.

SM: Were you and the Fed coordinating your policy? You were in agreement with what they were doing?

AO: If anything, we were pushing them harder for more easing, and we were off.

SM: So the idea was to touch the brakes and then let the economy go on.

AO: Yes, okay. I could try to put it a little more euphemistically, but I really can't argue with that. Yes, this was a big change in fiscal restraint. It was a major shift, because we did get a big expenditure cutback along with the surcharge. It did appear as though that would permit a further easing of monetary policy and still give us a slowdown. We got a slowdown in real economic activity. We didn't get as much of a slowdown as we expected.
    The more significant link of the chain, which became evident in 1969 and 1970 more than in 1968, was that a slowdown and even a recession didn't do much to slow inflation, and that was the bigger surprise. That was the first episode in a whole series of major shocks to the profession on the inflationary performance of this economy that have gone all through this decade—the upsurge in 1973-74, the resistance of inflation to the deepest recession of the postwar period in 1975, the failure of inflation to decelerate further despite an extremely slack economy in 1976 and 1977. What we know now is that we don't have an adequate inflation theory or inflation forecasting mechanism within the profession. We didn't know it then. We were really misled because exactly that touch of the brake worked so well in the first half of 1967. Inflation really did slow down on a couple of flat quarters in real GNP; we went from 4 to 2-1/4 percent or something like that. Why can't we do that again? Not within my day, but by mid and late 1969 we were down to 2 percent

growth rates again, and the inflation rate was not decelerating. I suppose you can find many reasons why by that time inflation had deeper roots in the system and there were lag forces from three years of inflation that were working throughout the system, whereas in the earlier case you really had had an inflation flareup that probably had not been built into institutions or expectations.

SM: It was never your intention to generate a more significant recession?

AO: Sure wasn't our game plan. I don't think it was the McCracken-Kennedy game plan in 1969. Gradualism was still the name of the game and McCracken was giving speeches on gradualism. Stein got into a great debate with Sol Fabricant on whether 1970 should be called a recession. I think the perception was still, "Yes, we want unemployment to go back from 3.6 to 4.1 percent but 2 percent growth for a couple of quarters is the way to do that. Then you go back to 4 percent growth and keep the unemployment rate 4.1 and everything's going to be fine." There's a great chart, I believe, in the 1969 Council Report, in our swan song Report, just doing a Phillips curve scatter diagram. As of that time there was absolutely nothing to suggest that there had been an upward shift of the Phillips curve, a structural deterioration in the labor market. If anything, when you compare 1956 and 1968, 1968 has a slightly lower inflation rate and a slightly lower unemployment rate. The years 1966 and 1967 also have slightly lower unemployment rates than 1956 or 1957, a better inflation performance. You could go down that curve just as you went up that curve. Why can't we get back to where we were in 1965, the good old days? That's exactly what we thought would happen. That's exactly what didn't happen.

SM: Did the election have any role in the choice of policy proposed for 1968?

AO: If any, probably in putting less pressure on the Fed to keep things easy. We probably got a tighter monetary policy sooner under the Republicans.

SM: I didn't mean that. I meant during the year 1968, during the campaign.

AO: Oh, that political theory of a business cycle is one of the most mythical myths that persist. I don't believe there was any difference in fiscal policy or monetary policy. I think 1972 is the only year in modern history where you could really identify a difference in macro policy associated with the divisibility of that year by four. The fact that Johnson wasn't running for re-election in 1968 conceivably may have had something to do with it. I don't know what he would have done differently if he had been running for re-election.

Certainly he would not have backed away from the surcharge. An administration has a set of policies, they have a momentum. Yes, there is a marginal tendency for people not to rock the boat during a campaign. If the Fed wanted to tighten, for example, it wasn't going to do that two weeks before election. If we were sufficiently smart about economic policy, we wouldn't have to make things look good just for election years, we could make things look good 48 months of every presidential term. This conspiratorial notion requires a degree of sophistication, a degree of competence that is so great that, if you had it, you wouldn't need to become conspiratorial.

SM: Did I read correctly in your book that the investment tax credit was put back at the end of 1967?

AO: In March of 1967, wasn't it? That proved to be a really brutal instrument. We got a tremendous impact of a very uneven kind from the suspension of the investment tax credit. On long duration equipment like railway cars and commercial airplanes, orders just dried up: an 80 percent decline in orders. On the shelf goods, there was barely any effect. The result was very lopsided. If businessmen really believe that the 7 percent investment tax credit is going back on next year the urgency about placing the airplane or the boxcar order is not great. I think the little fiscal program that suspended the investment tax credit in September 1966 really did break a log jam in financial markets, a real crunch in interest rates. The perception of reduced capital spending pressures and bond demand pressures had great influence in simmering that down for the next six months, but I would not recommend trying to play on and off games with the ITC on the basis of that experience. We started getting letters referred to us from boxcar producers--commercial aircraft wasn't a problem because most of the people who make commercial aircraft also had defense orders and they had loads of them--indicating that we were creating huge pockets of unemployment. That's not the way to get a decent anti-inflationary effect in the labor market, and it is terribly inequitable. So if you ever want to get an overnight relief for financial markets, suspending the ITC is the way to do it, but don't live with it more than a couple of weeks.

EH: In your book you advocate Congress' giving the president the authority to regulate tax rates within certain limits. If President Johnson had had that authority, would he not have acted just as cautiously as he did because of political reasons? Wouldn't politics constrain a president, even if he had such authority?

AO: It would, but I think it would have been harder for him to maintain the fiscal program he did in fact conduct through 1966, simply because it would have been clear to everyone that he was in a position to raise taxes. So if he wasn't going to use that lever, I think he might have been forced either to cut spending himself or maybe hold down Vietnam spending more. In a sense his inability to change taxes fast became an excuse for running a lousy fiscal policy.

AL: Political considerations might well have been such that he would have tried to reinforce his political popularity rather than take the medicine.

AO: But doesn't it change the terms on which you reinforce political popularity if everybody in the profession seems united in saying that this economy needs to be cooled off and the president has a lever at his hand by which he can do it? It's much harder for him to take the position that he's still thinking about the question and doesn't want to act precipitously, that, in addition, he hopes the need won't be there any more by the time Congress gets around to acting. The answer is, "If you think it's necessary today, Mr. President, do it today. If it's not necessary six months later, pull it off."

EH: Congress might want to give him such authority, in fact, to get it off their backs.

AO: Yes, you would think that and yet the jealousy about the prerogative is tremendous. Why does anybody want to have the power to do this bad thing, and yet they do. The only viable proposal in this area one could imagine being done within our lifetime would be a sort of compromise that Stanley Surrey devised: this would not be discretionary authority but a stipulative procedure by which the president could recommend a certain type of tax increase or reduction for urgent stabilization purposes, and it would take priority over everything else. It would be equivalent to having presidential discretionary authority with a thirty-day veto by either House of the Congress. But put it in the form that the Congress simply says, "We'll vote it up or down without amendment within thirty days." Then they have to legislate on a strict time schedule. We deal with these cyclical issues all the time and there have been several efforts to try to say what form a tax increase or cut should have for cyclical purposes. We ought to be able to make that decision and at least settle on that. Whether you're doing a uniform percentage surcharge, whether you're doing a dollar across the board, whether you're exempting low-income groups on an increase, let's settle that. Then we'll know what is the best counter-cyclical package and we'll debate it in terms of its need. Now every time a tax measure comes down the pike, we have to go through a great national debate on the distribution of the burden or the benefit and you can't make such a boilerplate package stand up.

SM: Given these difficulties with Congress, how do you come down

on the feasibility of pursuing a counter-cyclical fiscal
policy as a stabilization device?

AO: Well, it's limited.

SM: Are you still sufficiently optimistic that it's worthwhile to
try to sell this idea?

AO: I'm not sure I'd press hard for this discretionary authority
or accelerated procedures. Some of the trigger mechanisms
that we introduced in the last cycle have some promise as a
desirable feature, using unemployment triggers for jobs programs or for revenue sharing add-on. That's a way of getting
more automatic flexibility by building up the automatic stabilizers and allowing them to trigger off new programs. I
don't think we got much of a test in the last recession. The
real problem was deciding when we were fighting the inflation
and when we were fighting the recession.

AL: The whole argument we used to get from the economists was:
"We know how to handle these problems. Our problem is with
you damned political scientists who can't arrange the governmental decision making machinery in such a way so that we can
put the correct medicine into the bottle." You testified now
that economists don't know as much as they used to about how
to manage the economy.

AO: Oh, no, we don't know as much as we used to think we knew.

LS: How much did economists learn from the experience to contribute to revision of theory?

AO: I'll try to summarize that simply by saying that we know none
of our inflation theories really explained the behavior of
the price level in the last decade. That doesn't mean that
we now know the answers. A lot of us individually think that
we do have a better clue to what really goes on in the
economy and why it is as resistant to excess supply and
cooling off as it is, but there is no accepted new theory of
inflation that will do the job. The other thing we learned
really in 1972, 1973 and 1974 is that micro shocks, like food
and fuel, can have bigger macro impacts than we ever recognized before. We have also learned that the greater openness
of the U.S. economy makes international developments and
exchange rate developments more important than we realized
before. Any piece of experience gives us either some confirmation or amendment of our previous views, whether it's
the suspension of the investment tax credit, whether it's the
application of a combination of fiscal and monetary policy.
I would say that our ability to analyze the forces that
determine real economic activity, employment and output isn't
bad; it hasn't had any major improvement in the last twenty
years, but that's not where we have failed. In individual
instances, we were excessively optimistic about 1962 and

312

insufficiently optimistic about 1965--even prior to Vietnam--
but those weren't big errors. Even the mis-estimate of the
extent of deceleration of growth in late 1968 and early 1969
wouldn't have loomed large in perspective, had not the bigger
and more important inflation surprise been associated with
it. Many people in the profession have tried to explain
their failure to diagnose the recession in 1974, but, fortunately, I don't happen to be in that position. My diagnosis
of how inflation takes roots is heavily institutional.

EH: Does that suggest that the new theory will have strong institutional components to it, when it emerges?

AO: The profession is trying to cope with this problem in two
ways. One is a very expectational view. It's psychological
and it links the momentum of inflation to the perception of
government policy and so forth. The other links it to the
presence of explicit and implicit contractual relations in
the economy--that's the line I've been on.

7
The Council of Economic Advisers Under Chairman Paul W. McCracken, 1969-1971

Summary History

The incoming president, Richard Nixon, announced in late 1968 that his selection for Chairman of the Council of Economic Advisers was Paul W. McCracken, a member of the CEA during the Eisenhower years. Nixon characterized the University of Michigan economist as a "centrist." McCracken accepted the role of fiscal policy just as his Democratic predecessors had, but he also emphasized the equally important role of monetary policy. He was not willing to go as far as the monetarists in putting all his faith in the efficacy of monetary policy, but he was also critical of the excessively expansionist fiscal policy and erratic attempts at fine-tuning the economy in the 1960s. His goal was a stable combination of both fiscal and monetary policies that would focus on long-term, not short-term goals. Joining McCracken on the CEA were Henrick S. Houthakker, an authority on international economics, and Herbert Stein, a specialist in fiscal policy. In June 1971, Ezra Solomon replaced Houthakker, who returned to Harvard.

There were some changes in the structure of economic policy-making under the new administration. Nixon retained both the Troika and the Quadriad from the Kennedy-Johnson years, but they apparently functioned somewhat differently. The top level of the Troika, for instance, reviewed a range of forecasts, both judgmental and econometric, rather than working with a single forecast sent up from lower levels. The Troika also often worked through a White House liaison and did not maintain the direct links to the President that had existed earlier. Also, after Arthur Burns became Chairman of the Federal Reserve Board in February 1970, the Quadriad assumed a more important role in macro policymaking.

The CEA also participated in a number of other cabinet level groups, including the Cabinet Committee on Economic Policy. On occasion, the Council took part as well in the various task forces and working groups within the White House that were set up under John Ehrlichman's direction to formulate policy on such issues as welfare reform and oil import quotas. While this increasing emphasis on the role of the staff meant a lessening of the influence of cabinet officials, it is not clear that McCracken had as much difficulty as others, at least not in the first year or so of the administration. While he was of cabinet rank, he did not have the sort of competing role characteristic of department secretaries, against whom the administration's "counter-bureaucracy" was aimed. On the contrary, the CEA was included in the White House's daily staff meetings. But Ehrlichman's closer control over domestic policy matters after mid-1969 did limit the CEA's access to Nixon. Of even more significance was the creation of the Domestic Council and the Office of Management and Budget in July 1970, at the recommendation of the Ash Council. This reorganization shifted the focus of economic policy further away from the CEA, a trend evident as well in the central roles played by John Connally and George Shultz as administration spokesmen on economic policy from 1971 on. Generally, the CEA did not seem to have the central role in economic policymaking that it had under Kennedy and Johnson.

The central economic problem of the Nixon administration was clearly inflation. The McCracken CEA's analysis of the problem focused on excess demand that built up under the defense and Great Society expenditures of the Johnson years. According to their view, government policy had exacerbated the situation, both through delay in seeking a tax increase and through an easy money policy from mid-1967. Nixon's economic advisers rejected immediately any possibility of a sharp deflation and recession to halt inflation and bring the economy back to a noninflationary path. Such policy would be unwise if for no other reason than the political consequences of higher unemployment. But neither were we willing to accept the current rate of inflation in order to maintain a low unemployment rate, for there was much concern about built-in inflationary psychology and the instability of the Phillips trade-off. The course of action chosen was to try to cautiously approach the noninflationary growth path, avoiding as much increased unemployment as possible.

As developed in 1969, Nixon's program of "gradualism" focused first on stabilizing fiscal policy, but within the full employment surplus concept of the "New Economics" rather than traditional budget balancing. Fiscal restraint was to be carried out through moderate budget surpluses for FY 1969 and FY 1970 attained through budget cuts and extension of the surcharge. These surpluses would also help reduce the federal debt and release funds to ease the housing situation; this was to be accompanied by realignment of the Treasury debt structure to stretch out and lower interest rates and to ease strains on the private capital market. In line with the monetarists' emphasis on the need for controlling the growth of the money supply, the Fed was to continue its tight monetary policy at least through the first half of 1969. Other programs were to be established to cushion the impact of these policies, including manpower development and improvement of the income support system. Noticeably absent from the administration's 1969 program was an incomes policy. McCracken and the CEA were unconvinced that the wage-price guideposts of the previous administration had been effective enough to warrant the challenge to the free market principle. While jawboning and intervention in specific wage-price actions would be avoided, the CEA chairman did admit the possibility of government action in cases where the government's normal activities were directly related to such market developments, as in international trade policy, antitrust enforcement, government procurement, and application of minimum wage laws. But generally, intervention had little place in the administration's gradualist policy focused on fiscal and monetary policy.

The Nixon administration was determined to convince the public of the seriousness of its anti-inflation program. The emphasis was on restraint and preparation for what lay ahead. This was clearly evident in fiscal and monetary policy in 1969, with the shift from a FY 1968 $25 billion budget deficit to a FY 1969 $1.35 billion surplus and with the reduction in the growth of the money supply from 6.5 percent during 1968 to 2.8 percent in the first half of 1969. Nixon also called for extension of the surcharge for another six months, repeal of the 7 percent investment tax credit, postponement of reductions in automobile and telephone excise taxes, and budget cuts to reduce the Johnson administration's already very tight budget for FY 1970. Despite such efforts by the administration, the economy did not appear to be slowing down, as borrowing and investment actually increased. In September, McCracken continued to warn that a slowdown was indeed imminent, that the public should not expect continued growth, and that restraints would not be eased when the slowdown did develop. He emphasized that such a course was necessary to reduce excess demand and halt inflation. In November, it became clear that the boom had actually ended, and by early 1970 some economists were calling it a recession. The administration was charged with economic "overkill" much like that of the Johnson years. But the worst part was that wages and prices continued to rise.

The McCracken CEA's first Economic Report came out in early 1970. As during the JFK-LBJ years, the CEA had its own report, rather than returning to the anonymity of the Eisenhower years. Despite the problems that had developed in 1969, the report basically recommended following the gradualist policy that McCracken and the rest of the administration had advocated. The tone was low-key. While expecting inflation to continue through 1970, the Council hoped, through a moderate budget surplus and continued monetary restraint, to slow the inflationary rate and then in the last half of the year to rekindle growth. The CEA's view of 1970 rested on its emphasis on the role of excess demand and the problem of inflationary expectations in causing the continued inflationary pressures. As in 1969, wage-price policies were rejected in favor of fiscal-monetary actions.

Throughout 1970, Nixon and the CEA continued to back this analysis of the nation's economic problems despite doubts expressed both privately and publicly by other administration figures. McCracken repeatedly emphasized that disinflationary forces were at work and that controls would not be necessary to deal with the cost-push problem that critics suggested the administration was neglecting. In June, McCracken was instrumental in shifting attention away from such criticism for a time through a new focus on an administration program to increase productivity growth and through optimistic predictions of stronger gains in output, increased production, and a slowing down of inflation for the last half of 1970. As it turned out, however, the General Motors strike in late 1970 actually led to lower output and higher prices and wages (the price index up 5.5 percent from 1969 and the mean level of major wage settlements up 8.9 percent). Unemployment reached 6.0 percent, 1.5 percent higher than the CEA's forecast. The economy was not behaving as expected. The economic slowdown and increased unemployment were not stopping inflation.

With the economic downturn in 1969-70, pressure for intervention increased. Others within the Troika questioned the CEA's continued emphasis on demand rather than cost factors and its belief in the ability of monetary-fiscal policies to halt inflation. In April 1970, Burns publicly called for an incomes policy to deal with cost-push factors. Others followed this same line, but McCracken and the CEA emphasized that no wage-price controls would be forthcoming, although privately McCracken apparently began to consider the value of at least discussing some form of intervention. Open confrontation was avoided, however, when the focus shifted to the administration's new emphasis on productivity growth, as evident in the establishment in June 1970 of a National Commission on Productivity and a Regulations and Purchasing Review Board. More significant was the announcement that the CEA would begin to issue "inflation alerts" to inform the public about significant wage and price increases. It was stressed that the goal was to inform, not judge, and that this was not intervention. Accordingly, the subsequent alerts on August 7 and December 1, 1970, were simply accounts of past developments. It was not until April 13, 1971, that the CEA finally used the alerts for jawboning purposes.

In August 1970, Congress passed the Economic Stabilization Act of 1970 that gave the President the authority to freeze wages, salaries, prices and rents. Nixon insisted he would not use that authority. By December, however, he seemed more willing to intervene, first through liberalization of oil imports to keep fuel costs down and then through jawboning to influence construction industry negotiations. But while he was willing to take some limited action and resort to exhortation on occasion, Nixon still resisted both guidelines and controls. As inflation continued in January 1971 at the rate of 5.7 percent, it was clear that his economic policies were not paying off. Nixon then accepted the necessity of intervention in wage-price settlements, but only when absolutely essential. This was evident in Nixon's harsh criticism in early 1971 of a steel industry price rise and the CEA's April "inflation alert" focusing on the necessity of holding down upcoming industry wage increases. The administration also took action to hold down construction industry wage increases, culminating in the formulation on March 29 of the Construction Industry Stabilization Committee and craft dispute boards. McCracken admitted that these administration actions were elements of an incomes policy but insisted that they were limited, taken to restore market competition, and only supplemented fiscal-monetary policy.

When the CEA issued its Report in February 1971, it was still optimistic about reducing unemployment to 4.5 percent and lowering the inflation rate to 3 percent by mid-1972. The CEA also unenthusiastically accepted OMB forecasts of a $1,065 billion GNP for the year, a target few considered possible. By April such goals were clearly impossible and the Council revised its forecast, lowering the GNP target and predicting 4.9 percent unemployment by the second quarter of 1972. Although many within and outside the administration remained skeptical, an optimistic outlook was politically essential in light of Nixon's 1972 re-election plans.

Despite the slowdown in the economy, 1971 brought little relief from inflation. The level of wage settlements increased, while unemployment hovered at 6 percent. Although the rise in the consumer price index was the lowest since 1967, the rate of increase in wholesale prices and the private GNP deflator exceeded the 1970 level. The balance of payments problem worsened. The costs to the economy and to Nixon's political prospects were clear. Pressures for some sort of incomes policy mounted.

As calls for action from both Democrats and Republicans increased, disagreement continued within the administration in mid-1971 over the proper course of action. Burns continued to push for a tough incomes policy, while OMB Director Shultz opposed it. Shultz was also not favorably inclined toward McCracken's proposal for a stimulus to the economy accompanied by wage-price guidelines to control inflation. It was Secretary of the Treasury John Connally, however, who became the central figure in developing administration economic policy in the summer of 1971. Concerned with the political repercussions of continued poor economic performance, Connally tried to keep options open and urged Congress to extend the Economic Stabilization Act of 1970. He was not willing to reject the possibility of controls as the domestic economic situation worsened.

As the pressure for wage-price intervention increased, the international situation finally forced the administration's August 1971 action. As balance of payments deficits had increased in past years, the ratio of dollar liabilities to international reserve assets had grown. It was no longer clear that the U.S. could meet all the claims against its assets. The dollar was overvalued, but there was much concern about the effect that devaluation would have on the international financial system. The situation worsened throughout the summer culminating in Britain's request on August 12 for $3 billion "cover" for their dollar assets. Some action was clearly necessary, and it was generally agreed that the gold window would have to be closed, thereby suspending the convertibility of the dollar.

With a penchant for the dramatic, Nixon decided to also act decisively at the same time on domestic economic problems, thereby regaining the initiative for the administration in the entire economic field. On August 13, in a Quadriad meeting at Camp David, the decision was made to impose a temporary 90-day freeze on all wages, prices and rents (allowed under the Economic Stabilization Act of 1970), expansionary tax and expenditure cuts, the closing of the gold window, and a 10 percent surcharge on imports. The freeze was intended to give the administration time to develop a long-term program. Although the CEA and the Fed had done some independent staff work on incomes policy earlier that summer, the OMB had been given the initial responsibility for staff work, despite Shultz's opposition to incomes policy. Once the decision was made to act, McCracken, Burns, and Arnold Weber of the OMB worked out the details of the freeze, basically along the lines proposed by the OMB staff study. Other task forces worked on fiscal policy and international matters.

On August 15, 1971, Nixon made his dramatic announcement of the institution of the first peacetime controls program in the nation's history. The freeze was to begin immediately and last until November 14, at which time the as yet undeveloped Phase II of the administration's program would go into effect. The freeze was to be carried out through a hastily established organization focused on a cabinet level Cost of Living Council chaired by Connally, with McCracken as vice-chairman. The CLC was to determine administration policies for the freeze and work out the details of Phase II. Operational responsibility was given to the Office of Emergency Preparedness, with assistance from the Internal Revenue Service and the Agricultural Stabilization and Conservation Service. Throughout the freeze, CEA Chairman McCracken played a central role, first in the initial policy decisions before the CLC was set up and then as chairman of the Executive Policy Committee of the CLC that was responsible for interpreting existing policies and recommending new policies to the full CLC. This group became one of the most important units in the organizational structure, for it decided what issues would go to the CLC for consideration. The CLC itself often had trouble reaching agreement, for the constituency-oriented members' soft position on issues conflicted with the tougher stand taken by those like the CEA with broader responsibilities. Generally, despite criticism of the harshness of the policies and certain inequities, the freeze appeared to work, providing short-term restraint on wage-price increases. With the institution of Phase II on November 14, the nation then moved into the long-run controls program that was to continue until April 1974. Herbert Stein took the dominant CEA role in this phase of the controls program, beginning in December 1971 after the announcement of McCracken's resignation (as of January 1, 1972) and his own selection as Nixon's next CEA chairman. In the three years that McCracken served on the Council, economic policy had undergone a radical reversal, as the administration had given up its attempt to demonstrate the possibility of attaining both full employment and price stability through traditional fiscal-monetary policies and had instead instituted the nation's first peacetime controls program.

Oral History Interview

The Selection of the Chairman

EH: What do you know about your selection and whatever negotiations were involved in that process?

PM: I'm not sure that the person who has the job is a very good source for information on that subject. I mean this seriously because, obviously, the discussions that may have led to my selection occurred before I came on the scene. My impression is that the person who was probably as responsible as anyone else was Arthur Burns. When he was Chairman of the Council, he had become acquainted with then Vice-President Nixon, and Arthur suggested my name to Mr. Nixon after he was elected president.

After the election there began to emerge the usual scuttlebutt about who would get the job, and my name started to be mentioned for the chairmanship. A newspaper reporter whom I knew called me and asked me about it. I told him that I knew nothing about it and, paraphrasing Groucho Marx, I reminded him that I had been a member of the Council once and anyone stupid enough to have a second tour of duty would certainly not be smart enough to hold the job. When the announcement was made, he called me again, and I told him that I had not reckoned with the fact that if all three Republican economists in the country didn't do their duty, we couldn't have a Council at all.

EH: Had you had any personal relations with Nixon in the second Eisenhower administration?

PM: Not really. The Council at that time didn't have the pervasive activity in government that it did later on. Until I went down to the Pierre Hotel and talked to him, I had never formally met Mr. Nixon. At that time he said, "Can't we just settle this right now because I have to go down for a press conference? It's always helpful in a press conference if you have something to say." So we went down and he introduced me and reminded the reporters that, of course, we had known each other for ten years. But I had not actually met him.

EH: And you had not worked in the campaign?

PM: No.

ML: When Nixon met with you that first time, was there any explicit discussion of economic policy, planning or philosophy?

PM: Philosophy. Not really very much. There were the usual discussions about structure and logistics and how it would operate. One question that I suppose anyone is always inclined to raise under these circumstances is: how is the White House going to be structured; is the chairman going to report to the president or is he going to go through someone else? We had that discussion.

My impression is that presidents tend to tell each successive appointee that he will be particularly important in the administration.

EH: Did the President-Elect give you latitude to select the other two members of the Council?

PM: Yes, I remember quite distinctly as we walked to the door to go down to the press conference, he said, "Now, let's see, there have to be two other members of the Council. Do you have any ideas about this?" I said at that time, "Well, the first person I would like to talk to about this would be Herb Stein." As I recall, he said, "I don't think I know him personally, but I know who he is." I had no problem with either Herb or Houthakker, whom at that point I did not know as well as Herb. These names had to be cleared, but the selection was mine.

I think the chairman ought to be the primary person there. This is not just to make sure that life is nice, but because these people do have to work as a team. Moreover, many people are not aware that the executive authority of the Council of Economic Advisers is vested in the chairman, not the Council. Practically, it really doesn't make very much difference. Any chairman who's worth his salt is not going to try to throw his weight around or treat the other two people as second-class citizens. On the other hand, you don't want a debating seminar taking votes two to one in favor of a tax cut.

DD: You had no prior contact with Houthakker before you selected him?

PM: I'd had slight contact with him. I had nothing to do with the campaign, but in the summer we did develop quite a series of task force studies on various aspects of policy—agricultural policy, health, welfare. One of these was international economic policy, and Houthakker was a member of that resource group.

EH: What criteria were used to select these other two members?

PM: First, I obviously wanted people of demonstrated competence in what I would call the mainstream of economics. Second, I wanted some division; I didn't want two macro economists. I wanted someone who had substantial experience in the area of demand management policies, fiscal policy, monetary policy. Herb, of course, fitted that beautifully. Incidentally, I was not unmindful of the fact that Herb is a superb writer. One of the things you have to bear in mind about this job is that once a year you have quite a substantial literary problem on your hands. Then I wanted someone who would be competent to give direction to the international economic area, which was beginning to emerge as more important, to agriculture, and to the whole cluster of issues that, within the Council, we referred to as micro problems: programs such as price support programs in agriculture or trucking deregulation. Houthakker fitted that rather nicely. Actually, his appointment did come along a little later. We proceeded very rapidly with Herb. Frankly, I really had not thought about Houthakker. I was thinking of a few other people when Jim Dusenberry of Harvard called me and said, "You might want to give consideration to Houthakker," and I thought it was a good idea myself. This shows the political ecumenism. Jim, you see, had been a member of the Council under Kennedy.

Council members are primarily academics. That is, in general, a good policy, but the tendency in recent years to reach beyond academics—Alan Greenspan is a case in point—is good. Excellent people are out in the financial and business communities, and they ought not to be proscribed.

EH: Then you had to select a professional staff. How was that done?

PM: We essentially inherited a staff because the transition occurred in the middle of a year for the staff. The staff at that time, as I guess still is true, was part permanent and part academic. Many of the academic staff, I think, were not quite sure how they would get along with these troglodytes who were coming down, but that very quickly settled into place. When I arrived on the scene, it seems that we did have a vacancy in the monetary and financial area—I don't remember now who might have been holding that in the closing days of the Okun era—so we borrowed someone from the Federal Reserve for six months or so until we got that staffed. That was no real problem. Indeed, I recall one of the staff members—an academic—making the observation that, so far as what the staff does at the Council, it really doesn't seem to make very much difference whether it's a Republican or a Democratic administration. I think that probably is true. They're not doing political work. They're doing analytical work.

EH: What about the balance between temporary academic staff and permanent civil servants?

PM: I think it ought to be some of both. You have to have enough people around who understand how government operates, and they can be very helpful to the academics who come in on a short-term basis. My general experience was that it was better to get a mature young academic, not someone in his fifties, because it's very hard for the older scholar to shift gears. He may find at noon that he has to produce a memorandum by 3:00 p.m.—one that resembles a whole semester's project. The young ones can do it.

EH: Do you favor a small staff?

322

PM: Definitely. The larger the staff, the greater is going to be the structure, the more departmentalized it's going to become. The ideal CEA structure is a relatively small staff of about the size it presently has, and senior people on the staff who can apply their analytical disciplines over a fairly wide range of subjects. Take as an illustration the welfare proposals that finally did come to the Congress and missed in the House, I guess, by one vote. Fairly early in the game in meetings with the President, HEW was producing estimates of outlays and others were producing estimates, and they were so far apart that obviously the President couldn't make a decision. He didn't know what he was choosing. I was asked to have the CEA make an independent analysis or estimate of what the outlays would be. Bill Branson, whom some of you would know, and Dave Ott--both of whom had been brought to the staff by Art Okun--were a couple of fellows who weren't experts in welfare economics, but who understood how to apply their discipline to this sort of thing. They produced estimates. I suppose the CEA could have had a welfare department, but I would confidently predict that if we had had, we would have "struck out" on that kind of issue. As it was, we could tell two or three people with their juniors, "Just drop whatever you're doing and spend the next 24 hours on this." I would strongly oppose any major increase in the size of the Council. It's all chiefs, no Indians, and that's the way it ought to be.

EH: Does this mean the Council is very dependent on the agencies for data and other analytic work?

PM: Certainly for data. The CEA does not generate data, of course, and I certainly would be opposed to getting bogged down in that task. On occasion we might want BLS to do some analytical work for us, but it would be analytical work or statistical analysis. Whenever we really got in a bind, we would be more apt to turn to the Federal Reserve. They have so many economists over there that they wouldn't miss ten of them.

EH: But you never got into the business that Kissinger got into quickly, of directing that papers be written in the agency?

PM: Oh, no, no, because sooner or later, it's just going to create trouble. There are better ways to get things done.

DD: But in inter-agency groups, the Council, not necessarily the chairman but the Council member, might suggest that a logical place for a given paper to be developed would be at the Fed because of the size of the staff. In that process, the Council member would keep an eye on the paper and supervise it, so that he'd know what was going on in that area.

PM: Yes, that's quite true.

DD: The fact that the Council staff is small and their responsibilities aren't so specialized has been a positive inducement
to attract quality people.

PM: Yes, if you want these senior people, they have to be almost
stand-ins for the Council members.

EH: Did you have maxims in your mind, as you went into office,
derived from your earlier experience on the Council? Maxims
about operating in government, the role of economics in the
White House, and so on?

PM: Without trying to give any structured analysis, let me just
think aloud about this. One point that I had some fairly firm
views on and had done a little writing about was--let's use a
cliché--that attempting to fine-tune the course of the economy required continuing adjustments in economic policy that
were apt to build instability rather than stability into the
pattern. So I suppose I came to the Council with some bias
in the direction of a more steady-as-you-go management of
economic policy. I had not been impressed with the contributions that wage and price guidelines had made; the wage and
price guidelines approach to trying to solve or trying to
influence inflation struck me as one in which the arithmetic
was reasonably straightforward when the programs were not
needed, but in which the arithmetic became impossible when
they were needed. When we arrived, we were sometimes accused
of killing off the guideposts. That is, I think, factually
not correct. They were dead when we arrived. The prior two
Economic Reports had not even attempted to spell out the
arithmetic as to what the guideposts would be. Third, it was
becoming clear to me that we were going to have to move
toward a floating exchange rate system. I must say, however,
that a floating exchange rate system is easier to argue in an
academic seminar than it seems to work out in practice.
    Fundamentally, however--and here I think there was no
real disagreement within the administration--it seemed that
the clearcut economic policy problem was the rising rate of
inflation. The specific figures don't sound so startling any
more, but at that time they looked pretty troublesome.

EH: Were there maxims in your mind about cooperating in government as an economic adviser--things you had learned about the
institution of the Council earlier?

PM: Looking back over the history of the Council, I had been
impressed with the importance of the Council and the chairman
of the Council's trying to stay on that rather admittedly
ill-defined path that would enable him to maintain his status
as a professional economist, but also have the president
consider him a member of the team. The two extremes of the
Council, the two extremes of the spectrum were probably
staked out in the first administrations of the Council, if I
may use that term. Dr. Nourse, who was the first Chairman of

the Council, is no longer living. One must not make observations about his Council in a pejorative tone, because they had no charts to follow, but I do think that the Nourse Council and Dr. Nourse, in particular, probably took an excessively detached and Olympian view: that the Council would be a kind of economic policy supreme court dispensing pure advice from Mount Olympus to the people down below, such as the president. The problem there is that the president is apt to feel that the Council is not a member of the team. Now I would judge that the next time around the Council became excessively political and tended to discredit its professional status, without which it also limits its influence. Many in the Congress on the Democratic side of the aisle—Paul Douglas, for example—shared that view. After that somewhat uncertain beginning of wobbling from one extreme to the other, the Councils have pretty well stayed in the middle ground.

EH: The implication in regard to Keyserling is that if you go beyond the discipline too far your credibility is undermined?

PM: You're seen operating simply as a politician. If you go back and check the history—I think I'm correct on this—the Congress in 1952 gave the Council only about six months of an appropriation. And it was a Democratic Congress, so it wasn't a partisan issue. I don't think any chairman would insist that there was never a time when his toe didn't step over the line a bit one way or the other. But if one looks at the Councils thereafter—Burns, Saulnier, Heller, Ackley, Okun, up to the time I came on the scene—I would say all of those Councils pretty well maintained this kind of balance. Not easy to do, by the way. I think it's one of the difficulties of that job that probably is not appreciated by people who have not been there.

DD: In trying to keep your own Council on this line, did it become increasingly difficult to be a member of the team?

PM: No, in this kind of job, there are times when the situation goes better than others. There are times when you are going to be opposing policies that the president decides to implement. That doesn't mean he's wrong and you're right, but it means that you didn't intramurally support the policy.

EH: Does there not have to be an ideological fit between the economic adviser and the president for this relationship to work well?

PM: Sure, but that can sound as if it means more than it does. Obviously, if there were a Council of Economic Advisers in France and you switched from the Giscard d'Estaing government to a Mitterand government, the Council in one case is going to be totally different from the other. In this country— here I'm poaching on the domain of political science—we do have to keep two things in mind. One is that both parties are essentially mainstream. The second is--the political scientists and historians will probably object to this--that there is such a thing as a discipline of economics. This was partly what the staff person had in mind when he said, "We seem to do very much the same thing whether it's a Republican or a Democratic CEA." On the other hand, it's fair to say that there has to be a certain basic simpatico there.

ML: Could you give an example of how the so-called desire to be a member of the team actually molded certain aspects of your analysis of economic data?

PM: It's not a matter of molding your analysis, because, at least literally interpreted, that would suggest that you tailor your analysis in order to arrive at the right answer. Any CEA chairman who would tailor his analysis to arrive at some preconceived answer would not be very valuable to the president very long.

But what is the basic function of a CEA adviser? First, most of the CEA chairman's time will be concerned with micro economic problems. You don't spend all your time at the mountaintop contemplating the broad issues of fiscal policy. The most helpful thing you can do as an adviser to the president is to spell out the options he has and the implications of each option. Moreover, the CEA chairman is naturally going to be talking essentially about the economic dimensions of the decisions. Let me give you an illustration which has no quantitative significance but which illustrates this problem. At the end of 1960, three of us were asked by Dewey's friend, Bob Roosa, who was to be Under Secretary of the Treasury, to make a report to the then President-Elect Kennedy on the domestic economic situation and the balance of payments. (It shows how little things change.) The three were Alan Sproul, who had just retired at that point as president of the New York Fed, Roy Blough, who had been a member of the Council under Truman, and I. By the time the report was given to Kennedy--I think it was probably mid-February--he had been president perhaps a month. One of our recommendations, and the substance of it is not important, was that he ought to introduce legislation to reduce or remove the gold cover on Federal Reserve notes because it probably was going to be necessary and it would be better to do it before his back was against the wall. Well, you can argue this issue either way. But I remember we laid this out and Kennedy said, "Yes, I understand the logic of this. Now, let's see, that would have to go before the Senate Finance Committee, wouldn't it? And old Harry Byrd is chairman, isn't he? You know, if I propose that, old Harry Byrd would go right through the Capitol dome." I still remember that gesture. He said, "I don't want to start my administration that way." That is a good illustration of the adviser's role. I think we performed our function. It wasn't up to us to decide the issue. He had in mind other considerations and we weren't the experts on those. I'm sure he made the right decision.

AL: One of the problems I've never been able to understand is how economists see such a distinction between reporting to the president and then analyzing the state of the economy, which is clearly a technical and expert function. I take it that you don't mean that you are, in that sense, a member of the team. You're a part of the administration or of the government, rather than the inner circle.

PM: Yes, sure. What you're saying is that this concept is really a continuum all the way from not being a member of the team to being some combination, I guess, of a yes-man and a hatchet-man.

AL: How corruptible can you get?

PM: Obviously I would not use that term, but I think your comment does touch on one difficulty that anyone in that job is going to confront. You are going to find yourself occasionally before a congressional committee being asked about a policy decision the president has made and obviously you can't say, "Well, just between you and me I didn't like it very well either." You have to articulate the administration's position. Here the chairman of the Council really has to recognize—if I may use a football metaphor—that you are a member of the team and just because the quarterback doesn't happen to call what you think might be the right play doesn't mean that you absolutely won't run the play. It's been called, so you run it. But if you decide you don't like the whole damn game plan, then you get off the team. At what point do you metamorphose from one position to the other? It's a question of judgment. I suspect that most of us looking back can see points at which we wonder if perhaps we shouldn't have resigned. After all, there is a place for resignation in a democracy. In my own case, the point at which, in retrospect, perhaps I should have resigned was in the latter part of 1971 when the President went to wage and price controls. I had opposed that sort of thing, not only within the administration, but for a long period of time. I have no reason even yet to change my mind that these controls don't work, and I would have to say in all candor that perhaps the game plan had changed enough at that point that I should have said, "I've got to step off the team."

The President and Economic Policy

EH: How did the President think about economics, how did his values relate to it, how did he think politically about these questions?

PM: Well, there are two or three points here. Point number one: Nixon would have been ideologically—if one may use that

term--rather conservative, or liberal in the European meaning
of the term, in his general point of view regarding economic
policy issues. But, second, this would have to be interpreted in the context of Nixon's lack of interest in economics. Economics was never a public policy area of particular
interest to him. Nothing startling about that. Any man
arrives at the Oval Office with a background of interests and
experience in some things and not in others. Mr. Nixon may
even have had an almost psychological block about economics.
Let me compare him with Ford, for example. I did spend about
a month in the White House after Ford was somewhat uncere-
moniously dumped into the Oval Room and, of course, I had
known him for ten or fifteen years before that. I couldn't
help but see a startling difference between the men because
Ford found economic policy questions just intellectually
interesting. He enjoyed working with them. In fact, he once
said that he would have concentrated in economics instead of
becoming a lawyer except that he couldn't see any way to make
a living as an economist. (He's probably right.) I always
had the feeling that Mr. Nixon did not find economics so
interesting. At occasional White House dinners where businessmen and others would be brought in, the President would
give a round-up, an informal state of the union, I guess, and
he would dutifully go through the domestic issues, including
economic aspects, but when he got to foreign policy he got
animated and the lights went on. So there was a basic instinctive orientation in the conservative direction, but he
never really considered economics as inherently interesting
as some other subjects.

Actually the role of the Council in the administration
by the time of my second incarnation there was so totally
different from the first that sometimes I almost forgot that
I had ever been there, except that it was the same building.
For example, the Council had a much more pervasive role
within the Executive Office of the President the second time
around. I did, however, see President Eisenhower on occasion. He also had this rather conventional, conservative
approach, very much influenced at that time by his Secretary
of the Treasury, George Humphrey. Eisenhower didn't like to
have long memoranda as a modus operandi for briefing. He
wanted to have you brief him. Nixon was much more inclined
to want a paper that he could look at. When Eisenhower
interviewed me about being a member, he said, "Now people
around this White House understand that I don't like a memorandum that's over two pages long," but he then grinned and
said, "But I've about decided that's impossible for economists."

DD: I think that is an interesting distinction because my observation was that Kennedy was always intellectually interested
in the substance of economics. And Johnson just the reverse.

PM: That would be my impression.

EH: But was Eisenhower interested in the substance, do you think? Did he take to it?

PM: Oh, I think so. But just ranking the four presidents in terms of their inherent interest in economic policy, I guess I would put Ford first. I guess I'd put Kennedy in the same category, but I had such limited contact with Kennedy, I couldn't really speak to it.

EH: Did Nixon understand that macro economic policy was crucial for him politically? So he had to pay attention?

PM: Oh, yes.

EH: But it was a reluctant kind of attention.

PM: Well, yes, but of course that's not surprising. After all, a corporate CEO man may think that marketing is doggone important to the company, but it's not a subject he really is very interested in, so he has to force it. But he certainly understood its importance. I suppose one little piece of evidence was that early in 1969, the President sent a letter to George Meany--this letter no doubt is in the record-- assuring him that we were going to solve the problem of inflation without any increase in unemployment. That letter went to Mr. Meany without my having seen it. I discussed with the President that perhaps thereafter I'd better see such letters because it was not going to happen and it would not be politically smart to be making a promise that the technology of economic policy couldn't deliver on. On the other hand, since I realize that my tour of duty was during what some of you would consider to be the Mephistophelean age, you may find it hard to believe this, but at least as we saw it and I think as he saw it, the crucial task was to deal with the problem of inflation. Now that is not inherently an attractive problem within the political arena. Yet I can remember him, over and over, shaking his finger and saying, "Well, that would be very difficult politically but we do want to do what's right here."

DD: When he wrote the Meany letter and you let it be known that the technology of economics couldn't deliver, what was his reaction to your position?

PM: I don't recall any pyrotechnics as a result of it.

DD: In other words, he could take that kind of criticism?

PM: Oh, yes. Well, after he announced my appointment as Chairman, there was the usual flurry of news interviews, and I think a _Newsweek_ reporter asked me that question: "Is it going to be possible to counter the rising inflation without some increase in unemployment?" I recall quite explicitly saying, "No, it is not going to be. There is no way to do it without some increase in unemployment." And I called that to his attention. No, I don't recall having my ears pinned back because I brought the bad news.

Bureaucratic Politics and Economic Policy

EH: Let us focus now on the Council's relations with the White House staff. Walter Heller was very interesting in describing his initial relations with Sorensen and other all-purpose White House staff people close to the President who were lawyers. He said they were initially rather skeptical of economists, but that once he persuaded Sorensen and O'Donnell that he did have something politically useful to offer the President, then they became firm allies and helped cement him to Kennedy. What were the relations you and your colleagues had with the other White House staff in regard to making broad presidential policy? Were these obstacles?

PM: You started by posing the question, did I find them adversaries or allies. My answer is yes, both, which I suppose is inevitable. Of the three administrations that I had some significant experience with, namely Eisenhower, Nixon, and then Ford, I think clearly the most well structured of the three would be the Eisenhower administration. His experience had been operating within the context of large complexes, so he appointed a chief of staff and, on the whole, had a reasonably smooth operation. With the Nixon administration, it was something that evolved in a somewhat more uncertain way and over a period of time. The distinction, for example, between Haldeman and Ehrlichman. If one is talking about the people who, in the early period, were the very closest to the President, it would certainly have been my impression that it would have been those two. I suppose within the Cabinet it would have been John Mitchell, who had been chairman of his campaign committee in 1968. But it wasn't the kind of well-defined Eisenhower structure where everybody was told, "Now this is it." In the Nixon administration you had to find your way around, as it were. I never had to report to someone who would report for me to the President. When I wanted to see the President, I had to call the appointment secretary who was under Haldeman. If it was urgent, I usually would see him the same day. If it wasn't urgent, it might be a day or two later. By process of trial and error, the structures began to form. For example, a White House staff group would meet each morning at 8:00 or 8:30, presided over by Haldeman. Ehrlichman was there, as was Bryce Harlow, the Director of OMB, I, Peter Flanagan, and a few others.

EH: Were Moynihan and Burns initially part of this group?

PM: Moynihan was. This evolved as a more ongoing thing, as I recall it, only after a period of time. Arthur was not there during most of this period, and I suspect it emerged later on in 1969, about the time he was headed toward the Federal

Reserve. Now these meetings were just to keep everybody clued in on a wide array of issues; maybe the President was trying to get some bill out of the Senate and Bryce would report on how we were going to have to do that. If some economic data were coming out that day, I would usually alert them to what would be announced. This was not the more formalized structure—I suppose you want to get into that later on—of the Troika and Quadriad, which were more special-purpose or limited-purpose arrangements. Henry Kissinger, by the way, took part in that group.

EH: Did you find as Ehrlichman became more important as a domestic policy adviser, with the creation of the Domestic Council, that he was helpful or useful to you?

PM: No, he was, on the whole, useful. I don't recall feeling that Ehrlichman was in the way trying to thwart things. For example, just to pick one case, the CEA was not very enamored of AMTRAK. Ehrlichman was of the same view. Of course we didn't stop it. We were right, by the way. But this is just one illustration that we worked together very closely, although not successfully.

RF: Is the highly structured organization of the Eisenhower regime better or worse in the political context than the looser type of organization under Nixon?

PM: My own instinctive inclination is to say, "Oh, yes, of course, much better." In other words, a tidy arrangement is much better than an untidy one. Tidy is a better word than untidy. But I think it isn't quite so easily answered. The single most important variable is the guy at the top. At least as I understood him, Eisenhower would have been not only lost, he would have been enraged at chronic chaos around him; it just wouldn't have happened. If he'd inherited a looser structure, very quickly he'd have had this tidy structure. Nixon's experience, I think, more nearly typified what is apt to be the typical background of a president: namely, they will have had virtually no experience in managing large complexes. So there is apt to be a little more floundering around. Nixon, however, tended to move toward somewhat more structure. But I can envision a president who's a little more freewheeling, who might work very well with something that from the outside looks rather untidy. That might be his best method.

EH: Did not President Ford move in the direction of structure with the eventual creation of the Economic Policy Board and a highly collegial style?

PM: Yes. No doubt about that. At least when I went down there in late August or whenever it was, the board was meeting every morning at 8:00, so the old broad spectrum White House group that I was talking about apparently did not continue.

He also moved much more explicitly toward having the assistant to the president, a chief of staff, Don Rumsfeld and
then Dick Cheney. Certainly my impression was that this
wasn't the White House structure at the time I disembarked
and went back to Michigan.

EH: Were there any reasons why the EPB developed as it did, with
an assistant to the president as the secretary?

PM: Here I'm talking about something that was occurring while I
wasn't there. After Connally left at the end of 1972, I
believe, and George Shultz took over as Secretary of the
Treasury, it seemed from the outside, at least, that George
was the "chairman of the board," working very closely with
the CEA and OMB. George could perform that role as secretary
of the Treasury in part because he was just a very impressive
person. By the time Bill Simon came in, it probably was
necessary to have a somewhat more explicit structure. I
think it also helped to minimize the danger of internecine
struggles for power after George left. There could have been
quite a struggle for power between Bill Simon and Bill Seidman, for example. Alan Greenspan, of course, had actually
been appointed as Herb's successor by Nixon, but had not yet
been confirmed when Ford took over. So the whole thing was a
little uncertain.

EH: In reflecting on the problem of political balance on the
White House staff, could you say the White House staff is
split in two? In a sense you have professional cadre--NSC
people, CEQ, CEA, Domestic Policy staff--with a knowledge-
based skill. And then you have political cadre--legislative
liaison, press officers, close domestic policy advisers. Is
it really two White Houses in that sense?

PM: Well, no. Well, maybe two White Houses. After all, what is
the industry we're talking about? It's an industry in the
political arena, so naturally a good political operation is
going to be some uncertain mix of people who are very politically savvy. But it probably can't sustain itself as a good
political operation if it's always making technical mistakes
or analytical mistakes on the substance of policy. So it
requires both inputs. That really was the point of my little
parable about that report to President Kennedy. We made sure
that the President understood the economic aspect of it, but
there was a political dimension. For his own reasons--and he
was a political leader--he made a decision the other way.

EH: Turning now to bureaucratic relations, was there in fact an
informal Troika and an informal Quadriad in the Eisenhower
period?

PM: Yes, the roots of the Quadriad really do go back to the
Eisenhower period. Like some of the most useful institutions
in government, it emerged almost accidentally. It emerged

with the President inviting to the White House the Secretary
of the Treasury and the Chairman of the Fed and Steve Saulnier, who was Chairman by then of CEA, and the Director of
OMB who was, I think, Percy Brundage. He wanted to talk
about the economy, so he invited them to the White House for
cocktails one afternoon, but it was not a structured affair.
It started to develop a little more momentum. It really
became much more explicit, at least it's my impression, under
the Kennedy administration, which followed. Then in the
early part of the Nixon period, the Troika continued because
Dave Kennedy as Secretary of the Treasury, Bob Mayo as Director of OMB, and I knew each other quite well, and we developed a procedure of having breakfast about once a week at the
Cosmos Club, just to talk about things. You also had the
usual Washington structure of T1, T2, and T3. In other
words, T, the principals, met and agreed that they would
delegate the responsibility to their seconds in command who
would meet and agree what staff people for each of the three
agencies would finally do the work. I suppose the most
important part of this was trying to keep the administration
speaking reasonably with one voice on the analysis of the
economy and on certain obvious questions of policy and tax
policy, for example.

DD: When you got down to the T2, T3 level, the Fed got in somehow, didn't it, Paul?

PM: Oh, yes. Especially when, about once a month, the third
level would develop their views, their economic projections--
quite formal projects. I think Chuck Partee would participate in those sessions.

EH: Secretaries of Labor and Commerce were seen as second-class
citizens?

PM: They were not members when I was there. They were quite
explicitly not members. Because Dave Kennedy didn't want it.
And I think he was right. Once you go beyond the secretaries
of Treasury, the director of OMB, and the chairman of CEA,
you start to get representatives of interest groups in the
Cabinet. I think it was Ken Boulding who once said that we
really ought to call them secretary for Commerce and secretary for Agriculture and so forth. If you ask who in an
administration will more nearly have the general welfare
point of view that the president has to have, you almost
exhaust the list by the time you've nominated the secretary
of the Treasury and the chairman of the CEA and the director
of OMB.

EH: Would you apply that to both macro and micro policy questions?

PM: I would apply it to both macro and micro, but particularly to
micro policy.

ML: Why do you think that the Treasury Department is not as much interlaced with banking influence as Commerce with business or Labor with the AFL-CIO?

PM: If you look at what the secretary of the Treasury is doing most of the time, I don't agree. He's the secretary of the Treasury, not the secretary of Banking. He has certain regulatory functions (e.g., the comptroller of the Currency), and admittedly, the banking regulatory area is something that perhaps needs to be rationalized. But the secretary of the Treasury is going to be spending most of his time on such matters as tax policy, international financial and monetary developments. I don't see the synchronality, as it were, of the responsibilities of the secretary of the Treasury toward banking that I think a secretary of Commerce, for example, traditionally is apt to feel toward business. Indeed, he probably will be told by the president that his job is to represent business in the administration and the secretary of Labor's job is to represent the interests of labor.

WH: Did you discern in any of these direct channels to the president, to the closest people at the very top, any organization other than this Troika that did not serve special and limited constituencies but rather channeled in information about the general economy and the money policy?

PM: Yes. One source of advice that one ought not to overlook with any president is the people who, for one reason or another, have not been brought into government, perhaps didn't want to come in, who nonetheless may have a significant effect on the president's thinking. At least in the early Kennedy years, Paul Samuelson was considered to be a fairly influential person with the President but he never had a government job. I suppose there were such people when I was there, but I can't think of anyone who would stand out quite that sharply. I would urge a president to make sure that he keeps open whatever channels of communication he has. He needs different points of view.

EH: Would you not see the National Security Council staff and the president's science adviser, who got rubbed out, and even the Council on Environmental Quality, as a model at least, in the same vein as the Council?

PM: Well, yes. Of course, this was why I specified well within the general domain of economic policy. Let's take the CEQ as a case in point. If you are the head of that agency, how are you going to handle the inevitable trade-offs that will occur between measures to improve the environment and measures to ameliorate our energy problem? To be fair to the chairman of the CEQ, you cannot ask him to be the sacrificial lamb and keep this trade-off explicitly in mind. On the other hand, the director of OMB in making the analyses about actions and legislation is going to have to evaluate the cost-benefit calculus. For example, when I was there the proposal was made to have a tax on leaded gasoline. Here an economist's instinctive approach provided the disinterested variant: "No, if we're going to go in that direction, let's not have a tax on leaded gasoline of so many cents per gallon, but have a tax on lead used in gasoline." You could retain about 75 percent, as I recall it, of the value of lead in gasoline, even with about 25 percent of the lead that is used, but if you're going to tax leaded gasoline, then there is, of course, no incentive to reduce the lead content. Within the Executive Office of the President, it's pretty difficult to identify agencies, once you get beyond OMB and CEA, that will just instinctively start to think in terms of the cost-benefit of environment versus energy or whatever the trade-off. Some other agency will have one end of that trade-off and another will have the other.

DD: In influencing presidential decisions, how did you evaluate your own input from the CEA side vis-a-vis Treasury or OMB?

PM: Oh, it would vary. Of course, OMB had a markedly larger analytical staff than we did, so they knew much more than we about bill analyses. This will vary depending on the nature of the subject and on individuals. For example, in the last six or eight months of my tour of duty there, the Secretary of the Treasury was John Connally and not Dave Kennedy. Connally obviously had much more influence with the President than Kennedy did. Did that have any effect on the Council? Not in the sense that I found that suddenly I couldn't see the President, but our relative influence with the President was different when Connally rather than Kennedy was Secretary of the Treasury. I certainly would want the record to show that I had unlimited confidence in Kennedy's judgment on matters of concern, but on the question of directly influencing the President's thinking, this was simply not Kennedy's cup of tea. It was precisely John Connally's cup of tea. For example, it is certainly no secret that George Shultz and I were not enthusiastic about wage and price controls. John, being not primarily an economist but a politician, picked up the signals--I think correctly--that it was very important politically to move to wage and price controls. I recall that one of those public opinion polls--"Is the president doing a good job?"--taken right after wage and price controls were instituted showed that the percentage who thought the President was doing a good job had virtually doubled and held there. If I were John Connally, I would be saying, "Hell, I was right. You guys were wrong." We weren't making a judgment on the same basis, but, after all, it's a political arena. He was probably right on a more important matter than we were.

EH: If we were to admit Treasury, Bureau of the Budget and the Council didn't have external constituencies, did they have different institutional biases that continued over time by

virtue of what they had to do? They were their own constituencies in a sense. Did Treasury have certain things to
worry about, certain responsibilities that would bias the way
they would look at a given problem? The Budget Bureau the
same? Or not?

PM: Oh, yes. In fact, I recall saying once that if someone were
to have seen on TV the four-hour discussion of the economy at
Camp David and were asked, "Do you think you could pick out
the secretary of the Treasury, the Budget director, the
chairman of the CEA and the chairman of the Federal Reserve,"
my guess is that the result of his guessing would have been a
little better than just random. You could almost pick them
out by what they were saying. Let me start with the CEA
first. These people are going to sound as though they are
economists. They're going to think in terms of cost-benefit
calculus on a program. "If you move in that direction on
energy, you're going to have to give up some ground on environment and vice versa." I'm sure the CEA will probably
tend to be a little more concerned about the level of unemployment, for example. The central banker is going to be a
little more concerned about inflation than the CEA chairman,
although in my case I felt strongly in that direction. International monetary and financial institutional concerns are
going to be more evident to the central bank and probably to
the secretary of the Treasury than to these other two.
There's no universal man.

EH: Does the Budget Bureau have a continuing institutional bias
or does it just take coloration from the president?

PM: I suppose they tend to have an institutional bias that might
be characterized as: "You've got to prove it to me," because
the aggregate of all the good proposals add up to an excessive amount. They're certainly going to have a budgetary
concern much more evident in their thinking, I suppose, than
does the CEA chairman. It's not that in any of these cases
the other concerns are not present, but, if you listen, I
think you will get an orientation that probably reflects the
inherent orientation of the job.

DD: That doesn't apply either, Paul, does it, to just the three
we have mentioned? The clear confrontation reflecting institutional bias that I saw most in Washington was State vis-a-
vis Treasury.

PM: No question about that. Treasury considered the State Department to be the public relations consultant for the rest
of the world. I must say, by the way, there were times when
I felt the same way.

EH: The State Department has historically questioned the existence, the validity of the existence of the National Security

White House staff. Treasury never really felt that way about the Council?

PM: Well, Dewey, you´re the Treasury man here.

DD: No, I don´t think so. There were times, certainly more in the Heller period, where the Treasury point of view was so diametrically opposed to the CEA view. In Paul´s period, with Kennedy at the head of Treasury, I would suspect that there was no problem.

EH: People don´t write books about the Treasury-CEA conflict the way they do about the split between State and the National Security Council. It just doesn´t seem to be as salient to people, for reasons that quite elude me. It seems to me that they´re exactly the same.

PM: When Connally became Secretary of the Treasury, I noticed there began to be a spate of stories in the paper saying that Treasury believed that CEA ought to be done away with. They had all the earmarks of inspired stories. I think they were. I could see how a John Connally, who does not take a diminutive view of his domain, would think, "Oh hell, Treasury can handle all this." Moreover, I think this point that you´re making is all the more interesting because if you look at other governments, by and large, the ministries of finance are the three agencies really wrapped up in one.

DD: In my exposure to a number of secretaries of the Treasury, they were always very sensitive that the responsibility in the financial area was theirs and not the CEA´s. They always said, "We have the real operating responsibility. The CEA can go mouth off about these things anywhere they want to, but we´ve got the responsibility."

PM: Yes, I think Dewey has got a very good point. Here is an area where Treasury and the CEA had sticky relations. The Treasury, because they had these operating responsibilities for international financial or monetary policy matters, would feel that the CEA ought to "Keep its nose out of our business." The CEA mandate was not defined to exclude this, and they would consider that the Treasury didn´t see the policy issue. The question is not who´s right and who´s wrong; it´s just that there is at that point some overlap of the two circles. The two parts of the Economic Report that were always difficult were international economic matters and what we would say about monetary policy.

EH: Does the CEA have a comparative advantage, vis-a-vis Treasury and Budget Bureau, in the sense that it´s wholly disinterested, has no operating responsibilities?

PM: I think it has the advantages and the limitations. If you´re the operator, you are in a position, I suppose, to a greater extent to say, "Well, go to hell. This is the way we're going to do it." All an adviser can ask is, are the principals seriously listening to you? They may not agree with you.

EH: So there's no automatic leg-up for the CEA in this area of bureaucratic politics?

PM: No, as a matter of fact, I think that's an interesting, but not a terribly important, question, because their functions in the final analysis are different. If you're talking about totality of clout, obviously the CEA is de minimus in terms of agency size. But they have different roles to perform. If you're going to talk about an all-out power struggle, without knowing the principals involved, I suppose one would have to bet on Treasury. I'm not sure about that. Maybe the director of the OMB. Certainly not the chairman of the CEA. He has no inherent power base.

EH: Does the Council have an advantage in influencing the president, though, in macro policy as compared to micro, because there are more group politics in micro?

PM: Your point is that this general welfare type of approach is more nearly a macro issue. Yes, I'm sure that's true. On the other hand, I was talking with Charlie Schultze about this not long ago and he made the same point: you're not constantly sitting there on the mountaintop thinking about whether there should be a big tax cut or not. One of the things that any chairman of the CEA will find out, if he hasn't thought about it before, is that you arrive on the scene and for a very important instrument of macro policy, namely monetary policy, you don't have the dials in the president's office. Certainly, if Arthur Burns is Chairman of the Fed, then you find that out quite explicitly! Economists are sometimes surprised at my comment that most of my time, as I look back on it, was spent on essentially micro problems. Not the great vast issues. Well, maybe "most" is an overstatement. When the macro issues are open, I suppose they become issues of particular importance to the CEA, or the CEA is particularly important to those issues.

JJS: Is the CEA important in the micro issues that have built-in constituencies with a position you can almost predict ahead of time because in those issues the CEA is the only spokesman for the public welfare? The CEA, you know, typically speaks against minimum wage increases or for deregulation of trucking.

PM: Right.

JJS: And if they don't come in, everyone knows what the position of the Department of Transportation or the ICC is likely to be.

EH: But your resources are less there, and the president has less inclination to listen, doesn't he?

PM: No. Take the minimum wage as a case in point. That is interesting because the CEA will usually lose on that issue. I would be very surprised if the current CEA didn't take the same general position a year ago because economists pretty generally agree on what the effect of those escalations of the minimum wage is. But I do think that the president is very anxious to listen to someone who doesn't have an angle on these micro issues. When I had been on the job for just a few days, the Secretary of Agriculture almost slipped through something like a ghastly increase in the support price for soybeans. Of course, it got on the President's desk, seeming all full of motherhood and virtue. Henk Houthakker happened to have been talking to somebody in Agriculture and found out that it was there. I quickly explained what the implications were. I think this alerted him that perhaps on such issues he should listen to someone other than just the secretary for the interested department.

EH: Did you have to then ask or insist that such memos go through the CEA?

PM: For the next several months, the President sent a memorandum to the Secretary of Agriculture: "Any propopsal such as this must come through the CEA." Now you have to watch this because these agencies will make end runs if they possibly can.

EH: In ASPER [Assistant Secretary for Policy Evaluation and Research] at Labor, they regarded the program people in Budget as their allies, and the one CEA labor economist as an ally. But the program people in Manpower Administration or in OSHA [Occupational Safety and Health], for example, were seen as the enemy, the adversaries. So there is this link at the top. Your professional network extends beyond the Council.

PM: Oh, my word, yes. Anytime the CEA started to operate as a monastery, it would become almost irrelevant to the administration. I hope at some point we can discuss that more explicitly, because I think it a very important part of the influence that the CEA has had on policy.

DD: Even in the monetary area, you do have communication and you know very well what the monetary policy people are up to and you do make an input in that there is a continuing dialogue. So it isn't as if you're operating in a vacuum.

PM: No, and I'm sure this is an obvious point to students of government, but in evaluating whether it works well, you can't just look at the organization chart. On the whole, I think the coordination of monetary and fiscal policy over the years has been fairly good. You certainly would have difficulty inferring that from the way it is structured. When Arthur became chairman, for example, we had breakfast about once a week. And we had pretty candid discussions. We were discussing, in one way or the other, much of the time this morning the nature of the contribution of CEA to policy and what determines how influential it is, what the avenues of influence are. All of this is perhaps particularly inter- esting when one bears in mind the miniscule size of the agency. I used to say that I never had any difficulty with my budget with OMB: our agency was so small we came right in underneath their radar and they never perceived us.

One aspect of this subject that often gets inadequate attention is the extent to which policy and decisions are ultimately formed and made as a result of interdisciplinary or interdepartmental committees or groups. After all, most major policy issues in government do cut across departmental lines, and frequently there will be an interdepartmental task force or an interdepartmental cabinet committee. My own impression was that in those interdepartmental groups the Council played a more important role historically than is perhaps realized. Let me give you an illustration. Back in the fall of 1970, I believe, I received a memorandum asking me to be chairman of a cabinet committee on energy, which consisted of just those you would expect: secretary of State, Interior, Commerce, and so forth. I recall talking with one of my colleagues on the Council, probably Herb, and saying that as I looked over the list of members, I could think of only two reasons for my being chairman: one was that I would bring the objectivity that comes from total ignorance of the subject; the second was—and here I'm really somewhat more serious—that the protocol problem of designa- ting one of the cabinet members as chairman can be very sticky. But they could all agree that the chairman of the CEA constituted no threat to their protocol position at all. So in numerous ways like this, in man-hours that are not necessarily spent in the Oval Office, the CEA and the Chair- man of the CEA can have, cumulatively, a fairly significant influence on policy.

A second point I would make here—one that Dean Acheson has made—is that articulation makes policy, by which I mean that the Council of Economic Advisers writes the annual Economic Report. This should be seen as much more than just having to produce a damn book once a year. Dean Acheson made this point when he was explaining that one day when he was Under Secretary of State, George Marshall, who was Secretary of State, came in and said, "Dean, for God's sake, I've just remembered, I've got to give the commencement address at Harvard, so could you whomp up something for me to give." (The quotation is approximate.) Dean Acheson, who was re- lating the story to a little group at Michigan, said, "Of course, it's not essential, but it's helpful if in writing a speech you have something to say. So out of this came the Marshall Plan." Writing the speech made policy. Likewise the annual articulation of the president's case and how they

340

see things as they look ahead forces the administration once a year to focus quite explicitly on policy. And the person who puts the first pen to paper has a good deal of input. I wanted to mention those two points. Sometimes we get so engrossed in whether or how often the CEA chairman can see the president that we miss some of the significant avenues by which this little tiny agency can have a significant effect on public policy.

DD: How would you suggest improving the structural part of this policy process?

PM: I don't think government is very well structured for the making of economic policy and, therefore, I continue to be amazed at how well it works. In other words, I wouldn't worry very much about structure. The arrangement we have with the Federal Reserve could cause a president to say, "If, at the next election, I'm going to be held accountable for the results of economic policy, I at least have a right to have the instruments of policy." That would mean that he ought to have the last say. We have countries with it both ways. How does the record look? On the whole, it looks as if it works better to leave the Central Bank with a degree of remoteness. But if that is true, the individuals have to work out a modus operandi, and if they are smart enough to be there, good enough people to hold the job, they will. On the whole, I think it works out all right.

EH: The Ash Council, as you know, came forward with this notion of a Department of Economic Affairs. Did you speak to that at the time?

PM: No, but I think I would have if it had been seriously pursued. In fact, I recall writing in some paper that we also needed a Ministry of Economics. I guess I feel about that somewhat as I do about the telephone system. If it works, let's not mess it up. I think our system works. If you had a Department of Economic Policy, you would wind up with what is the Finance Ministry in most other governments. The CEA and the OMB and Treasury would all be rolled into one, and they would be less effective.

Reconstructing Policy Decisions

EH: What we have done in the past is simply to ask each Chairman to reconstruct the politics of policy formation of a major policy question. Usually it's been a macro question. I suppose we should begin with the situation you faced when you came into office, the legacy, how you began; the bottom line, of course, was the August 1971 decision on wage-price controls. What were the alternatives, who were the protagonists?

PM: To go back to the latter part of 1968 and early 1969, the

economic problem that we faced at that time was a rate of
inflation, which was rising rather rapidly from, as I recall,
a 1-3/4 percent per year rate in 1967; that rate itself had
been an interruption of an acceleration that really got
underway a little earlier. By 1968 it was, I think, in the
neighborhood of 4-1/2 percent, which, of course, illustrates
the extent to which one period's problem becomes the next
period's objective. In 1969 it was higher--I think over 5
percent--whatever the arithmetic, the rate of inflation was
itself rising; in other words the price level was accelerating in its pace. I recall that there was a kind of
"cabinet meeting" at the Shoreham Hotel not long before the
inauguration. Several people were asked to make very brief
statements as to what problems they saw. The thrust of my
comments was that the basic problem the administration would
have--and it would be a rather thankless problem--was to try
to retain a greater degree of stability in the price level.
Fundamental to that strategy would have to be significantly
more restrictive demand management policies, basic macro economic policies. I don't recall making any comment at that
time about income policies or guideposts or guidelines--those
were pretty well passé by that time anyway. I did, however,
discuss very briefly the external aspect of the problem: the
responsiveness of our current account position vis-a-vis the
domestic economy. As I recall it, on a so-called full employment basis our current account position was starting to
show a deterioration after 1966, approximately, and then we
actually went into the red in late 1969, I believe. You had
to go back a long time in our history to find another time
when our exports were falling below our imports--probably
back to 1923 or 1921, or 1920--almost fifty years. I do
recall discussing that very briefly. Now if I had this to do
over again, I would spend much more time on it, but at least
this external dimension of that complex of problems was
brought in.

The first basic statement of the administration on economic policy was the testimony I gave before the Joint Economic Committee about three weeks after the inauguration--I
suppose around the 10th to the 15th of February. The thrust
of the statement was that we would have to move steadily in a
restrictive direction--I suppose the term "gradualism" became
part of the lexicon here. On the other hand, we wanted to
avoid locking the brakes and producing a serious decline in
business activity. One of the very interesting analytical
issues, if I may comment parenthetically, is precisely whether it may not be better to lock the brakes and quash the
inflationary problem, which would be much more consistent
with the lore of central banking orthodoxy, for example, than
to try to move more cautiously.

SM: Could you be explicit in what you mean by gradualism here?
If a 4 percent unemployment rate is the norm, do you mean
cautiously moving back up to that rate or do you mean going
to a higher rate, say, 5 percent over a period of time?

PM: I guess I would put it not so much in terms of the unemployment rate, though it could be calibrated in that way, but in terms of trying to pursue demand management policies that would provide for an essentially lateral movement in the nominal volume of economic activity, or in any case a discernibly slower rate of expansion. I would not have advocated pursuing such severely and suddenly tight policies that you would get, in contemporary parlance, a V type recession chart—1958 would have been the prototype of a severe recession. This, of course, was discussed with the President; it sounded all right to him. Once again, he didn't approach this from the vantage point of a Ph.D. in macro economics or the virtues of the V type recession versus the other. Quite frankly, I think this strategy appealed to him because he was sensitive to the political problem that would be caused if he, a Republican, came in, locked the brakes and we promptly got unemployment, which is a politically sensitive issue anyway.

EH: But he had no real interest in the intricacies of what you were trying to do?

PM: Well, not in a highly technical discussion of whether the present value of future trauma is minimized by a V type recession or a shallower one of longer duration. But at that time, it certainly was my judgment that the pursuit of a firm, but gradual, policy of restraint was the better strategy. The case for that was articulated in that rather long statement before the Joint Economic Committee. That statement at least communicated that the administration was probably going to pursue an anti-inflationary approach. There was a very substantial decline in the stock market that day, which was attributed to my statement, so it was not dismissed as just rhetoric. It was, I think, interpreted that we were probably in for some slowing in the economy.

SM: How long did you think that the slowdown would take?

PM: At that time, I think we would have visualized it beginning around the middle part of the year. After a lag of a few months, we would have seen essentially a lateral or possibly a mild decline in the economy, but experiencing an upturn by somewhere around the second quarter or the middle part of the next year. The return to full employment, as it were, would have been somewhat later. I recall some memoranda with simulations as to how far out we'd get before we'd be back on the track—I don't remember precisely, but it was around 1971 or 1972.

But there is another dimension or implication to your question: how long would it take the price level to respond? You pursue policies of greater restraint; after a lag, you start to see the visible effects in terms of a slowing down in economic activity. But where in this sequence would history suggest that you might start to see an effect on the

price level? The analysis we did showed what we all know--
that the effect on the price level tends to lag a bit after
the economic slowdown. When we began to see some indications
that the economy was starting to respond, the fact that the
price levels didn't seem to be performing very well--by the
latter part of 1969, for example--was not unusually disturbing because, historically, the cyclical pattern would suggest
that something like that was to be expected. By the latter
part of 1969, however, I was becoming very much concerned
about the continued tight monetary policy on the part of the
Federal Reserve. I can recall being sufficiently concerned
in October or November of 1969 to send a rather long memorandum to the President, recognizing, of course, the monetary
policy was not in our domain, but that with this kind of
restraint we had to prepare for the possibility that the
decline in economic activity was going to be more than we had
been talking about earlier.

DD: Was the surcharge in place?

PM: The proposal to renew the surcharge had, of course, gone
forward much earlier. The legislation that finally came out
of the Congress landed on the President's desk around Christmas of 1969. I can recall a conversation where the President
was very much inclined to veto the whole tax bill, not so
much just on the narrow issue of the macro economics of it,
but because it had a lot of other things in there.

DD: This was 1969? Because the question of "overkill" came up
from the combination of these things.

PM: That would go back about a year earlier, because the tax
increase proposed by Johnson in the fall of 1967 finally got
passed--in fact it was signed, I think, at the end of June
1968. Then monetary policy eased. If you look at the literature, the term "overkill" was frequently showing up at that
point. Monetary policy eased up then in the latter half of
1968. Then as we moved through 1969, monetary policy became
more restrictive. We were also pushing pretty hard on the
budget--impounding expenditures. Indeed, I found myself
appointed to the construction area as well. I remember the
President issued a stop order on all new starts in federal
construction. Construction wage settlements were just wild
at that time; we were getting 50 percent increases per year
for the next three years. Many of the leaders of these
construction unions were just as concerned about this as
anyone else. I remember we did have the union leaders in for
a discussion with the President. This had been rather carefully set up. The President was to place before them his
concern and tell them that it would be much better if they
could develop a program of their own, but that if that were
impossible, the President then would use his authority to
suspend Davis-Bacon. These leaders thought that with that
whip behind them, they would then be able to come up with a

plan. Even so they were not able to agree, and the President did suspend Davis-Bacon for a while. Throughout this period there was a growing concern and a great deal of pressure to do what could be done on the expenditure side of the budget to try to move toward a more restrictive or less expansive fiscal policy.

Now what about the price level? After all, this was the key question. Since that was one of the more disappointing developments, let me comment on the positive side first. It would not be correct to say that this policy strategy had no effect on inflation. I would make the case that if the trend in the rate of inflation, beginning in the forepart of 1967, and continuing through 1969, had continued, then just simple extrapolation would suggest that the rate would have been up in the 8 to 10 percent zone by 1971. The fact is that the acceleration in the rate of inflation did pretty well get stopped. In 1970, for example, the rate of inflation was about 5-1/2 to 6 percent, and did not continue moving on up.

Moreover, let me turn now to the disappointing side of our policy strategy. First of all, we weren't getting the response in terms of the price-cost level that we had hoped for from this strategy of policy that was being deployed. I certainly don't want to give you the impression that I'm here to give you a biography of a great success in terms of the price level, although it wasn't a total failure either. I guess that's the point I do want to make. If you look at the non-food commodities, if you look especially at the wholesale price index, or if you look at the GNP deflator, it was less encouraging. If you look at the rates of increase in hourly earnings and compensation for manhours, those weren't showing the kind of deceleration that we would have pointed to as evidence that the strategy was working. By then, of course, we were in the summer at the beginning of the sequence of events that led up to Camp David, to Mt. Catoctin and wage and price controls.

Let us look at the external aspect of this problem for a moment. Our trade position went into deficit by late 1969, I think, certainly by early 1970. With the recession, the trade position started to strengthen, and as I recall, it strengthened enough so that our exports again exceeded our imports. But we weren't getting the comeback in our current account that would have undone the deterioration we had seen before. Not only did the current account not come back the way it should have, had that been the sole problem, but it turned around rather quickly and started to deteriorate again, even though by 1971 the economy was moving ahead only very cautiously. In other words, our current account position was not deteriorating because of an explosive domestic boom. It was deteriorating even though that was absent.

Now all through this period when the responses were disappointing, the administration was under a good deal of pressure to invoke an incomes policy. Here the President started to get much more involved. The President was not much interested in an incomes policy for two or three perhaps

not unrelated reasons. Given the President's instinctively
conservative orientation, he was not much inclined at the
outset to plunge in and want to be controlling, managing the
details of economic life. I think he did become more and
more persuaded that an incomes policy probably would not make
a significant difference, and I suppose I would plead guilty
to having encouraged him to think in that direction. But
another thing that is very important to understand about the
President--and it's something I'm sure political scientists
have noticed--and can be stated in the language of football
again: the President didn't have much patience with the Ohio
State four yards and a cloud of dust. He was the quarterback
who would go for the 50-yard pass, and I think that is just
beautifully dramatized in what he did vis-a-vis China, in his
decision to go to Peking. In the early part of 1971 I can
recall his saying, "We're not going to go to an incomes
policy. You and I know that that won't work anyway. If I
have to go, I'll go all the way." The 50-yard pass again.
So I wasn't overwhelmed with surprise when finally he had
made his decision. I'm sure it was partly a political decision. I rather suspect that if he'd had his druthers, he
would have preferred to put the decision off a little longer,
simply because if begun in August 1971, the liabilities of
wage and price control might start to become very evident by
November 1972, and he'd rather have waited a little longer
and had the plusses going for him. To his credit, I don't
recall his ever discussing it very explicitly in those terms.

We have here a theater with several stages. We had this
external problem that was deteriorating very rapidly. While
nominally the gold window was open and the formalities of the
old system were still there, anybody who wanted gold would
get quite a discussion out of it and would settle, we hoped,
for a nominal amount. Then in early July, I think, the
British indicated they might want some massive sum. And I
recall Paul Volcker, who was in my office one day in July,
saying, "Well, the question is not whether we're going to
close the gold window. The question is whether we do it this
weekend or the next weekend or maybe one or two after that,
but that's about what we now face."

You can see the various separable strands starting to
come together here. Camp David occurred right in the middle
of August, the 14th and 15th, but some days before that the
President indicated that he was inclined to go all the way.
OMB was doing primary work on the structure of this, but we
were doing some in the CEA. Then came the word to assemble
at Camp David on Friday afternoon. There we had a long
meeting--it was essentially the Quadriad. John Connally was
there with his deputy, Paul Volcker, who was the Under Secretary for Monetary Affairs for Treasury; George Shultz was
there with Arnie Weber, who was the Deputy Director of OMB; I
was there with Herb Stein; and Arthur Burns was there from
the Fed. And then the usual coterie of Haldeman and Ehrlichman were there, as was Bill Safire, who was the speechwriter.
We had this long meeting, which extended from about 4:00 p.m.

until 8:00 p.m. The separable issues were wage and price control, the closing of the gold window, tax reductions, and also the import surcharge. The President sat there, listening, participating, with the yellow legal size pad he always had, making notes. At the end of the meeting he told us: "Well, I´ve made my decision. We´re going to go for wage and price control. We´re going to go for tax reduction and the import surcharge. But on the closing of the gold window, I haven´t yet made up my mind." When we walked out of the meeting, we didn´t know what the President´s decision was going to be on that issue.

That was Friday. The President´s modus operandi in this kind of situation was that he would often sit there and mull over the question and think about it until the wee hours. When I went to breakfast the next morning at Camp David, Haldeman was there and said, "Well, the President called me at 4:00 this morning and said, `I´ve made up my mind. I´m going to go all the way. We´re going to close the gold window also.´"

DD: You were clearly against the freeze on wages and prices and argued that. Where did you stand on these other issues--the gold window, the import surcharge. Where did you come out on these issues?

PM: I think we were mildly opposed to the import surcharge. We were definitely for closing the gold window, and that would have been more consistent with my own predilection than for floating exchange rates. We were for the reduction of taxes.

DD: Was the import surcharge a negotiating instrument? In other words, did you contemplate that that would stay on for any length of time or was it just simply to get a better bargaining position?

PM: I think it was primarily a negotiating weapon. In fact there was some controversy as to whether the President had the power to do this or not. It seems to me Treasury´s legal opinion was that he did and Justice was not quite sure. There was a little uncertainty about this. The presumption was that the longer the surcharge stayed on the greater would be the chance that litigation would upset it anyway. But it was primarily a negotiating weapon, something you laid on the bargaining table that you´ll give up graciously, if they´ll give up something.

EH: Would you talk more about why you had so little confidence in guideposts.

PM: Oh, simply the evidence as to their effectiveness. In the early part of the sixties we had essentially a stable price level. At that point it was very easy to put forward the arithmetic of the situation: that if productivity is rising 2-1/2 percent per year, then wages can go up by that amount to maintain labor costs constant per unit of output. If I had to put a decease date on the guidelines, it would have been the settlement of the airline mechanics strike, about 1965. They had a very difficult strike: politically it became much more important to get the thing settled than to get it settled economically. I think if you'll go back and check the Economic Reports after that, the arithmetic essentially dropped out. The rhetoric remained, the importance of it. Peter Jay, who is the Ambassador from the UK, made the point--and he made it in the Wincott lecture he gave about a year ago--that nobody yet has been able to figure out how to control the average of a myriad of settlements so that the settlements can distribute themselves where they will. Now that's a very important point. Suppose we want to engineer wage settlements down now, leaving coal out of the count. Suppose, instead of 8 percent increases, we want them to average out at 6 percent. Does it mean all wage settlements should be 6 percent? Not necessarily. It means we want an average of 6 percent increases. The trap you get into is that the baker's union in Kansas City is settling and somebody asks, "What does it mean for us?" And you have to say that you haven't the foggiest idea. Or you could say 6 percent. Everybody gets 6 percent. But then you've frozen the labor market.

DD: From this experience, are you saying that the only way to get at the inflation problem is through macro policy, that you can't have an incomes policy--the Okun-Wallich carrot-stick ideas are just nonsense?

PM: No, I'm not saying that. But, I would say that far too much of the discussion about incomes policy through this period was, if I may draw upon Dennis Robertson's English, a grin without a cat. In other words, we must do everything else and then have a vigorous and effective incomes policy that provides sufficient flexibility for the pricing system to work. Nobody has been able to figure out what that means. Moreover, we've accumulated even more evidence on incomes policies, generally, and I don't find myself changing my mind greatly.

DD: So you don't think a tax-based policy is workable either?

PM: No, no, I want to leave that out. I'm just talking about the kinds of generalized types of restraint that we have seen in the UK or in various other countries from time to time. The Organization for Economic Cooperation and Development summarizes it pretty well in that volume on inflation--this is not the report that my committee produced, but we had pretty much the same thing in there--concluding that incomes policies seem to have a displacement effect for a short period. Whether it has any permanent effect in reducing the rate of inflation seems much more doubtful. I don't see anything in contemporary evidence to alter that. After all, wage and price control is nothing but incomes policy at the severe end of the spectrum. The Canadians have had it for three years and their rate of inflation is 9 percent. It didn't work for us.

DD: A little freeze worked.

PM: No. It had just the same effect. Did our wage and price effort leave us with a better performance in terms of inflation? I would say, "No, it did not." If the question is, "If you freeze prices for a month or two or three, will the index flatten out?" Of course, it will. The statistician can predict that if you freeze prices the next month's index will go down. The risers can't rise and the decliners will still decline, so the index goes down.

DD: But there are those who would argue that you filed that freeze too soon, that Phase II was done very ineptly.

PM: But you look at the whole history of these efforts—and I tend to look at this internationally, as I'm sure you do—and what impresses me is that they've gone through it and gone through the trauma of it and in the end don't have much to show for it. The governments are always criticized.

EH: In setting the policy of gradualism throughout 1970, George Shultz was with you. When did Connally arrive on the scene? Early 1971? When did opinion begin to diverge and who was beginning to diverge all of a sudden here?

PM: On that issue, the divergence would have been between Connally, on the one hand, and the rest of us, on the other.

DD: Actually, I'm not sure who led whom at the Treasury. It could have been Volcker; it would have appealed to Connally because he was a go-for-broke fellow.

EH: Well, is this the Treasury's institutional position? I thought this was Connally's political instinct.

PM: To some extent, the answer would be yes. By early 1971, approximately, Murray Weidenbaum was making speeches on the need for an incomes policy, presumably at least with the acquiescence of his principals in the Treasury. While I don't think that it was literally a Treasury view, there was a Treasury inclination in that direction.

SM: What about Arthur Burns? He publicly made talks about the need for an incomes policy at Pepperdine College.

PM: Yes, as a matter of fact, that was a bit of a problem, because that major speech came just a week before the President was to deliver a major economic speech to some business group. In essence, it seemed to put the President on the spot. I remember this. The President was very upset about it.

EH: Where was the President all the time this debate was going on? Was he soliciting points of view actively or was he rather in the background?

PM: The primary preoccupation of the President throughout most of this period was still foreign policy and, specifically, the Vietnam War. So I suppose the economic area wasn't dominating his thinking.

EH: You wouldn't say he was on top of it and anxious to get views quickly?

PM: Not in the sense that it was his primary interest. No, not at all.

DD: He didn't have the kinds of meetings, did he, that Kennedy did? Kennedy had quite frequent Quadriad meetings and looked at the economic issues. Johnson had bigger than Quadriad meetings. Nixon really didn't have those kinds of meetings, did he?

PM: The Quadriad meetings were supposed to be scheduled on a monthly basis. I think we pretty well met that schedule.

AL: Wasn't organized labor brought into this from February to August?

PM: The main contact with organized labor at this time was through George Shultz. George had the best personal relations with labor, better even than the secretary of Labor at that time.

EH: Meany was somewhat contemptuous of Hodgson, wasn't he?

PM: Yes, and so long as George Shultz was there, he was clearly the President's man vis-a-vis labor. When the decision was made, labor went along. There was, in fact, not even the kind of opposition that you saw in Canada two or three years ago, where the unions almost boycotted the program. That doesn't mean that they liked it, but I don't recall any major problems with organized labor.

DG: What was the posture of the Council during the process of this divergence? Did you people feel that you were being shunted aside or beaten down or that you weren't doing anything but presenting your position and that that was the way it should be?

PM: On the international aspect, we would have diverged from Treasury, and we would have preferred going to a floating exchange rate system. We were opposed to wage and price control or incomes policy. While there would be an ideological content--ideological in the sense that we couldn't see this program working without significant intrusions into the market mechanism--my primary sentiment was that it would be ineffective and that the President once again would be in a position of unloading a policy that would have no effect. That's tended to be the history of that kind of program.

EH: Did you not have a piece in the <u>Washington Post</u> not long before the fateful day in which you argued against the controls?

PM: I argued against wage and price controls. I don't withdraw a single word, by the way. I said this morning that I probably should have resigned when the decision was made to go to wage and price controls. Now why doesn't one resign? Well, if the occupant of the Oval Office tells you that it's important for you to stay around and help out, it's very easy to respond. The problem is that not infrequently, and it was true in this case, you will find yourself presented with a presidential decision that, so far as you were concerned, is right on a major issue of policy--namely the international--but has some baggage on the other side that you don't like. Now what do you do? I thought the decision on the external aspect was correct. The argument there was that we needed something like this to break inflationary expectations. That phrase was used repeatedly throughout this period. Even by economists. Given the fact that we weren't seeming to make much progress on the wage front, even if one wanted to take an optimistic view of what was happening in 1971, you couldn't rule out the fact that the rate of inflation was accelerating again. We'd gone through a fair amount of trauma, so I decided that I'd be willing to defend this as a part of the total package, even though it was well known that I did not want wage and price controls. The same was true for George Shultz.

EH: Could you talk a little bit more about Connally, how he perceived this, how it came to grow on him and how he prevailed upon the President?

PM: I don't think it would be unfair to say that Connally wouldn't see this primarily in terms of its economic aspects. He would see this first of all as a politician, a political leader. It was very clear that the President's popularity rating was low, in part because there was this almost tidal wave of demand for wage and price control. Even the Business Council was demanding wage and price control. Under these circumstances, I could see how a good political leader, not being excessively concerned with economic matters, would think that was the right way to go. Moreover, as I look back over the political record and the extent to which the program still seemed to be reasonably intact by the latter part of 1972, I expect he was right.

EH: Was Connally unschooled in economics, formal economic theory?

PM: Yes, but a very bright guy. He briefed well.

EH: But he understood your position?

PM: Oh, yes. But he would say, "It may be a good product but it won't sell." He was right. It wouldn't sell.

EH: Do you, in fact, think it was unnecessary, that things would have leveled out?

PM: My own view would be that we wouldn't have been any worse off--if we could have stayed with that policy a little longer, things would have leveled out.

DD: But you had to do something on the international side.

PM: No doubt about that.

SM: How many previous meetings or preparations for this Camp David meeting had taken place?

PM: Oh, they were more in the nature of incipient discussions, I think. The President had had some meetings with John Connally and also with George Shultz. I was not present. I can recall talking to the President on occasion about this. After he indicated that, "Well, if we have to go we're going to go all the way and you might want to be doing work on this," it was pretty clear.

DD: At Treasury there had been contingency planning right on through. There was the Volcker committee. There was an inter-agency group at Treasury chaired by Volcker. Henk Houthakker was the Council member on it. There was an inter-agency group within government meeting almost daily on this question of what to do about the international problem.

PM: Yes, that's right.

EH: Let's try to reconstruct the Camp David meeting just for the historical record. What was said, how long did it go?

PM: As I indicated, I think we gathered around the middle or latter part of the afternoon--3 or 4 o'clock. It went until 7:00 or 8:00 p.m. The President didn't begin the meeting by saying, "We're going to have wage and price controls," but it was pretty clear by that time that he had decided in favor of them. As I recall that meeting, I think the dominant discussion was in the international area. There wasn't really much argument about tax reduction. I think everybody was pretty well in agreement on that. Those would be the primary elements. On closing the gold window, Treasury supported it, George Shultz did, I did, Arthur opposed it. I can recall

Arthur saying, "Well, Mr. President"--and if Mr. Burns wants to give a performance worthy of Sophocles, he can do it-- "with this very strong program that you are now ready to deploy in the domestic area..." Mr. Burns felt there would be such a return of confidence in the dollar that it wouldn't be necessary to take this step. I don't think I would be misreading the tea leaves to say that it was Arthur's strong speech that led the President to say, "Well, I haven't quite made up my mind on that issue now," at the conclusion of the meeting. Had Arthur said, "Well, yes, all things considered, I support it, too," then I'm sure the President would have said at the end of the meeting, "Okay, we'll go with it all." Saturday morning we knew about it. Then there were discussions. The President was very much inclined to wait until Monday night, I think, to give his speech. A number of secondary issues had to be discussed: when should the speech be, who's going to run the wage-and-price-freeze machinery, how are we going to set it up. We had to have some task forces working on the different issues.

EH: These had not been anticipated. These institutional questions had to be faced fresh and new, is that right?

PM: Well, yes, there had been some discussion of them. We had done a little in the Council.

SM: Had the President called for memos from various people on possible wage-price programs that could be set up?

PM: I'm sure OMB had done some work. Treasury had done some work. We had submitted something; I don't remember just how much. I suspect in this case we had submitted less than some of the others. We were less enthusiastic about it.

EH: Could you describe what was set up and why it was set up the way it was?

PM: I'm not sure that I can give you the dramatis personnae in detail here. We had this international group and that clearly would have been Paul Volcker and you [Dewey], and Henk Houthakker.

EH: Setting up the actual institutions, the Cost of Living Council and so on: how did all this come about? What were the models?

PM: Let's see, didn't we have a Cost of Living Council prior to this? Well, we had some structure.

JG: I'd understood that you preferred some other name, such as "Economic Stabilization" but they thought Cost of Living would be a better sounding name.

PM: Yes. Once these decisions were made, of course, it was a rather frenzied place there for a day or two. I guess the structure got set up with the Cost of Living Council, the identity of the so-called Executive Policy Committee, which de facto really pretty much ran it. Arnie Weber and I and someone else--probably someone from the Office of Emergency Preparedness--were the counterparts of the international group working on the structure here. I did not come back down from Camp David until Sunday.

DD: Yes, neither did Volcker so you must have spent most of that time on these organizational questions.

PM: I think we did. But I'm sure that these sub-groups were working at that point. We decided that the structure through which we would operate would be the Office of Emergency Planning, and that was headed up by General George Lincoln-- "Abe." I think Herb Stein and Bill Safire were commissioned to work up drafts of the President's speech. Then on Sunday we had to get back down and get prepared, cue in aides, the press and television.

DD: By the time we had the briefing Sunday afternoon, President Nixon had documents on all of that, had a package all put together. That's the bureaucracy when it's working.

PM: That's the work you can do when the bureaucracy's not there.

JG: Had there been any consideration of what Phase II would entail or was it just simply something that would come later?

PM: No. That came along later. Obviously, when you're going to have this kind of program, the first thing you have is a wage-price freeze. The presumption was that you would use that time to get your more full-blown structure into place. The usual inter-agency group was constituted to develop this structure, and they developed it in terms of the freeze, phases, and so forth.
   My activity during that period--and this extends almost to the end of my tour of duty at the end of the year--was as chairman of this Executive Policy Council. Here was a situation where you didn't make rules and then look at the cases to see if they fit the rules. You looked at the cases, and after a while you began to see that you were making rules. If you're in any doubt about the complexity of the pricing system, then having this kind of experience...a freeze is a freeze. For example, I remember a little trucker who had concluded a contract with his drivers. His sole customer was A&P. A&P had agreed that once he concluded his labor contract, then they would establish rates appropriate to the higher costs. The freeze came right in the middle. He claimed that he probably would go bankrupt if he didn't get some immediate relief. Now I don't remember all the details, but the Internal Revenue Service, which we used for fielding, audited his books and corroborated that fact that he'd pro-

bably go broke. We still ruled against him. I don't know whether he went broke or not.

SM: How fast did these cases start coming in?

PM: Oh, my gosh, as of 8:00 the next morning. We didn't have nearly enough staff.

EH: These were appeals of people who were caught in particular crunches and who wanted exceptions?

PM: This does not pertain to the people in this room, but there is a simplistic lay view that price and wage controls are similar to a phalanx of Roman soldiers in step, that you blow the whistle and they stop. The methaphor I've often used is that it's much more akin to being on a playground of active children: you blow the whistle and tell everybody to stop. Some kid is hanging upside down with his toes up here, and many people can't hang on for more than just a day or two. I don't think there was a day that went by that I wasn't the defendant in at least one new suit. But, generally, we took a very hard line on the freeze. Our policy was almost, "The answer is no."

EH: Had you done otherwise, you would have been nibbled to death.

PM: And quickly it would have meant nothing.

DD: Here you have a division of labor because the Treasury and Fed really carried the international side in that period.

PM: Yes, they carried the international side and the financial side. Dividends controls and that sort of thing.

JG: Was there any conflict with the other members of the Council who represented constituents, such as the secretary of Labor or Secretary of Commerce?

PM: Actually, the Cost of Living Council didn't meet very much. This Executive Council met every morning for several hours. I should have looked up the specifics, but I was chairman, and "Abe" [George] Lincoln and somebody from Treasury, I think, was there. These cases would be coming in via "Abe" Lincoln's regional people.

EH: That's why you brought that office in, because he had a field staff?

PM: It was the only agency that had a structure with which to start working.

DD: In retrospect, do you think that as CEA chairman you should have been chairing this Executive Council?

PM: Probably not. I think it's not wise for the Council of Economic Advisers to be the agency that's arguing with people about wages and prices.

SM: That took up a tremendous amount of your time. You said two hours every morning.

PM: At least. And that was one of the major problems. Especially at the outset it probably occupied at least half my time. We were naturally having to keep track of these decisions; then we'd try to establish rules after the fact. But the pricing system is so incredibly complex, you can't make rules in advance.

JJS: Did the different members seem to be representing their constituencies?

PM: I don't recall that that posed serious problems. I can recall a few instances where somebody would come in and see the Secretary of Commerce because he had a problem, which is perfectly legitimate. We got, of course, all kinds of screams from people, but usually directly from the people adversely affected.

JG: But the Cost of Living Council itself really didn't make many decisions? They ratified decisions that were made?

PM: Yes, in the sense of the individual members who were sitting around the table. I wouldn't want to denigrate the role that they played. We did meet--I was there, too, as vice-chairman--in the early stages, probably once a week, and especially after generalized issues started to emerge.

EH: Was Connally interested in this process?

EM: Yes, he was interested, and of course he was chairman of the Council. However, the external or international dimension was taking a great deal of his time. As I recall, I probably presided over at least half of the Cost of Living Council meetings as well as at the Executive Council's meetings.

DG: During the rest of your term, were you involved at all in policymaking that looked toward lifting the freeze, or Phase II, or other policy changes?

PM: Well, there was Phase II. That would be the kind of issue that would have to come before the Council and be discussed. A task force consisting of people like Peter Flanigan, Herb Stein, somebody from OMB and Treasury--about a half dozen members, I think--was very importantly involved in developing the post-freeze structure. Our Council was probably the headquarters for that activity.

JJS: What effect did this have on other types of normal policy-

356

making? Did everything else come to a screeching halt for
the next several months?

PM: Yes. For a brief period, two to four weeks, this would have
been just about all-consuming because we were starting from
scratch. Later on, the normal processes of our role in
government began to reassert themselves and, of course, by
the latter part of the year, around mid-November, we had to
start our year-end trauma, the Annual Report. Now you'll
have to ask Herb about how it began to develop in 1972, 1973.

SM: At the same time that the controls were being put into place,
you had a more expansionary macro policy both from the fiscal
and I guess also the monetary side.

PM: Yes, I think so. Maybe excessively so. If I were going
around that track again, I would emphasize the crucial importance of coupling wage and price controls with a degree of
restraint in demand management policies that would have made
us uncomfortable at that time. If you don't it will certainly be--as it turned out to be--an abortive effort.

SM: Are you saying that the trouble with the wage and price
programs at that time was that they encouraged the expansionists to expand too fast?

PM: Yes. In other words, having "solved" the problem of inflation, we can proceed to deal with unemployment by expansion
policies. Internationally, that has been the route by which
these things explode at the end.

EH: Does economic theory begin to break down here in the explanation of the causes and remedies for inflation in this period?

PM: Now I think that's a very good question, and it's just as
pertinent today, maybe more so. Here, I would say, is a case
where economic theory is wanting. I think it's fair to say
that the theory of inflation is in a quite unsatisfactory
state. I would go even further and say that I think that
macro theory generally--and I've been generally in macro
theory--has a lower level of credibility with policy managers
than at any time since I've been an economist. And, I would
hasten to say, somewhat deservedly so. I guess I would say
that macro theory, and policy inferences thereby implied,
still produce reasonably predictable results for the nominal
volume of business activity. What we do not have is a good
theory that will tell us how that's going to divide between
real and price.

SM: At that time, were you talking in terms of Phillips curves
and shifting Phillips curves? What was your thinking about
this problem?

PM: It would have been more in terms of Phillips curves. The concept of the outward-looping Phillips curve came along a little later. Our theory of inflation, which would have been the underpinning of the strategy we were talking about, would have been pretty much just the Phillips curve logic of the approach to inflation, with possibly some emphasis on having to reverse this outward-looping process to get a little progress on the price level, which gives somewhat lower expectations, which gives you a little more elbow room.

SM: It appears to be very flat out there, way out to right, for reasons that nobody quite understands. You could say that the supply curve of the economy appears to be very flat and you just can't get the inflation rate down. Was there much discussion in 1970 and 1971 as to why this was?

PM: Yes, quite a bit, and, of course, the usual arguments: Do we have wages that are administered to such a degree that we have lost control on the cost side, so we are dealing with cost inflation? If so, what are the implications for policy? What can government do in its action directly to affect the price level? But the basic thrust--and here I would remain critical of those who oppose it--was an excessive tendency to argue that the problem is that government will not use an incomes policy or won't complement demand management policies with an incomes policy. As yet nobody has had much success in specifying what it was that was going to bring down the rate of inflation while at the same time leaving the pricing system free to operate. That's why I used the term, "a grin without a cat."

Let me speak to one of the last questions on your list: Do Republican administrations bear down harder on inflation than Democratic administrations, which are more concerned with unemployment? That is the kind of speech that one could more readily have given when we thought the Phillips curve would stay still. I think the major difference is the phase at which the administrations come into power. I recall Kermit Gordon introducing me once at Brookings when I was chairman of the Council, and he said if Nixon had won in 1960, I probably would have been the one to have gotten the credit for the 1962 tax reduction and then the Democrats would have had to come in to undo the overheating of the economy. As it happens, we got on the cycle the other way around. I don't see much difference in the parties on this issue.

8
The Council of Economic Advisers Under Chairman Herbert Stein, 1972–1974

Summary History

As a member of the McCracken Council of Economic Advisers, Herbert Stein had been perhaps the most ardent free-marketer and opponent of economic controls within the Nixon administration. By the time he took over as Chairman of the CEA in January 1972, however, he had come to accept the necessity of the administration's shift to a controls policy in 1971 and had taken a central role in the formulation of that policy, even serving as head of the task force that worked out the details of Phase II in the fall of 1971. A University of Chicago Ph.D. and respected authority on fiscal policy, he came to the CEA not from a university teaching position as had his colleagues but rather from a distinguished career in economic research and policy analysis at the Committee for Economic Development and the Brookings Institution. Joining Stein on the CEA were Ezra Solomon and the newest member, Marina Von Neumann Whitman, the first woman to serve on the Council. In the summer of 1973, Solomon resigned and was replaced by Gary L. Seevers. Whitman resigned in the fall of that same year; William John Fellner took her position on the CEA.

The reduced role of the Nixon CEA continued under Stein. As in the past, the CEA was represented on most relevant administration policy committees, including the Council on Economic Policy, the Domestic Council, the Cost of Living Council, and the Council on International Economic Policy, but the CEA was not the administration's spokesman on economic policy, a position it had yielded in 1971 to Treasury Secretary John Connally and then to his successor George Shultz in 1972. In January 1973, as Nixon's "administrative presidency" began to take shape, the CEA was clearly relegated to a second level role in policy development as well, subordinate to Treasury Secretary Shultz, who, as assistant to the president for economic affairs and Chairman of the Council on Economic Policy, became a sort of "super-secretary" overseeing the entirety of economic policymaking within the administration. After Shultz left the administration, Deputy Secretary of State Kenneth Rush became Nixon's chief economic counselor. Stein believed that these developments did not mean a decline in CEA influence but allowed the CEA to focus more closely on its analytic duties. He was not satisfied with the Council on Economic Policy that was established, however, and in early 1974 came to

believe that continued government intervention in the economy
would require the establishment of a larger-scale economic planning agency in order to assure effective policy coordination.

Stein became CEA Chairman during Phase II of the Nixon anti-
inflation program. Put into operation on November 14, Phase II
was a mandatory program designed to allow the economy to recover
after the ninety-day freeze and at the same time keep wages and
prices down, thus dampening inflationary expectations. As during
the freeze, the Cost of Living Council continued to maintain
overall responsibility for goals, coverage, coordination, and
policy, but a fifteen-member tripartite Pay Board and seven-member
Price Commission were established to administer the controls program. After labor representatives withdrew from the Pay Board in
March 1972, the board was reconstituted, much like the Price
Commission, with seven public members. The Committee on Interest
and Dividends, the Construction Industry Stabilization Committee,
the Rent Advisory Board, and the Committee on Health Services
Industry served in advisory capacities. The basic goal of Phase
II was to lower the inflation rate to 2-3 percent by the end of
1972. Since coverage was so broad (only raw agricultural products
were initially exempted), the standards were of necessity basically self-administered. For the wage sector, the Phase II standard
was to hold wage settlements down to 5.5 percent. For prices, the
controls program provided for cost pass-through within a profit
margin rule, with differing requirements for prior approval of
price changes and for reporting according to a three-tier system
based on size, scale, etc.

Up until late 1972, this program of controls appeared to be
effective, as both price and wage increases were moderated. Phase
II was not without problems, however, particularly in administration. The organizational structure was apparently not sufficiently defined, for the CLC and the Price Commission clashed several
times in disputes over policy responsibilities. The Pay Board
generally had autonomy, a concession to the constituent interests
represented on it, but the CLC indicated in November 1971 that it
felt that it had the authority to intervene in Price Commission
action, specifically delaying the effective date of certain price
regulations. The Price Commission insisted it had authority in
such matters and forced the CLC to reverse its position. Conflict
soon developed again over whether the CLC had the authority to
order full pass-through of Pay Board approved labor costs, despite
Price Commission objections. The Price Commission stood its
ground and allowed only a partial pass-through. Relations between
the two controls boards improved after that until June 1972, when
the Price Commission's attempt to alter controls policy in response to food supply changes forced the administration to reluctantly lift meat import quotas. From that point on, the Price
Commission's role in policymaking was effectively curtailed. Despite early emphasis on Price Commission authority and responsibility for price controls, it was made clear by the CLC and the
administration that the Commission's activities should be confined
to ensuring compliance.

In 1972 the Nixon administration was concerned with the
upcoming presidential election. When Stein reviewed the nation's

economic prospects in the spring of that year there was much criticism of his predictions of 2-3 percent inflation and 5 percent unemployment before the end of the year, a development Nixon's political advisers hoped for but few economic observers expected. The economy did appear to respond to the anti-inflation program, with the GNP deflator up only 2.9 percent by October. But high unemployment remained a serious problem. Therefore, although inflationary pressures had not yet been fully brought under control, the administration placed more emphasis in 1972 on stimulating rather than restraining the economy. Expansionist fiscal and monetary policies designed to increase output and curb unemployment were adopted. The Federal Reserve allowed an 8.3 percent growth in the money supply from December 1971 to December 1972. Federal spending accelerated, with a $23 billion deficit in FY 1972 and a $12.5 billion deficit in the first half of FY 1973, a drastic shift from the budget surplus secured by the Nixon administration in 1969. These expansionary policies bore fruit as the economy moved rapidly ahead during 1972 and 1973.

Once the election was out of the way and Nixon returned to the White House for a second term, the administration began to make plans to dismantle the controls program. It was with this purpose in mind that the administration announced the shift to Phase III in January 1973. Phase III was a transitional program designed to retain labor and business cooperation in holding down inflation while bringing the controls program to an end. Controls remained for food, health care, and construction, but the program relied otherwise on voluntary compliance with general wage and price standards. Both the Pay Board and the Price Commission were abolished, shifting the responsibility for remaining administrative functions to the Cost of Living Council. The President and his advisers were confident that this approach would work, predicting in the CEA's annual report that inflation would stay at 3 percent for the year and unemployment would decline to 4.5 percent.

Compliance problems turned out to be less important than world market problems that had begun to develop in late 1972. In 1972, worldwide crop failures had begun to exert pressure on the U.S. food supply, particularly grain and soybeans. Despite Price Commission concern, the administration and the Department of Agriculture had continued policies designed to keep the supply down and prices up. By December 1972 the pressures of world market demand were showing up in food prices, but it was not until 1973 that the full impact became evident, when farm and food prices became central to a resurgent inflation. By August, wheat prices were up 186 percent, corn up 163 percent, and broilers up 158 percent. Meanwhile the impact of Phase III had other repercussions that aggravated the situation in early 1973. The dollar had been devalued in December 1971 in order to improve the U.S. export-import situation, but the actual effect had been limited. Then with the shift to Phase III, international confidence in the dollar had declined in reaction to possible resurgent inflation. In February, the dollar was again devalued by 6 percent, but in contrast to 1971, the effect was startling, as import prices rose, export demand increased, and the dollar began to slide in value in the exchange markets. These problems were complicated by the strong domestic demand fueled by the expansionist policies of 1972. As a result, pressure on the productive capacity of basic-materials industries resulted in increased costs that were then passed on in price increases. In late 1973, the oil embargo and the increase in prices by the international oil cartel further aggravated the situation. By the end of the year, the Consumer Price Index was up 8.8 percent, wholesale prices were up 18 percent, and the GNP deflator had risen by over 5 percent, the worst peacetime performance since 1948.

There was widespread public perception that much of the problem was due to the voluntary nature of the Phase III program and that a return to controls like those of Phase II was essential. Non-compliance was not really the problem, however, so much as the fact that developments in the world market and excess domestic demand had altered the situation to the point that the administration's controls program was no longer suitable. As the price situation worsened in the spring and early summer of 1973, the administration attempted to revise its policies, on June 13 announcing a sixty-day price freeze. Wages were not included because structural developments had led to continued moderation that did not require action beyond the voluntarism of Phase III. Actions were also taken to increase supply through sales of stock-piled materials, expansion of the timber supply from national forests, and removal of beet import restrictions.

Beginning on July 18, 1973, the freeze was lifted on a sectoral basis and Phase IV began. Phase IV was a return to mandatory controls, and was accompanied by a more restrictive monetary and fiscal policy to slow down the economy. Phase IV was unpopular. Sharp shifts in relative prices, and the economy's first experience with supply-shock inflation inevitably created inequities and made the program very difficult to manage. Amid widespread unhappiness with the program, in early 1974 the economy slid into recession while experiencing its first double digit inflation since the Korean War. In the summer of 1974, Nixon struggled with Watergate; he also tried to restore his credibility on economic policy, holding well-publicized meetings with top economic aides. Yet as Watergate closed in on the President, so did the nation's economic problems. In August, when Nixon finally resigned, inflation was up to 12 percent, unemployment was at 5.3 percent, and output had dropped by 1.2 percent. Stein had already made plans to leave the CEA that fall to join the University of Virginia faculty, so with the new president also came a new CEA Chairman to deal with the mounting economic problems.

Oral History Interview

EH: You were a scholar before you served on the Council, a working economist, an historian of fiscal policy. Then you were
a member of the Council and eventually you were Chairman.
Did your perspectives of the Council as an institution
change as you moved in those three situations--first as a
scholar outside government, then as a member, and finally as
Chairman? And if so, how?

HS: I think it did change, but mainly in detail. By the time I
came to the Council, a lot of my ideas were set and many of
the ideas that I had in the book about how policy developed
in this country were confirmed by what I observed when I was
there. But I did not fully appreciate, when I was outside,
the enormous tempo of life at the Council and how rapidly
issues just swept over the government, were debated and
decided while people outside didn´t quite realize that there
was an issue up ahead. When I worked at the Committee for
Economic Development for twenty years, I had thought that we
were giving the government a lot of advice. We were always
writing policy statements about what to do on this or that,
and I thought we were really being very influential. But I
discovered when I was in the government that there really is
very little influence from the outside because the outside
never catches up with the speed at which things happen in the
government and in the Council. I, of course, did not fully
appreciate the range of the Council´s activities nor the
enormous and elaborate informal inter-agency network in which
the Council operated. My study of the Council had been
almost entirely about fiscal policy, and I had thought of the
Council sitting there deciding how big the deficit should be,
whereas that´s a question you decide only occasionally. Most
of the time you spend thinking about what the price of oats
should be. But my basic view that policy is determined by
the evolution of conditions and thinking in the country and
that the identity of the people who are there, either on the
Council or in the Oval Office at any moment, is of relatively
little importance was confirmed in a rather striking way. We
did many things that you could not at all have predicted from
the identity of the people who were there, but that you might
have predicted from a better understanding of the conditions,
the state of economic thinking, and the state of public
thinking.

DG: Arthur Schlesinger, Jr. made some observation about how confident he had been in writing about the American presidency
before he got into the government and how tentative he was in
what he had to say in the Kennedy book. The whole thing
seemed to be much more complex, intricate, after he got
inside government. Is your view similar to that?

HS: Of course, I´m not a student of the presidency in the sense
that he is. Certainly, my views about economics and economic

policy were considerably shaken, but I never believed that we knew how to do everything.

DG: You were less innocent than Schlesinger?

HS: I think I was. Never having been a member of the establishment, perhaps I was always more skeptical about what the establishment knew. That skepticism was not altered when I became temporarily a member of it. When I teach macro economic policy now, I say simply, "We just don't know that." But that is a very important admission. Many economists have the view that the economists know the answers; they come into Washington with a little briefcase in which they can look up the answer to any question and if the right answers are not given by the government, it's because something nasty called politics has intruded. That is not the situation at all. Our experience really confirmed how little economists know. Many of the difficulties of our experience are explained by the economists' inadequate understanding of the way the economy operates, especially in the rather new conditions we faced.

LS: Isn't it true that whenever you try to take a discipline and attempt to apply it, there's always going to be a great gap between the theory and the experience?

HS: That's because the theory is inadequate. The theory is satisfactory as long as it is an internal game played by the professionals in which their only concern is disproving the last journal article. But when you take it outside that milieu and try to work with it, then you see what a twisted cue you have.

EH: Given these limitations, what are resources of the economist without illusions?

HS: I don't want to say that we don't know anything or that we're just as well off consulting a medium or a palmreader, but the range of uncertainty has been very great and the range of disagreement among respected people is very great. The political figure making a decision has this great range from which to choose, and he has to make a choice on some basis other than what can be reported to him as the perceived wisdom of the economics profession because that perceived wisdom gives pretty wide range.

EH: You present a view of history in which the individuals are not crucial. We've been trying to pursue the point of view of presidents in relation to their economic advisers. Does the way a president thinks about economics make a difference? Do his values make a difference? How does the president incorporate the kind of analytic knowledge that you have to bring to bear? How did President Nixon do that?

The President and Economic Policy

IB: What model of the economy, if any, did President Nixon bring in with him? What were the critical variables that he iden- tified as "the economic theory?"

HS: I'll answer some aspects of that. I think Mr. Nixon realized that the economic problem was a large part of his task. He did not find it intrinsically the most interesting subject that he had to deal with. I very much doubt that any presi- dent does, but people have different views of that. I think that a person who becomes president is a person whose great skill is in dealing with people, and that gives him a natural affinity for the subject of foreign policy. He may think, for example, that he can handle the question of foreign policy by talking to Sadat or Begin. Some of them think they can handle the subject of inflation by talking to George Meany, but they really can't. The president would prefer to do it that way, but the economic problem is not a problem that you can handle by calling somebody in and having a chat with him or twisting his arm. There is a certain impersonal- ity about economic policy that makes it not very congenial to presidents.

President Nixon didn't consider economics his main strength or the subject to which he should personally devote a major amount of his time. He would rely more heavily on others in the case of economic policy than in the case of foreign policy. He also didn't believe that it was a terri- bly interesting subject to the country. He may have been wrong about that, but he never thought that a radio or TV speech about economics would have the same ratings or appeal in the country as a TV speech about his relations with China or even Vietnam.

I think he knew a good deal about the economy, about economics. I think he learned a good deal while he was Vice- President. He had been chairman of some committee that Eisenhower set up about economic growth and stability. He had known a number of economists. His service in the Con- gress and Senate had involved some knowledge. He also got some attitudes out of his experience as a lawyer. One of the fundamental points of his attitude towards economic policy derives from something that runs through his attitudes on many other things: he was very skeptical about the compe- tence of government, about the disinterestedness of the peo- ple who manage government policies. I think his belief in the free market came as much from this negative attitude toward government as from any understanding of the positive values of a free market that you might learn from an econo- mics textbook. He understood that, so he believed in letting the private system work. He also had a feeling, which was there at the beginning, but was certainly stronger at the end after our various experiments, that the government ought to set and stick with a course that the private sector could adapt to. We violated that very much, but that was his basic view. He was terribly impressed with the unemployment problem. As he wrote in <u>Six Crises</u>, he believed one of the reasons he lost the election in 1960 was because unemployment rose during the year. He attributed that in part to the Federal Reserve. He was always wary of the Federal Reserve and then the bankers.

LS: What was his attitude toward business?

HS: That is interesting. He did not have a great regard for the leaders of the business community, that is the Fortune 500 or the Business Council or the people who are now the Round Table. For one thing, they had never been his supporters. They had been Rockefeller Republicans, not his Republicans. I think he considered the small businessman and the medium-sized businessman his constituency. He was concerned about them. He did not have any deference to big business people, and especially not to big bankers. But this fear of unemployment was very much in his mind and had a considerable influence on our policy. This concern goes back to what I said about influences on the development of policy. If we look back at it now, not only Nixon but McCracken and I were excessively obsessed with the unemployment problem, and that's probably true of everybody who grew up in the 1930s. We never shook that off and we're only beginning now to have a more realistic view of that issue.

EH: In order to have good relations between an economic adviser and a president, there has to be some congruence in values and purposes, doesn't there?

HS: Yes, that's important. I think that we were very sympathetic on these matters. We shared this obsession with unemployment, although he had it more than I or McCracken did. I had never met Mr. Nixon until the day he announced my appointment as a member of the Council. When I went up to the Pierre to speak to him before my appointment was announced, he asked me to talk about economic problems, and I talked mainly about inflation. He said, "But we mustn't let that unemployment get up." That was more on his mind than on mine. But I shared with him his skepticism of the capacity of government, and I shared with him the free market orientation. Our most dramatic action was the imposition of the price-wage controls, to which I was opposed, but he always gave the impression that he also really detested having to do this and that we would make sure that we'd get out of it.

He was somewhat torn about international economic policy. He believed in free trade and he came to believe in floating exchange rates and thought that was a great thing that had been done. But he was also very nationalistic, rather inclined to believe that others were out to exploit us economically, and there was, I suppose, a struggle for his soul between the Connally forces and the University of Chicago forces about the matter.

AL: I've always had the notion that Nixon was an activist president. His personal preferences were to let the market work
where it could, but faced with a situation in which his
accession to power or maintenance of power was threatened by
economic circumstances, he was going to be a spender who
would outspend Roosevelt and everyone else. The importance
of the unemployment problem in his mind would suggest that he
had a philosophy that the powers of government were to be
used for the benefit of the whole people. Now doesn't that
raise a conflict here as to whether you can believe Mr. Nixon
is basically a free market man or whether he's going to be
President of the United States?

HS: Well, he was both; everybody has noted many paradoxes about
Mr. Nixon. He wanted to use the power of the presidency. He
just didn't believe that those other two million people in
the federal government were capable of doing anything, or
would do it if he told them. He really believed in the
government having minimum intervention in the economy, but he
was, as you say, an activist. He thought great presidents
were activist presidents. He always believed in throwing the
long bomb. That is, he used to describe the gradualism
policy, which was the policy of 1969-70, as the Ohio State
strategy of three yards and a cloud of dust. He loved football analogies. He accepted that and recognized that his
economic ideology and all of ours were really very moderate
and gray, but he shook his head about it, and he really
wished that he could do something more dramatic. Of course,
he finally found a guy who would throw a long bomb--Connally.
Another paradox that affected his attitude on many subjects
was the idea of conservative men with liberal policies.
Moynihan revealed that idea to him, and introduced him to
many books on the subject. I think he really believed that
he could be as Disraeli had been. He liked the idea that he
was this conservative president who put forth the family
assistance plan, but in his heart he was rather uncertain
about it.

Bureaucratic Politics and Economic Policy

EH: Did his style of authority, his way of structuring advisory
patterns, have an effect on those patterns and on the content
of policy?

HS: I'm not sure that it did. The pattern changed several times
during his administration. I don't know whether we would
have come to the freeze and to the wage-price controls if he
had not gotten into this very close relationship with Connally. But a number of external forces and situations were
leading him in that direction, and maybe Connally was a
consequence of those forces. He needed somebody who would
hold his hand while he was going there, and the rest of us
wouldn't. So I really don't know. I don't know what your
perception is of the advisory process that went on there.

We started with a very loose system. Of course, we inherited the Troika, and the Troika was a central body throughout the whole period. We started with the Troika of CEA, Budget Bureau (as it was then called), and Treasury, which continued to be the main influence in determining the government's official view of the economic outlook and remained the President's principal guide to fiscal policy. At the same time we set up the Cabinet Committee on Economic Policy, and the idea for that originated in the Council of Economic Advisers. This body was practically co-extensive with the Cabinet--everybody who had anything to do with economics. It was established for two reasons: some of the people whom the President had appointed to the cabinet, especially Maurice Stans, who was Secretary of Commerce, had been given the impression that they would have something to do with the formation of economic policy. There was no desire to admit them to the Troika, so we needed something else to take them in, and the Cabinet Committee on Economic Policy was established as a way of doing that.

But we also came in at a time when inflation was a big issue, and there was a feeling in the country that something more was needed to control inflation than the kind of fiscal policy that was the subject of the Troika; we needed some machinery that would show our concern with that and would, in fact, give an opportunity for other kinds of anti-inflationary policy to be considered, especially since such policies might involve the Departments of Commerce, or Labor, or Agriculture. So we had the Cabinet Committee on Economic Policy operating for about a year. It helped to introduce the President to his officials and allowed them to get some impression of what he was thinking. But it was an excessively large group; it allowed too many people to talk on too many subjects that they didn't know anything about and had no responsibility for. The President became bored with it and left it. It continued for a while with the Vice-President as its chairman, but he didn't have anything more to do with it, and it quickly faded away.

Then we went through a period--this is 1970--in which the President dealt with the Troika, dealt on a more or less equal basis with Treasury, Bureau of the Budget (as it still was), and the Council of Economic Advisers, but there was a feeling that things were at loose ends and not coordinated, especially in connection with international economic policy. The Secretary of Commerce and others were trying to promote some deals with the Japanese; advocates of incomes policy were also sprouting up all over the administration at secondary levels and needed restraint. During that period I believe the President felt that he didn't have any strong guidance. Then he brought in Connally, obviously a very strong character. The President, as I understand it, had not known Connally well before he worked on the Ash Commission, but he had been terribly impressed with both his persuasiveness and his understanding of political questions. He was a person he could rely on. I believe it was only during the

Connally period, and maybe not for all of that, that the President had a one-to-one relation with a single person in the economic field, as he had with Kissinger in the foreign policy field.

EH: Is that why he designated Connally as spokesman, then, in mid-1971? Did that follow from this?

HS: That followed partly from the fact that Connally was the dominant person, that he had most confidence in Connally, since he could discuss more things with Connally. Connally was also rather demanding; he did not take lightly to competition.

The occasion on which he designated Connally as his chief spokesman arose because the Council of Economic Advisers had an identifiable view in favor of a more expansionist policy. At a Camp David meeting in June--before the famous one on August 15--the question had been raised whether there should be a more expansionist policy; the Council was pushing that, but the decision was "No." I wasn't at the conference, but Paul was, and after they came back, the President called in the three members of the CEA--we were the problem--and told us that John Connally was going to be his official spokesman. He would welcome any memoranda from us, and internal comments, but we were not to promote contrary ideas in public. I remember a reporter coming to ask me about that shortly thereafter. I said, "Well, the President really cannot designate who will be his chief spokesman any more than he can designate who will write the country's songs. Whoever says interesting things will be reported." And this was not a serious restraint on anybody. It was a moment of pique, I suppose. Of course, then Connally went out and gave a press conference, talking about the four "no's": no price and wage controls, no tax cut, no closing of the gold window, no expenditure increase--all the things that we did. So we had a period in which the President worked fairly closely with Connally on a one-to-one basis. The Troika continued to function, however, and the Nixon-Connally relation was not nearly as exclusive as I believe the Nixon-Kissinger relation was. The degree of exclusiveness, even while Connally was there, faded after we got to the new economic policy and the Cost of Living Council was established. The Cost of Living Council, while it operated intensively in the first four or five months--during the remainder of 1971--was the closest thing we ever had to a real cabinet-style management of economic policy. This was a period of great intensity. The Council at first met every afternoon, all the members present--they were almost all cabinet people plus a consumer representative and a few others--and a quite broad range of economic policy got funneled into the Council. During this period Connally was operating with the advice and consent of the Council, and was really influenced by it. He was not a person who had strong preferences about policy. He just wanted to make a decision. Except when we got into budgetary

matters, he was operating pretty much as the chief decision
maker in the economic field--not in the role of an adviser to
the President, but in the role of somebody who has the President's authority in making decisions. But that did not last
beyond December, and then we moved into a period in which
Connally became more diverted to other things--preparing to
leave, I suppose.

The Troika continued to function, but this is the period
of Shultz's rise. From the time that Shultz took over we had
what I regard as the characteristic Nixonian style and the
ideal way to run this business because Shultz really was
delegated a good deal of the presidential authority. Shultz
was not only Assistant to the President, but a kind of assistant president for economic policy. Shultz always operated
through a committee system, and he was the most wonderful
manager of a committee you can imagine because he brought
everyone into the act, made sure that everybody had an opportunity to say his piece, did not dominate the discussion, but
always made sure that we came to a conclusion. Then the
relation to the President was this committee structure--a
kind of moving group.

EH: Was this before the creation of the Committee on Economic
Policy?

HS: Yes, the Committee on Economic Policy is just zero. It had
nothing at all to do with anything. So far as I can remember
it only met twice, and it, like the Cabinet Committee on
Economic Policy, had too many people with too little function. Its only usefulness was to have a few subcommittees
that did function, but as a Cabinet Committee it hardly ever
met. The main group was the Troika and then the expanded
Troika. In about 1971, the Troika was expanded to include
Peter Flanigan, who was the White House assistant concerned
with economic matters and who then became the executive
director of the Committee on International Economic Policy--I
can never remember whether it's committee or council, but the
initials are CIEP. He was there at first to represent the
political White House interests, but then as the representative of the international economic problem, which was very
important. After we got into the controls, Rumsfeld, who was
the director of the Cost of Living Council in Phase II,
joined the Troika. So you had an expanded Troika of five
people as the central body.

This Shultzian committee structure would present the
President with options on the important issues where a presidential decision was needed. We went through an excellent
process of synthesizing the arguments so that he was not left
with many insignificant issues to consider. We would really
boil the arguments down to the eligible options; he knew
where everybody stood on all the options, and he had a fairly
objective account of the options.

EH: This was done on paper, primarily.

HS: On paper, but then to be discussed with him. He would be presented with the options paper. I did a great deal of that options paper writing. Options paper writing is a great art, which I learned in the government, and I think it's a great responsibility. I try to teach my students about it.

This was the period after Shultz became Secretary of the Treasury--in about May of 1972--but before he became the Assistant to the President for Economic Affairs, which was only after the 1972 elections.

EH: And the President had the same quality of confidence in him that he had had in Connally?

HS: Perhaps more. Of course, he did not regard Shultz as the political magician that he regarded Connally as, but he had enormous confidence in Shultz, and I believe that's one of the things that came out of the early meetings of the Cabinet Committee on Economic Policy. He had not known Shultz before he appointed him as Secretary of Labor, but it was clear in those meetings of the Cabinet Committee on Economic Policy that Shultz had a great facility for taking everybody else's thinking into his mind and reaching a conclusion. The President could have complete confidence that Shultz was not grinding his own axe to the disadvantage of other contestants in the process.

LS: How does one square someone like Shultz, as you described him, with someone like Connally? These two people are quite different, yet Nixon responded to each one.

HS: Of course, they're both very high quality, very impressive people in different ways. Each of them could do something that the President needed. Connally was a terrific public spokesman for the President on economic policy, a great articulator, a very great persuader. But Shultz was a much better manager, especially from the standpoint of everybody else.

AL: You describe the Cost of Living Council as a marvelous vehicle for bringing people together and getting this consultation. Shultz performed that function admirably as a person. Why did that work when he was Secretary of the Treasury, but not when he was the President's man as Director of OMB or BOB?

HS: When he was the Director of OMB, he did not have that function. He was not the chairman of all these committees. He did not have that responsibility for coordinating economic policy. When he was Director of OMB, someone else was the secretary of the Treasury.

AL: So he had to be taken out of the budgetary area and get somehow closer to the President to do this job?

HS: As Director of OMB, he was close to the President. The President, I suppose, could have given that job to him then, but he didn't. While George was in charge of OMB, Connally was Secretary of the Treasury. If you have a strong secretary of the Treasury, he is the natural first reliance, the president's senior man. And he has some functions that nobody else has and that he doesn't share with anybody. When George was Secretary of the Treasury, he let other people in, whereas Connally did not. We're getting a somewhat exaggerated picture of Connally, however, because even with respect to international financial policy, international monetary policy, there was the Volcker group, in which you [DD] participated. This group was chaired by the under secretary of the Treasury and included representatives from the Federal Reserve, Council of Economic Advisers, State, OMB, and others, and it had a very large role in developing the government's international monetary policy, although that was finally the responsibility of the Treasury. It was a very good mechanism for discussing the problems analytically and politically, so we're exaggerating Connally's degree of exclusiveness, but his style was a great deal different from Shultz's.

Under Shultz we operated in this committee format. The options we developed would be presented to the President and if they were important issues, then a group would meet with the President. The Quadriad was still meeting with him; the Troika was still meeting with him. The core of this committee remained the Troika--the Treasury, CEA, OMB--but if we met with the President on something about controls, then the Director of the Cost of Living Council would be present. Later when energy became a problem, if we met on something about energy, the Director of the Federal Energy Administration would be present. We had, in effect, various circles. One was the Cost of Living Council circle and had to do with the price and wage controls with Shultz at the center. Another little circle had to do with international monetary matters. During 1972 we developed the administration's position on the reform of the international monetary system, which the President and Shultz presented to the IMF. That was developed in what seemed to be a very orderly way and was unusual in that the Secretary of State was brought into it, which as far as I know, had never happened before. Shultz was the leader, and the secretaries of the Treasury and State are traditionally rivals and coequals. Nevertheless, Rogers, who was then Secretary of State, accepted his position in this group along with CEA, OMB, Peter Flanigan, and Burns. So Shultz had this capacity for making everybody feel they were part of the group.

EH: How did the constituency departments relate to this group-- Labor, Commerce, Agriculture, Transportation, and so on?

HS: Mostly they were out, except Agriculture, because a large part of the inflation problem was the agriculture problem.

The Cost of Living Council had a food group in which the Secretary of Agriculture participated. All of these people were, of course, on the Cost of Living Council. I don't know that Transportation was, but Agriculture, Commerce, Labor, and HUD were on it, and they participated actively in the heyday of the Cost of Living Council, which was really through about the first three months of the control period. Otherwise they were not much involved.

I have not given the full flavor of the operation during this period because I haven't said anything yet about the 7:30 meetings, which were a very important aspect of the management of economic policy at that time. We used to meet every morning at 7:30 in Shultz's White House office, Shultz, I, Flanigan, the Associate Director of OMB, and Dunlop, who at that time was the Director of the Cost of Living Council, and when we got into the energy problem, whoever was in charge of energy. For a while it was Simon or Love. We would meet every morning for approximately half an hour, and everybody would tell what his problems were for the day, what he was supposed to do, anything he had on his mind. It was a wonderful opportunity for everybody to be informed about what everybody else was doing. Then most of us would go down to the 8:00 a.m. meeting with the White House senior staff, which was run first by Haldeman and then by Haig. The press people and the congressional relations people also attended this meeting. The economic problems that required consideration from these people and anything that arose in our 7:30 meeting could then be laid on the table there. By 9:00 a.m. we had done half of our day's work. But it's not a committee that you will find in a government manual.

EH: You don't give a picture of the policy staff interposing themselves between the President and the economic advisers. You haven't mentioned Ehrlichman's name at all in this regard.

HS: Ehrlichman really stayed out of our way pretty much. On a couple of occasions Ehrlichman made public statements about taxes for which he was reminded that that was not his business. When we were developing Phase III, we set up a group that was called T8 or C8--I've forgotten the initial, I know it was eight--Shultz, I, the Director of OMB (I think it was still Weinberger), some Cost of Living Council staff, and Marina Whitman. Before that was made final, we tried to get the contributions of the political people--Ehrlichman, first, and Bryce Harlow later when we were thinking about going to the second freeze. But that didn't work. They wouldn't sit still long enough. We had no problem with them, though, on the areas that were obviously economics. Some people were uncertain about what was economics, given the existence of the Domestic Council, but we never had any serious problem with them because they were basically not policymaking people on the Domestic Council.

EH: It never really became an analytic staff either, did it?

HS: No, it was a paper handling staff and an adjunct to the Congressional Liaison office, but they were primarily involved in making sure that the various departments submitted the necessary papers.

EH: Had it been a genuine analytic staff, would there have been problems of jurisdiction?

HS: Well, yes. I think that a logical line between the Domestic Council and economic policy was never clearly drawn. But the Domestic Council hardly ever met. There were some subjects that were recognized to be clearly their business. For example, the development of the family assistance plan was their business.

EH: You pretty much stayed away from that.

HS: I did personally, but Paul McCracken was involved heavily in it. The CEA did a great deal of work and when there was significant disagreement about the numbers and the facts, the President turned the job of resolving all that over to the Council of Economic Advisers.

LS: Was the role of the CEA in all of these administrative developments determined more by its institutional character, its original mission, or was it determined by the politics of whom the President responded to or whatever struck him as a good administrative arrangement? In all of this, for example, did the CEA feel itself overshadowed or threatened or downgraded?

HS: No, I don't think so. The influence of the CEA really derives from three things. First, it has a high class, technically competent staff. Other people, including the president, recognize that. Second, it has the ability to communicate with the president. Third, and this is something that I didn't really appreciate before, is the fact that it participates in so many inter-agency arrangements, committees, task forces. Hardly any important matter decided in the government isn't the subject of some inter-agency consultations because all the important matters involve more than one agency. If it's anywhere in the ballpark of economics, the Council will be represented, and that's where a great deal of work goes on. I don't know how it was in other administrations, but in the course of a year there may have been five or six important presidential decisions about economics: to draw up or revise the budget, to ask for a tax increase or cut, to impose controls, the phasing of the controls, to get out, to float or not to float. But most economic policymaking goes on below the level of the president, and most of what finally goes to the president always involves a great deal of hashing over before it gets to him. Contrary to the impression given in your report about the CEA's relation with Shultz, Shultz's elevation really enhanced the role of the Council because it meant very great power was given to a person with whom we could have very close relations, who understood us. I'd known Shultz for years; the first thing Shultz ever wrote about fiscal policy was a preface to my book. If Shultz had half the power of the President, we had much more influence over that half than we ever could have had directly with the President.

DD: So you felt quite comfortable in the Shultz period about the role of the Council and its input into the decision making process. What about in the Connally period? Was that more frustrating to you?

HS: Of course, I wasn't Chairman during much of the Connally period, though I was there. I had the feeling that Connally played things close to the chest. We didn't always know what was going on, but the Cost of Living Council somewhat miti-gated that because the Council had a very big role in the early development of the controls, both during the freeze and in the preparation for Phase II. Those extracurricular as-signments tended to bring us to the center of things. What I say about the difference between Connally and Shultz really applies less to the Council than it does to the other agen-cies of government. While Connally was exclusive, I didn't think that he was as exclusive in relation to us as he was in relation to, say, the State Department, which was totally shoved out of the international economic policy picture dur-ing the Connally period. Shultz brought them back in. I think that's true of other departments.

LS: Of the three sources of influence you mentioned, access to the president and technical expertise are interrelated. If a president has very high regard for your technical expertise, then it seems that your access will increase and that perhaps your influence in inter-agency councils will increase. So they're not three discrete variables.

HS: Oh, that's true. Your influence especially within the inter-agency councils depends very much on the fact that the others know that if you're really terribly dissatisfied with what's going on, you can send the President a memo and he will read it. All these other people are not always impressed with our technical competence. There were economists in the other agencies who thought they knew more than we did, and maybe they did sometimes. But because the President had a high regard for our judgment, they had to pay a good deal of attention to it.

LS: Would you rank that as the most important variable?

HS: Oh, yes, I think that is the most important. If you could not communicate to the President or to Shultz, his alter ego, then you might as well not be there; while the technical competence is an important aspect of influence, that's always a subject of jealousy.

DD: The picture emerges of great rapport with Shultz, but how did the Fed and Burns fit into that 1970-71 Troika reliance?

HS: The Quadriad existed, too. We had the Troika plus the Federal Reserve, which was the Quadriad which met only with the President. There was never any meeting of those four, aside from the meeting with the President. So it's true that Arthur did see the President. He also may have seen him on some other occasions. Once we got into the Cost of Living Council era, then Arthur was an adviser to the Cost of Living Council. He was offered a position as a member of the Cost of Living Council, but he decided that would be inconsistent with the independence of the Federal Reserve and agreed to be an adviser to it instead. He came to its meetings quite regularly and participated in all discussions about the management of the controls system and all those related aspects of economic policy. The Quadriad, however, functioned throughout, and at the Quadriad we would discuss the whole range of economic problems--not just monetary problems-- though, as you know, Arthur was not bashful about giving the President his view on any subject.

DD: What about the structural relations with the Fed and your rapport with Arthur?

HS: You know what the formal relations were. We used to come over every two weeks and have lunch with you. I believe that we told you much more about what we were thinking than you told us about what you were thinking. You used to tell us about your tennis scores and we used to tell you our thoughts about the GNP. You were all much, much more reserved. I suppose that's the nature of a decision making body and a collegial body. You didn't know what you were going to decide in three weeks at the next Open Market Committee meeting, so you had certain inhibitions about talking. We did discuss more substantive matters with Arthur than we did when William Martin was the chairman. The relations were, however, always rather touchy because of the Federal Reserve's independence and the feeling that we should not intrude in it, combined with the feeling that we were very interested in the Fed and ascribed probably more importance to it than most of our predecessors did. I don't recall any period when we had any grievances with respect to monetary policy. There were times in 1970 when we, especially Paul, were talking about the need for more rapid monetary expansion, and Arthur was somewhat annoyed about that. But we understood each other pretty well, and especially if you were appropriately modest about knowing how fast M1 should grow, it was hard to get into an argument about it.

SM: Previous chairmen have told us that even though the Fed was supposedly independent, it was in some sense a member of the president's team. Does that describe the Fed during the time that you were there?

HS: I would not regard it as part of the President's team. It certainly was not hostile--Arthur was not hostile--but we were unhappy about Arthur's campaign for an incomes policy during 1970 and early 1971. We thought--and I still think-- that his constant harping on the subject helped to get us involved finally in the controls. Everybody else, every editorial writer in the country, could say, "Even conserva- tive Arthur Burns, friend of the President, is in favor of incomes policy, so how can the President say that it's not a good thing to do?" That was very difficult. But he was a member of the team in the sense that we exchanged information with him. He could always communicate with us and directly or indirectly with the President. But he didn't feel any obligation to us; he operated in a very independent way. We never got any commitments from him about monetary policy because monetary policy is determined by a committee of thirteen people that meets every three weeks and can change its mind. We would get statements, which we could include in the Economic Report, saying, "With this fiscal policy and a complementary or accommodating monetary policy, we will a- chieve this result." We never got him to say, "We will give you a 6 percent rate of increase in the money supply." Of course, he's not a monetarist; he does not believe in fixing rates of monetary growth. He believes in more eclectic and flexible policies. We didn't have any problems about what the objectives of policy were, and I believe their objectives were pretty similar to ours.

DD: Were you at all troubled by Burns being the head of the Committee on Interest and Dividends? I always thought it very, very inappropriate for him to wear that hat and be trying theoretically to hold down interest and interest pay- ments, when to do the Fed's job properly, you had to be pushing interest rates up.

HS: I was not troubled by it at the time. Sometime I'm going to study that period more. I can see how in principle it creates a conflict. I don't know whether in fact the mone- tary policy was derailed because of that. I certainly would not have wanted control of interest and dividends to be put in the hands of the Price Commission or almost anybody else I can think of. I didn't think we should have had control of interest rates, anyway. I know there are these charges that we had an excessive monetary expansion in 1972 because the Federal Reserve or Arthur Burns had that responsibility, but you could explain it in other ways. I think we all made certain mistakes then about the condition of the economy.

RF: Dewey, in that case, I would think that the trouble was that

378

the policy was inherently contradictory, and in a situation like that it's better to have one person in charge to resolve the trade-offs rather than to have two different people operating two different agencies and conflicting.

DD: That's one view, but I still believe that the so-called independence of the Fed requires the chairman to walk a very fine line. Martin had a special skill and technique at doing that with five presidents; he kept an input into the president's thinking, but he maintained the Fed's independence. Burns didn't, as I saw it, right from the beginning. He tied himself too closely to the President's circles. He'd been the counselor to the President and this additional role with Interest and Dividends was reflected in his discussions in the Board's councils.

HS: Leaving aside the Committee on Interest and Dividends, Arthur maintained his independence in other relations. Maybe he was closer to Nixon than Martin had been to other presidents, but I never sensed any subordination or deference on his part. The Quadriad meetings were more often occasions for Arthur to lecture the President than for the President to lecture Arthur, so I don't believe that his intimacy was misused. If we had had a more distant chairman of the Federal Reserve, he might not have been at Camp David on August 15 when the decisions were made. I think it was a good thing that he was there and expressed his position. After all, we made a lot of decisions affecting relations with the rest of the world, but nobody from the Department of State was there.

EH: Could one argue that the Council has a greater comparative advantage in macro policy than in micro?

HS: Yes, I believe that's true. Just because there are so many micros.

EH: Is there a different politics of decision making in macro and micro?

HS: The micro decisions are much more decentralized and, of course, there are many more of them. But many of them are not terribly important, and the Council cannot keep track of all of them. This does relate to the point, which is quoted in the history, about my incautious statement once that maybe we should have a staff of 400 people. I was asked the question about whether we needed an economic planning agency such as they have in Japan or France, and I said that if the government was going to remain in this business of managing the economy in such detail then you would need something like that, but I hoped that the government would not remain in that business. The government's involvement in details of the economy has expanded, and, at least for the time being, it's not about to be reversed. I think that the ability of the Council staff to keep up with it is quite strained.

EH: People also look to the Council as having the primary prerogative in macro policy under the Employment Act, whereas in micro policy, every department is an advocate.

HS: Well, I don't think that's the situation. At some point in the history of the Council, and I don't know just when it was, the Council changed. The initial idea of the Employment Act was that all you needed to do was determine the size of the deficit and once you knew that, then everything else would follow. The Council was there to figure out the size of the gap using the Keynesian multiplier, and you didn't need many people to do that. But at some point the Council changed from doing that to being a kind of all-purpose economic analysis staff and developed some capabilities in a lot of other fields, particularly agriculture. I think of it as coming probably around Heller's time, but I'm not sure. The agriculture interest was always there, and there was always some labor interest, but I think of it as paralleling the expansion of the government. Now you need an energy man, you need somebody who can deal with environmental problems, you need somebody who can deal with health problems. Those weren't all big federal problems, even fifteen years ago. So the Council could stand a little expansion, but I don't mean anything approaching 400.

To some extent, the Council on Wage and Price Stability staff relieved the Council's burden in those areas, and I assume that those staffs work closely together. We also had some help in that field from the Cost of Living Council staff. But they had a special angle: they were just looking for ways to keep the prices down.

EH: With a small staff of this kind, do you really have the resources to take a look at a new problem, like inflation, when it emerges?

HS: Inflation is not a new problem. I was very impressed, when I was at the Council, with the great capacity of a highly qualified micro analyst to contribute something on almost any problem, even if it's one he's never heard of before. The outstanding example was the business about the law of the sea. No economist had ever heard of the law of the sea, but we had some people who were just good technical analysts and who contributed something to that. But so many of those issues come up that the Council could use some more people who are somewhat more specialized.

DD: Would you attract the same quality people, though? I've always thought that one of the attractions of serving in the Council was that you weren't so pigeonholed.

HS: They don't have to be. Instead of fifteen senior staff, I'm talking about having twenty. The range of problems has broadened, the White House's problems have broadened, so that means that these additional people would also have high-level problems to deal with. One thing that makes serving on the Council staff so attractive is that you get a very high stimulated rank. Even if you are a young associate professor from somewhere, you represent the Council on an inter-agency committee in which everybody else is an assistant secretary or under secretary. There's a certain thrill in that, and that should and could be preserved with a small expansion. The Council doesn't need a great deal of layering, but it should have enough qualified people to fill those spots and not be overburdened.

LS: How do you react to the thesis that the original sin was creating the CEA in the first place, that it was from the very beginning a planning agency and, as new problems developed and were directed to the White House, it was inevitably drawn into broadening its scope?

HS: Yes, after Mr. Carter was elected, one of his people consulted me about how the Council of Economic Advisers should be organized. I said, "How the Council should be organized depends on what kind of economic policy you're going to have. If you're going to have a Leontief economic planning policy, in which the government decides everything and in great detail, then you're going to need a large Council of Economic Advisers. If you're going to have Milton Friedman's economic policy, then you'll need a small Council of Economic Advisers." So the Council staff should be adapted to the nature of the economic policy that the government is following and to the requirements for advising the executive office—not just the president, but the executive office—on economic aspects of the decisions they have to make. Given the existing spread of government, you probably need more people.

As to the question about the quality of the staff and whether it is preferable to have a revolving staff or a permanent staff at the Council of Economic Advisers, I think that you need some of both. I was very impressed by how quickly a person could come in from the university and get on this rapidly moving train and play his part, get into the memo writing and the meeting attending and all that. You need some people there who will show them their way around, but academics can contribute a great deal. It was especially good to know that we had some people who brought us the latest word from the groves of academe. Whatever the latest econometric equation was in the journal, they knew it. I don't believe those are wonderful, but you wouldn't want to miss it.

EH: Most of us who study the presidency assume a necessary and valuable plasticity of staff, that each president is going to have to shape staff and authority relations according to his policy, which is in his own style. To what extent could one say that the Council, by its very existence and by performing its function, has institutionalized certain ways of approaching economic policy so that some things are done in a way that's predictable?

HS: There is a certain continuity in the kinds of things we look at and the way it's organized, even in the means of communication with the president. I don't know what the significance of that is. Maybe it does have something to do with the fact that economics is something of a discipline and that you draw people from somewhere near the mainstream of that discipline to be on the Council of Economic Advisers. You're not going to get somebody advising you to put a bomb in the basement of Exxon.

AL: Would it make that point more explicit if we were to look exclusively at what is happening institutionally over the years in the president's Economic Report? It's never been completely clear to me what the relation is under the statute. It's the president's report, but it is divided into parts: one, the president's report; two, the Council's, which professionally and disciplinarily is a report on the state of the economy, trends and problems. There's also a sense in which the president's report is the president's economic policy. To what degree is the president's economic policy different from or identical with the report that the Council gives?

HS: There is no inconsistency between them. The Council's report is an elaboration of the case for the president's policy plus a great deal more information, description, analysis. I can't think of any time when the Council's report has presented policies different from the president's report. In Eisenhower's day, the president's report was largely excerpts from the Council's report. In our time, we always wrote the president's report, except in the first year when he tried to have Bill Safire write it. There may have been a little difference of tone--we may have been somewhat more guarded in our own report than we were in his.

EH: There is an analogue for the CEA in the legislative clearance that OMB does with the agencies. The CEA performs clearance on agency proposals that call for more money. That's going to be done probably by every administration and every Council, and if we put our minds to it, I expect we could find eight or ten things that are done across time and done differently because there is a Council. In other words, there is an institution there.

HS: The OMB is the center of the agency clearance, and it exists because they exist, not because we exist. We just happen to get in on the list of people who cleared things. No, the Council gets to say something, but a lot of other people do also on the clearance of proposals or on the president's veto of legislative proposals. I'm really not clear about the answer to your question. Maybe one possibility--and this may be of some seriousness--is that if the Council of Economic Advisers did not exist, the president would have to get economic advice somewhere. God knows where he would get it. But it may be that the existence of the Council tends to reduce the range of sources from which presidents get advice. To go back to times before the Council existed, I think Roosevelt got advice from his business friends, from congressmen and other politicians, and from his general friends.

LS: He had Rex Tugwell, Ray Moley, Leon Henderson.

HS: Yes, sure, that's right. Of course, he had the so-called Brain Trust. But, even so, he was probably exposed to more diverse groups. Presidents have varied in that. I have the impression that Eisenhower got more advice from outside the executive office than subsequent presidents have done. That was partly because he had great esteem for business people, so he used to talk to them and get advice. But the existence of the Council may tend to make the presidency more ingrown. Now we recognized that, and I suppose others have, because we thought we had a responsibility to try to keep the president informed of what other people were thinking and not just what we thought. Every once in a while the President would ask to have some other economists brought in. Of course, he did speak to business people and others.

LS: But the whole mode of analysis of forecasting GNPs and gaps is something for which the Council is responsible. It never existed before.

HS: Oh, I know, but that's something for which the profession is responsbile. We just brought into the government what is the current mode of thinking of the profession. That would have been there even if there had been no Council of Economic Advisers. Somebody would do it: the Treasury would do it, or OMB would do it. In fact, you know, the original suggestion was that all this should be in the Budget Bureau.

EH: Did you favor the Ash Council proposal for a Department of Economic Affairs to pull together these diverse programs?

HS: I don't remember whether I did or not. I never thought it was going anywhere anyway. But I did not regard it as creating any problem for us.

LS: Supposing the OMB had succeeded in taking on that function. The CEA had a certain character as an organization that had a lot to do with the acceptance of this position. The OMB would have been perhaps more tainted with the notion of people who are permanent bureaucrats or excessively close to the president. But the CEA is an almost non-bureaucratic agency full of inner-outer people, more disinterested, perhaps.

HS: I don't know about that. I think you would have had a more internal staff. The OMB has always had a very high class staff, so it would not have been deficient in any way. And the staff has always been very nonpartisan. But without the Council the president would have had one less source of information. Now, on most matters, it's the Council, the OMB, and the Treasury. Perhaps one constant of the existence of the Council is that it gives the president the possibility of having three views. One of the great problems is to make sure that the president gets a sufficient range of views without giving him so many that he has to operate as his own economist. One of the great advantages of the Shultz arrangement was that the views were sufficiently refined and synthesized before he got them, but the process was not carried to the point where he was not left with any options.

DD: You talked about the Council representing the profession, bringing in the profession's view, and being nonpartisan. It's nonpartisan in a political sense.

HS: I never said it was nonpartisan. I said that the economics profession has a certain mainstream, but that mainstream has certain width. Maybe there's a spread from, say, Friedman to Heller, but it probably does not include Galbraith. But if you get two economists of different views together in a room with non-economists, in the end the two economists will be much closer to each other than they are to anyone else. In that sense, there is a certain neoclassical synthesis of economics. Even economists who are not worshipers of the free market have a certain respect for it. Of course, we did go to a kind of Galbraithean solution when we went to the freeze, but, by and large, there's a certain center to the profession.

AL: What's most fascinating about today's discussion is the assumption that the Council has a role to play beyond that of assessing the state of the economy and reporting on problems, trends, and policy options arising out of it. The office of the president, that whole machinery that you referred to earlier--the two Councils and the inner group, the staff level--are getting into operations that in administrative or political theory (in the old days) were supposed to be all wrong: staff functions were advisory, analytical, and they were never to get into offering policy options. What we need to learn here is this relation between policy analysis and advice and the business of administering controls through the executive office.

HS: All I'm saying is that the Council's capacities should match the president's requirements, and if the president is making decisions about the allocation of energy, which have an important effect on the economy, he needs some staff in the White House who are capable of giving him advice about that. If the government isn't in that business, then he doesn't

need that staff. I don't want to have the staff in order to
have the function, but if we have the function, I want to
have the staff to give him some advice. He should not be
entirely dependent on the Department of Energy to tell him
about that because they will always be a partied interest.
The role of the Council would still be purely advisory.

While the Council has been given this function that
initially emphasized the fiscal approach and stabilization of
the economy, I said that you also have staffs in the OMB and
at the Treasury who are involved in studying the same thing.
I said that they would be doing that even if the Council
didn't exist, but they might not, at least to the same extent, because they are there partly for competitive and
protective reasons. If the Council says, "You shouldn't have
a tax cut because it would destabilize the economy," the
secretary of the Treasury can ring up his economists and
they'll tell him, "You should have a tax cut because it will
stabilize the economy."

The Public Role of the Chairman

EH: We have not really focused on the public role of the Chairman
to any great extent. It's interesting and important, and I
thought I might ask you to talk about that a little bit.

HS: I don't know what the proper public role of the Chairman of
the Council is. I think chairmen have done what they've felt
temperamentally interested in doing. There are no rules
about it. Of course, I would like to say something about the
politicization business. At one of the first meetings of the
Cabinet Committee on Economic Policy, the President discussed
with the cabinet members and the Council the business of
public speaking about economic matters. He indicated that he
didn't intend to do much of it. He expected the Cabinet
members to do a great deal of it, to explain our policy in
all kinds of forums. Then turning to the Council of Economic
Advisers, he said, "Now you fellows should speak only in
small groups of professionals." We were not to be out in a
political arena; he didn't expect us to be carrying his spear
in the political process. I don't know whether he thought
that we weren't capable of it or that it wouldn't help him if
we tried, but he had a certain notion that we were professionals and experts and different from the Cabinet members,
many of whom were former governors or congressmen. I made
many speeches at all times because I like to make speeches,
but I was never urged to make any.

Then in 1972 the whole problem arose. During that time
I made four speeches that were considered political. The
first one was at the National Press Club. There was an
article in _Time_ about economics as a big issue in the campaign and how Muskie had Okun and Humphrey had Heller, I
guess, and McGovern had Galbraith. I thought it was a very
funny subject, and I gave a speech about Muskie saying to
Humphrey: "I'll trade you Okun for Heller and two draft

choices." Anyway, I thought it was very funny. It was not meant to be anything else. Then I gave a speech in a very secluded place--at the Homestead, Hot Springs, the Virginia Bankers Association--about Mr. McGovern's $1,000 per capita plan, the Demogrant, in which I said that his whole attitude was one of an aging balding fellow trying to be hip with the younger generation. It was very good. I made another speech at the Financial Analysts Federation, where McGovern had spoken previously, analyzing Mr. McGovern's economics. Then I made what was probably my most famous speech at the American Political Science Association meeting in Washington. On that occasion I held up this chuck roast and said that the price of the chuck roast has gone down 85 cents in the last month. Of course, somebody said, "Well, if you've been carrying it around in your briefcase for the last month, naturally it should cost less." People never believed prices went down and they never believed the statistics, so I thought I'd have some tangible piece of evidence. Then I got a lot of criticism for politicizing the Council because I made those political speeches. I don't have any record of what my predecessors did, but I felt that the President deserved the most forceful exposition that he could get of his economic policy, that the policy was working well and, certainly, by contrast to the alternatives offered, deserved a great deal of support. I didn't see anybody else around who was likely to do it any better than I did, and I enjoyed making those speeches. Nobody in the White House ever asked me to make them. In fact, the President, at some time during the campaign, appointed Pierre Rinfret as his economic adviser for the campaign. He did not regard me as his campaign spokesman. I was dismayed that he had done that but, nevertheless, he did do it. He didn't talk to me about it. Chuck Colson brought Pierre Rinfret in to see the President and they cooked that up.

But on the subject of politicization, I remember that I got a telephone call during 1972 from one economist who had been a member of the Council in the Kennedy days. He asked me what was going on. I said I was very busy because we had all these requests for economic information having to do with the campaign, and I felt that I could not ask the staff to do anything about it; all the assembling of the economic information for use in campaign speeches was done by the three members plus my administrative assistant because I wanted to preserve the purity of the staff. He said to me, "Well, we were not so fastidious."

It seems to me, however, that it is a legitimate and necessary function of the chairman to try to explain the president's policies. Every chairman has done it; some have spoken more and some have spoken less, but they've all done it. The president's Chairman of the Council of Economic Advisers is not a removed, impartial judge of the president, who can approve of some policies and disapprove of others and tell the public about that. The Chairman is the president's man. He's appointed by the president. Every president appoints somebody whom he feels will be sympathetic to him and supportive of his program. What is important is that the president should get the most objective economic advice that he can get. I don't see that speaking on behalf of the president's policies is inconsistent with this function. Of course, the chairman's speeches should be judged on the same basis as everybody else's speeches as to whether they are accurate and honest. If you want to read about it, this subject was aired at the meeting of the American Economic Association in December 1973. It was reported in <u>Challenge</u>. There were no Republicans among the people who charged me with politicizing the Council. Most of them were very deeply devoted to our predecessors and mainly journalists—people who do not disclose their own affiliations in writing about policy matters. The criticism was just a part of the fall-out of an intensely political atmosphere in which a large part of the writing and talking community felt itself extremely hostile to or at odds with the administration that I was serving. What is politicization by your adversary is honest exposition by your friend. Republicans, I guess, are no less political than Democrats.

LS: What are the boundaries, what's the function of the chairman and the members of the Council? Is it necessary to have a code? Is it necessary that some rules be formulated about where lines should be drawn?

HS: You mean a code that would be different from the code of the secretary of State or the code of the...no, I don't think so.

LS: Some would say, "If the chairman of the Council of Economic Advisers participates in election campaigns, then doesn't it in some way hurt the credibility of future Councils?" Is it therefore necessary to have some kind of code? Science advisers to the president, for example, got caught up in their advocacy.

HS: In the case of the science advisers, there was a board of people who came to Washington once a month and they were not the President's men. Members of the Council of Economic Advisers are the president's men, and I think that the Council members have a responsibility to behave in a way that is appropriate to their expertise. They should behave as economists first; they should not go around saying things that they could not defend as economists. But neither should the secretary of Agriculture say anything that he couldn't defend as a reasonable proposition, so if you just want a code that says people shouldn't tell lies, I agree with that. People think this problem has something to do with the political campaign. The political activity of a chairman is insignificant in a campaign. It is much more important at other times. When Charlie Schultze gets up and says the president's $25 billion tax cut is exactly what we need and without it, if it's more or less, the country will fall off the

edge of the cliff--that is a statement of great political
importance. The fact that he doesn't say it in the context
of a campaign doesn't change it or diminish it. In fact,
it's probably more persuasive when he doesn't say it in the
context of a campaign.

LS: But would you or any of the Council chairmen like to be
identified by people, economists, or elsewhere, as a Republican economist, a Democratic economist, a McGovern economist?

HS: Oh, there's no question that we always were. Of course, I
was not a Republican when I was appointed. I was a registered Democrat at the time and so was Arthur Burns when he
was appointed. But everybody in Congress knows when you come
up there and testify that you testify as the president's
spokesman, and of course, you give the economic rationale of
the president's policy. If you can't find an economic rationale for the president's policy, you're a pretty poor
economist.

AL: Our questions and your responses raise the issue of whether,
at the policy analysis level, there's no longer a significant
difference between the political appointee who is appointed
for political reasons and the standards of the professional
man or the scientific man in a controversial situation. I
hear you saying that a professional person can be hired or
bought to express any side of any issue. Doesn't this eliminate the distinction between what we used to think of as the
internalized standards of professional people who simply had
to avoid getting into the position of constantly defending
whoever their employer was.

HS: For one thing, it is not a case of whoever your employer was:
Kennedy would not have appointed me to the Council of Economic Advisers and Nixon would not have appointed Heller to the
Council of Economic Advisers, so you start off with a certain
affinity. Second, we are in the president's circle. We're
all appointed by the president, confirmed by the Senate, and
are president's men who are expert in what we are doing. The
fact that you are an expert in what you are doing shouldn't
disqualify you from participating in this process. There
probably are certain bounds relating to the character of the
activity, but they are probably associated more with the
capabilities and interests of the people. I didn't feel that
I was in the situation of defending whatever the President
had done. The President did things that I didn't talk about.
But I explained the prices and why the President did the
controls. I don't think anybody ever doubted that I was
opposed to it, so I don't believe that I prostituted myself
in any sense. I suppose I felt, particularly in our case,
that a very large proportion of the profession was hostile to
us, and that the President deserved an exposition of his
position from the standpoint of his economists.

SM: Did you get a lot of criticism from the members of the profession about these various speeches and interventions in 1972?

HS: Well, there was criticism in the press, which I suppose reflected criticism from the profession, although I don't know. The press who write in Washington about economics drink from a certain trough of economic opinion and I suppose that's where they got this notion. There was a hearing before the Joint Economic Committee at which Proxmire read something that I had said about McGovern and then commented that my statement was exceptionally out of line. I replied that what I had said was no different from what other economic advisers had said about the opposition, except that my statement was more colorful. And I think it's an entirely false issue. I was briefing the press two or three times a month on the state of the economy. There was great interest. I had plenty of public appearances. How do you distinguish which were political and which were not? The President's Report is a political document. Everybody understands that. That doesn't mean that it's a dishonest document. I'm just surprised that the word "political" has such a pejorative implication among political scientists.

But sometimes economic and political advice are just inextricable. Take, for example, the cases having to do with incomes policy and the various steps that might be taken. As the Communists say, whoever says A, must say B and think of what forces you will unleash by taking this step. The forces that you will unleash are in large part political forces; if you issue some guideline about wage and price increases, you not only have to ask, "Will that do any good in the economic sense?" but also, "Having done that, what impression are you conveying to the world about the efficacy of this way of attacking the inflation problem and therefore what will be the next political demand upon you? What will be the political repercussions of this economic step that will force you to some other economic step?" That's a political judgment, but there's nothing wrong with politics.

AL: If the Council chairmen and members can be relied upon to take policy positions depending upon the administration that is in power, does that, in the long run, injure the reputation and ability of economists or scientists to contribute to the process? Does it make people more skeptical of the role of knowledge, professional analysis, and experience?

HS: Well, maybe they should be skeptical, but as long as the situation is understood, there is no ground for complaint. That is true not only of Chairmen of the Council of Economic Advisers, but of all economists. Many economists are out talking to the world and to the country, and their political connections and allegiances should be known so that people can understand them and know how much weight to place on them. When the chairman of the Council of Economic Advisers speaks, everybody knows that he is the president's man. When a professor from the University of Minnesota speaks, they may or may not know that he is a high-ranking and closely linked Democrat. So there's less danger that the chairman of the Council is going to fool the people than that some other economist is going to fool the people. It is a subject on which there is a great deal of controversy because very few economic decisions come out of a computer. They're all judgmental, involve values and are political, and I think they need to be explained. I really don't see anything amiss in that process. Nourse tried to have it both ways; he tried to be the president's man and not be the president's man and that could not survive. When the Congress passed the Employment Act, they considered the alternative of setting up some kind of commission of disinterested, high-level citizens from business, labor, and agriculture. It's not the situation that Congress established, and that has its implications. Of course, we are still very much in need of some objective economists in this country, and I hope they'll turn up some day.

LS: The reason for creating the Council of Economic Advisers was that Congress was very distrustful of how the president was getting economic advice. They did want to institutionalize it. It seems, therefore, that all Councils do have a certain sensitive role to play.

HS: The Congress could have established something like the Federal Reserve—a board with a term of fourteen years, and at arm's length from the president—but they didn't. They put it next door to the president, to be appointed by him and serving at his pleasure. What could they have expected? You should look at the internal functioning of the Council for the answer to this question. You said the Congress wanted to establish some scientific source of advice and information for the president, and the question of whether the Council does that is not determined by the speeches we make.

EH: It's what's in the memos.

HS: Absolutely, it's what's in the memos. We have been focusing on a secondary aspect of the CEA chairman's job—communicating to the public—rather than on the primary aspect, which is communicating to the president and other inside officials. The key question is whether the chairman is independent, responsible and official in advising the president. Is he giving him an honest representation of what economics knows and thinks or is he telling the president only what he, the chairman, thinks, suppressing the range of opinions and uncertainties that exist in the profession, or is he telling the president only what he believes the president wants to be told? That is the real test of the professionalism of the CEA which distinguishes it from other agencies that are advocates within the decision making process.

Reconstructing Policy Decisions

SM: We've heard a little bit about the story of the controls in 1971. Perhaps it would be useful to start out with your work on the creation of Phase II.

HS: When we were at Camp David and the decision was made to impose the freeze for a period of up to ninety days, there was very little discussion about what would follow the freeze. The thinking seemed to cluster around the idea of something like the Wage-Price Review Board that Arthur Burns had been pushing: that we would retreat a long way from a comprehensive mandatory freeze and go to a system in which somebody would review wage and price increases proposed by large unions and corporations. It might or might not have mandatory authority, but it would be a fairly limited arrangement.

But when we had to start thinking about what to do next, I volunteered because my primary interest was in decontrol. A subcommittee of the Cost of Living Council, called the Phase II Committee, was set up, and I was the chairman of it. Jim Lynn represented the Department of Commerce and Larry Silberman represented the Department of Labor; they were the two other principal participants. To some extent Peter Flanigan participated, to some extent Arnie Weber, although not very much. Once in a while, Charlie Walker from the Department of the Treasury would appear, and Don Paarlberg from Agriculture. We were to write options for analysis and options for the Cost of Living Council. We were not making the decisions. I think this was the most effective and construtive piece of intensive work that I have ever engaged in. We met almost every afternoon. We would have a new paper turned out by the next morning, which generally I wrote, and it would go to the Cost of Living Council. The next afternoon there would be some discussion, and we would go back again and do some more. We were very intensely involved in that process. We started out with a very wide range of options, from just abandoning the whole thing to continuing something like the freeze. It soon became clear to us that the extreme decontrol options were out. They were just unthinkable because the public was so happy with the freeze. The public thought, "Well, at last, Washington has come to rescue me from my avaricious landlord." We could not withdraw the project all of a sudden, so it had to be a much more restricted system than any we were thinking of at Camp David.

There were a number of organizational questions: for example, should the Cost of Living Council control prices and wages directly? That seemed inevitable once you got started, but the labor people would not stand for that. Labor people tolerated the freeze rather reluctantly, but they would not stand for having the administration directly control wages. I think Meany was constantly remembering his World War II days when you had the War Labor Board, a tri-partite body,

and it was clear that we could not have a tri-partite body to
fix prices because business people would not stand for having
labor involved in fixing the prices. The organization that
evolved was a Pay Board and a Price Commission with the Cost
of Living Council above it.

EH: Was the fact that you had the Under Secretary of Labor and
the Under Secretary of Commerce--two constituency depart-
ments--very useful at this point for what you were trying to
do?

HS: Oh, yes, it was very important. Of course, they are both
very capable people. They are both lawyers. In addition,
especially Silberman had some feeling for what the labor
people would accept, and that was important. The Phase II
Committee, while very constructive and cooperative, was also
somewhat of a bargaining proposition. Silberman approached
this process as if he were engaged in collective bargaining:
he demanded things from the rest of us, and we were willing
to effect a compromise. Of course, we did talk to others
before we finished. We talked with Lane Kirkland from the
AFL-CIO. We talked with some business people. But there
wasn't much outside consultation.

Towards the end of the process, an issue arose between
the people who wanted to stay very close to the freeze and
those who wanted to allow more flexibility after the freeze
period ended, particularly to allow some room for wages to
rise. This became a kind of Burns vs. Shultz dispute.
Shultz's argument was that if you tried to hold the unions
very rigidly to the freeze standards, they just would not go
along with that, and the whole thing would break down, whereas Burns wanted to maintain the psychological advantage that
we had gained of getting a very low rate--practically zero--
of increases in the consumer price index for three months.

So we went through this process, which, I think, was
very professional and expert. Finally, we had all the options boiled down, and I got a call to go to Anchorage,
Alaska. The President was going to Anchorage to meet the
Emperor of Japan, who was en route to Europe. I was to go to
Anchorage and on the way back discuss the options paper with
the President. On the way back on Air Force One, the President was too tired to discuss the options paper, so I had a
long ride to see the Emperor of Japan. Then when Shultz and
I went in to see President Nixon in a couple of days, we went
over the paper, and he bought everything.

When we announced Phase II, a certain amount of flak
developed. The big issue is somewhat reflected in what you
have written about the relation between the Cost of Living
Council and the Pay Board and the Price Commission. They had
to have a certain autonomy, especially since they were a
somewhat representative group--certainly the Pay Board was.
We also wanted to keep the case-by-case decisions at a certain distance from the White House. Nevertheless, this was
being done under the President's authority and some control

had to be maintained in his behalf, so the executive order was drafted to give the Cost of Living Council authority to set the objectives of the program, to review the standards set by the Price Commission and the Pay Board, to assure their conformity to these standards, and to make decisions about decontrol. In a briefing about this Daniel Schorr asked me in seven different ways whether the Cost of Living Council could override the Pay Board and, finally, I said, "Well, we're not going to intervene in individual cases, but if they set up a standard that is inconsistent with the objective of getting the inflation rate down to 2-1/2 per-cent"--or whatever we had set--"then we do have that residual authority." So that was in the paper, and Mr. Meany went up the wall. We formulated a new treaty with Mr. Meany, a memorandum, which I always remember as the Columbus Day memorandum because we worked on it on October 12. George, I guess, took it over to Mr. Meany, and Mr. Meany initialed it. And then we went into Phase II.

SM: Did you get a lot of criticism from business about the dif-ferential treatment of business by size of business in Phase II?

HS: No.

SM: Was there any input by business, except from the Department of Commerce, in the construction of the program?

HS: Yes, we talked with a number of business leaders.

SM: At this same time you were already thinking about decontrol, about how you were going to get out of this thing?

HS: Phase II was a step back from the freeze.

SM: Yes, but were you thinking about it in terms of a transition back to a decontrolled economy?

HS: Absolutely. From the beginning. The President said that right at the beginning. Nobody in the country at that time, except Galbraith, wanted permanent price and wage controls. At least none of them said so. Did McCracken tell you the story of how we got the authority to impose price and wage controls?

EH: No.

HS: Congress enacted the authority in August 1970. It was an amendment to the Defense Production Act. About 200 words said the president shall have authority to set maximum prices and wages. That was all. No standards, no nothing. It was enacted with absolutely no expectation that he would ever use it. It was enacted to embarrass him, and members of Congress said that subsequently. To demonstrate that, one member of

Congress, a Republican from Georgia, proposed an amendment
that would have the Congress impose the controls right off--
not give the President the authority. He only got five
favorable votes for that. So that's how we got the authority. The authority was granted for six months and then later
extended. I don't know whether we would have ever gotten
into controls if we hadn't had the authority. For the President to have gone up and asked for the authority would have
been very difficult. For one thing, as soon as he asked, the
prices would have gone through the roof. So that was the
historical decision. By the time the authority expired--it
was enacted for six months--Connally was in as Secretary of
the Treasury. When the amendment was first enacted, the
President and everybody in the administration resisted it.
The President said he would veto it, except that it was an
amendment to the Defense Production Act, and he needed the
Defense Production Act extended. But he had no intention of
using it. Then when Connally became the Secretary and it
expired, he testified in favor of the extension of the au-
thority--again saying he didn't intend to use it, but he
didn't want to be in the position of being softer on inflation than the Democrats were. So we had the authority. Then
it was for a year at a time, and it expired in April 1972,
1973 and 1974.

SM: What was your expectation of how long Phase II would last?
Did you plan it to be a little over a year?

HS: We thought of it in calendar 1972 terms. We established a
goal for the end of the year, for the rate of a price increase. The standards as far as business was concerned
involved a calendar-year calculation of profits. But we
thought that we would be phasing out during the year, and, of
course, we did. We let out various categories of business by
size, and we phased out rent controls sometime during 1972.
We were decontrolling during 1972. Then we had the question,
at the end of 1972, of what to do next.

SM: I'd like to go back a little to the monetary and fiscal
situation that existed when the decision was made to go into
the controls and the freeze.

HS: From the time we came in, we had been saying, "We've got to
get the economy under restraint. We've got to develop a
certain amount of slack in the economy. When we do that, the
inflation rate will subside, and we will be able to regain
full employment without inflation." We had estimates of how
much slack and how much time would be required to get the
inflation rate down by a certain amount, and every quarter it
turned out that it was going to take longer. While there was
some evidence that the inflation rate was slowing down in
1971, it was rather mixed and insubstantial. We did know the
unemployment rate was up to 6 percent and we thought that was
a pretty high rate. Monetary policy became more expansionist

around the beginning of 1970; fiscal policy still remained rather restrictive during 1970, but during 1970 we faced the problem of the calendar 1971 and fiscal 1972 budget. It was clear that we needed a more expansionist policy; without it we could not get anywhere close to balancing the budget because the economy was so low. It was at that time that the President was sold on the idea of balancing the budget at full employment as a standard, and then he declared to Howard K. Smith, "Now I'm a Keynesian." So we had a moderately expansionist fiscal policy. But we had set a goal for calendar 1971 of a $1,065 billion GNP, which was a very famous forecast at the time, and some appropriate rate of monetary expansion was to get us there. We had a big dispute within the administration about what rate of monetary expansion would get us to $1,065 billion GNP. George Shultz was under the influence of Arthur Laffer, and Laffer had a model that demonstrated that we would get to $1,065 billion GNP with a 6 percent rate of growth in the money supply. The rest of us doubted that. We wrote a memo—a Kennedy, Shultz, McCracken treaty—that $1,065 billion was our goal, that we were not committed to the view that we would get there with a 6 percent rate of growth in the money supply, but that we would adapt policy to get there. Of course, we weren't in control of monetary policy, anyway.

SM: What would that have implied about the rate of growth of GNP—to get to $1,065? In real terms?

HS: I don't remember that. But we had a notion that we called the optimum feasible path—the path of the economy that would get the unemployment rate down to full employment, which we still thought of as 4 percent, in two years. We thought that was a path of gradual reduction of the unemployment rate that would be consistent with gradual reduction of the inflation rate. And $1,065 billion was on that path. What it meant in terms of numbers between 1970 and 1971, I don't remember, but it meant a slightly more expansionary policy than in 1970.

SM: How was it that you expected that inflation was going to wind down?

HS: By that time, the unemployment rate was about 6 percent, so even along this path, the unemployment rate would still be below full employment. We believed that we would have a situation in which the unemployment rate was falling, but was still sufficiently high to put some downward pressure on the inflation rate, and that was the way we hoped to work out of it. But as we came into the spring, it seemed clear that we were not on the track, that the inflation rate was higher and the output was growing less than we thought. The question then was whether we should have a more expansionist policy, since we were not growing on the upward track. George Shultz gave a speech that he called "Steady as You Go," and he sent

it to me for comment. What he meant by "steady as you go"
was that you should keep the policy constant. I maintained
that "steady as you go" meant that you should keep the goal
constant but that you should adapt the policy to it. Anyway,
he gave that speech, and we went through that period, which I
discussed earlier about the first Camp David meetings, where
the Council was pressing for more expansive policies and the
President and the Treasury would not go along with them.
   The evidence was very hard to interpret. If you look at
the Economic Report for 1972, you'll see that the rate of
increase in the cost of living was declining. But food
prices were rising very little and mortgage interest rates
were declining, so you could say that the true rate was not
declining. Wage rates also were not declining. Nevertheless, as long as the economy was in what we then thought was
such a slack condition, we thought there was room to expand.
Then when we went to the controls, part of that package was a
more expansionist policy. First, we needed it; second, we
thought the controls would hold the inflation down. The move
at that point, August 15, was very moderate. In fact, most
of the Keynesian economists said it was not stimulative at
all. They said we had a revenue reduction equaled by an
expenditure reduction, which not only gives you no stimulus;
but is negative, because of the balanced budget multiplier
theory. That was nonsense because it paid no attention to
the character of the revenue reductions and expenditure reductions. It was not, however, a very strong shot. Towards
the end of the year 1971 the inflation rate was very low, and
the unemployment was still stuck around 6 percent.

SM: At the end of the freeze?

HS: Yes. We are thinking about the budget for fiscal 1973 and
expenditure policy for the rest of fiscal 1972. We're still
at 6 percent, and we think we have a good distance to go. To
give the economy a shot in the arm, we proposed to increase
the fiscal 1972 expenditures, which by then meant the expenditures in the first half of calendar 1972, but to hold
fiscal 1973 because by that time we thought we would be
closer to full employment. So we were all out for increasing
expenditures in the first six months of calendar 1972. At a
Cabinet meeting the President--it must have been for the
first time ever--lectured the agencies and told them to get
out there and spend their budgets. He was somewhat sheepish
about it. He said, "Well, Herb tells me that's okay." But
they were very slow about it. We kept watching the monthly
figures, and the expenditures were not rising and finally the
Department of Defense came to our rescue when they expended
much money, which was probably some phony outlay. About May,
just shortly before Connally left, we decided this was enough
and we really had to get the fiscal 1973 budget under restraint. The President set a ceiling of $250 billion for the
fiscal 1973 budget and Congress was threatening to run over
that. Although there is a great deal of complaint now that

the policy in this period was too expansionist--and I think it was--the criticism then was that we were stepping on the brakes too soon, to use Walter Heller's expression at that time. We were accused of slowing down the economy before we were up to full employment. Somewhere in that period, after the middle of 1972, but most especially in the early part of 1973, we became reborn in the "old time religion" of fiscal and monetary restraint. By that time it was clear that the controls were not working, that the inflation was resurgent, and that there was no remedy.

SM: There was an enormous expansion in the money supply in 1972. What sort of role did the Council play in this? Did you coordinate with the Federal Reserve?

HS: We had discussions with them. If you're asking me, did we impose this on Arthur Burns, the answer is no. We never imposed anything on Arthur Burns. My explanation of it is that we all made the same mistake. We all thought, "We're a long way from full employment, we still have a lot of room for explaining the economy, and the inflation rate is low." We misinterpreted. Before we went into the controls, we argued many times that one of the great dangers of the controls was that they tempt you to an expansionist fiscal/monetary policy; that has been the universal history of controls. We fell into that trap again even though we said we never would. The whole theory of the controls was that we were going to wring the inflationary expectations out of the system so that we then would be able to let go of the controls and the inflation would not rebound. That was a total error, but we thought that some progress had been made in that direction by the middle of 1972.

SM: Of course, you were exceedingly unlucky with this tremendously unfortunate constellation of events in the beginning of 1973.

HS: We were unlucky, but if we hadn't been unlucky then, we would have been unlucky before it ended. We would have stuck with it until we were sufficiently unlucky.

SM: At the end of 1972 and the beginning of 1973 when you went to this more or less voluntary Phase III program, why wasn't it possible to predict what was going to happen to food prices with purchases by the Russians at that time and the predictions of the operators around the world? The year 1973 was going to see this tremendous explosion of food prices just at the time you were eliminating controls.

HS: There are two things to say about that. We didn't predict it. Agricultural farm production constantly has been predicted erroneously, and we established a study group under Karl Fox to find out why this was so. But I'm not sure what we should have done if we had predicted it because we did not

have farm prices under control. We had never controlled farm
prices at the farm level. It was just not feasible to do so.
You could argue that a prediction that farm prices were going
through the roof would have been a case for just giving up
the whole thing at that point, rather than struggling with it
anymore. But we did not predict it. I think a less pardon-
able mistake was not predicting the extent of the effect of
the devaluation of the dollar; in that case, some people had
better estimates than we did. The Federal Reserve thought it
would come to more than we did. But that was, of course,
after we had already made the decision to move to Phase III.
Shall I explain the reasons for the move to Phase III?

I don't remember all the options that were presented
there, but we did have a very intensive effort by this C8 (or
T8) group. There were a number of considerations. In the
first place, the act was going to expire on April 30, 1973.
We felt that if we were going to revise the controls system,
we should do it sufficiently in advance of that date so that
Congress, when considering the renewal, would know what our
plans were and would have some evidence of how they operated.
The labor people had left the Pay Board in the spring of
1972, so that we were operating with a Pay Board that included only public members. It had not been working badly,
but the labor experts involved felt that the continued fore-
bearance of the labor leadership could not be expected under
those conditions and that it was desirable to try to get the
labor leadership back on board. We had a meeting with them
in which it became clear to me what was troubling them: the
determination of what wage increases their members got was
made by a board in Washington in which they had no part; they
were not responsible for bringing home the bacon to their
membership. They would not tolerate the continuation of this
system. They had to be brought on board and in order to
bring them on board, it was necessary to get away from a 5.5
percent wage standard. That was too rigid for them. We
believed that this was an important part of the policy, but
we did not expect any wage explosion in 1973. A piece of
analysis done by Marvin Kosters showed that the structure of
wages was very well balanced so that some people weren't far
behind with a great case for catching up, thereby creating a
great deal of upward pressure.

On the price side, we saw increasing evidence that
investment in basic industries was being held back by the
squeezing of profit margins, by uncertainty about future
profit margins. We also found that the whole process of
controls was getting very much more complex and difficult to
manage because we were developing a body of price control
lawyers in the private sector who were there to contest us.
In the early days when it didn't seem that this was going to
go on forever, corporations were rather permissive. When it
seemed to be more durable, people began looking at the fine
print, figuring out ways to get around things.

Furthermore, our policy was to get out. The President
had said this was a temporary thing. We did not propose to

put the American economy in a permanent straitjacket, so we
had made some steps toward decontrolling, and, moreover, we
had lost control over about half of the wage sector. Congress had exempted from control all wages below a level that
was declared necessary for a reasonable standard of living,
so the system was disintegrating. We had to make a decision.
Because we were on a calendar-year basis with respect to a
profits standard, then it was desirable to make a decision
early in 1973. As I said, we didn't foresee the extent of
the food price increase, but we had been contending with food
price increases throughout 1972.

One thing I should mention is that the Council and the
OMB and later the Cost of Living Council had been in a per-
sistent struggle to get rid of the controls on agriculture
production and this was finally done, gradually, during 1972.
By the beginning of 1973 we were pretty much through with
them. This was not primarily due to the intervention of the
Price Commission, but had been a continuing fight on which
Agriculture slowly retreated.

I've asked myself, people have asked, Proxmire once
asked me, if I thought we had made a mistake in going to
Phase III at the time we did. I said, "No, I didn't think
so, except that we had given decontrol a bad name." It would
have been different if we had said, "We're going to be in
this business forever." Given the fact that we were determined to get out, I don't know when later it would have been
better to do it. As far as we could see, the economy was
going to be in a tighter and tighter position. We were also
encountering cases of shortages, and one of the revisions
that was made in the standard was that adjustments could be
made for shortages. In addition, the system was not entirely
voluntary. We were getting quarterly reports from the large
corporations about what their price and profit performance
was, and nothing really happened during 1973 that indicated
either on the wage side or on the profit margin side any
departure from the earlier standards. But once the food got
in motion and the industrial raw materials got in motion,
then everything else had to move. The fact that the second
freeze was such a flop indicates how difficult it would have
been to have kept the tighter controls.

SM: At the same time--the end of 1972 and the beginning of 1973--
     that you were going to be moving out of this controls system,
     Phase II, were you moving towards contraction? Did you
     believe that the economy was going up to the level that you
     were aiming for?

HS: Yes, fiscal policy and monetary policy both tightened at that
     time.

SM: At the end of 1972, beginning of 1973? What was your goal
     for unemployment and capacity utilization?

HS: At the beginning of the year we had 5 percent unemployment.

There´s a reference in this memo to the effect that I made these unrealistic forecasts about inflation and unemployment, but it is true that at the end of the year we had also reached the unemployment level that was forecast. We still believed we had room, but we were beginning to get concerned. In the 1973 Report we discussed the meaning of full employment, saying that it does not refer to any number, it just refers to the condition in which all the people willing to work at a wage equal to their marginal productivity are able to find work in a reasonable time. We were trying to get away from the 4 percent goal. I don´t remember the proposal for the fiscal 1974 budget, but we did succeed in holding the fiscal 1973 expenditures below the $250 billion ceiling that the President had urged. It came out under by about $3 billion. The fiscal side was that tight.

SM: How did you react in the beginning of 1973? Could you go through the chronology of what must have been a crisis in economic policymaking?

HS: It was a crisis, and we were dragging our heels. The price of food, especially meat prices, started rising, and the labor people complained that they couldn´t hold the wage level if something wasn´t done about meat. We decided to impose a ceiling on meat prices sometime in March, but things kept running along and we made some other rather token gestures. When we moved to Phase III, Shultz, I believe, had used the expression that we should keep a club in the closet, that we still had the authority and could swat somebody with it if it became necessary. So we swatted the oil industry, which was one of the worst choices to make, but that was going up the most in the non-farm sector at that time. As I remember, we reestablished pre-notification or did some minor steps of that kind.

 Then we had a big go around during May. John Connally was brought back to consult with the President; Bryce Harlow was around. We had a number of meetings about what we should do now. The President was very interested in going back into another freeze. We were all against it and thought of intermediate steps--I don´t really remember all the options. We would have meetings with him and he seemed to agree with us: "All right, you can´t do that. It´s just not practical. It´s not going to work again." Then we´d go away, he´d think about it some more, and he´d decide he´d like to do it. We would have another meeting and persuade him out of it. Shultz and I were supposed to go to Paris for a week to talk to the meeting of the International Monetary Conference and the OECD. We were going to go on the Treasury plane, and our wives were going to go with us. Every day the President would say, "Well, what do you need to go there for? We´ve got to discuss this thing. We´ve got to talk some more about it." The trip got narrowed down. Finally, we were going to go overnight, give our speeches, come back the next night. When we left, we thought he had agreed: "No freeze." When we got on the plane to come back, Shultz received a cable saying that the President had reopened this issue and asked for more papers. So he finally found somebody to go along with him and agree that the freeze was a good thing. But I won't go into all of that.

SM: How actively was Nixon involved in all these questions in that spring of 1973? Did he take a really active part?

HS: Yes, he did. When you remember what else was going on at that time, it's quite amazing. But, as I indicated earlier, we would have periodic spurts of intense activity with him. Every year three or four big economic issues requiring his attention would come up, and then we would have a lot of business with him. This was one of those occasions: what to do about the fact that the prices were running away at a rapid rate. We had frequent meetings and, as I say, John Connally was back in town. He was full of ideas, but, by and large, until the very end he was against going back into the freeze.

EH: Was that because he was listening to you all or because he had his own political thinking?

HS: I think he could see that it wasn't going to work again. The atmosphere was not right. It was a big entertainment the first time, but the second time around everybody would try to get out from under it, and you would have a great deal of trouble.

SM: Who were the people then who were in favor of it?

HS: Mr. Nixon was. Mel Laird was off on the Sixth Fleet in the Mediterranean, and he got a cable from him. I think he thought it was a good idea. But I think some people changed their minds just before the boat left and got on board.
     That was, however, quickly perceived to be a flop, and we very soon started making plans for Phase IV, the phase after the second freeze. That was a fairly orderly process. It was a very messy situation. I don't remember all the details, but we had so many problems about the dates on which we would restore the controls or dates on which we would relax the controls of this or that. This was the period in which the farmers were drowning little chickens, and all the cattlemen were swarming all over us and telling us that they were all going to move to Argentina. So some of these dates became important. We went back into the controls, but with the clear understanding that this move was on the way out. We went back to the more flexible Phase IV system, but we were not establishing a permanent system. All we were providing for them was an orderly transition, phasing some industries out step by step so that everything would not go out with a big bang on April 30.

JG: Did the Executive Committee of the CLC continue after the freeze?

HS: No. In fact, the Cost of Living Council, which I described earlier, had all these Cabinet people who attended regularly, but after we got through the exciting days and the television cameras went away, then they stopped coming. We then operated more with the central body, which was the chairman, the vice-chairman, and the director. A deputies group was set up with representatives of those three, and, I think, some under secretaries from some other departments, or maybe at least somebody from OMB. But that Executive Committee did not survive. We again went back to another one of these little committees circling around Shultz; the guiding committee was Shultz, Rumsfeld, and me at first, then later Dunlop and somebody from OMB.

SM: You referred to your shifting to the "old time religion" somewhere in the beginning of 1973. You had been somewhat expansionist in the previous two years, then you shifted. Could you tell us a little bit about that and what your new goals and scenario were for controlling inflation?

HS: We didn't have any numerical goals for controlling inflation. After all, the numbers were getting to be very high. But our determination was to hold down the growth of government expenditure, to get the budget deficit down, and this was accompanied by a more restrictive monetary policy. We believed that if we hung in there, the inflation rate would come down, and that would put us in a better position for the moment when the controls ended. Of course, we did not foresee the great explosion of the oil price, creating another problem. But still this policy was followed through 1973-74. There were internal disputes then between Simon and Ash about whether the budget should be cut $10 billion or $5 billion, which in retrospect was quite a trivial question. But a tight fiscal and monetary policy was carried on through 1974 and contributed to the recession, but also, I think, contributed to getting us down from double digit inflation.

SM: Do you think, in retrospect, that it may have been an excessively harsh or contractionary policy, or do you think it was about right?

HS: These questions are very hard to answer. Of course, we did not at all foresee that the unemployment rate was going to rise to 9 percent under this policy. If we had foreseen that, we probably would have backed off some. When Mr. Ford came in--I had 21 days with Mr. Ford--we had a meeting in which we discussed the economic outlook. Unlike Mr. Nixon, he liked these oral discussions, and they could go on for a long time. I told him it would be a good idea if each of the persons present--Burns, Simon, Ash, Seidman, and Greenspan (who had then been named as my successor but was not sworn in

until I left)--would write a memorandum so that the President
could see what everybody's forecasts and policies were, and I
would summarize all of this for him. Let me interject here
that Council Chairmen do have an important role in the selection of their successor and in the selection of the members.
Greenspan was one of three whom Shultz and I proposed. Within a week we had a meeting with all these memoranda and
President Ford read them and said, "This should be good
material for your economics class." I said, "May I take it
and use it in my class?" He said, "Yes." So when I went to
Virginia I had students reading all these memoranda. But
nobody then foresaw the unemployment rate rising above 6
percent. There was no disposition at that point to back off
from a restrictive policy, even though we did see that the
unemployment rate was going to rise, because we were obsessed
by the inflation. If we had known it was going to go to 9
percent, perhaps we would have retreated, but I'm not sure
whether that would have been the wise thing to do. I think
we may be better off now for not having done that.

DD: Was there any international dimension at all in any of this?

HS: Yes, it was always there. It comes in in various ways. One
of the sources of error, I believe, was in our failure to
have a proper understanding of what was going on in other
countries and to give sufficient weight to it. When I went
to the OECD meetings in Paris, people from all the other
countries seemed to know more about the United States than I
knew about any of the other countries. We did try to remedy
that by mobilizing some of the talent that existed in the
agencies, but we still are very deficient in our knowledge of
what's going on in other countries. I said earlier that we
underestimated the effect of the depreciation of the dollar
on the inflation rate in the U.S. Even if we had known it,
it probably would not have made any difference because most
of us--not the Federal Reserve--were religious floaters. We
were for flexible exchange rates and would have been even if
we had seen that it was going to add a few points to the U.S.
price level at that point. I am still a floater.

SM: Was there a difference of opinion within the Treasury, you,
and the Fed, vis-a-vis the amount of contraction? Were you
in favor of more or less contraction than these other groups
in 1973 and 1974?

HS: The only thing I remember is the Treasury-OMB dispute about
whether the budget should be cut $10 billion or $5 billion.
I was on the Ash side, in favor of the $5 billion cut. Simon
never came up with $10 billion worth of cuts. But we had no
disputes about the current policy. We did have a dispute in
the winter of 1973, 1974, talking about the budget for fiscal
1975 when some of my colleagues had gotten the old time
religion even more than I had. Simon and Burns were inclined
to say, "Balance the budget, no matter what." But that was

of no significance because when the recession came, we didn't balance the budget. As I said earlier, we could never have any dispute with the Federal Reserve about how restrictive monetary policy was going to be because they never described their future policy in terms that enabled us to criticize it.

SM: I'd like to go to the oil crisis in the fall of 1973 and learn what you did to try to deal with that.

HS: There were two or three decisions. The key decision concerned what to do about the price of oil. This came after they had started with the embargo. Earlier, when oil prices rose during 1973 before the embargo, we went to the two-tier system for controlling oil prices. That was an invention of the Cost of Living Council staff, which we and others objected to, but which we acceded to. Throughout this period-- I suppose still today--the Congress was very allergic to any increase in the oil price. That made it very hard for those inside who were opposed to maintaining a tight control on oil prices to resist because the other side could always run around to Congress and get some support. So the power does not always lie where it seems to. We got the two-tier system in the summer, but after the embargo and when the world price rose very rapidly, there was an issue of what to do about the U.S. oil price. We at the Council--and I, in particular-- were in favor of deregulating it for obvious reasons: it would conserve oil here, reduce our oil imports, and solve many problems. But some staff people in the Treasury were on the other side. By that time Congress had established a new act authorizing the control of oil prices--the Federal Energy Act, I believe--so it was no longer simply a matter of the Cost of Living Council. But the Director of the Cost of Living Council and the new Federal Energy Administrator were unwilling to raise the price, mainly for fear of the political reaction. We finally did get a $1.00 price increase for the old oil, from $4.25 to $5.25, but I think of our failure to deregulate as one of the great mistakes. Deregulation would have been a great shock and Congress probably would have enacted a ceiling the next day, but if we could have gotten rid of the ceiling in December 1973, the whole history of energy policy would have been different.

DD: Taking an even broader application, is it a matter, in our processes and the Council's role, of an inability to move toward a long-run solution to a long-run problem because of the short-run consequences? Deregulation would solve the long-run energy problem, but the short-run costs in terms of inflation or the private interests are great inhibitors to action. The Council is trapped by that, too, isn't it?

HS: There's a lot to that. You do not see for how long you are making a decision, and there is an unwillingness to grasp the nettle immediately. Aside from the price, we had questions of allocation. We thought, correctly, I believe, that we should try to maintain the supply of energy for industrial production and try to impose the conservation on oil for automobile and home heating use. That was effected pretty well. There was a running argument about whether we should have rationing, but there was very little sentiment for it in the administration. We somehow muddled through the crisis but we left ourselves with a terribly inefficient, cumbersome system for the future.

SM: At that time was there an expectation that this cartel would never hold together and that prices would go back down?

HS: There was a difference of opinion about that. Some people at the Treasury thought that the price was going to go down to $3.00 because of the demand and supply curves they had, but we were very skeptical about that. We did think that there was an equilibrium price around $7.00 because somewhere we got the notion that in time there would be a limitless supply of oil from shale at $7.00 a barrel. That always seems to be just beyond the horizon. So that was misunderstood, but if we had just decontrolled everything, the price would have been what it was going to be when all that shale came into the market.

EH: Was the President increasingly remote from your Council during this 1973-74 period and, if so, who was making the policy?

HS: No. This question is asked of me often, and I don't think so. He functioned very actively in the decision to move to the second freeze. When we made the arrangements about the move to Phase IV, he was in the Naval hospital for a while, but when we got into the energy crisis, he was quite active again, and we saw a lot of him then. He regarded energy as a very appealing issue. I think all the presidents do—Carter certainly does—as a vehicle for relating to the public. For the president it's the moral equivalent of war in that it lets him get on television frequently. President Nixon became very much involved in the energy issue. He sent up a number of messages and made some speeches about it. His last speech before he resigned was an economics speech that he made in Los Angeles around July 25. Just before that he held a number of meetings with business and labor people and other experts about the economy, and I went out to San Clemente for a week and worked on that last speech. I never felt that he was sloughing off his responsibilities in this sphere.

EH: His political capital was certainly diminished. Do you think that had any effect on things he might have done or might have done otherwise?

HS: The only thing I would attribute to the problem—and I'm not sure about that—was the move to the second freeze. He may have thought that would be another terribly popular move, as the first one had been, and that it would be helpful to him. Otherwise, he just tended to his knitting as far as economics was concerned.

EH: Was there a tendency for you and George Shultz and others to compartmentalize what you were doing and simply not worry about the Watergate business, much as Johnson's domestic advisers did in Vietnam?

HS: We worried about it, but there was nothing we could do about it. Every morning at the senior staff meeting it was the subject of discussion, and we would get briefings from Haig and Ziegler and the congressional liaison people on what was going on, but there was nothing we could do about it.

I had confidence in Mr. Nixon in the discharge of all his public functions. He screwed up in some rather trivial ones, but I do not accept the common view of him as a man who had vowed to overturn the U.S. constitutional system. He has my confidence still. I go to visit him.

DD: Applying all of this experience with wage and price controls, is there a way to avoid them in the future?

HS: I believe there is. But it's not easy. One of our big mistakes was in underestimating how difficult it would be and in not inducing the degree of patience in the American people that would have been required for the effective medicine to work. If you follow a policy of restraint--especially monetary restraint, but complemented by fiscal restraint--you will get the inflation rate down. You will go through some period of excessive unemployment, but you will end up with no more unemployment than you would otherwise have had. The period of strain, of excess unemployment, will be shorter, the more people believe in your policy and believe that you will stick with it despite the intermediate pain of it. I think that's the only way out. We certainly don't have any demonstration of the effectiveness of price and wage controls or of any of these intermediate things, like incomes policy or TIP. This is "old time religion," but I think that's the only effective medicine.

DD: Your prescription of using macro politics involved fiscal restraint. Yet when you say Simon's "balance the budget, period" was complete nonsense, and Carter's balance of budget in 1980-81 is complete nonsense, is there any possibility of getting fiscal restraint in the real world?

HS: You asked me whether there was any medicine, not whether people would take the medicine. I think that's one reason to have an independent Federal Reserve. We have given the Federal Reserve a certain degree of insulation from political pressures, and that's what they're supposed to use it for. I'm encouraged that they will, that they have recently, and that Congress seems to be willing to reduce the tax cut a

406

little bit, with more concern about the size of the fiscal
1979 deficit, than they seemed to be earlier. All you can do
anyway is try to sell these ideas. If people won't take the
medicine, then they'll have the inflation. The question is
how much inflation will it take to teach them?

DD: What's discouraging to me, and it applies to your earlier
period, too, is that our government really programs for an
excessively high rate of inflation. The programming involves
a 6 percent rate of inflation.

HS: We made many of these mistakes. My complaint about Carter is
not that he makes mistakes that we didn't make, but that he
makes the same ones eight years later, doesn't profit from
our experience. We constantly underestimated how much inflation we would get at any given level of unemployment. We
constantly were excessively optimistic about how quickly we
would get the inflation rate down.

LS: One of the effects of inflation is that it almost destroys a
sense of community or solidarity. Everybody begins thinking
simply about, "How am I doing as an individual?" And yet
phrases are uttered about the public's responsibility: "It's
up to the public."

HS: There is a great deal of confusion in those phrases. When
Strauss and Carter say things like that, they mean that it's
up to the public in their private capacities; it's up to the
wage earner to take a smaller wage increase or the business
man to take a smaller price increase. I don't think that's
any part of their responsibility in their private capacity.
But if you cannot elicit some kind of support from people in
their capacity as citizens for policies that are good for the
country, what hope is there?

AL: I was very impressed with your story about how you came back
from Camp David. Here you had a president, a public official, telling you what to do, and you went and carved out the
program. You now have in the executive office a machinery
for applying political and economic rationality to the
problems within the framework of a prior political decision,
if only you get that degree of leadership in the president.
Professional people cannot do much about the consensus in the
country, but you do have continuing and competent professional machinery to bring these issues up and get people to
talk in terms of the technical problems, protected from a
degree of political heat, which we simply lacked in the
Roosevelt and Truman administrations.

HS: We do have a very competent continuing executive office
staff. The OMB staff is really outstanding and there are
other pieces of staff around, so that good, technically
competent work goes on regardless of the complexion of the
political officers who are there. But the question depends

on the decisions at the top, and the decisions at the top are
very much constrained by what the public wants, or by an
administration's perception of what the public wants, which I
think is often quite wrong but is very important in their
decision making.

Improving the Council

DD: You mentioned earlier increasing the size of the Council
staff slightly because the problems have proliferated. Do
you see other ways that you could improve this piece of
machinery within the total machinery?

HS: I don't know the answer to that question. The basic problem
of the Council is that economists don't know enough and the
best way to improve the performance of the Council would be
for economists to learn something more than they do. There
is also very little machinery in government for any medium-
term or long-term research on economic problems. Perhaps the
Federal Reserve has a little more capacity, but there is,
generally, not much opportunity for such research in the
executive branch. I thought that we ought to have some
institution, perhaps modeled after the Industrial College of
the Armed Forces, with people there studying economic policy
questions for the longer run or with a view towards improving
our understanding of even short-run problems. You can say
that that's what all the other 14,000 economists in the
country are doing, but I don't think we mobilize very well
the talent of economists to solve problems. We have 14,000
economists each sitting in a little room trying to solve the
great problems, but of these isolated efforts only a tiny
fraction is going to make any contribution. Perhaps we could
establish an entity like the Army War College. Maybe put it
in Leavenworth, Kansas, or some place. Then you could send
somebody from the agency to spend a year there, just as we
send people from various departments to spend a year at the
War College or the Industrial College of the Armed Forces.

IB: Is it your supposition that, if one had the equivalent of a
war college or whatever, economic forecasts would look more
like those that you see and that this would get around the
problem of the lack of civic virtue and the resistance to
medicine-taking?

HS: No, no.

IB: What might be the Council's role if we had better long-range
analyses?

HS: If we had had better long-run analysis, we would have given
the President a more reliable, sharper picture of his options. But that doesn't change the other problem of how you
get the people to take their economic medicine. I don't

think the Council has any role in that. The president has a role in that, but all well-meaning citizens have a role. Nobody in the United States preaches civic duty anymore. Nobody preaches patriotism, work ethic, responsibility of any kind, and somebody needs to do that. I think the president is a person to do it, but he's not the only one.

SM: You don't really think that this reluctance to take the medicine that you're prescribing is only because the Americans are undisiciplined and unwilling to do it? Don't you believe that a number of people really don't think that these kinds of recessions to stop inflation were very effective? They read the record of your period as indicative that a good deal of unemployment really didn't have much of an effect on inflation rates and that it really was just a waste of many man years of potential output.

HS: Well, some years are doubtful and some are not. I don't think 1967-68 are doubtful cases, and we didn't act quickly enough then because government was unwilling to face the political problems of prescribing this bitter medicine. 1972 was probably a year like that, when we thought the public was very intolerant of the fact that we had 6 percent inflation and we were unprepared to tell them--partly because we didn't know--that this was going to be a long, slow process. Sure, there's disagreement about what you would teach people if you could teach them, but our inflationary errors cannot all be explained by errors of forecasting. I think we are unwilling to take the short-run costs for the long-run benefits. Only an extreme view would say that a policy of fiscal and monetary restraint will never work. We followed such a policy in 1973-74, and that inflation rate did come down, and it came down quite substantially. It would not have come down so substantially if we had not done that. There's a lot of evidence that this works.

9
The Council of Economic Advisers Under Chairman Alan Greenspan, 1974–1977

Summary History

Alan Greenspan was recruited as Chairman of the Council of Economic Advisers by Richard Nixon, but served in that role entirely under Gerald Ford. Greenspan's nomination was before the Senate when Nixon resigned in August of 1974, but Ford quickly renominated him. Previously the head of his own Manhattan business consulting firm (Townsend-Greenspan and Co.), Greenspan was not an academic economist and did not have a Ph.D., although he later completed his thesis and received a doctorate from Columbia University. His sound reputation as a forecaster and his plans for restoring the CEA to an advisory role easily won him the support of the profession. Although he was perhaps the most conservative chairman in the Council's history, even the more liberal past chairmen affirmed their respect for his abilities as an economist. He announced intentions to "depoliticize" the CEA and avoid a public role.

Greenspan became increasingly influential in the business-oriented Ford administration. He also had some experience in politics, having coordinated Nixon's panel of economic advisers during the 1968 campaign. He had then been the Nixon liaison with the Bureau of the Budget in the 1968-69 transition, turning down an offer to become the BOB director in the incoming administration. During the Nixon years, he had served as a consultant to the CEA and had participated in administration task forces and commissions studying foreign trade, the stock market, and other problems.

As an ardent advocate of laissez-faire, Greenspan criticized continued intervention by the government in the economy, even going so far as to oppose antitrust laws, the progressive income tax, consumer protection legislation, and subsidies. Consequently, he opposed any suggestion of controls and would agree to support a proposed revival of the Cost of Living Council only if it were limited strictly to a review function. He was critical of short-term political solutions to long-term economic problems. Refusing to be classed as either a Keynesian or a monetarist, he preached economic fundamentalism: less government spending, a balanced budget, and a stern monetary policy to deal with the inflation problem.

President Ford agreed with Greenspan's focus on the inflation problem, declaring it "Public Enemy Number One" when he addressed a joint session of Congress on August 12 on the state of the economy. Ford offered no real solutions but did call for bipartisan restraint in spending, approval of Nixon's proposal to reactivate an advisory Cost of Living Council, and support for a Senate proposal calling for a domestic summit meeting to consider the current economic problems. The reactivation in August of the CLC as the Council on Wage and Price Stability, when coupled with Ford's criticism of a General Motors price rise, seemed to indicate a revival of guidelines and jawboning, a possibility Greenspan resisted, but these developments only supplemented basic fiscal and monetary policies. More attention was actually focused on the September 27-28 "Conference on Inflation" and the series of twelve mini-summits leading up to it. The meetings allowed economists, labor, business, and various special interests to air their disagreements about the proper cures for the country's economic ills and, in the process, educate the public about the grim economic reality. Although some modification of the administration's program was expected, the "old time religion" remained firmly ensconced. Greenspan defended both the Fed's tight money policies and the proposed $5 billion budget cut, despite criticism that the first was excessive and the latter of little value. Skeptics insisted the summit was no more than a media event.

Ford was determined, however, to develop an effective and politically acceptable program before the November congressional elections. Within ten days, the new program was ready. On October 8, 1974, the President presented his ten point program to Congress, including a 5 percent income surcharge on individuals with higher earnings and on corporations, an increase in the investment tax credit, increased unemployment benefits, and public service jobs in depressed areas. Again, he urged the $300 billion budget ceiling. Proposals to deal with the energy shortage through an additional gasoline tax had been eliminated. The program was modest at best and not likely to have much effect. When Ford made that speech, however, he was wearing a lapel button that proclaimed the administration's new slogan: "WIN: Whip Inflation Now." He followed the October 8 speech with an address in Kansas City a week later in which he more fully developed the "WIN" program, reading recommendations and letters from citizens and his newly created Citizens' Action Committee to Fight Inflation. Voluntarism became the centerpiece of the Ford anti-inflation program.

The problem was that just as Ford announced his anti-inflation program, a recession was developing. Unemployment was over 6 percent, the GNP was off 2.9 percent for the year, and the Dow Jones industrial averages had dropped 200 points since August. Although Fed Chairman Burns admitted as early as October 10 that the nation was in the midst of a recession, the administration refused to concede such a development. The Ford anti-inflation program only served to worsen an already deteriorating situation.

Chairman Greenspan had wanted a tougher policy stand by Ford in October, and there was some speculation that he might get the increased budget cuts he desired, if public pressure to deal with unemployment did not force an increase in expenditures. However, he was actually one of the first administration leaders to urge a change in policy to deal with the evident recession. The administration did not even publicly acknowledge the existence of a recession until November 12, but by late November a small shift in policy was evident when Ford abandoned his $300 billion budget ceiling in favor of a slightly higher $302.2 billion goal. In early December, Greenspan then hinted at the possibility of a stimulatory tax cut, even though Secretary of the Treasury William Simon was still backing the October surtax proposal. He also chaired a December 19 White House meeting of ten private economists, from which came a recommendation for some form of government stimulus, preferably a tax cut. By this time it was clear that the economy was in trouble. Prices were continuing to climb, with the Consumer Price Index in November up 12.1 percent over the year before, the highest annual rate of increase since 1947. Meanwhile, unemployment reached 7.1 percent and the GNP was off 2.9 percent for the year.

It was within this context that Ford and his advisers formulated the administration's economic program for the upcoming year. In a speech on January 13, Ford indicated a major policy shift. Proposing a three-front "national recovery program," he called for $16 billion in tax cuts to slow the recession, tax increases to ease the energy crisis, and moderate budget restraint to cool the continuing inflation. This entailed an abandonment of fiscal conservatism in favor of deficit spending. Greenspan had reportedly hoped for more in the way of budget cuts to offset the tax cuts but yielded to a $51.9 billion deficit for FY 1976, the largest peacetime deficit in history, in order to secure the stimulus needed to end the recession. He was, however, adamant that any larger deficit would be excessive and only aggravate inflation.

By this time, the economic situation appeared even worse. The figures for the fourth quarter of 1974 indicated the second sharpest decline in the GNP since the depression (9.1 percent). Even worse, the 2.2 percent drop in real GNP for the year was the largest for any year since 1946. Meanwhile, inflation climbed to 12.2 percent and unemployment passed the 8 percent mark. Consequently, the President's State of the Union message and budget message were gloomy at best. The CEA's report in early February was likewise pessimistic about the near future, predicting that the recession would continue into the spring, with an upturn perhaps by the middle of 1975. The Council expected recovery to be slow and urged caution in order to avoid a boom and worse inflation.

Critics from both parties found the administration's program insufficient. Democrats demanded more action--more spending, tax cuts, and easier monetary policy. Even Nixon CEA Chairmen McCracken and Stein indicated that more stimulus was needed. Although the administration tried to hold the line on such proposals, Ford's release in mid-February of $2 billion in impounded federal highway construction funds indicated a lack of full commitment even within the White House to the restrictive budget policy. The White House was unconvincing, and so Congress, as expected, increased the size of the 1975 tax cut to $23 billion. Simon and Burns tried to persuade Ford to veto the bill, but Greenspan and James Lynn (OMB) were successful in convincing the President to sign it. Greenspan realized that some sort of stimulus was needed and that Congress was unlikely to approve anything less.

This advice went clearly against that given by Fed Chairman Burns, who had taught Greenspan at Columbia and had been instrumental in persuading him to accept the chairmanship. Still concerned with the inflation menace, Burns had been accused of trying to offset the administration's anti-recession policies by deliberately restraining the money supply. While the Fed had been perhaps overly cautious in restricting the money supply to an annual rate of 2 percent, by February some action had been taken to lower interest rates and add to the money supply, although the effect was meager.

By spring, there were indications that the recession was beginning to slow down. May was the bottom, and the upturn began in July, just as Greenspan and the CEA had predicted. Although there were fears in the fall that the recovery might weaken due to food and fuel price pressures, the CEA remained optimistic, revising its forecasts to take into account unexpected gains. By the third quarter of 1975, the GNP was up 13.4 percent (annual rate)—the highest quarterly increase in twenty-five years. Concerned with maintaining recovery without further inflation, Greenspan worked to come up with the proper budget estimates and deficit for the FY 1977 administration program. He determined that a $394 billion budget with a $43 billion deficit would be appropriate. Although the administration's program also included a surprising proposal to increase tax cuts to $28 billion, the overall shift to restraint in the budget received sharp criticism. The CEA's position on this point was made clear in its 1976 report, when it rejected a rapid return to full employment in favor of a more moderate and sustained recovery. Avoiding any direct forecast on unemployment, the report focused on the need to slow the inflation rate and restore confidence.

Unconvinced, Congress again acted as expected, setting federal spending at $413.1 billion, $17.3 billion higher than Ford had proposed. The deficit would be $50.6 billion. After repeated delays on the tax cut, Congress also extended the 1975 provisions, without passing Ford's recommended increase. Meanwhile recovery continued, with gains exceeding expectations. Unemployment was expected to drop under 7 percent by the end of the year, as inflation moderated. But as the November election approached, the figures did not actually look so favorable, for the leading economic indicators declined in September for the second consecutive monthly drop. As the President's economic advisers awaited more favorable economic reports, Ford lost to Jimmy Carter in the November presidential election.

Oral History Interview

EH: Why don't you begin by describing your first meeting with Ford--what you discussed and how you began to develop his confidence?

AG: Even though I had met Ford on social occasions previously, my first substantive meeting occurred when he was Vice-President. One of his secretaries called to ask me to drop by the next time I was in town. I don't recall whether it was before or after I was nominated for the CEA chairmanship by Nixon, but it was certainly in that period. I spent a good deal of time discussing my views on fiscal policy. Largely because he had spent so many years on the House Appropriations Committee, he was very knowledgeable about the details. As I recall, I discussed with considerable concern what we subsequently formalized in both budget documents and CEA reports: the seemingly inexorable rise in certain of the transfer payments in uncontrollable and controllable categories--at that point as I recall the transfer payments--or more exactly transfers to persons--were growing at a compound real rate of approximately 9 percent over the previous twenty years. The mere arithmetic of projecting that raised a major problem with respect to the level of aggregate expenditures in the subsequent five years and pointed out that the sharp rise in the most recent period and the most recent decade had been obscured by the peaking and then the decline in real defense expenditures subsequent to fiscal 1968. The decline in real defense expenditures had to come to an end at some point and when it did, unless there was a curbing in the rate of growth in this major sector of the non-defense outlay budget, we would find that what had been a relatively stable and surprisingly modest growth in real total federal outlays would all of a sudden run into an inflection point and a significant acceleration. We had an exceptionally long discussion, more than an hour, even though we had originally scheduled a relatively short period. We met in the Vice-President's office in the Capitol. I thought we got along exceptionally well. I told him what I believed. He told me what he believed. I thought we were very much in agreement. I had no other contact with him except peripherally, as I recall, until I was renominated by him and subsequently joined the administration in August 1974.

EH: Did you have another talk at that time, before the renomination?

AG: Not to my recollection. If so, it was strictly peripheral.

DD: Did Arthur Burns have a hand in this process of your nomination and your renomination?

AG: Oh, yes. The first nomination started, actually, with a call from Bill Simon. I said I was indeed honored by the thought,

but I would give him four other suggestions, and my answer
was no. When he called again I said, "Bill, I really appreciate it, but I really mean it." He said to me, "Well, would
you at least go speak to Al Haig?" I agreed to speak to Al
Haig. Haig called a day or so later and asked me if I would
come down to Key Biscayne. They put on the real White House
business for me. They had a special plane going out of
LaGuardia, and I said, "Boy, they must really want me." I
got there and had a long conversation with Al Haig. My
impression of Haig, as I suspect you may well know, is that
this country owes more to that man than it possibly knows.
This was now in June and July of 1974. I had a long conversation with Haig in which I said, "Look, you're making a
mistake. You really don't want me. I'm the type of chairman
who, if he gets involved in policy and finds that he cannot
agree with the policies being implemented, is likely to
resign. In fact, I will guarantee it. You don't need that.
I don't need that. I could not possibly stay, for example,
if there were some significant moves toward wage and price
controls." At the time we were unwinding from Phase IV, and
there was still a significant acceleration in prices and
great pressures from the Congress to reimpose some form of
either mandatory or at least tightening controls. He said to
me, "I think you're mistaken. That's not the direction in
which we are going. My best guess is that you won't feel the
need to resign as long as I know about it."

Two or three days later Arthur called me and said, "I've
got to speak to you." I said, "Arthur, I know what you want
to talk to me about--the answer is no." He said, "Come down
and see me." That was a mistake. I said, "Now look, I've
got this business. I'm not going to dissolve it. I'm not
going to break it up. It's a small, personal, very profitable, very effective business that I enjoy working in. I just
don't want to give it up." He said, "You've made that into a
personal business as big as you are, and you insist that
there is no one who could carry on without you. I know you
are afraid to leave for two or three weeks. You better find
out whether that thing can function." The convincing argument, strangely enough, was precisely that, for I had recognized it was a big problem. You either trust the people who
are working for you or not. So I began to think seriously
about whether it was feasible. With great reluctance and
great concern, frankly, about whether this was a wise move, I
finally said yes. First Bill Simon was very tenacious about
my accepting the appointment, then Haig, and, finally, Burns.
Throughout that period I hardly spoke to Nixon at all. He
and I never really got along very well together. One of the
reasons I didn't want to go to Washington was because I was
terribly concerned about what type of relations I would have
with him. As you know, I was fairly heavily involved in the
1968 campaign, and I think I was the only person in the
economic area who did not go to Washington. One of the main
reasons was that I felt very uncomfortable with the man, as

in fact most intellectuals or people like Burns and Bryce Harlow would feel uncomfortable with him.

The reason is that he himself somehow feels intellectually insecure, which is a great irony, because I´ve always maintained, and I still maintain, that Richard Nixon probably had the highest IQ of any president since Woodrow Wilson. I actually saw that man do remarkable intellectual feats. Yet there was this extraordinary attitude that made it very difficult to deal with him. I don´t know how McCracken and Stein related to him, but my dealings were very difficult. When Haig asked me in Key Biscayne whether I wanted to see Nixon, I said, "I don´t see any reason." No matter who the president is, saying no to the president is not an easy thing to do. In retrospect, Burns was unquestionably the key factor in my accepting the position; had I not had that conversation with him, I would have definitely said no.

EH: But what expectation did Haig hold out about Nixon´s future? After all, the House Judiciary Committee was going to work at this time.

AG: At that point--this was probably June--the general press expectation was still very mixed. In other words, the question of whether you could conceivably get a conviction in the Senate was very dubious. My guess is that the Senate was still sufficiently divided at the time that a two-thirds majority was not available.

EH: So this is actually before the House hearings, isn´t it?

AG: There´s no question. I remember that after I had said yes and my nomination had gone up, the whole thing began to unwind. It turned out, with some extraordinary irony, that I was before the Senate Banking Committee for confirmation on the day that Nixon resigned. Ford´s first official act, I was told, was to renominate me, and I learned subsequently that he did so because of the unanimous recommendation of the transitional task force, which had been headed by Don Rumsfeld. I´d known Don Rumsfeld and I knew a lot of the people who were on that task force. Apparently the only major meeting I had had with Ford was satisfactory. In any event, the nomination went up and, with the exception of Proxmire, it was confirmed relatively easily. I had made my acceptance of the post contingent upon certain conditions: that I was able to put the shares of Townsend-Greenspan & Co. in trust and not dissolve the company, with the sole requirement that I not deal with the people in New York while I was in office. That did raise some problems in my confirmation hearings, and I basically told them, "You either trust me or you don´t." I would be taking an oath of office that I took very seriously. I recognized the very significant potential conflicts of interest. My own personal view, however, was that there were conflicts of that sort with anyone, including a university professor.

EH: But Haig must have made a positive appeal. Was it to duty and to the need for the activity that you would be carrying on? There had to be continuity.

AG: Yes. Exactly. That's it. Especially during this period. Needless to say, the government must function, and the key area where continuous functioning of government was essential was in the economic area. He basically made a very strong pitch that, especially in times such as these, it was important for people like me to come down.

EH: In a sense, you could disentangle yourself from the then president, and say, "I'm going to go there and do certain things that need to be done for the country out of a sense of obligation."

AG: That's basically what I was planning to do, and my original view was that the role of the Council at that stage would be almost a caretaker operation. Just be certain that the thing holds together and that things don't fall through the cracks. My original view, when I went down, was that I would be there for a relatively short period of time. If Nixon had somehow continued in office through the end of his term, I probably would not have stayed more than a year.

EH: This suggests that had he been riding high, you might not have gone at all. You would not have felt the same obligation.

AG: That is true. It is very unlikely that I would have gone. The trouble with the Republicans, however, is that they have few choices. One of the arguments either Burns or Simon or somebody raised was that, "If you say no, we have no fallback position."

The President and Economic Policy

EH: Why don't we go back now to President Ford? How would you characterize President Ford's mode of thought about economic questions and the advisory relations that developed between you?

AG: First, you have to recognize what his background is. Clearly, he would not have had considerable experience directly in economics or in business. But he did, of course, have these many years on the House Appropriations Committee, which necessarily exposed him to a great many of the operations of the government and, peripherally, to how the economy affects government, and he had learned a considerable amount of practical economics. While I felt fairly close to his general point of view on economic policy problems, my initial impression was that he was not really capable of abstractly articulating a philosophy. Because of that, I sensed that he wasn't fully in control of the general framework of the policy decisions he was making on a day-by-day basis. But if you began to look at the concrete decision making process, what came through was a very sophisticated and consistent framework. Within perhaps a year, maybe even less, I was able to forecast how he would come out on individual issues with virtually zero error. I then began to conclude that this was not an accident. So, while he was not consciously or verbally in control of a general philosophy toward economic policy, he nonetheless had a fairly sophisticated view. Since my view was in most respects fairly consonant with his, it became rather easy for me to function. I could determine largely where he would come out under various scenarios, which meant that the analytical mechanism was very efficient. We didn't have to go back and keep checking. I could assist in creating options in a fairly complex way, knowing that most of what I was doing would be useful. Since I did have virtually unlimited access, I could just pick up the phone and say, "We're down to this problem. Here are your choices. How would you like to proceed, one, two, three, or four?" We could have a three-minute conversation and get significant instructions on what types of options he might want to pursue without a lengthy meeting or much work in detail with the President. Our economic policy group rarely, if ever, met for more than an hour and a half in any single sitting with Ford.

I should say parenthetically that the problems in economic policy in the Carter administration may be because such a consistent view does not exist. The President himself is quite generally articulate on most subjects, and yet if you look at the explicit policy decisions, it is very difficult to figure out where he comes out. His advisers have great difficulty in making judgments as to how the President will choose, granted a series of alternatives. This is a terribly inefficient way to function because the President himself is making not only the final option choices, but all the sub-option and minor choices as well; from a time point of view, that is not possible.

EH: What were the contours of this world view—Ford's and yours?

AG: Let me describe it in my terms, which are more analytical, and then merely try to indicate the extent to which he agreed or didn't. My view was that the fundamental cause of what then became known as stagflation and the underlying problems associated with it was that we were running into a period where the instabilities in the economy were creating increasing risk premium in the capital investment process; this led to a significant rise in the so-called hurdle rate of return, which was undercutting capital investment in a very pronounced way, both in the United States and abroad. A necessary condition for restoring balanced economic growth in the United States was to reduce the instabilities, thereby reducing the risk and hurdle rates, and a necessary condition for that was to bring down the rate of inflation. I believed the only way to do that in the long term was to bring down the rate of increase in money supply, which in turn required that the level of federal financing be brought down. I raised the original argument, which I think we exaggerated somewhat, on "crowding out" in House Budget Committee testimony in 1974--I believe it was September. In that testimony I discussed the role of on-budget financing, off-budget financing, and guarantees in the flow-of-funds context and tried to show why the effect on the capital markets of a borrower whose demand for funds is wholly inelastic is to put significant pressure on interest rates. The normal, semi-accommodative process of the Federal Reserve, which I find exists independent of who is there, leads in turn to an acceleration in money supply, which historically has always led to accelerated price levels. So my argument was that we gradually had to pull in the Treasury financing requirements, which are now perceived longer term as very substantial, especially in the context of this inexorable expenditure growth, which I mentioned in the beginning. My underlying policy thrust was to defuse instability in the system gradually and in a sense to be anti-activist because it was precisely the activism, both in the area of fiscal policy and in regulatory policy, which was creating the underlying elements of instability and risk in the system. In my view that activism was one of the reasons why, in Art Okun's terms, the discomfort index continued to rise, which in a sense is really a repudiation of a short-term Phillips curve. I believed that we should stop trying to engage in short-term fiscal fine-tuning, which, at best, we are poor at and, at worst, is counterproductive. We should try instead to focus on solving longer-term problems and in that process engage in as little policy as was both economically and politically possible. My view was that we had to slow down the pace of governmental policy actions, if we were to restore a level of risk in the system consistent with long-term non-inflationary growth.

I would say that Ford fundamentally agreed with that policy. As a consequence, he was, in many instances, willing to take extraordinary political actions. I remember a discussion we had with him in the fall of 1974 when there was grave concern that the economy was slipping badly. This was well in advance of any public discussion on this. I said, "We still don't know yet, but there's a very good possibility that we may have very severe problems in the spring of 1975." At that point, none of us would have forecast how severe, but we were expecting much worse problems than we were publicly able to talk about at that time. I said, "In April 1975, Mr. President, you're going to be under pressure to run $100 billion deficits, to blow the roof off expenditures. It's going to be very difficult to resist, but unless you do, you can forget this policy, because at the first sign of pressure, if it breaks, it will be almost impossible to pull it back together again." He said to me at the time that he fully understood that and he would do everything that he could to try to hold. I was very skeptical, as you can understand. In retrospect, that's precisely what he did. Things were worse than any of us told him was possible. Worse than I would have expected. Nine percent unemployment rate. If any of us had said there would be a 9 percent unemployment rate and the equivalent in Western Europe, and argued that there wouldn't be any significant social unrest in the United States or in Europe or Japan, they would have run us out of the country. We went through that period with a remarkable sense of cohesion in the country. Even more startling was Western Europe. Something fundamental had been happening. I think that was really the first sign of it, but clearly there was no way in the fall of 1974 even to remotely expect that to occur.

EH: Was the President receptive to the strategy you laid out because of values as well as because of his cognitive or his scientific understanding?

AG: My basic view is that it would start with values. His economic operational code was rooted in values, although, as I said, more subliminal than explicit. I always had the impression that Eisenhower was more value-oriented in a conservative sense than Ford. But there was also his pragmatic view that the system functioned best in the context I was outlining because his normal inclinations would always be to restrain federal government intrusion into the private sector. So it is both a value system and something that might be termed his pragmatic, economic theory.

DD: Was Ford interested in economics in depth or not?

AG: Yes, he was very interested, but more as a learning process for him than as a necessary input for a decision making option at that time. I spent a good deal of time discussing general economics with him, far beyond the need for any single decision. He once told me, as a matter of fact, that he very much appreciated Kissinger and me...he didn't use the word "tutor," but one got the impression that he was using both of us to facilitate conceptual absorption beyond the needs of the decision making process. Ford grew very significantly in his understanding as the months went on. Because he had such a detailed knowledge of government, he did have a handle upon which he could draw, and he could understand how the various forces within government and within the financial system functioned. It's difficult to know at what technical level he was able to be with you, but there's no question about his interest, and there's no doubt that he understood the effect of government guarantees and the effect of budget financing on the money markets.

DD: So he didn't get quickly bored?

AG: Oh, no. Never. In fact, it was the other way around; he was very interested in learning a number of the technical questions involved in the economic policymaking process.

EH: Could you sense or see how he was bringing this knowledge into a larger political framework and adapting it to that framework?

AG: Only in the sense that he recognized the need to bring down the level of governmental incursion into the lives of individuals. He made a very pointed question of deregulation. The deregulation issue obviously surfaced in the CEA and was sensed as something politically useful and important. He made a speech before small businessmen and got a tremendous response. I found him using as best he could his overall policy decisions to his political advantage. I think in many instances it was done poorly. I don't think that the Ford administration, in general, and the President, in particular, articulated as well as he should have. I think our speechwriting operation was Class B. And I'm being generous. This was one of the reasons why we much preferred to get Ford out without a piece of paper in front of him. He was scarcely what one would consider a great orator, but he did a lot better. What surprised the press more than anything is when we trotted him out to brief them on the federal budget in January 1976. That had never been done before. Was it 1975 or 1976? I can't remember which, but he went out there, and he knew every number in the budget.

EH: Not since Truman. The two men were much alike.

AG: That's correct. And it wasn't an act. He knew the material because he had been through the appropriations process in the Congress at great length, and that man really made his own budget. We would sit there session upon session on individual budgetary matters. The only time we had long sessions with Ford was when we went through the budget line by line. Ford understood why each decision was made. Fortunately, Jim Lynn and Paul O'Neil, both of whom knew Ford very well and held ideas very similar to what we were discussing, were very effective. I have never seen two people function in as administratively complex an area as they did as well as they did, integrating political, philosophical, and analytical skills.
    Paul O'Neil, now the vice-president of planning at International Paper Company, was Deputy Director of OMB. One of the reasons they were efficient is the same reason I was able to deal with Ford easily. We knew exactly where he stood. He had, as I said, a non-verbalized but very consistent policy, on which we could all hang in a relatively simple way.

EH: Could you change his mind by presenting new evidence and moving away from a predisposition?

AG: Yes. For example, I think we did that on national health
insurance. He was always in favor of it as a principle until
he began to look at the fiscal consequences. He definitely
moved back and decided it was desirable but that we could not
afford it at the time. I would say that there were innumer-
able issues of that nature where, if you gave him a very
strong argument, you could turn him around. The one area in
which I failed miserably was on the Energy Independence
Authority. I thought it was a bad idea. This was a $100
billion program to galvanize energy research development and
production. I had Rockefeller on the other side, and I think
this may have been the one case in which the President moved
in a direction that surprised me. It didn't strike me as a
consistent position and was, I thought, one of his very few
inconsistent policy decisions. The only other that I remember of even any minor substance was the release of a $2
billion highway fund. Paul O'Neil and I were on Air Force
One going into Topeka where he was about to spring this $2
billion thing, which was really in response to pressure from
the governors. I asked him--this is after the third time he
had said no--"Can we have a reconsideration of this thing?"
He said, "Sure," as the plane is going down into the airport.
So Paul and I marshalled our forces and reiterated our arguments. He said, "You haven't told me anything you haven't
told me before. If you had something new, I might listen.
But you haven't told me anything to change my mind." At
which point the plane landed, and he released it. I understand why he did it. It was the only time, aside from the
Energy Independence Authority, when I found him moving a-
gainst his own philosophical economic dispositions.

What really is important is that that was the only thing
he did. In the 1976 budget we originally had a long discussion on the types of employment policies we could engage in.
For example, we got involved in the issue of tax credits for
business for hiring teenagers or for hiring unskilled workers
as a potential training vehicle. When we really did an
analysis of the youth unemployment question, we realized that
it came down essentially to a corporate tax cut or a business
tax cut. I said to Ford, "Look, at worst all it does is cut
taxes. It may have some positive effect on teenage unemployment. It's a program that probably is not sensible from a
point of view of defining what a goal is, what type of program or policy or success you want. It won't work in that
respect. There's tremendous slippage in this type of program
and a potential for tremendous evasion of the actual policy
itself. Nonetheless, a lot of people will certainly support
it, think it's a significant move in the right direction, and
it could defuse many of the political pressures, which are
very strong." I frankly thought that he would buy it. And
he didn't. Finally, in a group of four or five of us, he
said, "I want your honest opinion. Will this work in the way
it's supposed to work?" I think Paul O'Neil said, "No. The
CEA staff told me no, and their analysis, as far as I could

see, was pretty solid." At which point Ford said, "Then I'm not going to do it."

EH: Now, public employment programs were revved up in the fall of 1974. The economists in ASPER [Assistant Secretary for Policy Evaluation and Research] in the Department of Labor were very skeptical about them, as were, I think, the CEA staff. But the Manpower Administration was pushing it. Was that a political act?

AG: Yes, it was mainly. The analysts in the Office of Management and Budget, CEA, and Treasury Department all thought that these were dead-end programs. In other words, the basic problem was that if the jobs were to be countercyclical they had to be self-destruct-type jobs, but self-destruct-type jobs, by definition, are jobs without a future, which meant that the job couldn't be anything that might be terribly useful for the person in his future employment. This led you to the expectation that you were dealing either with revenue sharing for permanent job slots, which is essentially what CETA has turned out to be, or with leaf raking. If we wanted to go for increased revenue sharing on job grants to state and local governments, our view was that we should call it what it was. Put it in as an item in the budget--at that point we were already dealing with $80 billion in grants. It's itty-bitty now; it was much less back then. It wasn't a question of breaking new ground; it was merely expanding old programs. But there is tremendous political power in a new program with capital N E W. One of the major problems we've always had in the White House and in government generally is that it's a public relations operation, how things are perceived, not what they are. I can say that Gerald Ford was very congenial to work with and always very relaxed, and I never got the impression that that was his central focus. It's not that there wasn't some of it, but I'd say far less than with any president in recent history. He eschewed that very consciously--he felt very uncomfortable with it.

DD: You suggest, in contrasting Ford and Nixon, that Ford had rather amazing flexibility, and that he was relaxed. Does this suggest that the man really had a lot of inner self-confidence, that he was not intimidated by intellectuals, for example? He didn't feel intellectually inferior?

AG: No, he was not. I wouldn't raise the issue of intellectual inferiority because I don't think it would surface in that sense. In other words, I think it might be more intellectual competitiveness. He is unquestionably a secure man, with fewer psychological hangups than almost anybody I've ever met. As a consequence, you never got negative emotional vibrations from the man, except when he was mad for reasons that were absolutely objective; there weren't any subtle or subterranean motives. One instance impressed me especially: at the time of the Mayaguez incident we were having an economic meeting and I was sitting next to Ford. Brent Scowcroft came in and put a note in front of Ford. He opened it up. He read it. This was the first time Ford heard of the incident. He turned to Scowcroft and said, "Okay, provided that we do not shoot first." Then he went back to the meeting and we continued the discussion. He struck me as somebody who had a sense of what it was all about, who had control of what he knew and what he didn't know. Nixon was more intellectually competitive and felt put down by people who were superior to him intellectually or more conversant with a subject; my impression of Ford was that the issue never came up. For example, he didn't believe that he was intellectually superior to Kissinger on foreign policy—he never would have suggested that—but he wasn't intimidated. Kissinger lost many internal battles in the administration. Ford was simply secure in that area, but not because he is an extraordinarily academically, intellectually gifted person. He's one of those extraordinary people who probably scored normal in psychology tests.

WH: Apart from the psychological foundations, isn't it also a matter of experience in his exchanges with people like Kissinger? He had had lifetime experience in government. He knew, as Truman did, that nobody else was going to assume the final responsibility for his decisions.

AG: I agree. I'm sure that explains a good part of it. I guess none of us will really have any feel for what it means to know you're President of the United States and your word on certain issues is final. It's an interesting introspective question.

EH: I wrote an essay in 1973 in which I said that we needed a president who loved himself in a biblical sense. And that's what Ford was. Great confidence in himself as a person. But some studies of politicians, some of which I've done, suggest that insecurity is positively linked to manipulative skill. You overcome low estimates of self by learning how to manipulate others, which is a disquieting thought, given some presidents we've had. Did you find that he thought about political leadership in skill terms? In talking about the Congress or public opinion did he think about skills, craftsmanship?

AG: Yes. Craftsmanship would be largely in his dealings with Congress, which he enjoyed working with because, as Minority Leader that obviously had been a very central part of his focus. He spent a great deal of time in the strategy of dealing with Congress and enjoyed that. He's not a manipulator in the conventional sense. I would say that Lyndon Johnson was a superb manipulator, and I don't think that Ford had those skills, probably not those inclinations. But he was definitely very much interested in how to swing a few votes, especially since in many instances he wanted to slow

things down and he needed only one-third of one House for
many of the things that he wanted to do. He vetoed many
things because a veto was actually a very key element of
economic policy. All he needed for sustaining himself was
more than one-third of any single House, which meant that a
few votes here and there made a considerable difference. He
was himself personally involved in trying to think of whom to
talk to, how that should be done. I have been in on numbers
of meetings with groups of people discussing things of this
sort and what types of arguments would be appropriate.

The Political Role of the CEA

EH: Let's move to the institutional questions. Did you seek to
depoliticize the Council, give it and yourself a low profile?

AG: Yes, for obvious reasons. Given the way things were evolving, I didn't think that the CEA in the very early stages
could get involved at the very high policy level. More
important, I still had residual concerns that the President
himself would make decisions that would be very difficult for
me to support. Having known Ford only superficially, I
wasn't quite sure how his policy positions would come out.
When the issue of who would be the chief economic spokesman
came up, I very clearly indicated to Rumsfeld, who at the
time was in the process of evolving the mechanism, that I
didn't want to be that spokesman and I didn't want the CEA to
be in on it. Not knowing what types of policies would
emerge, I was concerned that as chief economic spokesman I
would be out there taking political positions (1) with which
I felt uncomfortable personally and (2) which in my view is
precisely what the CEA should not be doing. I very consciously requested that we be dissociated from much of the
political decision making process. I cancelled the regular
monthly press meetings, and decided to make as few speeches
as feasible and have as few congressional associations as
were necessary. There were limits to how far I could go, but
there's still the question of conveying the logic underlying
the President's programs. I suspect I could have been the
chief economic spokesman very easily had I so chosen, largely
because it was then evolving--this was late August, early
September--and I was really the only economist in the operation. Rumsfeld and a number of the other senior people who
had been brought in, in a sense over the then vice-
president's staff operation, all were leaning on me for what
they should be doing in many areas, and I was very heavily
consulted on the original organization of the Economic Policy
Board and the whole posture of the structure by which economic policy was being created and implemented. I told them
that the Council of Economic Advisers should go back to its
original concept of being essentially a research, consulta-
tive operation for the President and that it was very difficult to be both a spokesman and an analyst.

I tried to pull us away as best I could and certainly in the early stages I was very pleased I was able to do so, because I would scarcely have wanted to go out and try to defend the WIN program. Its original version was far worse than the one that eventually came out. My first real experience in economic policymaking in the Oval Office occurred when I showed up at a meeting in which something had come out of the speechwriting department on a new "Whip Inflation Now" program, which included a voluntary national price freeze and a variety of other things. Sitting there I said, "What am I doing here?" Very fortunately, I was able to indicate--I was the only economist in the room, and it was mainly the vice-presidential staff--what would happen if you did that. So I was able to cut out a few of the proposals, but I was unable to scuttle that whole program. It was an unfortunate program from the beginning, precisely what Ford did not need, and probably the low point in economic policymaking in the administration.

DD: Were you able to avoid a public critical position on this or any other issues where you may not have been very happy with the resolution?

AG: I didn't say anything on WIN. That was the time, fortunately, when I cancelled all press conferences and I wouldn't comment on it publicly.

DD: You mean you never viewed that as an issue over which you would resign?

AG: Oh, no, it wasn't. The only thing that would have forced me to resign was to have to go out publicly and defend something that I didn't believe in. As a practical matter, it is very difficult to do that. Did you ever try to defend a position that you didn't believe in? When everyone starts popping the contradictions that you know are there and that you have raised yourself, you don't give a very effective performance. Needless to say, the WIN program reinforced my view that it was essential to maintain a policy that kept the CEA doing up and down option analysis and economic forecasting--not only for the President, but also for the White House and, in many respects, for the other agencies as well.

EH: Did the fact that you were not an academic person make any difference in your functioning?

AG: No. Well, it depends on what you mean. I'm more academic than anybody knows.

WH: Here's an economist who has been engaged in consulting on a monetary basis and on a firm basis as well. You were, therefore, broadly based, practical, but with less impetus toward getting power, more willing to serve in a technical consultant role, but also wanting a great deal more information about contextual matters and apparently relying much less on the exchange of paper. Other CEA chairmen emphasized the constant flow of memos; your emphasis was much more on access, the ability to give and take. I think that kind of experience is much better than academic experience.

EH: I would suggest that you had been socialized for the role perhaps more than you knew before you got there. Dealing with clients, dealing in a real world, political context. The model you developed in your own business as an adviser was quite appropriate.

AG: That´s true. I just shifted from a lot of clients to one. And that is a very important point. The very complex models that we would create for the clients were used for very explicit, practical purposes—facility planning or pricing policy or product forecasts. We used analytical techniques and data and theory to create an explicit proposal or set or options for action. That model is very similar to what is required in a political policymaking role or an economic policymaking role in government.

EH: An academic economist doesn´t necessarily develop those skills unless he´s been doing consultant work over some period of time. The academics have had a hammerlock on this job, by and large, and on the three positions and on the staff positions. Do you think that´s necessarily a good thing?

AG: I´m sure it isn´t. The only way you can be effective in this area is to have a very extensive institutional understanding of the way the system functions. The most effective staff people—even if they´re academics—are those who are either consultants or very specialized in an industry or a policy area. For example, in the energy area, our staff people from the university are very good in labor policy, if they fundamentally get to the data and see what´s happening. They are relatively poor in basic industrial analysis, forecasting, financial analysis, because they don´t know those institutions. In other words, the financial system is extremely complex and it´s unusual for an academic to have institutional knowledge that is essential to deal in that area. Frequently, economists start with Keynes and presume that that is an accurate description of the way the system functions, whereas, in fact, it´s an abstraction of one person´s view of the internal cause and effect mechanism that generates the aggregate system. A surprising problem is that a number of economists are not able to distinguish between the econometric models we construct and the real world. Even though they know that it isn´t the real world, their ability to go outside the modular structure is remarkably deficient. We really have a major effect on policy questions when we go outside that system.

I had a certain strange advantage. Having been an econometrician all my life, I knew where all the problems were, and it was very effective to say to some of the staff who would give me a printout from one of the internal models, "Give me the equation that generates this. Do you seriously believe that this captures what's going on now?" They'd look at it and turn red because they hadn't bothered looking at whether the system was really working. That is a very important advantage because it short-circuits the pressures that come up from the staff level. It's very important to have an institutional basis, but if you don't also have a fairly extensive academic background--I was the world's longest graduate student till I finally got my degree last year--the ability to know the literature, all the arguments and all the other things, you can't force the people on your staff to look in the direction you want them to look. Most people who show up on the CEA staff are, by definition, a lot better than average and they're not about to sit there and grind away at simplistic stuff. Unless you can direct them into certain areas for analytical reasons, you're going to have a very uninterested or rebellious staff or a staff that leaves. So while from a policymaking point of view there are many problems with having a strict academic as a CEA chairman, there are also problems in going the other direction. To have strictly a pragmatic economist without any theoretical or academic roots would be ineffective because of the huge political pressure that the academic fraternity in this area exerts through the Congress. If you cannot deal in that area, you'll be passing in the night.

DD: Without some academic credentials, if nothing else.

AG: Well, no, it's not even credentials. Credentials won't help you if you don't know the substance. What is really important is to be able to come to grips with the argument as to whether or not tax cuts are stimulative or counterproductive. Merely having credentials is not going to do that. Unless you can penetrate that surface argument and get to the foundation in a political-economic debate, which is really what the political arena is all about, you're going to be very heavily on the defensive. Unless you can counter the external arguments of the technician-experts, you will not get the confidence of the president. A pure academic usually has great deficiencies in this role. You cannot have this role, as it now stands and as I think it should stand, unless you have the technical capacity to handle those arguments. It's a complex mixture.

Bureaucratic Politics and Economic Policy

EH: Why don't we go back now and reconstruct the formation of the Economic Policy Board and then see how it came about and worked?

AG: It came about as part of the mechanism that had been evolving in the Nixon administration. There was a general recognition that the control of economic policy solely in the Troika and to a limited extent in the Quadriad no longer served the purposes of international economic policy or domestic policy generally, which very significantly interfaced with economic policy. As economics and economic policy surfaced as an ever-increasing political question, you could no longer hold economic policy tightly within the three key economic agencies. Economic policy, which was a relatively subordinate political question in government in the 1970s, became larger and larger until today it is the most profound political issue that everybody focuses on. This meant that other major Cabinet actors—Commerce, Labor, State, and a variety of peripheral groups—wanted to get into the system. There was also CIEP [Council of International Economic Policy] but that faded as an institution and became consolidated in the Economic Policy Board. We also had a special trade representative as an official member, and that in turn brought all of the economic policymakers into one basic group.

EH: You were going way beyond macro domestic policy, so you had to bring in other actors? There was a lot of micro policy involved with many questions of coordination of micro policy.

AG: Yes, but the essential reason was that an economic policy now became one of the key political questions in the country, and it could no longer be handled as a minor or marginal policy question. So all the actors wanted to get into the act; in a sense, they insisted.

EH: All your predecessors have said there was a front bench and a back bench. The Triad was the front bench, and the other fellows on the back bench were not really needed. "Commerce and Labor had no relative advantage, no competence. We didn't need them."

AG: I'm not saying I contradict them, but perspectives changed around this time. The key policymakers are still CEA, OMB and Treasury, with State quite heavily involved on international economic questions. Despite the enlargement of the Board, it was, I think, politically very effective because it had a mechanism by which conflicts within departments on economic issues could surface for resolution by the Economic Policy Board or a mechanism through which meetings with the President and option papers could be created for the purpose of decision making. Just to answer your question quickly, option papers are still done, they are still the formal mechanism through which the actual decision making of the president is made. He signs options on this and that, but a very great deal is decided through oral discussion. In any event, as part of the Rumsfeld transitional taskforce, this organization was instituted. The Secretary of the Treasury, who is the chief economic officer in the Executive branch, was made chairman, and Bill Seidman was Executive Secretary with a relatively small staff to handle largely administrative functions and administrative papers, which was done, I thought, rather well. Obviously, those papers were not constructed at that level; they originated in the CEA or in Treasury or in OMB or were a combined effort, which went in as the key option paper to the President with the White House staff--Seidman's staff--being management coordinators of papers rather than policy creators.

EH: The transition group--Rumsfeld, Laird, Morton, Scranton and Harlow--recommended this model.

AG: Certainly that group was originally involved in this mechanism. I've forgotten, frankly, whether that group developed the idea in this form, but certainly Rumsfeld was involved in it. I've forgotten whether that transition group dissolved at that point, but the initial concepts certainly came from that early group.

DD: How did Arthur Burns, as chairman of the Federal Reserve Board, fit into that large group, which obviously would embrace monetary policy questions? Did he attend?

AG: He attended when an issue of significance, not only monetary but anything, arose. He asked me always to tell him when he should show up, so I would·call him and say, "Arthur, there's an important meeting tomorrow morning on such and such. I think you ought to be there." And he would show up. Or he would call me and say, "I understand there's a meeting on such and such. Should I go?" I would say, "No. It's a waste of time." So I acted as his White House liaison as to when he should or shouldn't show, and I tried to keep him informed on what was going on as best I could. You know this old saw about coordination of Fed and White House policy? I could scarcely conceive of more discussion, more integration of policy, overall, than existed with Arthur. We didn't view it as monetary policy versus fiscal policy, and we considered Arthur an integral part of the whole policymaking apparatus, which he was. He had had extraordinary experience, which none of us had had--in a certain sense, not even Ford--and his insights were exceptionally valuable. Not that I agreed with him all the time--I didn't.

DD: Bill Seidman gave the view that many, if not most, issues were resolved right in that group rather than in option papers going forward to the President. Is that right?

AG: That's correct, but most of those issues were relatively small. Any issue in which there was not agreement among the interested parties within the administration would come before a meeting of the Economic Policy Board. For example, a question on housing policy, which might have inputs from HUD, Commerce and OMB, and on which there was not agreement, would come to the Economic Policy Board for discussion. If, at that stage, all the parties would agree and we had a unanimous vote, we would then send the President a memorandum recommending that he sanction that unanimous decision. Most of those were relatively small issues. On all major policy questions, there was an option.

DD: And did the Troika or Quadriad continue to function on the side?

AG: No. It really wasn't necessary. Troika III, which is the staff representatives, became the forecasting arm, which was then surfaced to Troika II, and then to the Economic Policy Board. Troika I--the chairman of the CEA, the secretary of the Treasury, and director of OMB--dissolved as a functioning administrative option.

SM: So macro policy questions were decided or discussed in the EPB?

AG: Yes. The so-called Executive Committee of the EPB. The Economic Policy Board, technically, included every cabinet member except the secretary of Defense, and all the other players, special trade representatives, CEA chairman. The Attorney General wasn't there. It was a group that rubber-stamped or was pro forma. The actual official functions were in the so-called Executive Committee of the EPB, which really was the EPB. This included the Troika, the Director of Energy Resources Council, which at that stage was Frank Zarb, the special trade representatives, subsequently the Secretary of Labor, Secretary of Commerce, and the Deputy Secretary of State.

DD: Your view was that this was a very efficient and effective mechanism for looking at the economic problems?

AG: No, I'm not saying that. It was a very efficient mechanism for surfacing and resolving minor administrative economic policy questions. On major macro policy questions it was not an efficient mechanism, and therefore we really worked around it in the key decision making processes. At least I did.

SM: Was this mechanism partly a result of an expansion of the CEA activities into more micro areas than under previous administrations, do you think?

AG: You mean EPB as such? No. First, the major reason, as I indicated, was that it was political. Secondarily, the government was so heavily involved in so many key areas at that point that any decision that was made, for example, by Commerce or by HUD or by HEW would have major political and economic significance and was, I believe, effectively discussed there because I was the only economist with the exception of some of the junior people and then John Dunlop when he came in, and John is not a technician in that sense. I would completely dominate the discussion, just on strictly technical grounds. Therefore, it was not a discussion. The real decision making processes would occur among the economists within the key administrative areas. I was perhaps exceptionally influential because I was almost the personal economist for Jim Lynn and Bill Simon, and they leaned on me very heavily. They nonetheless did get inputs from their individual economic operations which were fairly good. Significant disagreements were rare. So while economic policy was made formally in the Executive Committee of the EPB, as a practical matter an informal coalition developed the key options. Essentially, the President gave to the CEA an overweighing weight in what the forecasts would eventually be, and economic forecasts motivated significant key decisions throughout the whole system. What that forecast was and also what the presumed effects of alternative policymaking mixes were fell disproportionately to the CEA and as a consequence would carry a very great deal of weight into the meetings with the President. Where there were disagreements--and there were some--we would hammer them out individually. There was a lot of pressure, for example, from some of the senior people on the EPB, not to take negative forecasts and try to push them. They were very strongly against coming up with some of the CEA's rather pessimistic forecasts. We had to fight very hard, and we had to give in certain areas because the President said, "We will go with this. I don't want you to come out with a forecast that you cannot defend, but if the number were this instead of this, is that still a defensible number?" I said, "Less defensible but still defensible." But he would never say, "We're not going to do it this way. I don't want to take that forecast." He never put me in a position where I could not personally defend the forecast. That's what I did most of the time--try to tell the press why the forecast was, in our judgment, the most reasonable one. On several occasions, I went to him and said, "Mr. President, I cannot defend this position," and I explained to him why. He would reply, "Well, we'd better have another meeting." At the second meeting the whole thing resurfaced, and certainly on one occasion, perhaps on two, the tentative decision was reversed.

DD: You didn't have a Quadriad functioning, but when you came to macro issues the Fed was involved.

AG: Virtually every time the Economic Policy Board met with Ford, Burns was there, or Steve Gardner or someone.

SM: This was on the information basis that you described before, that you would call him up and say he ought to be here for this meeting.

AG: Well, yes. Legally, Burns could not be a member of the EPB. In fact, they had originally thought of putting him on, and I

said, "You cannot do that. Why don't we put him on as an
unoffical member who is invited to the meetings of the EPB?"
So he was invited. The EPB met formally at 8:30 a.m. every
morning of the week, for fifteen, twenty minutes, rarely more
than an hour. I found some of the meetings terribly tedious
and often sent other people. I thought there was an unnecessary amount of time for those meetings. Those sessions were
with the special assistants, not with the President. When we
had key meetings in which major policy options were being
constructed for purposes of sending them to the President, I
would inform Burns that he should be at the meeting. Burns
was at virtually every meeting that we ever had with the
President. He would express his views to the President as
he, in fact, expressed them to us. Burns never came out with
anything that surprised any of us because he had always told
us before what he believed and I would see Burns almost all
of the time. I would always tell the President, "Arthur
disagrees with this. His reasons are one, two, three, and
four. I think he's wrong or I think he's right. He will
tell you himself when he comes." He would show up and be
very effective. He'd come in there and get involved on most
subjects. This is a man who had been around government since
he was CEA chairman in 1953 and had an extraordinary store of
knowledge. He had a great deal of weight in the Ford administration, even on general policy on an unofficial basis. In
many respects, I would say that the Fed had very considerable
input into the administration's policies.

DD: Were those fairly large meetings with the President?

AG: It would vary. On many occasions Burns would meet with Ford
by himself. On a number of occasions I personally set up the
meeting. The EPB meetings on a major policy issue with the
President were very large, maybe twenty, twenty-five people.
Most there were observers and not direct participants. You
had a dozen principals, and these were not discussion meetings in which policy was essentially developed. They were
for final decisions on options for the President. But many of
those meetings—especially with regard to the economic forecasts—would rest upon the enunciation of the economic outlook as evolved by Troika III, and agreed to by Troika II.
We always knew who the Fed forecasters were, but they did not
get directly involved in the actual forecasts. Essentially
Burt Malkiel was chairman of Troika II for that session. He
controlled the staff inputs, and I would often sit in on
Troika III to give my views as to what was going on.

EH: Do you suppose Burns continued to try to play this general
resource role in the Carter administration and was rebuffed?

AG: No, strangely enough, he wasn't rebuffed. He saw Carter
quite often, one on one. I would assume he did try, as much
as he could, but he obviously did not have the entree nor the
sympathy.

EH: But he´s been criticized by people who have sat here before for trying to play that role. I don´t think we were aware of the fact that he had this all-purpose resource role in the Ford administration.

AG: Let me tell you this: Burns was very influential and extra-ordinarily useful. First of all, he´s an economist. Second, he´s an economist with very significant experience in the government. Let me also tell you, in many instances he had ideas that were not acceptable. In fact, Burns lost more than his share in respect to the positions he took relative to the decisions that Ford made. He was, nonetheless, excep-tionally influential and made, I think, very major contribu-tions to the economic policymaking process.

DW: Would you indicate some of the policy decisions over which he did have some significant influence?

AG: I would say he was very influential on the general policy of federal spending restraints. He was usually arguing for smaller budget deficits than the consensus. He would usually be advocating higher economic forecasts. In the broad policy discussions, I wouldn´t say that Burns carried the day inde-pendently above other people, but there was no doubt that his support for budget restraint was very important in the final decisions.

DD: Did he ever enter into any dialogue on the course of monetary policy?

AG: I would discuss it with him quite often. I happened to be quite supportive of his general point of view.

SM: You said that big macro policies were essentially decided by the old Triad or Quadriad. Did the Labor Department have any input on macro policy having to do with things that were obviously going to affect employment and unemployment rates?

AG: They tried. With the exception of their views on the minimum wage--largely a political question--which were contrary to the views of CEA, Treasury, and OMB, I would say their essen-tial input into the macro decision making process was not large.

SM: They just weren´t listened to, they didn´t have the staff to be credible, or what?

AG: They tried, but Dunlop took a position that was different from the surprisingly consensus decision making on the part of CEA, OMB, and Treasury. It had very little effect.

SM: I presume that his position was essentially to be more expan-sionary or more willing to countenance budget deficits than you were.

AG: No, or only marginally so. As I recall, Labor's forecasts would be more pessimistic than ours, implying the need for more stimulus. I did not come away with the view of John Dunlop as a major force for larger budget deficits, larger financings. Certainly Usery was very little involved in that at all. He stayed on the Economic Policy Board. But Dunlop was primarily involved with labor issues, and they did not have the supportive staff operations or a Secretary who was really conversant. Dunlop is not a macro economist. The Labor Department economic staff is not bad, but it doesn't have that expertise; they are micro economists.

SM: Yet these policies that you were making probably had more effect on the labor force and employment and unemployment than any of the micro policies.

AG: Oh, sure, unquestionably. That's correct.

DD: But Dunlop didn't have a strong view in these matters?

AG: Well, no, it's not that they weren't strong....Unfortunately, my memory is not as good as it could be on this. The impression I come away with is that he was more involved in the structural employment-unemployment programs, unemployment insurance programs, and the things that are directly Labor Department specialties. More often than not, he would prevail on the types of programs that he would be moving towards. He was not a maverick for big fiscal expansion, big expenditure, or tax cut. He was far more moderate in those discussions than I think the press was presuming he would be.

EH: I have the impression that over the years the policies of the Labor Department, which are micro, have never been plugged into a larger macro overview. They existed in a limbo--the manpower programs and others--without thought of their implications for macro policy.

AG: It's not to say that all these programs don't have a significant macro effect. The real question you should be asking is, if macro economic policy presumably has a far greater effect on employment and unemployment than all of the micro policies, why aren't they key players in the system? The major reason is that the Labor Department has a very strong constituency, and, as a consequence, does not produce the non-constituency policymaking output that, for example, CEA does. In other words, we did not have a constituency. In a sense, neither does OMB. The president is our constituency, but I mean somebody behind us pushing....Since the Labor Department felt it should in part at least advocate and support positions of its constituency, it had a certain partisan position, which may or may not have been consistent with the policy of the country as a whole or of the administration in general. That institutional limitation fundamentally inhibited their ability to deal in macro areas in the same sense that OMB and Treasury and CEA do. If Treasury had a significant constituency I think it, too, would have a problem.

EH: You don't think the bankers are Treasury's constituency?

AG: Not really. It's presumed that it has that constituency. It doesn't really. Commerce has an economic staff. There are some very good people there. But it has the same problem. The Treasury Department does not feel or in any way even marginally approach the need to advocate positions taken by bankers or the financial institutions in the same sense that Commerce is supposed to support business and the Labor Department is supposed to support labor. Historically, I believe Treasury did. In recent decades that is very fuzzy and, as far as I can see, internally largely nonexistent. As a consequence, Treasury has emerged as a key policymaker on the macro level. If you were to raise the argument, "If they had a good economic group on macro policy, would that change?" The answer is, "Commerce does and it doesn't." I don't think it's an accident; I think it would be very difficult. For example, it's not a Republican-Democratic question. You have the same problem regardless of the party in power.

WH: The network of people servicing Agriculture has continued to grow. Did they have no regular part to play the way Labor or Commerce did?

AG: We heard from Earl Butz, an agricultural economist, at length. Of course, Agriculture did not deal in the macro policy level, except peripherally. In other words, during Cabinet meetings, Earl Butz would put in his two cents, which was essentially quite supportive of Ford's general economic policy. But I would not consider they had significant input into the macro policy area.

EH: I would think you and your Democratic brethren might be agreed on many micro policy measures in regard to inflation, deregulation.

AG: Oh, yes.

EH: But none of you ever get anywhere. The Council doesn't have a comparative advantage on micro policy, does it?

AG: No, on a number of issues you align Democrats against Republicans and on a number of issues you align economists against politicians. To paraphrase Bob Strauss, politicians 10, economists nothing. The issue has, however, been brought into the public domain, and it's still functioning. Certainly the success of economists in restraining protectionist legislation has been really extraordinary. If economists were not out there discussing the abstract effects of protectivist legislation, I think we would find ourselves with "Son of Smoot-Hawley" very soon.

EH: Was the Economic Policy Board useful in the sense that you could catch these things in the net as they were coming from the departments? I remember Arthur Okun saying, "We have to be looking for them because they might go around us."

AG: Yes. Fortunately, it was very difficult to get around the Economic Policy Board. The administrative system worked in that respect. The chief of staff would throw the proposals back to the policy board; they wouldn't get to Ford. Not just everybody could come in and speak to Ford, unlike Lyndon Johnson who would go all over the place and ask to speak to everybody. Ford's time was pretty well allocated. I could always see him because I had fairly close personal relations with him, but that wasn't usual. As a result, it was very difficult to end-run the Economic Policy Board administration.

EH: I have a sense that a large part of the time of the CEA staff was spent commenting on departmental proposals, usually in a critical way.

AG: Oh, yes. That's correct.

EH: To what extent did the Council get into social policy, such as income maintenance, national health insurance, things coming out of HEW?

AG: There weren't terribly many proposals coming out of HEW at the time except national health insurance. A number of proposals on food stamps and the whole question of welfare reform did come through our operation. We did have extensive memoranda internally on that question.

EH: The Domestic Council never really took a grip on those questions, did it?

AG: They did not, much to everybody's surprise. The Domestic Council was set up under Nixon, and it was really a mechanism by which Ehrlichman could exert significant power. For some reason, it didn't move within the Ford administration. It was overshadowed by OMB in various forms of analysis, but why it never got off the ground politically, I don't know. It actually had considerable strength until Rockefeller took it over, then it seemed to fade. I may be mistaken on this, but my recollection is that there was no major initiative that originated in the Domestic Council and carried through the regular mechanism.

EH: How would you characterize the Rockefeller role in domestic policy?

AG: I think he was very significant in a lot of areas such as the New York City thing. His main interest was energy.

EH: Were there tensions between the Rumsfeld staff and the Rockefeller staff?

AG: Not the staffs. I think there was tension in a general way, but not real confrontation.

EH: You and Seidman really got along fine. How would you characterize the division of labor between yourself and Seidman? What did the President look to him to do? Why was he there?

AG: In part, Seidman and I did differ quite significantly on policy matters. Personally, we got along fine. Administratively, I thought he did a superb job. Basically, he was on the vice-presidential staff. He'd already been there. He was not a close friend of the President's.

DD: It sounds from your description as though there was very little confrontation. You were the central economist in this group, so you didn't have very much trouble.

AG: That's a very important point. One of the things I've learned about the system is how I would discuss the difference between Carter's administration and ours. The Ford administration had people whose essential policy philosophy, as best one could describe it, was very close to that of the President; whenever they would attend committee hearings, make public speeches, or even function within their own departments, they would very likely come out administratively pretty close to the President's position. There were unquestionably differences internally, which did surface in the press periodically, but it was remarkably tranquil. The Carter administration, in an attempt to get a broader spectrum, has an extraordinarily widespread set of philosophies, starting at the cabinet level and going down to the deputy assistant secretaries. And there really is a wide divergence between Carter and the people within his system. A deputy assistant secretary in the Ford administration, for example, would probably have held 80 to 90 percent of his views consistent with Ford's. In this administration, I would guess that the figure is closer to 30 percent. The whole structure of the Carter administration has a philosophy far more liberal than the President himself and, I would say, generally more liberal than the Cabinet. In other words, as you move from the top downward, this administration philosophically moves very significantly to the left. Now that is terribly difficult administratively. For the organization to function, you have to have people making decisions in the name of the president at all levels without direct consultation with their superiors. There's no way to have every single decision consistently measured up to the top. You have, therefore, a general state of inconsistency or paraly-

438

sis. In many instances, it's more the latter than the former. This means that managerially and structurally, economic policy is very difficult in this administration. Now, you may say, perhaps quite correctly, that the Ford administration lacked the internal debate that would focus on issues. But the debate has to be in the range of the president's knowledge because it's not possible for him to make judgments on technical issues when he has no personal judgment himself. What you need is ferment largely at the lower levels of the administration, in the press and in the Congress. You get your real conflicts, your policy debates largely by bringing in outside people. Periodically, I would have a meeting of outside economists, from Brookings, and we'd debate. Because I never knew and still don't have any view as to what the political organization of the CEA staff is, we also would have all sorts of views within the CEA. I used to get into very considerable debates with the CEA staff members. Those discussions were very useful because all elements of opinion would surface, not within the administration, but coming essentially from the outside. You cannot have debates on technical questions of policy between two people with the president there. I have a case in point: the issue of ownership of gold. Arthur was on one side. Bill Simon was on the other. The two of them debated the technical questions—excellent debate. After the meeting, Ford called me over and said, "I don't know what to do with this debate. I didn't understand it." And I said, "I'm sorry we couldn't resolve this before it came to you because I understand that it is a very technical question to be presented in that way." In most instances we were capable of harmonizing issues and there were almost never real debates between major antagonists. But we couldn't resolve a debate between Burns and Simon. I had no interest in doing it. Yet it was really unfair to ask the President to resolve it. The only type of decision the President could make was on an issue of basic value judgments within the context of his overall philosophy. You cannot have effective economic policy if there are major philosophical differences in the policymaking decisions among the policymakers or with the president. It won't work.

EH: Were there institutional biases in Treasury and the Budget Bureau that were different from the CEA? Could you predict where the Treasury would be coming from because of its institutional memory, its stakes in the government?

AG: Yes, but you could forecast the CEA also. We weren't less forecastable. Treasury, institutionally, is primarily free-market oriented, even in Democratic administrations. It varies on occasion and it depends on who is Treasury secretary. But because it's dealing with a set of financial institutions that depend upon free-market forces, its philosophical inclinations are free-market. The OMB, certainly in the last eight years, has been that way, but it's difficult to know whether or not that is institutional. My recollection is that it wasn't quite that way under Zwick and Shultz. OMB tends to reflect the political philosophy of the system, of the president, and it should. The CEA and OMB have got to be consonant with the philosophy of the president, or they will not be able to function. Treasury can function partly without it. Certainly in the Ford administration, you would find in the option papers an extremely high correlation on all issues between the positions of OMB, CEA, and Treasury. Before a paper went to the President, we would check the various sets of options and determine which agency supported which. We would very often find that the CEA, OMB, and Treasury chose the same option. When there was a large number of options, we'd split, but they would be close options.

EH: You were the leader?

AG: No. You have to distinguish between economic analysis of the staff operations and the principals. When I said that both Bill Simon and Jim Lynn would lean on me for economic information, it would be personal, but they would nonetheless be getting the feedback from their own economic operations. In many instances there were differences. I would often argue with some of their technicians and sometimes they would convince me, or sometimes I would convince them, and we'd end up in the same position. But it would be surprising how often we, Rudy Penner, who was the OMB economist, or any of a number of the assistant secretaries for economics or tax policy in Treasury would all come out the same way. There was a basic compatibility of philosophy between the President and all three of these key agencies. Going back to the Heller-Dillon-Kennedy triumvirate, you started quite differently, and you had a constant pulling and hauling.

DD: And with DOD.

AG: That was very significant. That's true.

SM: Isn't that largely because the previous chairmen tended to be more expansionist-minded than the Treasury or the OMB or the Fed, so that the CEA was always out front, pushing for a greater degree of expansion?

AG: I think that's probably right.

SM: So there is a fundamental conflict that you essentially didn't have.

AG: That's correct. I would have done better with the others in the administration.

DD: You've mentioned your staff analyses and that you didn't know the political biases there. What about your own Council

members? You had a changing Council. What was the input
from your own fellow Council members in the policy process?

AG: We set ourselves up so that each staff member reported organizationally to one of the other two Council members who were
in charge of different policy approaches. For example, Burt
Malkiel was in charge, as I mentioned before, of the internal
staff operation for economic forecasting and all related
macro policies. Von Furstenberg was working for Burt, and we
had many other very good guys in there. The technical
materials that would go in would go through that area. I
myself developed much of the material we used in forecasting
and analysis, so I worked with Burt in that group, feeding in
the basic materials. Paul MacAvoy would be in charge of all
the micro matters. He was in charge of the whole regulatory
and deregulation operation, plus energy and a variety of
other issues. For example, there were often very significant
differences between the Federal Energy Administration and the
CEA on energy questions. Paul would be basically in charge
of that, and I would work with Paul on trying to counter FEA
at various levels of government, including with the President. I would often send either of the Council members to
the EPB meetings especially when their areas were involved,
and I often brought them along, even though we weren't really
supposed to, to meetings where their speciality was involved
and I wanted to come, too. So they took roles in the development of CEA policy positions with the staff. They, of
course, did testifying when it was necessary, and they would
attend meetings with the President when it was important.

DD: Did one or the other of them take the international economic
policy input or did you reserve that for yourself?

AG: Technically speaking, Helen Yung and I dealt with the international area. Obviously, in an organizational sense, it was
Burt Malkiel's area, but the three of us really dealt with
it.

DD: International policy was all under EPB?

AG: Yes, that's correct. International economic policy became so
important that it couldn't go out on the side. It was discussed internally as part of the EPB process.

DD: There was no second level of any kind?

AG: No formal mechanism, except at the EPB level where Chuck
Robinson was a regular member as Deputy Secretary of State.

Reconstructing Policy Decisions

EH: Why don't we turn our attention to reconstructing policy
decisions. What purpose was served by the domestic policy
summit meetings in the fall of 1974?

AG: They were initiated by the Congress, really. The Senate.
     The major problem was that it wasn't clear what the policy
     options were. In other words, the Ford administration was
     just starting at the time and was trying to construct a
     national consensus on certain issues, of which this was the
     major one. It was originally the President's idea to go
     ahead with it. I was very heavily involved in the organiza-
     tion of the operation, who would be invited, the format. The
     basic purpose was to air all of the pertinent views of the
     groups that were somehow related to it. When you got every-
     body on the record, all the various ideas, there really
     wasn't very much. You will also find, if you go through the
     transcripts, that the economics panel did not foresee what
     was going to happen over the next twelve months.

SM: Were their forecasts based on erroneous assumptions about
     policy as well as about results?

AG: Many people advocated increased fiscal stimulus, but they had
     always advocated increased fiscal stimulus. A number of
     people called for tax cuts at the time or increased federal
     expenditures, but those were the people who had always been
     doing and saying this. And still are.

SM: Were there errors because the models were wrong or because
     the settings of the exogenous variables, like taxes or mone-
     tary policy, were wrong?

AG: In all instances, the models were wrong. You cannot con-
     struct what happened in the next year or the next six months
     from the structure of any model then extant. All of our
     models now have been re-jiggered to factor in that sequence,
     and the effect has been to increase very dramatically the
     effect of monetary policy in the models, and I might say,
     parenthetically, incorrectly. Monetary policy, in my view,
     was acting as a proxy for a number of other things and it's
     being captured in these models by sets of equations as
     though that's the cause; if you change the monetary policy
     input, therefore, the model will generate a certain GNP
     employment context. But that's true only if monetary policy
     still is acting as a proxy as it did back then. I'm not sure
     that we know that it will.
         The underlying structure is always the same. The ques-
     tion is: How do we infer what the significant elements of it
     are? We had a golden era of econometric analysis from the
     1960s on because prior to that, for about ten or fifteen
     years, we had had a situation in which inflation was not a
     critical issue. It apparently is a major factor in the level
     of economic activity. But during periods when inflation was
     a very minor factor, the models would not capture it as a
     significant variable and we were unable to make judgments as
     to its effect when it really became a large number. Now that
     we've seen what happens--we have an observation, a full
     cycle--we can draw some very significant conclusions about

the sensitivity of real demand on the basis of inflation and inflation changes and a variety of other things. That was not implicit in any of the models in 1974. They all missed it by large margins. The last forecast I made from my model before I left for Washington was for a mild recession in 1975. And I thought I was a pessimist.

SM: Did that have to do with all that was going on with oil prices or was it inflation expectations? What was it that was being missed?

AG: It was the vulnerability. Let me tell you what we knew at the time, because I remember having charts in that September summit in 1974. Of several key charts, one showed that the inventory levels were very high, but that unspent capital appropriations were exceptionally high. I went through an argument before national TV at the time explaining that if the capital appropriations figures weren't as strong as they appeared, the inventory level would be very dangerous. I went through the conclusion, which I believed, namely, that it would be very difficult to undercut that backlog so dramatically as to create anything other than a mild stagnation or weakness. As it turned out, there was a massive shutdown of the capital investment process. All of a sudden, capital investment collapsed and that triggered the inventory collapse. Consumer expenditures held up remarkably well in that period. So what was missing in all of the models was the ability to see what risk premiums could do to capital investments. We were all quite surprised at the dimension of the effect.

DD: You didn't factor in the inflation factor?

AG: You couldn't. We had no historical period from which we could infer what the parameters were.

SM: You had inflation rates up to 6 or 7 percent before the original price controls in 1970-71.

AG: No, we didn't. I think it went as high as 4-1/2. CPI was 4-1/2 when we put on controls. That's my recollection. Well, maybe it was higher for a very short period of time, but it never was picked up as a significant factor.

SM: Do you see a significant relation between a fixed capital formation and these inflation rates?

AG: I believe there's a very significant relation between hurdle rates of return and capital investment. I did a long article for the _Economist_ in August of 1977, I believe, in which I tried to define the state of capital investment here and abroad as a function of risk premium. I put a little bit of it in the Economic Report.

SM: If you expected higher rates of inflation, one would have thought that people would rush to buy or build machines and factories before the price went up.

AG: All it tells you is what the average expectation is. Inflation merely tells you where the average price is going, but it also creates a massive dispersion in price change, which means that it causes a massive dispersion in the rate of expected profits from any facility over the longer run. That is another way of saying that you're increasing the risk premiums implicit in the investment process. It is true that the average expectation of profitability rises, but the risk premium implicit in the dispersion increase apparently undercuts the present value. That's what the evidence shows us. That was not clear until we went through this experience.

EH: As you started in late summer and early fall of 1974, what did you think the problems were, the primary macro policy problems, and how did you proceed? You might want to weave the WIN program into that.

AG: As I said, I had expected negative growth in 1975, but very minor. I expected that inflation would simmer down. Remember inflation was coming down late in the year. My general view, as I said, and I gave congressional testimony on it, was essentially that we had to simmer down policy. But I sensed that it was going to be very difficult to implement that type of policy in the face of what would be considered rising unemployment, weakening demand, and the typical type of macro environment in which the ideal policy was more, not less. I didn't really know what types of short-term policies would be feasible politically, although my view of the long-term policy was that we had to simmer down the deficit, the rate of inflation, and eventually get to a stable, balanced economy, fully recognizing that there might be some considerable economic static for the next year or so. I thought that if the short-term policy became expansionary at this stage, it would prove eventually counterproductive, and I also recognized that long-term policy would be rather difficult politically. Fortunately, at the time I was not a key policymaker--I assumed I was merely supportive of Bill Simon, Roy Ash, and Arthur Burns--and while my views were clearly listened to, I wasn't called upon right at the beginning to be a key decision maker.

We became aware that the economy was getting a little shaky in the late fall. The first things I used to watch closely, when I was in New York, were the data we would get from the unemployment insurance system because we found that the initial claims weekly, seasonally adjusted, were usually the most sensitive barometer--perhaps the largest macro variable that we had. The levels of insured unemployment were beginning all of a sudden to tilt up, well before you had any other evidence. This was occurring in late September, early October. There was increasing evidence that the economy was in a shaky stage. The problem with the policy at that time was that Ford had just recently enunciated his mixed package of anti-inflation tools. Because there was some concern about what we could do as a minimum in the way of increased unemploymnent benefits, we advocated increased unemployment benefits plus an increase in the investment tax credit. Because we had argued that these were long-term policies, and long-term policies should not have a cyclical component in them, we also advocated a 5 percent surcharge, which made the package essentially fiscally neutral, slightly increasing the deficit, but nothing to speak of. But it became clear very shortly thereafter that the system was weakening, and the effect of the weakening showed up in prices fairly quickly and quite dramatically. The very heavy rhetoric about some form of incomes policies in August and September of 1974 just disappeared overnight, as the WIN program disappeared overnight.

One of our problems, which I´m sure you´ve heard in previous discussions with the CEA chairmen, is that you cannot turn on a dime. It´s a long, agonizing process before you can get the whole executive system turning. We finally turned after long discussions, but didn´t announce anything publicly until very late in the year, early 1975. As this process went on, I became more and more involved with things such as the State of the Union and a number of related, broad conceptual issues, which Rumsfeld very early pulled me in on. We had, I believe, an internal debate on the size of the tax cut, whether we should have a tax cut—the debate was well publicized. Our basic view was that whatever the President put out, the Congress would add to by $10 billion or more, so we decided what we thought was an absolute maximum and then subtracted 10. It came out roughly that way.

SM: Could you give us an idea of how you were going to fight this inflation? Were you going to be gradualist versus shock treatment? Were you aiming at a soft-landing on a 4 percent unemployment rate?

AG: It was a soft-landing scenario. Our general view was that you had to defuse the inflationary pressures very gradually, because if you tried to do it abruptly and generated large increases in unemployment, that´s a mistake in policy. It was considered then that 7-1/2 percent would be a large increase in unemployment. You wouldn´t be able to continue. You´d have to fumble your way back and it wouldn´t work. The choice wasn´t a real choice, especially in our type of system, so we concluded that the only way to do it was to support a marginally lower rate of monetary growth, which would require easier, longer-term smoothing down of the federal budget. It was always a gradualist approach.

SM: What did you expect would be the maximum unemployment rate that you would get with that policy? How long did you think that was going to take?

AG: Unemployment was never seen as a necessary condition for bringing down the rate of inflation. We always recognized that if the unemployment rate increased it was more an accident of policy or a failure of policy, but since the unemployment rate and inflation rate both went up together, we always argued that it was possible to bring them both down together. Over the longer run there's no question that that's right. The question is whether we could succeed in doing it over the shorter run. Our basic view was that that was the only choice we had and that was the policy goal we were going to take and try to fit our policies under. That soon became rather meaningless when the whole thing began to unwind very rapidly late in the year. Then the question shifted not to abandoning long-term goals, but to having a mix of short-term and long-term goals. George Meany was advocating $100 billion deficits and numbers of things that we all argued might be supportive in the short-run, but with vast long-term costs to the system. We essentially fended them off, and the major reason we were able to do so is that the response to these higher levels of unemployment was remarkably mild.

One of the columnists, it may have been Joe Kraft, wrote something on the unemployment situation here and in Europe, noting the great surprise throughout the world at the failure of social radicalism to emerge as a consequence. Essentially that political milieu enabled us to stay fairly well on stream. One of the things that enabled me to feel confident was that I knew we were looking at, aside from the drop in capital goods, essentially a sharp inventory recession. We were able to take the data, virtually on a week-by-week basis, to try to audit final demand to see whether we were getting a deterioration in final demand or whether the sharp drops in production and employment were wholly or almost wholly inventory correction. What was very encouraging was that as we got into January and February, it was very clear that final demand was holding up. It didn't take very much arithmetic to demonstrate that we were getting to a rate of liquidation that was fundamentally unsustainable, which meant that so long as final demand stayed up, production would have to start to close the gap. Not that inventory liquidation wouldn't continue, but that production would start to rise, employment would start to rise, and that would start to remove the political pressure. It wasn't until mid-February that I felt reasonably confident we were okay. From mid-December to mid-February, it wasn't clear what type of recession we were in. If I had seen retail sales, which had originally dropped and stabilized, start down again, or if capital investment had really begun to move down sharply, then I would have said we were in vast trouble. It's fortunate that that issue never surfaced because the data were unequivocal on that.

DD: Did you shift gears on your support of slower monetary growth or did you stick with that longer-run?

AG: No, I didn't shift gears. If we were looking at an inventory
      recession—and that subsequently proved to be correct—then
      the incredible level of unemployment was because production
      was so far below the level of consumption. You could account
      for the substantial decline in employment on the basis of the
      shift from inventory accumulation to liquidation. The rate
      of liquidation was at a maximum very early in 1975; in Febru-
      ary it stabilized and then started to narrow. The narrowing
      is what brought the production level back up, obviously, and
      started to bring the unemployment rate down. We were moni-
      toring very closely the levels of final demand on a day-by-
      day, week-by-week basis, and we saw no deterioration in
      housing or in consumer demand generally. We would have said,
      therefore, that the monetary policy did not have to become
      excessively expansive because it was not going to affect
      inventory liquidation, which had other causes, and there was
      no need on the final demand side. I remember a meeting in
      spring or summer of 1975 in which Arthur Burns took the
      position that the monetary growth levels at that time were
      adequate and that income velocity would accelerate. That was
      a tough forecast to make with all of our academic colleagues
      saying that if we didn't have 10 percent M1 growth, the
      economy would not recover from these levels. But he stood
      his ground and he was right. I think in the longer-run that
      it was a factor in the subsequent lowering of rates of infla-
      tion, which occurred in 1975 and 1976. So after what was
      clearly a rickety economic policy performance in the first
      six months of the Ford administration, I thought that policy
      came on rather sensibly and, even in retrospect, I find few
      things that I wish we had done differently.

SM: It has been said that you were in favor of more expansion
      during those first three or four months of 1975 than other
      members of the administration. This is the fight over the
      tax cut.

AG: That was the tax cut. My view was that we were going to get
      a tax cut larger than whatever we recommended. It was going
      to be larger, so I wasn't really surprised by what came back
      from the Congress. Others who felt very uncomfortable with
      it had recommended a veto. Looking at the aggregate level of
      financing requirements in the system, it struck me that while
      longer-term deficits of the type we were talking about were
      highly inflationary, in the short-run we could live with
      them, and provided we didn't throw off the long-term track of
      outlays, which was critical, a tax cut wouldn't be a great
      problem in controlling deficits over the longer-term. Even
      with 5 or 6 percent inflation rate, you get a very substan-
      tial increase in revenues at any normal growth level because
      of the graduated tax structure. The nominal increase in
      receipts is significantly above the programmed increase in
      outlays from what we call current services budget. As a
      consequence, if you hold yourself in position, you'll close

the deficit. That struck me as probably the best solution. I was not in favor of increased fiscal stimulus per se, but it didn't strike me as an excessively inflationary problem at that point. It would make it a little more difficult later on, but I was concerned that if the President vetoed the tax bill and the economy sagged, even for reasons other than the veto, that would throw off our long-term policy stance.

SM: Your long-term idea was that you would give a little on taxes now, so that you wouldn't generate a tremendous public outcry for a really expansionary policy?

AG: If the President had vetoed the tax bill, the economy might have recovered the way it recovered, which was one chance in 5 or 6. But if the economy slowed, for whatever reason including the failure to cut taxes, then there would have been tremendous pressure from the Congress--not only the Democrats, but I suspect the Republicans as well--for a massive cut in taxes beyond anything we had calculated or decided upon. From the standpoint of a cost-benefit analysis, the risk of vetoing the bill and, for whatever reason, having the economy sag would so upset our long-term strategy that it wasn't worth it; the costs of signing the bill, with regard to long-term strategy, were modest.

SM: If you had not had these political pressures from the Congress as you saw them, would you have been in favor of the tax bill?

AG: Yes, but probably somewhat smaller than the one that the Congress eventually passed.

DD: Before Carter took over, considerable concern was voiced at our CBO group that any tax cut--they were talking of $15 billion--would be offset by the Fed. I always said this was a nonsense view. They can be, in your words, semi-accommodative, they can be less accommodative, but to think of the two running counter is just not realistic.

AG: There was some of that sentiment in some elements of the staff in CEA and probably OMB and Treasury, but it was very muted. A good deal of that comes out of the macro models, the econometric models. In the type of period we're in now, and have been for the last five years, some of the key mathematical assumptions that are required to get appropriate fits are very seriously questionable. As a consequence, there are tremendous biases in our models, even though our statistical tests say that there are not. When you construct these models so that monetary policy becomes a key variable essentially to explain the 1975 result--having interest rates as a key variable in the system--then slight changes in monetary policy have vast effects on levels of aggregate demand and it's easy for very minor changes in your M1 targets to offset $30 billion in fiscal stimulus. Of course, it is nonsense.

It's nonsense only if you look at what's going on in the world and not what this modular structure is telling us. So yes, there was some concern, certainly in the CEA staff.

SM: Were you able to strike some sort of an understanding or a deal with the Fed about the size of the tax cut and the size of monetary expansion?

AG: Only in a very general way, because that implies a much more simplistic relation between monetary and fiscal policy than in fact exists. We're not sure within very wide ranges of the short-range effect of monetary policy. In the long run, there is a trade-off. If your purpose is to enhance capital expenditures, the ideal mix is for significantly less fiscal stimulus and more monetary. So my concern was with watching the federal funds rate at various levels of monetary growth and watching them evolve. So long as we had continuous eased money conditions at continuing lower interest rates, the short-term money supply growth was not a critical factor, in my view. We never said, "If we come up with a full employment deficit of X billion, which is 5 billion less than we would have, would you agree to increase the monetary growth rate by 1/2 or 1 percent?" Frankly, I wouldn't embark on that sort of negotiation because I think it's frivolous. The presumption that the economy works at that degree of fiscal and monetary fine-tuning is just not substantiated by reality. Any deal you make in government, if it gets beyond the two people who make it, becomes institutionalized and very difficult to unwind. The major problem you have in economic policy planning is that you cannot turn on a dime, that when you come up with the final economic forecast in mid-December, that sets into motion so many variables and so many relations, it is impossible to turn around.

SM: Could I return to the tax cut in 1975? Presumably, by March the word was really out that the economy was in a serious recession, and I'm curious about the pressures that you were getting, where they were coming from—Labor, Congress—to expand your proposed tax cut.

AG: Pressure was coming from everywhere. It was coming obviously from Congress. I used to put on my bullet-proof vest and armor when I'd go up to the Hill to testify. There was tremendous fear in the Congress. Economists' tools rarely give you firm conviction about an extraordinarily large world affair, but when I looked at the ten-day auto sales figures and the weekly retail sales, housing permits and starts, some of the new order series, and especially this insured unemployment system, I had enough conviction that we were looking at an absolutely incredible inventory phenomenon, as differentiated from a collapse in final demand. Having had that conviction and knowing that there is an absolute limit to the rate of inventory liquidation, I was sufficiently confident that I didn't waffle inside the White House. In Cabinet meetings I took the position that the bottom was in the spring: "I can't give you an exact date, but unless there is a collapse in consumer markets or in housing, it's got to happen that way." Every week we had a Cabinet meeting I'd get up and tell them what the last two figures were or the last figures. Fortunately, the data were never equivocal. It was one of the very fortunate times when the data were clear, were subsequently unrevised, gave a true picture, and you could figure out what was going on. That gave me strong conviction, and since I was the only analytical economist in the senior operation, I could hold sway on that question.

SM: Did the Labor Department clamor for tax cuts or for an increase in unemployment programs?

AG: I think just in unemployment programs. My recollection is faulty and I do not recall very explicitly.

SM: What about the Commerce Department?

AG: No, there was no big program. I can't say that anybody strayed very far off the reservation.

SM: What was Simon's policy recommendation?

AG: He had advocated vetoing the tax cut. His basic view was to keep the budget deficit down, stimulus down.

DD: He had the crowding-out theory, didn't he? Or did that come later?

AG: No, it didn't. The crowding-out theory originates in this testimony I gave at the House Budget Committee in September 1974, which got widely circulated within the administration.

DD: Maybe the reason you didn't get more pressure to act on the monetary side is because the credit and capital demands hadn't come in on that market from the private sector. You had easier interest rates than you might have had.

AG: If you do a flow-of-funds forecast, which we did, you find that at those levels of aggregated demand in the private sector, the throw-off of private savings was more than sufficient to absorb something fairly close to Treasury financing requirements without putting any significant pressure on the commercial banking system. Having concluded that, then by definition you're not going to get crowding-out. With inflation rates beginning to fall at the time, it was fairly obvious that inflation premiums in the long-term interest rates were beginning to ease. So the case for crowding-out is very important. In fact, it's a major case today, and it wasn't then. At that time, it was a conceptually correct case to make, but the numbers didn't support it.

EH: Would a Democratic economist and a Democratic administration, dealing with the same problem, have behaved differently?

AG: I suspect they would have, yes. I think that the tax cut and/or expenditure increase would have been significantly larger than ours. In fact, they were privately advocating that. We were meeting with these people.

SM: Would they have moved earlier?

AG: Yes, but remember, they didn't really move. The way to test somebody's policy stance is to look not at their absolute policy stance, but at how it changes. Their policy stance didn't go for more stimulus than they had originally been arguing. So there was no significant change at that point.

EH: They would read the data much as you would, and they would draw a different construction or have a different set of goals in mind?

AG: I would think so. I think there's a very big difference. There's less now than there used to be, but in 1973 and 1974 the ultimate inflationary effects of large monetary expansion would have been perceived far less by the average Democratic administration economist than by the Republican economist, if one can generalize in that way. I think you would have gotten tremendous pressure for very much more monetary expansion.

EH: An interesting question is where science leaves off and ideology begins.

AG: Well, theoretically, there shouldn't be any difference. In other words, one's ideology should merely be one's philosophy of the underlying views of how the world functions. The trouble is that it's not always easy to get evidence and one fills in the holes where one's knowledge is deficient on the basis of other sets of relations or general views of what the macro structure of the world is all about.

    I would define ideology largely as one's views where evidence is less than complete. There isn't a significant ideological difference in the sense that we're dealing with those who would like to see a collectivized economy and others who would not. The difference really lies in the effect of governmental actions--fiscal, monetary, and regulary policy--on the private decision making process. My view is that what was missing in Keynes' general theory is a significant negative effect on the marginal efficiency capital from the types of actions that are implicit in very large fiscal stimulus. I can argue, and do indirectly through the hurdle rate of return, that substantial fiscal stimulus, working through inflation and a number of other things, sharply depresses effective private demand; while it may be expansionary in the short-run, it is not over the long-run and usually is counterproductive. Very few economists in Democratic administrations would agree with that proposition. I suspect they would find that a mistaken view of reality.

We cannot capture in an appropriate way exactly what those risk premiums are. We do have various surveys of hurdle rates that do, in fact, show the rise in the rates, but we don't have the basic data that go from inflationary instability into a higher hurdle rate of return. If we did and we explicitly built it into our models, you would get this type of effect. Many of my Democratic friends argue that an increase in aggregative demand by increasing the level of economic activity will induce businessmen to invest. I say that the evidence of that is extremely faulty because you're asking them to make a twenty-year investment on the basis of five or three months of expansion in the demand for their product, and you're asking them to generate a facility that will not come on stream for a year to a year and a half.

EH: So that ideology really is not value judgment, it's a world view, the way you're using it.

AG: That's correct. For example, I often come out almost ad nauseum with free-market solutions not because I have an ideology, but because I believe it works. Where it doesn't, I recognize it doesn't. But my inclination would be to presume that the system works. There are others who presume that unless you prod it all the time, it will never function. Now that's an issue of evidence.

EH: Since there are gaps in knowledge, world view often substitutes for knowledge.

AG: Oh, indeed it does.

WH: But a world view that doesn't take account of contingencies is a hard-core ideology.

AG: I would agree with that. In reviewing a policy I always asked myself the question: What are the costs to the economy if we are wrong? If there is never any cost, you can argue very forcefully that you can try anything and should. But if you evaluate the cost of failure to be potentially very large, even though the probability of success of that policy is better than 50-50, the argument should be not to do it because you cannot accept the cost of failure.

SM: To what extent did the upcoming election in 1976 enter into your thoughts in 1975, vis-a-vis the tax cut and the President's discussion?

AG: To my knowledge, almost not at all.

SM: Wouldn't it be the case that it would take surely a year before that tax cut would have a big effect in the economy?

AG: No. We had had a big private rebate in April 1975, as I recall, and as a consequence, the essential focus of our tax cut policy at that stage was to get a quick effect, not a lingering effect, which is one of the reasons we opted for the rebate.

SM: The expectation was that you'd be back to an unemployment rate of 6 or 6-1/2 percent by 1976?

AG: The argument I made, and which, I believe, carried the day on the political side, was that the level of unemployment was not the critical variable. Unemployment is such a sensitive political question not because of those who are unemployed, but because of the majority of people who are concerned about becoming unemployed. Even with a 7 percent unemployment rate, 93 percent of the people are employed. The reason they are concerned about the unemployment rate is that they fear for their own job status. Once you conclude that, then you realize it's not the rate of unemployment that is significant, but the rate of lay-offs. I would much prefer to be running politically in an economy with an 8 percent unemployment rate that is falling--meaning the lay-off rate is low and the accession rate is high so that those who are employed have a great sense of job security--than with a 4 percent unemployment rate and rising. I argued, "I don't know where we're getting in the summer of 1976, but it is not nearly as important as what the direction of the unemployment rate is and what the lay-off rate is." That was consistent with our basic attempt at expansion. I would say that that argument was largely bought.

SM: Did you try to keep the rate of unemployment at a steady rate of X, Y, or Z to get the inflation rate gradually winding down?

AG: The reason we had that problem with the absolute target rate to resolve finally in the January 1977 CEA Annual Report was that the official full employment definition, as you know, was 4 percent. At that point very few economists were willing to buy that, but it was still such a hot political issue that in a period when the unemployment rate was very high, I recommended against revising upward the so-called full employment rate. It would have served no useful purpose. When we were required to make a long-term projection, we did project 4.8 as a four-year projection, but we were still declining at that point. We could always argue that it could continue to decline. In fact, there was a huge hullabaloo when we published our January 1975 long-term projections. It boggled everybody's minds that we were going out there with this high unemployment rate over a very long period of time. One thing I will say about Ford is that he bought it. I can't imagine that a Democratic administration could have done that politically. I didn't think that a Republican administration could do it, and I must say that when Ford was willing to buy that, my respect for the man rose immensely. We didn't really deal with that goal issue until we got into a redefinition of the full employment rate, which we then raised to 4.9.

SM: I wasn't really thinking so much of the goal of this so-called "natural rate," which is what you're talking about now, but in fact your own target of what would be required to bring the inflation rate down. In other words, 9 percent is obviously excessive.

AG: Yes. Over the next two years, I didn't perceive that we would get an unemployment rate sufficiently low to threaten the continued lowering of the inflation rate. In the two-year context, the issue didn't come up. Over the longer-run, the issue would come up, but we believed that if we could bring the rate of money supply growth down, in the context of rising real GNP growth or high real GNP growth, when we finally got to somewhere in the danger zone of, say, 5 to 6 percent, we would have the rate of monetary expansion at levels that would inhibit a major acceleration of a significant, more than cyclical, acceleration in inflation. My general notion was no more specific than that, because no action at that time required it to be more detailed.

SM: It would be quite interesting for the record if you were to comment on your insider's perception of the economic arguments in the election itself, because this is a terribly important part of the election.

AG: I thought that the campaign rhetoric implied a very significant policy change, one that would be a mistake and reignite inflationary forces. As it turned out, for the first nine months of the Carter administration, policies were not really very different from those Ford probably would have followed. They have been since, in my view, but not significantly. The arguments that there was insufficient demand, that the economy was stagnating, were wrong. The forecasts were wrong.

SM: It appeared that Ford really did take a bum rap in many ways, as you were saying. Demand was certainly increasing, and while it may not have been terribly high yet, it was certainly moving in the right direction and moving pretty fast. Employment was certainly rising. The fiscal stance had also become much more expansionary, so you could argue that the fiscal side was doing all that it could.

AG: Well, it was. In retrospect, from, say, April 1977, the implicit forecasts and the implicit policy prescriptions of the Carter campaign operation looked rather inferior to those we were making. Unfortunately, that was not the case in November.

SM: Were you asked to go out and make speeches, more or less trying to establish what the position was, what was going on?

AG: I told the President right at the beginning that I would not engage in the campaign as such. That shut off a vast amount. I don't believe the secretary of State, the Attorney General, the CEA chairman should be involved in campaigning. Some of the Cabinet members clearly have to and should be political. But when you're dealing in certain areas of policy, where institutions are supposed to generate information essentially of a bipartisan nature, I think it is most inappropriate.

SM: Presumably the main problem from the short-run stabilization point of view is that prices are so terribly inflexible downwards.

AG: Let me rephrase the question. In the longer-run, unit money supply will track the price level. In a sense, no significant long-term trend in income velocity is algebraically equivalent to that statement. If that is the case, then the question really is: If we somehow slow the long-term rate of growth in money supply, what will we reach as the rate of inflation? If we were able to reduce money supply growth to half of what it's been, would we necessarily slow growth and create unemployment? The anwer, I suspect, is not necessarily. In a period of relatively strong capital goods demand, I can envisage a case in which you can actually start reducing the rate of monetary expansion without creating unemployment or even the context of falling unemployment. Now that won't exist in any of the models because they define the structure in a manner that almost necessitates the type of response you're suggesting.

SM: Presumably there is a state of the world where in fact rates of inflation would fall. It's just that we haven't seen that state of the world in quite a number of years.

AG: In 1975 through late 1976 we did see both falling unemployment and falling inflation rates.

SM: We did, but with unemployment rates going to 9 percent.

AG: No, I'm talking about from the spring of 1975 to the fall of 1976.

SM: Well, the reduction is all in the year 1975. After March of 1976, the inflation rates start right back up to the 6, 7 percent range.

AG: It depends on what type of pattern you're looking at. If you adjust the inflation rate for the cycle, which you should in part, then there's a serious question about what has happened to that inflation.

SM: Were you looking at sectors of the economy in which there really did appear to be insensitivity of prices to demand or inflation rates that refused to come down?

AG: Oh, sure. We knew where prices were moving and where they weren't.

SM: Was there any question of intervening to try to push those prices down?

AG: If you're talking about jawboning as such, or any sort of intervention, I would say no. Of course, the original advocate of some form of incomes policy was Arthur Burns, and he did hold to that to a greater or lesser extent throughout that period, although in 1975, with the inflation rates falling, I perceived less of that discussion from Burns.

SM: Do you see any prescription that would increase downward flexibility of prices or inflation rates in response to demand?

AG: Sure. The Davis-Bacon Act would do wonders in construction. I'd say that is a remarkably effective price support mechanism.

EH: You mean to get rid of it?

AG: Yes. That would significantly increase construction costs flexibility, and, incidentally, it would lower aggregated capital costs and also would have that same effect.

EH: But it's probably not feasible.

AG: It was suspended for a short while. That's how we learned how potent it was. It was 1973, 1974. It started the sharp increase in open-shop construction. The extent of union construction was, I believe, two-thirds of the total construction labor force five, six years ago; now I think it's under 50 percent. It's been one of the reasons why construction costs in the non-residential area, where all the union activity is, have really slowed dramatically. I'm not a great advocate of administered price theory, which is really where your question is leading. I don't perceive any significant trend in market power between, say, 1959, '60, '61, and today. It doesn't strike me that the degree of price rigidities, which does exist, creates very much damage to the system. I don't believe that in the areas where they are critical—and there aren't very many—that they are a major factor in what may or may not be a short-term Phillips curve trade-off. The evidence is quite mixed on that question. What in fact was showing up in 1975 was that the areas where price inflexibility was the greatest were the areas with the lowest profit margins. And it does show up in a macro sense. You do find that the ratio of variable cost to price tends to rise as effective demand falls.

Profit margins fall because fixed costs are spread over fewer units. But if you actually take cyclically adjusted costs, then you find that that's what happens. Is there a structural policy that can significantly alter or should alter that? The logic of doing something is the basis of jawboning or various Tax Incentive Proposals. I think that the payoff from that is exceptionally small--maybe negligible. I don't know what the costs of failure are. One of the reasons I feel very uncomfortable with some of the current TIP proposals is that we're not aware of what some of the costs of failure are. In 1975 I envisaged the payoff from structural policies of the general type as being extremely small. But we did perceive potentially significant areas for effective action in some of the regulated industries. That's why we initiated the deregulation policy on trucks and airlines and raised very significant questions about the price effect of some of the environmental policies, seeking to make them explicit so that we knew what the trade-offs were. On the administered price side, I personally thought there was very little we could do. We did, as you know, significantly raise antitrust penalties, but my view was that economically it wasn't very effective.

DD: If you apply this approach and philosophy to the prevailing situation, with an inflation rate of 7, possibly 8 percent by year end, with productivity way down and with a tremendous number of wage contracts coming up in 1979, what can you do?

AG: I begin with the assumption that the economics profession does not have effective tools to fine-tune the system fiscally or for inflation. We can deal with confidence only in longer-term effects. I'm not sure we can do very much about inflation for the next year, year and a half. Policies now should be oriented toward 1980. I believe President Carter is doing the right thing, and they are moving towards getting federal financing requirements down. They can't do much for fiscal 1979, which means that their first shot at anything is the first part of 1980, and that's a year and a half away.

SM: What about a policy of indexing, i.e., learning to live with inflation, if you can't whip the inflation?

AG: I don't think you can.

SM: Was this ever discussed during this period?

AG: Oh, yes. It was discussed at great length early on. The problem with indexing, as I see it, is that the inflation problem is not strictly the issue of the rate of the average inflation but the dispersion question. Indexing cannot reduce dispersion. So long as it can't reduce dispersion, it does not significantly undercut the risk premiums that are implicit in the inflation rate.

SM: You could devise an insurance scheme where everybody would go into a common pool and could insure themselves.

AG: I think that such an insurance system would break down very quickly because the numbers of prices we're dealing with are horrendous. More important, we can't get a fix on a vast number of prices in the system. We don't really have a price index for women's dresses, for example. In 1971-73, we had Phases I, II, III, and IV of TIP, and my recollection is that there was no auditing of anything. All we did was collect paper and make believe everything was going on. TIP is in the Internal Revenue Service, which would legally require auditing. The problem of determining what a value-added price is for women's clothing I find absolutely statistically mind boggling. The tax courts would be flooded overnight, and the system would bureaucratically break down.

SM: I'm curious about the whole formation of the energy program. What administrative arrangements were set up to try to deal with it?

AG: The original focus of the energy proposal started with a weekend meeting at Camp David in which all of us got together. I think Frank Zarb was already Energy Administrator. Anyway, all the agencies that were involved went up there and talked through the whole question of strategy. We discussed energy resources; ERDA [Energy Research Development Agency] presented its appraisals of the aggregative levels of demand and supply of various types of fuels into the 21st century. The costs were discussed. It was a very extraordinary session in which we essentially pounded out the policy--in the total aggregate sense--to make the United States not only self-sufficient, but also with export capability and the net energy supplies. The general philosophy and basic approach was hammered out by a combination of FEA, CEA, OMB, and Treasury. I was heavily involved right from the beginning and spent a good deal of time on that project. Later Paul MacAvoy got involved in some detail. This is late 1974. Throughout the administration, CEA had very major inputs into energy policies. In fact, Frank Zarb and I, essentially, were the principals in all of the energy discussions. I don't know of a single major energy issue that we didn't get involved in. An Executive Committee of the Energy Resources Council included all the key participants. That was the mechanism--parallel to the EPB--through which energy policy formally evolved and from which the option papers were created and sent to the President. We worked to a substantial extent off the large model built up by FEA, which enabled us to test various proposals with respect to their effect on supply and demand. I don't know if I'm answering your question specifically, but that was the essential mechanism by which we functioned.

SM: You said Rockefeller had a major role.

AG: That was outside this operation with the idea of Energy Independence Authority, which was a huge $100 billion program for subsidies. The major issue was a lending bank to give huge government guarantees to help finance all of the energy, R & D and basic development. It was a huge study, basically by Rockefeller's people. Analytically, it was a very good job. But in our judgment--in fact, in most everybody's judgment--it was a blunderbuss that would have very major financial implications. I discussed this whole question of what guarantees do in the financial markets; when you interpose that type of institution into our system, the fiscal effect is horrendous. Fortunately, it made no headway. It went up to Congress and just died very quickly. I suspect somebody leaked the memorandum I wrote and how it would be a huge rip-off for industry, which it would have been.

SM: I presume you were going to rely on market mechanisms, higher prices, to increase supply and reduce demand?

AG: Yes. Our view was that we needed significantly higher prices to unwind the entitlements program. We had an excise tax with rebates. The notion of higher prices for demand suppression was largely picked up by the Carter administration, but their presumption was that the supply side was extremely inelastic. Our argument was that there was elasticity there and that we couldn't afford not to find out. Then our argument was that in natural gas the elasticity of supply must be terrific. Subsequent information suggests that we were not terribly far from the mark on the natural gas question.

SM: How did you avoid the outcry of consumers that Carter has been bedeviled with?

AG: Poorly. Our only argument--and it wasn't very effective--was to say that natural gas will be more expensive, but it's better than not having it. If you don't have it, you'll be forced to use distillate fuel oil, which is still more expensive. The illusion that raising natural gas prices increases consumer costs rests on the assumption that there is no supply elasticity from price. Our argument was that the evidence is very clearly in opposition to that. That's not an easy argument to make in the political framework. I say we did it poorly.

10
The Council of Economic Advisers Under Chairman Charles Schultze, 1977–1981

Summary History

Jimmy Carter became president at a time of 7 to 8 percent unemployment, a $66 billion dollar budget deficit and a 5 to 6 percent inflation rate. He had promised in the campaign to reduce both unemployment and inflation and to balance the federal budget in his term. Because the recession was the most salient problem in the fall of 1976 his economic advisers prepared a package of programs to stimulate the economy for submission to Congress in January. The newly appointed chairman of the CEA, Charles Schultze, was the principal author of the package, which had the support of Carter's other economic advisers and the Democratic congressional leadership. The intention was to give a quick stimulus to the economy in order to hasten recovery through public works, youth employment and training programs and increased public service employment. A fifty dollar tax rebate to each taxpayer was added to the package by Schultze as a temporary stimulant that would not deny the government needed revenue in terms of balancing the budget when the country later emerged from the recession.

Carter was personally skeptical of the need for such decisive action to rejuvenate the economy because he was a fiscal conservative and was already concerned that inflation would be his major problem. But he was carried along by the preponderance of his advisers who were reinforced by the most important Democratic national politicians. After the stimulus package had been introduced in Congress, Carter began to doubt the necessity for the rebate, particularly as indicators of economic recovery increased. In April, he withdrew the rebate from the program. This story is symbolic of one major difficulty of Carter administration economic policy: it was seldom clear whether the enemy was recession or inflation or both.

Charles Schultze, the administration's chief economist, was a veteran. He had been a CEA staff economist in 1952–53 and 1954–59 and had served in the Johnson administration as Assistant Director of the Bureau of the Budget from 1962 to 1965 and Director from 1965 to 1968. As a Senior Fellow at the Brookings Institution for many years, he was highly respected by his fellow economists and was well connected in the Washington world of "in and outers." It is difficult to imagine a selection for the CEA chairmanship who could have won more respect or have been more in the mainstream of pragmatic, liberal approaches to economic policy. Joining Schultze on the Council were William Norhaus, a Yale professor and expert on productivity, corporate profits and long-term energy supplies, and Lyle E. Gramley, Director of the Federal Reserve Board's division of research and statistics and an expert on economic forecasting.

The Carter administration took office in the early stages of recovery from the recession brought on by the first oil shock in 1973. Consequently its early policies were aimed at strengthening and guaranteeing this recovery process. However, as the recovery gathered momentum it became clear that inflation rather than recession would be the main problem. This was particularly obvious after the second oil shock in 1979, when OPEC prices more than doubled in response to the oil shortage caused by the Iranian revolution.

Managing a return to full employment without reigniting inflationary pressure was the central economic problem for the Carter administration. Since the economy was already in a recovery phase by 1977, the policy required a delicate balancing act between stimulus and restraint. This explains the frequent shifts in administration economic policy over time as the goal of recovery gave way to concern about inflation, to be succeeded by fears of recession.

In 1977 the administration complemented the stimulus package with an increase in social security taxes as a means of balancing future budgets. A potentially inflationary energy program was also introduced in 1977. But recession threats reappeared in late 1977 and the January 1978 administration budget request was expansionary with special attention to tax reform and tax cuts. However, in April, 1978 a new anti-inflation program of wage and price guidelines was announced and federal pay raises were cut. In fact, 1978 was a boom year. The January 1979 budget was, therefore, anti-inflationary and directed toward keeping the projected deficit down. Then by mid-1979, with a recession again threatening as a result of the oil shock of that year, stimulus proposals were developed. The January 1980 budget sent to Congress was an anti-recession plan. Yet by March 1980, the President and his economic advisers were so concerned about the galloping inflation, which approached 13 percent, that a new tighter, anti-inflation budget was introduced through a series of negotiations between the White House and the Democratic congressional leadership.

Carter and his advisers had been trying to adjust to the second oil shock without a real recession. They probably underestimated the buoyancy in the economy and the severity of inflationary pressures. By 1979 the inflation rate was accelerating and the economy stubbornly refused to respond to Carter's gradualist contractionary medicine. At this point, the administration had little choice but to step much harder on the brakes despite the upcoming presidential election and the virtual certainty that the country would be in a recession on election day.

By 1980 the President was determined to fight inflation in the full knowledge that his actions, when joined to new policies of the Federal Reserve Board, would hasten the impending recession. Chairman of the Board, Paul Volcker, had embarked on a policy in 1979 of controlling the money supply to check inflation. The administration took complementary action in 1980 to invoke the Credit Control Act, which checked consumer buying. Schultze tells in his interview how Carter strongly resisted advice to cut taxes and increase spending as the 1980 election campaign approached. The President entered the election campaign carrying the responsibility for both inflation and impending recession. While the President and his economic advisers thought that Volcker had acted too strongly, there was little they could do about it. Volcker had been appointed chairman in the summer of 1979 (to replace William G. Miller, who moved to the Treasury) because the administration felt that the national financial markets required reassurance that an anti-inflationary hand would be at the helm. And, within a year, the administration itself was engaged in an all-out battle against inflation.

In retrospect, there were four particular factors that forced the rate of inflation up. The first was the decline of the value of the dollar in international markets in 1977 and 1978. In those years the dollar lost twenty percent of its value against other currencies. This pushed up the prices of imported goods. The second factor was a continuing decline in industrial productivity which was accompanied by an expansion of the number of workers. The negative productivity in 1979 increased the inflation rate by several points. The third factor was the increase in oil prices stimulated by the Iranian revolution in 1979. World oil prices more than doubled, adding at least three points to the American inflation rate. Finally, a series of micro economic policy decisions contributed to inflation, in particular: increases in the minimum wage, farm price supports and workplace health and safety regulations. Carter did his best to hold these increases to what he thought to be reasonable levels but the political pressures from the groups in the Democratic coalition were strong and had to be accommodated. The President and his advisers believed that they had done a good job of holding the line on such increases and on budgets generally. In addition, administration policies of deregulation of airlines and banking, having been enacted and implemented, were intended, in part, as long-term anti-inflationary programs.

Carter entered office promising to expand the economy. The time to accept or deal with a recession never quite appeared as he and his advisers sought a precarious series of balances. A strong anti-inflation policy would have required Carter to challenge the ideas and values of the Democratic congressional leadership and the interest groups within the Democratic coalition. This was politically unrealistic. The shocks which made things worse—the decline of the dollar, fall in productivity, and oil price increases—added fuel to the fire.

Jimmy Carter tried to lead the Democratic coalition in a fight against inflation and thereby went against the strongest tendencies of his own party. It was the election of Ronald Reagan in 1980 that awakened Democrats to the need for examination of how the party of reform might deal with new economic conditions.

Oral History Interview
July 6, 1982

The President and Economic Policy

EH: There are three sets of questions. One set has to do with the President and his general style and then secondly the institutional patterns of advising and decision making and then third, some questions about policies. So we will start with the President. When Carter became President, did he have an economic philosophy that one could discern?

CS: It was fairly clear that his economic philosophy reflected two opposing strands and that dichotomy was representative of the essential problem, at least in the early stages of his administration. On the one hand, he was elected with a fairly strong commitment to taking steps to get the economic recovery going faster. This was made more dramatic by the fact that during a large number of months right in the middle of the campaign the recovery seemed to be faltering, kind of a lull, which made this particular promise even more central in his campaign. Over against that you have to remember that he was also a fiscal conservative who didn´t have the same attitude towards budget deficits, let´s say, that Lyndon Johnson had. And, therefore, there was always a certain amount of tension, particularly in the earlier stages, between a desire to stimulate the economy (which in turn meant tax cuts) and some expenditure increases (which inevitably led to larger budget deficits), and reconciling those strands was never easy. These are the inherent tensions that go on, it seems to me, in any similar situation; they were not peculiar to Carter except that the fiscal conservatism part of him was somewhat stronger than in many other recent Democratic presidents.

EH: It was deeply rooted evidently and went way back in his life.

CS: That´s right.

EH: And it would be fair to say that this tension was apparent in his early thinking about economic policy?

CS: That´s right, and interestingly enough in the early stages the need, the perceived need, both politically and economically, for economic stimulus ran against the grain of his fiscal conservatism whereas, conversely in what were objectively more difficult times, the last two years of his administration, the clearly perceived need for restraint and cutting back and so on ran in line with his fiscal conservatism even though paradoxically it was harder to do the second than the first.

EH: What did he expect economic analysis to do for him as President? And in particular the CEA as a source of economic analysis?

CS: I have never thought about any of it in that way.

EH: Another way of phrasing it, staff economists often talk about political executives as consumers--good or bad consumers of economic advice.

CS: In a sense here was a case in which supply creates its own demand, both from past experience and from being close to the Council and from observation. And I presume that it was true of my immediate predecessors but I don't know this for a fact. First, you know, I never even questioned it. I fed him a steady diet of short memos--very short usually--on the latest statistics. That is, it wasn't so much that he said I want this, that or the other thing; it was something that we established from Day One. Every new important piece of data we would get the night before it was released, and then he would have a memorandum on his desk ranging anywhere from one paragraph to two pages explaining the number and usually a little bit of its significance and occasionally the dramatics of the development. So the first thing he got (and of course he became used to it and expected it) was a very steady stream of very current data analysis.

EH: You got some sense that he appreciated this, that he was using this in some way?

CS: That's right. He obviously read it, stayed aware of it. If you told him one thing one month and forgot and told him something different the next month he would pick it up. That happened, occasionally, to my embarrassment. The second thing we gave him, more in the early years of the administration understandably, were several, relatively lengthy pieces. I can recall two of them, both on different aspects of economic policy, not the standard macro. He liked both and sent them around to all the other Cabinet members. One was done early by Barry Bosworth, of the Council on Wage and Price Stability, attempting to cost out, in terms of inflation increments, price level increments, the effect of all of the decisions made during the first year in micro economics-- regulation, minimum wage, and farm prices. Bosworth put that all together, explained how this ran through the system, how an increase in regulations, say, would show up as a price increase and ultimately maybe as a wage increase. We put it all together, totalled it up and sent it to him. That proved to have a fairly big impact on him, I think. The second thing we did was to give him an essay on what the unemployment statistics mean, who is unemployed, what's it like. It was about twenty pages. It was done with a lot of headings, tables and charts and so again he got this analytic memo, liked it, and talked about it at some length at the next Cabinet meeting. Thirdly, at least twice a year, he got

fairly organized briefings on the economic outlook, the risks
in the outlook, both long- and short-run, and how particularly the budget policy related to that as preparatory both in
the very early stages and then nearer the end to making his
budget decisions. This was fairly formal, organized, jointly
done by CEA doing this part of it and the OMB coming in with
budgets. This is rambling but it gives you some sense....

EH: Now as Governor he had presumably dealt with what one might
call micro issues although they didn't call them that in
Georgia. But we presume that he never dealt with macro
policy, never had that responsibility. Did he approach those
two areas differently insofar as one could separate?

CS: Yes, as far as I could tell his interest and participation in
micro matters was clearly, I might say, more to his liking.
There was more verve there than when you got to relatively
broad macro sorts of things. By the way, this I don't think
is necessarily peculiar to Carter, and I have never been able
to understand that, to tell the truth. He had to work at
macro. He seemed on the one hand fighting for it and on the
other hand almost resisting it.

EH: Would he put in personal interpolations in the micro? You
know the Lynn and Whitman case study of welfare reform in
which they were talking about public employment and he was
talking about three people in Plains, etc. Would he do that?
Would he see real people, real institutions?

CS: That was part of it. You could always watch his mental
process dealing in a fairly logical, in fact quite logical,
principled rigorous way with micro concepts. I remember once
watching him invent for himself the concept of marginal
opportunity cost, you know, no small thing. I can't remember
the incident. I wish I could, but it was a pleasure to watch
him. We did something one time dealing with probability. It
was snapped up, just gobbled up. It was natural to him.
Macro, you had to fight for. He was less inherently interested in it. For example, the notion that from a macro
economics standpoint a wasteful expenditure could nevertheless be employment creative. He used to josh me about that
all the time and I used to josh him back saying that public
service employment was the most wasteful conceivable expenditure that I could imagine but we were buying it for employment creation; the idea that however wrong it was to spend
money inefficiently, that in doing an economic forecast the
inefficient expenditure of money, at least in the short run,
was nevertheless employment creating.

EH: There was a capacity of mind that was sharp and analytic on
discrete problems.

CS: Although again it is not quite so much the abstraction versus
the concreteness, this may be part of it, but that isn't

quite the distinction, maybe all encompassing versus focused style.

EH: Except you can find evidence that he had a proclivity for comprehensive solutions, can't you?

CS: Well, the Energy proposals....Again, you have to take this in context. I remember explicitly with Lyndon Johnson, going in to try to brief him on next year's budget (mind you it wasn't what we did with Carter); the budgets were five years out. This was next year and I never got past this year's. The abstract notion and the way the economy and everything is going to look several years out wasn't the same reaction but I thought it was alien also to Johnson. He had to fight for it.

EH: What was your working relationship with him day in and day out, week in and week out.

CS: It was basically threefold--or more than that. First: very frequently we saw him on all kinds of occasions ranging from very small to much larger groups hammering out some particular policy. That could range from two other people to a much larger group. It would obviously vary depending on the work load and the time of the year. Second: we had regular, scheduled one-on-one short twenty-minute sessions. Initially, it was twice a week but it was clear that we didn't need it twice a week. It was once a week for quite some time and then I think it was after 1979 sometime, trying to free up more time, we cut it down to once every two weeks. So I would see him one-on-one on a regular scheduled basis. Third: a very ad hoc sort of thing. Something would come up. You wouldn't call it highly infrequent but you wouldn't call it frequent. I would pick up the phone and call over to Phil Wise and say, "Can I get in to see him for five minutes?" I would say the most frequent were the sessions, say, with Eizenstat and McIntyre or Blumenthal and Bob Strauss and one or two other people. If something would come up like minimum wage, then there would be Ray Marshall and Eizenstat and the President and maybe one or two other people. That was the most frequent. Finally in the last two years of the presidency there was something called the "inflation breakfast," initially under the aegis of Fred Kahn because so many of the things in the incomes policy kept coming up all the time. In fact it became an economic breakfast every two weeks at which there would be the main players with the major economic advisers, plus Mondale, plus Eizenstat and the President. They met pretty regularly every two weeks, and, as I say, it changed from just inflation to anything in economics.

EH: Did you get the impression overall that he regarded successful economic policy as crucial to his administration, his programs and his political future or that perhaps his stronger interests were in other areas?

CS: I can't answer that. I don't have any way of....If by economic policy we mean macro policy as opposed to domestic...
Certainly through most of the period of both Lyndon Johnson
and Jimmy Carter one got the feeling that there were other
things that were more urgent. Now there is a reason for
this—a case of different men and different situations. Lyndon Johnson was completely wound up on domestic areas—he
went up and got a lot of new legislation...but foreign policy? I think, he got a lot of things under control. The real
point being that you may play all the diplomatic and strategic games but never have to face reality until the world
comes to an end. Reality doesn't come up and bite you in the
face. In domestic economic policy of a micro kind—win or
lose—it's very easy to see an outcome to the struggle; you
can do something, get a piece of legislation through or
something like that. Macro economic policy is much more out
of your control, in the sense that how often does the President get a chance to make macro economic policy? Not very
often; when he does his impact is relatively modest. He gets
an agreement with Menachem Begin, we get the SALT talks, he
gets the Panama Canal treaty through Congress, gets the new
foreign aid bill by, makes new arrangements with Taiwan or
PRC and domestic legislative policy is also concrete. But
macro economic outcomes are much harder to come to grips
with.

EH: You can have symbolic victories in the other areas. It is a
little more difficult, maybe.

CS: Yes, I mean, for example, tax reform as opposed to tax cut.
If you had gotten the tax reform it would have been a very
concrete specific thing. We changed capital gains, we
changed a loophole here. Whereas with fiscal policy impact
(a) if you see it, it's sometime later and (b) you don't know
how much would have happened anyway, and finally (c) it was
particularly difficult for Carter because I think he was, in
the last two years, fighting a lot of outside events and at
best could have had only "damage limitation."

EH: Let's move on to the second category, institutional patterns.
A decision was made not to keep the Economic Policy Board of
the Ford administration. Who made that decision and why was
it made? How was it made?

CS: In all honesty, I don't remember very much about that. I
have some general impressions that may need to be corrected
by other observers. First, we believed that having a group
which met formally, as I understand the old Economic Policy
Board did every day to pass on virtually everything coming
through it, would possibly be useful for the small stuff but
not very useful for the big stuff. It was too formal, would
likely get routinized; it wasn't needed. Secondly, we wanted
initially to have a smaller group and also a continued presence in the international arena. And finally, my recollec-

tion is that Mike Blumenthal, having heard of Kissinger's influence on foreign economic policy, wanted a group in which Treasury would be _primus_ _inter_ _pares_ on international economic issues as opposed to the Security Council. What resulted was the EPG, the Economic Policy Group. Paradoxically, initially at least, everybody and his or her brother was on it. It was unwieldy. I have an impression, though not certain knowledge, that Juanita Kreps and Ray Marshall, before they came on board, got a promise from the President that they would be involved. Pat Harris got involved by a route I no longer remember. You had State, you had the economic agencies; they each initially came with their assistants, assistant secretary level who in turn brought staff and it was a circus. It took various experimentations and changes in "ad hockery" over the first two years to get that group down to a smaller, workable committee. And I no longer remember all the steps but there was initially a lot of dissatisfaction both on the part of the people running it, Blumenthal and (my impression is) the President. He walked into one meeting for the first time and he sits and looks around the room and, while I never heard him say it, I'm sure he was shocked by the huge attendance.

EH: And then the question does become how are all these diffuse micro issues handled and what are the processes for dealing with them?

CS: By the time we finished we had a very good process for making sure that any question that was generally considered economic would go to the EPG, come through, get staffed, the papers get to the President and the right people get consulted, usually. The problem was what was or was not economic. There was always a little bit of jockeying. In my recollection of the Kennedy/Johnson years we ran somewhat differently, but that was a different era. The Troika was very limited--three agencies at various levels. Macro economic policy and nobody else was involved. And conversely they didn't handle a hell of a lot else, international economic policy, same people involved--but much differently. And all of the domestic economic stuff got staffed out jointly between CEA and OMB as the routine matters came over. Whereas in the Nixon, Ford, and Carter administrations there was, one way or the other, a much more formal dealing with the EPB, the EPG and its various advisers.

EH: Does that reflect some kind of interlacing, a perception of greater interlacing, do you think?

CS: There probably is some of that and I think it is a combination of that plus the weight of tradition and the power of Bob Strauss' personality--the special trade representative began to come to all our meetings--then of course we had Fred Kahn. I must say I like the older Troika system better.

EH: Did the formal Troika disappear as such? But an informal Troika plus one or two continue?

CS: It never quite settled down exactly; an informal Troika plus Eizenstat plus occasionally someone like Mondale, for example, would form an inner core, and Fred Kahn would be involved in most things, and then it would get enlarged for some questions. I remember one time, and I can't remember which year it was, there was a group we called the "eleven" group. It was "sub rosa" to try to prevent leaks from too many people being involved. Actually it was a Troika plus Eizenstat, and for some period of time McDonald who was Ham Jordan's deputy.

EH: Would this group at any given time consider micro issues?

CS: Oh yes. You could never be quite sure what would and wouldn't come to you. For example, National Health Insurance was handled by another group although the individual players in EPG were involved.

EH: The rationale was that NHI was a domestic policy staff matter, almost by tradition coming out of HEW--like welfare reform?

CS: I am trying to remember. The regulatory stuff may have come occasionally through EPG but foreign and international policy did except when it came to some very technical trade stuff like trigger price mechanisms, which was done by Tony Solomon of Treasury.

The Structure of the Council

EH: One of the things that came up over and over again in our interviews with your predecessors was the question of whether the Council is sufficiently staffed to deal with the whole host of micro issues that departments are pushing toward the president.

CS: I no longer remember the numbers--it would be useful to look at the administrative part of the annual Report to count the staff. We had to take a cut and we may have lost one or two people. On the one hand I think it is too small, but I wouldn't want to expand it very much. There is no logic to this, but it seems to me that it is absolutely critical to have a good working relationship between CEA and OMB. And if there is a small, competent CEA staff, a little larger than it now is (three or four additional people), each really covering some major area, generally working very closely with OMB, it is a marvelous salt. There is no inherent limit if you say CEA should get involved in all micro issues and be staffed up heavily. Where do you stop? When OMB and CEA are sympatico at the top levels then the second levels work well together.

EH: And the OMB top people are drawing on their program people who have knowledge.

CS: That's right, exactly right. If it works well, CEA and OMB are normally sympatico on most issues. CEA can provide very often the technical economic knowledge that the program people don't have when it comes to a very complicated piece of analysis. There are usually at OMB, and should be at the top level in the fiscal area, a few first-class economists. So it works together very well; it is a good complement. As I say, if you start to expand CEA so it alone, on its own with no relationship with anyone else, tries to handle all these questions, I think you've got yourself a real problem.

EH: Would you apply the same principle to the Domestic Policy staff or NSC or....

CS: Yes, as a matter of fact, I think the Domestic Policy staff ought to be a little bit like the CEA, a first-class, small number of people who heavily work with OMB. Since Nixon there has been a very heavy Domestic Policy staff layer, a very large number, who tend to do a lot of things themselves, and you develop OMB-Domestic Policy staff collisions on issues that I don't think need to be there. The OMB staff are involved heavily in things that aren't just budget cutting. OMB is a better staff. So a relatively few, I'll pick a number out of the air, I am not sure it's the right number, ten Domestic Policy staff... CEA at its present size of eleven senior people (it depends upon how you count the numbers) plus three or four new people working closely with OMB is ideal.

EH: Did Califano do this when he was putting together the Great Society?

CS: Yes. There was a lot of OMB, CEA input.

EH: Does OMB give you something more than just their maxims? They have a number of maxims; everything has to be under a department and all that business.

CS: There is that. Some of this feeds on itself. You get OMB people actively engaged in writing a piece of legislation, new legislation, new programs, broaden their interests; it makes a difference.

EH: What is the comparative advantage of the CEA in this arena with Treasury and OMB and a few other players. What does the CEA bring that is distinctive?

CS: Well, on the one hand, it brings what OMB should bring, which is, it supposedly has no client. Treasury has less client than most. Nevertheless the secretary of the Treasury is supposed to represent the business and financial community in some very broad sense. That makes a difference in attitude. The CEA can bring to this (unlike OMB which is an institutional, career repository of a lot of knowledge) a protection for the presidency, an ability if you can get really good people, in the framework of this non-representative approach, some first-class economic analysis when it comes to sticky issues. The practice (which I suspect grew like Topsy and does not at first sound like a good way to run a place) of bringing in different people every year, in fact given what CEA is, is usually worthwhile. Now there are some people who just turn out never to be too suited for this. And ideally my guess is that if we could get people for two year stints it would be better. You can't and the choice is between having a staff that is almost all career and a staff which does have to spend some time breaking in. I'll take the latter, because it adds something—which by itself is by no means enough—but something important. Where you stand depends upon where you sit, and we don't really sit anywhere, in the sense of client or bureaucratic interests.

EH: But it's got to be harnessed to the regular government in some constructive way to multiply its energies.

CS: Well, I don't know if I have used it before with you, but I probably have because I use it all the time, it's the idea of realistic hair shirts. On the one hand it is the responsibility of CEA, and I think of OMB too, to say that the Emperor has no clothes, or by God you don't do this without a cost— cost in the broad sense. You know, getting rid of inflation ain't free, Mr. President, no matter what you say and conversely you stimulate the economy right now and you can promise inflation-hair shirts. Simultaneously, realistically, if you are going to play the hair shirt role well, it has to be realistic in the sense that if you are always at the purest end of everything you lose all your clout. Obviously the terms "realism" and "hair shirt" don't go together, but I haven't found better terms.

Bureaucratic Politics and Economic Policy

EH: How would you fit the President into this general broad picture of economic advising that you presented earlier. How did his style of authority shape it? What were the interactions between the President and this loosely clustered group of advisors?

CS: My single clearest impression is that there were too many options and sub-options. Everything became a long string of, "Well, if on the one hand, if on the other hand." It became a very tortuous process.

EH: Was that because he wanted it that way or was that because he didn't make an effort to guide it in any other way?

CS: In my judgment there is ultimately where Blumenthal and then Miller, and or Eizenstat, actually both, ought to have had the presidential authority to tell a Cabinet officer, "No, that option is not going to go to the President. I am not going to have option 6a in there. Here is what we all agreed on. There are three possible ways to do it. Sure, there can be some minor changes. If you want to appeal to the President, go see him." That's what I thought was needed. It isn't so much the authority to sign off on the part of Eizenstat or Blumenthal but rather the authority to say, "This is what is going in the presidential memo. I'm running this process for the President and we are going to do it this way." Now, everybody tried and we would end up with four or five different options.

EH: You could develop a hypothesis that he liked that because he liked to do his homework or you could say he just simply, for whatever reason, didn't impose order on it--chose not to.

CS: Yeah, that's right. Which one I don't know.

EH: Okay. Either hypothesis is plausible.

CS: In order to impose order you have to resolve to be a little bit of a son-of-a-bitch. There have to be some occasions when you tell a Cabinet officer "no." I may be overstating this particular aspect of it, as I say when you say lack of delegation--that's right--what clearly is needed. Now again you don't want to give Eizenstat the authority to say yes and no ultimately to the final choice, but you do want to give him the authority to manage the process so he has some control. If he abuses it you can chew him out, but some control over how much is going to come in to the President so he is not completely overloaded. Now you may be right, maybe the President wanted that. It is quite possible.

EH: Did you ever hear him complain about having too many options?

CS: Yes, he did. Either too many or too much but whether that was because some days you don't feel good and you mumble about things like that. If he really meant it, I don't know.

EH: Did you also perceive that he did the work? That he read the papers?

CS: Oh, yes. But there is a limit. God knows, it's a matter of human energy, but towards the end of the day, there is a limit to how much you can really absorb. He did it. And he was not a person as far as I know who stayed up until two or three in the morning. He worked solid and hard and had very good work habits. He particularly used to work quietly alone in the morning--come in at six and work until nine or something like that, or eight, before he started the day.

EH: It is clear, isn't it, that Eizenstat would have been the person?

CS: Oh yes, clear.

EH: Even in economic policy?

CS: Well, no. Again, it seems to me, there would have always been problems around the edges, but I would say that the ideal way to have done it was simply to give more authority to the structure that was already there, the basic structure. On fundamentally economic things, it should go to the core of EPG headed by the Secretary of the Treasury, and on domestic policy, to Eizenstat. You always have some little friction as to what goes where but that is not critical. I think you can settle that.

EH: What would you say were the principal economic policy initiatives across the four years?

CS: Well, it depends on how you define economic, but clearly the initial one was (a) the so-called stimulus package, (b) energy, and (c) the tax reform/tax cut of 1978. Let's take as a separate one the whole incomes policy and relate it to the last two years of fighting the inflationary problem both on the incomes policy and the fiscal front. Let me add to that, energy and you can break energy into two parts: one was the initial energy program and the second was decontrol. Obviously I should throw into this the whole regulatory reform.

EH: Were there any persistent underlying themes?

CS: Clearly the major concerns of economic policy changed from stimulus to inflation fighting. One description that would apply to many areas is "middle of the road," i.e., if you compare the Carter regulatory reform in the non-economic (environmental) area with Reagan's, it is middle of the road. There was a lot of emphasis in the last two years of Carter on getting at the budget, but when you compare that with Reagan it is middle of the road. The one area where we were not middle of the road was in economic deregulation. It was a fairly radical change. In my judgment, at least, it was both politically and economically successful. The implication is not that this is the way to do anything else.

EH: You have talked about the dilemma of this fiscal conservative who was beholden to a constituency, a party of liberal constituencies making lots of demands. How did this manifest itself? Did it manifest itself in lots of little bits and pieces of micro policy, but how about the big macro issues, too?

CS: One way to characterize it that I haven't thought about until just now is in the macro area. We went against our traditional constituencies in the last two years, particularly shown by the fact that despite its being the middle of a presidential primary (when it wasn't all that sure that it was a shoo-in for Jimmy Carter) and later on in the general election, we had no tax cut, even in the middle of a recession, in the middle of an election year, and no significant budget expansion. It was a very conservative non-constituency oriented campaign, both the primary and the general election, coupled, however, in those last two years with the continued, understandable inability on little micro issues to say no.

EH: In the micro issues was it a question of the President's not having criteria by which to take a stand?

CS: The answer to that is yes and no. On substantive grounds, generally, the President wanted to be tight: on farm price supports, on regulatory reform, on the environmental side; he wanted to be fairly tough despite constituency interests. The problem was by what criteria did you decide case after case, since you can't thumb your nose at your constituencies all the time. You have to have some balance. What criteria do you use for that balance? And there is where I don't think we had any; I'm not sure any exist. It isn't that there is something nice and obvious sitting out there....

EH: Even the orthodoxies that most economists would subscribe to were not helpful.

CS: Well, it wasn't so much that. That might give you the substantive answers, looked at from an economist's standpoint. But that doesn't tell you where you come down as president when you are doing a lot of things. So one day it was the liberal solution, give a little and satisfy our constituents, and the next day we have to be tough because we are fighting inflation. It is a little hard to figure out in advance "which day—which way" and that may be inherent in the nature of that particular time and game and place and everything else. I don't know what the politico-economic criteria should have been.

EH: That was a hard time for a Democrat to be president, wasn't it?

CS: In my judgment, that's right. Very much so. Possibly if he had been Hubert Humphrey, he would have played that game quite differently.

EH: Right. A Humphrey or Udall would have been more in tune with the constituency.

CS: Right. On the other hand, you know, where would you have been in substance?

EH: Could anything have been done differently on the inflation front to have reduced the political damage the President eventually suffered?

CS: Hindsight. I think it would have been worth taking a bigger risk--again, this would have been a problem with the constituency--having an explicit tough incomes policy earlier, and being willing to be "presidentially unfair." I mean by this, again from hindsight, we never did have a nice dramatic steel confrontation, I don't mean steel per se. Why? It turns out that everytime something like that came up the rules of this game were almost always set by the accountants and lawyers. The company which was presumably doing something wrong could really tell you, "Well, it isn't that open and shut, Mr. President. Fred Kahn tells you we are violating the guidelines but you press him hard and he will admit that there is at least some chance that his interpretation is wrong." Is the evidence 85 percent and to hell with it, Company X or whoever, you violated the guidelines. You, or a given union, are going to get presidentially excoriated. We needed to be more willing to take a real risk to heat it up and stir up the animals, taking a risk when somebody is going to accuse you of being unfair, when in fact, the evidence is never 100 percent anyway in these sorts of things. How much good a tough incomes policy would have done in the face of an oil price explosion, I am not sure. The problem with that is that in the case of the big explosion in oil prices that came along just about this time, a highly successful program of this type would not have kept inflation from rising, and only an econometrician could say (and I wouldn't trust them to tell you), "Well, if you hadn't done that you would have had so much more inflation." So what does a president do when a highly successful policy keeps the increase of inflation down (instead of going from 6 to 9 percent it went from 6 to 8). In the real world no president has been able to point and say, "Look how successful I was." At least if he tries it they are going to laugh at him. So having gone through all this, yes, I think we could have done better, but I don't think anybody really believed that we would have done better.

EH: It doesn't do any good to say, "The English are worse off..."

CS: Oh, we always say that. We have been writing speeches saying that 50,000 times, but the proof of the pudding is that it's much easier to say, "Look how much worse off. Were you better off than you were four years ago?"

EH: Did Carter undertake to persuade people that his economic policies made sense?

CS: No. I have a lot of admiration for the guy on some things. It seems to me in this particular case, however, he could have done a much better job particularly during the campaign.

He could have done a much better job but it still would have
been a very difficult job. He would still have been on the
defensive and indicating the rationality of his economic
program, not the success of it, because unfortunately success
is absolute and success in damage limitation in this particular case is in doing a much better defensive job. Maggie
Thatcher came in clearly at the height of an inflation. You
can say that it is going to be difficult and painful as hell
to get it down. Let me tell you it is much harder to take an
inflation that has gotten worse while you were there. It is
going to be a difficult thing and painful to get it down.
Yes, he could have done better, but even a genius would have
been operating under some difficulty.

December 5, 1983

Reconstructing Policy Decisions

SM: Why don´t we start with the stimulus package that you came
into 1977 with--maybe you could just summarize the way you
decided on it and what its main provisions were.

CS: You are obviously at this stage interested in more or less
the pure substance of it, not the interesting sidelights of
who struck John--that´s not your main interest, I presume.

SM: I would say not the main, except it´s relevant to what you
decided and what you had to forego.

CS: Let´s see. I think there were three or four major strands.
(a) Fairly general agreement, right or wrong, that under the
then current policy, the recovery would be too slow, therefore we needed some "stimulus." (b) A strong view on my part
(which I pushed as hard as anybody else--but I don´t want to
say I was the only one) that, particularly given Carter´s
position on tax reform which we thought was clearly going to
require tax cuts as well later--permanent tax cuts, we did
not want to give away any more permanent revenue loss than we
had to. The combination of those two led to the idea of the
rebate which, of course, had been tried and, on what I
thought at least was relatively decent economic ground, was
found to have been somewhat effective in ´75. So that was
one part. Secondly, although I cannot recall exactly the
timing of all these elements, it was clear that the traditional idea particularly on the part of the Congress (Jim
Wright, Tip O´Neil and the like) that we have to spend our
way out of this led to some substantial pressure for putting
in some accelerated public works as part of this. And my aim
on that was to keep that as small as possible, knowing that
it was impossible to kill it. There was a lot of back and
forth on exactly how to do that. My recollection is that we
had sold Carter on keeping it to a two billion dollar public
works package and, in a session with the Congressional lead-

ers at Plains before the inauguration, he agreed to put another two billion dollars in but with some kind of contingency
concept that you would not necessarily use it until you saw
what the economy was doing. The third strand that evolved
was something that Ray Marshall--more or less over my objec-
tions--when I say more or less I don't think that I objected
to all of it but I objected to the emphasis on it--had a
fairly sizable public service employment program and additional spending on training and the like. Fourth, sometime
fairly early on after the election, Larry Woodworth, who had
agreed to come over from being the chief of the Joint Internal Revenue Taxation Committee to be the Assistant Secretary
of the Treasury for Taxes, came to a meeting and very much
impressed Carter with his arguments for a particular revision
in the tax code which I have forgotten by now but it had to
do with taxation on lower income which amounted to a three to
four billion dollar a year revenue component that was permanent. Carter bought that so you then had the initial idea of
a temporary stimulus tacked on to a public works program,
mainly on congressional initiative, the public service employment part mainly under Marshall...

SM: That's different than the part that the Congress supported?

CS: Yes, they were interested in it, but their big interest was
in public works projects, widely spread--everybody gets a
little bit--spent three years later. Although they did get
the grants distributed pretty quickly this time; they did a
good job on that. In any event it got to be that four-part
package, and the idea then was the negotiation among all
parties back and forth about how big each one was, partly
before inauguration and partly after. We finally came back to
Carter with a package which (finally having done overall
macro economics of) had, I think, an eleven billion dollar
rebate. One other element got into this. Somebody came
along with the idiotic idea you've got to do something for
small business. Some people, and I am fairly sure I was one
of them, wanted a modest improvement in depreciation allowances for some investment incentives. Then along came the
idea we had to do something for small business and there was
a countervailing proposal which was a very small credit on
employer taxes for the employer's share of the payroll tax.
That was a small amount, around a billion. We couldn't get
agreement on it, and I finally came up with the brilliant
suggestion to give people an option, and the small businessman with less capital could take the payroll tax deduction
and the others could take depreciation, and it will cost you
a little bit more, but not a lot more unless we get an
argument about it. We adopted that rather idiotic proposition, so we really had a fifth element. In the early stages
of this exercise, we were doing a lot of the calculations
first with some of the transition team. We had been working
on costing out the employment part of this--the public service employment--and secondly with Barry Bosworth and I work-

ing on the back of an envelope and then gradually getting control of the CEA´s machinery trying hastily to do economic impacts, revenue impacts, cranking those into the budget, and all this business.

SM: Now the economy was already in the middle of an expansion—— why did you feel that you needed more push?

CS: Well, as of the latter part of 1976, there was a lull, partly abated later but not completely. Unemployment stopped going down, the economy grew slowly for a couple of quarters, and then it began to go up with a fairly substantial pace again, just about January. But if you look at the last six months—— really from the second to the fourth quarter——of 1976 on then unrevised numbers, there was a lull, and there was probably an excessively ambitious view at the time that you could, without pushing too far at the other end, go up steeper and then settle down. And to that you´ve got to add the straight, raw political fact of life that Carter had based a big chunk of his campaign on getting the economy moving again.

SM: What was Carter´s position on the packages?

CS: Like most presidents, and politicians, they like micro econo- mics and don´t like macro economics. Macro economic concepts are foreign; you cannot get your hands on them. Carter was, in the long run, a fiscal conservative. My impression was he realized that he was the leader of the Democratic party, and they all told him he had to do these things which meant a bigger deficit. He wasn´t sure he liked that. He would go along with it; he liked the idea of making the tax cut only temporary at first. But the idea of the rebate really grated on him, I think. It was like giving somebody something for nothing. I don´t think he ever said that. I think he was talked into that by me, his macro economist, more than any- thing else. He immediately liked the idea of the employment programs. It would get people back to work in a way you could see concretely. But he was no great enthusiast for public works, and I agreed with him. He played a straight political role on that, but he was not pushing that. He did like the Ray Marshall program. You could see his eyes light up when Ray would go into all this stuff about putting people to work and training them, and giving them work skills and all these marvelous things you could do. So, on a more general basis, Carter, in his first two years was a fiscal conservative who (in the first year particularly) was going along with deliberately beefing up the deficit because he guessed he had to. He turned with more conviction to auster- ity during his last two or two and one-half years, even though it was much messier. Even though it was a lot tougher politically, it suited his own inherent views better.

SM: Was there a concern about inflation at this time?

CS: Of course, but less so than later, there was less inflation.
We were always, in terms of an anti-inflationary program, six
months to a year behind the game. At the same set of meetings at which economic policy had been decided, it was agreed
(and I was the one who finally gave voice to it) that we
didn't want stand-by wage and price controls. We did give a
lot of lip-service to all sorts of micro stuff and voluntary
incomes policies, but never did much about it until later and
were always too afraid to tackle organized labor on this. We
always were six months behind, were always too late. Initially Marshall and some of the others sold the President on
the idea that incomes policy was a dirty word and guidelines
were dirty words and all that, so to whatever extent they
would have done any good, they were late. There was a lot of
experience in the Nixon years and controls weren't a very
good idea. All standby controls are going to do is possibly
make you subject to more inflation, to the extent that there
was discretion in pushing up prices, you get more of it as
people position themselves. I remember explicitly there was
a big debate back and forth between the businessmen and Larry
Klein and a few of the other more liberal economists and the
President. By that time I think he probably knew he was
going to ask me to be CEA chairman, as he turned to me and
said, "What do you think?" In the meantime I had been waf-
fling on the subject, but finally I had to come down and say,
"Don't put in anything like standby wage and price controls.
It's not an easy call, but don't do it." I had a feeling I
was right. Guidelines are a Democratic president's problem,
among others--he's always scared to take on organized labor,
and when we finally did do guidelines--which I think worked
for a while, they were late and they weren't tough enough--
and then we blew them up ourselves the next year.

SM: By that time things were a little out of control anyway so it
was pretty difficult. But do you regret the failure to ask
for standby controls?

CS: No, I don't regret that. I don't think we would have used
them. I was against them all the way through. And if you're
not going to use them then having them there in a period in
which inflation is just going to go up is just an invitation
to a businessman to raise prices, which means either use them
or don't use them.

SM: Yes, particularly when a lot of this inflation was supply
side stuff and it's not obvious how to handle the controls
anyway. There's no doubt about that. What was Blumenthal's
position on that original stimulus package?

CS: I don't remember any major dissents. You have to remember
Blumenthal was a quick learner, but he came into this never
having played in the macro policy game so he felt his way for
a while. And I don't blame him. And hence, while I have

strong recollections of his later views, I don't have any strong recollections of that time. I'm sure he had them. Mike was seldom reticent.

SM: What was the position of business leaders?

CS: I don't know. Business leaders, like almost everyone else, disliked the rebate. I think the only person in town who liked a rebate was Charlie Schultze. Earlier it was always me selling the idea...I exaggerate somewhat. I had a fixed idea in my own head that you didn't want to give up those long run revenues until you were ready. But I didn't want a lot of stimulus occurring later.

SM: But all the economists say temporary things are what you want.

CS: But all the Congress hated it. For some reason it struck them as immoral. You just hand a fifty dollar check to people. That's terrible! Very peculiar, really. There's something about attaching something to it. However, a permanent tax cut is understandable. Also there is a good chunk of inchoate supply side ideas mixed up with this; that is, if you structure the tax cut right, you can get good things out of it, but a fifty dollar rebate, well, that's immoral. It was intriguing. There was a legitimate economic question as to the marginal propensity to consume out of windfall income, but that wasn't really the issue. In any case, everybody heaved a sigh of relief except me, I think, when it was gone. That's not true, Mondale and Eizenstat fought for it, but I mean you got a sense that people were glad to get rid of this thing.

SM: When was it finally dropped?

CS: April, very quickly, mainly because inflation temporarily heated up in the early part of 1977. You may remember that in 1976 (between December and December) food prices actually dropped. I remember that there was a 4.8 percent CPI inflation rate while in fact the underlying rate was near 6 to 6.5 percent. Depends on how you measure it. Otto Eckstein's measurement was even higher. A lot of that was a temporary drop in food prices as farmers sold off their herds. Unfortunately because we got that in 1976, in 1978 we got a big burst of inflation. You could say that Richard Nixon four or five years later murdered Jimmy Carter, i.e., what Nixon did with those beef price controls got cattlemen to the point where quite literally, if you look at the chart on herds, it's incredible. In any event, what happened in early 1977 was that we got a flurry of inflation which was mainly food prices. Some of it was a permanent pickup, i.e., you're just picking up what was temporary and what wasn't there anyway. And there was additionally a flurry on food prices and the economy was doing well and it was clear there were going to be large political credits that would have had to have been used up to get the rebate. Even Hubert Humphrey apparently called (I don't remember the details on this) and in effect said, "For God's sake, drop it." Both Bert Lance and Blumenthal, I think independently, began to have qualms about it and went to Carter; and then I remember we had a big debate around the table with Carter one day and we dropped it. From hindsight I don't think it either hurt or helped; I can't say it made a big difference.

SM: It wasn't an enormous revenue measure under the best of circumstances.

CS: Eleven billion dollars, in current dollars now maybe twenty; but it wasn't nothing. The one thing that was clear, however, and should have been from foresight for a good politician, was that there were a lot of people who really didn't like it but who had taken a political position on it to please Carter. Then the first thing he did was suddenly to reverse course. I know Muskie was absolutely outraged.

SM: Because he left Muskie out on a limb?

CS: Two things: he left him out on a limb and he didn't discuss it with him. All kinds of people who wouldn't have given you two cents for the rebate either were left out on a limb or began to think, "Well, this guy, you can't count on him." From that standpoint it was bad news. If we wanted to drop it we should have done a lot more homework.

SM: Did you lose a lot of political capital with Carter over the thing?

CS: I don't know. It's hard to know how much I had anyway.

SM: You happened to be in office at a time when the economy was going right up towards full employment and you didn't have a whole lot of leeway for a lot of spending programs.

CS: Plus the fact that sectorally you probably expanded the non-defense civilian sector of the federal government as much as the popular will was going to let you expand it. So (a) on a macro economic fiscal policy basis you have to move into austerity and (b) from a long-term share of government basis you have to move towards finally saying, no more net new programs or at least not many; if you give one you have to take one, and the two together get all mixed up. It's great for Ronald Reagan in one sense. He didn't have to make any choice. And poor Jimmy Carter, who was not the world's greatest politician anyway, got stuck with this tremendous problem that I don't think any Democrat could have solved.

SM: It reminds me, did you even consider (this is not so relevant at this point as later) the role that monetary policy was supposed to play?

CS: Initially we wanted to be accommodating.

SM: How much slack did you think you had in the economy at this point in early 1977?

CS: At the time several things had happened. (1) Greenspan, just before we got there, had semi-officially recalculated the high employment GNP at a five percent unemployment rate instead of four. They had a new estimate of full employment and we reluctantly came around to accept that.

SM: Over the time in the CEA Report you kept adjusting the full employment/unemployment rate upwards.

CS: In the first year.

SM: You kept adjusting it upwards and reducing downward the full employment output level.

CS: You have to remember at the time how much slack I thought I had. I wasn't sure but it became clear to us by the end of 1978, which made it too late, that not so much the level of unemployment but the speed with which it had come down was a problem. We had an argument among ourselves whether it was a speed limit problem as well as a level problem and we pretty well reached the conclusion that one of the problems in late 1978 (it wasn't a massive problem) was that we had pulled the rate of unemployment down too fast. Back in 1977 we still thought we had a good bit of room. And I still think we had some.

SM: But in fact if you look at the GDP deflator, it's already creeping up. All the way through 1976 and 1977.

CS: The GDP deflator and Eckstein's core rate of inflation still has farm prices in it. My recollection is that you actually got some relative energy price cuts. Relative at that time. And if you look at Eckstein's core rate, it does not look like that; it's pretty flat.

SM: What was Burn's position on the stimulus package?

CS: I am sure he was far from enthusiastic; my general impression is he went out of his way without ever doing anything explicitly to indicate, as far as he was concerned, the less of this we had the better.

SM: Now, I take it that there wasn't a whole lot of explicit coordination with the Fed.

CS: No, no. Not with Burns. Much more with Volcker. Even

though Volcker did some things I disagreed with, but in terms of talking to him about it, much more communication.

SM: Do you think that a greater degree of coordination makes sense; do you think that Burns was right, that coordination...

CS: No, I think it depends on what you mean by coordination. If you mean really talking together frankly, it makes great sense. Sometimes people mean more formal mechanisms. If you ask me how we might coordinate, let me give an example. In March of 1980 we went back up to the Congress (our budget having been there only two months) and said rewrite the budget. Volcker sat in on all the major decision sessions on that, and he gave and he took. But you never had to worry; he wasn't posturing.

SM: That is different. It would be my impression as an outsider that that's different than had been the case under Burns.

CS: That's correct.

SM: In writing about the need for a stimulus package in January of 1978 in that CEA Report, you forecast a slowdown by late 1978. Again the expectation was that the economy, if left alone, was going to slow down. But in fact 1978 was a boom year, despite the rise in farm prices. Do you feel that you were over-forecasting the degree of slowdown in the economy?

CS: Some, yes. My own view is that in 1978 we probably added, by excessive demand stimulus, perhaps one-half percent, perhaps a bit more and one percent to the rate of inflation. And that was a mistake. But in the context of going from what I considered to be core 6 percent to core 10 percent rate, that stimulus was a relatively modest part of it; yet it was probably a fatal mistake. We would have been better from hindsight to have played it slower. Our program probably was right in terms of our own forecast, i.e., if we had gotten what we'd forecast we probably would have been right in asking it. My recollection is that we were surprised on the upside. I haven't gone back and looked. I was surprised about the strength in the upside.

SM: If you read the CEA Reports, that is what it looks like. There is a continual surprise about the underlying strength of the economy, in the face of really fairly massive shocks that should have slowed it way down. In thinking about it now, do you have any reasons, do you understand what might explain that unexpected strength in the economy?

CS: No, I haven't gone back and analyzed it.

SM: Or the failure of the forecast, I guess, is the other question?

484

CS: You have to put all this in context. Where we really failed in the forecast was on inflation. My recollection in going back and looking at the forecast is that the main times we got in trouble on the forecast were when we redid the originals. If you go back and look at the January forecasts for each year, they weren't bad on real activity; they were bad on inflation. It is the ones we did in the mid-years that were excessively optimistic. For example, in 1980 we forecast a recession, then in March we proposed the revised budget and pushed up our forecast again. We forecast more activity. My memory is unclear here, but the thing I do remember is explicitly going back and looking at the annual forecasts. They were not bad if you didn't take into account the mid-year ones, or the special ones.

SM: In 1979, as I remember, you forecast a slowdown, but of course that was before all the oil shocks, so in fact you were about right except that there was this enormous amount of constraint imposed by higher oil prices.

CS: I think it was in mid-year 1979 we forecast implicitly a recession which we didn't get.

SM: You had this continual thing, and that turns out to be important, I guess, in your deciding what mix of policies to use.

CS: I think the big decision, which was more an implicit decision than anything else, was not to use demand policy sufficiently to offset the oil shock enough to keep it from getting built into inflation, because it would have cost us very substantially in unemployment. We hoped to rely more on incomes policy to control inflation, but I think we may have kidded ourselves to some extent about it. When faced with a difficult trade-off, whichever way you go in a trade-off, you probably kid yourself you're going to get a better trade-off. Just as I think the Fed kidded itself in 1981 and 1982 about how bad the trade-off was going to be in one way. We kidded ourselves probably the other way.

SM: You mean there are two ways to go, one is the incredibly severe sharp slowdown in 1975 and 1981, but you understandably opted for a different sort of package.

CS: Well, a somewhat different one. Yes. In order to avoid the supply shock inflation from getting built into inflation you have to do exactly the same thing you have to do to wring out inflation once you have got it. And when I say we chose that, I don't think it ever became an explicit choice. At least in that administration, it wasn't. Nobody was really arguing to be Draconian enough to do what would have had to be done to keep that inflation rate from rising.

SM: How did you think you were going to control inflation? How were you going to keep the oil shock from getting imbedded in higher inflation rates?

CS: I thought we were trying importantly to do it through the incomes policy. Also by late 1978 and into 1979, the emphasis became austerity. The budget submitted in January 1979 was very different from the budget submitted a year earlier. I no longer remember specifics but it was sure supposed to be. This was a matter of degree. And you know (you have to face up to it, I guess) from hindsight it was probably a little bit of closing one's eyes. There is a human tendency (when faced with a difficult choice, and having made it part way) possibly not to spell out the full horrors to yourself. Probably something of that in there, even though I never recall having done that consciously; it probably has to be there.

SM: It must have been very difficult because when you talked to Carter at that time, all the news was bad. And the choices were very unattractive.

CS: Nobody, but nobody was willing to say quite explicitly, yes, we are going to force the unemployment rate up.

SM: I would think it more difficult for a Democratic administration to do that.

CS: Sure, but I say "no" administration. Now they may let it happen, you know; I mean, obviously we all do. We did. In 1980 with the recession, absolutely no stimulus, no nothing. But to sit there in 1979, not facing "natural" recession, simply facing an increase in oil prices, do you then tighten up in conjunction with the automatic tightening you get from that to the point of forcing a recession so that you won't get the inflation? We never considered it.

SM: Did you consider using the Fed? This gets back to this coordination with the Fed: one way to take the heat off yourself would be to have the Fed do it, since they are more insulated from the political process.

CS: For a short period, at the turn of the year in 1978-79, Blumenthal and I carried on a leaked campaign in the press to try to pressure Miller into tightening up. There were leaked stories about how administration officials think the Fed ought to tighten up—normally it's the other way around—and we got a very nasty note from the President at one time in effect saying, lay off. Democratic presidents, even fiscal conservatives, are also populist on interest rates. But there was a period (it could have lasted two to three months) in early 1979 when we thought the economy was going too fast and monetary policy was too easy. I remember explicitly on a Saturday morning sitting down on a background basis with John

Berry of the <u>Washington Post</u> and just laying it all out, the basis on which the President blew up.

SM: That´s got to be one of the only times in all of the record that we have of the CEA in which the CEA chairman is actually asking the Fed to slow down.

CS: At least under a Democratic president.

SM: No, I think under any administration.

CS: And then, of course, late in 1978, together with the Fed, we engineered the dollar rescue operation which included a tightening of money. And in 1979 when Volcker did his famous revolution. While I was dead set against it, I very much agreed he had to do something dramatic on interest rates. I wanted him to do something dramatic on conventional policy.

SM: What did you want him to do?

CS: Raise interest rates. I didn´t want him to adopt, to go to a monetarist set of targets. In other words, I wanted him to continue to target interest rates, in effect, just raise them a lot, at least by historical standards.

SM: But didn´t his policy have somewhat the same effect?

CS: Oh sure, except that once he got himself into monetarist rhetoric, it took him a very long time to be able to bow out. And if you convince the world that virtue consists in sticking with those money targets, even when they don´t make sense, then you have a hard time getting out of it, and he did. He finally did. But we went through more than we needed to, and in late 1981 and into 1982, incredible interest rates in the middle of the recession, partly on that account. Now, the response to that, which is perfectly valid, is that what monetarism really is for the Fed (and I´m morally certain this is what Volcker thinks, too) a political cover. They´re not monetarists, but it allowed them to do what they could never have done. They may be right from a broad political standpoint and I was wrong. They could never have done what had to be done if it looked as if they were the ones raising interest rates, when they were targeting interest rates, per se. But with fixed monetary targets they could just say, "Who, us? There´s nobody here but us chickens. We´re just keeping the money supply within bounds. The market´s driving the interest rate up." That let them do what might have otherwise been impossible, and I must admit that from that standpoint it made sense. I just think (a) the system is wrong, and (b) they overdid it. But politically the old system might not have been able to stand what would have had to be done.

SM: In 1978 you started with a new round of inflation. What

caused it; was it excess demand?

CS: Otto Eckstein has explicitly gone back to try to look at this. There were three elements although one of them I suspect in 1978 was small. One was that meat prices just went up tremendously. Allen Blinder has a very nice piece which takes that period apart. It's a history of inflation from 1973 to 1980. And my recollection is if you look at Eckstein and Blinder on this, a very small amount was demand inflation, but there was some though not a lot. I don't remember what their numbers were. My guess is it would be a good bit less than one percent, but it may be as much as one percent. There was a massive run up in meat prices in late 1978 (I think it was late '78). That made a big difference, and then there was also the effect of government actions, something we used to jump up and down about all the time, but I doubt now if the quantitative significance was that much. There were a lot of things coming on such as regulatory policy and minimum wages. Now Bob Gordon insists that that was very important. But my recollection of the numbers was that in no one year was it important. But it contributed.

SM: It's hard to imagine that regulation could cause such a big sharp jump up.

CS: Well, it depends on from what. From 1976 it was. You take the underlying rate at 6 to 7 percent. My recollection is by the end of 1978 we had something less than 7 percent inflation. Take the meat prices...

SM: You are speaking of the core rate of inflation and I am thinking of the GDP deflator. You really get a big jump up in the CPI, which is going to end up getting into wages, sometime, if you don't do something about it.

CS: That's right.

SM: Yet in the 1979 report, you still were making an effort to show that there was slack. What I'm interested in is whether at the time you didn't perceive it as an excess demand situation?

CS: No, except, I think in the January 1979 Report you will see recognition tentatively on our part that we may have violated a speed limit. Also, I remember struggling for hours over a paragraph which implied recognition that you sure couldn't get much lower than 6 percent unemployment. You have to remember that all this time we'd been negotiating with the left wing of the Democrats on the Humphrey-Hawkins bill, who had been trying to get us to endorse 4 percent unemployment as a goal. But my recollection is that in the January 1979 Report there were two things. One was the recognition of the speed limit; it was pretty delicate, that we'd overshot, and it was going to be very hard to get any lower than a 6 percent unemployment. Again, without ever saying that explicitly.

SM: Even though I believe that the full employment, unemployment rate was still calculated at around 5 percent at that point.

CS: If you look at the original Greenspan Council's calculation, which in effect is still used, the rate is 5.1 percent. It is a complicated, demographic calculation, and they explicitly say it doesn't tell you what the rate of unemployment is at which inflation starts accelerating. It is not a natural rate (or whatever you want to call it). But we stay away from that. You will find most Economic Reports of the President were fairly vague in that. For very obvious reasons, we were reluctant to come down and put a number on it.

SM: What were the policy responses that you took in the beginning of `78 to cope with inflation--for example, the April package?

CS: My recollection is that the only thing that was really in the April package (but my memory is vague on this) was this attempt to come up with a somewhat more concrete incomes policy with the concept of "deceleration." It was Barry Bosworth's very clever way of getting around numerical guidelines, i.e., at the moment, there was an insuperable administration reluctance to go for numerical wage guidelines. The deceleration idea was that people had generally gotten out of line with each other and, where they had, we could not do much about it. And so if everybody decelerated this rate of wage and price increases, leaving aside for the moment the question of ultimate income realignments, inflation would generally move down. Since we wanted to get a deceleration of wages and prices, we had to make noises about how those who had gotten the most ought to decelerate the most. It was a fairly clever way of trying to have guidelines without a specific number, but of course it was too vague. We preached and promoted and jumped up and down, but with little effect.

SM: Was that when you set up the Council on Wage and Price Stability?

CS: No, that had been there for years. That was when we put Bob Strauss in as the President's inflation adviser. We were trying to use "Mr. Negotiator" to help us negotiate some of this stuff. And then in October 1978 we went to full blown numerical guidelines. That was when Kahn came in.

SM: At that point were you talking about coordinated monetary and fiscal policy, about using more restraints to slow down spending?

CS: We had already submitted a budget, and we were not about to pull it back. I'm sure we made noises about restraint and all of this, and I think at that time we weren't pushing the Fed to ease. But at the time (my recollection is in early 1978), it was our feeling that the problem of inflation wasn't fundamentally a demand problem. We didn't see it warranting any additional slack in the economy.

SM: To change the budget, I presume, would be regarded as a tremendously severe action.

CS: And I have a vague recollection that the real speed up of inflation in 1978 came later in the year as meat prices heated up.

SM: That isn't the way it looks from the GDP deflator. It's the second quarter, the spring.

CS: This was April; we didn't know the GDP deflator until July. And while I am very fuzzy, my recollection is it was later than this and even then we didn't latch on to the idea; we still did not agree (that is, I didn't agree) by late 1978 that the level of activity was too high. We did come around to the "speed limit" idea, but it was only late in the year, trying to ask ourselves why what happened occurred, because there was a creep up in the core inflation rate speed limit. And what we did was not pulling unemployment down to too low a level, although we probably couldn't get any lower. I think we knocked a full percentage point off in a year. I mean if you're at 7 percent and take it to 6 percent. In fact, we reduced unemployment by 1-3/4 points in two years.

SM: If you look at it in terms of capacity utilization, which is another way of measuring inflationary pressure, you were getting up there around 85-86 percent capacity utilization, so, from that point of view, you were getting awfully close to a turning point where inflation would accelerate.

CS: That's right, but it was our judgment, right or wrong, that we were not at any excessive level, but we pretty well had to flatten out so we did not go too fast.

SM: Your idea of what you were going to do was just a slight pullback?

CS: Yes. Again, I no longer remember what we forecast for growth in 1979, but I would doubt it was a lot more than the potential.

SM: That's where you said that from this point on the only thing we can do is grow with the potential of the economy and that's going to be around 3 percent, as I remember.

CS: Something like that. Whatever it was, I can't remember, but much slower.

SM: Much slower rate. This is a new world. Did you think of trying to bring in the Fed to help slow down the economy since you obviously couldn't change tax rates in the middle of the year?

CS: Again, we didn't think we were overdoing it until late 1978 and early 1979. That's the point. It is true that late in 1978 and early 1979 we explicitly thought that the Fed was too easy. We tried to get them to change, but undercover. We never went out and had a public fight with them. That was in late 1978, early 1979. It may have been that we did not start until January, it may have started in December, but it only lasted for about two months or so, until the President decided he wanted no more of that.

SM: How did you expect the guidelines to work? Was there any evidence that excessive wage settlements were causing the upsurge in inflation?

CS: No, it wasn't so much that. Again, you see, we did not think of it as an upsurge in core inflation. We were trying to get inflation down. And the whole point of this was to decelerate the rate of wage increases. Not because they'd been responsible. In fact, there were some areas where they had gone ahead. But as a general proposition, you couldn't argue that real wages had been running ahead of where they should have. But it was just a momentum going. This was our way of hoping we could ease the core rate of inflation down. If everybody decelerates, nobody will lose; that was the idea. Now what happened, of course, is we no sooner got that promulgated and fighting through all sorts of nitty-gritty on it, when the oil thing blows up on us. Obviously when you get a blow-up in oil prices, labor has to take it in the neck, but that's hardly solving the problem. What we had been telling them (not thinking about oil prices) was play ball and you won't lose. Now we're telling them play ball with us, and by the way, if there is a price increase, don't get it back in your wages. And that becomes a much tougher game. Now, in addition, we were faced with many other problems. First thing we did, once you go into guidelines, you have to be somewhat specific about how you cost out settlements. How do you judge in advance a settlement with a cost of living clause (COLA)? You obviously can't judge how big a wage increase there will be until you price out the COLA, at some assumed rate of inflation. Well, the lower the assumed rate of inflation, the smaller that settlement looks. And hence in 1978, but particularly in 1979, that got to be a massive bone of contention. It gave an unfair advantage to organized labor over everybody else, when we agreed to price the COLA out at a rate of inflation that was obviously too low. This meant that if you then calculated wage increases based on what you really thought inflation was going to be, they could meet the guidelines and still have a juicy contract. That became a massive problem, partly in 1978, but mainly in 1979 and 1980. The guidelines, I think, had some restraining effect in 1978 and 1979. It does turn out that in the U.S. (I think I´m right on this) oil shock, real wages absorbed the loss that they had to absorb faster than in most other countries. That is a generally valid phenomenon comparing U.S. and Europe; the workers of Europe keep up with the cost of living much more quickly and regularly than our workers do. The main point is that since we did not see the core rate accelerating very much, we wanted both (a) to try to prevent any of that acceleration from happening and (b) to pull the rate of inflation down. And then when we were hit with the oil shock, we had this whole problem of how to isolate that shock.

SM: Democratic administrations have been charged with being too soft on inflation. And because of their constituencies they do have a problem with anti-inflationary measures. Do you think that would be a fair criticism of the Carter administration?

CS: Well, up until Ronald Reagan came along, I guess so. Sure. Let me put it another way. If you actually look back at it, you get a mixed record. For example, Richard Nixon pump-primed and inflation-be-damned in 1972. The Federal Reserve in 1972 had the largest rate of increase in the money supply we had seen for a long time. Eisenhower, on the other hand, was much more cautious. Kennedy was cautious. In terms of rhetoric, you´re right. In terms of actual performance, when the chips are down especially in election years, it´s a mixed bag. As a general proposition Democrats find it a lot harder to cut spending. Democrats tend to be more populist on interest rates. But when both parties sit down and take a cold evaluation of what they really are willing to do in an election year or in two years, to deal with inflation, different presidents have different records and it´s a mixed bag. Probably the best was Harry Truman. In a sense, he wasn´t all that successful, but Harry, by God, went to a tax increase even in 1949 in a recession. He immediately got two tax increases to finance the Korean War. He had one bad year of inflation, but he hit it in the head. Eisenhower was pretty good; Kennedy was good; Johnson was good up until Vietnam, then he wasn´t any good. Nixon was no good on it when the chips were down. Carter overdid it. Our trade-off was, from hindsight, not austere enough. With Reagan, it has really been Volcker who has done it, not fiscal policy. Now what Reagan did was to sit still for Volcker. Jimmy Carter might well not have done that—although I can´t be sure.

SM: Is it because you weren´t willing to take drastic measures; in other words, that you really wanted fine-tuned response, that you ended up in this trouble?

CS: Oh, I don´t know how fine tuned a response it was. I guess somebody could argue we should have taken really drastic action, and it wouldn't have been so drastic later. One could make that argument.

SM: You could compare the 1974 and 1975 response with your response.

CS: I don't think it was our response, I just think it was timing on that. I don't think our response would have been any different. If Jimmy Carter had been president, you would have had in 1981 and 1982 a fairly sizable recession. It would have been less than we got, but what would have happened is we would not have come in with any big tax cuts. Unlike Reagan, we would have been fiscally austere. The Fed would have been tight, but probably not quite so tight. We just don't know how to get rid of inflation without putting the country through the wringer. Carter would have had a recession too, since on the one hand he could not have had a stimulative budget and since he wouldn't have been able to control Volcker. You can't second-guess Volcker when he is the only anti-inflation game in town. My guess is that if Carter had been re-elected, you would have gotten a pretty sizable recession, although I think less than we actually experienced.

SM: Carter was really worried about inflation by this time?

CS: Oh yes. You see he was a fiscal conservative anyway. He would have vetoed a big tax cut for different reasons. I don't think he had a great big grand idea any more than Ronald Reagan has on controlling inflation. He would have been tough on his budget, as he was. But always colored by the fact (and this was a problem with Carter) that when he got down to the nitty-gritty and each of the interest groups of the coalition came in, he'd give a little here and give a little there. So he would never have been able to cut spending as Reagan did, but he would never have cut taxes like that. My guess is you would have had a recession as Volcker leaned on the economy; you would have had a tax cut on business and not so much on individuals so you would have had a much smaller tax cut, but you would have had some. Smaller expenditure cut, too. Smaller defense increase, a tighter budget. No stimulus, or not very much. Probably would have to give in, just as Reagan did, to some kind of public works symbolism. But you would have had a recession. We would have pulled inflation down a little slower and had a little less unemployment, but there would have been a recession. So I don't really think that that's the point....I don't think any president has deliberately chosen to have a recession. The real way each of them has had to face up to the question is that the Fed has done it and then they have to decide the extent to which they're going to fight it with a budget stimulus. Fundamentally, and I'm overstating this but, the Fed let the real money supply fall sharply in 1974. It was very tight and they threw us into a recession. And then the question was do you or do you not have a fiscal stimulus. In 1981, had Carter been re-elected, I'm convinced Volcker would have thrown us into another recession. Volcker's policy would have. It's the only way to get inflation down. And we would have accepted it. It would have been a great stress and I'm glad I wasn't there. A great stress with the administration, and when you start jumping on Volcker publicly, it would have been a terrible time to have been there. My guess is that Volcker, sensing that, wouldn't have gone quite so far. Conversely, we wouldn't have had as much of a stimulative budget as we got with Reagan. So you would be facing a different world now, but you would have gone through a recession.

SM: Yes, it does seem to me that somewhere along there the budget got much more contractionary. The full employment surplus increased.

CS: We were finding out a little bit of the same problem that Mr. Reagan is finding out and with a vengeance. Something which I hadn't realized until very recently is the tremendous leverage of the interest on the debt in periods of both high interest rates and recession. It's scary. None of us realized that. So, we would have submitted a pretty tight budget. We did in 1981 in the outgoing budget. We would have busted that budget by interest expense alone as the deficit got much bigger and interest rates got much higher. But you're right. Remember in January 1980 Carter submitted a budget and then all of a sudden for the first time since I've been around this town, it looked to me as if inflation was getting out of hand. We had temporary rates of 18 percent. I think we actually panicked a little. But that probably did us good. And we then negotiated what now is a piddling change in the budget, but at the time seemed like a very large one, of a $13 billion reduction. It was a very useful performance with the Congress by the way. It is an analogue to the Greenspan Commission's action on Social Security. It is kind of a way of getting some of the advantages of a parliamentary government by precooking some things before you send them up to the Hill. So we precooked for seven straight days, in twelve-hour-a-day sessions with the Democratic congressional leaders. We precooked a package on budget cuts and resubmitted the budget in March of 1980, along with an ill-fated request for a tax on gasoline or energy which would have made a big dent in the deficit.

SM: Was it a wise idea to go back with the budget so soon after you had submitted the other one?

CS: By now, I don't know. Oh, I guess on balance it was. We did some silly things along with it, however. I'll never forgive myself for sitting still for those things. I let some of the political types persuade us that while we were doing so many illiberal things in this package, cutting so much out of spending, putting a tax on energy which would hurt the poor people, all this business--that we should do something liberal. And the something liberal was selected credit controls. What happened was absolutely fascinating. We got the steepest decline in GNP in one quarter in our history, I would guess. Something nobody could ever figure out in advance. The American people felt guilty about using credit, I'm convinced, and as soon as the President said something about credit, they didn't bother to read the regulations, or what they meant. They were actually very mild, but the public just stopped using credit. We had merchants calling in to complain that all their customers thought that the President declared consumer credit illegal, immoral, unpatriotic. There were huge temporary drops in appliance sales. It had an incredible impact on real demand. Interest rates went right down, but then right back up again. It had an incredible impact. It wasn't going to last. It gave us a quicky recession, which didn't do much good.

SM: It did, however, make it appear that you were taking firm steps and there may be something to be said for that.

CS: Maybe.

SM: Did you coordinate with the Fed on that?

CS: Oh, yes, we pulled them kicking and screaming into that. Volcker was there. He had full access to the Councils. He sat with the President while we discussed all this. And he didn't want this. He didn't want those credit controls. But having gotten himself into the process one of the prices of a gentlemen's agreement is that you play by the outcome. You make your case and if you lose you still play good soldier, which he did. But obviously he didn't like them. I was lukewarm, mildly hostile, but not enough to come down hard on it. I think I made a mistake. In any event, we did cut the budget. By the time the Congress got finished with it, the cuts ultimately eroded some. Not only didn't we get the energy tax increase, Congress yanked the President's power-- he had some standby power to put some energy taxes on--they yanked that power. There was a big fight with the Congress on that. Nevertheless, the revised budget was still a good thing to do.

SM: This was a terrible time to have to put the economy into a recession. How much did the political question of the elections dominate thinking at this time?

CS: Carter was very good. I no longer remember the specifics, but about August of 1980 we all wanted an economic program for the second term that would be something for Carter to run on. Also in the mid-year projection of the budget, we wanted him to put in a contingency line on a business tax cut. It was a very complicated argument. On the grounds that if it was a modest, business oriented tax cut, we ought to do it or be prepared to do it. I forget the details. He said no, no tax cuts, no fiscal action whatsoever, not even on a contingency basis because of inflation and the fear of inflation, even though the economy was just beginning to recover from that sharp downturn. He wasn't going to do anything. This was August. I remember going down to Sea Island, the hottest day I ever spent in my life. And my memory is now vague but he overruled all of his economic advisers in terms of having a contingency tax cut. He had to send to the Congress a mid-year budget estimate, that's what gave him this occasion. I remember pleading up to the very last minute for him to put a small business tax cut in the economic program that was finally announced in September or something like that, something to be an answer to Reagan's supply economics. But he wouldn't do it. And he became very adamant that we were not going to do anything that gives the budget a stimulus. In my judgment, even going too far the other way. He would have vetoed the capital gains tax that went into effect in 1979 if I had given him one ounce of encouragement on macro economic grounds. It passed in 1978. You may recall the initial Carter plan to reform the tax system which finally turned out to be a tax cut, easing taxes on capital gains. He would have vetoed it. Now he would have vetoed it because he felt he had been double-crossed and instead of getting tax reforms he got more tax loopholes--that was his reason for vetoing it. I kept saying we needed the tax cut. From hindsight, even though his reasons for vetoing were wrong, if I had told him we could get by without a tax cut, he would have vetoed that tax cut and we would have had more restraint in 1979 and more unemployment and mildly less inflation. It might have given you fractions of a percentage point on inflation and somewhat higher unemployment.

SM: We've mentioned the continual problem of forecasting demand, and it leads me as an outsider to wonder how good are the projection models, the econometric models; are they adequate for the task?

CS: I will be a little bit cynical and say in the first place it doesn't matter. Only on grounds as the Reagan people found out; you simply cannot afford to get very far outside the consensus projection. Now, if you actually get way outside the pack and get lucky and turn out to be right, that's marvelous, but basically one can't. You lose your credibility. Now you can edge one way or the other. So that's my first proposition: if Data Resources, Wharton and all the other blue chip forecasters are fairly close together (and they very often are), you pretty much have to be within their forecast range.

SM: How do you use them?

CS: All sorts of different administrations have different ways of

doing it. When I was Budget Director with Johnson, we did it
formally, the so-called Troika, at three levels, staff there
to forecast, the Assistant Director, Council member second
level vetted it, approved it, and then the principals discussed it. The Council of Economic Advisers took the lead,
but it was a joint effort with the three main economic agencies. I don't know how the Nixon people did it. All I know
is when I came to the CEA, for reasons I will never understand, my counterparts at Budget and Treasury somehow assumed
the CEA really held the responsibility for the forecast, and
they never questioned my sole authority there. And I never
told them otherwise. Strangely enough, while we did it as a
team at the lower level with different agencies participating, when it got up to higher levels the CEA took it over
and it was our forecast. And once in a while, the Treasury
Secretary, or Budget Director complained. As I say, really
that's not the way it had been done, but that's what they
assumed and I never questioned it. What it was was a blend
of using the models and more informal methods. In the first
place the models are only a vehicle for tracing out the
implications of the assumptions which are factored in. They
can't just run them cold. So the main use of the models is
to simulate anyway; it is not so much to forecast. We would
put in judgmental decisions about a lot of things on the
basis of a lot of discussion such as the strength of investment. We'd run models, but then do our own assumptions, and
run them through the models again, because you get a lot of
implications out of them. And then look at the results and
iterate it and look at the results and chew and argue and
scrap. It was a complicated process. Where the models were
used much more was to see what would be (in a simulation
process) the implication of raising taxes by ten billion, or
lowering taxes or changing oil taxes; thus much more for
simulation, than for forecasting, per se.

SM: In 1978 Carter proposed a TIP plan. Who were the proponents?
Maybe you could describe the process.

CS: Absolutely fascinating. Number one, it basically stemmed
from Art Okun's ideas, but Barry Bosworth dreamed up this
particular idea. We then had it staffed out. Both the
Treasury and Budget Bureaus, and CEA had people working on
this, really examining it. I remember we had a principals'
meeting to try to put together the October 1978 anti-
inflation package. Barry Bosworth was out of town and the
staff came up with what I would say was on balance a very
lukewarm to negative attitude on the TIP; they didn't come up
with a flat recommendation. It was clear, if you looked at
all of their objections and all the problems, that if you'd
forced the staff to vote, they would probably have voted
against it. By staff I mean Council members and staff—same
thing in Budget and Treasury. Barry Bosworth who, it turns
out, was more amenable to it, was out of town. I presented
that report to the assembled Economic Policy Group which was

like a floating crap game. It got bigger and smaller depending on turf fights, who got the President's ear and got
himself inserted into it. This was a fairly large group
including Bob Strauss and Fred Kahn and the Budget Director,
some White House staff and everybody. And the TIP idea was
presented, and all of a sudden Bob Strauss' eyes started
glowing and all the politicians in the room and everybody
else got all excited. "Great idea; we've got something new
now. Don't drop it. It's the only new thing we have and
everything else in the package has been leaked but this is a
marvelous idea. We have a new Carter initiative." They
brushed aside all the technical objections. Mind you, I was
for it, so I'm not objecting. But I was for it with a lot of
questions. But all of a sudden it just swept the room. It
was incredible. I couldn't believe it. The staff almost
dropped dead. They'd expected objections and discussion. It
had been pretty well staffed out, but there were still a lot
of difficulties. The Treasury staff were particularly dead
set against it, because, of course, all the lawyers could see
the problems of defining wages, but lo and behold it was
accepted. We couldn't check it out politically because of
this idea of absolute secrecy; we didn't want this to leak.
And then, on the Hill it ran into a very lukewarm reception.
The day before the entire package was released we had the
assignment of calling people to find out whether they would
agree with it. But you never find out that way. You can't
just pick up the phone and call Russell Long and say, "Russell, what do you think?" He's not about to commit himself
so hard he can't uncommit himself. And it's new to him. I
don't blame him. And so you get all kinds of semi-cautious,
lukewarm, "well, maybe." So you go in and tell the President
nobody objects. In fact, they are simply waiting to see what
the reaction would be. On something new like that, you have
to lay the groundwork over a long period of time. This is
where you need the hearings and the public statements for
things to get kicked around in public for a year or two
before you can move. In any event, what happened just blew
me off the wall. The proposal ran into an absolute lukewarm
to hostile reception, ranging from hostility to indifference.
People said if you really want me to I might vote for it. It
became clearer and clearer it was going nowhere. And then
all of a sudden, all of the people who were in favor of it
began to back off and in particular the Treasury Secretary
started. He didn't sabotage us (he was too loyal to do
that), but he wasn't plugging for it very hard. He kept
bringing back all the reasons why it wasn't going to go
anywhere. He kept telling these to the President, then
finally, it just died. It would have died anyway. But all
these people who had unthinkingly jumped on it as a great
gimmick ran as soon as it got into trouble. So it went
nowhere. A funny thing that I do remember that embarrassed
the economic advisers was a probability run that we did. The
key thing on the TIP was what are the probabilities of inflation going high enough above our threshhold that you really

would have a big fiscal payout. For that to happen you had
to get a fairly sizable growth in prices relative to wages.
A large drop in real wages had to happen, the way we had
rigged it. I remember we had run the numbers, and we went to
the President with this probability distribution which had
been run off the past data. We said, "Mr. President, the
chances are one in a hundred that you'd ever have to pay off
as much as X. You'd have to have another oil price increase
as big as the last one, and we all know that's not going to
happen." If you look at the probabilities on the straight
history. It was one case, nothing else in history like that.
It would never happen. Now we also made the argument that if
we ever did get into a great big oil price hike, if we should
by some freak ever hit this probability, it would drive the
economy down and you'd need the stimulus. In fact, we didn't
need the stimulus. Because in fact if it did drive the
economy down, we should probably have let it be driven down,
to stop the inflationary consequences. So we wouldn't have
wanted whatever would have been the extra stimulus. But in
any event, the basic idea was a good one. It was just the
wrong year, the one year you should never have done it. I
liked the idea.

SM: In terms of your relations with the Fed, what sort of policy
coordination was there between the fiscal and monetary side?
Were you using the Quadriad sort of arrangement that had been
used before? How did it work?

CS: Sure, there was the Quadriad; there was a periodic meeting
more or less every six weeks, two months, or whatever. It
wasn't as much as every month, but maybe every six weeks. At
the meeting the Fed Chairman, first Burns, then Miller, and
then Volcker, the President, the main economic advisers, very
often the Vice-President. But they were like two dogs sniff-
ing around each other. I never found it very useful. You
don't coordinate by having the principals sit down, particularly when one of the principals, namely the President,
doesn't really know very much about the technical part of
this. He gets a briefing paper the night before. Nor did
they know each other all that well. I found this to be a
very constrained, rather symbolic thing. When we actually
had some major thing to discuss, for example that March 1980
budget policy, we had not the Quadriad but rather meetings of
the relevant people with the President, at which Volcker
came, and that was fine. I mean you get to the substance of
something. But to meet every six weeks because the President
and the Fed Chairman ought to meet, that doesn't do you any
good. What you need is a kind of ongoing dialogue. Paul
Volcker, with whom on occasions I disagreed very vigorously,
was a joy to work with. I always got the impression he
wasn't out to bullshit us anyway. He was just interested in
discussing what ought to be done. Now I'm not saying he told
me everything, exactly. He had his own internal policies
with the Board. We had vigorous discussions when he insti-

tuted the new revolution. And, I told him I thought he was absolutely wrong. But he said, "I'm going to do it." I said, "We are not going to fight you in public. I know you have to do something strong, but I think you are wrong to do it this way." I know Miller and I agreed that there was no use in carrying the fight on in public. That was in October or November of 1979. But in any event I never had any qualms about Volcker. I used to breakfast with him every two weeks.

SM: Never any discussion of "we'll give you more on taxes if you give on monetary policy"?

CS: It doesn't work that way. The occasion doesn't come up that often. That's the point. Sure, once a year, at budget time or maybe occasionally, but not often. There is undoubtedly a better way to do this, probably, but I don't know what it is. It's inherent in the nature of the game that so long as the Fed is independent, then to some extent, and I can't quite put my finger on it, they are going to preserve a bit of independence of staff action. With the staff, we would talk and have good relations most of the time. But there was always a little bit of a feeling that our objectives were not the same as their objectives, which is true. Their role is precisely not to have in their social objective function all the arguments that the politicians do. And that carries over in all sorts of ways, so in the best of worlds if you're going to have them independent, I really think they ought to be. I could think of some ways to change it. But basically you have to just live with the fact that there's always going to be a bit of dog-sniffing arrangement. Because the institutions answer to different clienteles and social objectives.

SM: Doesn't that mean that the President loses or has only some control over one of the main instruments of policy.

CS: I'm getting conservative in my old age, I guess. I guess I would say on balance even though I vigorously disagree with part of what the Fed did in the last couple of years that that is a constraint maybe the President ought not to have control of. Now, my point is that whenever the President has a strong anti-inflationary policy of his own (for example, he is running a great big budget surplus), he can argue publicly with the Fed. He could go on television and say these willful men are destroying us. He would win. The Congress would go for it immediately. But if the Fed has the only anti-inflationary game in town the President can't do anything about it. Jimmy Carter would never have let us attack the Fed strongly in the last days of the campaign. I think the President is faced with all kinds of constraints, constitutional constraints, human nature; it's very hard for him to manipulate the printed press, etc. The Fed is another. I would, for example, put the secretary of the Treasury as a non-voting member of the Federal Open Market Committee. Just so he'd be there to make his point and then make sure that

500

whatever he said wasn't in the minutes. You don't want that record of disagreement to be entered in the minutes. But let him have his say before the board. But beyond that I'd take my lumps, which means that a lot of things happen you don't like.

SM: One final question. What do you think the role of the CEA chairman should be? Do you think that the chairman has been losing clout? Has there been a trend down over time?

CS: No, I don't think so. Different chairmen have had different influence depending on a whole host of things that we haven't had enough obervations on even to run a regression with all the stuff in it yet. Depends on the personal relations with the president, depends on the times. Greenspan was very close to Jerry Ford. But at that time and from the outside, it was Simon who was the big spokesman. It was only people really in the know who realized Greenspan was the one. I had less influence with Carter but apparently had more influence than Marty Feldstein has with Reagan, somewhere in between. Heller had a major influence, ultimately bringing Kennedy around to getting the tax cut, though it was 1964 before we got one. Arthur Burns had a good bit of influence; his successor had much less. So there is a lot of variance, but I don't see a trend.

SM: It seems that the CEA chairman has gotten more and more into micro issues?

CS: I'm not sure of that. I'm sure if you go back to the late '40s and early '50s, that's right. I spent, in terms of time, much more than they did on that. I mean how many times do macro decisions come up anyway? We were active all over the place. We didn't expect to win most of them, but had some influence. I spent a tremendous amount of my time the first year and a half on regulatory management. Trying to organize an administration which essentially had a lot of hostages among the environmentalists. To get some balance into it. And that took a tremendous amount of time, an incredible number of legal problems. I won't bore you with them, but what is the role of a presidential adviser in talking to regulatory agencies? I was sued a number of times. All sorts of things: the minimum wage, agricultural prices. We spent a lot of time on agriculture. Lot of time on trade. Spent a lot of time in welfare reform. The role of the Council is a bit different on micro than on macro. On macro you are the President's economic adviser, on micro you are too, but much more a hair shirt in the councils of government. It's important to have an independent hair shirt. You are seventy-five percent of the time on the losing side. The fact that you're there sometimes makes the protectionism a little less. We won some twenty percent or thirty percent of the fights with Agriculture. But never a majority. It is very important. Ultimately in the macro economic arena your successes and mistakes get washed out as the events go on. Micro stuff can live for for years. It has much smaller impact but accumulates. The CEA's micro role probably has grown some but I think it's been pretty big for quite a while. I have no idea from Council to Council how that's gone. I put a lot of time on it. But different chairmen have had different attitudes. I thought micro was very important.

Bibliography

General

Ackley, Gardner. "The Contribution of Economists to Policy Formation." The Journal of Finance XXI (May 1966): 169-77.
Bailey, Stephen K. "Political Elements in Full Employment Policy." American Economic Review 45 (May 1955): 341-50.
_____. Congress Makes a Law: The Story Behind the Employment Act of 1946. New York: Columbia Univ. Press, 1950.
Bach, G. L. Making Monetary and Fiscal Policy. Washington, DC: The Brookings Institution, 1971.
Blough, Roy. The Role of the Economist in Federal Policy Making. Urbana: Institute of Governmental Public Affairs, Univ. of Ill. Bulletin No. 51, 78, 161; 1953.
_____. "Political and Administrative Requisites for Achieving Economic Stability." American Economic Review 40 (May 1950): 165-78.
Bonnello, Frank J. and Thomas R. Swartz, eds. "Macroeconomic Performance and Policy: A Thirty Year Perspective." In Alternative Directions in Economic Policy, pp. 1-34. South Bend, Ind.: Univ. of Notre Dame, 1978.
Baskin, Michael J., ed. The Economy in the 1980s. Transaction Books. Rutgers, NJ: State Univ., 1980.
Buchanan, James M. and Richard E. Wagner, Democracy in Deficit: The Political Legacy of Lord Keynes. New York: Academic Press, 1977.
Burns, Arthur F. Prosperity Without Inflation. New York: Fordham Univ. Press, 1961.
Canterbury, E. Ray. Economics in a New Frontier. Belmont, CA: Wadsworth, 1968.
Colm, Gerhard, ed. The Employment Act, Past and Future: A Tenth Anniversary Symposium. Washington, DC: National Planning Association, 1956.
Destler, I. M. Presidents, Bureaucrats and Foreign Policy. Princeton, NJ: Princeton Univ. Press, 1972.
Feldstein, Martin. The American Economy in Transition. Chicago: Univ. of Chicago, 1980.
Flash, Edward S., Jr. Economic Advice and Presidential Leadership. New York: Columbia Univ. Press, 1965.
Goodwin, Craufurd D., ed. Exhortation and Controls: The Search for Wage-Price Policy, 1945-1971. Washington, DC: The Brookings Institution, 1975.

504

Graham, Otis L. Toward a Planned Society: From Roosevelt to Nixon. Oxford: Oxford Univ. Press, 1976.

Heller, Walter W. New Dimensions of Political Economy. Cambridge: Harvard Univ. Press, 1967.

_____. "What's Right with Economics?" The American Economic Review 65 (March 1975): 1-26.

_____. The Economy, Old Myths and New Realities. New York: Norton, 1976.

Hess, Stephen. Organizing the Presidency. Washington, DC: The Brookings Institution, 1976.

Hoadley, Walter E., ed. American Assembly. The Economy and the President: 1980 and Beyond. Spectrum Books. New York: Prentice Hall; 1980.

Hobbs, Edward H. Behind the President: A Study of Executive Office Agencies. Washington, DC: Public Affairs Press, 1954.

Jacoby, Neil H. "The President, the Constitution and the Economist in Economic Stabilization." History of Political Economy III, 2 (Fall 1971): 398-414.

Lewis, Wilfred, Jr. Federal Fiscal Policy in the Postwar Recessions. Washington, DC: The Brookings Institution, 1962.

Livingston, J. A. "Economic Research and Public Policy." American Economic Review 45 (May 1955): 296-328.

Naveh, David. "The Political Role of Academic Advisers: The Case of the U.S. President's Council of Economic Advisers, 1946-76." Presidential Studies Quarterly 11 (Fall 1981): 492-510.

Norris, S. E. The Economics of the Political Parties: With Special Attention to Presidents Eisenhower and Kennedy. New York: Macmillan, 1962.

Norton, Hugh S. The Employment Act and the Council of Economic Advisers, 1946-76. Columbia, SC: Univ. of South Carolina Press, 1977.

Nourse, Edwin G. Economics in the Public Service: Administrative Aspects of the Employment Act. New York: Harcourt, Brace, 1953.

Nourse, Edwin G. and Bertram M. Gross. "The Role of the Council of Economic Advisers." American Political Science Review 42 (April 1948): 283-95.

Okun, Arthur. The Political Economy of Prosperity. Washington, DC: The Brookings Institution, 1970.

Pechman, Joseph A. and N. J. Simlev, eds. Economics in the Public Service, Papers in Honor of Walter Heller. New York: Norton, McLeod, 1982.

Porter, Roger B. "Economic Advice to the President." Political Science Quarterly. (Fall, 1983): 403-26.

Porter, Roger B. Presidential Decision-Making: the Economic Policy Board. Cambridge: Cambridge Univ. Press, 1980.

Puth, Robert C., ed. Current Issues in the American Economy 1978-79. Boston: Heath, 1978.

Saulnier, Raymond J. The Strategy of Economic Policy. New York: Fordham Univ. Press, 1963.

Seligman, Lester. "Presidential Leadership: The Inner Circle and Institutionalization." Journal of Politics 18 (August 1956): 410-426.

Shultz, George P. and Kenneth W. Dam, Economic Policy Beyond the Headlines. Boston: Norton, McLeod, 1977.

Sichel, Werner. Economic Advice and Executive Policy: Recommendations from Past Members of the Council of Economic Advisers. New York: Praeger, 1978.

Silverman, Corinne. The President's Economic Advisers. Inter-University Case Program. Tuscaloosa: Univ. of Alabama Press, 1959.

Stein, Herbert. The Fiscal Revolution in America. Chicago: Univ. of Chicago Press, 1969.

Stein, Herbert, James Tobin, and Henry Wallich. "How Political Must the Council of Economic Advisers Be? A Discussion." Challenge 12 (March-April 1974): 28-42.

Strayer, Paul J., Ray Blough, and George Bach. "Stabilizing the Economy: The Employment Act of 1946 in Operation." American Economic Review 40 (May 1950): 144-90.

Sundquist, James L. Politics and Policy: The Eisenhower, Kennedy and Johnson Years. Washington, DC: The Brookings Institution, 1968.

Thomas, Norman C. "Political Science and the Study of Macro-Economic Policy Making." Policy Studies Journal 4 (Autumn 1975): 7-15.

Tobin, James. "Stabilization Policy Ten Years After." Brookings Papers on Economic Activity 1 (1980): 19-71, 72-89.

_____. "The Intellectual Revolution in U.S. Economic Policy Making," Univ. of Essex, Noel Buxton Lectures. London: Longmans, 1966.

Tufte, Edward R. Political Control of the Economy. Princeton, NJ: Princeton Univ. Press, 1978.

Turner, Robert C. "Problems of Forecasting for Economic Stabilization." American Economic Review 45 (May 1955): 329-40.

U. S. Congress, Joint Economic Committee, 89th Cong. 2d sess., Twentieth Anniversary of the Employment Act of 1946: An Economic Symposium. Feb. 23, 1966. Washington, DC: Government Printing Office, 1966.

U. S. President. Economic Reports.

Wallich, Henry C. "The American Council of Economic Advisers and the German Sachverstalentigerat: A Study of the Economics of Advice." Quarterly Journal of Economics 82 (August 1968): 349-79.

Keyserling (1949-1953)

Acheson, Dean G. Present at the Creation. New York: Norton, 1969.

Bernstein, Barton J. Politics and Policies of the Truman Administration. Chicago: Quadrangle Books, 1970.

_____. "Economic Policies." In The Truman Period as a Research Field, pp. 87-148. Ed. by Richard Kirkendall. Columbia, Mo.: Univ. of Missouri Press, 1967.

Colm, G. "The Executive Office and Fiscal Economic Policy." Law and Contemporary Problems 21 (1956): 710-723.

Cornwell, Elmer E., Jr. "The Truman Presidency." In The Truman Period as a Research Field, p. 213-55. Ed. by Richard Kirkendall. Columbia, Mo.: Univ. of Missouri Press, 1967.

Donovan, Robert. Conflict and Crisis; the Presidency of Harry S. Truman. New York: Norton, 1977.

Flash, Edward S., Jr. Economic Advice and Presidential Leadership. New York: Columbia Univ. Press, 1965. Chaps. 2, 3.

Gross, Bertram and John P. Lewis. "The President's Economic Staff During the Truman Administration." American Political Science Review 48 (1954): 114-30.

Hamby, Alonzo L. "The Clash of Perspectives and the Need for New Syntheses." In The Truman Period as a Research Field: A Reappraisal, 1972, p. 1-14. Ed. by Richard Kirkendall. Columbia, Mo.: Univ. of Missouri Press, 1974.

_____. "The Vital Center, the Fair Deal and the Quest for Liberal Political Economy." Americal Historical Review 77 (1972): 653-78.

Hansen, Alvin. The American Economy. New York: McGraw-Hill, 1957. Chapter 6, "The Employment Act of 1946 Under Truman."

National Industrial Conference Board. "The Council of Economic Advisers: Retrospect and Prospect." Studies In Business Economics 38. New York: National Industrial Conference Board, 1953.

Sitkoll, Harand. "Year of the Locust: Interpretations of the Truman Presidency Since 1965." In The Truman Period as a Research Field: A Reappraisal, 1972, p. 75-112. Ed. by Richard Kirkendall. Columbia, Mo.: Univ. of Missouri Press, 1974.

Burns (1953-1956)

Adams, Sherman. Firsthand Report: The Story of the Eisenhower Administration. New York: Harper and Row, 1961.

Donovan, Robert J. Eisenhower: The Inside Story. New York: Harper, 1956.

Eisenhower, Dwight D. Mandate for Change. New York: Harper and Row, 1960.

Flash, Edward S., Jr. Economic Advice and Presidential Leadership. New York: Columbia Univ. Press, 1965. Chaps. 4, 5.

Goldman, Eric F. The Crucial Decade and After: American 1945-1960. New York: Knopf, 1965. p. 349 ff.

Gordon, H. Scott. "The Eisenhower Administration: The Doctrine of Shared Responsibility." In Exhortation and Controls: The Search for a Wage-Price Policy, 1945-1971, p. 95-134. Ed. by Crauford D. Goodwin. Washington, DC: The Brookings Institution, 1975.

Hansen, Alvin. The American Economy. New York: McGraw-Hill, 1957.

Holmans, A. E. "The Eisenhower Administration and the Recession, 1953-1954," Oxford Economic Papers 10 (February 1958): 413-37.

Murphy, C. J. V. "The Eisenhower Shift." In Eisenhower as President, p. 50-66. Ed. by Dean Albertson. New York: Hill and Wang, 1963.

Saulnier (1956-1961)

Adams, Sherman. Firsthand Report: The Story of the Eisenhower Administration. New York: Harper and Row, 1961.

Eisenhower, Dwight D. Waging Peace: The White House Years, 1956-1960. New York: Harper and Row, 1962.

Flash, Edward S., Jr. Economic Advice and Presidential Leadership. New York: Columbia Univ. Press, 1965.

Gordon, H. Scott. "The Eisenhower Administration: The Doctrine of Shared Responsibility." In Exhortation and Controls: The Search for a Wage-Price Policy, 1945-1971, pp. 95-134. Ed. by Crauford D. Goodwin. Washington, DC: The Brookings Institution, 1975.

Hansen, Alvin. The American Economy. New York: McGraw-Hill, 1959.

Lewis, Wilfred, Jr. Federal Fiscal Policy in the Postwar Recessions. Washington, DC: The Brookings Institution, 1962.

Murphy, Charles V. J. "The White House and the Recession." Fortune 57 (May 1957): 124-27, 266-80.

Norton, Hugh S. The Employment Act and the Council of Economic Advisers, 1946-76. Columbia, SC: Univ. of South Carolina Press, 1977.

Stein, Herbert. The Fiscal Revolution in America. Chicago: Univ. of Chicago Press, 1969.

Heller (1961-1964)

Canterbery, E. Ray. Economics on a New Frontier. Belmont, CA: Wadsworth, 1968.

Cochrane, James L. "The Johnson Administration: Moral Suasion Goes to War." In Exhortation and Controls: The Search for a Wage-Price Policy, 1945-1971, pp. 193-204. Ed. by Crauford D. Goodwin. Washington, DC: The Brookings Institution, 1975.

Evans, Rowland and R. Novak, Lyndon B. Johnson: The Exercise of Power; A Political Biography. New York: New American Library, 1966. p. 597 ff.

Gettleman, Marvin E. and David Mermelstein, eds. The Great Society Reader: The Failure of American Liberalism. New York: Random House, 1967. p. 551 ff.

Goodwin, Craufurd D., ed. Exhortation and Controls: The Search for Wage-Price Policy, 1945-1971. Washington, DC: The Brookings Institution, 1975. Chapter on JFK years, by William J. Barber, pp. 135-91.

Fairlie, Henry. The Kennedy Promise: The Politics of Expectation. Garden City, NY: Doubleday & Co., 1973. p. 376 ff.

Flash, Edward S., Jr. Economic Advice and Presidential Leadership. New York: Columbia Univ. Press, 1965. Chaps. 6, 7.

Harris, Seymour E. "Economics of the Kennedy Years." In John F.
     Kennedy and the New Frontier, pp. 61-87. Ed. by A. D. Donald.
     New York: Hill and Wang, 1966.
     . The Economics of the Kennedy Years and a Look Ahead. New
     York: Harper and Row, 1964. p. 273 ff.
Heath, Jim F. John F. Kennedy and the Business Community. Chi-
     cago: Univ. of Chicago Press, 1964. p. 198 ff.
Heller, Walter W. New Dimensions of Political Economy. Cam-
     bridge, Mass.: Harvard Univ. Press, 1966. p. 203 ff.
Kershaw, Joseph A. and Courant, Paul N. Government Against Pov-
     erty. Washington, DC: The Brookings Institution, 1970.
Lander, Byron C. "Group Theory and Individuals: The Origin of
     Poverty as a Political Issue in 1964." Western Political
     Quarterly 24 (Sept. 1971): 514-26.
Miroff, Bruce. Pragmatic Illusions: The Presidential Politics of
     John F. Kennedy. New York: David McKay, 1976, p. 234 ff.
Norton, Hugh S. The Council of Economic Advisers: Three Periods
     of Influence. Columbia, SC: Univ. of South Carolina, 1973.
Paper, L. J. The Promise and the Performance: The Leadership of
     John F. Kennedy. New York: Crown, 1975. p. 406 ff.
Rowen, Hobart. "The Big Steel Crisis: Kennedy vs. Blough." In
     J. F. Kennedy and Presidential Power, pp. 95-115. Ed. by
     Earl Latham. Lexington, Mass.: Heath, 1972.
     . "Kennedy's Economists," Harper 223 (Sept. 1961): 25-32.
Schlesinger, A. M., Jr. A Thousand Days: John F. Kennedy in the
     White House. Boston: Houghton Mifflin, 1965.
Sheahan, John. The Wage Price Guideposts. Washington, DC: The
     Brookings Institution, 1972.
Sidey, Hugh. John F. Kennedy, President. New York: Atheneum,
     1964.
Slesinger, Reuben E. National Economic Policy: The Presidential
     Reports. Princeton, NJ: Van Nostrand, 1968.
Sorenson, Theodore C. Kennedy. New York: Harper, 1965. p. 783 ff.
Stein, Herbert. "Tax Cut in Camelot." In J. F. Kennedy and Pres-
     idential Power, pp. 81-94. Ed. by Earl Latham, Lexington,
     Mass.: Heath, 1972.
     . The Fiscal Revolution in America. Chicago: Univ. of
     Chicago Press, 1969.
U.S. Government. General Services Administration. National Ar-
     chives and Records Service. John F. Kennedy Library Oral
     History Program. Interview with Walter Heller, Kermit
     Gordon, James Tobin, Gardner Ackley, Paul Samuelson and Jo-
     seph A. Pechman, August 1, 1964, Fort Ritchie, Md.
Wilkins, B. H. and C. B. Friday, eds. The Economists of the New
     Frontier. New York: Random House, 1963.

Ackley (1964-1968)

Cochrane, James L. "The Johnson Administration: Moral Suasion
     Goes to War." In Exhortation and Controls, pp. 193-294.
     Ed. by Craufurd D. Goodwin. Washington DC: The Brookings
     Institution, 1975.
Kearns, Doris. Lyndon Johnson and the American Dream. New York:
     Harper and Row, 1976.

Rowen, Hobart. The Free Enterprisers: Kennedy, Johnson and the Business Establishment. New York: Putnam, 1964, p. 319 ff.
Stein, Herbert. The Fiscal Revolution in America. Chicago: Univ. of Chicago Press, 1969.

Okun (1968-1969)

Cochrane, James L. "The Johnson Administration: Moral Suasion Goes to War." In Exhortation and Controls, pp. 193-294. Ed. by Craufurd D. Goodwin. Washington, DC: The Brookings Institution, 1975.
Hall, Robert E. and Gordon, Robert J. "Arthur M. Okun, 1928-1980." Brookings Papers on Economic Activity 1 (1980): pp. 1-5.

McCracken (1969-1971)

Ackley, Gardner. "Observations on Phase II Price and Wage Controls." Brookings Papers on Economic Activity 1 (1972): 173-90.
Bosworth, Barry. "Phase II: The U.S. Experiment With an Incomes Policy." Brookings Papers on Economic Activity 2 (1972): 343-83.
Evans, Rowland, and R. Novak. Nixon in the White House: The Frustration of Power. New York: Random House, 1971. pp. 431 ff.
Fiedler, Edgar R. "The Price-Wage Stabilization Program." Brookings Papers on Economic Activity 1 (1972): 173-90.
Goodwin, Craufurd D., ed. Exhortation and Controls: The Search for Wage-Price Policy, 1945-1971. Washington, DC: The Brookings Institution, 1975.
Houthakker, Hendriks. "Thoughts on Phase II." Brookings Papers on Economic Activity 1 (1972): 195-98, 207-9.
Kareken, John H. "FOMC Policy, 1970 and Beyond." Brookings Papers on Economic Activity 3 (1976): 474-84.
_____. "Monetary Policy in 1969." Brookings Papers on Economic Activity 1 (1970): 152-61.
Lerner, A. P. "1971 Report of the President's Council of Economic Advisers: Priorities and Efficiency." American Economic Review 61 (Sept. 1971): 715-23.
Okun, Arthur. "The Personal Tax Surcharge and Consumer Demand, 1968-70." Brookings Papers on Economic Activity 2 (1971): 167-204, 205-11.
Poole, William. "Thoughts on the Wage-Price Freeze." Brookings Papers on Economic Activity 2 (1971): 429-43, 450-51.
Silk, Leonard S. Nixonomics. New York: Praeger, 1973, p. 224 ff.
Teeters, Nancy H. "Outlook for Federal Fiscal Policy." Brookings Papers on Economic Activity 2 (1972): 467-77.
_____. "The 1973 Federal Budget." Brookings Papers on Economic Activity 1 (1972): 221-32.
_____. "The 1972 Budget: Where It Stands and Where It Might Go." Brookings Papers on Economic Activity 1 (1971): 226-33.
Weber, Arnold R. In Pursuit of Price Stability: The Wage-Price Freeze of 1971. Washington, DC: The Brookings Institution, 1973. p. 137 ff.

510

Stein (1972-1974)

Dusenberry, James S. "Some Observations on Monetary Policy." Brookings Papers on Economic Activity 2 (1973): 508-14.
Enzler, Jared J. and James L. Pierce. "The Effects of External Inflationary Shocks." Brookings Papers on Economic Activity 1 (1974): 13-54, 55-61.
Goodwin, Craufurd D., ed. Exhortation and Controls: The Search for Wage-Price Policy, 1945-1971. Washington, DC: The Brookings Institution, 1975.
Grayson, C. Jackson, Jr. and Louis Neeb. Confessions of a Price Controller. Homewood, Ill.: Dow Jones, 1974.
Kosters, Marvin H. and Ahalt, J. Dawson. Controls and Inflation: The Economic Stabilization Program in Retrospect. Washington, DC: American Enterprise Institute, 1975.
Lanzillotti, Robert F., Mary T. Hamilton, and R. Blaine Roberts. Phase II in Review: The Price Commission Experience. Washington, DC: The Brookings Institution, 1975. p. 209 ff.
McCracken, Paul W., moderator. The Economy and Phase IV: An AEI Round Table Held on 19 July 1973 at the American Enterprise Institute for Public Policy Research. Washington, DC: American Enterprise Institute, 1973.
Osborne, John. The Fourth Year of the Nixon Watch. New York, NY: Liveright, 1973. p. 218 ff.
Schnittker, John A. "The 1972-73 Food Price Spiral." Brookings Papers on Economic Activity 2 (1973): 498-507.

Greenspan (1974-1977)

Carter, Harold O. "1975 Report of the President's Council of Economic Advisers: Long on Analysis, Short on Policy." American Economic Review 65 (Sept. 1975): 539-47.
Ford, Gerald. Lettters. Ed. by Robert N. Winter-Berger. Secaucus, NJ: L. Stuart, 1974.
Okun, Arthur. "Unemployment and Output in 1974." Brookings Papers on Economic Activity 2 (1974): 495-505.
_____. "A Postmortem of the 1974 Recession." Brookings Papers on Economic Activity 1 (1975): 207-21, 235-37.
Poole, William. "Interpreting the Fed's Monetary Targets." Brookings Papers on Economic Activity 1 (1976): 247-59, 280-82.
Porter, Roger B. Presidential Decision-Making: The Economic Policy Board. Cambridge: Cambridge Univ. Press, 1980.
Reeves, Richard. A Ford, Not a Lincoln. New York: Harcourt, 1975. p. 212 ff.
Tobin, James. "Monetary Policy in 1974 and Beyond." Brookings Papers on Economic Activity 1 (1974): 219-32.

Schultze (1977-1981)

Anderson, Bernard E. "The Carter Economics: A Symposium." Journal Post Keynesian Economics I (Fall 1978): 31-33.

Cecchetti, Stephen G., Davis S. McClain, Michael J. McKee, and Daniel H. Saks. "OPEC II and the Wage Price Spiral." In What Role for Government? Lessons From Policy Research, pp. 137-54. Ed. by Richard J. Zeckhauser and Derek Leebaert. Durham, NC: Duke Univ. Press, 1983.

Calleo, David P. The Imperious Economy. Cambridge: Harvard Univ. Press, 1982. Chap. 8, "The Carter Cycle."

Davis, David Howard. Energy Politics. New York: St. Martin's Press, 1982.

Heineman, Jr., Ben W. and Curtis A. Hessler. Memorandum for the President: A Strategic Approach to Domestic Affairs in the 1980s. New York: Random House, 1980. pp. 251-266.

Poole, William. "The Monetary Deceleration: What Does It Mean and Why Is It Happening?" Brookings Papers on Economic Activity 1 (1979): 231-40.

Schultze, Charles L. "Carter's Economic Policy." Business Horizons 21 (June 1978): 5-10.

Verleger, Philip K., Jr. "The U.S. Petroleum Crisis of 1979." Brookings Papers on Economic Activity 2 (1979): 463-76.

Viscusi, W. Kip. "The Political Economy of Wage and Price Regulation: The Case of the Carter Pay-Price Standards." In What Role for Government? Lessons from Policy Research, pp. 155-75. Ed. by Richard J. Zeckhauser and Derek Leebaert. Durham, NC: Duke Univ. Press, 1983.